BOTTICELLI

BOTTICELLI

PAINTER OF FLORENCE

BY

HERBERT P. HORNE

INTRODUCTION BY
JOHN POPE-HENNESSY

PRINCETON UNIVERSITY PRESS
PRINCETON, NEW JERSEY

Published by Princeton University Press, Princeton, New Jersey
In the United Kingdom: Princeton University Press, Guildford, Surrey

LCC 79-5481
ISBN 0-691-00323-8 pbk.
ISBN 0-691-03949-6

Printed in the United States of America
by Princeton University Press, Princeton, New Jersey

Originally published as *Alessandro Filipepi, Commonly Called Sandro Botticelli, Painter of Florence* by
George Bell and Sons, 1908.

TO WHOM I OWE
MY INITIATION IN THESE STUDIES
D. B. B.
W. H. P.
FOR REMEMBRANCE

CONTENTS

LIST OF PLATES

¶ *With a few exceptions, all the pictures have been photographed for this book by Mr. Emery Walker.*

INTRODUCTION

(1979)

More than seventy years after its publication, it would be generally conceded that this book is the best monograph in English on an Italian painter. It was issued in 1908 in a small edition of two hundred and forty copies, most of which were bought up by libraries. Fastidiously produced, it was from the outset an expensive publication and it is, as a result, more familiar to students at second hand than in the original. Nonetheless, it is the well from which later books on Botticelli one and all are drawn.

The volume was, the author tells us in his introduction, "written at leisure during a period of many years, and with no other thought than to satisfy the curiosity of the writer." It is a long, discursive book—it totals three hundred and thirty-five pages with thirty pages of supporting material—and its text is continuous and not broken down into chapters or subsections. The single span in which it is conceived is, however, symptomatic of its intellectual character. It moves with easy mastery from biography to political and social history, from history to literature, and from literature to the works of art, whose connotations are analyzed with unfailing consistency and thoroughness. Resident in Florence, Horne cohabited with the pictures he described, getting to know them with an intimacy that must put modern art historians to shame. One has the impression that his knowledge of Florence and Florentine art in the fifteenth century was so profound that he was incapable of formulating judgments which were unhistorical.

Herbert Horne was born on February 18, 1864.[1] His interest in art was aroused at a very early age by one of the masters at his day school, the art critic Daniel Barron Brightwell, and the Botticelli monograph is dedicated jointly to Brightwell and to Walter Pater, whose *Renaissance* he had read as a young man. Horne's father was an architect, and in 1882 he joined the architectural firm of Mackmurdo, one of the creators of English *art nouveau*.[2] He was appointed a partner-designate of Mackmurdo in 1883, and became a full partner in 1885 when he reached the age of twenty-one. His association with Mackmurdo coincided with the founding in 1882 of the Century Guild. One of the objectives of the Guild was to effect a cross-fertilization of the arts, such as had occurred in Florence in the fifteenth century, and the medium through which its influence was exerted was a periodical, *The Century Guild Hobby Horse*. For the first two years of its existence, Mackmurdo edited the magazine, and in 1886 Horne succeeded him as editor. In his early twenties, Horne already enjoyed a considerable reputation. Meeting him in London in 1888, Bernard Berenson hailed him in a letter as the successor of William Morris, "the great man of the next generation, an architect, painter, poet, fine critic, and editor of the *Hobby Horse*."[3]

We can no longer reconstruct the stages by which the poet, typographer,

1. Ian Fletcher, "Herbert Horne: The Earlier Phase," *English Miscellany* 21, 1970, pp. 117-157.
2. Nikolaus Pevsner, *Pioneers of Modern Design: From William Morris to Walter Gropius*, London, 1949, p. 90.
3. Ernest Samuels, *Bernard Berenson: The Making of a Connoisseur*, Cambridge (Mass.), 1979, p. 62.

and architect became an art historian. All we know is that in the 1890s Horne reacted strongly against Mackmurdo and the principles of *art nouveau*, devoting his energies increasingly to criticism, and that from 1895 he spent part of each year in Italy. According to Berenson, in a diary entry written more than half a century later,[4] he was commissioned by a London publisher, George Bell & Sons, to prepare a short book on Botticelli. Arriving in Florence for the brief stay its preparation would entail, he discussed the project with Berenson, who "convinced him it would take years to do one," and Horne thereupon threw up his contract and started work upon a very different type of book. This telescoped account may be essentially correct. George Bell & Sons (by whom the Botticelli monograph was eventually issued) were engaged at this time in sponsoring a series called *Bell's Handbooks of the Great Masters in Painting and Sculpture*, some of which were entrusted to such reputable scholars as Weale, Perkins, and Maud Cruttwell. Horne may therefore have contracted to undertake the volume on Botticelli, which was later entrusted to a writer called Streeter. More important than the advice he received from Berenson must have been the fact that conditions in Florence in the middle of the eighteen-nineties were, in a special sense, conducive to original art-historical research. In 1895, Berenson himself was preparing the paean to Botticelli and the list of Botticelli's works that were published a year later in *The Florentine Painters of the Renaissance*. At the same time a native Florentine, Giovanni Poggi, was embarking on a lifelong study of the Florentine archives, and an adoptive Florentine, Aby Warburg, was engaged in examining the literary and cultural background of Florentine painting. For the next few years Horne saw Berenson frequently, bicycling with him through the country round Mantua as well as to Volterra and San Gimignano. To judge from a letter to Robert Trevelyan, Berenson was more than a little irked by Horne's unflagging serious-mindedness.[5] No doubt points of connoisseurship were discussed between them—among the attitudes they shared was a common mistrust of German scholarship as it was represented in the standard Botticelli monograph of Ulmann[6]—but Horne's Botticelli when it at last appeared was strikingly un-Berensonian. The documentary research behind it is first-rate, and its approach reflects the thinking of Warburg, who mistrusted Berenson but admired Horne.[7] Horne was a writer of distinction and a critic in his own right, and when he speaks it is with a voice of remarkable individuality—literate, astringent, and skeptical.

As work on the book progressed, Horne led an increasingly withdrawn and solitary life. From 1904 he lived exclusively in Florence, where in 1912 he bought a small palace by Cronaca, Palazzo Corsi, in the Via de' Benci. An inveterate collector, he had formed in London a collection of English watercolors, which he sold in 1904 to Edward Marsh, and in Florence he assembled a new collection of primitives, Renaissance furniture and applied art, and Old Master drawings. When he died, on April 14, 1916,

4. Bernard Berenson, *Sunset and Twilight: From the Diaries of 1947-1958*, London, 1964, p. 316.
5. *The Selected Letters of Bernard Berenson*, edited by A. K. McComb, London, 1965, pp. 64-65.
6. H. Ulmann, *Sandro Botticelli*, Munich, 1893.
7. E. H. Gombrich, *Aby Warburg: An Intellectual Biography*, London, 1970, p. 96.

the palace and the collection it contained were bequeathed to the municipality of Florence. They form the present-day Museo Horne.[8]

Horne's *Botticelli* has stood the test of time better than almost any other book about art history. Subsequent research has added very little to the documents Horne knew. One of the few new references of consequence is a passage in the will of Giorgio Antonio Vespucci of March 23, 1499, in which provision is made for frescoes of scenes from the lives of St. Denis the Areopagite and St. Paul, to be painted by Botticelli in one of the Vespucci chapels in the Ognissanti.[9] There is no evidence, however, that the frescoes were executed, and if they were, they do not survive. Another document, published by Mesnil in 1914,[10] proves that the Munich *Lamentation over the Dead Christ* was painted for the church of San Paolino, not far from Botticelli's house, and is therefore more closely associable with the artist than Horne supposed. The publication of the inventories of Lorenzo and Giovanni di Pierfrancesco de' Medici[11] shows that the *Birth of Venus* was not painted for Lorenzo di Pierfrancesco as Horne supposed—though it was indeed at Castello in the mid-sixteenth century—and that the *Allegory of Spring* had a white frame and stood over a bed. Thanks to the researches of Mesnil, it is established that the *Adoration of the Magi* from Santa Maria Novella, now in the Uffizi, was commissioned by Guasparre, not Giovanni del Lama,[12] and our knowledge of the patron and his chapel has been much extended by Hatfield.[13] It is now known that the donor of the *Annunciation* from Cestello in the Uffizi was Benedetto di ser Francesco, not Benedetto di ser Giovanni, Guardi.

Horne possessed preternatural powers of observation. Thanks to his experience as an artist, he knew how the pictures he described were painted—his account of the technique of Botticelli's mentor, Antonio Pollajuolo, is by far the best that has been written on that difficult and enigmatic artist—and without laboratory aid he formed a clear and almost always accurate impression of their physical state. The only instances in which Horne was deceived are with Botticelli's and Ghirlandaio's frescoes in the Ognissanti (where the elegiac distichs at the top have been found to date from the middle of the sixteenth century, not from the fifteenth)[14] and the Aynard *Crucifixion*, now in the Fogg Art Museum (which was completely overpainted in Horne's day, but has been proved by cleaning to be a damaged autograph original). Of one work and one only is Horne's discussion inadequate. This is the fresco of the *Annunciation*, now shown in the Uffizi, which he knew in the loggia of San Martino alla Scala where its artistic

8. For the Museo Horne and its collections see Carlo Gamba, *Il Museo Horne a Firenze*, Florence, 1961, and Filippo Rossi, *Il Museo Horne a Firenze*, Milan, 1967.

9. Ronald Lightbown, *Botticelli: Life and Work*, London, 1978, vol. 1, pp. 129-130, 179.

10. Jacques Mesnil, "Le Pieta botticelliane," *Rassegna d'Arte*, vol. 14, 1914, p. 207.

11. J. Shearman, "The Collections of the Younger Branch of the Medici," *Burlington Magazine*, vol. 117, 1975, pp. 12-27.

12. Jacques Mesnil, "Quelques documents sur Botticelli," *Miscellanea d'Arte*, 1903, pp. 91-96. In the present book, Horne retains the form of the name given in an earlier article (H. Horne, "The Story of a Famous Botticelli," *Monthly Review*, February 1902, pp. 133-145).

13. Rab Hatfield, *Botticelli's Uffizi Adoration: A Study in Pictorial Content*, Princeton, 1976.

14. Millard Meiss, *The Great Age of Fresco*, London, 1970, pp. 169, 170.

quality could not be assessed. A number of paintings have changed hands since he discussed them—the Hermitage *Adoration of the Magi* is in the National Gallery of Art in Washington, the Farinola *Last Communion of St. Jerome* is in the Metropolitan Museum of Art, the Kaufmann *Judith with the Head of Holofernes* is in the Rijksmuseum, and three of the panels with scenes from the legend of Nastagio degli Onesti are in the Prado in Madrid. A fourth panel with scenes from the life of St. Zenobius, now in New York, came to light in an English private collection three years after the publication of Horne's book. The Convertite altarpiece, the documents for which he published, was identified by Yashiro in 1925[15] and is now in the Courtauld Institute of Art. It was, however, Horne who, seven years after his monograph appeared, identified and published its predella, in the John G. Johnson Collection of the Philadelphia Museum of Art.[16]

Long as it is, this is no more than the first part of a much longer book. Horne recognized that Botticelli was not simply an artistic personality in our modern sense, but the head of one of the most productive workshops in Florence in the later fifteenth century, and he believed that any monograph dealing with his work should discuss "the productions both of his immediate disciples and of those painters who fell indirectly under his influence, or who were associated with him in some way or another; in short, the productions of his school in the widest sense of the word." It is a cause for continuing regret that he did not complete the second part. We may be confident that, had he done so, the characters of many of the minor painters who worked in Botticelli's studio would have been more clearly defined than they are now. Horne had an unrivaled sensibility to quality in execution. What other scholar has dared to question the autograph status of part of the *Birth of Venus* ("In point of execution, the whole of this painting is not, perhaps, of equal excellence, I seem to detect the hand of an assistant in some of the draperies, especially in the white dress of the nymph, which, however admirable in design . . . is, nevertheless, a little mechanical in many of the details of its folds")? What other scholar could have achieved the just and wonderfully precise analysis of the handling of the *Coronation of the Virgin* executed for San Marco? In reading the present book, it is important for this reason to distinguish between two types of omission, that of pictures Horne did not know (like the Granada *Agony in the Garden*, the Pallavicini *Transfiguration*, and the Abegg *Portrait of a Friar as St. Dominic*) and that of pictures he knew (like the *Smeralda Bandinelli* in London, the Santa Maria Novella fresco of the *Nativity*, and the Filangieri *Male Portrait* formerly in Naples) but deliberately relegated to the second section of his book. Berenson tells us, in the preface to the first volume of *The Study and Criticism of Italian Art*, that when he was engaged in reconstructing the synthetic figure of the Amico di Sandro (part Botticelli, part early Filippino Lippi, part the unknown artist he was claimed to be), Horne followed his studies "with benevolent interest." There can be little

15. Y. Yashiro, "A Newly Discovered Botticelli," *Burlington Magazine*, vol. 46, 1925, pp. 157-167.

16. H. Horne, "La tavola d'altare delle Convertite dipinta da Sandro Botticelli," *Rassegna d'Arte*, vol. 13, 1913, pp. 147-154.

question but that Horne's unpublished book would have been a contribution of real significance to the methodology of Florentine painting.

The excellence of the present book is not restricted to the plane of fact. As an interpretation of Botticelli and his work it has never been surpassed. Warburg's great study of the literary sources of the *Allegory of Spring* and the *Birth of Venus* appeared in 1893, a year or two before Horne started work,[17] and though it unquestionably influenced Horne's thinking, there is much in the passages on the mythologies that is original. Later expositions of these paintings, by Panofsky,[18] Wind,[19] Gombrich,[20] and Chastel[21] have plowed the furrow of Neoplatonism, but whether they are correct or simply represent an intellectual fashion current in the middle of the twentieth century is debatable, and even if they were accepted they would not invalidate Horne's highly persuasive interpretations. The book is founded on an intuitive understanding of the artist's intellectual processes, and on an acute visual sensibility which makes many of its pages—especially those on the illustrations to Dante's *Paradiso*—classics of art criticism.

Fritz Saxl in a lecture describes Horne as "perhaps the most accomplished historian of art whom [England] has ever produced."[22] Let us hope that the reissue of his monograph on Botticelli will exercise some influence outside the area of its speciality, and that young art historians will pray, to whatever deity they may believe in, to grant them the stamina and the unflagging concentration, the accuracy and the flawless sense of relevance, the all-embracing curiosity, the culture and the grasp of probability, the delicacy of perception, and the urbanity and eloquence of Herbert Horne.

John Pope-Hennessy
June 1979

17. Aby Warburg, *Sandro Botticelli's 'Geburt der Venus' und 'Frühling,'* 1893, reprinted in *Gesammelte Schriften*, vol. 1, 1932, pp. 1-61.

18. E. Panofsky, *Renaissance and Renascences in Western Art*, vol. 1, New York, 1960, pp. 192-200.

19. E. Wind, *Pagan Mysteries of the Renaissance*, Oxford, 1958, pp. 113-127.

20. E. H. Gombrich, "Botticelli's Mythologies: A Study in the Neoplatonic Symbolism of His Circle," *Journal of the Warburg and Courtauld Institutes*, vol. 8, 1945, pp. 7-60; reprinted in *Symbolic Images*, London, 1972.

21. A. Chastel, *Art et humanisme à Florence au temps de Laurent le Magnifique*, Paris, 1959.

22. F. Saxl, *Lectures*, vol. 1, London, 1957, p. 332.

INTRODUCTION

IN 1550, forty years after the death of Sandro Botticelli, the earliest account of the painter appeared in the first edition of a famous book, "Le Vite de' piu eccellenti Architetti, Pittori, et Scultori Italiani, da Cimabue insino a' tempi nostri: descritte in lingua Toscana, da Giorgio Vasari, Pittore Aretino." This edition was printed at Florence, in two volumes, by Lorenzo Torrentino. The notices of Botticelli, which Vasari collected, were for the most part singularly correct, having regard to the historical methods of his time. The only material errors of commission to be found in this account, consist in the substitution of an imaginary goldsmith, called "Il Botticello," for the painter's eldest brother, Giovanni; the attribution to Sandro, of the altar-piece painted for the chapel of Matteo Palmieri, in the church of San Pier Maggiore, a work now in the National Gallery, at London, No. 1126, and generally admitted to have been painted by Francesco Botticini; and the statement that the painter died in 1515. Vasari, in writing these "Lives," appears to have made use of the notices of Florentine painters, sculptors, and architects, collected apparently by one Antonio Billi, between the years 1516 and 1530. These notices, of which the original manuscript, known as "Il libro di Antonio Billi," is now lost, have come down in an epitomized form, in two manuscripts: but only one of these, the "Codice Petrei," contains notices of Botticelli. Another early collection of similar notices, compiled by some anonymous writer, between 1542 and 1548, appears to have been unknown to Vasari. This anonymous writer, who was probably a member of the Gaddi family, and who is, therefore, known as the "Anonimo Gaddiano," appears to have been exceptionally well informed in all that relates to Botticelli. He recounts two anecdotes, and describes six works, besides other particulars, to which Vasari makes no allusion. Other early notices of importance are to be found in the "Memoriale di molte Statue et Picture sono nella inclyta Cipta di Florentia Per mano di Sculptori & Pictori excellenti Moderni & Antiqui, tracto dalla propria Copia di Messer Francesco Albertini prete Fiore*n*tino Anno d*omi*ni 1510"; the earliest guide book to Florence, of which an unique impression is preserved there, in the Biblioteca Riccardiana.

App. I, Doc. I.

App. II, Doc. I.

App. II, Doc. II.

In 1568, the second edition of Vasari's "Lives" was published at Florence, in three volumes, by the Giunti. The account of Botticelli, as it stands in this edition, differs considerably from that which appeared in the edition of 1550. Vasari has cut out the introductory paragraph, modified several statements, and inserted two anecdotes and a number of additional notices. These additional notices, for the most part, either lack ulterior confirmation, or refer to works of art which have long since disappeared. In one of these passages, Vasari states that Botticelli "painted two angels, in the Pieve of Empoli, on that side, where is the St. Sebastian of Rossellino." These two panels, painted with the figures of two angels, and of the kneeling donor and his wife, form the lateral decorations of the carved and gilt, wooden tabernacle which still contains the marble statue of St. Sebastian by Antonio Rossellino. This tabernacle is now preserved in the little gallery attached to the Pieve of Sant' Andrea, now the Collegiata, at Empoli. Like the altar-piece painted for Matteo Palmieri, and ascribed by Vasari to Botticelli, these two panels have by common consent, and first by Signor Cavalcaselle, been attributed to Francesco Botticini. Indeed, neither these paintings, nor the altar-piece in the National Gallery, betray any trace

App. I, Doc. II.

Cavalcaselle e Crowe, Storia della Pittura in Italia, ed. Le Monnier, VII, 120.

b

of Botticelli's influence: a comparison of the latter picture with Sandro's illustration to Canto XXVIII of the "Paradiso" of Dante, will show how entirely different they are in manner. But Vasari's error is not difficult of

Vasari, ed. Sansoni, III, 52.

explanation. "Many," he says, in a certain passage, in the second edition of the "Lives," "having found written the name, Melozzo, and having compared the times, have believed that for Melozzo was intended Benozzo." Although he does not acknowledge it, Vasari had himself made that very

Id. ed. 1550, I, 422.

mistake, in the first edition of the "Lives": in the same way, having found written the name, Botticini, he appears to have thought it an error for Botticelli.

One other writer of the sixteenth century may be mentioned here: Raffaelo Borghini, in his book, called after the villa of his patron, "Il Riposo," and published at Florence, in 1584, although he does little more than epitomize the account of Botticelli as it stands in the second edition of Vasari's "Lives," and even reproduces a clerical error of the press, adds to that account three notices of value. During the seventeenth and eighteenth centuries, most writers upon art appear to allude to Botticelli only because he is mentioned by Vasari. Such repetitions need not detain us: but as a curiosity of criticism, I may cite the following passage from the notice of the painter, given in the "Abecedario Pittorico" of Pellegrino Orlandi, first published at Bologna, in 1719, and again at Venice, in 1753: "Sandro Botticelli, Fiorentino, cervello stravagante, e bizzarro, che da Filippo Lippi riportò tutti i necessari documenti per la pittura, sichè gran Maestro comparve." Even Filippo Baldinucci, who first essayed to commentate Vasari, in his "Notizie de' Professori del Disegno da Cimabue in qua," published at Florence in 1681-1728, adds nothing of real value concerning Botticelli, to what he has taken from that writer.

In the notes by Giovanni Gaetano Bottari, to the editions of Borghini's "Riposo," published at Florence, in 1730; and of Vasari's "Lives," published at Rome, in 1759, and again at Leghorn and Florence in 1767-72, an attempt was first made to trace the vicissitudes which various works by Botticelli had undergone, since the sixteenth century. But the trend of circumstance which chiefly went to arouse a wider interest in early Florentine painting, had its origin in the reforms of the Grand Duke Pietro Leopoldo. The suppression at Florence, of a number of the smaller parish churches, in 1768-69, and again in 1783-87, of the once powerful "Arti," or Guilds, in 1777, and of the Religious Companies, in 1786, led to the desecration of numerous churches and oratories. These buildings, like the guild-halls of the "Arti," were, for the most part, turned into dwelling-houses, or put to other secular uses; and the works of art which they contained, were dispersed. A mass of early paintings thus found their way into the hands of dealers, or private persons: and attention was called to many a work of the thirteenth and fourteenth century, which had lain neglected in the corner of some house or palace. An advertisement issued by a Florentine picture-dealer of the time, illustrates how quickly an attempt was made to turn to account these works of the earlier masters, which had thus been thrown upon the market. This pamphlet is entitled: "Catalogue Raisonné de Tableaux Originaux des meilleurs Maîtres; Avec une Collection separée de precieux Morceaux Depuis l'année 1220. iusques en 1712; qui font l'histoire de la Peinture en Toscanne, où chaque ouvrage est décrit selon l'ordre des tems; [&c.] par M. le Chevalier Menabuoni jadis Menabuoi. Le tout se trouve à vendre chez M. Vincent Gotti Peintre Florentin demeurant à Florence dan la rüe

Val-fonde près de la Forteresse d'en bas au Numero xxx. A Florence MDCCLXXXVII." The "collection separée" comprised seventy-seven pieces; including putative examples of Cimabue and Giotto, of eleven painters of the fourteenth century, and sixteen of the fifteenth century. That attributed to our master is thus described: "No. xxv. Un Tableau qui représente le Portrait d'une Femme, peinte par Alexandre Botticelli disciple de Frère Philippe Lippi."

The invasion of Italy by the French, the spoliation of churches and public galleries and the straitened circumstances to which the Italian aristocracy were reduced by the Revolution, contributed to bring about a new and a greater dispersion of works of art. Foreign, and especially English, buyers were quick to seize the occasion; and a vast number of paintings and sculptures left the country. It was under these circumstances, that William Young Ottley, afterwards keeper of the Print Room of the British Museum, acquired at Rome, "about the end of 1798, or the beginning of 1799, when the principal families were in the acutest stage of their misery," the first genuine painting by Botticelli which left Italy, the "Adoration of the Shepherds," now in the National Gallery, No. 1034. This was the only painting bearing Botticelli's name, to which Dr. Waagen alludes in his "Works of Art and Artists in England," as having seen here, during his first visit to this country, in 1835. Ottley, he tells us, had formed a collection of paintings of the Tuscan school, "with few exceptions, excellent works by masters the most eminent of their time," and "in a pure state"; whereas in the greatest galleries were then to be found, "only the rudest performances of those ages." But his enthusiasm for such early pictures was exceptional; and he told Dr. Waagen that nobody had paid so much attention to them, as his visitor. When after an interval of less than twenty years, Dr. Waagen revisited this country in 1854, he saw a large number of paintings ascribed to Botticelli, though for the most part the works of his school, which had, in the meantime, been acquired by such collectors as Lord Northwick, Rev. Walter Davenport Bromley, Mr. Alexander Barker, Mr. Fuller Maitland, and others: these he describes in his "Treasures of Art in Great Britain."

l.c., London, 1838, II, 125.

In this same interval, Botticelli was first recognized to be more than a mere name in the pages of Vasari. "The merits of this great artist," says Morelli, in his "Studies in the Munich Gallery," "have only been recognized again in recent years, and first of all in England." A recent writer has stated that Botticelli was one of the early masters of whose work Ruskin in his letter of January, 1847, addressed to the "Times" newspaper, urged the trustees of the National Gallery to purchase examples. No allusion, however, to Botticelli occurs in that letter. As Ruskin afterwards confessed in "Praeterita," his sympathies chiefly lay with Fra Angelico and Ghirlandaio at that time; "Lippi and Botticelli being still far beyond me." His first public allusion to Botticelli occurs, if I mistake not, in the course of the Slade lectures on "Landscape," which Ruskin delivered at Oxford, during the Lent Term of 1871.

J. Cartwright, Sandro Botticelli, London, 1904, p. 2.

l.c., ed. 1885, II, 224.

Among the first to realize in some definite measure the peculiar character and charm of Botticelli's art, were Dante Gabriel Rossetti and the Pre-Raphaelites. "In 1849," Mr. W. M. Rossetti writes to me, "when my brother, with Holman Hunt, first visited Paris, he observed in the Louvre, with particular pleasure, one or two pictures by Botticelli, and talked about them on his return. [The charming panel of the Virgin and

Child with St. John, No. 184, was by far the finest of the pictures then ascribed to Sandro, in that collection.] After that, Botticelli remained in abeyance with him for some years; but certainly not forgotten. In 1860, I for the first time visited Florence, and was greatly struck by the Botticellis —very specially by the 'Birth of Venus.' On my return, I spoke about these works to my brother and others. This refreshed his interest in Botticelli; and in March, 1867, he bought that little picture of which you speak, [the portrait of Smeralda Bandinelli, now in the Ionides Collection, in the South Kensington Museum.] Of the Spring, he had, I think, no direct knowledge at all, until a friend, towards 1879, sent him a well-sized photograph of it. He wrote his sonnet, I am sure, not earlier than 1879: more likely in 1880, or even in 1881." The sonnet in question was first printed in the volume of "Ballads and Sonnets," which appeared in the course of the latter year.

FOR
SPRING
BY SANDRO BOTTICELLI.
(In the Accademia of Florence.)

What masque of what old wind-withered New-Year
  Honours this Lady? Flora, wanton-eyed
  For birth, and with all flowrets prankt and pied:
Aurora, Zephyrus, with mutual cheer
Of clasp and kiss: the Graces circling near,
  'Neath bower-linked arch of white arms glorified:
  And with those feathered feet which hovering glide
O'er Springs brief bloom, Hermes the harbinger.

Birth-bare, not death-bare yet, the young stems stand,
  This Lady's temple-columns: o'er her head
  Love wings his shaft. What mystery here is read
Of homage or of hope? But how command
  Dead Springs to answer? And how question here
  These summers of that wind-withered New-Year?

Attached to this sonnet in the first edition, is the note: "The same lady, here surrounded by the masque of Spring, is evidently the subject of a portrait by Botticelli, formerly in the Pourtalès collection in Paris. This portrait is inscribed 'Smeralda Bandinelli.'" Rossetti here alludes to the painting which he had acquired in 1867, and which he regarded as a genuine work of the master; although it is now generally admitted to be an admirable production of his school.

Meanwhile, an essay by Walter Pater, entitled "A Fragment on Sandro Botticelli," had appeared in the "Fortnightly Review," for August, 1870, and was reprinted in 1873, in the first edition of his "Studies in the History of the Renaissance." Although the "legend" of the painter, as told by Vasari, goes unchallenged in this essay, (indeed, one of the main contentions of its writer turns on the mistaken attribution to Sandro of the Palmieri altar-piece,) it remains the subtlest and most suggestive appreciation of Botticelli, in a personal way, which has yet been written. The apologetic touch with which this "Fragment" draws to a close,—"Is a painter like Botticelli, a secondary painter, a subject for general criticism?"—may serve to remind us how largely this very essay has contributed towards the discovery of the unique place which Botticelli holds among the great masters of the Renaissance.

The appearance of this "Fragment" was followed by the publication, in 1873, of "Ariadne Florentina," containing six lectures on wood and metal engraving, which Ruskin had delivered, as Slade Professor, at Oxford, the previous year. The last of these lectures, on "Design in the Florentine Schools of Engraving," is, in effect, a criticism of Botticelli. Although Ruskin starts out with the fantastic assumption that the prints of the Sibyls and Prophets, traditionally associated with the name of Baccio Baldini, had been designed by Sandro, as studies for an unrealized project for the decoration of the vault of the Sistine chapel, he does not fail to say many admirable and suggestive things by the way, concerning the painter and his work. Both this book and "Mornings in Florence," published some two years later, in which Ruskin again returns to speak of Sandro, were widely read, and contributed not a little (though nothing was further from the intention of their writer) to bring about that peculiarly English cult of Botticelli, which now became a distinctive trait of a phase of thought and taste, or of what passed for such, as odd and extravagant as any of our odd and extravagant time. With the "Aesthetic Movement" and the classic epoch of "1880," the name of Botticelli grew to be a catch-word among persons for whom early Italian Art could never possess any real significance. And so it became possible for Mr. Du Maurier to perpetrate his joke in "Punch," (I quote like the prophets,) of the reproof of the one young man of fashion to the other, who when asked if he liked Botticelli, had replied that he preferred Chianti,—"Botticelli isn't a wine, you juggins, it's a cheese"; and for Mr. W. E. Henley in his verses, "Culture in the Slums," to make his hero, whose form was "the Bloomin' Utter," often do "a quiet read at Booty Shelly's poetry."

Throughout the last century, English collectors had shown a great partiality for the purely ornamental qualities of early Italian painting: the pictures of Botticelli and his school, like those of Crivelli, were sought out for their decorative beauty, before their finer and more artistic traits had been duly appreciated, or even realized. Hence, little or no attempt had been made to distinguish between the genuine works of Sandro, and those of his imitators. At the time, when Pater's essay first appeared in 1870, Botticelli was nominally represented at the National Gallery by three "Madonnas" of his school, two of them being "Tondi": and the only genuine works by him then in the collection, passed under the names of Masaccio, No. 626, and Filippino Lippi, No. 592. No wonder then that those "circular pictures, into which the attendant angels depress their heads so naively," those "peevish-looking Madonnas" who conform "to no acknowledged or obvious type of beauty,"—the school-pictures, in short, in which the imitators of Botticelli exaggerate his mannerisms, in the attempt to reproduce that peculiar sentiment which is inseparable from his personality and art, should have come to be regarded as the typical works of the master himself. And it was but natural that the bizarre vein of feeling, and the obvious, though very real, decorative qualities of such school-pieces, should appeal strongly to a time when an art, chiefly pre-occupied with detached ornament which had no direct relation to architecture, and with detached sentiment which had no direct relation to actual life,—

for such essentially was the art of Morris and Burne-Jones—was all the vogue.

Meanwhile, the scientific criticism of the Vasarian "legend," a criticism based alike upon connoisseurship and documentary research, had been slowly making progress. The research of documentary evidence had its beginnings in the publication of the "Carteggio inedito d'Artisti dei secoli XIV, XV, XVI," by Johan Gaye, at Florence, in 1839-40; and of the edition of Vasari's "Lives," copiously annotated by Vincenzo Marchese, Gaetano and Carlo Milanesi, and Carlo Pini, which was issued at Florence by Felice le Monnier, in 1845-57. The first critical account of Botticelli and his work appeared in "A New History of Painting in Italy, from the second to the sixteenth century," by J. A. Crowe and G. B. Cavalcaselle, published at London, in three volumes, in 1864-66. This work became "the foundation of all study of Italian painting," and has not yet been superseded. Although the chapter on Botticelli added much to our knowledge of the painter, it is not one of the more fortunate portions of the book. Not only do its writers fail to discriminate sufficiently between Sandro's authentic productions and those of his school, but they accept without sufficient discrimination, what had become the orthodox view of the painter. In the Sistine Chapel, for instance, they find "Sandro inferior to Domenico and to Perugino, and only preserving superiority over Cosimo Rosselli"; in the frescoes of St. Augustine and St. Jerome in the Church of Ognissanti, at Florence, Ghirlandaio, in their opinion, displays "more nobleness and decorum" than Botticelli. These are judgements, I think, which have since been reversed. At a later time, Sir J. A. Crowe sought to palliate, in some measure, this scant appreciation in a couple of articles which appeared in the "Gazette des Beaux-Arts," in 1886.

In the studies entitled "Die Werke italienischer Meister in den Galerien von München, Dresden und Berlin," which Giovanni Morelli first published at Leipzig in 1880, under the pseudonym of Ivan Lermolieff, and which afterwards appeared in a revised and amplified form, with the addition of a volume on the Borghese and Doria-Panfili Galleries, in 1890-93, a new spirit was introduced into the criticism, not only of Botticelli, but of all early Italian Art. Although much that Morelli had to say of Sandro was both acute and suggestive, he, too, was strangely mistaken in several of his judgements, but he gave a new impetus to such studies which has not yet died out. In 1893, the first monograph on Botticelli, by Dr. Hermann Ulmann, appeared at Munich. Since the publication of that book, "Lives" of the painter have appeared in English, German, French, and Italian; and the number of scattered essays and studies, already formidable at that time, has increased tenfold.

In the present volume I have endeavoured to bring together whatever throws any real light on the life, or work, of Sandro Botticelli, in a historical, antiquarian or aesthetic view; but without losing sight of the fact that the only valuable function of the connoisseur is to distinguish the genuine productions of a master (especially in the case of Sandro) from those of his imitators, and to disengage and note the significant qualities of such genuine works. In a future volume, I propose to discuss the productions both of his immediate disciples and of those painters who fell indirectly under his influence, or who were associated with him in some way or another; in short, the productions of his school in the widest sense of the word. This second volume will, also, contain a catalogue of all the known works of the master and his imitators, and a full index to both volumes.

I take this occasion to acknowledge my indebtedness to owners of paintings, and directors of galleries, too numerous to be mentioned here, who have afforded me facilities for studying, or photographing, the works of art in their possession, or keeping: to Sig. Eugenio Casanova, for much invaluable assistance when I first began my researches among the Florentine Archives; to Dr. Georg Gronau and Mr. William C. Ward, for references to printed books; to Dr. Warburg, for calling my attention to various inventories, and for help on several questions of archaeology; to Mr. Berenson, for notes of many school-pictures, for the loan of photographs, and for any hints which, in the course of conversation, I may unconsciously have taken from him and not elsewhere acknowledged; and, lastly, to my sister, for help in reading the proof-sheets.

This book has been written at leisure, during a period of many years, and with no other thought than to satisfy the curiosity of its writer. Perhaps, the student who has himself made the attempt, alone can appreciate the difficulty of writing such a book, upon such a plan, as this. The study of early Italian Painting is still at a stage of research and analysis. Much, indeed, has been found out since Crowe and Cavalcaselle first published their "History of Painting in Italy"; but much remains to be discovered. And until every field of research has been duly explored, any attempt at reconstruction must, of necessity, to some extent or another, prove to be of a provisional character. The student, then, will best understand me, if, with one of the earliest writers upon Florentine Art and a contemporary of Sandro's, I end these pages of introduction in the distich:

Si nunc errarem, fateor me errare libenter:
Nam sine censore, nullus in orbe fuit.

ALESSANDRO FILIPEPI, COMMONLY CALLED SANDRO BOTTICELLI, PAINTER OF FLORENCE.

ALESSANDRO, the Florentine painter, says Vasari, was "called according to our usage Sandro, and nicknamed 'di Botticello' for the reason which we shall presently see. He was the son of Mariano Filipepi, a Florentine citizen, by whom he was diligently brought up, and caused to be instructed in all those things, which are usually taught to children before they are placed at the workshops. Although he readily learned whatever he had a mind to, he was nevertheless always restless; nor would he content himself with his schooling at all, either with reading, writing, or arithmetic; so that his father, weary of this wilful humour, in despair put him to the craft of a goldsmith, with a gossip of his called Botticello, then a very competent master of the art. There was at that time a great familiarity, and almost a continuous intercourse, between the goldsmiths and the painters; by which means, Sandro, who was a ready youth, and wholly attracted to drawing, growing enamoured of painting, resolved to devote himself to it. So that having freely opened his mind to his father, who knew the bent of his inclination, he was taken by him to Fra Filippo of the Carmine, at that time a most excellent painter, and placed with him to learn the art, as Sandro himself desired."

Vasari, ed. 1568, I, 470.

Such is the one account of the youth of Sandro Botticelli which has come down to us; an account which Vasari prints in both his editions of the "Lives," without any material variation. Elsewhere, he adds that the painter died in the seventy-eighth year of his age, in the year 1515: "d'anni settantotto, l'anno 1515:" implying that he was born about the year 1437. Vasari's account went unquestioned until Johan Gaye, in 1839, cited a document in his "Carteggio inedito d'Artisti," according to which the birth of Botticelli took place about the year 1447: more recently the Florentine commentators of Vasari have shown that the death of Botticelli occurred in 1510. The document cited by Johan Gaye is one of the many "Portate al Catasto" returned at various periods by Mariano Filipepi, the painter's father, which, strangely enough, have hitherto remained unedited and unused, although they enable us to correct more than one statement of Vasari, and add not a little to our knowledge of the origin and earlier years of the painter. The "Portate," or "Denunzie al Catasto," as the returns, or declarations, to the officers of the taxing were variously called, date from the year 1427, when, in order to distribute with greater equality the burden of the heavy taxes, which were levied for the war with the Duke of Milan, it was enacted that henceforth the personal estate, to the value of a hundred florins and upwards, should be chargeable as well as the real: and because both kinds of property were then first "heaped together" for the purposes of assessment, for which the Florentines used the word "accatastare," this tax was called the "Catasto." In order to give effect to this new enactment, every citizen was required to make a declaration, according to a prescribed form, of his possessions in land, houses, goods, and money; his rents and charges; his debts and credits; together with an account of his family, under the official heading of "bocche," or mouths, for the maintenance of whom certain abatements were allowed: and upon this declaration or "Denunzia," his taxes were assessed.

Id., I, 474.

Vol. I, p. 343.

The "Denunzie" of Mariano Filipepi are preserved in the vast "Campioni," or registers, of the Gonfalone Unicorno, in the quarter of

Santa Maria Novella; each "gonfalone," or ward, being named after the banner and its charge, under which its citizens assembled. From these documents it appears that the father of Sandro Botticelli was a younger son of Giovanni, and a grandson of Amedeo, Filipepi; and that, like the father of St. Catherine of Siena, he was by trade a tanner, "choncjatore di cuoja, overo galigajo." Jacopo, one of the brothers of Mariano, followed the same calling, and the two brothers rented successively the same shop, if, indeed, they did not work together. The worthy, but distasteful, craft of Mariano may yet be seen practised with all the primitive art known to him, in the tanners' quarter, the Via delle Conce, at Florence; as at Siena, in Fontebranda, near the birthplace of St. Catherine. Mariano appears to have been born c. 1396-7, and his wife, Smeralda, c. 1403-4: but both their ages, and the ages of the other members of their family, are given so variously in these several "Denunzie," that it is not possible, for the most part, to determine them with any precision. On the "Denunzia" returned by Mariano in 1431, he compounded his taxes in a sum of three soldi: "Conpostosi dacordo Jn s*oldj* tre ao*ro*." On the "Denunzia" returned by him two years later, in 1433, he compounded in a sum of two soldi: "Chonposto In s*oldj* 2." His family had increased; another daughter had been born to him, and his means had decreased. He then rented a house in Borgo Ognissanti, at a yearly rental of ten florins, from one Durante, a retail cloth-dealer: the position of the house is not indicated. In this document the names, and ages, of himself and his family are given thus: "Mariano, annj 36; [Smeralda] sua donna, annj 27 [in error for 29]; Giovannj suo figluolo, annj 12; Antonio suo figluolo, annj 3; Lisa sua figluola, annj 7; Beatrice sua figluola, annj 1."

Appendix II, of the present volume, Document III. App. II, Doc. IV.

App. II, Doc. V.

According to a third "Denunzia" returned by Mariano some eight years later, his affairs had, meanwhile, gone from bad to worse. This document, which is of the briefest, is dated 17th August, 1451: the gist of it lies in a single, unfinished sentence. "Sustanza: No*n* si truoua nulla di vasente, siche abbiate p*er* rachomanda p*er* la pace dj . . .": as to his substance, nothing is found of value; and the rest of the sentence, which appears to be a recommendation to the "Signori Ufficiali del Catasto" that Mariano should not be troubled more about the matter, breaks off abruptly, as a thing not worth the writing. Perhaps, not too grave an interpretation should be placed on this document: the records of the "Catasto" show that the Florentine of the fifteenth century was not altogether unlike the Florentine of to-day, in his readiness to avoid the payment of his taxes. Meanwhile, in the interval which elapsed since the return of the "Denunzia" of 1433, Smeralda, amid circumstances which, if not actually necessitous, were of the slenderest kind, had borne her husband four other children, of which the youngest but one was Sandro.

App. II, Doc. VII.

Unlike this fragmentary declaration, a fourth "Denunzia" returned by Mariano in 1457, is a document of several folios, which throws no little light on the early years of the painter. It appears from a note written on the folio preceding this document, that it was returned "on the 18th day of February," 1457, that is, 1458, new style. "I find myself," says Mariano, "at the age of 65 years, able to make little at my craft [cholla mja arte posso pocho fare]; my wife of the age of 53 years. Giovanni, my son, a broker [sensale almonte], of the age of 37 years. Antonio, my son, works at the craft of a goldsmith [sta allorafo]: he had a salary of 25 florins a year, now when he has anything to do, he works as a journeyman, and I draw small profit by it. Simone, my son, of the age of 14 years, I am sending him to Naples with Pagolo Rucellai." Then follows the entry: "sandro mjo figlolo detta dannj 13 sta allegare ede malsano." The word "legare" is faded and indistinctly written; yet it certainly appears to be spelt in this way. And so the question arises, whether the phrase "sta allegare" is to be read literally "sta a legare," that is, "he works at book-binding;" or, as I think more probable, as an error for "sta allegere," that is, "sta a leggere," a phrase which I find used indifferently, in these "Denunzie," with the phrase "sta alla squola," that is, "he is at school." Had the former meaning been intended, the word, in all probability, would have been spelt with an h, "leghare." Moreover, the fact that the boy was in indifferent health, that his family were living in a villa without the city, and that his brother, Antonio, who was a year older than himself, had not, until then, been put to any occupation; all these circumstances tend to show that the passage in question should be read: "Sandro, my son, of the age of 13, is at his books and is in ill health." According to a later "Denunzia," one of Sandro's nephews was still at school, at the age of fourteen. Mariano continues his account of his family: "I have a girl of the age of 15 years, without a dowry. Another of the age of 10 years, who in time will have a dowry of 200 florins. And further Nera, the wife of Giovanni, my son, of the age of 17 years, and the said Giovanni has a daughter at nurse 5 months old, costing 1 florin the month."

In the former part of this "Denunzia," Mariano enumerates his various holdings. First, he says, there are two houses, which he held as dwelling houses; the one situated "in the quarter of Santa Croce, Gonfalone Bue," at a rent of 16 florins a year, "which house," he adds, "I have let at the same rent, until the feast of All Saints next, 1458, since I hold it till that time;" the other, in the quarter of Santa Maria Novella, Gonfalone Lionrosso," at a rent of 11 florins a year, the term of which "expired at the time of All Saints last past, 1457." Although the boundaries of these houses are given, in both cases the name of the street is omitted in which they stood. Meanwhile, for economy, perhaps, or for the health of his family, he had taken a villa: "a house situated in the parish of San Piero a Careggi, in which my family lives, or part of them, which I have hired from Ser Niccolo Valentini, at the rate of 6 florins the year; sanza sustanze," that is, without the produce of the farm, or "podere." The little church of San Pietro a Careggi lies a couple of miles beyond the Barriera del Romito: it was then approached by the Porta Faenza; and within the boundaries of its parish lay the famous villa of Cosimo de' Medici. "And further," Mariano continues, "I have a shop where I tan the leather, at the foot of the bridge at Santa Trinita, in the quarter of Santo Spirito, which is the property of Giovanni di Sandro Capponi, for which I pay 40 lire a year." The boundaries of the shop, which follow, have enabled me to identify it with the tanner's shop rented by Jacopo, the brother of Mariano Filipepi, in 1451, from the same landlord, and at the same rent. In the "Denunzia" of Jacopo, the boundaries of this shop are given thus: "ap*ri*mo via d*j* App. II,
lungharno aijº chiassolmo aiijº mª pichina." The shop, therefore, stood at Doc. VI.
the angle of a "chiasso," or alley, facing the Arno, at the foot of the Ponte Santa Trinita. The name, Chiasso Olmo, is no longer borne by any of the neighbouring streets, but I conjecture that that part of the present Via de' Coverelli, between the Via Santo Spirito and the Lungarno Guicciardini, which in the last century bore the name of Chiasso Coverelli, may have

originally borne this name, or an adjoining blind alley, which has been since built over.

Other portions of this "Denunzia" show that the slender circumstances, in which Mariano found himself shortly after the birth of his son Sandro, were not, perhaps, wholly due to the increasing needs of his family. He gives the names of eight debtors who together owe him some 100 florins; but these assets, he adds, are of small account, since "questj djsopra sono tuttj falljtj," these persons have all failed. On this "Denunzia" of 1457, he compounds his taxes in a sum of "s*oldj* tre ao*ro*," although he is allowed an abatement of 2,000 florins for the "x bocche," or mouths, which he has to feed; which was twice the amount of the abatement allowed him in 1431, when he compounded his taxes in a similar sum of 3 soldi. The more thriving condition to which the affairs of Mariano had, meanwhile, been brought, appear to have been largely due to the success of his eldest son, Giovanni, who was already on his way to become a prosperous broker. Indeed, although the "Denunzia" of 1457 is drafted in the name of Mariano, it was Giovanni, on whom the cares of the family had chiefly fallen, that actually made the return. This appears not only from the wording of the request with which the document closes: "p*r*ego chesemjnjate le boche emjo pad*r*e vec*c*hio ella fancjulla sanza dote;" but, also, from a note, on the folio preceding the "Denunzia," to the effect that it was returned on the 18th February by Botticello, the broker: "Ad*j* 18 d*j* feb*r*ajo *recho* Botticello sensale." This "Botticello sensale" and Giovanni are, without doubt, the same person. Not only has Signor Milanesi already declared that no memorial is to be found among the Florentine records of any goldsmith called "Botticello," as Vasari would have us to believe; but in a Latin document recording the sale by auction of certain lands and houses of Renato de' Pazzi, which had been confiscated to the State on account of his share in the Pazzi Conspiracy, the name of Giovanni occurs thus: "Johannes marianj vocatus botticello." The "Denunzia" of 1457, therefore, proves that while Sandro was still a boy of thirteen, and before he had been put to any trade, certainly before he had been put to the trade of a goldsmith, his elder brother, Giovanni, was commonly known by the nickname of "Il Botticello." To the present day, in the country around Florence, such nicknames, often bestowed in a way which is characteristic enough of Florentine humour, are frequently used in lieu of proper names. Nor is the meaning of Giovanni's nickname difficult to divine: whether, like Falstaff, he was "out of all compass, out of all reasonable compass," or whether he resembled the friends of the worthy Gianesse, who broached the "botticello di vin" in the opening verses of the "Beoni" of Lorenzo de' Medici, the point of the raillery remained much the same. As early as 1472, the painter is called "Sandro di Botticello;" and it is remarkable that in the same document, and in an entry of the same date, his elder brother, who was some seven or eight years his senior, is called by his proper name, Antonio di Mariano Filipepi. We have here, I think, an indication that Sandro was brought up by his brother Giovanni, rather than by Mariano, their "padre vecchio;" and so the boy became associated in the popular mind with "Il Botticello." At the time of Sandro's death, this nickname had come to be adopted as the surname of the family, as "de' Botticelli," or merely "Botticelli." Francesco Albertini in his "Memoriale," published in the year of the painter's death, alludes to him as "Sandro Bocticelli;" and in the endorsement of a

Vasari, ed. Sansoni, III, 310, note 1.

App. II, Doc. VIII.

App. II, Doc. XI, fol. 56 tergo, and fol. 5 tergo.

document of the year 1512, the painter's nephew, Mariano, is called "Mariano Botticellj."

Sandro's second brother, Antonio, is described in the "Denunzia" of 1457, as a journeyman goldsmith; but he appears to have chiefly followed the craft of a "battiloro," or beater of the gold-leaf which, at that time, was still largely used by the Florentine painters, not only for the gilding of the frames of their pictures, but also for the gold backgrounds, the aureoles, and other such embellishments. He belonged both to the "Arte della Seta," the Guild of the Silk Weavers, among whose members the "Orefici," or Goldsmiths, were enrolled; and to the "Compagnia di San Luca," the Painters' Company, which included many of the "battilori." The books of the Matriculations of the "Arte della Seta" record that he took the oath, upon matriculating as a goldsmith, on 20th May, 1462: "Antonius Mariani Amidei Vannis juravit pro aurifice die xx maii 1462." About this time, or perhaps earlier, Antonio seems to have set up as a master gold-beater, in partnership with others. Neri di Bicci, the Florentine painter, has recorded a business transaction which passed between himself and "Antonio di mariano battiloro echonpagnj," on 4th April, 1467, in his book of "Ricordi." Furthermore, the "Libro Rosso," an account-book of the "Compagnia di San Luca," shows that Antonio paid fees, as a "battiloro," to the guild in 1472, and again in 1482.

App. II, Doc. IX.

App. II, Doc. X, fol. 124.

App. II, Doc. XI, fol. 5 tergo, and 6 recto.

Thus it would seem that Vasari's story of how Sandro became attracted to painting, like his explanation of the name "Botticello," is not so much a mere stroke of fiction, as a misconception; an actual piece of history mistaken in the tradition, as not a little that is erroneous in Vasari proves to be. It is by no means impossible that Sandro was actually put to the craft of a goldsmith, in the workshop of his brother Antonio; it is still more probable that, through Antonio, Sandro first fell under the spell of the painter's art, and became, as Vasari says, "enamoured of painting."

Simone, his third brother, who was but one year older than himself, appears to have passed the greater part of his life at Naples: he was still there in 1493, "in the service of a rich and very great merchant of our city," as he himself tells us. Shortly after that time he returned to Florence, where he became the intimate companion of his brother, Sandro, during the troubled times of Savonarola, of whose rise and death Simone has left a "Chronicle."

P. Villari, etc., Scelta di Prediche di Savonarola, p. 459.

Since Johan Gaye cited in his "Carteggio inedito," the "Denunzia" of 1480, which states that Botticelli was then thirty-three years of age, the date of his birth has been invariably given as 1447. But, according to the "Denunzia" of 1457, he was born some three years earlier. Of such contradictions these "Denunzie" are full; everywhere they furnish proofs of the carelessness of the Florentines about such details. Moreover, Giovanni, who drafted the "Denunzia" of 1480, appears to have put down the ages of the various members of his family from memory. Thus, he states that his brother Simone was "of the age of 40 years or thereabouts," "deta dannj 40 in circha," but in the earlier "Denunzia" of 1457 he had stated that Simone was but one year older than Sandro. Again, it is difficult to think that Giovanni, in drafting the "Denunzia" of 1457, would have made a mistake in regard to the ages of four children who were severally of 15, 14, 13, and 10 years. Every circumstance and probability points to the earlier "Denunzia," as the weightier authority on this point of Sandro's age. And if the statement of this earlier "Denunzia," that

Sandro had at that time, 18th February, 1457-8, completed his thirteenth year, is to be understood literally, it follows that he was born during the twelve months which began on the 18th February, 1444. For the rest, there is no reason to doubt Vasari's statement that Botticelli's schooling was of that elementary kind, which the son of a working tanner would ordinarily have received in Florence, in the fifteenth century: his real education began in the workshops of the painters.

ed. Sansoni, II, 627. App. II, Doc. I, fol. 49 tergo & Doc. II, fol. 83 recto.

Vasari, ed. Sansoni, II, 87-9.

Cavalcaselle and Crowe, ed. Le Monnier, V, 188.

G. Guasti, Quadri di Prato, p. 48.

Vasari, ed. Sansoni, III, 490.

The assertion of Vasari that Botticelli was the disciple of Fra Filippo Lippi: "stette con fra Filippo, in sua giouentù, Sandro Botticelli," is borne out by two of the writers who preceded him, by Antonio Billi according to the epitome of the "Codice Petrei," and the "Anonimo Gaddiano." Although the many paintings which have come from the workshop of the Frate, do not contain so much as a figure, or even an accessary passage, which could be ascribed to Botticelli, there is better evidence that Fra Filippo was the master from whom, as a boy, he learned the elements of his art, in the way in which the influence of that painter reasserts itself in the forms and technical methods of Botticelli's pictures, when he comes to mature his manner, after freeing himself from the conflicting influences of his youth. Whether we altogether reject Vasari's story of Sandro and the goldsmith, or whether we attempt to reconcile it in some way or another, with the "Denunzia" which Mariano returned in January, 1457-8, we are led to conclude that Botticelli was placed with Fra Filippo at no great interval after that date. Such documents as the "Ricordi" of Neri di Bicci, show that a boy was commonly placed with a painter, "per discepolo," at the age of thirteen, and often at the age of ten or eleven; but rarely after his fourteenth year. The latest date, then, at which the apprenticeship of Botticelli with Fra Filippo could well be placed, would be the year 1459. At that time Fra Filippo was living, unconcerned as ever, amid all those scandals and disorders which his "beati amori," or his other and less pardonable indiscretions, had brought upon him. He had then settled for some years at Prato, where he had first gone for the purpose of painting in fresco the choir of the Pieve, now the Cathedral. The commission for these paintings appears to have been given to him shortly after Messer Gemignano Ingherami became "Proposto," in 1451: in a document of 29th May, 1452, Fra Filippo is already alluded to as the painter, "che dipigne la chapela del altar magore." In 1455, he bought from the wardens of the "Opera" of the "Sacro Cingolo," the house near the Cathedral at Prato in which he chiefly lived and worked during the remainder of his life, and to which Sandro must have come as a boy. When the Via Magnolfi was constructed in 1865, the fabric of this house was incorporated in the new building, marked by a modern inscription, at the beginning of the street. Meanwhile, the frescoes in the choir at Prato, which had proceeded well enough for a time, appear to have been gradually brought to a standstill through a series of interruptions. In 1455, we hear of the lawsuit begun by the painter's assistant, Giovanni da Rovezzano, for the recovery of his salary; of the consequent confession of Fra Filippo, when put to the torture, that he himself had forged what purported to be the quittance given by Giovanni, for the sum in dispute; and of the brief of Calixtus II., pouring the pains and penalties of the Church upon the head of the luckless painter, "qui plurima et nefanda scelera perpetravit." Next, it appears from certain letters preserved among the Medicean archives, that Fra Filippo was at Florence, from the earlier part of the year 1457, until the spring of 1458, working on certain paintings at the instance of Giovanni di Cosimo de' Medici. An erroneous interpretation has, certainly, been placed upon these letters, both by the Florentine commentators of Vasari, and by Messrs. Cavalcaselle and Crowe, who print them at length in their new edition; it is, however, an easier matter to point to their mistakes, than to put a correct interpretation upon the documents, which are both obscure and fragmentary. The whole of the four letters refer, in part at least, to the same picture, a triptych executed by Fra Filippo for the King of Naples. The first of these letters is addressed by the painter to Giovanni de' Medici, at Fiesole, at whose instance the commission was procured: it is dated 20th July, 1457, and is signed, "Frate filippo dipintore in firenze." "The Saint Michael," writes the painter, "is in such perfection that, since his armour is to be of silver and gold, as also his wings and dress, I have been about it to Bartolommeo Martelli: he said he would speak with Ser Francesco about the gold and what I have need of; and that I should do everything in accordance with your wish; and he reproved me greatly, declaring that I had acted wrongly towards you. Now, Giovanni, I am here to be your slave in everything, and I will work to good purpose. I have had from you fourteen florins, and I wrote to you that there would be thirty florins of expense, and it must be so, because [the picture] is fine with ornaments." In this vein, the painter continues: he has no money; and he prays that he may not be hindered on that account: for three days he has done no work. In conclusion, Fra Filippo says that the cost of the picture, entirely finished, will be sixty florins, including the woodwork, the gold, the gilding and the painting; and that it shall be finished, "for his own part," by the 20th August. "And," he adds, "in order that you may be properly informed [as to the price asked for the picture], I send you the design according to which the woodwork has been made, with the height and the breadth." On the lower margin of the letter, Fra Filippo has sketched a triptych in a Gothic frame. In the central panel the Virgin is seen kneeling, with two angels by her side, in adoration of the Young Child: in the wings are two other kneeling figures; in the left wing a monk, and in the right a partially nude figure of a saint. Whether the latter figure is intended for the St. Michael alluded to in the first part of this letter, as Messrs. Cavalcaselle and Crowe have suggested, or whether the St. Michael formed part of a different painting, is a point not to be decided: the sequel, however, seems clearly to show that the triptych was the painting executed for the King of Naples. From a passage in another letter, of the 31st August, 1457, addressed by Francesco Cantansanti, the "Ser Francesco" of the former letter, to Giovanni de' Medici, at Cafaggiuolo, it appears that the picture was still unfinished, although the time fixed by the painter for its completion had gone by. Fra Filippo, writes Cantansanti, owes for the gilding of the tabernacle-work of the panel. "I have urged him on every day; till Saturday evening I stayed with him an hour to make him work. [Some work yet] remained for him to do; afterwards, as I parted from him, he took what was done [? gli prese quel fatto] and went home, and yesterday evening whipped himself off. Those things [*i.e.* the various parts of the unfinished picture] remain in pledge for the rent. I leave this tangle to Serragli [the agent for the King of Naples in the matter] to unravel; if not, at my return, I will try my hand at it myself. But see at what peril the man goes!" In the event,

Cavalcaselle and Crowe, ed. Le Monnier, V, 162, note 1, and 163, note 1.

the picture was redeemed, finished, and sent to Naples; for on 27th May, 1458, Giovanni de' Medici writes to Bartolommeo Serragli at Naples: "I have had your letters some days past, by which I understand that you have presented the picture to the King's Majesty, and that it has greatly pleased him: and so of the error of Fra Filippo we have laughed a good while." The allusion, I think, is plainly to some escapade of the painter in which the picture was involved; and not, as Messrs. Cavalcaselle and Crowe would have us believe, to the abduction of Lucrezia Buti. In a fourth letter, of 10th June, 1458, Giovanni de' Medici writes that another picture might, with management, be obtained from the painter, "especially now that Fra Filippo has been obliged to return to Prato."

The researches of modern criticism have done much to dispel the romance of Vasari's story of how Fra Filippo, taken by "the beautiful air and grace" of Lucrezia Buti, the nun of Santa Margherita, contrived at length, "per via di mezzi e di pratiche," to carry her off, on the feast of the "Sacro Cingolo," from the convent on the great Piazza del Mercatale, of which Fra Filippo had been appointed chaplain. Signor Milanesi has
Vasari, ed. Sansoni, II, 633. published in his commentary on Vasari's "Life of Fra Filippo," many valuable documents relating to this period of the painter's career; but here, as elsewhere, that distinguished archivist did not think it always necessary to clearly distinguish between statements founded upon documentary evidence, and statements which were merely conjectural. In order to reconcile Vasari's story with the evidence of contemporary documents, Signor Milanesi would have us believe that Fra Filippo, being chaplain of Santa Margherita, contrived to carry off Lucrezia Buti from the convent, on the feast of the "Sacro Cingolo," 1st May, 1456; that Lucrezia lived with the painter in his house, near the convent, for nearly two years; that Filippino was born there in 1457; and that, in spite of these open irregularities, Fra Filippo not only escaped ecclesiastical censure, but was allowed to retain his chaplaincy of the convent for several years, in spite of renewed complaints against him. Such a state of things was, I think, improbable even in Italy in the fifteenth century; nor does this attempt to recast Vasari's story really accord with the documents, which Signor Milanesi discovered, when we come to examine them.

Id., II, 634. We have it on the evidence of these documents that Lucrezia Buti, and her sister, Spinetta, were the daughters of a small shopkeeper in Florence, who died in 1450, leaving twelve children by his second wife. Antonio, the eldest son of this marriage, on whom the burden of this numerous family was cast, succeeded in marrying one of his sisters, but not meeting with the same good fortune in regard to the others, sent Lucrezia and Spinetta, shortly before 1454, to be nuns in the Franciscan convent of Santa Margherita, on the Piazza Mercatale, at Prato; a life for
Id., II, 636. which they did not possess the least vocation. We know, also, that on the 23rd December, 1459, Lucrezia and her sister, Spinetta, with three other nuns of Santa Margherita, in the habits of their order, with their heads veiled, and lighted candles in their hands, renewed the vows of their order, "et solepniter promiserunt &c. stabilitatem, conversionem suorum morum et castitatem, et obedientiam debitam, &c., facere et observare." This reformation of the manners of the convent proved, however, to be rather in form, than in fact and in deed. On the 8th May, 1461, a "tamburazione,"
Id., II, 637. or secret accusation, sent anonymously, as the Florentine custom was, to the "Ufficiali di Notte e Monasteri," states that the procurator of the

monastery of Santa Margherita had had a child born to him in the convent, who had been secretly sent out of the city by night, and the next morning carried back to Prato to be baptized; and, the informer adds, Fra Filippo, the chaplain, has had a male child by one of the nuns called Spinetta, and this child is in his house, and is growing up [è grande], and is named Filippino. That Fra Filippo was still chaplain of the monastery, and that the birth of Filippino was not, as this document shows, a thing generally known—indeed, the informer himself supposes Lucrezia's sister to have been the mother—are circumstances which suggest that Fra Filippo used the surreptitious and cautionary methods in this intrigue adopted by the procurator, rather than the romantic, but perilous, mode which Vasari imputes to him. Vasari says that Filippino was ten years old at the time of his father's death, and that he died at the age of forty-five: in other words, that he was born in 1459. Signor Milanesi conjectured, though on what grounds he has omitted to say, that Filippino was born in 1457. One piece of evidence which has been adduced to bear upon the point, is the supposition that the phrase in Giovanni de' Medici's letter of 27th May, 1458, "lo errore di Fra Filippo," refers to the seduction of Lucrezia Buti; an hypothesis, it seems to me, which is entirely gratuitous. If Signor Milanesi's conjecture be correct, the seduction of Lucrezia must have taken place in 1456; and, therefore, it is unlikely that Giovanni de' Medici would have thus alluded to it, in a letter written nearly two years afterwards, in 1458. What slight indications we have, go to bear out the conjecture that 1457 is the true date of Filippino's birth. Finally, we are led to surmise, with Signor Milanesi, that, in spite of Vasari's assertion to the contrary, Pius II., the delightful and humanistic Aeneas Sylvius, granted the painter a dispensation, releasing him and Lucrezia from their religious obligations, and allowing them to take one another as lawful man and wife; for in 1465 a daughter, named Alessandria, was born to him, and in 1466 his assistant, Fra Diamante, had succeeded him in the chaplaincy of the monastery of Santa Margherita.

Vasari, ed. Sansoni, II, 629, and III, 475.

Id., II, pp. 629, 637-8 and 640.

This digression, if it has served no other purpose, has enabled us to catch by the way, "glimpse-wise," some unmistakable traits in the character of the painter who profoundly, and ineradicably, left his impress on Botticelli's genius; who determined so much in his life, not only as an artist, but as a man. What colours do these dusty documents show at the light, even of this distant day! What contradictions, as some may think, are there between the man as we here catch sight of him, and the painter as we see him in his works! Perhaps, after all, that inordinate love of pleasure, which stopped at nothing to gratify itself, and to which all his faults and failings are to be traced, was but the counterpart of that sensuous preoccupation with mere physical beauty, grave and exquisite as it always was, which finally distinguishes his art, in spite of its ostensible character. But I stay too long in coming to discuss the paintings which Fra Filippo is known to have executed at this time.

In February, 1459-60, Fra Filippo undertook to paint a Virgin and Child, with certain saints, in four lunettes, "above the vault, which is above the tomb of Messer Gimignano" Inghirami, in the cloister of San Francesco, at Prato; a work which has unfortunately perished. These frescoes were proceeding during June and July, 1460; the painter having undertaken to finish them by September. The same year, Messer Carlo de' Medici became "Proposto" of Prato on the death of Messer Gimignano Inghirami; and the work of painting the choir of the Pieve appears to have been presently

G. Guasti, I Quadri di Prato, p. 108.

resumed. But even then Fra Filippo, in his wonted fashion, appears to have made slow progress with these frescoes; for on the 6th April, 1464, the persons deputed to overlook the accounts, reported that there was little prospect that he would finish the work, unless Messer Carlo intervened; and they proposed that the painter should be bound to complete the frescoes by the following August. The whole work was probably finished by the end of the year, or the beginning of 1465. To this time must be ascribed the lower series of stories: the "Beheadal of St. John the Baptist," and "Salome dancing before Herod," in cornu epistolae, and the "Stoning and Burial of St. Stephen," in cornu evangelii. The portrait of Messer Carlo de' Medici, appointed "Proposto" in 1460, which the painter has introduced into the "Burial of St. Stephen," and the marked difference in manner between these lower stories and the upper paintings, go together to determine their date. That Botticelli acquired the grammar of his art from Fra Filippo, while these frescoes were in the course of execution, is, perhaps, the only thing that can be asserted about him, at this time, with any certainty. The influence of these frescoes is to be traced, in an unmistakable way, in all Botticelli's earliest history-pieces, and especially in the pictures of the "Adoration of the Magi" in the National Gallery at London, and in the Gallery of the Uffizi, not only in their execution, but also in their design and composition. But in order to fully understand the influence of the master upon the disciple, it is necessary to take a more general view of Fra Filippo's art than is afforded by the frescoes at Prato.

Vasari, ed. Sansoni, II, 625, note 1.

Every writer on Florentine painting, following Vasari, had assumed that Fra Filippo was a disciple of Masaccio, until Mr. Berenson pointed out that Fra Filippo's pictures show some late Giottesque painter, probably Don Lorenzo Monaco, to have been his first master. When Masaccio came to the Carmine, c. 1427, to continue the paintings in the Brancacci Chapel, begun by Masolino, Fra Filippo, then a young man of twenty-one, must have already become an accomplished painter. The pictures of Lorenzo Monaco reveal his influence upon Fra Filippo in many ways; in the type of his Madonnas, the forms of his hands, the composition of his "predella" panels: and the splendid choir-book filled with miniatures by Don Lorenzo and his school, in the Laurentian Library at Florence, shows that Fra Filippo owed much of his art as a colourist, to this master. Like Ghiberti, Lorenzo Monaco fell under the spell of those incomparable masters of decoration, the Sienese painters. Parallel, but how removed from the perfunctory art of the Giottesque painters of Florence, the art of Siena presents the unique spectacle in Italy, of manner fastidiously refined upon manner, during a period of more than two centuries, but constantly, with an individual hand, and with distinguished taste. Like Ghiberti, Lorenzo Monaco learned the secret of the nervous, undulating, rhythmical line of the Sienese painters, imitating it with a grace of his own: and it is this quality of line, like a strain of the blood which reasserts itself in an after-generation, that recurs with a new significance, and a finer power of expression, in the paintings of Botticelli.

Florentine Painters, ed. 1896, p. 44.

Fra Filippo, in his youth, fell deeply under the influence of Fra Angelico, as we see in the lovely "tondo" of the "Adoration of the Magi," in the collection of Sir Francis Cook at Richmond; but it is chiefly through the influence of Masaccio that he becomes one of the masters of the new "Naturalistic" school in Florence. Unlike Masaccio, who so transmutes the old methods of the Giottesque painters that they become for him, as for Paolo Uccello, a new form of pictorial expression, Fra Filippo elaborates and refines upon them, till they grow perfectly expressive of his ideas. For him, this new "Naturalism" is but a graft on the old Giottesque stock. But before I attempt to make my meaning clear, let me indicate, by the way, in what sense the term of "Naturalism" is applicable to that school of Florentine painters in the fifteenth century which had its rise in Masaccio. Such a term, like that of "Realism," is commonly used by us to denote the aim of certain modern painters to render the effect of some particular "show" of Nature, with all that is accidental to it under particular conditions: that, at least, is the central idea lying, it may be, beyond many other lesser distinctions, which we would commonly convey by such a term. But, in this sense, the term is in no wise applicable to the school of Masaccio: on the contrary, the "Naturalism" of the Florentine painters, to borrow the phrases of Leonardo da Vinci, lies in the endeavour so to order the "inventions of the imagination," when the artist comes to express them by design, "that nothing is left in the work which is not sanctioned by reason and by the effects of Nature." And so that idea of universality, which dominated all antique art, lies at the root of the "Naturalistic" art of Florence, in the fifteenth century. Plotinus, thinking of the Greeks, says: "We must know that the arts do not merely imitate that which is apparent to the senses, but recur to the principles from which Nature herself proceeds; and further, that they do many things from themselves alone, and supply what is wanting to perfection, as possessing in themselves the Beautiful;" and Leonardo, thinking of Florentine painting, says: "Il dipintore disputa e gareggia colla natura."

L. da Vinci, Literary Works, I, 252.

Ennead V, Bk. 8, Sec. I.

L. da Vinci, Literary Works, I, 332.

We must turn to the studies and sketches of a painter, and especially to those of a Florentine master, whose paintings are essentially but coloured drawings, or rather cartoons, if we would trace the characters of his art to their source. Just as a writer, in an occasional letter, is discovered in his undress; so in a sketch, or study, we take a painter unawares, without his disguises, his premeditated effects: we see him as he is in himself. The genuine drawings of Fra Filippo are as rare, as those which bear his name are numerous. Three only are known to me, which could be attributed to him with any degree of certainty: the drawing in silver-point, on a red ground, of a draped female figure in the British Museum, among the drawings of the Malcolm collection, No. 6; a drawing to which Mr. Berenson has called my attention, in the Museum at Hamburg, a composition of several figures in pen-and-wash, of a saint casting out a devil; and the sketch of a triptych on the margin of the letter of 20th July, 1457, addressed by Fra Filippo to Giovanni de' Medici, which has already been described. It is preserved in the Archivio di Stato at Florence, among the "Carteggio Mediceo innanzi il Principato," Filza VI, No. 258. Slight and faded as it is, this little drawing is, perhaps, the most important piece of evidence which we possess, of the real nature of Fra Filippo's influence over Botticelli. It is drawn with the pen, with an admirable ease and precision of touch. Unlike the sketches of Domenico Ghirlandaio, or Andrea Verrocchio, and their followers, the delicate, unbroken stroke of the pen is here used only to express actual form, without the use of shading, or cross-hatching, in order to render relief. The little sketch for a figure of "Fortitude," in the "Libro Resta" at Milan, one of the earliest, extant drawings by Botticelli, technically differs in nothing from this little sketch by Fra Filippo; and the splendid series of pen-drawings, which Botticelli executed at a somewhat later time, in illustration to the "Divina Commedia," though more elaborately designed, are done, precisely, in the same technical method. Certainly, these drawings in illustration to Dante show that one of the chief secrets of Botticelli's art lay in the power, which he possessed in an unrivalled way, of representing by definite, linear form, a mental image as it rises in the mind, with that vivid sense of reality which is the prerogative of a great imagination. All that was communicable in that way of drawing, Botticelli acquired from Fra Filippo, both in the use and the quality of his line. The parallel might be carried farther in the case of the pen-drawing at Hamburg, by Fra Filippo, and such a drawing by Botticelli as the figure of St. John the Baptist in the Uffizi, Frame 55, No. 188; but it is enough to have suggested the comparison.

Passing from the drawings to the paintings of Fra Filippo, especially those which he executed after he recovered himself from the influence of Masaccio, and reverted more nearly to the forms and technical methods of the Giottesque master from whom he acquired his art, we see how largely the habit, shown in the drawings, of conceiving and defining form in terms of pure line, goes to determine the execution of the paintings; and how the modelling is but an additional means of expression to the precise, linear definition of the forms. Unlike Masaccio and Paolo Uccello, who break away from this linear, Giottesque tradition of draughtsmanship in their attempt to render the mass of a figure entirely by its relief, Fra Filippo remains, in the middle of the fifteenth century, a painter of Giottesque descent, not only in his method of draughtsmanship, but also in many of his forms, such as his hands and draperies, the rocky backgrounds of his pictures, the convention of his trees; and these, precisely, are among the characters of his art which Botticelli seizes upon, and imitates, in his own works. It is in his use of line, especially in the contours of his heads and hands, in the subordination of the modelling to this linear definition, and still more in the forms of his draperies, which descend in long unbroken curves to the feet, and fall sharply on the ground in broad, angular folds (forms of a purely Giottesque origin), that Botticelli most plainly reveals from whom he acquired the elements of his art. Other influences, especially in the earlier part of his career, obscure, and even disguise the influence of Fra Filippo, but technically Botticelli always remained his disciple.

As yet, I have only touched upon some of the external characters of Fra Filippo's art which went to determine the genius of Botticelli, but these were not the only traits of the master which left their impress upon the disciple. "Fu fra Philippo," says Christoforo Landino, "gratioso et ornato et artificioso sopra modo:" Fra Filippo was full of grace and ornament and art, beyond any of his time. True it is, that he paints always God, and the Mother of God, and his saints, as becomes a religious; but the ostensible subjects of his paintings veil the real interests of the artist, as scantily as the habit of the monk hides the real nature of the man, which peeps out in him like one of those odd faces, half-imp, half-angel, which peep out from the corners of his pictures. He is the first among the Florentine masters to paint for its own sake that beauty of the creature,

"Whose action is no stronger than a flower:"

and he paints it with an incomparable sense of its charm and delicacy, as becomes an age that has sought to fashion itself after the blithe, humanistic civilization of the antique world. And yet the clean air of the cloister clings to him in spite of himself; in spite of himself he remains the child of Lorenzo Monaco and the Beato Angelico; and he depicts this beauty of the creature as it were some outward manifestation of the spirit. That "Sacred Conversation" of the Medicean saints, seated in a row, is one of the lovelier possessions of our National Gallery; and in those frail, flower-like people, whose characters we seem to tell like the characters of flowers, we have a perfect example of the etherealized, but earthly, beauty which Fra Filippo delighted to paint. That "appetito di bellezza," to use a phrase of Lorenzo, Il Magnifico, which led Fra Filippo to make all his paintings "beautiful with ornament," in the delicately imagined vestments of his saints and angels, their rosy garlands and lily wands, the ordered cloisters and chambers, the cool, green woods where they walk, the flowers carpetting the earth, or growing between the crannies of the rocks; all that sentiment of beauty, Botticelli also inherited from his master. In what manner this delicate and ornate temper reasserts itself in Botticelli's work, and in what degree he was influenced by Fra Filippo as a colourist, I shall show as I come to discuss his earlier pictures. But although Fra Filippo was perhaps the greatest colourist among the Florentine painters of the fifteenth century, his influence in this regard over Botticelli is of all such traits the hardest to distinguish.

It has lately become the fashion among certain critics of Italian art to deny that Fra Filippo was the master of Botticelli; and recently Dr. Richter has gone so far as to assert that he must have learned his art from Pesellino. Although the "Denunzia," returned by Mariano Filipepi in 1457, sufficiently controverts such an opinion, since Pesellino died on 29th July, 1457, when Botticelli was still a boy at school, I would point out that none of the peculiar forms of Pesellino are to be traced in any of the drawings or paintings of Botticelli. Both the evidence of documents, and the internal evidence of Botticelli's own pictures, entirely go to prove that Vasari was preserving a real tradition when he wrote in his garrulous way that Botticelli, "giving himself wholly" to the art of painting, "followed and imitated his master in such a manner, that Fra Filippo conceived an affection for him, and taught him to such good purpose, that he rapidly arrived at a height which none would have foretold."

ed. 1550, I, 491.

Of the earliest years of Botticelli's career, when he was wholly the disciple of Fra Filippo, nothing is extant; but there remains one very early painting, an "Adoration of the Magi," in the National Gallery at London, No. 592, in which the influence of Fra Filippo far outweighs any other. This painting was one of thirty-one pictures which were bought at Florence, out of the Lombardi-Baldi collection, in 1857, for £7,035. It had previously been in the collection of the Marchese Ippolito Orlandini, at Florence, in the Palazzo Orlandini del Beccuto, in the Via de' Buoni, adjoining the church of Santa Maria Maggiore. In the National Gallery, this picture still bears the name of Filippino Lippi, although Morelli long since pointed out that it was unquestionably by the hand of Sandro Botticelli. In the Palazzo Orlandini, it bore, with far more reason, the name of Fra Filippo Lippi. The picture is painted on a panel, measuring 1 ft. 8 in. in height, and 4 ft. 7 in. in length; and no doubt formed the decoration of some piece of furniture, though not necessarily of a "cassone," or coffer. It is, unfortunately, in an indifferent

Italian Masters in German Galleries, ed. 1883, p. 236.

F. Fantozzi, Guida, p. 488.

state of preservation: the original pureness and clarity of its colouring is much darkened by heavy, brown varnish; the surface has been much scaled by over-cleaning, and in many places the picture has suffered from repainting. Many of the heads, for example, to the left of the composition, have been coarsely retouched.

Botticelli painted the "Adoration of the Magi" many times. Besides this picture, four other versions by his hand have come down to us; and of a sixth we possess some partial copies. In this early painting alone does he observe the traditional composition of the scene, placing the Virgin in profile, with the young Child and St. Joseph by her side, on the extreme right of the picture, as the Magi with their followers approach them from the other side. The scene is contrived within the ruin of an antique building, against whose slender marble piers has been built the rude pent-roof of the stall, where the Virgin has laid her first-born. One of the Magi, bowed to the earth, kisses the foot of the holy Child, as a courtly page by his side looks upward in astonishment at the star that had gone before them, "till it came and stood over where the young child was." Round about these wise men, stand their counsellors in solemn, stole-like raiment, and their courtiers and pages in rich habits of the time; and to the left of the picture, through the narrow defile of the rocky gorge which forms the background of the picture, still presses on their splendid and innumerable retinue. For these kings from the East have come (in the phrases of a religious writer of the time, who is describing such a scene out of Holy Writ), "in su grandi chaualli, et con molta compagnia et leggiadra giente, diuedere le nouitade": as some prince, or cardinal, would have come to Florence, to make his offering at the Servi, attended by a great rout of followers in gay, Burgundian habits. On the other side of the picture, in contrast to all the press and stir of this worldly crowd, St. Joseph, warned of the angel in a dream, leans in meditation upon his staff, knowing "all this was done, that it might be fulfilled which was spoken of the Lord by the prophet;" while beside him, unobserved, two shepherds with their bagpipes and mountain-horn break in upon the scene.

In this, perhaps the earliest of his extant paintings, Botticelli already appears an artist of immense accomplishment: few of the works of his maturer years surpass this early picture in the beauty and invention of its composition. "Fu copioso di figure nelle storie," says Vasari of him: and into this painting he introduces some threescore figures, without confusion, and without loss of pictorial effect. In the design of all the central part of the picture, in the large composition of the draped figures which stand around the Magi, in the group of the Virgin and St. Joseph, the influence of the painter of the fresco of the "Burial of St. Stephen," in the choir at Prato, is unmistakable; and yet there is a certain largeness and sculpturesque simplicity of relief which is beyond anything to be found in the frescoes at Prato, and which directly recalls the master who had inspired Fra Filippo in their design. Vasari relates that "Sandro di Botticello" was one of the many Florentine painters who in their youth studied the frescoes of Masaccio in the Brancacci Chapel in the Carmine; and, indeed, in the bowed figure of the Magi who kneels before the Virgin in Botticelli's picture, we seem to detect a reminiscence of the then unfinished fresco of the "Raising of the King's Son." But an examination of this "Adoration of the Magi" in greater detail, shows that the influence of the painter's first master is the predominating element in it.

Vasari, ed. Sansoni, III, 323.

Id., II, 299.

THE ADORATION OF THE MAGI *National Gallery, London*

The head of the Virgin, the whole conception of the figure of St. Joseph, the motive of the shepherds, the design of the ruined wall and pent-roof, and especially the forms of the long, flowing draperies of the Magi and their courtiers, have, among other things, been directly imitated from Fra Filippo. In the figure of the last of the Magi, who stands with his back turned to the spectator, the bunched draperies, and the long fold descending in an unbroken curve to the heel, may be cited as forms especially characteristic in this regard. On the other hand, there is everywhere running throughout the picture, an element which is left unexplained by the influence of Fra Filippo. The involved composition of the group of horsemen to the left of the panel, the types of many of the heads, with their sinuous contours, and accented modelling of the brow and cheek-bone, the forms of the horses, the rich habits of the time in which the pages and grooms are dressed, are among the more obvious traits and forms which mark the influence of a painter of a very different character to Fra Filippo, and for the interpretation of which we must elsewhere turn.

The writers who preceded Vasari, Francesco Albertini, Antonio Billi in the epitome of the "Codex Petrei," and the "Anonimo Gaddiano," all agree with him in recording that Botticelli painted one of the seven panels of the Theological and Cardinal Virtues, which formerly adorned the Hall of the Mercanzia, in Florence. "I omit to mention," says Francesco Albertini, writing in 1510, "the six figures of the Virtues which are in the Guild of the Mercanzia, by the hand of Piero Pollaiuoli: the seventh is by Sandro:" "Non fo mentione delle sei figure delle Virtu sono nellarte della Mercantia p*er* mano di Pietro pull. La septima e di Sa*n*dro." The epitomist of the "Codex Petrei" adds that the picture which Sandro painted was a "Fortitude," and that it was done by him in his youth: "fece da giouanetto nella merca*n*tia una forteza belliss[a]." Elsewhere this writer says that Piero Pollaiuoli executed the other six Virtues that were to be seen "in una spalliera in sala della Mercantia." The "Anonimo Gaddiano repeats these statements: Botticelli, he says, "dipinse nella merchata*n*tia la forteza, nella spalliera de sej, che l'altre sono dimano dipiero dell pollaiuolo." Vasari, writing in 1550, varies his account in one important particular: Botticelli, he says, "dipinse essendo giouanetto nella mercatantia di Fiorenza vna fortezza fra le tauole delle virtu, che Antonio, & Piero del Pollaiuolo lauorarono." And, again, he repeats in the life of the Pollaiuoli, that Antonio and Piero together "fecero nella Mercatantia di Fiorenza alcune virtù, in quello stesso luogo doue siede pro Tribunali il magistrato di quella." About few other pictures by Botticelli are so many early authorities in agreement, as about this panel of the "Fortitude."

Memoriale, fol. 6, recto.

App. II, Doc. I, fol. 49, tergo, & fol. 50, tergo.

App. II, Doc. II, fol. 83, tergo.

Vasari, ed. 1550, I, 491, & 500.

These seven pictures of the "Virtues," then, according to these authorities, were originally placed "nella spalliera di sei," in the wall-panelling above the bench, or tribunal, where the "Sei," or six magistrates, "used to sit for the hearing of causes" in the Hall of the Mercanzia. This court was erected, as the inscription over the door of the court-house in the Uffizi Lunghi has it, "mercatoribus ut bona fide agant:" in other words, it was a court for the trial of disputes arising out of commercial transactions. In the fifteenth century this court was held in the Hall of the Palace of the Mercanzia, an early Florentine building adorned with the arms of the Florentine "Arti," or Guilds, which still remains on the east side of the Piazza della Signoria, at the corner of the Via de' Gondi. Upon the completion of the "Uffizi," or Palace of the Public

Offices, from the designs of Vasari, during the latter part of the sixteenth century, the tribunal of the Mercanzia was removed to a new court-house in the Uffizi Lunghi, which is still marked by a marble bust of Christ above the doorway. The paintings of the "Virtues" were brought to this new court-house; and here they were seen in the seventeenth century by Giovanni Cinelli, who, in his edition of the "Bellezze di Firenze," published (p. 98.) in 1677, says that "in the court of the Mercatanzia are painted the Theological and Cardinal Virtues, by the hand of Antonio Pollaiuolo." On the suppression of the Mercanzia, in December, 1777, these pictures were taken to the gallery of the Uffizi, where for nearly a century they remained stored away in one of the magazines. At length, in 1861, they were thought worthy of a place in the gallery. Five of them are now hung together in the corridor: "Hope," No. 69; "Justice," No. 70; "Temperance," No. 71; "Faith," No. 72; and "Charity," No. 73; the other two are hung in the third Tuscan Room: "Prudence," No. 1306; and "Fortitude," No. 1299, the picture which all the earlier authorities ascribe to Botticelli. (Die Galerie Borghese, ed. 1890, p. 107.) Morelli went so far as to deny that Botticelli had any share in this picture; but he omitted to say on what grounds he based this opinion. Other critics have cast doubts upon the authorship of more than one early painting by Botticelli; while some have turned to Verrocchio, and even to Pesellino, to account for the influences which they found in them. None, however, has troubled to study methodically this painting of the "Fortitude," in the connection in which it occurs with the other "Virtues" of the Pollaiuoli. Briefly, then, the earlier phases of Botticelli's art become intelligible only in the light of the influence which Antonio Pollaiuoli exercised over him. But before that influence can be understood and estimated, it is necessary to rehabilitate the character of Antonio as a draughtsman and painter. The mistaken notion that "painting was for Antonio a mere pastime and a proof of his various skill"—to use the expression of the Florentine commentators of Vasari—that Piero Pollaiuoli was the painter, and Antonio the goldsmith and caster of bronzes, may be traced back to the end of the fifteenth century. Ugolino Verino expressly says as much in his Epigrams; and Francesco Albertini, in his "Memoriale," published in 1510, attributes no less than six different works, which then existed in the churches and public buildings of Florence, and which the two brothers had executed together, entirely to Piero; while he only once alludes to the work of Antonio, as a goldsmith. Antonio Petrei, in his epitome of the "Libro di Billi," and the "Anonimo Gaddiano," both repeat these misconceptions, which Vasari has, in a great measure, perpetuated. And so it becomes necessary, before these paintings of the "Virtues" can be really understood, to collect what is to be known about Antonio Pollaiuoli, as a draughtsman and painter, at the time at which Botticelli fell under his influence.

(J. Gaye, Carteggio, I, 265. Vasari, ed. Sansoni, III, 286.) Antonio was born, according to a "Denunzia" of his father, in 1429. Vasari says that he was placed as a boy with Bartoluccio, the stepfather of Lorenzo Ghiberti, to learn the craft of a goldsmith; and that he was one of the youths who assisted Lorenzo in the modelling of the bronze doors of the Baptistery at Florence. A quail, which is yet to be seen on the left architrave of the third door, the "Porta del Paradiso," was modelled by Antonio, if we may believe Vasari. The commission for this architrave, together with the ornaments of the frame of the door, was given to Ghiberti in 1447; and the whole work appears to have been finished

FORTITUDE *Uffizi Gallery, Florence*

in 1451. Antonio was then in his twenty-third year. "Whereupon," adds Vasari, "his skill and reputation increasing, he parted from Bartoluccio and Lorenzo, and opened a goldsmith's shop in the Mercato Nuovo." So far, Vasari's story is credible enough; several notices are extant which show that Antonio was in great vogue as a goldsmith, at this time. On the other hand, his account of how the goldsmith turned painter will hardly bear to be examined. "Antonio," says Vasari, "knowing that that art did not vouchsafe a long life to the labours of its craftsmen, resolved, from a desire of a more lasting memory, not to give himself longer to it; and so, having Piero, his brother, who was occupied with painting, he applied himself to that art, in order to learn the methods of managing and working the colours." Elsewhere, Vasari states that Piero had been placed as a boy, to learn painting with Andrea da Castagno; but none of the paintings of Piero Pollaiuoli bears out this assertion. Besides Andrea da Castagno died in August, 1457; and according to a "Denunzia" of that year, returned by Jacopo Pollaiuoli, Piero was then a boy of fourteen. The pictures executed by Piero unquestionably show, as Morelli long since pointed out, that not Andrea da Castagno, but Alessio Baldovinetti was his master. On one point Vasari is certainly incorrect: there is ample proof that Antonio did not abandon the craft of a goldsmith, either at this, or at a later time, in order to become a painter. On the contrary, he continued until the end of his life in great repute, both as a goldsmith and a caster of bronzes. Furthermore, there is every reason to suppose that in 1457, he was already an accomplished draughtsman; and, judging from the pictures which he is known to have executed in 1460, he must have then had some considerable practice in painting. Indeed, it is far more probable that Piero was put to learn painting, in order that he might become his brother's assistant, than that Antonio, already in great repute as a master of design, turned to a boy of fifteen or sixteen in order to acquire the difficult art of a painter. As a draughtsman, Antonio fell deeply under the influence of Andrea da Castagno; as a painter, he must have studied in the workshop of Alessio Baldovinetti. We see that in the types of some of his heads, in his preoccupation with movement, in his love of landscape, and in the technical methods which he employs in his painting.

Id., II, 261.

Id., III, 290.

Id., III, 286.

J. Gaye, Carteggio, I, 265.

I. Lermolieff, Die Werke Italienischer Meister, etc., 1880, p. 389.

The earliest paintings by Antonio Pollaiuoli, of which any notice has come down to us, are the lost "Labours of Hercules," which were executed for Cosimo de' Medici. Antonio, in a letter of the 13th July, 1494, writes that "it is thirty-four years ago that I made those 'Labours of Hercules' which are in the hall of the palace," then belonging to Piero di Lorenzo de' Medici, adding "that we made them between us, a brother of mine and I:" "che le facemo tra un mio fratello ed io." In the inventory of the goods of Lorenzo de' Medici, taken at the time of his death in 1492, these pictures, three in number, are described as hanging in the "sala grande" of the Palazzo Medici, now the Palazzo Riccardi. They were painted on canvas, and measured six braccia "per ognj verso," some eleven and a half feet, either way. They represented Hercules and Hydra, "erchole chammasa Lidra;" Hercules and the Lion, "erchole che sbarra el Lione;" and Hercules and Anteus, "erchole che schoppia anteo." After the flight of Piero de' Medici in 1494, they were taken to the Palazzo della Signoria, and hung in the "Sala del consiglio antiquo," where they were seen in 1510 by Francesco Albertini, who erroneously ascribes them in his "Memoriale,"

Archivio Storico dell' Arte, V, 208.

App. II, Doc. XXV, fol. 13, tergo.

to Verrocchio. After that time, nothing more is heard of them. In the Gallery of the Uffizi, are two little paintings on panel, in a single frame, No. 1153, of "Hercules and Hydra" and "Hercules and Anteus;" and in the print-room of the British Museum is a slight, but very masterly, pen-drawing, of "Hercules and Hydra," which closely agrees with the little panel in the Uffizi. Both the panels and the drawing are unquestionably by the hand of Antonio Pollaiuoli. This design of "Hercules and Hydra" is repeated on the cuirass of a bust in terra-cotta of a young knight, also by Antonio, which is in the Museum of the Bargello, at Florence, No. 161. In the same museum is a small bronze of "Hercules and Anteus," a contemporary copy of some original by Antonio Pollaiuoli, the composition of which closely recalls that of the panel in the Uffizi. This bronze, a sketch of the composition of "Hercules and Hydra" on a sheet in the Louvre, in the His de la Salle Collection, No. 111, from the sketch-book long attributed to Verrocchio, an engraving of the same subject, and another of the "Hercules and Anteus" by Robetta [Bartsch, vol. xiii, p. 404, Nos. 21 and 22], among other things, when studied together leave but little doubt that the two panels in the Uffizi, and the drawing in the British Museum, were the preliminary studies for the paintings which Antonio and his brother executed in 1460, for the Palazzo Medici. The two little panels are touched in with great freedom of hand, especially the distant landscapes which form the backgrounds. They are the work of a master who has long practised the art of painting, not of a man who had turned to it with difficulty within the last three or four years, as Vasari would have us believe. "L'animo mio alla pittura era in grande parte volto," says Lorenzo Ghiberti; and perhaps Antonio Pollaiuoli already might have used the expression of himself, in the workshop of Lorenzo.

Side by side with these "Labours of Hercules," should be studied some ruined wall-paintings which were discovered in the autumn of 1897, in the Villa Galletti, adjoining the Torre del Gallo in the Arcetri, a suburb of Florence. They had been painted in tempera; but successive house-painters and paperhangers had so scraped and scoured them down to the plaster, that little or nothing remained, except the outlines of the figures which had been traced from the cartoon on to the fresh "intonaco." They had originally covered the walls of a vaulted room, on the ground floor; but only portions of the paintings in two of the bays remained. These paintings represented a plinth rising some two and a half feet from the ground, and pierced by a series of circular-headed openings, which appeared to have been originally filled with perspectives: in the spandrils, between the heads of these openings, were figures of naked "putti," of which two only remained. On the plinth was a dance of naked men, some three parts the size of life; and behind these figures, at the level of the corbels supporting the vault, was hung a curtain, or tapestry. The lunettes of the vault above had been filled with fruit and foliage. Of the nude figures, there remained in the fragment to the left, the naked figure of a man in profile, rather leaping than dancing, and the upper portion of another dancing figure; both wearing those scroll-like head-dresses which occur in the embroideries executed from Antonio's designs for the vestments of San Giovanni: in the fragment to the right, was the nude figure of a youth standing between two dancing figures of men. The fine, nervous outlines of these figures, the vigorous, sinewy forms, the rough, hirsute character of the male heads, the "claw-like" hands turned back sharply at the wrists, closely recalled the fine pen-drawings of Adam and Eve by Antonio, in the Gallery of the Uffizi, Frame 31, Nos. 95F and 97F. The writer had the good fortune to see these wall-paintings when they were first uncovered, and before the outlines of the figures had lost the original beauty of their draughtsmanship; but they have since been barbarously daubed over by the proprietor of the villa, in order that they may be exhibited to credulous strangers as the work of Botticelli. These paintings were probably executed shortly after 1464, in which year the villa and the adjoining property were sold by the widow of Lamberto Lamberteschi to Jacopo Lanfredini. The drawings of Adam and Eve belong, no doubt, to the same period of Antonio's art: of a later time are the pen-drawing in the print-room of the British Museum, a composition of eight nude figures, and the engraving of the ten naked men, known as the "Battle of the Chain," which bears the inscription "OPVS ANTONII POLLAIOLI FLORENTINI." This splendid print, perhaps the finest representation of the nude which Florentine art can show before the rise of Leonardo da Vinci, must always remain one of the chief authorities on which our knowledge of Antonio Pollaiuoli as a draughtsman is founded.

G. Carocci, Dintorni di Firenze, p. 239.

Bartsch, vol. xiii, p. 202, No. 2.

Vasari says that Antonio Pollaiuoli understood the nude more "modernly," than the masters who preceded him had done; that he dissected many bodies to study their anatomy, and that he was the first to show the method of finding out the muscles that have form and order in the human figure: "fu primo a mostrare il modo di cercare i muscoli, che avessero forma ed ordine nelle figure." But this, again, is a statement which needs some sort of qualification. Other artists before Antonio had turned to the study of anatomy in the pursuit of their art: Lorenzo Ghiberti, for instance, in his "Commentary" includes "Notomia" among the "arti liberali" necessary to a sculptor. Rather, let us say, then, that Antonio Pollaiuoli was the first to draw the nude figure in accordance with an idea of its anatomy, expressing something more of the forms and attachments of the muscles, than actually meets the eye in the living figure. It is by virtue of this new thing which he brought into Florentine art, that he becomes the original father of that school of the nude of which Michelangelo is the incomparable master, and Luca Signorelli the precursor. But, unlike Michelangelo and his followers, Antonio Pollaiuoli sees the "naked, human form divine" with a directness and spontaneity of vision which is almost antique in its freshness. No veil of tradition or prejudice, no "idol" of the mind, comes between him and the human figure, to diminish or distort his view. With the great artists of antiquity, he divines that the supreme beauty of the human form is "rather male than female." But for him there is nothing delicate, or desirable, in this beauty of the naked creature: it lies wholly in the health and vitality, in the order and offices, of the firm, knit, sinewy frame; in the sharp, virile contours; in the ever-varying planes of the muscles, on which the light falls, as they move, as on a gem; in the bony frame subtly asserting itself at the attachments of the muscles, at the temple, at the joints at the wrist or knee. He draws the human form as he found it in the sinewy, almost uncomely Tuscan type around him; but he always represents it transfigured, in some moment of its greatest energy, or under the stimulus of some high passion, such as had not yet wholly died out of Florence. And so his nudes are not those of Greek athletes, but of mediæval antagonists in feud, inspired by that spirit of discord and revenge, which had ruled all in Florence during the age of the Guelfs and Ghibellines. In the expression of this virile sentiment, Antonio

Vasari, ed. Sansoni, III, 295.

Pollaiuoli continues the art of Andrea da Castagno, who, with an energy and power unknown, strangely enough, to any Florentine painter of the fourteenth century, has imbued his works with that mediæval, savage temper which found its highest expression, in Italy, in the "Inferno" of Dante. That temper, which, lingering on, chilled and inflated in the works of the later Florentine painters, Vasari sought to distinguish by the term "terribilità," Antonio Pollaiuoli refines upon, by his employment of the nude as a means of its expression in painting, lending to it a new significance, which was not without its influence on the art of Botticelli.

Vasari, ed. Sansoni, III, 95, note 1.

Contemporaneous with the paintings in the Villa Galletti is the altar-piece of the chapel of the Cardinal of Portugal, in the Basilica of San Miniato al Monte. The order for the tomb of the cardinal was given to Antonio Rossellino in 1461; and the chapel was consecrated, according to the inscription over the arch opening into the chapel, in October, 1466. This picture, which has been removed to the gallery of the Uffizi, No. 1301, represents St. James the Great, St. Eustace, and St. Vincent, at whole length, against a landscape background. It was undoubtedly executed from a cartoon by Antonio: his peculiar forms are to be seen in the head of the St. Vincent, and in the hands and in the fine angular folds of the draperies of the three figures. But the execution, which is somewhat dry in quality, seems to have been largely carried out by Piero, whose hand may be detected in the head of the St. Eustace, and in the elaborate painting of the rich velvets and brocades. On the wall of the recess, above the altar of the chapel, in the Basilica of San Miniato al Monte, from which this altar-piece picture was removed, is a damaged, but admirable fresco of two angels drawing back a curtain, which, even more clearly than the panel, shows the hand of Antonio. Another picture of St. Raphael, the Archangel, and Tobias, formerly in the church of Or San Michele, at Florence, and now in the gallery at Turin, No. 117, shows a joint execution: the cartoon was undoubtedly by Antonio, the painting largely by Piero. Of a somewhat later time is the altar-piece of the Martyrdom of St. Sebastian, formerly in the chapel of the Pucci, in the church of the Annunziata, at Florence, and now in the National Gallery at London, No. 292. This famous picture, which had so great an influence on Florentine art, appears to have been not only designed, but in a great part executed, by Antonio: his hand is especially to be seen in the figures of the archers in the lower part of the painting. According to Vasari, it was finished in the year 1475.

Vasari, ed. Sansoni, III, 293.

App. II, Doc. XI, fol. 13 tergo, 14 recto, 144 tergo, and 111 tergo.

To these notices of Antonio Pollaiuoli as a painter, which are drawn chiefly from an examination of his works, I will add a piece of documentary evidence. The "Libro Rosso" of the Compagnia di San Luca, an account book begun in the year 1472, of which I shall hereafter speak at length, shows that "Antonio diachopo delpollaiuol° orafo edipintore" paid fees to the guild, "p*e*lla soue*nz*ione deluogho earte," etc., on the 16th October, 1473; and that on 2nd February, 1472, the Feast of the Purification, he, in common with the other principal "men of the body," offered a candle to the value of "2d." in their church of Santa Maria Nuova. This entry shows beyond question that Antonio, at that time, was one of the foremost painters who were then practising their art in Florence. It appears from other entries in the same book, that "Piero diachopo delpollaiuol° dipintore" did not pay any fees to the guild, although called upon to do so; excusing himself, perhaps, upon the ground that he was his brother's assistant. In the light of these notices, Antonio Pollaiuoli is seen to be the great "maestro di disegno" which his age reputed him; and the character which Benvenuto Cellini draws of the poulterer's son in his "Trattati dell' Oreficeria e della Scultura," becomes intelligible. "This man," says Cellini, "was a goldsmith, and so great a draughtsman that, with scarce an exception, all the goldsmiths made use of his most beautiful drawings, which were of such excellence that many sculptors and painters (I say, some of the best masters of those arts,) still use his drawings, and acquire by them the greatest honour. This man produced few other things: only he drew marvellously well, and always devoted himself to this great art of design." The numerous old copies of lost drawings by Antonio Pollaiuoli, not to speak of the many works of art in which Pollaiuolesque motives occur, serve to bear out what Cellini here says of him and his imitators. His continual employment as a goldsmith prevented him producing few things, beyond his drawings and cartoons. In his larger paintings he was invariably forced, as we have seen, to seek the assistance of his brother, Piero: the few pictures which are entirely by his own hand, are all of a small size. Besides the little "Labours of Hercules" in the Uffizi, there exist but four: the "Apollo and Daphne," in the National Gallery at London, No. 928; the "Hercules and Nessus," in the Jarves Collection, No. 64, at Yale College, New Haven, U.S.A.; the "David with the head of Goliath," in the Museum at Berlin, No. 73A; and the portrait of a lady, in the Hainauer Collection, at Berlin.

Vasari, ed. Sansoni, III, 286, note 3.

Such a view of Antonio necessarily restricts our view of Piero; indeed, the few independent works by him, which have come down to us, show him to have been a painter of a very different character from his brother. In the large panel of the "Annunciation," in the Museum at Berlin, No. 73, everything in the picture is sacrificed to the elaborate rendering of the jewelled brocades and rich tissues with which the figures are draped, and the florid ornaments of the Virgin's chamber. The attitudes are heavy and immobile; the faces over-fleshy, and wanting in form and expression; the draperies hiding, rather than expressing, the figure. The large altar-piece of the "Coronation of the Virgin," now in the choir of the Collegiata, at San Gemignano, is a far finer painting; the figures are more animated, the heads better constructed; but the painter is here more dependent upon his brother, than in the panel at Berlin. This picture is signed, and dated 1483. The painting in which Piero is seen to the greatest advantage as an independent painter, is the fine portrait of Giovan Galeazzo Sforza, in the gallery of the Uffizi, No. 30, which was painted for Lorenzo de' Medici, probably on the occasion of the duke's visit to Florence in 1471. It is, then, as the able executor of his brother's cartoons and designs that this painter is chiefly known to us.

Let us now turn to discuss, in the light of this excursus, the "Virtues" of the Mercanzia. It needs no practised eye to see that the five panels, Nos. 69-73, which hang by themselves in the corridor of the Uffizi, are in a very indifferent state of preservation; and that the "Prudence" and the "Fortitude," which hang apart, in the third Tuscan Room, are fairly well preserved. The "Prudence" and the "Fortitude" are painted in tempera, in the ordinary way, on a panel prepared with a "gesso" ground, "in tavola ingessata." The other five panels, on the contrary, appear to have been thinly painted in tempera immediately upon the unprepared panel, and to have been finished with glazes applied with an oil, or varnish, medium, probably with a view of obtaining greater depth of tone than

was obtainable with the ordinary methods of tempera painting. This medium having perished in the course of time, the tempera under-painting has cracked and flaked away. The little picture of "David" at Berlin, No. 73A, is a well-preserved example of a picture executed in this way. The colour of the wood has been left here and there, in the shadows of this picture, in a way that seems to anticipate the use which the seventeenth-century painters made of the dark "priming" of their panels and canvases. The portrait of Giovan Galeazzo Sforza, in the Uffizi, No. 30, is another,
Id., III, 291. but far less well-preserved example of the same method. Vasari speaks of more than one picture which Antonio executed "a olio:" he alludes, doubtless, to some method of glazing in oil upon a "tempera" under-painting, which Antonio probably learned, not from Andrea da Castagno as Vasari states, but from Alessio Baldovinetti, the disciple of Domenico Veneziano, who certainly employed some such method. At an early period, probably at the end of the sixteenth century, when these pictures of the "Virtues" were taken to the new court-house of the Mercanzia in the Uffizi Lunghi, the five panels were restored, and so largely gone over, that it is now impossible to form any opinion regarding their execution. On the back of the panel of the "Charity," No. 73, is preserved a large "cartoon," or, more strictly, a drawing preparatory for the under-painting of the same composition, done in charcoal on the wood, and here and there heightened with white. In design it differs from the painting only in the action of the child, and in the omission of the jewels and ornaments of the figure, and of the brocades of the draperies; but in the vitality of its conception, and in the beauty of its draughtsmanship, it is beyond measure superior to the painting. These fine qualities of design and draughtsmanship, the exquisite modelling of the flesh over the bony structure, the forms of the hands, the angular disposition of the long, narrow folds of the draperies, show conclusively that Antonio Pollaiuoli was the author of this cartoon. That Antonio gave the sketches for the other panels of the "Virtues," including the "Fortitude," appears, I think, from the attitudes and general conception of these figures, on comparing them with this cartoon and the bronze reliefs of the same "Virtues" on the tombs of Sixtus IV. and Innocent VIII., by Antonio, in St. Peter's at Rome. In designing these various "Virtues," Antonio has taken the traditional conception of them as draped and seated figures of women, holding their allotted symbols, as they occur in many an earlier work of Florentine art; in the reliefs, for instance, on the Loggia de' Lanzi, at Florence. That Antonio, also, gave the cartoon for the "Temperance," No. 71, as well as for the "Charity," is, perhaps, to be seen in the forms of the draperies. For the rest, Piero certainly drew the cartoons of the "Faith," No. 72, the "Justice," No. 70, and the "Hope," No. 69: the immobile pose of the figure, the rounded, fleshy, structureless faces, the heavy folds, as of some thick, woollen stuff, of the draperies that fall over the knees of these figures, betray altogether his hand. An additional piece of evidence of the part which Piero took in preparing the cartoons for these panels, exists in the drawing by his hand for the head of the "Faith," done in black and red chalk, and pricked for pouncing, which is preserved among the drawings in the Uffizi, Frame 43, No. 14506F. The state of the five panels which hang in the corridor of the Uffizi, precludes any judgment being now formed as to their execution; they contain, however, nothing which would go to prove that they may not have been originally executed by Piero. On the other hand, both the cartoon and the

painting of the "Prudence," No. 1306, are unquestionably by him: all those traits which I have remarked in his pictures, the absence of movement, the heavy, rounded forms, occurring in this painting side by side with the skilfully executed brocades and tissues, and the delicate, variegated colour, render it a very characteristic work.

But to come at last to the panel of the "Fortitude:" an examination of this picture, in its sequence with Botticelli's other early works, leaves no doubt that he executed both the cartoon and the painting. The disciple of Fra Filippo unmistakably betrays his hand in the forms of the draperies, in the long, fluted folds of the purple robe as it falls over the knees of the figure; in the unbroken curve of its embroidered hem as it descends from the knee to the foot; in the broad angular folds which rest on the ground: forms wholly dissimilar from those of the draperies of Antonio and Piero Pollaiuoli. The fantastic armour on the breasts and shoulders of the figure, and the ornaments of the throne, show the passing influence of a school of engravers connected with the name of Maso Finiguerra, a goldsmith, and a "maestro di disegno," who imitated Antonio Pollaiuoli, and who had died in 1464. As the legendary inventor of the art of engraving upon metal plates, Finiguerra has acquired a reputation which is not supported by any extant works which can be attributed to him. The plates of the "Sibyls," which came from the workshop of these engravers shortly after the death of Maso Finiguerra, afford examples of the kind of ornament which Botticelli had in his mind while designing this figure of "Fortitude." Some years after, Botticelli gave the drawings for more than one cut which came from the workshop of these engravers, as I shall relate in its place. On the other hand, the attitude, proportions, and relief of the figure, the forms and modelling of the head, hands, and feet, betray, as unmistakably, the influence of Antonio Pollaiuoli. Indeed, the attitude and the general conception of the figure suggest, as I have said, that Antonio gave the sketch from which the cartoon was elaborated. As a representation of the virtue of Fortitude, this painting is as inadequate an one as the "Prudence" of Piero Pollaiuoli; of all these designs, the cartoon of Antonio alone expresses its subject. But while Piero sacrifices everything in his picture to the skilful rendering of the rich brocades, tissues, and jewels, Botticelli attempts to produce a figure which shall unite in itself the delicate beauty of Fra Filippo, with the vitality and "naturalism" of Antonio Pollaiuoli. What Botticelli chiefly learned from Antonio, as this painting of the "Fortitude" reveals, was the art of rendering the relief and movement of a figure; of expressing the mass of a figure by its relief, and the "passions of its mind" by its movement. To reconcile these new qualities of painting with the method of draughtsmanship, with its nervous, rhythmical line, and the delicate sense of beauty, which he had acquired from Fra Filippo, "gratioso et ornato et artificioso sopra modo;" to unite these purely pictorial qualities in his own manner, had entirely engrossed the thoughts and sympathies of the painter, to the exclusion of the real subject of the picture. Exquisitely conceived and finely realized as this figure is, from its own limited point of view, it shows, nevertheless, that the elements of Botticelli's art, thus variously derived, had not, as yet, become perfectly fused and expressive.

A. Bartsch, Peintre-Graveur, XIII, 72, Nos. 25-36.

There is one piece of invention in the picture which is peculiarly characteristic of Botticelli; I mean the fastidious fancy with which the hair is tricked with pearls, and brought down in two long plaits over the shoulders, and between the breasts. Such an arrangement of the hair is found repeated in one of the figures of the Graces, in the picture of the "Spring" in the Florentine Academy; in the figures of the daughters of Jethro, in one of the frescoes of the Sistine Chapel at Rome; and again in the person of Venus, in the picture of "Mars and Venus," in the National Gallery at London. This piece of invention was especially seized upon, and exaggerated, by the imitators of Botticelli. In colouring, the simple scheme of the picture, the purple robe, the white under-dress, the smalt azure of the sleeves and bodice, contrasted with the cool, silver armour, the subdued hues of the marbles and porphyry in the throne and pace, is peculiarly characteristic of certain early pictures of Botticelli. The arched panel on which the picture is painted measures 6 ft. 1 in. in height, by 2 ft. 0½ in. in breadth. Although fairly well preserved, the picture has suffered from restorations, necessitated by the tendency of the colour to flake from the ground; and in a few passages, especially in the hands, it has also been damaged by retouches. The indications afforded by the meagre notices of the painter's life at this time, and by the internal evidence of the painting, alike point to the conclusion that the panel of the "Fortitude" was painted *c.* 1468-9.

Somewhat later, in point of time, than this panel of "Fortitude," are two little paintings, of which Raffaello Borghini, the first writer to speak of
p. 352. them, has left in his "Riposo," a miscellany of painting and sculpture both ancient and modern, published at Florence in 1584, the following account: "Not long since Messer Ridolfo [Sirigatti, a knight of Santo Stefano, and a great *amateur* of those times] had two little pictures framed together, in one of which was painted Holofernes on the bed with his head cut off, and with his barons standing around him in astonishment, and in the other Judith with the head in a bag; but he gave them to the most serene Lady Bianca Cappello de' Medici, our Grand Duchess, hearing that her Highness, as became the great lover of vertu that she is, wished to adorn a writing-cabinet with pictures and antique sculpture, and judging that little work of Botticello worthy to be seen near the other things which had been placed there by her Highness." These little paintings, which from that time have always remained in the Grand Ducal Collection, are now in the gallery of the Uffizi, No. 1156, "Judith with the head of Holofernes," and No. 1158, "Holofernes found dead in his tent by his barons." They are painted on panels, measuring 10⅝ in. high, by 8¼ in. broad, and are now framed separately, in heavy, carved frames of the seventeenth century.

In the first picture, Judith in her "garments of gladness," her hair braided and tired, descends the rising ground on which the Assyrians are encamped. In her left hand she bears an olive-branch, in token of the peace she brings to her people; in her right hand the "fauchion" of Holofernes, the sword of their deliverance. Her serving-maid hurries in her footsteps, bearing the head of "the chief captain of the host of Assur," wrapt in a linen cloth, in a basket which she carries on her head; and the wine-flask with the oil-flask slung about her wrist. Below, in the valley girt round by distant hills, lies the city of Bethulia. The whole country-side is alive with a troop of horsemen that makes its tortuous way up the hill-side, followed by a company of lances swarming out of the city gate. It is characteristic not only of Botticelli, but of his time, that he should neglect the outward circumstances of the story (for in the story Bethulia was on a mountain), and represent the city, with its walls and towers, lying

JUDITH WITH THE HEAD OF HOLOFERNES *Uffizi Gallery, Florence*

in a valley by a river, like Florence by the Arno, with the enemy encamped on the neighbouring hills, as they were in actual warfare at Florence. Of the same kind, is the piece of invention by which Botticelli, departing again from the story, represents Judith bearing an olive-branch, like "un tronbetto coll' ulivo a notificare la pace," to use a phrase of the time, as a herald or trumpeter used to do, when sent to Florence to declare a peace, during the intestine wars of the fifteenth century.

With the exception of something in the type of the serving-maid, the colour of her saffron dress, and the odd, Giottesque convention used in the drawing of the cypress-tree, there is little in this painting which directly recalls the manner of Fra Filippo. On the contrary, the most striking trait in these figures of Judith and her serving-maid, their tall proportions and alert movements, has no counterpart in the short, stolid figures of the Frate. The "document" which explains this and much else in these two little paintings, which, perhaps, interprets more clearly than anything else which we possess, the nature and extent of Antonio Pollaiuoli's influence over Botticelli, is that incomparable series of embroideries, executed, as Vasari tells us, from the designs of Antonio for the apparel of a chasuble, a cope, and two dalmatics, for San Giovanni, the Baptistery of Florence. These embroideries, some twenty-seven in number, have been cut from the rich vestments, "di broccato riccio sopra riccio," which they once adorned, and are now preserved in frames in the Museum of the "Opera" of the Cathedral, No. 110 p°. According to the Florentine commentators they were executed in 1470, by Paolo da Verona and other embroiderers. Vasari says, in his characteristic way, that "the figures were not worked less well with the needle, than they would have been had Antonio painted them with his pencil;" and the outlines of Antonio, which may be seen here and there traced upon the linen, where the silk has worn away, together with a school-copy of the original drawing for the embroidery of "St. John preaching in the Desert," in the collection of Herr Beckerath at Berlin, show that Vasari is here using a very pardonable piece of hyperbole. Let us set this figure of Judith beside the figure of Salome to whom a soldier offers the head of the Baptist in a charger, in the embroidery of the "Feast of Herod:" not only in the attitude, but in the whole conception of the form, proportions, and movement of the tall, alert figure, in the way in which the head is set upon the slender neck, the shoulders and elbows thrown back, the draperies caught by the drooping torso in its rapid motion, is Sandro clearly imitating Antonio. Where the peculiar temperament of the disciple of Fra Filippo asserts itself, is in the invention of the outer dress of translucent lawn, twice girdled at the breasts and loins; of the under-dress of pale grape-purple shining through it, against the azure sky; of the elaborate tire of the hair—things designed with a certain fastidious delicacy which formed no part of the genius of Antonio Pollaiuoli.

Vasari, ed. Sansoni, III, 299.

Id., note.

The picture is indifferently preserved; it has been stripped in many places of its glazes, and it has not escaped retouching. The lights on the dress of the Judith have been gone over by a skilful hand, and the figure of the serving-maid has been freely retouched. The painting has thus lost something of the original glow and clarity of its colouring. A "pentimento" may be traced in the figure of the Judith, which was originally taller; the right foot having been set back by half its length. Some two years ago an early school-copy of this picture was acquired by Signor

Cavalcaselle and Crowe, ed. Le Monnier, VI, 286.

Bardini, of Florence, from the Palazzo Fondi at Naples. This copy contained several variations from the original, especially in the background, which had been freely altered, the cypress-tree on the right being omitted. These variations betrayed the hand of an able, but somewhat colourless imitator of Botticelli in his earlier years. The picture was not in perfect condition; but, unlike the original in the Uffizi, it had not been retouched.

In a far better state of preservation is the second picture in the Uffizi, a composition of ten little figures, of Bagoas and the captains of the Assyrians discovering Holofernes in his tent, "dead and his head taken from him." In this, more than in any other painting, Botticelli appears undisguisedly as the imitator of Antonio Pollaiuoli. Sandro deliberately exchanges here the simpler, and more sculpturesque way of composition, which he had learned from Fra Filippo and Masaccio, for the more involved and naturalistic method which Antonio had founded upon the intricate complexity of figures as they occur in actual life. When placed beside some of the embroideries from the vestments of San Giovanni, beside that of the "Entombment of the headless body of the Baptist," for instance, it would seem that Botticelli was here attempting something in direct emulation of those designs. In the conception and composition of the painting, as in its actual forms and details, the heads of the figures, the dead body of Holofernes, the habits and "harness" of the Assyrian captains, the imitation of these embroideries is unmistakable. And further, both the forms of the horses in the background of this picture, and the way in which they are introduced into the composition, closely recall the horses in the embroidery of the story of how Herod, having heard of the fame of St. John, came into the wilderness to hear him preach. The colouring of this panel of Holofernes, the preponderance of the cherry-reds tending now to a deep purple, now to a blonde vermilion, and contrasted with the white horse, the pallid body of Holofernes, the white bed-clothes, the smalt blue of the tent-curtain, the grape-purple robe of the knight at the foot of the bed, is but an elaborate variation on the scheme of the "Fortitude." In criticising these two little paintings, it must be remembered that they were originally framed together, as Borghini records; that they are parts of the same picture: viewed as a single work, they show that Botticelli, at the very outset of his career, already possessed in a high degree the power of seizing upon the pictorially significant moment of a story, and of expressing it pictorially. In this lovely figure of Judith, radiant, and rejoicing that her "countenance hath deceived him to his destruction;" the men of Bethulia already issuing in the distance from the city gates to pursue the Assyrians, and the captains of the army of Assur finding the headless body of Holofernes, "their minds wonderfully troubled," Botticelli presents to the eye, "nel suo tutto in istante," according to the accepted tradition of historical painting in his time, the whole drama of the story of Judith. Masterly as these paintings are in conception, in execution they betray some immaturity of hand in the drawing, as, for example, in the lower limbs of the serving-maid, and in the figures on the horses in the tent of Holofernes. In handling, however, they are executed with an admirable largeness and freedom of touch, although they are scarcely above the size of miniatures. In point of date, these little panels must have been executed shortly after the designs for the embroideries of the vestments for San Giovanni, which, as we know, were executed in 1470.

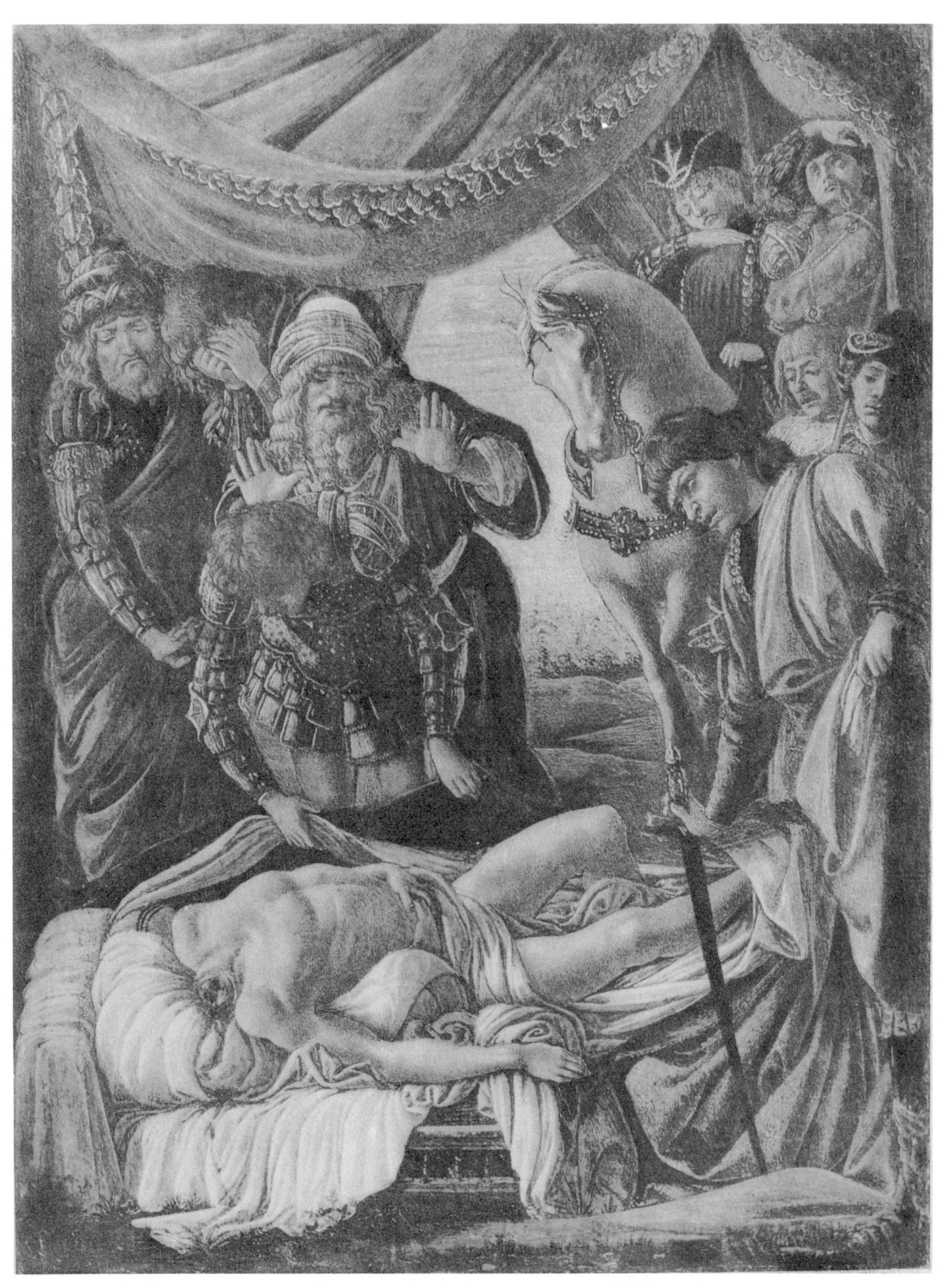

HOLOFERNES FOUND DEAD IN HIS TENT *Uffizi Gallery, Florence*

Let us turn back, for a moment, to review the early "Adoration of the Magi," in the National Gallery, No. 592, by the light of these panels and embroideries. We now see how the group of horses and horsemen, with its involved composition, to the left of the picture, the types of many of the heads, the forms of the horses, the habits of the grooms and pages have been derived from Antonio Pollaiuoli. Observe, for example, how the white horse in the foreground of the "Adoration of the Magi," on the left, closely recalls the white horse in the background of the "Holofernes," and how both have their prototype in the horses of Antonio's designs. The early date of the picture in the National Gallery is clearly shown by passages imitative of Fra Filippo and Pollaiuoli occurring side by side, and revealing the hand of the disciple who has not yet assimilated the various influences under which he has fallen.

Of the same early period of Botticelli's art is a portrait in the gallery of the Uffizi, No. 1154, of a young man holding a medal of Cosimo de' Medici, the elder, which formerly passed as the work of some unknown Florentine painter, until Morelli, in his studies of the Borghese Gallery, pointed out that it was unquestionably by Sandro Botticelli. This portrait still retains its original "encadrement," a narrow carved and gilded fillet, framed upon the panel of the painting, which measures 21½ inches in height, by 14½ inches in breadth, not including the fillet. The actual painting is in a very indifferent state of preservation: the head has been much scaled by successive processes of cleaning, and has been freely retouched, especially on the left cheek and the neck. The hands are in a still worse condition; indeed, they have been so much repainted that they now appear distorted. The medal of Cosimo de' Medici, the elder, which the figure holds, is modelled in relief in "gesso" and gilt, like the ornaments of the older Giottesque pictures; an actual cast, it would seem, from a medal attributed to Michelozzo, bearing the legend, "MAGNVS . COSMVS . MEDICES . P.P.P.," some of the letters of which may yet be traced in the picture. This medal, which exists in more than one version, was probably first struck to commemorate the decree of the Signoria bestowing the title of "Pater Patriæ" on Cosimo, shortly before his death in 1464.

J. Friedlaender, Die Italienischen Schaumünzen, pl. XXVII, No. 4.

No male portrait by Antonio Pollaiuoli, such as undoubtedly formed the prototype of this picture, is now known to exist. The portraits by Antonio, once in the Arte del Proconsolo, disappeared at the time of the suppression of the Florentine Guilds at the end of the last century; but the fine portrait of a man holding a ring, by some follower of Antonio Pollaiuoli, in the collection of Prince Corsini at Florence, No. 210, remains to attest how much, both in the conception and treatment of the portrait in the Uffizi, Botticelli owed to Antonio. Unlike the earlier portraits by Masaccio, Paolo Uccello, Andrea da Castagno, and Domenico Veneziano, where only the head and shoulders are shown, without the hands, and often in rigid profile, against a background of a single colour, the panel by Botticelli is one of the earliest to anticipate our modern way of portraiture, the portrait itself being introduced incidentally, as it were, by the gesture of displaying the medal. Especially Pollaiuolesque are the forms and relief of the features, the sinuous contour of the face, the accented modelling of the cheekbone; and so, also, the hands, which in their original condition must have closely resembled the hands of the "Fortitude," both in the modelling and in the attempt to unite that expressiveness of gesture so characteristic of Antonio, with that beauty of form which is proper to fine hands. The

Vasari, ed. Sansoni, III, 292.

colour of the picture, moreover, the blonde vermilion "biretta," the olivaster features set in the thick masses of dark, reddish-brown hair, the stately black habit edged with a fine cord of green, and tied at the neck with a green lace, shows how greatly the disciple of Fra Filippo had come to modify his sense of colour under the influence of the Pollaiuoli and the "naturalistic" painters.

This picture was formerly said to be a portrait of Pico della Mirandola (who, by the way, was born in 1462), by some unknown Florentine painter working about 1440. When Morelli pointed out that it was a work by Botticelli, he called it the portrait of a medallist; whereupon Professor Eugène Müntz rushed to the rescue of that distinguished critic, and declared the painting to be a portrait of Piero di Lorenzo de' Medici, who was born in 1471, and, therefore, of the last period of Botticelli's art. As my purpose is not to form a museum of other people's conjectures, but to invent a few of my own, I must leave the student of such things to consult the exhaustive works of Dr. Ulmann and Professor Steinmann, where he will find surmises as learned as contradictory, collected and arranged with an industry which I will not be rash enough to emulate. Now the only thing which can be asserted about this portrait, beyond the question of its authorship, with any certainty, is that it was painted shortly after the panel of the "Fortitude;" and that it is, therefore, a work of the earliest period of Botticelli's art. The insistent way in which the medal, held by the fastidiously designed hands, is introduced into the picture, the whole Medicean cast of the features, the powerful jaw, the keen eyes, alike suggest that it is the portrait of some immediate descendant of Cosimo de' Medici, the elder. Of his sons, Piero and Carlo, and of his grandsons, Lorenzo and Giuliano, numerous portraits remain which dispel at once any notion that this may be a portrait of any one of them. Of Giovanni, the younger son of Cosimo, only one painting of the fifteenth century has come down to us, in the "Adoration of the Magi," by Botticelli, now in the gallery of the Uffizi, No. 1286. In that painting, Giovanni, strangely enough, is portrayed as a young man about the same age as the person seen in this portrait, although he died, at the age of forty-two, in 1461. "Era di natura caldissimo," says an old biographer of Giovanni, and in the alert, sensuous face of the figure holding the medal, I seem to see the same person represented as in the "Adoration of the Magi;" though, in the latter picture, the treatment of the head is less Pollaiuolesque, the hair less abundant. But the question remains, why did Botticelli represent Giovanni, the patron of Fra Filippo, as a young man in the painting of the "Adoration of the Magi," and not, as he must have seen him, when a boy in the workshop of the Frate, a man of forty or more?

In the background of this portrait, Botticelli has conveyed by a few easy strokes of the pencil, one of those bird's-eye views in the valley of the Arno which are elaborated with infinite care and detail in the paintings of the Pollaiuoli. The sense of the shining river, as it meanders through the green valley which runs out level to the hills, is admirably introduced into the picture, merely as a background, and by way of relief to the figure. A passage in the "Trattato della Pittura" of Leonardo da Vinci has been often quoted to show that Botticelli had no care for landscapes, and that he painted them indifferently. "That painter," says Leonardo, "cannot be universal, who does not equally delight in all the things which appertain to painting: thus, if he do not take pleasure in landscapes, he accounts

Trattato, ed. Ludwig, I, 116.

PORTRAIT OF A MAN HOLDING A MEDAL *Uffizi Gallery, Florence*

them to be a thing of slight and simple research; as our Botticello, who said that such a study was vain, since by merely throwing a sponge full of divers colours against a wall, it left on the wall a stain wherein was seen a fine landscape. It is indeed true, I say, that the various inventions which a man wishes to find in that stain may be seen in it, such as heads of men, divers animals, battles, rocks, seas, clouds, woods, and other such things; and that it produces its effect, like the sound of a bell in which one is able to hear that which it seems to say to you: but although those stains may give you invention, they do not teach you to finish any one detail; and of these [stains] such a painter makes wretched landscapes."

Such is the passage as it occurs in the best manuscript of the "Trattato," the Codex Vaticanus 1270. It is not to be found among the portions of the "Trattato" which have come down to us, in the holograph of Leonardo; and in the edition printed at Paris in 1651, the text of this passage is very corrupt. Leonardo wrote the "Trattato della Pittura," according to Dr. Richter, in 1492, during his first settlement at Milan, when Botticelli had already passed the zenith of his career; and in using the expression, "il nostro Botticello," Leonardo alludes to him as one of the acknowledged masters of Florence at that time. What Leonardo here says, truly enough, of Botticelli, is that he accounted the painting of landscape for its own sake "a vain study;" and this, from the point of view of Leonardo, was a great fault, or, at least, a great limitation: but Leonardo does not assert that Botticelli himself painted wretched landscapes. The saying of Botticelli's which Leonardo here preserves, was obviously said in that paradoxical spirit which characterizes more than one of his sayings which have come down to us. No Florentine painter had a finer eye for nature in his landscapes than Botticelli, yet his landscapes are always introduced into his pictures, in an accessory way, as backgrounds to his figures. For him, inanimate nature is but the scene of the Human Spirit. As his manner develops, he exchanges the lovely distances of his earlier paintings for the austere landscapes of his last pictures, in which "blank ranges of rock," and great unbroken spaces of sky and sea, predominate. In this he seems to anticipate the genius of Michelangelo, of whom it was finely said that "when we speak of him, woods, clouds, seas, and mountains disappear, and only what is formed by the spirit of man remains."

Side by side with these unwritten documents of Sandro's history, the delicate traits and characters of his art, which must always appear, to the true student of the master, the more significant and assured facts of his life, occur certain written documents, which also have their value and their place in his story, although they preserve for us but the merest fragments of its outward circumstance. The "Compagnia di San Luca," the Company of Design, as Vasari calls it, had been founded at Florence about the year 1350, by the successors of Giotto, to minister to the needs, both spiritual and bodily, of its members. In obedience to mediæval notions, the painters of Florence were enrolled among the Guild of the Physicians and Apothecaries, the "Arte dei Medici e degli Speziali;" and this Company of St. Luke, evangelist, physician, and painter, had its "residenza," or seat, in the great hospital of Santa Maria Nuova; the "cappella maggiore," the chapel of the high altar, of the church of the hospital having been granted to its members for their oratory. "From this beginning," says Vasari, "sometimes meeting together, and sometimes not, this Company continued until it was reduced to the form in which it exists to-day." It

Vasari, ed. Sansoni, I, 673.

appears to have already declined during the latter half of the fifteenth century, and in the course of time the Company was brought to such a pass that at length, "abandoned by nearly everyone," it was transformed, in the year 1562, through the exertions of the sculptor, Montorsoli, into the "Accademia di Belle Arti," which exists to the present day, a venerable monument of the influence of academies on the arts of design.

Id., VI, 655-6.

In the year 1472, a general effort appears to have been made to revive the "Compagnia di San Luca," to replenish its members, and to renew its interests. The names of all the painters who then practised their craft in Florence were entered in a ledger, called, for the sake of distinction, the "Libro Rosso." Besides the gold-beaters, the wax-figure makers, and a few carvers, the names of some hundred and twelve "dipintori," including decorators, miniature-painters, glass-painters, painters of stained cloths, coffers, playing-cards, etc., were thus entered in this account book. On the debit side of the account were set down in common form, the fees due to the Company; on the credit side, the moneys received by them. The greater number of the craftsmen whose names were entered in this way, duly paid fees to the Guild; but in many cases no fees appear to have been paid. Among the names of the painters thus entered in the "Libro Rosso" is that of "Alesandro dimariano dett° Botticello dipintore." The first entry under his name on the debit side of the account is the sum of 6 soldi, by way of composition, made on 17th June, 1472, through the chamberlain, of every debt due to the Guild, until 1st July next following. Then follow, for his yearly offering on St. Luke's day, 18th October, 1472, the sum of 5 soldi; for his fee for the maintenance of the Guild and its "luogo" or place of assembly, for the year beginning 1st July, 1472, at the rate of 1 soldo 4 denari the month, 16 soldi; and for the impost levied on 18th October, 1472, "for the pennons of the trumpets," the sum of 5 soldi. These were the bannerets, bearing the arms or "impresa" of the Company, which hung from the trumpets used at their processions and assemblies. Such trumpets with pennons may be seen in the "Desco da Parto" by Masaccio, in the Museum at Berlin, No. 58[c], and in the "Adoration of the Magi" by Botticelli, in the National Gallery, No. 1033. The other side of the account shows that on 18th October, 1472, Botticelli paid in cash to the chamberlain of the Guild, 6 soldi for his composition-fee, 5 soldi for his yearly offering, and 5 soldi 4 denari on account of his Guild-fees. On the 7th February, 1472-3, he paid a further sum of 9 soldi; on 4th June, 1473, one lira; on 24th September, 2 soldi 8 denari; and in October of the same year a final sum of 5 soldi. After that time the entries in the "Libro Rosso" cease until the year 1482; whether the Guild lapsed into its former state of neglect, or whether its transactions were recorded in the other account books mentioned in these entries, the "Libro della Sovvenzione" and the "Libro Vatorno," we are unable to ascertain owing to the loss of those ledgers. Towards the end of the "Libro Rosso" is an "Account of the candles offered on the day of Santa Maria Candellaia, the 2nd day of February, 1472," in the church of Santa Maria Nuova. The four captains of the "Compagnia di San Luca" offered each a candle to the value of 4*d.*; the four counsellors, among whom was Antonio Filipepi, the elder brother of Botticelli, each offered one to the value of 3*d.*, as did the chamberlain, Andrea della Robbia; while the stewart, Cosimo Rosselli, and "the men of the body," to the number of thirty-two, each offered one to the value of 2*d.* Among the latter are the names of Botticelli,

App. II, Doc. XI, fol. 14 tergo, and fol. 15 recto.

App. II, Doc. XI, fol. 144 tergo, and fol. 145 recto.

"Alessandro di Mariano dipintore," and "Ant° dijachopo del pollaiuolo." Such a document serves to remind us that both in its form and scope, the "Compagnia di San Luca" was purely a religious society.

Another entry in the "Libro Rosso" is of value, since it throws a ray of light upon the early relations of Botticelli with the most famous of his disciples, Filippino Lippi. It appears from this entry, which was begun in the month of June, 1472, that Filippo, the son of Fra Filippo, from Prato, painter, was then working with Sandro di Botticello: "Filippo di filippo dap*r*at° dipintore chonsandro di botticello." Vasari, in his life of Fra Filippo, relates how that master being overtaken by death before he had brought the frescoes at Spoleto to a conclusion, "left by will, to Fra Diamante, the guardianship of his son Filippo, who, being then a child of ten, learning his craft from Fra Diamante, returned with him to Florence; Fra Diamante carrying with him three hundred ducats, which remained owing from the commune for the work done; out of which, having bought some property for himself, he made over but a small part to the child," who, he adds, "was placed with Sandro Botticello, then held to be an excellent master." In his life of Filippino Vasari repeats that the boy was placed with Botticelli, "notwithstanding that the father had, at the point of death, recommended him to Fra Diamante, 'suo amicissimo e quasi fratello.'" What independent evidence has come down to us entirely bears out Vasari's story. At the time of Fra Filippo's death, on 19th October, 1469, the frescoes in the choir at Spoleto wanted little for their completion: in the "Nativity" alone, the last fresco in the order in which they would naturally be painted, is the journeyman hand of Fra Diamante clearly distinguishable alike in the design and in the execution. But whatever remained to be done was finished in the course of a few months; and Fra Diamante returned to Prato before the spring of the following year had passed; for on 24th May, 1470, payment was made to him for the arms of the late Podestà, Cesare Petrucci, which he had painted in the loggia of the Palazzo Pubblico at Prato. Shortly after this time Fra Diamante appears to have removed to Florence, ridding himself of his ward by placing him with Botticelli, and investing the better part of the money which he had received for the frescoes at Spoleto in real property ("alcuni beni" is the phrase Vasari uses) at Florence. A document of the year 1478, which I have found among the Florentine archives, probably relates to this very property: it shows that Filippino, on coming of age, successfully resisted the attempts of Fra Diamante to deprive him of the possession of a house, in the parish of San Pietro Maggiore, in Florence, presumably a part of his inheritance under his father's will. Certainly, all that is to be known about Fra Diamante proves him to have been as unscrupulous a man as he was an indifferent painter. The entry in the "Libro Rosso" affords an actual indication that Filippino was placed with Botticelli, probably in 1470, and certainly not later than 1471; for although the first entry on the debit side of the account is of the month of June, 1472, the first entry of receipt is dated 24th September, 1473, at which time, as I take it, Filippino, having finished the ordinary term of two to three years as "discepolo," or apprentice, first began to pay his fees in the quality of a "garzone," or journeyman. The mere fact that a boy of fifteen, as Filippino was, at the most, in 1472, should be called upon to pay fees as a painter to the "Compagnia di San Luca," proves that he had already had not a little practice in his art, and that he had shown the promise of his

App. II, Doc. XI, fol. 56 tergo.

Vasari, ed. Sansoni, II. 628.

Id., III, 461.

G. Guasti, Quadri di Prato, p. 107.

future ability. In the workshop of Botticelli, Filippino must have worked in company with that fascinating painter, whose name has not come down to us, but whom I shall seek to identify with Berto Linaiuoli, when I come to speak of the disciples of Botticelli.

App. II, Doc. XI, fol. 44, tergo.

As for Fra Diamante, we learn, from another entry in the "Libro Rosso," that in the year 1472 he had become a monk of the order of San Giovanni Gualberto, in the monastery of San Pancrazio: "Dondiamante dipintore Monarcho dellordine di S° giouannj ghualbert° fatt° in Sanbranchazio." He had already exchanged the habit

Vasari, ed. Sansoni, II, 640.

of a Carmelite, for that of a Benedictine, monk before the death of Fra Filippo, apparently after he had been imprisoned by his religious superiors in 1463.

During the latter part of the year 1473, about the time of these last payments to the "Company of Design," Botticelli was working upon a picture which formerly adorned one of the Florentine churches. The

App. II, Doc. II, fol. 85, recto.

"Anonimo Gaddiano," the earliest writer who speaks of this painting, has preserved the date, taken apparently from some inscription on the frame, at which it was finished, or, more probably, dedicated; the feast of the saint falling on the 20th January. "In Santa Maria Maggiore," he says, "there is by his hand a St. Sebastian on panel, against a column, which he made in January, 1473:" "In santa Maria maggiore e di sua mano v*n*° sa*n* bastiano intauola, che e invna colonna, il quale fece dj

ed. 1550, I, 492.

Gie*n*naio nel 1473:" that is, January, 1474, new style. Vasari, in the first edition of the "Lives," also records that Botticelli painted "a St. Sebastian in Santa Maria Maggiore, at Florence." Upon adding, in the second edition

ed. 1568, I, 471.

of 1568, a notice of a "Pietà" by Botticelli, in the same church, Vasari appears to have misread what he had formerly written, and re-punctuated the passage, inserting a full stop after the word "Sebastiano." The passage in its altered form purports that Botticelli painted this picture of St. Sebastian, among other things in Casa Medici, for Lorenzo the Magnificent. A comparison of the text of the two editions, however, leaves no doubt that this altered reading is only a "lapsus calami." No other authentic notice of the picture has come down to us, though many later writers, like Raffaello Borghini in his "Riposo," reproduce Vasari's slip of the pen. The church of Santa Maria Maggiore, one of the most ancient in Florence, was rebuilt in the thirteenth century. The Gothic fabric, which was erected at that time, still remains in the Via de' Cerritani; although its fine vaults and arches are almost hidden by the "stucchi" and marbles, with which the church was encrusted in the seventeenth century. The "colonna" against which the painting of St. Sebastian hung was, doubtless, one of the simple, quadrangular piers of the arcades that divide the nave from the aisles. When Giovanni Cinelli published

d. 212.

his edition of the "Bellezze di Firenze," in 1677, this panel of St. Sebastian, together with "the many ancient paintings of the excellent masters," works by Agnolo Gaddi, Masaccio, Paolo Uccello, Pesello, and others, had already been taken away from the church, or destroyed, when

Del Migliore, Firenze Illustrata, I, 426.

the side chapels were renewed by Gherardo Silvani, in the earlier part of the seventeenth century. From the time of its removal from the church, the picture was entirely lost sight of, until Messrs. Crowe and Cavalcaselle

Crowe and Cavalcaselle, ed. 1864, II, 396.

recognized the hand of Botticelli in a panel of St. Sebastian in the Museum at Berlin, No. 1128, which then passed as a work by Antonio Pollaiuoli. This picture had been acquired by the Prussian Government in 1821, with the collection of Mr. Edward Solly, an English banker, who was one of

ST. SEBASTIAN *Berlin Gallery*

the first "amateurs" to collect early Italian paintings. It is painted on a tall, circular-headed panel, measuring 6 ft. 5 in. in height, and 2 ft. 5½ in. in breadth, such as might well have hung against one of the piers of Santa Maria Maggiore. It bears no inscription; but it no longer retains its original frame. With the exception of a few unimportant restorations, it is fairly well preserved.

The old attribution of the painting to Antonio Pollaiuoli is intelligible enough, on account of the exterior resemblance which it bears to the figure of St. Sebastian, in the great altar-piece by the Pollaiuoli, now in the National Gallery at London, No. 292. According to Vasari, this altar-piece was finished in the year 1475. If that date be correct, Botticelli must have seen the picture while it was being executed; for he certainly appears to have taken from it some hint for his own painting. There is more than an accidental similarity between the attitudes and forms of these two figures of St. Sebastian; in the device by which they are placed upon the lopped branches of the tree to which they are bound; in the way in which they are relieved against the sky. But if there are points of resemblance between the two pictures, still more are there points of difference. Antonio Pollaiuoli attempts, in his direct, naturalistic way, to realize the scene as it might have happened, and to depict the passions of suffering and resignation in the figure of the saint. In Botticelli's painting, on the contrary, there is no suffering, no degradation of pain; the martyrdom of the saint is expressed only by the symbolism of the tree to which he is bound, the arrows which transfix him, and the figures of the archers who retreat across the distant landscape. The real subject of the painting is the Divine Image in this serene and radiant God, the portrayal of the naked, human creature in all the beauty of its form and structure. Unlike Antonio Pollaiuoli, Botticelli never acquired that knowledge of the nude which a study of anatomy alone can give; he knew little of the underlying forms of the muscles, of their attachments to the bony frame, of their offices of flexor and extensor. The mechanical processes of anatomy which revealed much to Antonio Pollaiuoli and Leonardo da Vinci, could have signified little to him who largely divined the nature of things by "vision." The convention of the nude which, in the figure of St. Sebastian, Botticelli had already founded upon the learned draughtsmanship of Antonio Pollaiuoli, served him for the purposes of his art throughout his life; he still employs it, with scarcely any change, more than thirty years after, in the figures of the giants in his illustration to Canto XXXI. of the "Inferno" of Dante. And so, also, in his later paintings of the nude, the outlines become more rhythmical and expressive, the relief of the figure less Pollaiuolesque in its emphasis, but the conception of the forms remains unaltered. The peculiar sentiment of beauty which Botticelli here attempts to express in this picture, is emphasized by the refinement of the colouring of the olivaster flesh, the black hair, the white loin-cloth with its delicate embroideries, seen against the pallid, almost gray sky. Two things may be noticed in the brown landscape, besides the Pollaiuolesque figures of the retiring soldiers; of the one archer who brings down a bird with his bow, and of the other who reclines on the sward, watching the saint from afar; things touched in with an admirable freedom of hand: I mean the fantastic character of the towers and bastions which guard a bridge over a port or estuary in the distant landscape, unlike anything which Botticelli could have found in Florence, seem to have been imitated from the landscape of some

Vasari, ed. Sansoni, III, 293.

Flemish painting. Both this and the peculiar, circular touch by which the underwood near the pond to the right of the picture, and the tall slender tree, in front of the estuary to the left, are painted in, mark the connection of Botticelli with Jacopo del Sellaio, a painter with whom he may have worked as a youth, in the workshop of Fra Filippo, and of whom Vasari has left a brief notice.

During the same month of January, 1473-4, in which this picture of St. Sebastian had been brought to a conclusion, Botticelli was called to Pisa, to confer with the wardens of the "Opera" of the Duomo about certain frescoes which they had proposed that he should paint in the Campo Santo. Benozzo Gozzoli, who had been called to Pisa in 1469, Pisan style, to decorate the Campo Santo, had already in 1474, Pisan style, completed the first eight of his famous series of stories from the Old Testament, and had received the commission to proceed with the four next frescoes in the series. Foreseeing no very certain end to this stupendous undertaking, which, as Vasari, in his characteristic way, says "might justly have frightened a whole legion of painters," the wardens of the "Opera" had invited Botticelli to Pisa, with a view to taking part in these decorations of the Campo Santo. In a volume of "Ricordanze" of the "Opera," which is preserved among the public archives at Pisa, at fol. 130, tergo, is this entry of the month of January, 1473, Florentine style: Mcccc° Lxxiiij° [Pisan style], "to Sandro botticella, painter of Florence, one gold florin, which was given him because he came from Florence to see where he was to paint in the Campo Santo, [for his expenses] until 27th day of January." The Pisans and Florentines, I may add, dated the beginning of the year "ab incarnatione," that is, from the 25th March; but the Florentines dated it from the 25th March following, and the Pisans from the 25th March preceding, the commencement of the year as we now reckon it, according to the new style, from the 1st January. From the cross-entry on fol. 136, tergo, of the 30th May, 1475, Pisan style, it appears that Botticelli then came to an agreement with the "Opera" about these paintings: "chesacordo poj conlop*er*a adipingniere Incamposanto." This agreement, as we gather from a third entry, was that Botticelli should first paint a story in the Cathedral, "per uno paragone," as a paragon of his skill, by way of comparison with, I doubt not, the productions of their admired Benozzo. This entry of 20th September, 1475, Pisan style, occurs in another volume in the public archives at Pisa, of "Entrata e Uscita" of the "Opera," fol. 70, tergo: "To Sandro, called Botticella, painter, lire 130 soldi 10, in part for the painting of a story commenced in the Duomo, in the chapel of the Incoronata, that is, the story of the Ascension of our Lady, which he is making for a paragon, which, if it please, he is then to paint in the Campo Santo [laquale fa p*er*vno paragone che piacendo apoj adipingniere Incamposanto]." According to various entries, which occur in other documents preserved among the chapter archives, Botticelli was engaged upon this painting in July, 1475, Pisan style, when the carpenter, Jacopo di Giovanni, called Soppetta, was ordered to make the scaffold for the painter, "che dipinge in duomo nella Incoronata." From other entries of payments, in grain and money, made to "Sandro detto Botticello" (or "Botticella," as the name is variously spelt, out of a confusion with other persons of that name at Pisa), and for ultramarine brought from Florence, it appears that the work proceeded until the following month of September; after which time the entries which relate to it cease, the work apparently having been

L. T. Centofanti, Notizie di Artisti, pp. 87, 88.

App. II, Doc. XII.

App. II, Doc. XIII.

I. B. Supino, Archivio Storico del l'Arte, VI, 153.

left unfinished. Vasari states in one of the passages which he added to the life of Botticelli in the second edition, that "in the Duomo of Pisa, in the chapel of the Impagliata, he began an Assumption with a choir of angels; but afterwards, not pleasing him, he left it unfinished." It is more probable that Botticelli abandoned the fresco when he saw that it was little likely to satisfy the good wardens of the "Opera," whose taste in such matters is shown by their constant employment of Benozzo Gozzoli, during a period of more than seventeen years. Benozzo had lived and worked nearly all his life away from Florence and its new ideas; and we are apt, in our admiration for the great decorative beauty and the admirable design and draughtsmanship of no few passages in Benozzo's frescoes, in the Campo Santo at Pisa, to overlook the half-bourgeois, half-rustic naïvety of their conception. In comparison with the provinciality of Benozzo's art (for it is nothing else) the strange, modern ideas of Botticelli must have proved little intelligible to the Pisan wardens.

Vasari, ed. 1568, I, 474.

No vestige of Botticelli's painting is now to be seen in the chapel of the "Incoronata," or of San Ranieri, as it has been called since the "urna" of the saint was placed upon its altar in the seventeenth century. The vault of the apse of this chapel, which is in the head of the right transept, "in cornu epistolae," is still encrusted with the early mosaic of the "Coronation of the Virgin," which Vasari ascribes to Gaddo Gaddi, and the wall below, on which Botticelli probably painted his fresco, is now covered by the marbles, among which is a relief of the "Assumption," begun by Francesco Mosca, and finished after his death by his son Simone. Botticelli's unfinished painting, which was probably still in existence when Vasari wrote in 1568, must have been destroyed by the erection of these marbles in 1583.

L. T. Centofanti, Notizie di Artisti, p. 204.

One other early work, painted by Botticelli under the immediate influence of Antonio Pollaiuoli, remains to be discussed. This picture was lately in the collection of Prince Chigi, at Rome, but as these sheets go to the press it has passed into the collection of Mrs. John L. Gardiner, of Boston, U.S.A. It is painted on panel, and represents the Virgin seated, turned towards the left, with the Child on her knee, and an angel by her side, in three-quarter figures, about half the size of life. The genre-like treatment of the subject was already a commonplace among the Florentine painters; but Botticelli transfigures it by a touch of really imaginative symbolism: he represents the angel offering to the Child a dish of corn and grapes, the fruits of his Passion; while the Virgin plucks one of the ears of corn to give to her Son. Behind the figures, seen through an opening in a kind of pierced parapet, is a distant landscape. The way in which the architectural lines of this parapet are introduced into the picture in order to relieve the figures, recalls the backgrounds in certain paintings by Andrea da Castagno and Alessio Baldovinetti. Very Pollaiuolesque in form are the heads of the Virgin, and still more that of the angel, "crowned with olive green." Despite a certain immaturity, seen in the disproportion of the Virgin's hands, and a thinness of quality in execution, the picture is among the more lovely and solemn of Botticelli's earliest works. It is well preserved, and admirable in colour. The azure and purple of the Virgin's dress are very pure and luminous; the angel is in white, and the cloth in which the Child is wrapped of that pale grape-purple which Botticelli, in his earlier paintings, borrows from Fra Filippo. An old copy, or rather a free version of this picture, in which the largeness of the original composition is much spoiled by the exaggeration of the details, and by the introduction of some meaningless ornament, is in the Gallery of the Palazzo Panciatichi, at Florence, No. 89. Another picture which has much in common with the Chigi panel is in the Museum at Naples, No. 32, where it passes as a work by Botticelli. The Virgin is seated, as in the Chigi picture, against an architectural background, with two angels on her left, one of whom presents the Child to her. Mr. Berenson has suggested that this may be an early work by the anonymous painter whom he calls Amico di Sandro, an attribution which I shall discuss in its place. Dr. Ulmann cited this panel, and another in the Gallery of the Hospital of Santa Maria Nuova, at Florence, No. 23, among the most characteristic of Botticelli's earliest works. In the picture at Santa Maria Nuova, the Child is partly held by the Virgin, and partly by an angel who stands beside her; and the figures of another angel and the young St. John, in the background, complete the composition. This picture may originally have been by the same hand as the panel at Naples; but Dr. Ulmann, in speaking with so much confidence about it, omitted to remark that the entire surface of the picture had been repainted in the sixteenth century. The motive of the Child supported by an angel is derived from Fra Filippo, like much else in these paintings; but the heads and draperies, especially in the panel at Naples, unmistakably show the influence of Verrocchio and his school. These Verrocchiesque tendencies, coupled with the assumption that the two pictures were early works by Botticelli, have contributed to a source of confusion in the criticism of the painter. A certain school of German critics, among whom

H. Ulmann, Sandro Botticelli, p. 36.

are Dr. Bode and Dr. Ulmann, has sought to insist upon the influence which Verrocchio, in their opinion, exercised over Botticelli; indeed, Dr. Ulmann goes so far as to assert that he worked for some time as an assistant in the "bottega" of Verrocchio. The erroneous attribution to Botticelli, dating from the time of Vasari, of certain paintings by Francesco Botticini, the imitator and assistant of Verrocchio, a blunder which Dr.

Id., p. 77.

Ulmann attempts to explain by the supposition that Botticelli gave the design for such a picture as the Palmieri altar-piece, in the National Gallery at London, No. 1126, has, no doubt, tended to give colour to this theory; and the very real points of resemblance in manner which the Pollaiuoli and Verrocchio owe to their common master, Alessio Baldovinetti, have served to increase the confusion. The only passages in the works of Botticelli, which can be taken as evidence of Verrocchio's influence, are the regular, embossed folds of the dress of the Virgin in the painting lately in the collection of Prince Chigi, and of the cloak, as it falls over the left shoulder of the "Fortitude," in the Uffizi, No. 1299; and, above all, the head of that figure. The forms of these draperies occur rather in the works of Verrocchio's school than of Verrocchio himself, and are, perhaps, to be traced to Fra Filippo and Pesellino. The head of the "Fortitude," however, remains undeniably a Verrocchiesque trait. I will not go so far as to say that it is an accidental trait, but it is certainly an exceptional one, which marks only a passing influence. What is really remarkable, is that Botticelli should have been so little influenced, either by Verrocchio, or his school. Altogether, these early works of Botticelli show their author, in the clearest way, to have been a disciple of Fra Filippo, who was attempting to form his manner under the dominating influence, for the moment, of Antonio Pollaiuoli.

THE VIRGIN AND CHILD WITH ANGEL *Collection of Mrs. J. L. Gardner, Boston, U.S.A.*

The panel of the Virgin and Child, lately in the collection of Prince Chigi, was probably executed shortly after the panel of the "St. Sebastian" at Berlin; but I have discussed it in this place, in order that I might speak of it in connection with two "Adorations of the Magi," the earliest of a certain group of pictures in which the development of Botticelli's mature manner, out of his early Pollaiuolesque manner, is shown in its successive phases.

The earlier of these two pictures of the "Adoration of the Magi" is the "tondo," in the National Gallery at London, No. 1033. It was acquired in 1878, for the sum of £800, from the collection of Mr. W. Fuller Maitland, where it had passed as a work by Botticelli. The authorities of the National Gallery, however, thought fit to attribute it to Filippino Lippi, a name which it still bears; although Morelli long ago observed that Botticelli was undoubtedly the author of it. This painting is probably the "tondo" formerly in Casa Pucci at Florence, to which Vasari alludes in one of the passages which he inserted into the second edition of the "Lives": "in Casa Pucci fece . . . in vn tondo l'Epifania." If that conjecture be correct, it was probably executed for Antonio Pucci, for whose chapel in the Annunziata, the Pollaiuoli painted the altar-piece of St. Sebastian, which is also in the National Gallery. Of the Pucci, I shall speak when I come to discuss the other paintings which Botticelli afterwards executed for them in 1487. The "tondo" in the National Gallery is painted on a panel, measuring 4 ft. 3½ in. in diameter. It is in a very indifferent state of preservation; it has suffered much from over-cleaning, and the surface, in many places, is cracked and blistered. What is worse, the whole of the picture has been gone over, and disfigured by retouches; the heads have especially suffered, and the purity of its colouring has largely been lost. But the original beauty of the painting may still be seen in a few of the figures in the foreground, which are among the better preserved passages of the picture.

Italian Masters in German Galleries, ed. 1883, p. 236.

Vasari, ed. 1568 I, 471.

Here, as in the earlier "Adoration of the Magi" in the National Gallery, Botticelli represents these kings from the East like princes of his own time, attended by their courtiers, their pages, their dwarfs and apes, their trumpeters, who blow a clarion as they present their gifts, their rout of grooms and horses, and guards. In designing this picture, Botticelli seems to have had in his mind the "tondo" which his master, Fra Filippo, had painted in his youth under the spell of Fra Angelico. In that incomparable piece of pure Florentine art, now in the collection of Sir Francis Cook, at Richmond in Surrey, Fra Filippo had taken the traditional composition of the scene, in which the Virgin is seated, with the Child and St. Joseph, on the right hand, as the Magi approach her from the left, and adapted it, with exquisite art, to the difficult space which a "tondo" presents to the designer of pictures. Botticelli, on the other hand, with his gift for real invention, which was so rare a thing among the Florentine masters of the fifteenth century, has attempted in this picture an altogether novel and original composition. He has placed the Virgin in the centre of the picture, with the young Child on her knee and St. Joseph by her side: the Magi are kneeling before her, while their courtiers stand round about them, on either side, and below, in the foreground of the picture, their servants and horses await them. Here, as in the "tondo" of Fra Filippo, the rustic roof of the stall is contrasted with the regular lines of the ruined building against which it has been raised, and, what is surely no accident in either picture, a peacock is conspicuously perched on some ruined wall or pier. But unlike anything in Fra Filippo's painting is the ruin, which forms the scene of Botticelli's picture —a strange, indescribable piece of antiquity, as of some vast, cruciform church, the roofless arches of which rise into the clear air and measure out the space of the heavens. The building, temple or basilica, or whatever it may be, is raised above a vaulted under-croft; and below, in the foreground of the painting, among its shattered piers, Botticelli has grouped the figures of his story, to the number of seventy or more, which have ascended from either side into the nave or body of the ruin. It is in the design of this architecture, and in the art with which the figures are disposed before it, and proportioned to it, that, what is now the chief beauty of the picture, its imposing effect of courtly spaciousness, largely consists. I cannot stop to analyze all the intricate beauties of this composition, but I would notice the device by which the figure of the arch seen in perspective through the arch above the Virgin is echoed in the groups of figures which encircle her in a double rank. In originality and subtlety of design, Botticelli certainly never afterwards surpassed himself in this kind of composition. The drawing of the figures wants, perhaps, the largeness and breadth of Botticelli's later works, but his manner is here already more formed and of a piece. Of the few directly imitative passages which this picture contains, one only need be noticed: the distant town in the landscape to the right, like the buildings in the landscape of the "St. Sebastian" at Berlin, is distinctly reminiscent of the background of some Flemish painting. This "tondo" seems to have been executed about the year 1476.

The other painting of the "Adoration of the Magi" was the famous picture, which originally stood "between the doors" of the great Dominican church of Santa Maria Novella, at Florence. Francesco Albertini, in his
Fol. 4, recto. "Memoriale" published in 1510, is the earliest writer who alludes to "la
App. II, Doc. I, fol. 49 tergo. tauola de' Magi, fra le porte, di Sandro Bott.," in the church of Santa Maria Novella. In Antonio Petrei's epitome of the "Libro di Billi," the picture is mentioned in the same brief way, "Vna tauola in s[ta] maria nouella alla porta del mezo." The "Anonimo Gaddiano," however, speaks
App. II, Doc. II, fol. 85 recto. of it somewhat more precisely, "Et [in] santa maria nouella dipinse vna tauoletta di altare che e acanto alla porta del mezo, de magi che vj sono piu p*er*sone ritratte alnaturale." But it is to Vasari that we must turn for
Vasari, ed. 1568, I, 472 a description of this painting. "A small picture on panel," he says, "with figures of three-quarters of a braccio each, was given to Sandro to paint at this time, which was placed in Santa Maria Novella between the doors of the chief façade of the church to the left on entering by the middle door. And in it is represented the Adoration of the Magi; where so great a love is seen in the first old king, who, kissing the foot of our Lord, and overcome with tenderness, plainly shows that he has accomplished the end of his long journey; and the figure of this king is the portrait of Cosimo de' Medici, the elder, the most lifelike and natural of any that are to be found of him in our own day. The second, who is Giuliano de' Medici, father of Pope Clement VII., is seen, with all his soul intent, devoutly to do reverence to the Child and present to him his gift. The third, who also kneels, and who appears while adoring him to render him thanksgiving and confess him the true Messiah, is Giovanni, the son of Cosimo. Nor can the beauty be described which Sandro has shown in the heads

TONDO OF THE ADORATION OF THE MAGI *National Gallery, London*

which are to be seen there, turned in various attitudes, one in full face, others in profile, another in three-quarter face, another bowed, and others in other ways, nor the diversity of airs both of young and old; with all those rare inventions that are able to make known the perfection of his skill, he having distinguished the retinues of the three kings in such a way that one is able to recognize which are the servants of the one and which of the others. It is certainly a most admirable work, and in colouring, drawing, and composition so beautifully concluded, that every craftsman remains to-day astonished at it." With the exception of the sentence stating that the figure of the third Magi is a portrait of Giovanni di Cosimo de' Medici, this passage had appeared, almost as it stands, in the first edition of 1550. According to these various accounts, this picture originally formed the "tavoletta d'altare" of an altar which stood in the nave, beside the principal door of the church; Vasari alone asserts that the painting was "to the left on entering by the middle door." But there is more than one inaccuracy in his description of its design, which shows that he was writing from memory; and his memory, also, played him false in regard to the original position of the painting in the church. I read in a "Sepolcrario," or register of all the chapels, tombs, and inscriptions in the church of Santa Maria Novella, preserved among the manuscripts in the Biblioteca Riccardiana at Florence, that this picture of the "Adoration of the Magi" formerly stood, not as Vasari says to the left, but to the right, of the middle door of the façade on entering the church. In other words, the altar, above which it was placed, stood against the wall of the façade, where is now Masaccio's fresco of the "Trinity"; this painting having been removed here, from its original position above the altar of the "Madonna del Rosario," in the left aisle, during the "restoration" of the church in 1858-61. According to this "Sepolcrario," "diligently copied," so runs the title, in 1729, from the original, compiled in the year 1617, which was then in the possession of the Fathers of the church, the altar, beside the middle door, "was anciently erected by Giovanni Lami, a Florentine citizen, together with a sepulchre of marble [in the pavement before it], and it was called the altar of the Magi, because there had been painted in the 'Ancona' by Sandro Botticelli, a most excellent painter, the story of the three Magi, held by all to be an admirable work; which, in the rebuilding of the altar, was removed by Fabio Mandragoni, a Spaniard, and placed in his palace which he had built not far from the church." "This altar," adds the writer of the "Sepolcrario," "was, the first time, adorned with the richest marbles and the noblest carvings by the aforesaid Lami, and it afterward came into the family of the Fedini. They, after having held it many years, sold it to Fabio Mandragoni, who then renewed the altar, destroying the old one, that it might follow the order of the altars." This Fabio Mandragoni was, probably, one of the many Spanish merchants who settled in Florence, after the marriage of Eleanora da Toledo with Cosimo I.; and the allusion to the "ordine delli altari" enables us to fix the date at which he removed Botticelli's picture from the church. Vasari in his own "Life," published in 1568, records how by the order of Duke Cosimo, he had taken away the "tramezzo," or choir-screen, from Santa Maria Novella, and formed a new choir behind the high altar: and, he adds, that since the altars in the aisles of the nave "have no common order and proportion," he had begun to replace them with new altar-pieces "with rich ornaments

App. II, Doc. XIV.

Vasari, ed. Sansoni, VII, 710.

of stone in a new fashion," according to a regular design. The "tramezzo" was removed in 1565, and these lateral altar-pieces were erected, at intervals, by the owners of the altars during the following ten or more years. The writer of the "Sepolcrario" goes on to say that Fabio Mandragoni covered "the burying place of the first founder of the altar, by the steps of the new altar, intending to make his own in front of it, as the other patrons of the altars had done: but that intention was not accomplished, for what reason I know not, and he sold the altar to Bernardo di Giovanni Vecchietti," who placed there a painting of the "Annunciation" by Santi di Tito, who died in 1603, and "finished the chapel left imperfect by Fabio Mandragoni." This altar with the painting by Santi di Tito, and the stone altar-piece from Vasari's design, were removed during the barbarous "restoration" of the church in 1858-61.

The painting which Botticelli executed for Giovanni Lami appears, then, to have been still in its original position, when Vasari published the second edition of his "Lives" in 1568, and to have been removed from the church by Fabio Mandragoni, c. 1470-75. After that time the picture passed out of memory, until Signor Carlo Pini pointed out, in a note to the edition of Vasari, published at Florence in 1845, of which he was one of the editors, that Botticelli's "Adoration of the Magi" still existed in the gallery of the Uffizi, where it had hitherto passed as a work by Domenico Ghirlandaio. According to a label on the back of the panel, it came to the gallery on "13 Maggio 1796," from the ducal villa at Poggio Imperiale, beyond the Porta Romana, at Florence. This villa had been bought and rebuilt by the Grand Duchess Maria Maddalena of Austria, in 1622; and here, in the seventeenth century, Richard Lassels saw "in one gallery," as he tells us in his "Voyage of Italy," published in 1670, "the true pictures of divers late princes of the house of Austria, of the house of Medices, and of other princes their allies." And so I conjecture that this "Adoration of the Magi" had already in the seventeenth century passed into the Grand Ducal Collection, and had been placed in this gallery at Poggio Imperiale, on account of the portraits of the Medici which it contained.

Vasari, ed. Le Monnier, V, 116, note 1.

Of the family of the Lami, or da Lama, as they were more anciently called, I find few notices, and those of little interest: none of this name appears to have attained to the honours of the Republic. One member of the family had been buried in Santa Maria Novella in the fourteenth century. Of Giovanni Lami, I can find nothing; but I surmise that he was a merchant who had built up his own fortunes, and wished to ingratiate himself with the Medici: his issue, perhaps, failing early in the male line, the altar and chapel may have descended by marriage to the Fedini.

The painting in the gallery of the Uffizi, No. 1286, which closely agrees with Vasari's description, is now generally accepted as the picture formerly in the church of Santa Maria Novella; indeed, it is impossible to come to any other conclusion. Framed upon the actual panel of the painting is a carved and gilded fillet, or architrave moulding, a member for which there was no need when the frame of the altar-piece was of wood, but necessary to bring a painting into relation with a marble frame. This detail thus appears to explain what the writer of the "Sepolcrario" says of the original altar, "fatto di ricchissimi marmi, e nobiliss[i] Intagli." In the inventory of the goods of Lorenzo, Il Magnifico, the frame of an altar-piece is described as made of white marble, carved.

THE ADORATION OF THE MAGI—THE ALTAR-PIECE OF SANTA MARIA NOVELLA *Uffizi Gallery, Florence*

Both in design and manner, this painting recalls the damaged "tondo" of the same subject, in the National Gallery. The composition which Botticelli so fortunately contrived within the circular space of that picture, he now adapts to the quadrangular panel of this; placing the Virgin in the centre of the picture, the Magi kneeling before her, and their followers disposed in two groups on either side of the painting. That conception of the scene which was implied in the "tondo," and in the other earlier "Adoration" in the same gallery, is here frankly realized: the Medici, already lords of Florence in all but the title, are the kings which "have seen his star in the east, and are come to worship him, with their court." Before the Virgin, in the act of kissing the foot of the young Child, kneels, as Vasari says, Cosimo de' Medici, the elder, in a black habit, richly embroidered with gold and lined with ermine. In the foreground below the figure of the Virgin kneels, not Giuliano di Piero de' Medici, as Vasari asserts, for he was murdered at the early age of twenty-five, but a much older man. It is not, however, difficult to recognize in the shrewd, sharply-cut profile, the powerful jaw and thick-set neck, the head of Piero, Il Gottoso, the son of Cosimo de' Medici, as he is represented in his bust by Mino da Fiesole, No. 234, in the museum of the Bargello, at Florence. He turns to the third Magus, who kneels beside him on his right, in a white habit, embroidered with gold. According to the passage which Vasari inserted into the second edition of the "Lives," this figure is a portrait of Giovanni, the second son of Cosimo de' Medici: that Vasari was here repeating what was generally believed at the time he was writing, is shown by the fact that the portrait of Giovanni, No. 5, among the portraits of the Medici, which Cristofano dell' Altissimo painted for Duke Cosimo I., and which now hangs in the gallery leading from the Uffizi to the Palazzo Pitti, was copied from this head by Botticelli. The other extant portraits of Giovanni, an inscribed medal figured in Dr. Friedlaender's work, "Die Italienischen Schaumünzen," plate XXVII, No. 6, and the bust by Mino da Fiesole, No. 236, in the museum of the Bargello, represent him as an older man, he having died in 1461, at the age of forty-three. If Vasari's statement be correct, it is strange that Botticelli should have painted Giovanni as a youth, when he lived till middle age. Around these kneeling figures of the Magi stand their courtiers and servants disposed in two groups, on either side of the picture. The heads of some of these figures are undoubtedly portraits, and this has led certain writers, and Dr. Ulmann conspicuously among the rest, to attempt their identification. The arguments, however, which Dr. Ulmann has advanced in support of his theories, appear to me, for the most part, to be entirely notional and gratuitous: let me give an instance of my meaning. In the figure of the young man who stands with his hands crossed before him, beside the kneeling figure of Giovanni de' Medici, on the right, Dr. Ulmann would see a portrait of Giuliano de' Medici; but if the head of this figure be compared with that, immediately below it, of the crouching youth who looks up towards the Virgin, it will be seen, I think, that neither is a portrait, but that both are heads of the same manneristic type. The features of Giuliano, in the portrait of him ascribed to Botticelli, in the Morelli Collection at Bergamo, No. 21, and on the medal commonly attributed to Antonio Pollaiuoli, which was struck to commemorate the Pazzi conspiracy in 1478, are seen to have closely resembled those of his father, Piero, but to have been marked by an individual and unmistakable

H. Ulmann, Sandro Botticelli, p. 59.

character. Again, Dr. Ulmann's supposition that a portrait of Lorenzo Tornabuoni is to be found in the head of the young man with a cap and feather, to the extreme right of the picture, and a portrait of Lorenzo de' Medici in the whole-length figure of a youth, of much the same age, who stands to the left of the picture, with his hand clasped on the hilt of a sword, which he holds before him, is still more untenable; since Lorenzo Tornabuoni was a mere child, and Lorenzo de' Medici a man of twenty-eight, in 1477, about which time this picture was certainly painted. If the portraits of Lorenzo and Giuliano de' Medici are not to be found in this picture (and none of the heads in the picture resemble at all their portraits on the medal, struck to commemorate the Pazzi conspiracy), then most of Dr. Ulmann's other conjectures become still more improbable. Indeed, many of the heads which Dr. Ulmann has taken for portraits, such as those in the group of three figures to the extreme left of the picture, which, according to Dr. Ulmann, represent Lorenzo, Il Magnifico, and Poliziano, are, in my opinion, no portraits at all. Two portraits, however, have been introduced into the picture with very evident intention; in both cases the figures look out of the picture, towards the spectator; one on the extreme right, and the other on the extreme left, of the painting. That on the left, the head with the full, rounded face and dark hair, seen immediately above and behind the figure of the youth resting upon his sword, may possibly be a portrait of the donor. That on the right, the full-length figure in the foreground, completely draped in a saffron cloak, has long been recognized as a portrait of Botticelli himself. The one other portrait which exists of him, in the fresco of the "Crucifixion of St. Peter," by Filippino Lippi, in the Brancacci Chapel, in the Carmine at Florence, was painted some five years later, after Botticelli's return from Rome in 1482. Filippino's portrait represents a man of a highly sensuous temperament; whereas Botticelli paints himself of a nature scarcely less sensuous, but of greater intellectual power and force of character, such as his works show him to have been.

In its composition, this picture is more largely designed, and in drawing more simply and firmly executed, than the earlier "tondo" of the same subject in the National Gallery. The figures of the Virgin and Child closely recall the picture lately in the collection of Prince Chigi, at Rome; not only in the type of the Virgin's head, and the design of the veil and dress, but even in the disproportion of the hands, and the odd drawing of the Child. Again, the peacock perched on the ruined wall to the right, is a close repetition of the bird in the "tondo," in the National Gallery. The rendering of the heads, and especially those of Cosimo, and Piero, de' Medici, is very masterly, in its drawing and modelling: but although a greater tendency to naturalism is shown in the drawing of the figures, the draperies are still designed according to the tradition which Fra Filippo had handed down from the Giotteschi. Not the least beautiful passage in the picture is the landscape, in the background, in which some distant, blue hills are seen beyond the ruins of a temple, the pale, marble arches of which rise against the blue sky. Botticelli certainly never painted a more lovely, or more delicate, piece of landscape than this distance, which is executed with a breadth of handling, and a sense of light and tone, which seem to anticipate not a little of the achievement of our modern schools of landscape painting. In its colouring, this "Adoration of the Magi," more than any other early work by Botticelli, recalls the peculiar beauty and gaiety of Fra Filippo's colour. The delicate, clear purple, azure and green of the Virgin's dress, which are repeated in the bending figures on the right, here changing into scarlet or warm purples, olive greens, deeper azures, or delicate grape-purples, form the key of the colour scheme. Notwithstanding its minute finish, the painting is executed with an astonishing freedom and directness of handling. The panel on which it is painted measures 4 ft. 5 in. in width, and 3 ft. 7¼ in. in height. On the whole the picture is well preserved; but the surface has been damaged by "scrubbing," and the colour has been much darkened by successive coats of varnish. The gold ornaments, for example, on the red robe of the figure of Piero de' Medici, and the vessels which he and Giovanni are holding, have almost been obliterated in the process of cleaning. Again, other passages, such as the tunic of the youth holding his sword before him, have suffered from local retouches. Some partial restorations may also be detected at the top of the picture, on the pent roof, where the colour has flaked away: but from the worst of evils, that of repainting, the panel is fortunately free.

Such is the picture which established Botticelli's reputation as a painter in Florence, and which largely went to fix the character of his art in the popular mind. Vasari thus concludes his life of the painter in the first edition: "Sandro truly merited great praise in all the pictures that he made, in which the love and care of his art constrained him: and although he was led away, as I have related, by the things through which the excellences of art are by hypocrisy brought to nought [Vasari is alluding to his adhesion to Savonarola]; it does not therefore follow that his works are not both beautiful, and greatly extolled; and above all the picture of the Magi in Santa Maria Novella." The popularity of the picture (for the crowd is the same in all ages) was, no doubt, largely due to the admirable portraits of the Medici which it contained: but, as Vasari adds elsewhere, "every craftsman to-day is left astonished at it." Any critical attempt to trace the development of Botticelli's art must largely be based upon a study of this painting, which forms the chief link between the pictures painted in his early Pollaiuolesque manner, and those which he executed when his manner was entirely formed. In this "Adoration," the elements of his art first become perfectly fused and expressive: his manner is no longer disfigured by imitative passages introduced into a picture, merely because his predilection lay with such things. A writer who has done much to insist upon those traits of manner and sentiment in Botticelli's works, which were seized upon and exaggerated by his imitators, has said with more truth than, perhaps, he himself was aware of, that "Botticelli lived in a generation of naturalists, and he might have been a mere naturalist among them." In this picture, more nearly, perhaps, than in any other, Botticelli is seen working in accordance with that tradition of naturalistic art in Florence, of which Domenico Ghirlandaio was, at that time, the chief interpreter; the tradition of the unconstituted, but not, therefore, the less real, Academy of the Florentine "botteghe." Of all the great pictures of Botticelli, it is the dryest in conception, the most learned in execution: the painter, to use the phrases of Leonardo, lets nothing pass in the work which, in his view of things, is not "sanctioned by reason, and by the effects of Nature." Nowhere is Botticelli's peculiar temperament obtruded into the painting; its grave and reasonable beauty nowhere disturbed by those "bizzarie," that "strange-

Vasari ed. 1550, I, 496.

ness in the proportion," by which such works as the "Spring" and the "Calumny" are distinguished. In this "Adoration of the Magi," Botticelli deliberately measures himself against his contemporaries, and seeks to display all the resources and accomplishment of his art. Nothing, certainly, by Domenico Ghirlandaio, with whose works the picture obviously suggests a comparison, approaches it in the vivacity of its conception, or in the variety and beauty of its design and colouring. Ghirlandaio, admirable master though he was of heads and single figures, constructed and modelled with consummate ability, was never able to compose and execute a story of this kind, at once with the same force and spirituality in the presentation of the subject as a whole, and with the same invention and beauty of design in the details.

I will take this occasion to speak of another painting of the "Adoration of the Magi," by Botticelli, which seems to have been painted about this time: but it had already disappeared in the sixteenth century, and the only record which we have of it, is a brief notice preserved by the "Anonimo Gaddiano." "There is by his hand," says that writer, "in the Palazzo de' Signori, above the staircase that leads to the 'Catena,' the story of the three Magi." This public staircase, which was on the north side of the Palazzo Vecchio, formed a part of the original fabric of the palace, but it was almost entirely rebuilt by Michelozzo Michelozzi, at the time when he secured the campanile, rebuilt arches in the courtyard, and carried out other works there, shortly after 1450. Vasari, in the second edition of the "Lives," has left the following account of this staircase, which he himself had then lately replaced by the present staircase of the palace: "One thing alone the ingenuity of Michelozzo was unable to remedy, namely, the public staircase; since, from the first, it had been ill-contrived, ill-placed, and badly constructed; steep and without light, and with wooden steps from the first floor upwards. Nevertheless he set to work in such a way, that at the entrance in the courtyard he made a flight of circular steps, and a doorway with pilasters of 'pietra forte,'" etc., "and, moreover, he made all the steps of 'pietra forte' up to the floor where the Signoria was lodged; and he fortified them at the top, and in the middle, with two portcullises, in case of tumults; and at the head of the stair he made a door which is called the 'Catena,' where was continually stationed a 'tavolaccino,' who opened and shut it according as the order was given him, by whoever was in office." Elsewhere, Vasari records that Antonio Pollaiuoli "executed in the Palazzo della Signoria, at the door of the 'Catena,' a 'St. John, the Baptist';" and that the bronze statue of "David," by Andrea Verrocchio, now in the Museum of the Bargello, No. 22, was originally "placed at the head of the stair where stood the 'Catena.'" This statue was finished in 1476; and here, perhaps, we may have an indication of the date of Botticelli's painting of the "Adoration of the Magi," which, from its position, would seem to have been a fresco on the wall above this staircase. Vasari concludes his account of the works executed by Michelozzo in the Palazzo Vecchio, by relating that, when the Duke Cosimo I. took up his residence in the palace, in 1538, he sent for Vasari from Rome, in order that he might prepare the designs for the various alterations and additions to the building which were afterwards carried out. Among these, Vasari prepared a plan for the entire reconstruction of Michelozzo's staircase. In lieu of the lower portion leading to the first floor, Vasari constructed a

App. II, Doc. II, fol. 84, recto.

Vasari, ed. 1568, I, 341.

Id., ed. Sansoni, III, 293.

Id., III, 360.

G. Gaye, Carteggio inedito d'artisti, I, 572.

new flight of stone steps opposite to those which Cronaca had built as an approach to the Sala de' Cinquecento; and the upper part of the old staircase, leading from the first floor to the Sala de' Gigli, he entirely reconstructed in the form in which it now exists. These works, which involved the removal of the "Catena," and the destruction of the paintings by Sandro Botticelli and Antonio Pollaiuoli, were carried out in the interval which elapsed between the publication of the first and second edition of Vasari's "Lives;" for in the first edition, which was printed in 1550, he says that the "David" of Verrocchio "fu posta & è ancora oggi nel palazzo Ducale [as the Palazzo Vecchio was then called] al sommo della scala doue sta la catena;" but in the second edition, printed in 1568, he alters the passage thus: "fu posto in palazzo al sommo della scala, doue staua la catena."

Vasari, ed. Sansoni, IV, 451.

Id., ed. 1550, I, 462.

Id., ed. 1568, I, 481.

It is possible that we may possess some slight and partial copies of this lost fresco of the "Adoration of the Magi" by Botticelli. In the Gallery of the Uffizi are two little panels which originally formed parts of the same "predella:" one, No. 58, represents an "Adoration of the Magi;" the other, No. 57, contains two stories of the "Preaching and Death of St. Peter, Martyr." This "Adoration of the Magi" appears to have been taken from some lost painting by Botticelli, recalling in its manner and composition the "Adoration" in the Uffizi, No. 1286, which came from the church of Santa Maria Novella. The other panel of the "Preaching and Death of St. Peter, Martyr," although by the same hand, does not suggest any such original. Both panels, in short, are by one of the many feeble, and colourless, eclectic painters, who were working in Florence at the beginning of the sixteenth century; by some painter who, although not of the school of Botticelli, happens, in the case of the "Adoration of the Magi," to borrow the composition from him. This conjecture is borne out by a drawing once in the collection of William Young Ottley, who has given a fac-simile of it in his work called "The Italian School of Design," published at London in 1823. In the text which accompanies this plate, the drawing is described as a study "in chiaro-scuro in distemper," by Fra Filippo Lippi, for part of a picture of the "Adoration of the Magi." The present possessor of the drawing is unknown to me; but from the admirable fac-simile engraved by F. C. Lewis, it is seen to be an old copy of a portion of some finished painting by Botticelli. It represents a group of five whole-length, standing figures of men, with the indications of a sixth kneeling figure, in the lower left-hand corner. On comparing this drawing with the little panel of the "Adoration" in the Uffizi, No. 58, it is seen that the principal figure in the drawing is identical with the foremost figure of the group to the right in the painting, a man in a red cap and robe, who leans with his right arm on the shoulder of the figure behind him; and that the kneeling figure, which is partially indicated in the drawing, is found entire in the painting in the figure of a youth in a green tunic and red hose. The remaining four figures in the drawing have, in the painting, been replaced by three feeble figures of the copyist's invention. The real character of the panel is thus explained: unlike the drawing, which must have closely followed the original, the painting is seen to be a free version of it, in which the general composition, and many of the principal figures appear to have been preserved, but in which some figures have been omitted, and others freely varied. The existence of these two early copies, by artists who were not of the school of Botticelli,

l.c., facing p. 14.

points to some original which was well known in Florence at the beginning of the sixteenth century.

The passage in the little panel in the Uffizi, No. 58, which appears to preserve most nearly the character of its original, is the central group of the Virgin, the Child and St. Joseph, with the crouching figure of the Magus, who is kissing the foot of the Christ. The composition of this group of figures is found repeated in an unfinished painting of the "Adoration of the Magi," by Botticelli, which within the last few years has been exhibited in the Gallery of the Uffizi, No. 3436. The picture had long been stored away in the magazines of the Uffizi, when, in 1880, the Commission appointed to examine the vast stores of the gallery, selected it among the number of pictures to be added to the collection. Nothing is known of its history beyond the date at which it came to the Uffizi, which is recorded on a label affixed to the back: "20 Aprile 1779 di Sandro Botticellj." It is painted on an oblong panel, measuring 5 ft. 7 in. in length, and 3 ft. 5½ in. in height: and it appears to have been lightly sketched by Botticelli, in tempera, in monochrome, and afterwards to have been abandoned. At a later time, in the earlier part of the seventeenth century, it was in great part gone over in oil-colours, by some indifferent hand. No portion of the original painting is now perfectly preserved; but Botticelli's hand may still be detected in the distant groups of horsemen, in the middle distance, and in some figures of the lateral groups in the foreground. Excepting in a few passages, such as the head of the Virgin and the distant breaks of landscape, the character of which have been entirely changed by the seventeenth-century painter who attempted to colour the picture, Botticelli's manner is everywhere to be recognized in spite of the repainting, especially in the composition and attitudes of the figures, and in the forms of the heads and draperies. The general design and conception of the painting as a whole, just that aspect of it which suffered least at the hands of the painter who sought to finish it, form, perhaps, its most remarkable traits. Of all the elaborate compositions of this painter, who was so lavish of figures in his stories, this astonishing composition is the most elaborate: in the foreground alone are some eighty figures, not including the groups of horsemen in the middle distance. Although the mass and perspective of many parts of the picture have been destroyed, or thrown out of focus, by the clumsy retouches which disfigure it, this composition remains an extraordinary instance of Botticelli's power of introducing a vast number of figures into a story without confusing its issue, or detracting from its effect. The quiet expectancy of the Virgin and St. Joseph, the profound devotion of the Magi, the zeal of some of their courtiers, the wonder of others, the interminable crowds of their followers, who stream over the distant landscape with eager haste, the fighting soldiers, the restive horses,—are all woven by the painter into a single, entire conception, as if he sought to cast into visible shape the images of Isaiah: "Tunc videbis, et afflues, et mirabitur, et dilatabitur cor tuum quando conversa fuerit ad te multitudo maris, fortitudo gentium venerit tibi."

When the picture was first discovered among the stores of the Uffizi, Mr. C. Heath Wilson, in a notice which appeared in the "Academy," for
l.c., p. 372. 20th November, 1880, declared that the picture contained the portraits of Lorenzo, Il Magnifico, and Savonarola. This absurd suggestion, which has been gravely accepted by Dr. Ulmann and Signor Venturi, has caused

the painting to be generally regarded as one of the last works of Botticelli. Perhaps, the only certain thing which can be said of the picture, in its present state, is that it contains certain Pollaiuolesque motives and forms, which are especially characteristic of the pictures known to have been executed by Botticelli before his journey to Rome in 1481. The figure of the man on horseback, with his right arm raised above his head, to the extreme left of the picture; the head of the man who is holding a restive horse in the opposite corner of the panel; his attitude, which recalls that of the Mercury in the picture of the "Spring"; the forms of the horses in the same group; such things may be cited as peculiarly characteristic of Botticelli's early manner, while he was still under the influence of Antonio Pollaiuoli. Nor are the crouching and tilted figures, by which Botticelli in this "Adoration" seeks to express rapid movement, necessarily a characteristic of his later manner, for they occur already in the cuts, executed from Botticelli's drawings, in Cristoforo Landino's edition of the "Divina Commedia," published at Florence, in 1481. Indeed, these cuts present several points of analogy with this painting, which, in my opinion, was one of the last works executed by Botticelli, before his journey to Rome, in the earlier part of the year 1481.

Dr. Ulmann states that he saw, in the collection of Mr. George Salting, at London, a repetition of the group on the left, with the rearing horse, behind the figure which he took to represent Savonarola, in this unfinished "Adoration." It was executed on canvas, and appeared to have formed part of a larger work. I have not been so fortunate as to see this fragment, which Mr. Salting parted with, some time ago, to a London dealer. Dr. Ulmann took it to be an original work by Botticelli, which had been greatly retouched; but it would seem that it was merely an old copy. It had, I suspect, formed part of the same copy, as the fragment once in the collection of William Young Ottley.

H. Ulmann, Sandro Botticelli, p. 147.

What explanation, then, is to be put upon the analogy of these various paintings and drawings? The little panel, No. 58, in the Uffizi, and the fragment once in the Ottley Collection, may possibly be partial copies of the lost fresco of the Palazzo Vecchio, which, in design, possessed certain points of resemblance with the unfinished "Adoration" in the Uffizi. But the two compositions must not be confused; for whereas the unfinished painting has all the richness and multiplicity of parts, which Botticelli loved to introduce into his smaller panels, the two copies of what I take to have been the fresco in the Palazzo Vecchio possess the simplicity and largeness of design which is necessary to the effectiveness of a wall-painting. There is another circumstance, slight and problematical though it be, which may possibly illustrate the similarity of these two compositions. Vasari in his description of the "Adoration of the Magi," formerly in the church of Santa Maria Novella, says that the painter "distinguished the retinues of the three kings in such a way, that one is able to recognize which are the servants of the one, and which of the other;" a remark which is without meaning, applied to that picture. In the unfinished painting in the Uffizi, however, the companies of the three kings have followed the star by three several roads, which wind over the distant landscape from different quarters of the heavens: so that here, as in many other passages of Vasari's Lives, the mistake, it would seem, is to be traced to some confusion, or misconception, of fact. I have already pursued these conjectures further, perhaps, than their grounds warrant me;

Vasari, ed. 1568, I, 472.

but they will have served their turn, if they lead other students of Botticelli to look into this question of the fresco once in the Palazzo Vecchio.

Botticelli's unfinished picture of the "Adoration of the Magi," is, at present, placed on an easle in front of the unfinished painting of the same subject by Leonardo da Vinci, No. 1252, in the Gallery of the Uffizi. Although these two pictures differ widely from one another in point of drawing and technique, there is much in their conception of the subject which is analogous, and which recalls the contention of certain critics that Botticelli fell, also, under the influence of Leonardo da Vinci. Professor Eugène Müntz, following in the steps of Herr Müller Walde, propounded

l.c., Ser. II, Vol. III, p. 1.

this theory at length in his "Studi Leonardeschi," which appeared in the "Archivio Storico dell' Arte" for 1897. A sufficient proof of the contention, according to Professor Müntz, is afforded by a silver-point drawing of a woman's head in the Library at Windsor Castle. This drawing, we are told, is not only a genuine work of Leonardo's, but it is, also, a study for the no less genuine painting of the "Ascension" in the Museum at Berlin: and in order to prove how deeply Botticelli was influenced by Leonardo, Professor Müntz has reproduced the drawing at Windsor, side by side with the head of the Virgin in Botticelli's "tondo" of the "Magnificat," in the Uffizi, No. 1267 bis. To all this I would merely reply, that the drawing at Windsor is no more a work by Leonardo than the painting at Berlin; and that both must be ascribed to one, or another, of the many Milanese imitators of the Florentine master. Indeed, the drawing at Windsor is nothing else than a free copy of some head by Botticelli, or one of his pupils: it may even be a reminiscence of the head of the Virgin, in the "tondo" of the "Magnificat;" but it was certainly executed, at the least, some twelve or fifteen years after that picture. But as I would not presume to disillusionize either Professor Müntz, or Signor Venturi, of the least of their convictions, let me turn to what appears to be a real analogy of motive between these unfinished paintings of the "Adoration of the Magi." The whole question of whether Botticelli was influenced by Leonardo or not, depends, obviously, upon the relative dates

Vasari, ed. Sansoni, IV, 27, note 3.

of their works. It has long been suggested that the unfinished "Adoration," by Leonardo, in the Uffizi, is the picture which the monks of San Donato a Scopeto, in the suburbs of Florence, commissioned him to paint in March, 1481, for the High Altar of their church. Not only did Filippino Lippi paint the same subject in the picture which afterwards, in 1496, took the place of Leonardo's unfinished painting; but the form and dimensions of Filippino's panel are almost identical with those of Leonardo's panel, which is of the very unusual form of a perfect square. The best argument, however, that the unfinished "Adoration" is the picture begun for the monks of San Donato lies in the fact that the numerous studies by Leonardo which exist for this painting are all of the master's early Florentine period, before his first journey to Milan; their analogy with the few dated drawings of this period which we possess, is, I think, to be clearly demonstrated. But that is a point which I may well leave to Mr. Berenson to establish, in his forthcoming work on Florentine drawings. If Leonardo's unfinished "Adoration" was the picture commissioned by the monks of San Donato, it was begun and abandoned during the time that Botticelli was at Rome, working in the Sistine Chapel: and if I am right in my conjecture that the whole of the "Adorations" by Botticelli which have come down to us, with the one exception of the picture at St. Petersburg, were executed before he went to Rome, in 1481, they are all, therefore, with one exception, earlier in point of date than Leonardo's panel. To this there is but one conclusion, namely, that just as Leonardo has borrowed the motive of the horses and horsemen in the background of his picture, from Antonio Pollaiuoli, so he has taken the motive of the crouching figures of the Magi from one of the many "Adorations" of Botticelli. This theory will not, of course, commend itself to those critics who argue, that since Leonardo was a greater artist than any of his contemporaries, therefore he could have borrowed from none of them: but "the difference between a bad artist and a good one," as William Blake said, "is, that the bad artist *seems* to copy a great deal, the good one *does* copy a great deal."

If the "Adoration of the Magi" formerly in the church of Santa Maria Novella were painted, as I conjecture, in 1477, no considerable interval could have elapsed between the execution of that picture and of the famous painting called the "Spring." Much speculation, but little research has been made in regard to the history of the latter picture. It has been generally assumed that the "Spring" and the "Birth of Venus" were painted for Lorenzo, Il Magnifico; a theory which, if not invented, was first launched upon the world with the semblance of authority by the late Sir Joseph Crowe, in the "Gazette des Beaux Arts," in 1886. "C'est probablement," that writer remarked, "pour Laurent le Magnifique que Botticelli exécuta le Printemps et la Naissance de Vénus, qui ont survécu aux holocaustes de Savonarole parce qu'on les avait envoyés à la ville du vieux Côme, à Castello." It would be idle to attempt to trace all the mistaken assertions that have arisen from this tissue of misconceptions, not one of which is founded on any tittle of evidence. Had these pictures been painted for Lorenzo, Il Magnifico, they would have been described in the elaborate inventory of all the works of art, furniture and other household goods, which were found in his various palaces and villas at the time of his death in 1492. Furthermore, the villa of Castello never belonged to Cosimo, Pater Patriæ, or even to Lorenzo, Il Magnifico. The earliest notice which we possess of the "Spring" and the "Birth of Venus" is that of the Anonimo Gaddiano, who was writing in 1542-48, but who is here quoting some earlier writer. "At Castello," he says, "in the house of the Sig. Giovanni de' Medici, [*i.e.*, Giovanni delle Bande Nere, who died in 1526,] he [Botticelli] painted several pictures which are among the most beautiful works that he made." The only other original notice is that of Vasari, who in the first edition of the "Lives," published in 1550, thus describes these pictures by Botticelli: "Throughout the city," he says, "in various houses, are many 'tondi' and naked women, done by his hand; among which, at the present time, there are still at Castello, a seat of the Duke Cosimo of Florence, [the son of Giovanni delle Bande Nere,] two allegorical pictures; the one of the birth of Venus, whom those airs and winds bring to land, with the Loves; and the other, also a Venus, whom the Graces trick with flowers, signifying the Spring; which are expressed by him with much grace." These two notices, when taken together, show that the "Spring" and the "Birth of Venus" were already at Castello whilst it was in the possession of Giovanni delle Bande Nere, between the years 1503 and 1526, long before that branch of the house of Medici succeeded to the Duchy and possessions of the elder branch, after the murder of the Duke Alessandro. Vasari, in his "Life

l.c., 2e Pér., Vol. XXXIV, p. 184.

App. II, Doc. XXVI.

App. II, Doc. II, fol. 85, recto.

Vasari, ed. 1550, I, 492.

Id., ed. Sansoni, VI, 72.

H

of Tribolo," says that this villa was "originally erected after a very good design by Pier Francesco de' Medici:" but in this Vasari is in error. I read in the "Denunzia" returned in 1480-1 by Lorenzo and Giovanni, the sons of Pierfrancesco de' Medici, that they possessed among their vast estates, "a farm [podere] situated at L'Olmo a Castello, in the parish of San Michele at a place called Il Vivaio, with its boundaries and confines, and with a palace [palagio dasignore], and with a walled garden, and with its appurtenances of household goods, which we hold for our habitation and use; bought in the year 1477 from Niccolò di Andrea di Lotteringo della Stufa; the deed drawn up by Ser Giovanni da Romena." This villa, it seems, had been sold to Niccolò della Stufa, in 1454, by Dionigi Da Mangona; and earlier in the century it had been in the possession of the Del Milanese. Vasari's error in regard to its origin is, perhaps, to be explained by the fact, that he more than once confuses Lorenzo with his father, Pierfrancesco: and in Vasari's assertion, that the palace of Castello "fu murato" by Pierfrancesco, may linger some tradition of the reparations and embellishments which the house underwent when it came into the possession of Lorenzo. Nor is it difficult to discover the motives that led to the purchase of this villa. Pierfrancesco de' Medici, the son of a natural brother of Cosimo de' Medici, Pater Patriæ, had died in 1476, leaving his immense fortune to his two sons, who were still youths; Lorenzo having been born in 1463, and Giovanni in 1467. Lorenzo, Il Magnifico, relates in his "Ricordi," that when Pierfrancesco came of age, in 1451, his father being dead, the property of their family was divided; a half of all their goods and estates, and a third part of their trading interests, falling to the share of Pierfrancesco. In this division of the property, besides the house in the Via Larga, adjoining the palace of Cosimo de' Medici, the villa of Trebbio, and houses in Prato and Scarperia fell to the share of Pierfrancesco; but no villa in the vicinity of Florence. It was to remedy that want, that Lorenzo di Pierfrancesco, after his father's death, bought the villa of Castello in 1477. There is evidence, as I have shown, that the pictures of the "Spring" and the "Birth of Venus" were never in the possession of Lorenzo, Il Magnifico, and that they were already at Castello before 1526. When Piero de' Medici fled from Florence in 1494, the works of art, furniture, and household stuff, which he had inherited from his father, Lorenzo, Il Magnifico, were confiscated and sold by the order of the Signoria; but Lorenzo and Giovanni di Pierfrancesco de' Medici, who had joined the popular party, were allowed to continue in the full enjoyment of their property. From the time that Castello came into the possession of the sons of Pierfrancesco de' Medici, until the time at which the notice, preserved by the "Anonimo Gaddiano" was written, the villa, with its furniture and works of art, had remained undisturbed. To these premises there is but the one conclusion, that the "Spring" and the "Birth of Venus" were originally painted at the instance of Lorenzo di Pierfrancesco de' Medici for the decoration of the Villa of Castello: and this conclusion is borne out in the case of the "Spring" by the internal evidence of the painting, which undoubtedly shows that the picture was executed c. 1478, shortly after the "Adoration of the Magi" once in the church of Santa Maria Novella. Messrs. Crowe and Cavalcaselle had long since expressed the same opinion: the "Birth of Venus," however, which they consider to be a work of the same period, is of a later time, as I shall endeavour to

App. II, Doc. XV, fol. 412, tergo.

G. Carocci, Dintorni di Firenze, p. 145.

App. II, Doc. XV.

Cavalcaselle and Crowe, ed. Le Monnier, VI, 215.

AN ALLEGORY OF SPRING *Gallery of the Academy, Florence*

show in its place. Another indication of the date of the "Spring" is afforded by the figure of Flora, which seems to have been suggested by one of the figures in the relief of the "Birth of the Baptist" by Antonio Pollaiuoli, in the silver altar of San Giovanni, which is now preserved in the Museum of the Opera del Duomo, at Florence. The commission for this relief was given to Antonio on the 2nd January, 1477.

Lorenzo di Pierfrancesco de' Medici has long been known as the patron for whom Botticelli afterwards executed one of his greatest works, the series of drawings in illustration to the "Divina Commedia" of Dante; but few notices have been collected regarding his patronage of the artists and men of letters of his time. Vasari mentions him on one occasion only, as the patron for whom Michelangelo executed his early statue of the young St. John: but for Lorenzo di Pierfrancesco, Filippino would seem to have painted the "Adoration of the Magi," formerly above the high altar of the church of San Donato a Scopeto, near Florence; and for him, also, I suspect, Leonardo da Vinci began the painting of the same subject, which had been intended for the same altar, but which was left unfinished, and of which the picture by Filippino finally took the place. Lastly, it would seem that Signorelli painted more than one picture for the Villa of Castello. The grandfather of Lorenzino de' Medici, who by his murder of the Duke Alessandro unintentionally placed his cousin Cosimo, the son of Giovanni delle Bande Nere, on the throne of Tuscany,—the memory of Lorenzo di Pierfrancesco was little acceptable at the time at which Vasari wrote. The portrait of Lorenzo di Pierfrancesco is not to be found among the portraits of the Medici, which were executed by Cristofano dell' Altissimo for Cosimo I.; and Vasari was too accomplished a courtier to remind the world unnecessarily of a branch of the Ducal family whom the reigning Duke could only regard, at least officially, with horror and detestation.

Vasari, ed. Sansoni, VII, 147.

Id., III, 473.

Id., IV, 27, note 3.

Id., III, 689.

Of the relations of Lorenzo di Pierfrancesco with the men of letters of his time, I will here only stay to speak of the poems which Angelo Poliziano addressed to him. Already in 1482 he had dedicated one of his "Sylvæ," the "Manto," to Lorenzo; and at a later time an elegy and some epigrams. In the dedicatory letter prefixed to the "Manto," Poliziano requests Lorenzo not longer to delay the publication of his own verses, "quæ tibi musæ amatoria carmina vernaculæ suggerunt": but in spite of the compliment, both his amatorious and his pious pieces have hitherto remained in manuscript. Several are to be found in a manuscript of the Biblioteca Nazionale, at Florence, Cl. vii., Cod. 1034; and in another volume in the same collection, Cl. vii., Cod. 374, may be seen a "Sacra Rappresentazione" of the "Invention of the Cross," as well as a "Lauda." Another "Lauda" has been printed by Francesco Cionacci, in his collection of the "Rime Sacre" of Lorenzo, Il Magnifico, and various members of his family, published at Florence, in 1680: and other pieces are among the manuscripts of the Biblioteca Laurenziana, at Florence. These verses show that Lorenzo di Pierfrancesco possessed, at least, no little taste, and reading, and literary art.

A. Ambrogini, Prose Volgari, etc., ed. Del Lungo, pp. 287, 253 & 124.

On the death of Lorenzo di Pierfrancesco de' Medici, in 1503, the villa of Castello fell, as we have seen, to the share of his nephew, Giovanni delle Bande Nere; and after his death, during the siege of Florence, the house was fired, and narrowly escaped destruction. Here Cosimo, the son of Giovanni, chiefly lived before he became Duke of Florence, in 1537. He then began to enlarge the house, and alter the gardens; and finally undertook the erection of all those elaborate fountains and water-works, which Vasari has described at length in his life of Tribolo. The villa and gardens of Castello, which still remain at the foot of Monte Morello, some two and a half miles from the Barriera del Ponte all' Asse, on the road to Prato, can now show little that is earlier than the time of Cosimo I.; even the original house, which was then incorporated with the new villa, is to be traced with difficulty. The pictures of the "Spring" and the "Birth of Venus" were permitted, however, to remain among the ornaments of the house. In an inventory, taken in the year 1598, of all the household goods then in the palace of Castello, I read that "in the salotto, where the Great Duke eats," hung "one large picture on panel, on which are painted three Goddesses who are dancing, and Cupid above, and Mercury, and other figures, without a frame, antique"; and "in the chamber of the Duke, on the ground floor," was "one large picture on canvas, antique, in which is painted a Venus above a shell, with other figures, in a gilt frame." According to a later inventory of the year 1638, these two pictures, which had been reframed, then hung with the "Pallas" of Botticelli, which had been brought from the Palazzo Medici, "in the salotto," leading out of the "Sala of the Palazzo Vecchio," or older part of the house, "with the window looking over the meadow, in front of the Vivai," which Vasari describes lying between the villa and the Arno. Both pictures remained at Castello until 1815, when they were brought to the Uffizi: for a long time the "Birth of Venus" hung in the first corridor, and the "Spring" in the then private corridor of Vasari, leading from the Uffizi to the Palazzo Pitti, where it remained unnoticed and almost unknown. At the time that Messrs. Crowe and Cavalcaselle published the first edition of their "History of Painting in Italy," in 1864, the "Spring" had been taken to the Gallery of the Florentine Academy, where it still remains.

Vasari, ed. Sansoni, VI, 71.

App. II, Doc. XVI.

App. II, Doc. XVII, fol. I, tergo.

Vasari, ed. Sansoni, VI, 73.

l.c., II, 418.

Before I pass on to discuss the subject of the picture, which commonly goes by the name of the "Spring," I will attempt to dispel a legend which has grown up about this, and other paintings by Botticelli, according to which these pictures contain the portraits of Simonetta, the mistress of Giuliano di Piero de' Medici. I will not trouble to trace this legend beyond a note by a Mr. Tyrwhitt, which was published by Mr. Ruskin in 1873, in his "Ariadne Florentina." In that note, Mr. Tyrwhitt sought to prove that Simonetta Vespucci, after the death of Giuliano, "must have been induced to let Sandro draw from her whole person undraped, more or less"; and that she is represented in the "Spring," the "Birth of Venus," the "Calumny," and other paintings by Botticelli. This legend was afterwards revived by Signor Venturi in the "Archivio Storico dell' Arte," amongst other writers; and more recently by Dr. Richter in his "Lectures on the National Gallery." According to the last writer, the painting of "Mars and Venus," in the National Gallery, is among those pictures which contain portraits of Simonetta and Giuliano de' Medici. But what is it that we really know about Simonetta and Giuliano?

l.c., p. 257.

In the year 1475, on the 28th of June, at the yearly jousts in the Piazza di Santa Croce, with which the festivities in celebration of the feast of St. John the Baptist, the patron saint of Florence, were concluded, the prize was carried off by the brother of Lorenzo, Il Magnifico, Giuliano de' Medici, who wore the favour of Simonetta, the beautiful wife of Marco Vespucci. According to the notions of mediæval chivalry, ladies were as

A. Neri, Giornale Storico della Letteratura Italiana, V, 131.

indispensable to a joust, as were arms or horses; and it would be entirely unhistorical to necessarily imagine in the attentions of Giuliano to Simonetta anything beyond an elaborate piece of ceremonial compliment. Angelo Poliziano, then a young man of twenty-one, desiring to obtain the protection of Lorenzo, Il Magnifico (or in the phrase he addressed to Lorenzo, "porre il nido in tuo felice ligno"), began the "Stanze" celebrating this joust, in imitation of those in which Luca Pulci had celebrated the joust won by Lorenzo, Il Magnifico, in 1469. While Poliziano was still engaged in composing the "Stanze," and while all the brilliant pomp and circumstance of the joust of Giuliano were fresh in the popular mind, Simonetta, who had been born of a Genoese family, c. 1453, and who had married Marco Vespucci at the age of sixteen, was seized by some tisical malady, and died on the 26th April, 1476. If the joust had been an occasion of compliment to Giuliano, the death of Simonetta proved a still greater occasion of condolence. Poliziano, who has meanwhile been received into the family of Lorenzo, Il Magnifico, as the tutor of his children, turned from the unfinished "Stanze," to express the sentiments both of Giuliano and himself on her death, in epigrams of a choice latinity. Bernardo Pulci wrote an elegy, "de obitu divæ Simonettæ ad Iulianum medicem": and Luigi Pulci, and Michele Marullo, amongst others, addressed an epigram to the knight of Simonetta. In less than two years, her death was followed by the murder of Giuliano. At the time of Simonetta's death, none of the pictures which are said to contain her portrait were painted, or even invented: and at the time of Giuliano's murder, in 1478, one only, the "Spring," could possibly have been begun. All historical evidence is thus entirely opposed to this legend: but there is one circumstance which is more damaging to this pretty fiction than any such historical evidence; and that is that none of these paintings contain a single portrait. Indeed, the explanations of Signor Venturi and Dr. Richter are pictorially not less absurd, than are historically Mr. Tyrwhitt's conjectures.

This fantastic medley of misconceptions seems to have had its origin in one of those notices, for the most part of doubtful authenticity, which Vasari inserted into the second edition of his life of Botticelli. "In the Guardaroba of the Duke Cosimo," says Vasari, "are two heads of women by his hand, which are very beautiful; one of these is said to have been the 'inamorata' of Giuliano de' Medici, the brother of Lorenzo, and the other Madonna Lucrezia de' Tornabuoni, the wife of the same Lorenzo." I find in an inventory of the Guardaroba, taken in the year 1553, the second picture correctly described as a portrait of Lucrezia, the wife of Piero de' Medici, though the name of the painter is not given, but no portrait which can be identified with the other head of the "inamorata" of Giuliano. It is possible that the head in profile which now hangs in the Gallery of the Palazzo Pitti, No. 353, as a portrait of "La Bella Simonetta" by Botticelli, may be the picture which Vasari saw in the Guardaroba of Duke Cosimo. This beautiful portrait, which has been much descried because it represents a plain and unattractive person, is certainly a work of the school of Botticelli, and must have been painted about the time of Giuliano's death. But be that as it may, is it not far more probable that the portrait of the "inamorata" of Giuliano, which Vasari saw in the Guardaroba, was a portrait of the mother of his son, afterwards Pope Clement VII., a lady of the Gorini family, rather than of Simonetta, the

Vasari, ed. 1568, I, 474.

wife of Marco Vespucci? At any rate I have shown how entirely devoid of any foundation is the assumption that portraits of Simonetta, or Giuliano, are to be found in these paintings by Botticelli. I would add, that no portrait of Simonetta is known to exist. The head of a woman in profile, bearing the legend, SIMONETTA JANVENSIS VESPVCCIA, now in the Musée Condé, at Chantilly, No. 13, has been recognized as a head of Cleopatra by Piero di Cosimo, which Vasari saw in the collection of Francesco da San Gallo. The head is clearly an ideal head of Piero di Cosimo's manneristic type; and the inscription was, no doubt, added after the panel was seen by Vasari.

Vasari, ed. Sansoni, IV, 144.

The only indication which we possess of the subject of the picture called the "Spring," beyond the evidence of the painting itself, is the description of Vasari, who, in his easy fashion, speaks of it as an allegorical picture of "a Venus whom the graces trick with flowers, signifying the Spring." That the central figure is Venus, draped, like other earlier representations of the goddess in Florentine art, is shown by the figure of Cupid who hovers about her: that the three Graces are represented, as Vasari says, and Mercury, as the writer of the old inventory noted, might easily be demonstrated; but not so the three figures on the right of the picture. The similarity has been remarked between this painting and the description of the realm of Venus, in the first book of the "Stanze" of Poliziano:

l.c., St. 68, ed. Bologna, 1494.

"oue ogni gratia si diletta,
Oue bilta di fiori al crin fa brolo,
Oue tutto lasciuo drieto a Flora
Zephiro uola, et la uerde herba infiora."

Here, no doubt, in these images of the Graces, of the wanton Zephyr flying after Flora, and of the green grass breaking into flower, as elsewhere in the "Stanze," we find many of the details, and much of the sentiment of the painting. But the subject of a great picture, such as this picture undoubtedly is, does not lie in its details, but in its central idea: and the central idea of this picture manifestly consists, as Vasari says, in a certain conception of Venus expressed as an allegory. In vain do we search the "Stanze" of Poliziano for any conception of Venus which may explain the picture: the Venus of the "Stanze," followed by Cupid and his crew, Pleasure and Deceit, vain Hope and vain Desire, Quarrels, Truces, Tears, Suspicions, and fifty such, may be the Venus of Anacreon, or the Anthology; but it is not the Venus of the "Spring."

Now that the Greek and Latin poets, as well as the Italian, have been searched for some passage which might explain the subject of Botticelli's picture, (we owe this labour to Dr. Warburg, the author of that admirable little work, "Sandro Botticellis 'Geburt der Venus' und 'Frühling,'") it would seem that the painting is no mere illustration of some particular passage, but a cento of many ideas, suggested chiefly by certain passages out of Lucretius. The poem "De Rerum Natura" had been recovered by Poggio Bracciolini from some German monastery about the year 1417; and the numerous copies transcribed during the century, of the manuscript discovered by Poggio (eight are preserved in the Laurentian Library alone, at Florence), testify to the eagerness with which it was read and studied. In the age of Lorenzo, Il Magnifico, the works of the antique Latin and Greek writers were among the modern literature of Europe; and this

J. A. Symonds, Renaissance in Italy: The Fine Arts, ed. 1877, p. 251.

poem by Lucretius was newer and younger than Dante. A passage in the Fifth Book, one of the many splendid, starlike passages which shine out from the obscure and sombre texture of this magnificent poem, contains a description of the procession of the seasons, which is introduced in illustration of a theory, that, as the seasons are renewed in a regular order, so the moon is daily renewed in regular, successive phases. In this passage the Spring is thus described:

"It ver et Venus, et Veneris praenuntius ante
Pennatus graditur, zephyri vestigia propter
Flora quibus mater praespargens ante viai
Cuncta coloribus egregiis et odoribus opplet."

l.c., V, 737-740.

"Spring and Venus go their way, and the winged harbinger of Venus [Cupid], steps on before; and close upon Zephyr's footsteps Flora, their mother, strawing all the way before them, covers it with rarest colours and odours." It is this goddess whom Lucretius invokes in the magnificent exordium of his poem, the Venus Genetrix of Universal Nature, by whom

"genus omne animantum
Concipitur visitque exortum lumina solis,"

Id., I, 4-5.

by whom every kind of living creature is conceived, and brought forth, beholds the light of the sun. This is she at whose advent, the Spring, the winds and clouds flee away, the earth manifold in works puts forth sweet-smelling flowers, the levels of the sea laugh, and the heavens grown calm shine with diffused light:

"Te, dea, te fugiunt venti, te nubila caeli,
Adventumque tuum, tibi suavis daedala tellus
Summittit flores, tibi rident aequora ponti
Placatumque nitet diffuso lumine caelum.
Nam simul ac species patefactast verna diei
Et reserata viget genitabilis aura favoni,
Aeriae primum volucres te, diva, tuumque
Significant initum perculsae corda tua vi.
Inde ferae pecudes persultant pabula laeta
Et rapidos tranant amnis: ita capta lepore
Te sequitur cupide quo quamque inducere pergis.
Denique per maria ac montis fluviosque rapacis
Frondiferasque domos avium camposque virentis
Omnibus incutiens blandum per pectora amorem
Efficis ut cupide generatim saecla propagent."

Id., I, 6-20.

These passages from Lucretius not only explain, as I think, the conception of Venus, which forms the central idea of this picture, but, also, the three obscurer figures of the composition, namely, Spring, Flora and Zephyr. In regard to the remaining figures of the Graces and Mercury, it is not difficult to account for their introduction into the allegory. Their association with Venus is one of the commonplaces of Roman mythology; and the passages out of the Latin authors, which might be quoted in illustration of it, are many. Two of the most characteristic sort must suffice. The conception of the Graces accompanying Venus at the approach of Spring, occurs in Horace, in one of the Odes:

Lib. I, car. IV.

> "Solvitur acris hiems grata vice veris et Favoni, &c.
> Tam Cytherea choros ducit Venus imminente luna,
> Junctaeque Nymphis Gratiae decentes
> Alterno terram quatiunt pede, &c."

Again, the conception of the Graces and Mercury, with Cupid, among the attendants of Venus, is found in another Ode of Horace, in which the poet calls on the Goddess to visit the house of his mistress, Glycera, adding:

Lib. I, car. XXX.

> "Fervidus tecum puer, et solutis
> Gratiae zonis, properentque Nymphae, &c.,
> Mercuriusque."

These two passages are sufficient to illustrate the kind of reminiscence of antique mythology which suggested the introduction of these figures into the painting of the "Spring." Other passages might be quoted from the Italian poets of the Renaissance, such as the passage out of the "Rusticus" of Poliziano, v. 210-220, which Dr. Warburg has cited: "Auricomæ, jubare exorto," etc.; but a multiplicity of such instances would hardly serve to elucidate further the subject of the picture. The conception of Venus which is embodied in its allegory, whether or no suggested by Lucretius, is not to be mistaken; reverting as it does to the conception of the Goddess in its origin, as the personification of the fructifying powers of Nature, which are yearly renewed with the Spring. Perhaps, in the two paintings of Venus, which Botticelli executed for Lorenzo di Pierfrancesco de' Medici, are to be traced that double conception of Aphrodite; of Aphrodite Urania, the Heavenly Venus, the daughter of Uranus, born of the sea without mother; and of Aphrodite Pandemos, the daughter of Zeus and Dione, the Venus of universal nature, spiritualized by Botticelli in his painting of the "Spring," which certain later writers have sought to emphasize; and notably Franciscus Junius in his work "De Pictura Veterum," out of certain passages in Pausanias and Lucian. But from such debatable interpretations, let us turn to examine the details of this picture in the light of the passages which I have cited.

A. Warburg, Sandro Botticellis 'Geburt der Venus' und 'Frühling,' p. 37.

The scene of the picture is a grove of orange-trees, starred with blossom, and heavy with fruit, recalling the trees which Paolo Uccello introduces with so much decorative effect, into the backgrounds of his battle-pieces, where the fruits glow among the leaves,

> "Like golden lamps in a green night."

Botticelli may have intended by it the tree which, in the "Stanze" of Poliziano, grew before the entrance of the Palace of Venus:

Stanze, I, 94.

> "una gran pianta,
> Che fronde ha di smeraldo, e pomi doro."

In the centre of the painting, in a gap in the wood, is a bush of myrtle, flecked with white blossom, which forms a kind of aureole about the figure of Venus, who is standing before it:

Id., I, 85.

> "El mirtho, che sua dea sempre uagheggia,
> Di bianchi fiori e uerdi capelli orna."

Behind the trees, the level distance stretches away under the serene heaven. The foreground is most elaborately and exquisitely painted with flowers.

Unlike Poliziano, who prefers the flowers which recall allusions to antique fable or poetry, Botticelli paints those only which he found in the woods and fields around Florence; such as the rose, the violet, the daisy, the wood-strawberry, the purple iris, the wild orchid, the colts-foot, or the wood-spurge. For representations of flowers more beautiful than these, we must turn to the drawings of Leonardo da Vinci.

The mediæval conception of Venus, as a stately draped woman, was, perhaps, more familiar to the Florentine mind in the earlier part of the fifteenth century, than the antique conception of her in the nude. Leon Battista Alberti, in his second book, "Della Pittura," speaking of propriety of invention in Painting, says, "sarebbe cosa non conveniente vestire Venere o Minerva con uno capperone da sacomanno:" and in a "Judgment of Paris," on a "desco da parto" in the Carrand collection, in the Museum of the Bargello, at Florence, the three Goddesses are attired, in long, trailing dresses of the time. In the "Spring," Botticelli represents Venus veiled and draped in solemn, stole-like raiment; and of a grave beauty, scarcely to be distinguished from that of his Madonnas. Her robe, which falls about her with something of a studied disorder, is of purple diapered with gold; her white dress is embroidered about the neck and breasts with a flame-like ornament; and over her shoulders falls a jewelled necklace, from which hangs an ornament in the form of a crescent moon.

l.c., ed. Janitschek, p. 115.

Above the figure of Venus flies Cupid, blindfold, who shoots from his bow an arrow barbed with flame. In this figure alone is there any reminiscence of antique design in the picture: the attitude is to be traced to one of those flying "putti" of the Roman sarcophagi, which Donatello imitated on the tomb of Giovanni and Piccarda de' Medici, in the old sacristy of San Lorenzo, at Florence.

"It ver et Venus:" on the left of the Goddess, Spring precedes her, with Zephyr and Flora. Departing, on the one hand, from Lucretius' image of the wind, "Veneris praenuntius," and on the other, from that common conception of Zephyr and Flora, which Milton enshrined in the line:

"Mild as when Zephyrus on Flora breathes,"

Botticelli, by a piece of his own invention, represents the Spring, a half-naked figure, clad in a loose, diaphanous drapery, and flying before the Wind, who forces his way down through the trees, and attempts to take her with both his hands. As he breathes on her, flowers fall out of her mouth into the lap of Flora, who goes forward beside her. The figure of Zephyr is coloured a faint, bluish hue, to represent the airy body of the wind. As for the figure of Flora, her attire is as bizarre as her person:

"Candida e ella, et candida la uesta,
Ma pur di rose et fiori dipinta e dherba."

Stanze, I, 43.

Her white dress is elaborately embroidered with knots of roses, cloves, corn-cockles; her head and neck are wreathed with flowers; a girdle of roses is about her waist, and her lap is filled with the roses and flowers of Spring, with which she straws all the way before them:

"praespargens ante viai
Cuncta coloribus egregiis et odoribus opplet."

The group of the three Graces, on Venus' right hand, is, perhaps, the most lovely passage of the picture. The translucent draperies in which these figures are clad, are caught back against them, as they move in a stately round; their lithe, boy-like limbs gleaming through the folds of the lawn:

Martial, VIII, 68.

> "Femineum lucet sic per bombycina corpus,
> Calculus in nitida sic numeratur aqua."

This conception of the Graces, with its exquisite design of the interlocked hands, was probably suggested to Botticelli by a passage in the Third Book, "Della Pittura," by Leon Battista Alberti, where, after quoting Lucian's description of the "Calumny" of Apelles, which at a later time suggested to Botticelli the picture in the Uffizi, Alberti proposes as a subject for the painter "those three sisters, to whom Hesiod gave the names Aglaia, Euphrosyne and Thalia, with their hands entwined, laughing, and clad in ungirt, diaphanous vesture." This description is borrowed from Seneca, "De Beneficiis;" and in the Latin version of his treatise, Alberti quotes, *more prophetarum*, the actual words of the Roman writer: "implexis inter se manibus, ridentes, solutaque perlucida veste ornatas."

De Beneficiis, I, 3. L. B. Alberti, De Pictura, MS. Riccard. 767, fol. 81, recto.

To the extreme left of the picture, turning away from the other figures, is the god Mercury. A purple mantle, powdered with golden tongues of flame, is caught about his naked body by a girdle, from which hangs the "herpe," or short sword of the god. On his head is a helmet, and on his feet, in the form of winged "socci," are the "talaria aurea" of the poet. Conceived in the character which the ancients always held of him, "lucri auctor et negotiator," the god of increase, by ways fair or foul, his left hand resting upon his hip, he easily lifts above his head, with the right, his "serpent-rod," about which gathers a little cloud, "like a man's hand," the harbinger of coming showers. The painter seems here to be refining upon the virtues which Virgil ascribes to the Caduceus in the Æneid, where he speaks of the power which it brought the god over the winds and rain-clouds:

l.c., IV. 245.

> "Illa fretus agit ventos, et turbida tranat
> Nubila."

This power of the god over the wind and rains is symbolized in the earlier marble relief of Mercury, by Agostino di Duccio, in the third chapel on the right in the temple of the Malatesta, at Rimini, by little clouds which are represented gathering about the knees of the figure.

Although so large a portion of the imagery of this picture of the "Spring" has its counterpart in the imagery of the "Stanze" of Poliziano, the conception of Venus, which forms the central idea of the painting, is not to be found in, nor explained by, the verses of Poliziano. This similarity of detail running through the painting and the verses, the undeniable resemblance in the imaginative quality of their invention, can only be explained by the supposition that Botticelli, like Michelangelo, "consigliato dal Poliziano," in the design of the relief of "Hercules and the Centaurs," according to Vasari, had the idea of the "Spring" given him by the great scholar. The conception of the "Birth of Venus" was certainly suggested by Poliziano, as I shall show in its place; whether personally or not, is another question. But there is a further circumstance which seems to lend colour to this theory. Botticelli's picture of the "Spring," and the

Vasari, ed. Sansoni, VII, 143.

so-called picture of "Pan," by Luca Signorelli, in the museum at Berlin, confessedly stand apart by themselves, among the paintings of antique story, or mythology, which as yet had been produced in Florence, on account of the learned and highly imaginative conception of their subjects. When such subjects occur on the earlier "cassone," and furniture panels, they are either closely related in conception with the triumphs and public shows, which were made in Florence on the feast of St. John, the Baptist, or on the feasts of the patron saints of the various quarters of the city, or they are to be traced directly to some classical source, which was well known at the time. But the "Pan," like the "Spring," offers no such points of comparison, nor can it be traced to any single classical source. Indeed, the allegory of Signorelli's painting, which embodies some antique personification of the primæval forces of nature, akin to that in the "Spring," yet remains to be elucidated in its finer meanings. Vasari says Id., III, 689.
that for "Lorenzo de' Medici," Signorelli painted "in una tela, alcuni Dei ignudi"; doubtless, the picture of the "Pan": and, adds Vasari, Signorelli also painted for Lorenzo, "a picture of our Lady with two small figures of prophets in monochrome, which is now at Castello, a villa of the Duke Cosimo." Now, neither of these two pictures could have been painted for Lorenzo, Il Magnifico; for neither are set down in the inventory taken at the time of his death: and the picture of our Lady, with the two small figures of Prophets, remained at Castello until the beginning of the present century. I suspect, then, that for "Lorenzo de' Medici," in Vasari's account, we should read "Lorenzo di Pierfrancesco de' Medici"; and I also suspect that, like the "Spring," the painting of the "Pan" was done by Signorelli, for the decoration of the Castello, upon the advice of Poliziano. Without such an explanation both paintings remain singular and inexplicable among the works of their authors. The one early notice, which I have been able to discover in regard to the App. II,
"Pan," is, that in the year 1598, it was in the Palazzo Medici, now the Doc. XVI.
Palazzo Riccardi, where it may have been removed by Cosimo I at the time that he enlarged and remodelled the villa of Castello. It is to be hoped that Dr. Warburg will illustrate for us the obscure but fascinating allegory of the "Pan," in the way that he has illustrated the allegory of the "Spring": but whether any evidence will be forthcoming, to substantiate, or refute, my theory of the origin of Signorelli's picture is a matter, I fear, of the greatest uncertainty. But I stay too long in discussing the outward meaning of a painting in which, it has been finely said, "an under-current of original sentiment" occurs "as the real matter of the picture through the veil of its ostensible subject."

With so much in that "real matter" of the "Spring" which is the expression of what was most intimate, and individual, in the painter's moods and habit of perception, communicable only in the precise pictorial form in which he expressed it, we may well pause at the attempt to speak even of its more tangible traits. That "appetito di bellezza," which Lorenzo, Il Magnifico, urged as a sufficient ground and justification of his amatorious verses; that pre-occupation with beauty in its rarer qualities, which is the real source of the "Stanze" of Poliziano, occurs in the "Spring," but inseparably from its naturalism on the one hand, and its fantastic temper on the other, as the real source of its inspiration. In no painting which possesses the sentiment of beauty at all in the same degree, are there so many forms and traits so far removed from the accepted ideas of beauty. "There is no excellent Beauty that hath not some strangeness in the proportion;" and to this element of strangeness in the beauty of the "Spring," is to be traced not only its excellency, but the charm and fascination which the picture has exercised in our own time. In conception antique, solemn, religious; in expression modern, as it then was, Florentine, bizarre, fantastic; it is in the dexterous fusion of these opposite elements that the strangeness in the proportion of the thing chiefly lies. In common with the other Florentine painters and sculptors of the fifteenth century, Botticelli dimly divines the antique world in the dawning light of the Renaissance, and seeks to realize it, unconsciously perhaps, with the help of his imagination, and of the world around him. He derives the subject-matter of his picture wholly from antiquity; but of Greek or Roman sculpture, or painting, he knows little or nothing; nothing, at any rate, that can hinder or distort his vision. And so just that which chilled and destroyed Post-Raphaelite art, served only in Botticelli, to quicken his vision of the world around him, to see it with younger and fresher eyes. Such were the elements and chances that went to make the "Spring" the most original and inventive picture which Florentine art had as yet produced. The mere circumstance that the subject-matter of Florentine painting was in so large a measure traditional or prescribed, forced the Florentine painters to expend their powers on purely pictorial qualities of treatment. But in the "Spring" we have an imaginative subject treated with great imagination, apart from its pictorial originality.

For the composition of the picture there is no precedent. Although it represents but a single scene, the subject is treated in a series of incidents. The figures move over the background like the figures in a tapestry: perhaps, the composition was suggested by one of those "panni fiandreschi," which are found described in the inventory of the goods of Lorenzo, Il Magnifico, and in other such documents of the time. In coming to examine the technique of the "Spring," in its sequence, in order of time, with the "Adoration of the Magi" formerly in Santa Maria Novella, and the earlier "tondo" in the National Gallery, we must not forget that in executing a painting of the dimensions of the "Spring," Botticelli would necessarily modify the technical method which he employed in a composition of small figures. In order to find a parallel instance, in point of execution, with the "Spring," we must go back to the larger panels of the "Fortitude" in the Uffizi, and the "St. Sebastian" at Berlin. Apart from the simplicity and largeness of design, which is necessary to the due effect of nearly life-sized figures, Botticelli, in all these larger panels, not only worked from an elaborate cartoon, and relied far more than in his smaller panels upon his particular use of line as his principal means of expression, but he also adopted a colour-scheme of the simplest character, which greatly differs from that of his smaller panels. Such a painting as the unfinished "Adoration" in the Uffizi, affords grounds for the conjecture whether the pictures of this character were executed from a finished cartoon at all, or merely from studies and sketches, in the same way as his "predella" panels? But the question is too large and difficult to be discussed in this place. The "Spring" is painted on a panel measuring 6 ft. 8¼ in. in height, and 10 ft. 4 in. in breadth. It is executed in tempera unvarnished, on a "gesso" ground; and is in an extraordinary state of preservation. Just that coat of dirt, which has robbed it of its original freshness, and left it a little sombre in colour, is the best proof of its fine condition: the few retouches, which may here and there be detected, being local restorations of little moment.

The picture of the "Spring" still belongs to the early period of Botticelli's art, by reason of the Pollaiuolesque character of much of its design and draughtsmanship, especially in the drawing of the nudes, of the heads of Mercury and Zephyr, and of the figure of Flora. This last figure, as I have noted, closely recalls the figure of the woman who steps forward, almost with the same movement, in the panel of the "Birth of St. John, the Baptist," which Antonio Pollaiuoli executed for the silver altar of the Baptistery, now preserved in the Museum of the "Opera" of the Cathedral at Florence. It was from Antonio Pollaiuoli, also, that Botticelli learned to perceive the solemn, magisterial beauty of gravid women, of which he has expressed his sense with so much sweetness and dignity, in the figure of Venus, in the "Spring." This trait in Antonio Pollaiuoli is, perhaps, to be traced to some Flemish or German influence: or it may even mark the influence which the splendid altarpiece, painted by Hugo Van der Goes, for the church of the Hospital of Santa Maria Nuova, in Florence, seems to have exercised over him.

If there is much in the picture of the "Spring" which recalls the early, Pollaiuolesque period of Botticelli's art, there is much, also, which anticipates his later and matured manner. In this picture, Botticelli displays for the first time, perfectly arrived, that rarest and most individual quality of his art, his peculiar and unrivalled use of line as a means of expression, not only of form, but also of mass and movement. All the elements of Botticelli's method of draughtsmanship were, no doubt, already present in his earliest works: in such a painting as the panel of "St. Sebastian," at Berlin, the perfect fusion of these elements "by the spirit upon them by which they become expressive to the spirit," was alone wanting to the achievement of what was rarest and most individual in him. In the peculiar quality of his line, Botticelli unites the grace and sweetness of Fra Filippo's pencil, with the virile and nervous quality of draughtsmanship, which, in the drawings of Antonio Pollaiuoli, becomes profoundly expressive of movement and structural form; and in this way Botticelli, while still following in its essential elements the technical method of Fra Filippo, outruns the ideas of his master, and learns to express in the outlines of his figures more form and structure than is elaborated, or even suggested, by their modelling. Like Antonio Pollaiuoli, Botticelli constantly employs forms which are not beautiful in themselves, and sometimes even ungainly; such as the right hand of the figure of Spring, or the left foot of Flora: but such things, which mark his observation of the human figure as he found it in the Tuscan type around him, are the "salt" of his manner, which lend force and virility to his draughtsmanship, and correct that unalloyed sweetness of line, which is apt to cloy a little, even in the works of so admirable a master as Fra Filippo. In the same picture, we find a passage as harsh and powerful as anything by Andrea da Castagno, concluding in another which recalls the sweet, rhythmical design of Lorenzo Monaco, or the Sienese. It is by reason of this so various a quality of expressive line that Botticelli stands apart among the great Florentines of his time; and the secret of the charm and fascination which his paintings and drawings have exercised in our own time, is largely to be found in a form of art which inimitably expressed a temperament not less complex and bizarre.

In its colouring, the "Spring" recalls that of the earlier painting of the "Fortitude;" a scheme in which only white and purple and blue form the colours of the principal masses, relieved in the one case, against deep green foliage, in the other, against the subdued marbles of the background. In these panels, as in the one other large panel of his early period which has come down to us, the "St. Sebastian," at Berlin, Botticelli designedly avoids the richly variegated colouring of his smaller paintings: the brilliant azures, the varied cherry purples and vermilions, the golden olive greens, with which he colours those intricate compositions. The larger paintings of the "Spring" and the "Fortitude" doubtlessly demanded a simpler scheme of colour, which should have relation to the proportions of the figures, and to their decorative purpose; but such considerations were not the guiding element in the determination of the colour scheme. In the "Spring," especially, we see how subtly that scheme has been subordinated to the design; how careful the painter has been that the colouring of the picture should present nothing which might detract from the expressiveness of its line.

A. Poliziano, De conjuratione Pactiana.
L. Landucci, Diario, p. 17, etc.

It is at this time that the story of Botticelli first becomes inseparably interwoven with the contemporary history of Florence. On the 26th April, 1478, while High Mass was being celebrated in the cathedral church of Santa Maria del Fiore, at Florence, in the presence of Cardinal Raffaello Sansoni, the nephew of Count Girolamo Riario, Giuliano de' Medici was, at a given sign, stabbed in the breast, by one Bernardo Bandini, and despatched by Francesco de' Pazzi, within the choir of the church: Lorenzo de' Medici was attacked at the same time by two priests, but escaped with a slight wound into the sacristy; and Bernardo Bandini, seeing that the chief part of their design had failed, killed Francesco Nori, in his attempt to get at Lorenzo. While these events were proceeding, Francesco Salviati, the Archbishop of Pisa, with his brother, Jacopo, and another Jacopo Salviati, a relative of his, and Jacopo, the son of the famous humanist, Poggio Bracciolini, with a number of Perugian exiles, whom the Pazzi had drawn to their party, attempted to possess themselves of the Palazzo della Signoria. The Archbishop having entered the palace with some of his company, and pretending to impart a matter of state from the Pope to the Gonfaloniere, met him in so distracted a way, that the Gonfaloniere, suspecting the worst, called the guard to arms, and, upon the Archbishop attempting to escape from the room, sprang at Jacopo Bracciolini, and threw him to the ground. At this, the Signori retired with all haste into the Campanile of the palace; while the Gonfaloniere defended the entrance to it, as best he could, with a spit which had been taken from the kitchen. Meanwhile Jacopo de' Pazzi, seeing the plot miscarry, rode as a last resource into the Piazza, and called the people to arms; but he got no other response than the shower of heavy stones, which those who had retired to the top of the Campanile hurled down upon him. At length, some of Lorenzo's party having forced the gates and retaken the palace, killed most of the Perugians there and then, and secured the Archbishop and the rest of his company. The same evening, says Luca Landucci, Francesco de' Pazzi, naked and wounded as he had been dragged from his bed, and the Archbishop of Pisa, and Jacopo Bracciolini, were hanged at the windows of the Palazzo della Signoria, with about twenty others at the windows, either of the Palazzo della

Signoria, or the Bargello, or the Palazzo del Podestà. And they hanged the Archbishop at the same window as Francesco de' Pazzi; and as he fell, he bit at the dead body of Francesco, and the halter tightening round his throat, his eyes open and fixed with terror, he held on to the body with his teeth. On the following day, the 27th April, the two Jacopi Salviati were hanged at the windows, with many others of the families of the Cardinal and the Archbishop. And on the 28th April, Jacopo and Renato de' Pazzi, who had been taken, the one at Falterona, the other at Belforte, were hanged at the windows above the Ringhiera, with a great number of their men. Excepting the Cardinal, who had been made prisoner, only two of the conspirators escaped with their lives: Bernardo Bandini, who, thinking himself secure at Constantinople, fled there; and Napoleone Francesi, another creature of the Pazzi, who escaped by the help of Piero Vespucci. Even the Count of Montesecco did not escape, but was beheaded on the same day that the two priests who had wounded Lorenzo de' Medici, were hanged. It was this scene of unhesitating, inexorable retaliation, that Botticelli, "come seruitore, & obligato alla casa de' Medici," perhaps at the instance of Lorenzo himself, was called upon to perpetuate.

The custom of painting the effigies of those persons who had been declared traitors to the State, on the front of some public building, in order to perpetuate their infamy, had long prevailed in Florence. In 1343, when the Duke of Athens was banished from the city, he and the creatures of his misgovernment were painted on the tower of the Palazzo del Podestà, "et in aliis locis;" to wit, in the prisons of the Stinche, and upon the face of the Grand Brothel. In 1425, Niccolò Piccinino, with five other "condottieri," who had sold themselves to the enemies of the Republic, were painted upon the Palazzo della Condotta, hanging by one foot; and again, in 1434, the figures of Rinaldo degli Albizzi, his son, Ormanno, Ridolfo Peruzzi, Palla Strozzi, and others, who had been banished after the return of Cosimo de' Medici, were painted on the Palazzo del Podestà by Andrea da Castagno, who henceforth went by the name of Andrea degli Impiccati. These figures, like those of the "condottieri," were represented hanging by the foot, to denote that these persons had been outlawed, and not executed. After the miscarriage of the Pazzi conspiracy, the task of painting the effigies of the conspirators on one of the public buildings was committed to Botticelli: and within the space of some twelve weeks, these frescoes were commissioned, executed, and paid for, as appears from this entry in a volume of the "Deliberations and Resolutions" of the Otto di Balia for that year: "On the 21st July, 1478, Item, the Signori Otto, in due form and order, etc., deliberated and paid to Sandro di Botticello for his labour in painting the traitors, 40 gold florins, etc." The Anonimo Gaddiano alone, among the early biographers of Botticelli, has left any description of these paintings. "Botticelli," he says, "painted, in 1478, on the façade where formerly was the Bargello, above the Dogana [or custom-house], Messer Jacopo, Francesco and Renato de' Pazzi, Messer Francesco Salviati, Archbishop of Pisa, and the two Jacopi Salviati, one the brother and the other the kinsman of the said Messer Francesco, and Bernardo Bandini, hanging by the throat, and Napoleone Francesi, hanging by one foot, who were discovered in the conspiracy against Giuliano and Lorenzo de' Medici; and for which Lorenzo then made the epitaphs at the feet, and among the rest, the one for Bernardo Bandini, which ran in this wise:

Vasari, ed. Sansoni, I, 625, note 3.

Studi sul centro di Firenze, p. 133.

S. Ammirato, Istorie Fior., II, 1023.

Vasari, ed. Sansoni, II, 680.

App. II, Doc. XVIII.

"'Son Bernardo Bandinj un nuovo Giuda,
Traditore micidiale in chiesa io fuj,
Ribello p*er* aspettare morte piu cruda.'"

The other "epitaphs" have not been preserved; but at the end of a rare, and undated, edition of the "De Coniuratione Pactiana Commentarius," of Angelo Poliziano, printed at Florence, probably in 1478, there are three Latin epigrams upon Francesco Salviati, which appear to have been composed for these paintings, and rejected, no doubt, upon the ground that inscriptions in the vulgar tongue were more likely to serve their turn. The first of these epigrams on the Archbishop must suffice as an example of the rest:

"Quid tam, furca, doles, laqueus cum gestiat? Heu, heu!
Salviatum eripuit celsa fenestra meum."

The position of Botticelli's frescoes is more precisely recorded by Jacopo Nardi, in his "Istorie Fiorentine," where he says that the figures of the rebels of 1478 were painted above the door of the Dogana, "sopra la porta della Dogana." In the fifteenth century the door of the Dogana was below the Bargello, or official residence of the Capitano di Giustizia, at the upper end of the Via del Dogana, now the Via de Gondi, near the Piazza, adjoining the original Palazzo della Signoria. In 1495, the part of the Bargello above the door of the Dogana was removed to make way for the Sala de' Cinquecento, which was built by Il Cronaca, for the Great Council of Savonarola. Luca Landucci records in his "Diary," on 18th July, 1495, "si faceva nella Dogana e fondamenti per la sala grande;" and again, he adds that, on 12th August following, "fu finita la volta della sala grande, quella parte che copriva la corte del Capitano." This vault, which was erected upon the site, partly of the Dogana, and partly of the courtyard of the palace of the Capitano di Giustizia, remains below the Sala de' Cinquecento; and the doorway which leads to it from the Via de Gondi, and which was built by Il Cronaca in place of the old "porta della Dogana," still bears a marble slab on the key-stone of its arch, inscribed with the word DOGANA, and the arms of that office.

l.c., ed. 1582, p. 43, tergo.

L. Landucci, Diario, pp. 112 and 114.

But the frescoes which Botticelli had painted on the front of the Bargello removed by Il Cronaca in 1495, had already been destroyed after the flight of Piero di Lorenzo de' Medici from Florence in 1494. On the 14th November, 1494, three days before the entry of Charles VIII into Florence, Lorenzo di Pierfrancesco de' Medici, and his brother, Giovanni, who had been banished by Piero di Lorenzo de' Medici, and those who had been exiled by Piero, Il Gottoso, in 1466, and the remnant of the Pazzi who had been exiled in 1478, made their public entry into Florence; and, at the same time, says Giovanni Cambi, in his "Istorie," the outlaws of the year 1434, who had been painted on the Palazzo del Podestà, and those of the year 1478, on the Palazzo del Capitano, were destroyed: "e furono chanciellati quegli chonfinati del anno 1434. dipinti al Palagio del Podestà, e quegli del anno 78. al Palagio del Chapitano." Jacopo Nardi, amongst other writers, records the destruction of the frescoes, both of Andrea da Castagno and of Botticelli. "At the same time," he says, "were destroyed the effigies of those who had been declared rebels in the year 1434, painted on the front of the Palazzo del Podestà, and those of 1478, painted above the gateway of the Dogana."

l.c., printed in Delizie degli eruditi Toscani, XXI, 80.

Historie Fior., ed. 1582, p. 43, tergo.

No little confusion has arisen in regard to these frescoes, in consequence of an error which Vasari made in describing the figures painted by Andrea da Castagno, on the tower of the Palazzo del Podestà, as those of the Pazzi conspirators. That Vasari is describing the paintings of Andrea, and not those of Sandro, is shown by the passage in which he says that these figures "were hanging by the feet in strange attitudes:" whereas, with a single exception, all the figures of the Pazzi conspirators were represented hanging by the neck, to denote that they had been actually hanged. Another circumstance, which has added to the confusion, is that, in 1574, the Palazzo del Podestà was converted to the uses of the Bargello, and still commonly goes by that name. But Vasari, who could never have seen these frescoes, is, no doubt, preserving some account of them which had been handed down in his time. He says that the figures painted by Andrea da Castagno were larger than life, and that the work was done with such art and judgment, "che fu uno stupore." It would seem that Botticelli had studied these frescoes, when he came to paint his own figures of the Pazzi: certainly, the influence of Andrea da Castagno first asserts itself in his work about this time. This influence is shown in an unmistakable way, in the fresco of St. Augustine, which Botticelli executed in the church of Ognissanti, in 1480; and it must be reckoned among those which went to determine Botticelli's mature manner, as we see it in the frescoes of the Sistine Chapel at Rome. The loss of these effigies of the Pazzi, a subject which must have especially commended itself to the virile genius of Botticelli, cannot be sufficiently deplored. Vasari, ed. Sansoni, II, 680.

The true nature of the Pazzi conspiracy was disclosed by the events which followed its miscarriage. At first, Sixtus IV went so far as to send letters of condolence to Florence, protesting that the plot had been contrived without his knowledge, or complicity. But the delay in releasing Cardinal Raffaello, and the manner in which Montesecco was handled, soon furnished excuses for the Vicar of Christ to pursue his real purpose. On 1st June, 1478, a Papal Bull was issued anathematizing Lorenzo de' Medici and the magistrates of Florence, and threatening to lay the city under an Interdict, unless the offending persons were punished according to their deserts, within a month. The chief grounds for this sentence were stated to be the enmity of Lorenzo to the Holy See, and especially his violation of the rights of the Church, by the execution of the Archbishop of Pisa, and the retention of Cardinal Raffaello. The Cardinal was allowed to leave Florence; but the Bull was followed by an Interdict before the month had elapsed: and upon the refusal of the Florentines to banish Lorenzo, Sixtus and the Count Girolamo resolved to attempt by open war what they had failed to effect by intrigue and priestcraft. The following winter, during the customary suspension of hostilities, Lorenzo appealed to the King of France; and Philip de Commines was sent with an embassy to Rome, to mediate between the Pope and the Florentines. A letter of the 9th February, 1478-9, addressed by the Dieci di Balia to Tommaso Soderini, the Florentine Orator at Venice, who had been sent there in the hope of better disposing the Venetians towards the cause of the Florentines, relates that one of the French ambassadors at Rome, had arrived in Florence, sent by the others to discuss the terms of a peace; and that among the conditions which the Pope sought to impose upon the Florentines, was the stipulation that the effigy of the Archbishop of Pisa, which Botticelli had painted among those of the other conspirators, on the front of the App. II, Doc. XIX.

Bargello, should be destroyed: "che si cancellassi la pictura dellarciuescouo." According to Scipione Ammirato, the painting of the Archbishop was actually destroyed in 1479, shortly after these overtures: "Fu bene il Papa compiaciuto," he says, "circa il leuar via la pittura fatta dell' Arciuescouo di Pisa." In spite of this concession, the negotiations came to nothing; and the war, which was renewed in the spring, dragged on a whole year, to the damage of the Florentines. When, at the end of November, it became evident that the Florentines would be unable to hold out much longer against the joint armies of the Pope and the King of Naples, Lorenzo de' Medici resolved to stake everything upon a single stroke of diplomacy; and on the 6th December, 1479, he set out from Florence, upon his famous voyage to Naples.

S. Ammirato, Istorie Fior., III, 136.

During the absence of Lorenzo, Bernardo Bandini, the assassin of Giuliano de' Medici and Francesco Nori, was brought prisoner to Florence. He had been handed over to the Florentines by the Sultan, at the instance of Antonio di Bernardetto de' Medici, who had been sent to Constantinople for that end; and on 28th December, 1479, five days after his arrival, the wretched man was hanged at the windows of the Capitano di Giustitia. As his body hung dangling above the frescoes of Botticelli, Leonardo da Vinci made a pen-and-ink drawing of it, carefully noting on the margin his name, and the stuff and colour of his clothes. This drawing, which is now in the collection of M. Leon Bonnat, of Paris, led Dr. Ulmann to suppose that Leonardo executed a painting of Bernardo Bandini, for which this drawing was a study, and that this painting replaced the figure which Botticelli had executed in 1478. The mien and lineaments of such a man at the moment of violent death was just such a spectacle as would have attracted the serious curiosity of Leonardo: but it is very unlikely that, had he painted the figure of Bandini upon the Bargello, no notice of the work should have come down to us. The German professor, however, omitted to make one conjecture that he might well have made. In 1478, the figure of Bernardo Bandini, like that of Napoleone Francesi, must have been painted hanging by one foot, for both had escaped from Florence alive: and in 1479, after Bandini had been taken and hanged, his effigy would seem to have been repainted, hanging by the neck, for the epigram by Lorenzo de' Medici, which the Anonimo Gaddiano has preserved, was certainly written after Bandini had been taken and hanged in 1479. If that was so, it is unlikely that the work should have been given to anyone except Botticelli. I may add that the portrait of Giuliano de' Medici, No. 21, in the Morelli Collection, in the Accademia Carrara, at Bergamo, which Morelli himself attributed to Botticelli, is undoubtedly by that anonymous painter of his school, Amico di Sandro. An old copy of this portrait is in the Museum at Berlin, No. 106[B].

L. Landucci, Diario, p. 33.

L. da Vinci, Literary Works, I, pl. lxii.

H. Ulmann, S. Botticelli, p. 48.

From the time of the completion of the frescoes of the Pazzi conspirators, we possess no notice of the painter until the year 1480, when Botticelli was painting in the church of Ognissanti, in Florence, in company with Domenico Ghirlandaio; the first of several occasions on which they worked together. A number of early notices of the frescoes which they executed, have come down to us. "In Ogni Sancti sono picture antique," says Francesco Albertini, in his "Memoriale," "et sco Aug. di Do. G. et sancto Hiero. di Sandro." Antonio Petrei, in his epitome of the "Libro di Antonio Billi," says that Botticelli painted "uno s[to] agostino, in ognis*an*ctj nelpilastro del coro dinanzi." The Anonimo

l.c., ed. 1510, fol. 5, recto.

App. II, Doc. I, fol. 49, tergo.

ST. AUGUSTINE *Church of Ognissanti, Florence*

Gaddiano, among his notices of Botticelli, speaks of this figure of St. Augustine, "on the pilaster before the choir," in similar words, adding, that it was done in rivalry with Domenico Ghirlandaio, who painted a figure of St. Jerome opposite to it: "Nella chiesa d'ogni santj nel Pilastro dinanzi al coro dipinse in frescho vn s^to^ agostino, al ri*n*contro del sa*n* girolamo fatto a co*n*correnza co*n* Domenicho del grillandaio." [App. II, Doc. II, fol. 83, tergo.] Among his notices of Ghirlandaio, the same writer says more precisely that the two frescoes were executed at the same time: "Nella chiesa d'ogni santj dipinse [Ghirlandaio] in fresco v*n* san girolamo nel pilastro del coro fatto a co*n*correntia co*n* sandro di Botticello che al rinco*n*tro i*n* vn medesimo tempo dipinse il santo agostino." [Id., fol. 86, recto.] The ambiguous phrase "nel pilastro del coro dinanzi," by which the position of the frescoes is indicated in these notices, is explained by the account which Vasari gives of them. In the second edition of his "Lives," that writer thus amplifies what he had written in the former edition: [Vasari, ed. 1550, I, 492.] "In Ogni Santi he [Botticelli] painted in fresco, on the 'tramezzo' [or screen], near the door which leads to the choir, for the Vespucci, a St. Augustine, in which, seeking to surpass all those who were painting in his time, and especially Domenico Ghirlandaio, who had executed on the other side a St. Jerome, he exerted himself not a little: which work, when finished, was greatly extolled on account of his having shown in the head of the saint that profound habit of thought, and acute subtilty of mind, which are wont to be seen in persons continually absorbed and abstracted in the investigation of the loftiest and most difficult things. This painting, as I have said in the 'Life of Ghirlandaio,' was moved this year, 1564, from its place, without harm and entire." [Id., ed. 1568, I, 471.] In the 'Life of Ghirlandaio,' Vasari repeats the statement that the fresco of St. Jerome, which Domenico painted "in rivalry with Sandro di Botticello," had, together with the fresco of St. Augustine, "(the friars having occasion to remove the choir from the place where it was,) been bound with irons and carried across the middle of the church, without damage, in the very days that these 'Lives' are being printed for the second time." [Id., I, 458.] The two frescoes, shorn of their original framework, and inclosed in painted borders of the sixteenth century, still remain in the position in which they were then placed, against the lateral walls of the nave, between the third and fourth of the side altars, on entering the church by the principal door; the St. Augustine of Botticelli being on the right, and the St. Jerome of Domenico Ghirlandaio on the left wall.

The choir of the church of Ognissanti, like the choirs of Santa Croce and Santa Maria Novella, anciently extended into the nave of the church; being raised somewhat above the level of the rest of the church, which lay between it and the great doorway. This choir was inclosed, in the phrase of an old chronicle of the monastery, "da muraglia alta," by a high wall, or screen, which stretched across the nave, dividing it into two portions. [R. Razzòli, Chiesa d'Ognissanti, p. 5.] The position of this screen appears to be marked by the present position of the frescoes of Botticelli and Ghirlandaio. In the centre of the screen, leading to the choir, was a doorway; and on either side of this doorway, facing the great door of the church, was erected an altar. A similar arrangement, on a small scale, still exists in the Chiesina degli Angioli, at La Verna, in the Casentino. Over the altar to the right, on entering the choir of Ognissanti, was the little painting of the "Death of the Virgin," by Giotto, which Michelangelo used to extol. [Vasari, ed. Sansoni, I, 396.] On either side of the doorway into the choir, and between it and these two side altars, were the frescoes of St. Augustine and St. Jerome, the former on the right, the latter on the left hand. The painted architectural ornaments, the "pilastri del coro dinanzi" of the early notices, by which these figures were inclosed, and of which some portions remain, formed the enrichments of this doorway; so that the two figures of St. Augustine and St. Jerome were parts of a single work, and were doubtlessly executed, as the Anonimo Gaddiano asserts, at the same time. The fresco of St. Jerome bears the date "M°CCCCLXXX." But another circumstance serves to determine the date of the "St. Augustine:" Botticelli repeats the attitude of the upper part of this figure, and much of the detail, in one of the figures of the Popes which he executed the following year, 1481, in the Sistine chapel at Rome.

In the fresco in Ognissanti, St. Augustine is seated, almost in profile to the left, at a table in his cell. He is attired in the white rochet of an Augustine canon, over which he wears a red cope, lined with saffron: his white mitre lies beside him. The table at which he sits is covered with a chequered cloth; and upon it is placed a movable desk, supporting a book which lies open before him. Above the desk stands an armillary sphere of the heavens: and behind the saint is a clock, the dial of which is marked by the twenty-four hours of the day and night. On a shelf running around the walls of the room, are ranged a number of books with their boards exposed, as the fashion then was, in the case of large volumes; the title being written on the upper lid. One volume, which is open, seems to be a manuscript of Euclid. The painting is inclosed on either side by a fluted pilaster with a Corinthian capital, above which rises the springer of a semicircular arch: behind this arch runs an entablature. The remains of a similar architectural frame are seen in Ghirlandaio's fresco of St. Jerome; but it is not possible, from such slight indications, to reconstruct the entire design of these architectural ornaments. On the architrave of this entablature, in Botticelli's fresco, is painted a shield bearing the arms of the Vespucci: Gules, on a bend azure a semé of wasps or. The frieze above it is inscribed with the legend:

"SIC AVGVSTINVS SACRIS SE TRADIDIT VT NON
MVTATVM SIBI ADHVC SENSERIT ESSE LOCVM"

The St. Jerome in Ghirlandaio's fresco is seated in the habit of a cardinal, and, like the St. Augustine, is writing at a desk in his cell. The head and figure are drawn and modelled with great mastery; and the background and accessory parts of the picture are as admirably done as anything of their kind in Florentine painting: but the multifarious details; the books ranged on shelves against the wall of the room, as in the fresco of St. Augustine, and protected by a green curtain; the hour-glass, penner and ink-horn, glass water-bottles, rosary, jars, books, and the cardinal's hat, on the shelf above the curtain; the spectacles, scissors, rule, candlestick and pounce-box on the table; although of great interest in themselves as illustrations of the furniture of the cell of an ecclesiastic in the fifteenth century, detract the attention from the real subject of the fresco. On the frieze of the entablature, in the upper part of the fresco, is inscribed the distich:

"NE TIBI QVID PICTO HIERONIME SANCTE DEESSET
EST NVPER MIRVM MOTVS AB ARTE DATVS"

Movement expressed by art! Had the distich been inscribed above the fresco of Botticelli, one might have read into the lines a meaning hardly intended by the writer. "That figure is most admirable," says Leonardo, "which by its action best expresses the passions of its mind." Judged by such a canon of art, the St. Jerome of Ghirlandaio must unquestionably yield to the St. Augustine of Botticelli. Annihilation, extasis, exolution,—we will not stay to inquire by what name the theologian would distinguish that "handsome anticipation of heaven," which the painter has represented in this figure of St. Augustine; but rather observe with what directness and power he has rendered the trance of the saint, as he pauses in his writing, by the simple, unaffected movement of the figure. The art by which Botticelli has, in his painting, made the outward, physical significance of the body expressive of the mysteries of the spirit, was worthy of one who had set Dante before him as the inspirer of his ideas. It is not, perhaps, until we have placed this "St. Augustine" of Botticelli beside some later rendering of an equally transcendental subject, such as the Italian and Spanish painters of the sixteenth and seventeenth century loved to paint, that we fully perceive with what a masculine turn of thought Botticelli has conceived, and with what simplicity and directness he has handled, a subject of the kind which afterwards proved a pitfall to the greatest of the academicians. We, at the present day, are apt to think of that "undercurrent of original sentiment" which runs through his works, and even the exaggeration of that sentiment in the many works of his school which pass under his name, as the distinguishing character of Botticelli's manner; but for the Florentines of his own day, this forcible, this Dantesque air, which in the fresco of St. Augustine is first clearly shown, this "aria virile," as the Florentines themselves called it, was that which distinguished his work, from the work of his disciples and contemporaries. But there is another trait to be noticed in the development of Botticelli's manner as seen in the fresco of St. Augustine; the presence, namely, of a new influence in his art, the influence of Andrea da Castagno. Already in such a passage as the head of the Flora in the "Spring," the influence of Castagno might, perhaps, be suspected; but in this figure of St. Augustine, the powerful, accented drawing of the beetling brows, the distended nostrils, the powerful, bony hands with their large joints and square nails, show that Botticelli had made a profound study of Castagno, probably at the time when he was painting the effigies of the Pazzi conspirators. Such a work as the fresco of the "Last Supper," by Castagno, which remains in the Refectory of Sant' Appollonia, at Florence, affords in the figures of the apostles the type which Botticelli has refined upon in his figure of St. Augustine. The greatness of Andrea da Castagno as a draughtsman, his science and naturalism, the largeness, force and severity of his manner, have yet to be estimated at their proper value. More than any other early Florentine painter, does he reflect the temper of mediæval Florence, when every one of the great houses which thronged its narrow streets was a fortress, munitioned with its tower, and its load of stones, against its neighbour. The legend of the murder of Domenico Veneziano by Andrea da Castagno, which had already grown up at the beginning of the sixteenth century, though without the least foundation in fact, really prefigures his character as an artist: and in spite of the researches of the commentators, we still think, as we look at his pictures, that one who drew as he drew, could not have done less.

L. da Vinci, Literary Works, I, 295.

The same year that Domenico Ghirlandaio painted the "St. Jerome" in the Church of Ognissanti, he executed a large fresco of the "Last Supper," which is still in existence, in the Refectory of the Monastery. Vasari and other early writers, duly ascribe the work to its real author; but the "Anonimo Gaddiano," probably by an error of transcription, attributes it to Botticelli. This, as I have elsewhere said, is the one error to be detected in the invaluable notices of Botticelli which that writer has preserved. Vasari also mentions a figure of St. George, which Ghirlandaio painted in the Church of Ognissanti. The "Anonimo Gaddiano," transcribes a notice of this "St. George," which is now lost among the paintings of Ghirlandaio, but adds in the margin, "Credo sia di Sandro." It would not seem that the Anonimo had any grounds for believing that the painting was by Botticelli, excepting his personal opinion, which was contrary, not only to his own authorities, but also to Vasari.

App. II, Doc. II, fol. 83, tergo.

Vasari, ed. Sansoni, III, 259.

App. II, Doc. II, fol. 86, recto.

The question remains: for which of the Vespucci were these paintings of St. Augustine and St. Jerome executed? The family of the Vespucci, which had their origin at Peretola, a village near Florence, early settled in Borgo Ognissanti, and had their chapels and burial-place in the church of Ognissanti. Ugolino Verino, in his "De Illustratione Urbis Florentiæ," celebrates the family for the many illustrious men which it had produced and for its patronage of the arts:

l.c., ed. 1790, II, 92.

"Egregiis ornata viris, nec inhospita Musis."

During the latter part of the fifteenth century, there were two principal branches of the family in Florence: the descendants of Simone Vespucci, the founder of the Spedale de' Vespucci, whose chapel, erected in 1386, is in the head of the right transept of the Church of Ognissanti; and the descendants of his first cousin, Stagio. Among the descendants of Simone, were his son Giuliano, whose chapel is in the left transept of Ognissanti, beside the high altar; his grandson, Guidantonio, many times "orator" of the Florentine Republic, at the court of the King of France, the Pope and the Italian States, and more than once Gonfaloniere; Marco di Piero di Giuliano, the husband of "La Bella Simonetta," and his brother, Piero, who was banished from Florence on account of his part in the Pazzi conspiracy. At a later time, Guidantonio Vespucci employed Botticelli on the decoration of his house in the Via de' Servi, which he bought in the year 1498. Of the descendants of Stagio, the most famous was his great-grandson, Amerigo, the navigator, who gave his name to the Continent of America. Ser Nastagio, the father of Amerigo, was one of the foremost notaries of his age; and Giorgio Antonio, his uncle, was an eminent scholar, and a follower of Savonarola. Ser Amerigo, the grandfather of the navigator, had his family burial-place in the cemetery, in which Botticelli himself was afterwards buried, on the east side of the church. The little slab, bearing the name of Ser Amerigo and the arms of the Vespucci, remained in its original place, against what had once been a wall of the cemetery, until some two years ago, when it was barbarously removed into the church, as an attraction for tourists. After the death of Ser Amerigo, his son, Ser Nastagio, acquired an altar in the church, at that time the only one erected against the right wall of the nave, between the "tramezzo" and the wall of the façade. This altar, which is now the second to the right, on entering the church, was anciently entitled the altar of the Pietà. In the earlier part of the year 1898, on removing the sixteenth-century painting of Saint Elizabeth of Portugal, to whom the altar had been re-dedicated, some ruined frescoes by

Domenico and David Ghirlandaio, which, according to Vasari's very dubious assertion, contain a portrait of Amerigo Vespucci, were discovered in a recess behind the picture. The sepulchral slab, which in the seventeenth century was still in its original position, in this chapel, was then brought from the chapel of Giuliano Vespucci, where it had long been, and replaced in the pavement, beside the altar, in the nave. The inscription, which bears the name of Ser Amerigo Vespucci, and the date 1472, was, at the same time, entirely renewed. The proximity of this altar to the fresco of Botticelli on the "tramezzo," coupled with the circumstance, that the branch of the Vespucci who owned the altar, were living in the Via Nuova, in a house adjoining that of the Filipepi, in 1480, afford some grounds for the conjecture, that Botticelli may have executed the fresco of the "St. Augustine" for Ser Nastagio Vespucci. Vasari, ed. Sansoni, III 255.

The peace which Lorenzo de' Medici effected with the King of Naples, on the occasion of his voyage to Naples, at the close of the year 1479, served only, in the event, to enflame the intrigues of the Pope against the Florentines. During the summer of 1480, the Duke of Calabria, who occupied Siena, seemed fostering a design to make himself master of Tuscany, when all Italy was startled by the news that the city of Otranto had been taken by the Great Turk, on the 28th July. This sudden incursion forced the Italian States to lay aside their plots and intrigues, and unite in the common defence of their country. The Duke of Calabria was hurriedly recalled from Siena; and the King of Naples formed a new league with the Florentines, and urged them to make their peace with the Pope. The time was judged to be opportune, and twelve of the chief citizens of Florence were dispatched to Rome to obtain a reconciliation: on the 3rd December, in the Portico of St. Peter's, they made their formal submission to the Pope, who ordered them, as a penance for their offences, to furnish and maintain fifteen galleys for the war against the Turks. On 11th January, 1480-1, Guidantonio Vespucci, and Pierfilippo Pandolfini, were appointed ambassadors to Rome, to confirm the peace; and on the following day, a new tax was levied by the Signoria, in order to meet the charges which had been imposed upon the state. L. Landucci. Diario, p. 37.

The "Denunzia" which Mariano Filipepi returned on the occasion of this tax, is one of the few documents which touch upon the family life of Botticelli. This "Denunzia" bears no date, but it would appear from others in the same series which are dated, that it was returned about the 30th January, 1480-1. Although drawn up in the name of "Mariano di Vanni," tanner, "choncjatore di quoja, overo galigajo," this declaration, like the earlier one of the year 1457-8, was drafted by his eldest son, Giovanni. It states that their family consisted of twenty persons, who are thus described: App. II, Doc. XX, fol. 244, recto.

"Our Mariano is aged eighty-six years, and no longer works. Monna Vangelista, kinswoman of the said Mariano, and sister of our mother, and wife of the late Amideo, brother of our father, aged seventy.

"Giovanni, my son, aged sixty years, formerly a broker [sensale djmonte]: Beninchasa, his son, aged nineteen years, is at Rome with Salutati, hitherto he costs me more than he earns. Amideo, son of the said Giovanni, aged sixteen years, is at the bank, and as yet has no salary. Jacopo, son of the aforesaid, aged fourteen, is at school. Alessandra, aged ten, daughter of the aforesaid, without dowry. Agnoletta, aged eight years, daughter of the aforesaid, without dowry. Nannina, aged five years, daughter of the aforesaid, without dowry. Smeralda, aged one month, without dowry.

"Antonio di Mariano, aged fifty-one years, was a goldsmith; now he is at Bologna, selling books in sheets [lib*r*i *in* forma]: and receives two ducats the month, and his expenses. The wife of the said Antonio, is seven months gone with child, she is named Bartolommea, daughter of the late Filippo Spigliati. Lisabetta, his daughter, of the age of nine years, without dowry. Mariano, his son, aged seven years. Bartolommeo, his son, aged five years. The wife of Giovanni, Monna Nera, daughter of the late Beninchasa di Manno de' Cori, has been omitted [from among the foregoing].

"Simone di Mariano, of about the age of forty years, without employment, at Naples.

"Sandro di Mariano, of the age of thirty-three years; he is a painter, he works in the house when he will [edjpintore lavora *in* chasa quando evole].

"I have a daughter, which I have to marry in three years from now."

In the interval which had elapsed since the return of the earlier "Denunzia" of Mariano, in the year 1457-8, his wife, Esmeralda, and his brother, Jacopo, had died; and his eldest son, Giovanni, had retired from his business of a broker. Giovanni's family now consisted of his wife, three sons, and three daughters. Antonio, the second son of Mariano, had given over his business of a gold-beater, in order to turn to the more lucrative trade of travelling for the printers, with books in sheets, for which the demand was daily increasing. Meanwhile, Antonio had married, and had a daughter and two sons, the elder of whom, Mariano, afterwards became a painter. Simone, Mariano's third son, was still at Naples: and Sandro, who is said to be thirty-three years of age, a statement which I have already discussed, had his workshop in the house. The account concludes with the mention of another unmarried daughter, who had been born since 1458. The two daughters of Mariano, and Giovanni's baby-girl, mentioned in the "Denunzia" of 1457-8, had probably, in the meantime, grown up and were married. Other passages of this "Denunzia" contain a description of the house, or rather houses, in which this numerous family lived in common, in accordance with Florentine usage. One of these houses Mariano, or rather Giovanni, owned: "a house for our dwelling, situated in the Via Nuova, in the parish of Santa Lucia of Ognissanti, [boundaries] on the first [side], the street; on the second, [the property of] Lorenzo, the strap-maker; on the second, the Prior of San Paolo, and previously was [the property] of Giuliano Manieri; on the third, Ser Nastagio [Vespucci]; on the fourth, the hospital of the Vespucci, that is to say the Bigallo; on the fifth, Simone di Pietro Guiducci." The other house was hired: "and because we are many in family, I rent another house adjoining mine, for which I pay the Prior of San Paolo a rent of nine florins the year, and which has the same boundaries as the above:" or rather, the boundaries of the two houses seem to have been put together. In the margin, against the description of the former house, is a note stating, that, according to the "Denunzia" returned by Mariano in the year 1469, it was then occupied by him as a dwelling-house. The "Campione" containing the "Denunzia" of 1469 is, unfortunately, one of the many volumes that were lost, or destroyed, during the Napoleonic invasion of Tuscany. In 1498, Sandro, and his brother Simone, were living in the former of the two houses, which had descended to Benincasa and Lorenzo, their nephews: the second house was then rented by their brother, Antonio.

The Via Nuova was that portion of the present Via del Porcellana, which lies between Borgo Ognissanti, and Via Palazzuolo; formerly the name of Via del Porcellana was given only to the continuation of the street from Via Palazzuolo to the Via della Scala. That portion of the present Via del Porcellana, which was formerly the Via Nuova, runs out of the Borgo, between the church of Ognissanti, and the Hospital of San Giovanni di Dio: and the house in which Botticelli lived, and painted, from 1469 to 1498, if not until the time of his death in 1510, was on the right hand, on entering the street from the Borgo; the third house before a narrow by-street, which now bears the name of the "Via San Paolino." The houses at this point of the street, then backed upon the Spedale de' Vespucci, which had been founded in the year 1400, by Simone Vespucci, for the shelter of indigent persons by night, and placed by him under the control of the Compagnia di Bigallo. In 1587, this hospital was, by the command of the Grand Duke Ferdinand I, ceded to the Fathers of San Giovanni di Dio, an order who especially devoted themselves to the care of the sick. In the seventeenth century, the old fabric of the hospital underwent many changes; and at the beginning of the eighteenth century, it having become necessary to further enlarge the Spedale di San Giovanni di Dio, as it was now called, a quadrangle was erected between the original building, and the church of San Paolino, which reached "as far as the Via Rosa." In Ferdinando Ruggieri's map of Florence, published in 1731, the present Via San Paolino is called the Via Codarimessa; but in Francesco Magnelli's map, published in 1783, the Via Rosa. It would seem that the latter name was originally applied to the portion of the street, which runs by the side of the church of San Paolino, and that anciently, the Chiasso di Codarimessa was the portion between the church and the Via Nuova. The new quadrangle of the hospital, which was finished in the year 1735, thus involved the reconstruction of all the houses on that side of the Via del Porcellana, between the Via San Paolino and Borgo Ognissanti, including those in which Botticelli and his family had lived.

G. Richa, Chiese Fior., IV, 26.

Id., IV, 29.

In the year 1480, the house at the angle of the Via Nuova, and the Chiasso di Codarimessa, towards Borgo Ognissanti, was the property of Ser Nastagio Vespucci, the notary, the father of Amerigo, the famous navigator. In the "Denunzia," returned by Ser Nastagio in that year, he thus enumerates the boundaries of this house: "da j°, detta via [*i.e.*, Via Nuova]; a ij°, chiasso; a iij°, Simone dj piero guiduccj; a iiij°, fratj dj settimo in*par*te, et in*par*te mariano dj uannj amidej galigaio:" and adds, that he had bought the property on 23rd December, 1474, from the heirs of Antonio Bertini. In an earlier "Denunzia" of the year 1457, at which time Ser Nastagio rented the house, the chiasso is specified by name, "Chiasso di Codarimessa." From these and from other "Denunzie," it is clear that the house which Mariano rented from the Prior of San Paolo, adjoined that of Ser Nastagio; and that the other house, which Mariano owned, was the third house from the "chiasso," and the house of Lorenzo, coreggiaio, the fourth, in the direction of Borgo Ognissanti. Their site is now occupied by the houses numbered 4, and 2, in the Via del Porcellana. In 1480, as I have already said, the Prior of San Paolo, or San Paolino, as it is commonly called, then a college of secular priests, was Angelo Poliziano.

App. II, Doc. XXI.

The "Denunzia" of Mariano continues: "I rent a 'podere' which I took on account of the plague: I hold it for two years: it is situated in the parish of San Piero a Careggi, the property of Riccardo di Papi di Michino. I pay 30 lire the year for it," etc. This "podere," or parcel of land, with its villa, was situated in the same parish as the villa which Mariano had rented in 1457-8. The plague broke out in Florence during the year 1478. Luca Landucci records in his "Diary" for 14th September, 1478, that it was then already making great ravages in the city, that some forty persons were lying sick of it in the Spedale della Scala, where all infected persons were taken, and that seven or eight deaths occurred there every day, and on one day eleven deaths. On the following 6th October, he says that there were about one hundred sick of the plague in that hospital; and in December, 1478, and April, 1479, he again speaks of the ravages, which the disease was making. It is not until March, 1481, that he notes the decline of the mortality. The Spedale della Scala was situated within a hundred and fifty yards of the houses of the Filipepi, in the neighbouring Via della Scala. An inscription, now in the Museum of San Marco, was afterwards erected on the wall of the cemetery of the hospital, recording that twenty thousand bodies of those who had died in this hospital, of the pest, were buried here in the year 1479. The mortality was very great; but this pious inscription is, perhaps, a truer record of the terrors of those who survived its ravages, than of the actual numbers of the dead.

L. Landucci, Diario, pp. 27, 28, 30, 31, and 37.

G. Richa, Chiese Fior., III, 340.

Besides the house in the Via Nuova, the "Denunzia" of 1480-1 states that Mariano was possessed of six parcels of land in the parish of Santa Maria a Peretola, a village near Florence, some two or three miles beyond the Porta al Prato. This property, like the house in the Via Nuova, would seem to have been bought by Giovanni with his own gains, for both descended to his sons, Benincasa and Lorenzo. Under the head of "Benj alienatj," or property which had passed out of the possession of the person making the return, are set down two houses in the parish of San Frediano, one "in sul chanto dj via maffia," and the other adjoining it, which had belonged to Jacopo, the brother of Mariano, and which had been sold in the year 1470. The same document, also, states that by his will, dated 18 February, 1462, "Jacopo di Vannj Amidej" had left a yearly sum of ten lire, to be paid in perpetuity to the Friars Observant of San Francesco al Monte, for a "piatanza," or mass to be said for the repose of his soul.

The "Denunzia" of 1480-1 shows that Botticelli, at this time, was possessed of no real property; but his condition seems to have been more prosperous than this document allows. It appears from other "Denunzie," which were returned the same year, that he then had, at least, three "discepoli," namely, Jacopo di Domenico Toschi, aged seventeen, Giovanni di Benedetto Cianfanini, aged eighteen, and Raffaello di Lorenzo Tosi, aged eleven. Of these disciples, I shall speak at length when I come to discuss the school of Botticelli. They were, probably, among the assistants whom Botticelli carried with him to Rome, to work on the frescoes of the Sistine Chapel. The "Denunzia" of 1480-1, moreover, proves a point of some importance in that regard, namely, that Botticelli was still in Florence in January, 1480-1, but indications are not wanting to show that he must have gone to Rome in the earlier part of the year. Macchiavelli, among other Florentine historians, relates that Guidantonio Vespucci, who had been sent as Orator to the Pope after the submission of the Florentines, by his prudence and management brought the terms of peace to be tolerable, and

Vasari, ed. Sansoni, IX, 258.

obtained many marks of favour from the pontiff in token of their reconciliation. I suspect that the Florentine envoy, at the instance of Lorenzo, may have had a hand in this matter of obtaining painters from Florence for the Pope's chapel: an act of courtesy which could only have served to ingratiate the envoy at the papal court.

In the autumn of the year 1481, while Botticelli was in Rome, working on the frescoes of the Sistine Chapel, an edition of the "Divina Commedia" of Dante was published at Florence, with a commentary by Cristoforo Landino. This edition, according to the usage of the time, is without a title-page, and begins: COMENTO DI CHRISTOPHORO LANDINO FIORENTINO SOPRA LACOMEDIA DI DANTHE ALIGHIERI POETA FIORENTINO. The colophon concludes thus: IMPRESSO IN FIRENZE PER NICHOLO DI LORENZO DELLA MAGNA ADI .XXX. DAGOSTO. M.CCCC.LXXXI. It was the first edition of the poem which had been printed in Florence; though many earlier ones are known to have been published in various parts of Italy, the first having appeared at Fuligno in 1472. The edition of Cristoforo Landino, however, was the first in which any attempt was made to purge the text of the "Divina Commedia" from the gross errors which had abounded in the earlier, printed copies of the poem. Landino's commentary is chiefly valuable on account of the notices contained in the "Proemio," of Florentines famous in arts and learning, and as an illustration of the study of Dante in the fifteenth century. In every paper copy of this edition, so far as I am aware, at least two engravings are found printed from copper plates, on the paper of the text. The first occurs on the tail-margin of the first page of the text; no space having been left for it at the beginning of the canto: and in consequence, it has, in most copies, been more or less cut away by the binder's shears. The second engraving occurs at the beginning of the second canto; and in many copies, a third is found printed at the beginning of the third canto: while at the beginning of each of the remaining cantos of the poem a space, intended for a similar engraving, has been left blank. In some copies, however, a variable number of these spaces from the third to the nineteenth canto of the "Inferno," contain additional engravings which have been pasted upon the paper of the text. In one copy in the British Museum, the engraving in illustration of the second canto is printed a second time, at the beginning of the third canto. The same peculiarity occurs in a very remarkable copy preserved in the Biblioteca Riccardiana at Florence; but in this example, the engraving in illustration of the third canto had been inserted in its place, pasted over the repeated engraving. In the same copy, the ensuing cuts up to the nineteenth canto of the "Inferno" have been pasted in, according to their order; and on the space at the beginning of the twentieth canto, another engraving had been laid down, which from its subject appears to be an alternative cut in illustration of the third canto. No other impression of this apparently rejected cut is known to exist. The experimental character, as it would seem, of these illustrations is further shown by another circumstance. In the splendid copy printed upon vellum, which Cristoforo Landino presented to the Signoria of Florence, and which is still preserved there, in the Biblioteca Nazionale, these engravings are omitted; the spaces for them in every instance being left blank. The binding of this copy, which was renewed in the year 1785, retains the silver bosses and corner-pieces of the original boards, which were covered with white and red satin. The boss in the centre of the upper board contains a silver disc, 2½ in. in diameter, worked in

Press mark: 639. M. 2.

No. 106 bis.

Ed. Sec. XV, No. 273.

"niello," with a figure of the Marzocco; and that on the lower board, a similar disc engraved with a figure of Hercules with a club, standing astride, in a landscape. This figure, like the Marzocco, was one of the devices of the Florentine Republic. The corner-pieces, also, are engraved in "niello," with the shields of the republic: one of them, on the upper board, has been renewed. These "nielli" were certainly executed in the same workshop as the engravings which occur in the paper copies of this Dante: the double bar on the brow of the Hercules, the Pollaiuolesque form of his figure, the convention of the trees in the landscape, indeed, the style generally of the engraving, leave no doubt on this point.

Vasari, ed. 1550, I, 494.

Vasari, in the first edition of the "Lives," says that after Botticelli had returned to Florence from Rome, "being of a restless turn of mind, he commentated a part of Dante, and figured the Inferno, and put it into print; in consequence of which he consumed much time, so that not working was the cause of infinite disorders in his life." Vasari could scarcely have intended the expression "comentò vna parte di Dante," to be understood as some writers have understood it, in the sense that Botticelli actually wrote a commentary on a portion of Dante: the passage, "comentò vna parte di Dante, & figurò lo inferno, & lo mise in stampa," must be taken, I think, as a single, pleonastic expression, of the kind Vasari commonly uses, which plainly has reference to the 1481 edition of Landino's "Dante," with its unfinished illustrations to the "Inferno." The value of Vasari's statement was not fully realized until the series of drawings in illustration of the "Divina Commedia," which are now at Berlin, was acquired with the Duke of Hamilton's manuscripts, by the German government in 1884, and eight of the missing leaves were discovered by M. Strzygowski in the Vatican Library, in 1886. Of the drawing for the first nineteen cantos of the "Inferno," for which there are engravings, only eleven are known to exist: those for Cantos I, IX, X, XII, XIII, XV and XVI, are at Rome; those for Cantos VIII, XVII, XVIII and XIX, at Berlin; while the drawings for Cantos II, III, IV, V, VI, VII, XI and XIV are wanting. These drawings, as I shall seek to show when I come to discuss them, were undoubtedly executed at a later period, than the engravings in the edition of 1481: they were probably begun shortly after 1492. On comparing the one series with the other, it is seen that, although there is everywhere a close similarity between them, both in their general conception and design, in the choice of the incidents illustrated, in the forms and movements of the figures, and in the accessory details, yet there is little or nothing in the drawings which has been merely transcribed, or repeated, in the engravings. It is evident that the two series are independent of one another; and that the engravings were executed from an earlier, and smaller, set of drawings. The experimental character of these cuts, which is indicated not only by their incomplete state, and the variant of the cut for Canto III, but, also, by their entire omission from the vellum copy presented by Landino to the Signoria, may have been one cause of their abandonment; but the departure of Botticelli for Rome, in the spring of 1481, at a time when these cuts had been newly begun, was probably the chief reason why they were never finished. They show, at least, that already in 1481, Botticelli had spent no little time over the study of Dante: and, perhaps, in the phrase of his father's "Denunzia" returned in 1480, "lavora in casa quando evole," we may detect an allusion to this time of apparent idleness, to the days and weeks squandered in this vain study, as his family no doubt thought, and as Vasari, who seems to preserve a tradition of the opinion then current in the workshops, records. But for us, Botticelli's study of Dante begins with, and is inseparable from, the development of what is rarest and most individual in his art: for us, it brings him into the company of two of the greatest intellects in the annals of Florentine art, of Brunelleschi and Michelangelo, who were both profound lovers and students of Dante. Indeed, we might apply to Botticelli the phrase which Vasari applies to Michelangelo, "il suo famigliarissimo Dante." The influence of the "Divina Commedia," by virtue of which Signorelli stands alone among the painters of Umbria, lent scarcely less colour to the genius of Botticelli, than it lent to the genius of Michelangelo. Of the actual designs of these cuts I shall omit to speak until I come to discuss the later series of drawings at Berlin and Rome, for not only do the two series of designs interpret one another in regard both to subject and style; but the drawings also enable us to judge how far the engraver, who was not of Botticelli's school, or even of his following, varied from his originals in the process of rendering them "in stamp." For the moment, let us only attempt to learn what is to be known about the engravers, or shop of engravers, to whom the execution of these plates is to be attributed.

Vasari, ed. Sansoni, II, 333, and VII, 213.

In the notices prefixed to the "Life of Marcantonio Raimondi," Vasari states that the art of taking impressions on paper from engraved metal plates owed its origin to "Maso Finiguerra, the Florentine, about the year 1460;" and that it arose from his practice of taking casts in sulphur of the silver plates which he had engraved for his "nielli," which led him to take impressions on moist paper in the same way. Finiguerra, adds Vasari, "was followed by Baccio Baldini, a Florentine goldsmith, who not having much gift for design himself, all that he made was from the invention and design of Sandro Botticelli." In his introduction to the "Lives," Vasari roundly asserts that all Italian and German copper-plate engraving had its origin in the "nielli" of Maso Finiguerra. This legend of the origin of engraving, and the assertion that Baccio Baldini, who followed Finiguerra, constantly worked from the designs of Botticelli, have given rise to a mass of notices, for the most part entirely uncritical, which deal with the early Florentine "nielli" and engravings on copper. These notices, which began with the appearance of Filippo Baldinucci's "Notizie de' Professori del Disegno," in 1681, and extend almost to the present day, have resulted in ascribing more than a hundred engravings, besides the "Dante" cuts, to Baccio Baldini, working from Sandro Botticelli's designs: and it was not until Mr. Sidney Colvin recently brought together, and examined, all the known evidences which bear upon this subject, in the admirable introduction to his "Florentine Picture-Chronicle by Maso Finiguerra," London, 1898, that the real character of Finiguerra's art, and, consequently, of the prints commonly ascribed to Baldini and Botticelli, became apparent. Here, it is necessary to touch upon this intricate subject, whose antiquarian interest far outweighs, as I think, its artistic value, only in so far as it enables the student of Botticelli to distinguish between the few engravings, which were undoubtedly executed from his drawings, and the numerous other prints by the same engraver, or school of engravers, the design of which are commonly attributed to Botticelli.

Id., V, 395.

Id., I, 209.

Maso, the son of Antonio Finiguerra, a Florentine goldsmith, was born in 1426. Already, at the age of twenty-three, he was in repute as

S. Colvin, Chronicle of Finiguerra, p. 21, etc.

an engraver of "nielli," and the sulphur casts of his plates brought no inconsiderable prices: for Alessio Baldovinetti had entered among his "Ricordi" on the 23rd July, 1449, the exchange of a dagger, for "uno zolfo" of Maso Finiguerra, valued at 1 lire, 13 soldi. In 1452, Maso received payment for the famous pax of San Giovanni, to which Vasari and Cellini allude. According to a "Denunzia" returned by Antonio Finiguerra, in 1457, his family was then living in a house in Borgo Ognissanti, and his son, Maso, was in partnership with Piero di Bartolommeo di Sali, goldsmith. The same year, Antonio Pollaiuoli appears to have been associated with Maso and his partner, in the execution of a pair of silver-gilt candlesticks, for the church of San Jacopo, at Pistoia. In 1461-2, we hear of him supplying Cino Rinuccini with the silver ornaments for a girdle worked in niello: a couple of years later, he died prematurely, at the age of thirty-eight, and was buried on the 24th August, 1464. Such, briefly, is the tenor of the principal documents which relate to this artist. The only existing works, which, on the evidence of contemporary documents, are known to be by Finiguerra, are the figures executed from his cartoons in "intarsia," by Giuliano da Maiano, for the Sagrestia Nuova, in the cathedral at Florence. It appears from an entry of 21st February, 1463-4, among the "Ricordi" of Alessio Baldovinetti, that Maso Finiguerra designed the cartoons for the figures of San Zenobio and the two deacons, in the panels, now in the Museum of the Opera del Duomo, No. 108, and of the Virgin and the angel in the three panels forming an "Annunciation," which are still in their place in the sacristy of the cathedral. Besides these panels, Filippo Baldinucci states in his "Notizie de' Professori del Disegno," that he had seen a great number of drawings by Maso Finiguerra, in the collection of Cardinal Leopoldo de' Medici, which afterwards went to enrich the Gallery of the Uffizi. These drawings, no doubt, are those to which Pierre Mariette alluded in a letter of the year 1723, where he speaks of "un volume intero di disegni di questo Maso," among the drawings of the Grand Duke of Tuscany. On the 17th August, 1793, forty-six drawings were stolen from the Uffizi, which appear to have formed part of the contents of this volume, already attributed to "Pollaiuolo." A portion of these stolen drawings is, perhaps, to be identified with the twenty-two drawings in the collection of M. Leon Bonnat, at Paris, which still bear the name of Pollaiuoli; and others, with a number of drawings by the same hand, which are scattered among the public and private collections of Europe. Of the remaining drawings of the series, which are still preserved in the Uffizi, the majority are now labelled "scuola di Pollaiuolo," and only four of them ascribed to Finiguerra. Two of the series, however, bear the name "Maso Finiguerrj" written in a sixteenth century hand. Lastly, in the Print Room of the British Museum, there is a series of ninety-nine drawings on folio paper, which form a pictorial chronicle of the first ages of the world, from the Creation to the Birth of Christ. These finished drawings, as Mr. Colvin has shown in the introduction to his admirable volume of facsimiles of them, are clearly by the same hand as the studies traditionally ascribed to Finiguerra in the Uffizi. In one instance, the kneeling figure of a woman in one of the studies in the Uffizi, has been used, almost without alteration, for a figure in the "Chronicle." On comparing these two series of drawings with the "intarsia" panels, executed by Giuliano da Maiano, for the sacristy of the cathedral, at Florence, it is seen that the similarity between them is such, that they

Vasari, ed. Sansoni, V, 444.

Id., III, 288, note 4.

S. Colvin, Chronicle of Finiguerra, pp. 23-24.

l.c., ed. 1681, II, 107.

G. Bottari, Raccolta di Lettere, II, 314.

A. Gotti, Gallerie di Firenze, p. 256.

S. Colvin, Chronicle of Finiguerra, p. 2.

Id., p. 27.

Id., Pl. XCIV.

might well have been designed by the same draughtsman: while on the same wall of the sacristy as the "Annunciation," are two other panels with full-length figures of "Isaiah" and "Amos," which so closely recall certain figures in the "Chronicle" that it is impossible to doubt the close connection between the drawings and these panels, which are known to have been designed by Finiguerra. From these, Mr. Colvin goes on to point out the relation between a certain small group of rare impressions on paper of "nielli," of which the greater number are in the collection of Baron Edmond de Rothschild, at Paris, with the drawings in the Uffizi and the British Museum. And here again he remarks that one of the studies in the Uffizi, of a naked "Putto" blowing a horn, has been used by the engraver of one of these "nielli." Lastly, Mr. Colvin turns to discuss the connection between these various drawings and "nielli," and the group of engravings, executed in what is technically known as the "fine manner," which have been commonly ascribed to Baccio Baldini and Sandro Botticelli. Mr. Colvin points out that the "fine manner" of these engravings is identical in technique with the engraving of these "nielli." To a certain point, then, Vasari was correct in his statements; for this particular group of prints was certainly executed by engravers in "niello," and appears to have originated in their practice of that art.

Id., p. 31.

The earliest of these engravings, to which a date can be assigned, are the series in illustration of the "Planets," which are known to have been executed before 1465. Others were certainly executed many years after Maso Finiguerra's death; such as the plates in the "Monte Sancto di Dio," printed in 1477, and those in the "Dante" of 1481. None of these engravings in the "fine manner" could have been executed, I think, before 1460: the greater number of them were certainly done after Finiguerra's death, and, therefore, not engraved by him. But I will attempt to briefly characterize the more important cuts of this group. Adam Bartsch, in Volume XIII, p. 158, etc., of "Le Peintre Graveur," published at Vienna in 1811, attributes to Baccio Baldini, working from the designs of Botticelli, a series of twenty-four plates of the Prophets, and another series of twelve plates of the Sibyls. Of both these series of cuts, there exist at least two states of the plate executed in the "fine manner," as well as a set of copies done in the "broad manner." The designs of the former series of the "Prophets" have been drawn from two distinct sources. In the case of the greater number of the cuts, the figures are entirely Pollaiuolesque in character, and the accessory ornaments in the manner of Maso Finiguerra. This category includes the plates of "Noah" [Bartsch, Vol. XIII, pp. 165-7, No. 1], "Moses" [id., No. 3], "Aaron" [id., No. 4], "Samuel" [id., No. 5], "David" [id., No. 6], "Solomon" [id., No. 7], "Elijah" [id., No. 8], "Elisha" [id., No. 9], "Jeremiah" [id., No. 10], "Baruch" [id., No. 11], "Joel" [id., No. 14], "Jonah" [id., No. 17], "Nahum" [id., No. 18], "Haggai" [id., No. 20], "Zachariah" [id., No. 21], and "Joshua" [id., No. 23]. The design of the "Samuel" especially recalls certain drawings in the "Chronicle" of Finiguerra; and the attitude of the "Joshua," the figure of "Hope," executed by Pietro Pollaiuoli, among the "Virtues," formerly in the Mercanzia at Florence. The figures in the remaining plates of this series have been copied, wholly, or in part, from earlier, German prints. Herr Max Lehrs, in an article entitled, "Italienische Kopien nach Deutschen Kupferstichen," printed in the Prussian "Jahrbuch," has pointed out that the figure of the "Ezekiel"

l.c., Vol. XII, p. 126.

[Bartsch, Vol. XIII, pp. 165-7, No. 12], has been closely copied, in reverse, from the figure of "St. John," in a series of plates of the Apostles by the "Master E. S." [Bartsch, Vol. X, pp. 20-2, No. 31], while the head has been taken, in reverse, from the head of "St. Peter" in the same series [id., No. 28]; that the figure of "Amos" [id., Vol. XIII, No. 15] has been copied, in reverse, from the "St. Paul" [id., Vol. X, No. 38], the "Obadiah" [id., Vol. XIII, No. 16] from the "St. Peter" [id., Vol. X, No. 28], the "Malacchi" [id., Vol. XIII, No. 22] from the "Thaddæus" [id., Vol. X, No. 36], and the "Isaiah" [id., Vol. XIII, No. 24] from the "St. James the Greater" [id., Vol. X, No. 30], all, likewise, in reverse, and from plates in the same series. In every case, the Florentine engraver has adapted these designs to his purpose, and added some accessory ornament in the manner of Maso Finiguerra. Again, the plate of "Jacob" [id., Vol. XIII, No. 2] is clearly reminiscent of some German original: indeed, the action of the right leg appears to be taken from the "St. Matthew" of the "Master E. S." [id., Vol. X, No. 39]. The right hand and drapery over the right arm of the "Habakkuk" [id., Vol. XIII, No. 19] has clearly been copied from the "Thaddæus" of the "Master E. S." in the same series [id., Vol. X, No. 36]; and some German original appears to be behind the design of the "Daniel" [id., Vol. XIII, No. 13]. In the plate of the "Habakkuk," especially, do we seem to gain an insight into the methods of the engraver of these plates, who, "having no gift for design himself," copies here, imitates there, and then overloads his patchwork with ornament, in order to hide his want of invention.

On the other hand, the designs of the series of the Sibyls [Bartsch, Vol. XIII, pp. 172-5], have been derived from, at least, three distinct sources. The "Elispontic" Sibyl [id., No. 30] has been copied, in reverse, from the plate of "St. Thomas," in the same series of Apostles by the "Master E. S." [id., Vol. X, No. 34]. Three other plates of the Sibyls have been taken from another series, by the "Master E. S.," of the Evangelists [Bartsch, Vol. VI, pp. 23-4], namely, the "Libyan Sibyl" [id., Vol. XIII, No. 26] from the plate of "St. John" [id., Vol. VI, No. 65], the "Delphian Sibyl" [id., Vol. XIII, No. 27] from the "St. Mark" [id., Vol. VI, No. 64], and the "Tiburtine Sibyl" [id., Vol. XIII, No. 34] from the "St. Matthew" [id., Vol. VI, No. 66]. The design of certain of the other plates are clearly of a Pollaiuolesque character; such are the "Cimmerian Sibyl" [id., Vol. XIII, No. 28], the "Erythræan Sibyl" [id., No. 29], the "Cumæan Sibyl" [id., No. 31], the "Phrygian Sibyl" [id., No. 33], and the "Sibyl Agrippa" [id., No. 36]. Two of the other plates, the "Persian Sibyl" [id., No. 25], and the "Samian Sibyl" [id., No. 32], seem to have been derived from some French or Burgundian source; from some miniature, perhaps, or tapestry. In all these plates, the accessory ornament has been added in the manner of Finiguerra: in one instance, that of the "European Sibyl" [id., No. 35], while the ornament has thus been contrived in the manner of Finiguerra, the scarf has been imitated from some German print, and the petticoat from some French or Burgundian design. In spite of their miscellaneous origin, these two series of prints are, certainly, not only among the earliest, but also among the best engraved plates of this series of prints in the "fine manner."

Besides the cuts of the Prophets and Sibyls, Adam Bartsch attributes the following plates to Baldini, working from Botticelli's designs: The twenty cuts in illustration to the "Dante" of 1481 [id., Vol. XIII, pp. 175-187, Nos. 37-56]. Although engraved in the same workshop as the foregoing plates, these cuts are much inferior to them in point of execution: indeed, as Mr. Colvin says, they "represent the decline, and to all appearance the last production, of this style and this workshop in Florence." Three plates in illustration of the edition of "Il Monte Sancto di Dio," by Antonio Bettini, Bishop of Fuligno, printed at Florence in 1477, by Nicola di Lorenzo della Magna, the printer of the "Dante" of 1481 [id., Vol. XIII, pp. 187-190, Nos. 57-59]. The plates, again, are undoubtedly the production of the same workshop. Their feeble designs would appear to be the unaided productions of the engraver: the figure of the youth in a tunic and hose in the first cut, is reminiscent of the draughtsman of the "Chronicle;" and the cut of the "Inferno" of some earlier traditional illustration to "Dante." Eight plates of the "Planets" [id., Vol. XIII, pp. 190-200, Nos. 60-67]. In the British Museum is a set of copies of this series, with a calendar dated 1465. These plates, the engraving of which closely recalls that of the cuts in the "Monte Sancto di Dio," are not, in my opinion, from designs by the draughtsman of the "Chronicle," but by some other Florentine artist of far less individual character.

To this list of plates, ascribed by Bartsch to Baldini and Botticelli, J. D. Passavant added the following in his "Peint-graveur," which was published at Leipsic in 1864: the twenty cuts known as the "Otto" prints [Vol. V, p. 27, Nos. 68-91]. These prints, which exist for the most part in unique impressions, the greater number of which are in the British Museum, seem to have been intended as working patterns for the decoration of the tops of small boxes. In several instances [id., Nos. 80, 81, 83, etc.], as Mr. Colvin has pointed out, the designs of these prints have been adapted from drawings in the "Chronicle." In one case [id., No. 71], a figure of Cupid has been copied, in reverse, from a "St. Sebastian" by Martin Schongauer, and in another instance [id., No. 82], a design of a squire and lady, with boy playing on a pipe and tabor, has clearly been taken from some Burgundian original. To these, Passavant adds some thirty miscellaneous prints, which he attributes to the same engraver, if not to the same designer [Vol. V, p. 39, Nos. 92-121]. Among them, however, are included many plates belonging to an entirely distinct group, and executed in a wholly different technique, known as the "broad manner," by some engraver, or school of engravers, who were working at Florence during the last few years of the fifteenth century. Among such cuts are the large stories from the Old and New Testament: "Moses and the Tables of the Law" [id., No. 93], "David and Goliath" [id., No. 94], "Solomon and the Queen of Sheba" [id., No. 95], and the "Adoration of the Magi" [id., No. 96]; things certainly neither engraved by any follower of Finiguerra, nor designed by Botticelli. To these, Passavant adds the fine print of the "Assumption," in two sheets [id., No. 100], which was unquestionably done from a design by Botticelli; but this plate, and some others which are executed in the "broad manner," I discuss later on, in their place. Other plates were added to Passavant's catalogue, in the article on "Baccio Baldini," in Dr. Julius Meyer's "Allgemeines Künstler Lexicon," published in 1878 [Vol. II, p. 586, etc.]; and others have since been described in various scattered articles; but a catalogue of these prints, which shall not only describe their various states, but also enumerate the

Chronicle of Finiguerra, Pl. XXXIX and LVIII.

impressions of them that exist in public and private collections, still remains among the many *desiderata*, the want of which perpetually hinders the student of early Italian art. All that I can attempt here is briefly to characterize some of the more important of these miscellaneous prints, engraved in the "fine manner." Mr. Colvin has pointed out that the design of one of these prints, the large plate of the story of "Theseus and Ariadne" [Passavant, Vol. V, p. 44, No. 105], has, with certain variations, been directly copied from a drawing in the "Chronicle." Other prints, such as the plate of the "Hunting party encountering a wild man and his family" [Passavant, Vol. V, p. 45, No. 111], and the so-called "Battle of the Hose" ["Jahrbuch der K. Pr. Kunstsammlungen," Vol. VII, p. 73] appear to have been engraved from drawings by the draughtsman of the "Chronicle," and in the same category should, perhaps, be placed some other plates, among which are the "Christ before Pilate and the Flagellation" [Passavant, Vol. V, p. 41, No. 98], and a plate of "Ships" [Bartsch, Vol. XIII, p. 140, No. 72]. The larger number of these plates, however, show the influence of Maso Finiguerra rather in the execution than the design. Thus the design of the large plate of the "Conversion of St. Paul" ["Künstler Lexicon," Vol. II, p. 586, No. 42], which exists in an unique impression, betrays the hand of some Florentine draughtsman who was influenced both by Antonio Pollaiuoli, and still more by Paolo Uccello. Such a print as the "Allegory of Eternal Life and Death, with the Nativity" [Passavant, Vol. V, p. 70, No. 71] closely recalls the cuts in the "Monte Sancto di Dio," the design having probably been put together by the engraver. The "Nativity" in two sheets [Passavant, Vol. V, p. 40, No. 97, *a* and *b*], is another print of the same order which has been adapted from some design of the school of Fra Filippo.

Chronicle of Finiguerra, Pl. XLVI and XLVII.

These instances are sufficient to show from what various sources the engraver, or engravers, of these prints in the "fine manner" derived their designs: but in spite of Vasari's story, with the exception of the series of cuts in illustration to "Dante," in one instance, and in one instance alone, has a print engraved in the "fine manner" after a drawing by Botticelli, come down to us; that, namely, in two sheets, of the "Triumph of Bacchus and Ariadne," which exists in a unique impression preserved in the British Museum. The two sheets together form a frieze-like composition, and in their untrimmed state, measured at least 22½ inches in length, by 8¼ inches in height. The right-hand sheet, which is described by Passavant [Vol. V, p. 44, No. 104], was formerly in the collection of Sir Mark Masterman Sykes; and at the sale of the third portion of his collection of prints, at Messrs. Sotheby's, on 24th May, etc., 1824, it was bought by William Young Ottley, Lot 1054, for £13 13*s*. On the dispersion of the Ottley collection of prints, on 17th May, etc., 1837, this sheet was again sold by Messrs. Sotheby, Lot 1827, for £5: it then passed into the collection of the Rev. H. Wellesley, D.D., Principal of New Inn Hall, Oxford; at the sale of the second portion of whose collection, on 2nd June, 1860, at the same sale-rooms, it was bought by the Trustees of the British Museum, Lot 99, for £15. The left-hand sheet, formerly in the collection of the Marquis of Masclary, was acquired for the Museum in 1872.

The car of Bacchus is preceded by five Mænads with dishevelled hair, partially clad in loose, flying raiment, who, possessed of the god, go

THE TRIUMPH OF BACCHUS AND ARIADNE (2 Plates) *From the unique print in the British Museum*

forward with wild gestures. The foremost of them is holding the rent body of an animal; the bacchante beside her bears on her shoulder a boar's head; and the rest follow, clashing together the richly-wrought wine-vessels. Their train is brought up by a man girt about the loins with vine leaves, who is playing on a double pipe. Following upon him is the car, drawn by two centaurs, on which reclines the horned and drunken Bacchus, who, with his head fallen on his breast, embraces Ariadne. She is lying naked and crowned beside him, and looks askance for the moment as she fondles him. Two young fauns are seated on the front of the car; beside them a satyr clambers up the overhanging vine-stock to gather the grapes; while a Mænad, who holds up the gashed body of a sacrificial animal, follows after the rout.

The Triumph of Bacchus and Ariadne was a subject which Botticelli was not alone among the Florentines in handling. It occurs in the "Stanze" of Poliziano, in the description of the carvings on the gates of the Palace of Venus, in the stanza beginning:

> "Vien sopra un carro dhelera e di pampino
> Couerto Baccho: il qual dui tigri guidano," etc. Lib. I, St. III.

Again, one of the finest lyrics of Lorenzo de' Medici, Il Magnifico, celebrates this triumph of the God of vines; but Lorenzo's treatment of the theme shows that it was probably written for one of the "Trionfi" which formed part of the public shows in Florence, on great festivals. The nature of these "Triumphs," in the invention of which many of the ablest artists of the time took a part, appears to be largely reflected in the various "Trionfi," with which the Florentine "cassone-painters" of the fifteenth century loved to decorate their coffers. With such things, Botticelli's design of Bacchus and Ariadne has little or nothing in common: on the contrary, this print must be reckoned among the few motives which he directly derived from antique sculpture. On a famous sarcophagus in the British Museum, which came from the gardens of the Villa Montalto, at Rome, to take an example at hand, Bacchus and Ariadne are represented, as in Botticelli's design, seated in a car with four wheels, which is drawn by two centaurs, one of whom is playing on a lyre, and the other on a double pipe. Among the drunken rout of Mænads which accompany the progress of the god, is a satyr, and a Silenus playing on a double pipe. On another well-known sarcophagus in the Louvre, the vine spreads over the car, as in the print. Possibly, some other Roman relief exists, which contains all the exterior elements of Botticelli's design: but the spirit in which the Florentine painter has handled once again the old theme, is very different from the antique. The car of Bacchus, and even the trappings of the centaurs who draw it, are actually formed of the clambering vine-stock, which, rising up high overhead, embowers the god and the "cast mistress" of Theseus. Other vines which crawl about two elm-props on either side of the group of Mænads who go before, mingle with the vine of the car, and inclose the heady actors of this Triumph, beneath great festoons, thick with the "lustful clusters" of the grape. The Bacchus of this scene is the exile, at last returned among men, who has been centuries long under the ban of Christianity. If we would find some literary parallel which should interpret the spirit of Botticelli's design, we must search, not among the poets of antiquity, but among those of his own time. The chorus of Mænads with which Angelo Poliziano concludes his "Orfeo," possesses that strain of the mediæval spirit, the sense of something noisome and overheady in the wine-cup, which permeates Botticelli's design. Take two of its verses:

A. Poliziano, Cose Volgari ed. 1494.

Ognun segua, Baccho, te!
  Baccho, Baccho, eu hoe!

Chi uuol beuere, chi uuol beuere,
  Vegna a beuere, uegna qui!
  Voi imbottate come peuere:
  Iuo beuer anchor mi:
  Glie del uino ancor per te;
  Lascia beuere prima a me.

Ognun segua, Baccho, te!
  Baccho, Baccho, eu hoe!

Imi moro gia di sonno,
  Sonio ebria, o si, o no?
  Star piu ritti e pie non ponno:
  Voi siet' ebrie chio lo so.
    Ognun facci, comio fo:
    Ognun succi, come me!

Ognun segua, Baccho, te!
  Baccho, Baccho, eu hoe!

The splendid design of this print of Bacchus and Ariadne has suffered not only from the feebleness of the engraving, but also from the florid manner in which the engraver has exaggerated some of the decorative details, and added others. A comparison of the print with the drawings of the

l.c., Pl. IV.

"Drunkenness of Noah," in the "Chronicle" of Maso Finiguerra, shows that the engraver has treated the vine-stock entirely in the florid manner of Finiguerra; and that on the chlamys which Bacchus wears he has introduced a pattern of pine-cones which occurs in more than one plate in the "fine manner," and notably in the print of the Samian Sibyl [Bartsch, Vol. XIII, p. 174, No. 32], where the same pattern occurs on the dress. In spite of these exaggerations of the ornaments, and in spite of the feebleness of its execution, which is scarcely better than that of the "Dante" cuts, the power and invention of this design is such, that this print remains an incomparably greater work of art than any of the other prints in the "fine manner" which pass under the name of Baccio Baldini. It is possible that Botticelli may have seen some Roman relief of the "Triumph of Bacchus and Ariadne" in Florence; but it is more probable that he was first acquainted with the antique treatment of this theme during his stay in Rome; and that the print in question was executed shortly after his return to Florence, in 1482.

What, briefly, then are the conclusions to be arrived at concerning the origin of these prints? The drawings of the "Chronicle" in the British Museum, as Mr. Colvin has shown, are clearly by the same hand as the studies in the Uffizi, traditionally ascribed to Maso Finiguerra: and both these series of drawings closely recall the intarsia panels, in the sacristy of the Cathedral at Florence, which are known to have been designed by Maso. The one conclusion to be drawn from these resemblances, namely, that both series of drawings, like the designs for the intarsia, were the work of Finiguerra, is not inconsistent with his character, as an artist, which has come down to us. Giovanni Rucellai in his "Zibaldone," begun in 1459, speaks of him as a "maestro di disegno:" while Benvenuto Cellini, who was writing nearly a century later, says, in his "Trattati dell' Oreficeria, e della Scultura," that "Maso Finiguerra followed only the art of engraving in 'niello': he was a man who never had a rival in that profession, and always worked with the aid of drawings by Antonio [Pollaiuoli]." No "niello," or impression of any "niello," which is known to exist, bears out the reputation which Cellini attributes to Finiguerra: none, certainly, is from a design by Pollaiuoli. The few extant impressions in the style of Finiguerra recall the later "nielli" on the binding of the vellum copy of Landino's "Dante," in the Biblioteca Nazionale, at Florence, and were, no doubt, executed by the same shop of engravers. On the other hand, we know that Finiguerra was associated as a goldsmith with Antonio Pollaiuoli: and the studies in the Uffizi show how entirely their draughtsman had founded himself on that great master. Again, it is as an executive and not as a creative artist that Cellini extols Finiguerra: and the drawings of the "Chronicle" show that Finiguerra was a skilful and facile imitator. In such a design as the charming "Rape of Helen," pl. 57, we see how well he could enter into the spirit of Pesellino; and in other drawings of the same series, he appears no mean imitator of Antonio Pollaiuoli and Alessio Baldovinetti. But when he is thrown back upon his own resources he seeks to hide his want of invention by the copious use of meaningless and florid ornament: his line and forms become coarse and mannered; and we begin to understand Vasari's assertion that though Maso Finiguerra "drew very well and much," Antonio Pollaiuoli "equalled him in diligence, and surpassed him in design."

G. Marcotti, Mercante Fior., p. 68. l.c., ed. 1857 p. 7.

Vasari, ed. Sansoni, III, 287.

On the other hand, it is difficult to attribute any extant print in the "fine manner" to Finiguerra's own hand. Vasari, we must remember, does not attribute any engraving in the ordinary sense of the word to him; but only impressions on sulphur and paper of his "nielli." It is to Baccio Baldini that Vasari attributes such engravings. One thing, however, is abundantly evident, that some disciple, or disciples, of his, who after his death inherited his drawings, and continued to engrave in his manner, produced such plates as the illustrations to the "Monti Sancto di Dio" of 1478, and the "Dante" of 1481. Such mannerisms as the use of a double line across the bridge of the nose to represent age, the peculiar convention employed for the herbage and trees, the Pollaiuolesque forms of the figures and draperies, show that such engraver or engravers did not merely work from Maso Finiguerra designs, but were actually his disciples, taught in his workshop. More than this, these prints show that after Maso's death their art gradually deteriorated; until at length, in 1481, they produced such poor examples of the engraver's art as the cuts in Landino's "Dante" undoubtedly are.

The question remains: by whom was the workshop of Maso Finiguerra carried on, after his death, in 1464? to whom are the later plates in the "Monte Sancto di Dio," of 1477, or in the "Dante" of 1481, to be ascribed? Are they the work of Francesco, the brother of Maso Finiguerra, who with Tommaso and Antonio, the sons of his late brother, Stefano d'Antonio di Tommaso Finiguerra, rented a goldsmith's shop, in the Via Vacchereccia, "bottegha dasercizio dorafo jnuacherecja," in Florence as late as 1498; or are they the work, as Vasari would seem to assert, of Baccio Baldini? The commentators of the edition of Vasari, published at Florence by Le Monnier, in 1845, state that Baccio Baldini "was born in Florence in 1436, and that he was still living about the year 1480": but no authority for this statement has been forthcoming, and Signor Milanesi, in the later Florentine edition of Vasari published by Sansoni in 1878, was unable either to correct or add to it. Again, the "Matricole" of the Arte della Seta, the Florentine Guild of the Silk Mercers, with whom the goldsmiths were associated, record the matriculation about this time of nearly a score of goldsmiths of the name of Bartolommeo, of which Baccio was the colloquial form; but it is not possible to identify Baccio Baldini with any one of them, since the family name is rarely, or never, given in these "Matricole." Yet there are some indirect indications that a goldsmith of this name may have existed. Scipione Ammirato, in his Florentine Histories, mentions a "Bernardon Baldino," "intendentissimo gioielliere," in connection with the melting down of the treasure of San Giovanni at the time of the siege of Florence: and there was a Baccio Baldini, a celebrated Florentine physician of his time, who wrote a life of Duke Cosimo I, among other things in print, and to whom Vasari alludes in the "Life of Filippino" as an "amatore di tutte le virtù." And so, in spite of the doubts which have been cast on the very existence of Baccio Baldini, I cannot help thinking that some one, more fortunate than myself, may yet chance upon his "Denunzia" among the labyrinthine recesses of the Florentine archives. But until evidence to the contrary be forthcoming, we must accept Vasari's statement, and continue to ascribe this group of prints to Baccio Baldini. That nomenclature is, at least, as convenient as any other, and may, as I say, after all prove to be correct.

App. II, Doc. IX.

Istorie Fior., ed. 1841, III, p. 394.

ed. Sansoni, III, 475.

We had broken off our story at the moment when Botticelli had been called to Rome to paint in the Pope's chapel.

It had been well for the memory of Sixtus IV, had he left no worse monument of himself than the innumerable churches and public buildings which he founded, rebuilt, or restored throughout Rome and the Papal territory. Of all these, none has brought him greater renown than the chapel in the Palace of the Vatican which bears his name. The precise date of its erection has not been ascertained, but it was no doubt begun subsequently to the completion of the library, a work undertaken by Sixtus IV, shortly after his election to the Papacy. The fabric of the library was already finished in 1475; for the accounts of Platina, the Pope's librarian, show that Domenico Ghirlandaio and his brother David were engaged from November, 1475, to May, 1476, upon certain paintings in the library which have perished. According to Vasari, Baccio Pintelli, or more correctly Pontelli, was the architect of the Sistine Chapel. From his designs, says Vasari, were constructed "sotto le stanze di Niccola," below the "stanze" of Pope Nicholas V, which were afterwards painted by Raphael, "the great library, and in the palace, the chapel called after Sixtus, which is decorated with fine paintings." It appears, however, from a document which M. Eugène Müntz discovered, that Giovannino de' Dolci, a Florentine, was the architect of this chapel. This document, which is dated 26th February, 1486, sets forth that certain sums of money were

E. Müntz, Les Arts à la Cour des Papes, I, 121-5.

Vasari, ed. Sansoni, II, 652.

Les Arts à la Cour des Papes, I, 137.

then owing to Cristoforo de' Dolci, as the son and heir of Giovannino de' Dolci, "pro expensis fabricarum capellæ majoris et arcis civitævetulæ ac diversorum [laboreriorum] in palatio factorum:" "for the expenses of the fabrics of the great chapel, and of the fortress of Civita Vecchia, and of divers [works] executed in the [apostolic] Palace." It appears from other documents which M. Müntz has cited, that this architect came to Rome during the pontificate of Nicholas V, and was employed both by Pius II and Paul II: by the latter pope he was engaged on the building of the Palazzo di S. Marco, now the Palazzo Venezia, as well as upon the fabric of the Vatican. Upon the election of Sixtus IV, Giovanni de' Dolci was appointed "suprastans," or surveyor, of the Papal Works, at a salary of eight florins the month. In 1476, he was surveying the fortifications of Ronciglione: and on the 14th November, 1481, he was appointed "commissarius" for the erection of the "arx" or fortress of Civita Vecchia. The fabric of the Sistine Chapel was certainly finished by the beginning of the year 1481: I suspect that it may have been begun shortly after the completion of the Chapel of the Choir in St. Peter's, which was consecrated in 1478, and that its decoration had been delayed by the want of painters, occasioned by the papal war with the Florentines. Sandro Botticelli, as the "Denunzia" of 1480-1 shows, was still in Florence in January, 1481, and a document discovered by Signor Gnoli, a few years ago, among the archives of the Vatican, establishes the fact that the work of decorating the building must have been begun within a few months after that date. In this document, as in other contemporary documents, the chapel is called the "capella magna," the great chapel, to distinguish it from the "capella minor," which also led out of the "Sala Reggia" or "aula magna" as it was then called. The site of the "capella minor" is probably occupied by the Pauline Chapel.

Id., I, 86, 240-1; II, 17-18.

This instrument, which is dated the 27th October, 1481, in the eleventh year of the Pontificate of Sixtus IV, sets forth how on that day, in the presence of a Public Notary, and two witnesses at Rome in the Apostolic Palace, "Master Giovanni di Pietro de' Dolci, of Florence, living at Rome, surveyor, or commissary, of the fabric of the Apostolic Palace," acting at the command, and on the commission, of the Pope, gave out on contract "to Cosimo di Lorenzo di Filippo di Rossello, to Alessandro di Mariano, to Domenico di Tommaso di Currado, of Florence, and to Pietro di Christofano of Città della Pieve, in the diocese of Perugia, painters, sojourning at Rome, the painting of the new Great Chapel of the said Apostolic Palace, from the head of the altar downwards, that is to say, ten histories of the old and new testament with the curtains below, to be painted to the best of their ability, well, diligently, and faithfully, by them, and any one of them and their assistants, in the same manner as the work has been begun. And the said painters agreed with, and promised, the said master Giovanni di Pietro," etc., "to paint and finish the said ten histories with their curtains before the 15th day of the month of March next following, at the price of payment and estimate at which the histories already executed in the said chapel by the same painters were estimated, under a penalty of fifty gold ducats for any one of them failing therein," etc. The document concludes with an obligation, in legal form, of their "goods, both present and future," in the event of their failure to fulfil the terms of the contract; and the names of two papal notaries are appended as witnesses to the deed. It is clear, then,

App. II, Doc. XXII.

from this instrument, that Giovannino de' Dolci was the architect of the chapel; that the Florentine painters, who were engaged upon its decoration, were Cosimo Rosselli, Sandro Botticelli, and Domenico Ghirlandaio, together with Pietro Perugino, who had then settled at Florence: and it would seem that four of the fourteen Histories from the Old and New Testaments, on the lateral walls, and the wall above the entrance of the building, were already finished in October, 1481; and that the paintings on the wall above the altar, together with the figures of the Popes and the decorative paintings between the windows, in the upper part of the chapel, were, also, finished at that time. The completion of so large a part of the work would argue that it had been begun in the earlier part of the year 1481: but the political relations of the Pope and the Florentines were such, that it is extremely unlikely that so large and important a body of Florentine painters would have been called to Rome before the month of March, 1481.

Certain learned professors of the science of pictorial criticism have detected the hands, not only of Filippino Lippi and Fra Diamante, but also of Melozzo da Forlì, in the frescoes of the Sistine Chapel. Professor Schmarsow has informed us exactly which of the figures of the Popes were painted by Melozzo: but as I am unable to follow the arguments of the egregious Professor, not having studied in the Academy of Lagado, I must leave his conclusions undiscussed. Dr. Ulmann, again, has attributed to Fra Diamante definite portions of the paintings between the windows of the chapel; and to Filippino, the landscape and architecture in the background of Botticelli's fresco of the "Temptation of Christ." The former of these attributions is based upon a document, which Signor Milanesi discovered in the Public Library of Poppi, in the Casentino: the other upon a notice of the Sistine Chapel, which Signor Milanesi cited in connection with that document, from the "Opusculum de Mirabilibus novæ & veteris urbis Romæ," by Francesco Albertini, which was published at Rome, on 4th February, 1510-11. The passage in question, which occurs in the chapter, "De nonnullis ecclesiis et cappellis," was written at the time at which Michelangelo was still engaged in painting the vault of the chapel. The writer, who is addressing himself to Pope Julius II, thus describes the chapel of Pope Sixtus IV, in the Palace of the Vatican: "Capella P. P. Syxti IIII in palatio perpulchra, in qua sunt picturæ novi et veteris testamenti cum pontificibus sanctis, manu et arte mirabili nobilium pictorum concertantium, videlicet: Petri de Castro plebis, et Alexandri et Dominici et Cosmæ atque Philippi Floren. quam tua beatitudo ferreis catenis munivit: ac superiorem partem testudineam pulcherrimis picturis et auro exornavit, opus præclarum Michaelis Archangeli Floren.", etc. An examination of the document at Poppi, such as Dr. Ulmann does not appear to have made, led me to establish the fact, that the frescoes, which Fra Diamante painted for Sixtus IV, were not among the decorations of the Sistine Chapel, but were executed in another, and entirely distinct building; and that they were already finished in 1478. But as this question properly forms no part of my present subject, I must postpone its discussion. As to the share which Filippino Lippi is said to have had in the paintings of the Sistine Chapel, a document which has lately come to light, a report of an agent of the Duke of Milan, written prior to the death of Lorenzo de' Medici in 1492, expressly states that Filippino Lippi did not work in

A. Schmarsow, Melozzo da Forli, p. 208.

H. Ulmann, Sandro Botticelli, pp. 92, and 97.

Vasari, ed. Sansoni, II, 641.

App. II, Doc. XXVIII.

the Sistine Chapel with Botticelli, Perugino, and Ghirlandaio. Indeed, it would seem that Francesco Albertini was acquainted with the contract of 27th October, 1481, or with some similar record; and that his expression, "et Cosmæ atque Philippi," is but a misreading of the name of Cosimo Rosselli as it stands in that instrument, "Cosmo Laurentii Phylippi Rosselli." But the best proof of all that neither Fra Diamante, nor Filippino, worked on the chapel, is that not the least trace of their hands is to be found in its paintings.

Among other early notices of the paintings in the Sistine, is the statement which the "Anonimo Gaddiano" derived from the "Libro di Antonio Billi," that Botticelli "nella cappella di sixto fece 3 faccie o quadrj;" a statement, which was erroneously copied by Antonio Petrei. And there is, also, the account of Vasari, who, in the first edition of his "Lives," relates that the picture of the "Adoration of the Magi," which Botticelli painted for the church of Santa Maria Novella, "brought him both in Florence and abroad, such fame that Pope Sixtus IV, having caused the chapel in the Palace at Rome to be built, and wishing it decorated, ordered that he should become overseer of the work; whence it was, he executed in that chapel with his own hand the following stories, namely, Christ tempted of the devil, and Moses slaying the Egyptian, and drawing water for the daughters of Jethro, the Midianite, likewise the descent of fire from heaven while the sons of Aaron were sacrificing, and some canonized popes in the niches above the stories." But let us rather turn to the paintings themselves.

App. II, Doc. II, fol. 85 recto.

App. II, Doc. I, fol. 49, tergo.

Vasari, ed. 1550, I, 490.

The Sistine Chapel, even in its original state, could never have been among the great achievements of Florentine architecture in the fifteenth century. Like many another building which Sixtus IV erected, it was admirably contrived for the purposes for which it was intended to be used: and in that, perhaps, its chief merit, as a piece of architecture, consists. In construction, it was defective: the walls were not strong enough to resist the thrust of the vault; and already before Michelangelo began to paint in the chapel, Julius II had been obliged to strengthen the building with iron ties, "ferreis catenis," as Francesco Albertini records in the passage which I have cited. The work was probably carried out in 1504, when the chapel was closed for repairs from April till October, as Burchard records in his "Diary." One of these ties is still to be seen running immediately above the gallery, or cornice, along the wall, over the principal entrance. Vasari, also, relates that at a later time, Antonio da Sangallo, the younger, restored one side of the chapel which threatened ruin; and the left wall of the chapel remains bulged several inches out of the perpendicular. Much as the building and its original frescoes have been damaged by the subsidences brought about by faulty construction; the paintings have suffered still more in their effect, through the introduction of the later frescoes of Michelangelo. The crazy walls seem unable to support the astonishing pile of storied architecture, and hurtling forms, which his genius has projected beyond the vault: and the fresco of the "Last Judgment," on the wall above the altar, opens upon a scene, in comparison to which the space of the building appears cramped and narrow. And not only has the architectural effect of the building been destroyed by the frescoes of Michelangelo, things incomparable and apart, which would have dwarfed any building except it had been designed by the master himself; but the paintings which were executed for Sixtus IV,

J. Burchardus, Diarium, III, 356.

Vasari, ed. Sansoni, V, 465.

no longer keep their place, and produce their due effect, in the building. In its original state, the chapel must have produced an effect of light and space, of symmetrical design and complete decoration, which is now difficult to realize. But let me attempt to restore it in words.

The Sistine Chapel is a quadrangular, vaulted hall, planned upon a triple square, some forty-five feet in breadth and one hundred and thirty-one feet in length. The entrance is in the centre of one of the end walls, immediately opposite to the altar. The walls are divided in the direction of their length, by two cornices; and of their height, by three orders of shallow pilasters, which are separated from one another by the cornices. Upon the highest tier of pilasters rest the pendentives of an elliptical waggon-vault. These pendentives, with the pilasters on which they rest, form a series of circular-headed spaces which are pierced by a corresponding series of circular-headed windows, at regular intervals around the walls of the buildings; namely, six spaces with their windows on each of the lateral walls, and two on each of the end walls. At the foot of the pilasters dividing these spaces ran the upper cornice, at a sufficient projection to form a narrow gallery round the four walls of the building. Below this cornice ran a series of sixteen histories in fresco, divided by the second order of painted pilasters, and corresponding to the circular-headed spaces with their windows above them; namely, six on each side, and two at each end of the building. Below the stories ran a shallow cornice, or stringcourse; and below this stringcourse a series of sixteen spaces, painted in imitation of hangings, and divided by the lowest order of painted pilasters. These spaces were interrupted by the altar and altar-piece above it, by the principal entrance, at either end of the building; and by the "cantoria," or singing gallery, in the right wall.

Vasari, ed. 1550, II, 962.

In its original state, the vault of the Chapel was not painted: Vasari, in the first edition of the "Lives" (repeating, no doubt, what he had heard directly from Michelangelo,) states distinctly, that Julius II, "moved by the love which he bore to the memory of his uncle, the roof of the Chapel of Sixtus not being painted, (sendo la volta della cappella di Sisto non dipinta,) ordered that it should be adorned with paintings." In the course of the execution of that work, begun in 1508 and finished in 1512-3, Michelangelo destroyed the paintings in the lunettes surrounding the heads of the windows, in order to complete the scheme of the vault by a series of figures setting forth the genealogy of Christ. The paintings destroyed by Michelangelo would seem to have been wholly of an architectural and decorative character. Among the drawings by Michelangelo in the University Galleries at Oxford, is a large sheet drawn with the pen, and washed with bistre, of his paintings on the vault and in the lunettes of the Sistine Chapel. This sheet, which appears to be some engraver's drawing, No. 36 in Sir J. C. Robinson's Catalogue, shows the frescoes originally painted by Michelangelo in the two lunettes above the windows in the wall over the altar, which he himself afterwards destroyed, when, in c. 1535-6, he prepared the wall for the fresco of the "Last Judgment"; and at the same time removed the whole of the older frescoes, filled up the two windows, and took away the cornices, on that side of the chapel. At a later time, during the pontificate of Paul III, when the Sala Reggia was erected from the designs of Antonio da San Gallo, the two windows in the wall above the entrance were also filled up, and painted in imitation of the original lattice.

Id., ed. Sansoni, VII, 352-4.

The wall spaces between the splays of the windows, and the pilaster supporting the pendentives of the vault, are still decorated, on the three sides of the Chapel, with a series of painted niches with circular shell-heads, containing the whole-length figures of the popes, to which Vasari alludes. The pilasters between these niches, and the splays of the windows, are painted with grotesque ornament; and the lunettes above the windows were probably decorated in the same way. Some notion may yet be formed of the paintings which originally covered the wall above the altar. It is no longer possible to say precisely in what way the central space between the two windows was treated; but we may conclude with certainty that it contained a figure of St. Peter. In the niche to the left of the left window, facing the altar, was doubtlessly painted a figure of St. Linus, the successor of St. Peter; and in the niche to the right of the right window, another figure of St. Cletus, the third bishop in the see of Rome. The existing figures, on the lateral walls, continue the series in the same order. St. Clement, in the first niche to the left; St. Anacletus in the first niche to the right; and so forth to the number of twenty-eight figures, the last of which, representing St. Marcellus I, the 31st Pope according to the orthodox computation, is painted in the centre of the wall above the entrance.

The two "histories" in fresco, below the principal cornice on the wall above the altar, which were destroyed by Michelangelo, seem in their arrangement, to have repeated those which remain on the wall above the entrance. The fresco on the left represented the "Finding of Moses"; and that on the right, the "Birth of Christ": according to Vasari both were painted by Perugino. These frescoes were, severally, the first of the two series of "Histories of the Old and New Testaments," specified in the contract of 1481, which are continued around the other walls of the chapel. In the stories from the Old Testament, on the left side of the chapel, facing the altar, was set forth the life of Moses; and in those from the New Testament, on the right side, the life of Christ: in each case story echoed story, the type in the life of Christ answering to the antitype in the life of Moses. The twelve stories which remain on the lateral walls occur in the following order: The first story to the left, beside the altar, represents "The Journey of Moses and Zipporah into Egypt, and the Circumcision of their First Born." The first story to the right immediately opposite, "The Baptism of Christ." Vasari attributes the latter fresco to Perugino; but as Morelli has pointed out, both this and the fresco of the "Journey of Moses," are undoubtedly by Pinturicchio. The second story on the left, which represents "Moses slaying the Egyptian, and drawing water for the daughters of Jethro, and his trials in the land of Midian," and the second story on the right, of "The Temptation of Christ," are by Sandro Botticelli. The third story on the left, "The Destruction of Pharoah and his host in the Red Sea." Vasari attributes this fresco to Cosimo Rosselli. It is clearly Ghirlandaiesque in character; and its execution has been ascribed wrongly, as I think, to Piero di Cosimo. Third story on the right, "The calling of St. Peter and St. Andrew," by Domenico Ghirlandaio. Fourth story on left, "Moses receiving the Tables of the Law on Mount Sinai, and the Worship of the Golden Calf," by Cosimo Rosselli. Fourth story on right, "The Sermon on the Mount, and the healing of the Leper," by Cosimo Rosselli. Vasari attributes the landscape of this fresco to Piero di Cosimo. Fifth story to left, "The Destruction of the Company of Korah," by Botticelli. Fifth story on the right, "Christ giving the Keys to St. Peter,"

Vasari, ed. Sansoni, III, 579.

Id., III, 188.

Id., III, 259.

Id., III, 188-9.

Vasari, ed. Sansoni, III, 578.

by Pietro Perugino. Vasari states that Perugino was assisted by Don Bartolommeo della Gatta; but the fresco thoughout is obviously by Perugino. Sixth story to left, "The Last Days of Moses." This story, which represents Moses giving the law to the children of Israel, his sight

Id., III, 691.

of the promised land, and his death, is attributed by Vasari to Luca Signorelli. It must, however, be ascribed to the painter whom Vasari in the first edition of the "Lives," rightly calls Don Piero della Gatta, but erroneously in the second edition, Don Bartolommeo, and whose real

Vasari, ed. 1550, I, 468. Id., ed. 1568, I, 448.

name was Don Piero d'Antonio Dei, abate of San Clemento, in Arezzo. This conclusion is evident, as I think, from a study of the works traditionally attributed to him; especially those paintings which, like the fresco in the Sistine Chapel, show the influence of Signorelli: namely, the fresco of "St. Jerome" in the sacristy of the Cathedral at Arezzo, the altarpiece over the third altar in the right aisle of the Collegiata, at Castiglione Fiorentino, the "predella" pictures belonging to this altarpiece, which are now in the sacristy of the church, and the painting of "St. Francis receiving the Stigmata," in the Church of San Francesco, in the same town.

Cavalcaselle and Crowe, ed. Le Monnier, VIII, 537, etc.

Vasari, ed. Sansoni, III, 188.

The sixth and last story on the right wall of the Sistine Chapel, the "Last Supper, with scenes from the Passion," is by Cosimo Rosselli.

The two stories on the wall above the entrance, have both been repainted. The one to the left, on entering the building, representing the "Archangel Michael and Satan contending over the body of Moses," is said to have been twice repainted; the existing fresco was executed during the pontificate of Gregory XIII, by Matteo da Lecce. The story to the right of the entrance, representing the "Resurrection," was repainted at

Id., III, 259.

the same time by Arrigo Fiammingo. Vasari records that the original of this fresco by Domenico Ghirlandaio, had already in his time been in great part destroyed in the process of replacing above the entrance a lintel which had been fractured by the subsidence of the building. Below this series

Id., III, 579.

of frescoes, over the altar, was originally "la tavola in muro," (to use Vasari's phrase,) painted with an "Assumption of the Madonna," by Perugino, "in which Pope Sixtus was represented kneeling." This painting, like the other frescoes on the wall above the altar, was removed to make way for Michelangelo's "Last Judgment." The painted pilasters and the hangings in the spaces between them, which completed the scheme of decoration, still remain on the lateral and end walls of the building. The painted hangings, the "cortinia" of the contract of 1481, are powdered with the arms of Pope Sixtus, surmounted by the Papal Keys and the triple tiara. The same shield is repeated among the ornaments of the pilasters, which are painted with richly contrived candelabra and grotesques, like those on the upper pilasters and the splays of the windows. These ornaments do not, however, contain anything which suggests that Botticelli had a share in their design. They were, probably, the work of some painter, who made the execution of such things his chief business, like Andrea di Cosimo, the disciple of

Id., III, 189.

Cosimo Rosselli, who, as Vasari relates, "attese assai alle grottesche."

If I am right in my conjectures as to the original state of the Sistine Chapel and its decorations, the interior of the building, considered as a whole, must have produced a very different and far finer effect than that which it now produces. The symmetrical plan and arrangement of the architecture; the simple vault, undisturbed by any paintings, and contrasted with the rich decoration of the walls; the pierced clerestory admitting the light on all sides; produced, as I surmise, an effect of space, and fine proportion, such as can only proceed from an entire and consistent scheme of architecture and decoration. In such a scheme, the continuous band of splendid decoration around the chapel, formed by the stories from the Old and New Testaments, doubtlessly kept its place and produced its due effect as the chief feature of the chapel, in which all the other frescoes and ornaments culminated. Now these stories are completely overshadowed by the frescoes of Michelangelo; and the eye which should have rested upon them, is drawn upwards to the vault.

But let us now examine in greater detail the frescoes which Vasari attributes to Botticelli. With the exception of the paintings between the windows in the wall above the altar, all have fortunately been preserved; notwithstanding the intention of Julius II to have the whole of the earlier frescoes repainted by Michelangelo. Of the figures of the popes in the niches between the windows twenty-eight remain; twelve on each of the lateral walls, and four on the wall above the entrance. The niches themselves fill the whole of the spaces between the upper cornice and impost mouldings of the window-arches in height, and the splays of the windows and the pilasters below the pendentives of the vault in breadth. They are of the simplest Florentine architecture, ornamented with the echinus, and other such Roman ornaments. In each case, the panel of the plinth below the niche, bears an inscription recording the name of the pope commemorated, the number of years he occupied the chair of St. Peter, and the year in which he suffered martyrdom. These inscriptions, which follow a common form, are in an indifferent state of preservation, and many of them have been carelessly restored. For instance, the name of "S. LVCIVS" has been turned into "S. VOIVS"; and other errors have been made in repainting the numerals. The inscription below the figure of St. Anacletus, the first in a fair state of preservation, may be cited as an example of the rest:

"S · ANACLETVS · GRECV[S] · EX ATH
ENIS · SE · AN · VIIII · M · II · D · X · MAR°.
CORONATVR · AN · XPI · CXII · M · IIII · D · XIII."

The figures themselves are somewhat larger than life, and, like the niches which contain them, are drawn in perspective from the point of view of an imaginary spectator, standing upon the floor of the chapel below. Upon examining these figures in detail, we find that they are not only very unequally preserved, but also very unequal in execution. One or two of the finest might well have been executed by Botticelli himself; others recall, especially in some of the heads, the hand of Domenico Ghirlandaio; but many appear to be of an indeterminate character, recalling at once the manners both of Ghirlandaio and Botticelli. Let us take them categorically, one by one, in their historical order, beginning with the figures next to the wall above the altar:

Pilaster at angle:

1st niche to left. S. CLEMENS ROMANVS. In purple cope. The head, in my opinion, is by Domenico Ghirlandaio; the figure by an assistant of Ghirlandaio, working, apparently, from a sketch by Botticelli.

1st niche to right. S. ANACLETVS GRECVS EX ATHENIS. In purple cope, with red apparel. The head is again by Domenico Ghirlandaio; but the hands and draperies are distinctly Botticellesque.

Window:

2nd niche to left. S. EVARISTVS GRECVS PATRE IVDEO EX BETHLEEM. In red cope, with apparel embroidered with saints. The design of the figure is thoroughly Botticellesque, especially the head, which, however, has been much retouched.

2nd niche to right. S. ALEXANDER ROMANVS. In a saffron chasuble and black dalmatic. The head seems to have been executed by an assistant of Domenico Ghirlandaio; but the figure and draperies are designed in Botticelli's manner.

Pilaster:

3rd niche to left. S. SIXTVS ROMANVS. In processional habit. The head and shoulders have been entirely repainted; the draperies are Botticellesque.

3rd niche to right. S. THELESPHORVS GRECVS. In purple cope. The underlying design of Botticelli is very apparent in this figure; the head, especially, is fine.

Window:

4th niche to left. S. IGINVS GRECVS EX ATHENIS. In blue chasuble. The head is by Domenico Ghirlandaio; the design of the draperies is Botticellesque.

4th niche to right. S. PIVS ITALVS EX AQVILEIA. In saffron cope. The head is by Domenico Ghirlandaio; the hands, and even the draperies, are more in Ghirlandaio's than in Botticelli's manner.

Pilaster:

5th niche to left. S. ANICETVS SIRIVS. In saffron cope. This figure is entirely in the manner of Botticelli; the head wants only some more virile quality of drawing to be his.

5th niche to right. S. SOTHER ITALVS EX FVNDIS. In white chasuble, with yellow apparel. This admirable figure must have been executed from Botticelli's cartoon; the head may even have been painted by the master himself.

Window:

6th niche to left. S. ELEVT[HERIVS GRECVS EX NICOP]OLI. In blue chasuble. The head is Ghirlandaiesque; the draperies, which recall in character those of S. Alexander in the second niche to right, are Botticellesque.

6th niche to right. S. VICTOR AFER. In purple cope and white surplice. By an assistant of Domenico Ghirlandaio, working from a drawing by Botticelli; the head especially is Ghirlandaiesque.

Pilaster:

7th niche to left. S. ZEPHERINVS ROMANVS. In grape-purple cope. By an assistant of Ghirlandaio, working from Botticelli's drawing; the hands especially are Ghirlandaiesque.

7th niche to right. S. CALISTVS ROMANVS. In green chasuble. The figure is entirely in the manner of Botticelli; the head has been much retouched.

Window:

8th niche to left. S. VRBANVS ROMANVS. In white cope, richly brocaded in black and gold. The head and hands are Ghirlandaiesque; but the figure was probably executed from a sketch by Botticelli.

8th niche to right. S. PONTIANVS ROMANVS. In grape-purple cope, with red and gold apparel. All that part of the head above the upper lip, with the tiara, has been entirely repainted; this figure was probably executed by some assistant of Ghirlandaio.

Pilaster:

9th niche to left. S. ANTHERVS GRECVS. In purple chasuble, with blue apparel. The head is of uncertain character, but the draperies show that a drawing by Botticelli was employed.

9th niche to right. S. FABIANVS ROMANVS. In red chasuble, with green apparel. The mitre has been restored; the figure is of an uncertain character.

Window:

10th niche to left. S. CORNELIVS ROMANVS. In blue chasuble, with green apparel. This fine figure is entirely in the manner of Botticelli; the head is probably by his own hand.

10th niche to right. S. LVCIVS ROMANVS. In purple chasuble, with green apparel. The cartoon of this figure was probably done by Botticelli; the execution by one of his assistants; but the head, which is somewhat damaged, may have been painted by the master himself.

Pilaster:

11th niche to left. S. STEPHANVS ROMANVS. In a green cope, with orange apparel. The cartoon and the execution, in part, of this figure were probably the work of Botticelli himself.

11th niche to right. S. SIXTVS SECVNDVS GRECVS EX ATHENIS. In saffron cope, with green and red apparel. The head, and action of the right hand and arm, are repeated from the figure of St. Jerome in the church of Ognissanti, at Florence. The cartoon of this figure, and perhaps the execution of the head and hands are to be ascribed to Botticelli himself.

Window:

12th niche to left. S. DIONISIVS ROMANVS. In white chasuble, richly brocaded in gold. The head has been much repainted; the draperies are Botticellesque in character.

12th niche to right. S. FELIX ROMANVS. In green cope, lined with red. The head and hands are Ghirlandaiesque. This figure has been much retouched.

Pilaster at angle:

Niche to left of left window. S. EVTICHANVS ITALVS EX TVSCIA. In red cope, lined with green. Executed by an assistant of Ghirlandaio from a drawing by Botticelli: the head and hands are Ghirlandaiesque.

Niche to right of right window. S. [CAIVS EX] DALMATA. In orange chasuble, shot with green, and green apparel. Executed by an assistant of Ghirlandaio, from a drawing by Botticelli; the draperies are very Botticellesque in design.

Window:

Niche to left above entrance. S. MARCELLINVS ROMANVS. In cope and surplice, processional habit. The cartoon and the execution of the head, and in part of the figure, are by Botticelli. This is, perhaps, the finest and best preserved of all these figures.

Niche to right above entrance. S. MARCELLVS ROMANVS. This figure was entirely repainted in the seventeenth century. The original fresco was, probably, ruined by the settlement which fractured the lintel of the door below it.

A careful scrutiny of these frescoes goes, then, to bear out Vasari's statement that Botticelli was appointed "capo," or chief, of the work of

decorating the Sistine Chapel; since by far the larger number of these figures of the popes, if not actually executed by him, were evidently done from his sketches, and in many cases by his own assistants. To Botticelli, therefore, must be attributed the general scheme of the decoration of the chapel, in so far as it was not predetermined by the architecture of the building, or by the orders of the pope; for the subjects of the paintings were, no doubt, dictated by Sixtus, or his theologians. If the contention that Botticelli was assisted by Domenico Ghirlandaio and his disciples in the execution of these figures of the popes, required any other evidence but that of the paintings themselves, it might be found in the fact that Ghir-
App. II, Doc. XXIII. landaio and Botticelli, upon their return to Florence in 1482, were jointly commissioned by the Signoria to decorate the same wall in the Palazzo Vecchio. Taken as a whole, these figures of the popes are by no means equal in quality of execution, to the paintings by Botticelli and Ghirlandaio on the walls below them; indeed, they are no more than their greater height from the floor, and the part which they played in the original scheme of the decoration of the chapel, required them to be, namely, decorative figures, designed in a large and sculpturesque manner, and executed with good effect. At the same time, the heads are full of character, and the attitudes admirably varied. In order to obtain a greater effect of richness, the tiaras and vestments of the majority of these figures have been studded with raised "gesso" points, gilt. This mode of treatment in itself shows that these figures were chiefly intended to be judged as decorative paintings, and as such they are admirable.

Let us now turn to the three Histories from the Old and New Testament, which Botticelli executed among the series of paintings which still remain on the lateral walls of the chapel, below the cornice at the foot of the clerestory. These paintings are difficult to examine in detail, on account of their height from the floor of the chapel, and the faulty lighting of the building, due partly to the blocking up of the windows in the end walls of the chapel, above the altar and the entrance. Darkened as they are by age and restoration, these frescoes are so obscured by the glare of the clerestory windows immediately above them, that they may be better studied in good photographs, than in the originals. Like the figures of the popes, these stories can best be examined from the narrow gallery, formed by the projection of the cornice at the foot of the clerestory. The first, in order of subject, of the three stories by Botticelli, represents the trials of Moses, in seven distinct incidents, or scenes. In the foreground, to the right, Moses is seen in the act of slaying the Egyptian, whom he has thrown to the ground. He kneels, brandishing a short sword in his right hand, as he holds the Egyptian down by the throat, who, with a face distorted by agony, clutches helplessly at the air: behind them, the figures of a man and woman turn away in fear, near an open loggia. In this naïve, direct manner, Botticelli translates, into the terms of painting, the story as
Exodus, II, 11-14. it stands in Holy Writ: "And it came to pass in those days, when Moses was grown, that .... he spied an Egyptian smiting an Hebrew, one of his brethren. And he looked this way and that way, and when he saw that there was no man, he slew the Egyptian, and hid him in the sand. And when he went out the second day, behold two men of the Hebrews strove together: and he said to him that did the wrong, Wherefore smitest thou thy fellow? And he said, Who made thee a prince and a judge over us? Intendest thou to kill me, as thou killedst the Egyptian?" Following this

MOSES SLAYING THE EGYPTIAN, AND THE TRIALS OF MOSES IN THE LAND OF MIDIAN *Sistine Chapel, Rome*

incident, in the distant landscape beyond the loggia, Moses, with a club
over his left shoulder, is seen fleeing into the land of Midian: "Now Id. II, 15.
when Pharaoh heard this thing, he sought to slay Moses. But Moses fled
from the face of Pharaoh, and dwelt in the land of Midian: and he sat
down by a well."

The next two episodes of the story form the subjects of the two scenes
which fill the central portion of the fresco: "Now the priest of Midian Id. II, 16-17.
had seven daughters: and they came and drew water, and filled the
troughs to water their father's flock. And the shepherds came and drove
them away: but Moses stood up and helped them, and watered their flock."
In the middle distance, before a clump of trees, Moses drives off with
his club a couple of shepherds; and again, in the foreground, he is represented
filling a trough with water, which he has drawn out of a well; while
two of the daughters of Reuel, or Jethro, stand by with their flock. The
painter passes over the marriage of Moses with Zipporah; and in the fifth
and sixth episodes, which occupy the middle distance of the fresco, on the
left, represents the stories of Moses keeping the flock of Jethro, his father- Id. III,
in-law, and of God appearing to him out of the burning bush. On the 1-5.
right, Moses seated on the ground in the midst of the flock, puts off his
shoes from off his feet; and on the left, he is represented kneeling before
the bush, out of which God, the Father, issues in a halo of light. Below
these two episodes, in the foreground, is a group of thirteen figures
descending by a road which passes over some rising ground, which
represents the return of Moses with his wife Zipporah, his sons, and
their family, into Egypt: "And the Lord said unto Moses in Midian, Go, Id. IV,
return into Egypt: for the men are dead which sought thy life. And 19-20.
Moses took his wife and his sons, . . . and he returned to the land of Egypt."

In no other single work, is that power of dramatic painting which Morelli noted as one of the chief characteristics of Botticelli's manner, shown more variously, or significantly, than in this fresco. With unfailing mastery, the painter has successively rendered the passion and vigour of the Pollaiuolesque group of Moses slaying the Egyptian, the quiet, pastoral beauty of the scene at the well, the spiritual fervour of the story of the Burning Bush, the splendid and varied character of the heads, one of them a portrait, in the return of Moses into Egypt; weaving with consummate art, episodes so different in motive into a single and entire composition. The bare hill-side with its grove of ilex trees, against which these various figures are set in large relief, is admirably imagined, heightening as it does, not only that sentiment of primitive piety which transfigures the group of Moses talking with God out of the burning bush, but also the very different beauty of the scene by the well, with the two daughters of Jethro arrayed in white, the one with her spindle and distaff, the other with her sheep-skin and shepherd's staff; figures which, in charm of conception and beauty of line, recall the most lovely passages in the "Spring," or the "Birth of Venus." The sheep, and the lapdog which a boy is carrying, are among the few, yet admirable, representations of animals which we have by Botticelli.

The second fresco by Botticelli in the series, in order of subject, is the second painting on the right wall, representing the "Temptation of Christ," and corresponding to the fresco of the "Trials of Moses." The principal subject of the painting is represented in four episodes of little figures, in the middle distance of the picture; but in the foreground is a composition of larger figures, the meaning of which remained unexplained until Dr. Steinmann in an article published in the "Repertorium für Kunstwissenschaft," [l.c., Vol. XVIII, p. 1.] pointed out the nature of its subject. In the centre of the fresco stands the Temple of Jerusalem, in the midst of a mountainous and watered landscape. On a rocky height in the middle distance, to the left of the picture, Christ is seen with the devil disguised as a hermit, with clawed feet and bat-like wings, carrying a crutch and rosary, who points to the stones before him, with the words: [Matthew, IV, 3, &c.] "If thou be the Son of God command that these stones be made bread." In the middle of the picture, on a pinnacle above the pediment of the Temple, Christ is again represented with the devil in the same guise, who tempts him a second time: [Id. IV, 5-6.] "If thou be the Son of God, cast thyself down." Lastly, on a high rock, to the right of the picture, Christ, after being tempted for the third time, [Id. IV, 8-11.] unmasks the devil, who, as he flies away with his hermit's habit blown open, discovers his dugged breasts, goat-like haunches, and clawed feet. Behind the figure of Christ, three angels, who have come to minister to him, prepare a table set with food and wine. Lastly, on the other side of the picture, but nearer to the foreground, Christ is seen returning [Luke, IV, 14.] "in the power of the spirit into Galilee," accompanied by four angels, one of whom bears a wand of lilies. Besides these episodes, there is the episode in the foreground of the fresco, a composition of more than forty larger figures, which, as Dr. Steinmann has shown, represents the purification of a leper, in obedience to the Mosaic Law, as set forth in the fourteenth chapter of the Book of Leviticus. In the court before the Temple is the altar of burnt sacrifice. On the right, the leper, accompanied by two friends (one of whom, incredulous of his recovery, lifts his garment to assure himself), stands upon the steps of the altar: on the left, a woman, intended perhaps for the wife of the leper, hurries forward with an earthen bowl on her head, in which are the [Leviticus, XIV, 4.] "two birds alive and clean," that the law commands to be offered for him that is to be cleansed. In front of the altar stand the high priest with an acolyte in a white surplice, who holds a dish filled with the blood of the bird that has been killed over the running water; [Id. XIV, 6.] while the high priest dips the cedar wood and the hyssop, bound into a bunch with the scarlet, into the blood in the dish. Explanations such as those by which Dr. Steinmann has attempted to connect the painting in a symbolical sense, with the death of the Sultan, Mahomet II, or in a complementary sense, with the Hospital of Santo Spirito which had been refounded by Sixtus IV, must be rejected, I think, as altogether fantastical. The Hospital of Santo Spirito was not a lazar house, but a general hospital and orphanage; nor is it necessary to turn to the death of the Grand Turk in order to elucidate the symbolism of the purification of the leper in this connection. On the contrary, the introduction of this incident into the picture is to be explained on purely theological grounds. The purification of the leper, which is here understood symbolically of the purification of the heart by faith (leprosy having been always interpreted by the Church, as the symbol of sin), is introduced in direct allusion to the command, related in all the synoptical gospels, which Jesus laid upon the leper whom he healed: "Show thyself to the priest, and offer the gift that Moses commanded, for a testimony unto them." [Matthew, VIII, 4, &c.] The cleansing of the leper is one of the first miracles related of Jesus after the temptation; and the significance of the miracle as completing in a theological sense the story of the Temptation, is too self-evident to need any further comment.

THE TEMPTATION OF CHRIST *Sistine Chapel, Rome*

Of the many admirable figures and portraits in the foreground of this fresco, I must notice only the chief. On the extreme right of the picture, stands a man somewhat past the prime of life, wrapped in an ample cloak, and holding a baton in his hands. Dr. Steinmann has suggested that this may be a portrait of Girolamo Riario, the nephew of Sixtus IV, who was created Count of Forli in 1480, and shortly after Gonfaloniere of the Church. Somewhat behind this personage, on the left, is the portrait of another ecclesiastical dignitary; and on the right, the figure of a youth in a cap and long robe, one of the most beautiful portraits which Botticelli has left us. To the left of these portraits is the figure of a woman in flying draperies, who steps forward, almost in profile, with a bundle of oak faggots on her head. In the blithe, exuberant sense of life which animates this incomparable figure, Botticelli approaches more nearly to the spirit of Greek art than, perhaps, even Donatello himself had done. Beside this figure is a half-naked "putto," laden with bunches of grapes, who starts at a snake which has crept out from the fruit. This figure, as Dr. Steinmann has remarked, closely recalls, in its motive and attitude, an antique statue of a draped figure of a girl carrying a dove, and startled at a snake, which is preserved in the Museo del Campidoglio at Rome; having been added to the collection by Pope Clement XII. More than one antique statue of a naked "putto" starting at a snake is extant; but none, so far as I am aware, in this attitude: it would seem, however, that some such statue in the pose of the Capitoline marble was known to Botticelli. On the left of the woman carrying the bundle of faggots stands a group of ecclesiastics, containing four admirable portraits. The foremost figure wears the habit of a cardinal, and it has been suggested by Dr. Steinmann that it is a portrait of Giuliano della Rovere, the nephew of Sixtus IV, who afterwards became Pope Julius II. The suggestion is by no means improbable: Vasari expressly states that besides the portrait of Sixtus in the altar-piece by Perugino, Piero di Cosimo painted Virginio Orsino and Ruberto Sanseverino in one of the frescoes in this chapel. Immediately behind the figure of the high priest is another admirable portrait of an ecclesiastic; and the rest of the foreground of the picture, on the left, is filled by a series of figures, of young men and maidens, of delicate pages and fine courtiers, alike admirable for their invention and draughtsmanship.

E. Steinmann, Sandro Botticelli, p. 49.

Vasari, ed. Sansoni, IV, 132.

For beauty of individual passages, this fresco is surpassed by nothing of Botticelli's; but considered as a whole, it is in its composition, the least satisfactory of the three stories by him in the Sistine Chapel. In representing the three incidents of the "Temptation" in the middle distance of the picture, and in amplifying their symbolical meaning by the introduction of the story of the "Purification of the Leper" into the foreground, Botticelli hit upon what was, pictorially, a most ingenious device for the solution of the problem by which he was confronted; for two of the three incidents of the "Temptation" were of such a nature that they could not, in the same painting, be represented in the foreground, and were, therefore, by themselves inadequate to fill so large a space, in a way that would accord with the other frescoes in the series. But the device was happier in its conception than in its execution; for the principal figures in this incident of the "Purification of the Leper" are outbalanced by the more effective groups of portraits and accessory figures by which they are surrounded. The composition is confused; indeed, so little does this part

of the picture explain itself, that the real meaning of its subject was lost
sight of for centuries.

The third and last fresco by Botticelli, in the series, represents the
story of the destruction of Korah and his company, in three scenes, or
Numbers, incidents. On the right of the painting is a group of eight figures, repre-
XVI, 1-3. senting how Korah, Dathan, and Abiram "took men," and "gathered
themselves together against Moses and against Aaron, and said unto them,
Ye take too much upon you, seeing all the congregation are holy, every one
of them, and the Lord is among them: wherefore then lift ye up yourselves above the congregation of the Lord?" Korah and his company,
with stones in their hands, gather themselves against Moses, who raises
his hands with a gesture of admonition. One man, with a scroll-like,
Pollaiuolesque head-dress, steps forward to restrain a youth about to stone
the patriarch; and a hand is laid on the arm of the man behind them,
who is in the act of throwing another stone. Immediately behind this
group are ranged eight other figures of which little more than the heads
are seen. The greater number of these are portraits of ecclesiastics; but
I much doubt whether the head, the last but one on the right, which Dr.
Steinmann has reproduced in his little book on Botticelli, is a portrait at all;
certainly, it cannot be regarded as a portrait of the painter. In the centre
of the picture is another group of eight figures, surrounding the altar of
Id. v. Burnt Sacrifice, as the painter conceived it: "And Moses said unto Korah,
16-17. Be thou and all thy company before the Lord, thou, and they, and Aaron,
to-morrow: and take every man his censer, and put incense in them, and
Id. v. bring ye before the Lord every man his censer." Moses on the right of
18-19. this group, lifts his rod towards "the door of the tabernacle of the congregation," which is seen in perspective on the extreme left of the painting,
and behind him, Aaron, in a triple tiara, turns in the same direction as he
swings his censer; while Korah and his company are confounded by the
flames of their censers, which are miraculously blown against them; one
of the men covers his face with his cloak as he attempts to extinguish the fire,
and another, overcome, has fallen to the ground. It is thus that Botticelli
translates into the language of the painter, the story of Holy Writ: "And
there came out a fire from the Lord, and consumed the two hundred and
Id. v. fifty men that offered incense." The third incident is represented in the
20-21, 32-33 group of seven figures on the left: "And the Lord spake unto Moses and
unto Aaron, saying, Separate yourselves from among this congregation,
that I may consume them in a moment." . . . "And the earth opened her
mouth, and swallowed them up, and their houses, and all the men that
appertained unto Korah, and all their goods." In the fresco, the earth is
seen to open before Moses, who raises his right hand with a maledictory
gesture, as Korah and two of his company go down "alive into the pit."
Behind the figure of Korah, two of the sons of Aaron are miraculously lifted
up on little clouds; and behind the figure of Moses are two admirable
portrait-figures of ecclesiastics.

Immediately behind the altar of Burnt Sacrifice, in the centre of the
picture, raised upon a stone pace, approached by steps, is a triumphal arch,
copied in its architecture from the arch of Constantine at Rome. It is only
in the details of the reliefs that its design varies from the original. Instead of the dedicatory inscription on the panel of the attic over the central
Id. v. 40. arch, the painter has placed the admonition, "that no stranger, which is
not of the seed of Aaron, come near to offer incense before the Lord":

THE DESTRUCTION OF COMPANY OF KORAH *Sistine Chapel, Rome*

NEMO SIBI ASSVMMAT HONOREM NISI VOCATVS ADEO TANQVAM ARON. This representation of a piece of antique Roman architecture, figuring for the first time in the paintings of Botticelli, serves to remind us how the painter, previously to his journey to Rome, had derived his conception of classic architecture entirely from such buildings, as the early Romanesque churches of San Giovanni and Sant' Apostoli, in Florence. To the right of the arch is seen the ruin of another Roman building, a Corinthian portico, with the remains of an upper "loggia." In the distance, behind these buildings in an ample landscape, is an estuary flowing between broken and mountainous shores. On the right, through the columns of the portico, is seen a walled town with architecture of that Flemish character which I have remarked in the fresco of the "Temptation;" and on the other side of the fresco, to the left of the arch, where the water runs into the shore, are two ships lying at anchor before a cliff on the farther bank, above which is a church, "bosomed high in tufted trees." The truth with which the ships are drawn, the hawsers and anchors on the quay, the stratification of the cliff, and indeed all the details of this landscape, which is one of the most beautiful passages of the kind Botticelli has left, show it to have been carefully studied from nature.

In design, this fresco is the most vigorous and Pollaiuolesque of all Botticelli's paintings in the Sistine Chapel. The gesture of the hand raised above the head, which is used more than once here with varying intention, the open mouth expressive of violent passion, the scroll-like head-dress which one of the figures wears, are traits which show how forcibly the manner of Antonio Pollaiuoli was present in his imagination while designing this story.

Among the drawings exhibited in the Gallery of the Uffizi is a slight sketch, in pen and ink, of the composition of this fresco, Frame 55, No. 146, which is attributed to Botticelli, but which is seen from the handling to be by Filippino Lippi. Dr. Ulmann cites this drawing as a proof of the old assumption that Filippino worked in the Sistine Chapel in company with Botticelli; but I have already shown the fallacy of such a contention. On the contrary, this little drawing must be regarded as a sketch done from memory; for not only does it differ from the fresco in the grouping of the figures, but the draughtsman has introduced part of the Colosseum into the background, on the left of the arch of Constantine. It dates, no doubt, from the time when Filippino was in Rome, working on the frescoes of the Caraffa chapel, in the church of Santa Maria sopra Minerva.

H. Ulmann, S. Botticelli, p. 99.

In colouring a series of stories such as these, certain traditional usages were observed: thus, in the various incidents of the two frescoes from the life of Moses, the figure of the patriarch is represented throughout in a saffron dress, with a green outer robe, in order to make the sequence of the several incidents the clearer to the spectator. The use of gilding has been occasionally resorted to, for burnishing the lights and ornaments: for example, the reliefs on the triumphal arch in the story of "Korah and his company" have been heightened in this way. But these frescoes are by no means overloaded with gold, as Vasari, in a passage which has often been quoted, would have us believe. Despite the processes of cleaning and retouching which these paintings have undergone at various times, they remain in a far better state of preservation than the majority of such frescoes. The figure of Moses slaying the Egyptian, in the first painting of the series, is one of the passages which have suffered most,

Vasari, ed. Sansoni, III, 188.

apparently from damp; and a closer examination of their surface than I have been able to make, would doubtlessly disclose other such passages.

The day has gone by when the frescoes in the Sistine Chapel, by Botticelli and his contemporaries, were stigmatized as a "Gothic medley;" but even later and more tolerant critics have objected that Botticelli's compositions want the unity of Perugino's and Ghirlandaio's paintings. A work of art, however, must properly be judged from its own point of view; and the frescoes by Botticelli in the Sistine Chapel were designed in accordance with the canons of taste accepted by his age. Even Leonardo da Vinci, in his "Tractate of Painting," lays down the principle that if the life of a saint, divided into several stories, is to be painted upon a wall, instead of representing it in so many different pictures, each with its own point of sight, in the mediæval way, the painter should arrange the various stories in a single picture, (as Botticelli has done,) so that there may be only one point of sight. On the other hand, a picture composed on these principles was a concession to the traditions of the Church; and the student of painting must always feel that in the frescoes of the Sistine Chapel, as in his larger altar-pieces, Botticelli was hindered by the ecclesiastical prescriptions of subject which were imposed upon him. Fortunately, however, the rarest qualities of painting are not necessarily hindered by a mere prescription of the subject, or by a traditional arrangement of the figures which it contains; and in their presentation of all the finest and most individual qualities of Botticelli's painting, the incomparable air of his figures, his rendering of form and movement, his beauty of line, his wealth of invention, these frescoes are unsurpassed in their kind.

L. da Vinci, Literary Works, I, 271.

In the decoration of the Sistine Chapel, the great opportunity of his life was given to Botticelli at the very moment when his genius had come to its full maturity. Aware of what fortune had brought to him, he produced a series of frescoes which stand apart from the rest of his works, by reason of the unique occasion on which they were painted, and their monumental character. But not only do these paintings form his most imposing work; they present in epitome, the entire range of his art, and they illustrate more completely and more significantly than any other single work of his, that side of his genius which the influence of Antonio Pollaiuoli chiefly went to develop; the aspect of it which revealed, in the estimation of his contemporaries, the distinguishing characteristics of his manner, but which in our modern criticism of the man has been largely overlooked. For the student of Botticelli, they must form the centre of all his studies; the masterpiece from which the character of the painter must primarily be argued. Judged as part of the original decorations of the chapel, executed for Sixtus IV, they remain unquestionably the finest of the early frescoes in the Sistine. They may want the simplicity and decorative effectiveness of Perugino's fresco of "Christ giving the keys to St. Peter," or the unity and academic sanity and accomplishment of Ghirlandaio's story of the "Calling of St. Peter and St. Andrew," qualities which Messrs. Crowe and Cavalcaselle so much admired; but in their spirit, invention, and beauty of draughtsmanship, these three paintings by Botticelli remain unsurpassed. As one looks at the "Stories of the Old and New Testaments" still preserved in the Sistine Chapel, one cannot but be impressed by the incomparably greater, and more various, genius of the man.

Vasari, ed. Sansoni, III, 188.

Vasari, in his life of Cosimo Rosselli, has preserved an anecdote of Sixtus IV and the painters who worked for him in the chapel in the

Vatican, which is a characteristic piece of the kind of gossip then current in the Florentine workshops. "It is said," writes Vasari, "that the Pope had ordered a prize to be given to the painter who, in the judgment of the Pontiff, should best acquit himself in the execution of those pictures. When the stories were finished, his Holiness went to see them; each of the painters having striven so to bring it about, that he should deserve the prize and the honour of it. Cosimo, conscious of his want of invention and design, had sought to hide his defects by covering his work with the finest ultramarine blues, and other bright colours, and by heightening the lights of the picture with a great quantity of gold; so much so that there was not a tree, a blade of grass, a piece of drapery, nor a cloud that had not been thus lit up; he having persuaded himself that the Pope, who understood little of that art, would on that account give the prize to him. When the day arrived on which the works of all the painters were to be uncovered, his were shown along with the rest, and amid much laughter and many jests, were scoffed and jeered at by the other painters, everyone bantering him instead of having compassion on him. But in the end, the laugh was turned against themselves; for those colours, as Cosimo had imagined, so dazzled the eyes of the Pope, who did not understand much about such things, although he greatly delighted in them, that he decided that Cosimo had acquitted himself in the work better than all the others. And so, having caused the prize to be given to him, he ordered the rest to cover their pictures with the finest blues that could be found, and to heighten them with gold, that they might resemble those of Cosimo in colouring and richness of effect. Whereupon the poor painters in despair at being forced to comply with the narrow intelligence of the Holy Father, began to spoil what they had well executed. Thus Cosimo had the laugh of the very men who, a little before, had laughed at his own work." Although the story cannot be accepted in its literal sense, for all the painters in question had, long before they worked in the Sistine Chapel, freely employed gold for heightening the lights of their pictures; it yet preserves, no doubt, the tradition that Sixtus preferred the gaudy and unimaginative works of Cosimo Rosselli, the least meritorious of all the paintings in the Sistine Chapel, to the masterpieces of Botticelli, Ghirlandaio, and Perugino. But if Sixtus knew little, and cared less, for the finer qualities of art, it should at least be conceded to his memory, that the public works and buildings erected by him, even when they are wanting in design, are invariably characterized by that admirable sense of use and fitness which marks the better side of his character.

The Anonimo Gaddiano records one other work, which Botticelli executed in Rome, besides the frescoes of the Sistine Chapel; a painting on panel of the "Adoration of the Magi." "In Roma dipinse anchora, et faceuj una tauola dj magi che fu la piu [? bella] opera che maj facessj." An epithet has dropped out of the sentence; but the writer is plainly speaking in great commendation of the picture. No other early writer alludes to this painting; but the picture is, perhaps, to be identified with a panel of the "Adoration of the Magi," No. 3, in the gallery of the Hermitage, at St. Petersburg. This painting is the latest in point of style of all the extant paintings of the "Adoration of the Magi," by Botticelli; and undoubtedly belongs to the same period of his art as the Sistine frescoes. It was bought in France, for the gallery of the Hermitage, by the Czar, Paul I, on the advice of Baron Vivant Denon, in 1808,

App. II, Doc. II, fol. 85, recto.

from the engraver Peralli, who is said to have obtained it from one of the great collections in Rome. For many years it passed as a work by Andrea Mantegna, until Dr. Waagen, in 1861, pointed out that its author was, undoubtedly, Sandro Botticelli. It is painted on a panel measuring 3 ft. 5 in. in width, by 2 ft. 4 in. in height. Of the earlier paintings of the "Adoration of the Magi" by Botticelli, this picture recalls most nearly, in its composition and general design, the little altar-piece, once in the church of Santa Maria Novella, and now in the gallery of the Uffizi, No. 1286. The Virgin is seated with the Child on her knee, in the centre of the picture, before a ruined hall of antique architecture, over which a rough, framed roof has been thrown to afford a shelter for the cattle. St. Joseph stands leaning upon his staff, by the side of the Virgin; as one of the Magi, who kneels before her, is about to kiss the foot of the Child. Another Mage kneels on their left; and the third Mage approaches from the other side of the picture. The courtiers of the three kings are disposed in two ranks, on either side of the central group, so as to lead the eye up to the perspective of the ruined building; and the servants of the Magi, with their horses, are seen in the middle distance, in smaller figures, on either side of the ruin. In the background is a wooded landscape, with roads winding between the hills and rocks. It is the one genuine work by Botticelli which is only known to me by a photograph; but I gather from those who have seen the picture, that it is tolerably well preserved, though somewhat darkened by varnish, and that its colouring is no less characteristic of the painter than its design. Of all the "Adorations of the Magi" by Botticelli which are extant, it is the most largely composed, the most simply and severely designed; and, although it contains upwards of forty figures, it is the version of all others which possesses the greatest repose and grandeur of scale. In the monumental composition of this picture, in the large relief and structure of the figures, in the fine naturalism of its draughtsmanship, the noble character of the heads and the avoidance in it of all ornament, we again seem to detect the influence on Botticelli of Masaccio, "optimo imitatore di natura, di gran rilieuo, universale, buono componitore, et puro sanza ornato."

C. Landino, Dante, ed. 1481, fol. V, tergo.

The passage with which Vasari concludes his account of Botticelli's work in the Sistine Chapel, certainly possesses the ring of veracity. Having, says Vasari, on account of the frescoes which he executed there, "acquired, along with the many rival painters who worked with him, both natives of Florence and other cities, greater fame and name, he had from the Pope a good sum of money, which he all ran through and consumed out of hand, during his stay at Rome, by living at chance, as was his wont; and at the same time that part of the work which had been allotted to him having been finished, and uncovered, he returned forthwith to Florence." There is no reason to think that the frescoes of the Sistine Chapel were not duly completed, in accordance with the terms of the contract, by 15th March, 1481-2. At least, we know that Botticelli and Ghirlandaio had returned to Florence before the 31st August, 1482; and the remaining works in the Sistine Chapel having been brought to a conclusion, the building was consecrated by Sixtus himself on the feast of the Assumption, 15th August, 1483.

Vasari, ed. 1550, I, 494.

J. Volaterranus, Diarium, in Muratori, Rer. Ital. Scrip., XXIII, col. 188.

Two events stand out sharply in the life of Botticelli: his journey to Rome, and the death of Lorenzo, Il Magnifico; the latter by reason of its

THE ADORATION OF THE MAGI *Gallery of the Hermitage, St. Petersburg. (From a photograph by Braun, Clément et Cie.)*

effect, not only on Sandro's career, but on the whole course of Florentine art and events. The paintings and drawings, which he executed during the ten years which elapsed between these two events, may be determined with tolerable certainty; but the precise order in which they were executed remains the most difficult problem in the criticism of his works. There are few dates, or exterior indications, which go to prove their sequence; and the changes in the painter's manner were brought about so gradually, not to say imperceptibly, that an analysis of the internal evidences which his pictures afford, becomes a matter of the greatest delicacy and fineness of perception. After Botticelli's return to Florence, in 1482, he remains singularly independent of the art around him: no new influence breaks in upon his art, to interrupt its gradual and steady course. Leonardo da Vinci had been called to Milan, perhaps as early as the latter part of the year 1482. After the death of Sixtus IV, in 1484, Antonio and Piero Pollaiuoli settled in Rome, in order to cast the tomb of the Pope; and in 1485, Andrea Verrocchio went to Venice, where he died, to make the statue of Bartolommeo Colleoni. From that time until the return of Leonardo to Florence in 1500, the only serious rivals of Botticelli at Florence, were Domenico Ghirlandaio, Perugino, and Filippino, his own disciple. Ghirlandaio certainly surpassed Botticelli in business and capacity for work; and Perugino and Filippino were less harassed by the poetic temperament than he: but Botticelli unquestionally possessed the greatest genius. For nearly twenty years after his return from Rome, indeed almost till 1504, when Leonardo and Michelangelo changed the whole course of Florentine art, by their cartoons for the Sala de' Cinquecento in Florence, Botticelli remained the most popular, if not the most prosperous, painter in Florence. No painter in Florence before or after him, not even Michelangelo, could boast of so many imitators, who exclusively followed his manner; and we must turn to the Milanese school of Leonardo da Vinci, for a more remarkable instance of the predominant influence of a single master.

An attempt to analyze the course of Botticelli's art from 1482 to 1492, leads us to note certain general tendencies and characteristics, which may serve to guide us in determining the order of his works. His peculiar forms, during this period, tend to become more mannered, and his figures more energetic in their movements; but at the same time, the masses of his pictures are composed with a greater simplicity and largeness of design, which lends to his compositions a greater air of repose. His design, in short, after his return from Rome, becomes more "antique": I mean that he relies more and more on the essential, significant elements of form, and mass, and movement; gradually discarding much of that mediæval richness of ornament, especially in the elaborately wrought flowers and foliage, in the backgrounds and foregrounds of his pictures, which is characteristic of his earlier works. Again, the landscapes in his pictures tend to become more barren and severe: in place of the lovely distances in such a picture as the "Adoration of the Magi," once in the church of Santa Maria Novella, we find great spaces of still water enclosed by bare shores, which are broken by bleak, cliff-like masses of rock. The background of his "Calumny of Apelles" in the Uffizi, a work executed not long after 1492, consists of a cloudless sky, above a stretch of water unbroken by a wave. But it is, perhaps, in the quality of his line, and the increased mannerism of his forms, that the course of his art is most clearly to be traced. His line tends to become more rhythmical, nervous, and accented; and in his later works, more and more expressive of movement, and less of constructed form and mass. In his forms, he reverts more frequently, towards the close of his career, to that rugged Castagnesque character of the heads and hands, which he derived from Antonio Pollaiuoli; and develops such mannerisms as the long, finger-like toes, the undue emphasis of the joints, and the hard, fluted Giottesque folds of the draperies. Again, Botticelli tends more and more to employ the device of tilting a figure, in order to express rapid movement. Mere comeliness of form is sacrificed to the expression of character, of the passions of the mind: he grows less preoccupied with the beauty of the body, than with the health of the spirit. But from such generalizations let us pass to discuss in detail the works themselves.

Among the works, for the most part of a decorative nature, which were carried out in the Palazzo della Signoria, during the latter half of the fifteenth century, after the restorations of Michelozzo Michelozzi, was the construction of a new audience chamber for the Priors, with a large hall, or ante-chamber, leading to it from the public staircase of the palace. In the time of Vasari, this hall was called the "Sala dell' Oriuolo," from a famous clock by Lorenzo della Volpaia, which formerly stood there, and now the "Sala de' Gigli," from the decoration of its walls. These two rooms, which are upon the second floor of the palace, were formed within the space of the old Sala dell' Udienza of the Priors, by the erection of a party-wall, carried upon a wooden girder of elaborate construction, in order that the original extent of the "Sala de' Dugento" below, might be left undisturbed. Vasari, who describes the construction of this party-wall at length, attributes the work to Benedetto da Maiano. The project was approved by the "Operai," or wardens of the works, of the palace, in 1473; and various payments were made to Giuliano da Maiano and Il Francione, between 1475 and 1480, on account of the beautiful door, which still remains in the party-wall between the two rooms. After the return of Botticelli, Ghirlandaio, and Perugino, from Rome, in 1482, the "Operai" of the palace resolved to employ them on the decoration of the new rooms. The Sala dell' Udienza is at the angle of the building above the fountain of Neptune, and the Sala de' Gigli adjoins it on the north side of the palace. The latter room, which is called the great hall of the Priors, "sala magna dominorum," in the records of the "Operai," is lit by three windows, which look out across the narrow part of the Piazza della Signoria. On entering the room from the staircase of Vasari, by the sixteenth-century doorway opposite the windows, the party-wall and the door of Giuliano da Maiano are on the left hand.

Vasari, ed. Sansoni, III, 341.

J. Gaye, Carteggio Inedito, I, 571-7.

App. II, Doc. XXIII, fol. 13, recto.

It appears from the Deliberations of the "Operai," that those officials having assembled in the "camera armorum" of the palace, on the 5th October, 1482, "gave out and placed on contract, by the virtue of the enactment approved by them on 31st August last past," etc., "to Domenico di Tomaso del Ghirlandaio," etc., "the face of the hall of the palace of the Florentine people, towards the Dogana, (faciam sale palatij p*o*p*u*li flor*entinj* versus doanam,) to be worked and painted with an image of St. Zenobio and other figures, for the ornament of the said palace," etc. And at the same time they gave "to the said Domenico, and to Sandro di Mariano, painters, present and accepting the same, etc., the wall-face towards the audience-chamber of the Priors, (faciam sale audientie d*omi*nor*um*,) in the said palace, to be painted and ornamented for the ornament of the said palace," etc. Item, "to Pietro, called Perugino, and Biagio di Antonio Tucci, the face of the hall of the said Priors towards the Piazza, that is to say, the window-face, (facia*m* sale palatij dict*orum* d*omi*nor*um* *ver*sus plateam, v*idelicet* faciam finestiare*m*,) to be worked and painted for the ornament of the said palace," etc. Item, "the face of the said hall on the side towards the well (facia*m* putei dict*e* sale,) to Piero di Jacopo del Pollaiuolo, painter, to be worked and painted for the ornament of the said palace," etc. A few weeks later, on the 31st December, 1482, the "Operai" gave "to Filippo di Fra Filippo, although absent, the painting of that part of the hall which they had formerly placed on contract with Perugino, the painter:" at the same time, the "Operai" resolved that the price of the painting of St. Zenobio, to be executed by Domenico Ghirlandaio, was to be sixty florins. The entries of payments at the end of the volume containing these Deliberations, show that various sums of money were paid to Ghirlandaio, on account of the painting of St. Zenobio, between the autumn of 1482 and 1485. The long intervals which elapsed between the last payments were, no doubt, due to interruptions which the work underwent.

Id., fol. 14, recto.

The fresco of St. Zenobio by Ghirlandaio, to which these documents relate, is still to be seen on the east wall of the Sala de' Gigli, on the side towards the Sala de' Cinquecento, which stands on the site of the old Dogana. The painting represents the saint enthroned between the two holy deacons, Eugenio and Crescenzio, under an archway of antique architecture, and with a view of Florence in the distance of the background: in the lunettes of the side arches are full-length figures of Brutus, Scævola, Camillus, Decius, Scipio, and Cicero. The head of San Zenobio shows that Ghirlandaio had not escaped the influence of Botticelli, during the time that they had worked together in Rome. The other three walls of the Sala de' Gigli are now decorated with a semée of gold lilies on a blue ground: it is to the decoration of these walls that the Deliberations of the "Operai" have reference. The phrase, "faciam putei," used in the Deliberations to describe the wall which was given to Piero Pollaiuoli to paint, undoubtedly refers to the wall of the Sala de' Gigli, on the side of the well which existed between the Sala de' Gigli and the courtyard, for the supply of the Priors' lodgings; since none of the walls of the Sala dell' Udienza answers to the description. Again, the expression "faciam sale audientie," used of the wall which was given to Ghirlandaio and Botticelli to paint, is clearly a loose phrase of the same kind as the expression "faciam putei;" and must be taken, I think, as I have taken it, to refer to the wall of the Sala de' Gigli, on the side towards the Sala dell' Udienza; and not, as Signor Milanesi and others have held, to one of the walls of the Sala dell' Udienza itself. Understood of the Sala de' Gigli, the phrase becomes a specific description; but understood of the Sala dell' Udienza, it remains vague, since it does not specify which of the four walls is intended. The same argument might be applied to the phrase which describes the wall at first given to Perugino and Biagio Tucci, and afterwards to Filippino, to paint: there being two window-walls in the Sala del Udienza. The wall in question was, plainly, the window-wall of the Sala de' Gigli; for the same phrase, "faciam sale palatij," etc., is used to describe both it and the wall given to Ghirlandaio. Read in this way, these entries become coherent and precise; the whole of them referring to a single scheme, the decoration in its entirety of the Sala de' Gigli. The

Vasari, ed. Sansoni, III, 322, note.

records of the "Operai" contain no further references to the projected paintings by Botticelli, Piero Pollaiuoli, and Filippino: delayed for some reason or another which is now unknown, the painters appear to have been called away on other work, and the scheme to have been abandoned.

Another fragment of evidence, an entry of debit and credit in the "Libro Rosso," the account book of the "Compagnia di San Luca," which I have cited many times, goes to prove the presence of Botticelli in Florence at this time. (App. II, Doc. XI, fol. 14, tergo, and fol. 15, recto.) The one side of the account shows that on 25th November, 1482, "Alessandro dimariano, dipintore," was debited with a sum of ten soldi, "placed to the debt of all the men of the company in accordance with a resolution [entered] in the book of resolutions, at folio 35;" the other side of the account, that the money was paid the same day. The "libro de' partitj," referred to in this entry, has not been preserved among the records of the Florentine Academy; and so, it is no longer possible to say on what occasion this resolution was passed by the company.

Shortly after Botticelli's return from Rome, if I mistake not, Filippino Lippi painted his portrait in one of the frescoes of the Brancacci chapel, in the church of the Carmine, at Florence. Vasari, in his description of the paintings of this chapel, which had been left unfinished by Masolino and Masaccio, (Vasari, ed. Sansoni, III, 462.) says that Filippino introduced a number of portraits into the fresco of the "Raising of the King's son," begun by Masaccio; and among them those of Antonio Pollaiuolo and of himself, youth as he was: and, adds Vasari, "in the story which follows, he drew Sandro Botticello, his master, and many other friends and great persons; and amongst the rest, Raggio, the broker, a person of much wit and spirit, who carved in relief on a shell the whole of the 'Inferno' of Dante, with all the circles and divisions of the pits and the shaft exactly proportioned, and all the figures and particulars which the genius of that great poet had imagined and described; a thing held to be marvellous in those times." But Vasari corrects himself; for the portraits of Botticelli, Pollaiuoli, and Filippino are to be recognized from the woodcuts with which he illustrated the second edition of his "Lives of the Painters," published at Florence, in 1568. (Id., V, 441.) These portraits were cut on the wood by Cristofano Coriolano, from drawings which Vasari, and his disciples, had made from the various originals. On turning to the frescoes of the Brancacci chapel, we find that the portrait of Botticelli occurs in the lower fresco, on the right wall of the chapel, in the group of three whole-length, draped figures, which stand in the centre of the picture, watching the crucifixion of St. Peter. The figure of Botticelli is seen in profile to the left, in a black cap and red cloak. (Id., ed. 1568, I, 470.) In Vasari's cut, the head is reversed. If, as I conjecture, these frescoes were painted in 1482, this portrait represents Botticelli at the age of thirty-eight: the earlier portrait of the painter by himself in the little altar-piece of the "Adoration of the Magi," formerly in the church of Santa Maria Novella, having been painted, as I have shown, c. 1477, when Botticelli was thirty-three. In both these portraits the brow is broad and prominent, the nose large and aquiline, the mouth full, the hair dark and curled; but the head of Botticelli done by himself shows a man, if not of a less sensuous temperament, than the head of Filippino does, at least of a greater intellectual vigour, such as his pictures show him to have been; the eye is clearer and more piercing, the jaw more powerful, the character of the head more resolute. The portrait of Antonio Pollaiuoli occurs in the same fresco as the portrait of Botticelli, but in the story of "St. Paul before the Proconsul," to the right of the composition; the keen, almost ascetic man in the red cap, who stands beside the seated figure of the proconsul. The head of Filippino by himself is in the same story, to the extreme right of the fresco, looking out of the picture.

Vasari, in a passage which he added in the second edition of the "Lives," says that, for Lorenzo de' Medici, Botticelli, "besides many other things, had worked much at the Spedaletto, near Volterra." (Vasari, ed. 1568, I, 473.) Elsewhere, Vasari states that Domenico Ghirlandaio painted "at the Spedaletto, for Lorenzo de' Medici the elder, the story of Vulcan, in which many nude figures are at work, forging with hammers the thunderbolts of Jupiter." (Id., ed. 1550 I, 466.) These paintings were evidently executed in fresco, for no mention is made of them in the Inventory of the goods of Lorenzo de' Medici, taken at the time of his death, among the movable furniture then at the Spedaletto. (App. II, Doc. XXVIII, fol. 119, recto.) From the Medici, the Spedaletto passed to the Cibò, with the portion of Maddalena, the daughter of Lorenzo, Il Magnifico, who married her in 1487, to Francesco Cibò, the son of Pope Innocent VIII: and at the beginning of the seventeenth century, it was bought from the Cibò, by the Corsini, of Florence, in whose possession it has since continued. One other notice of these frescoes, dating from the seventeenth century, has come down to us. Giovanni Bottari, in the notes to his edition of Vasari, published at Rome, in 1759, says that Ghirlandaio's painting of the story of Vulcan was then "under a portico exposed to the damp air, on account of which it had suffered much." (l.c., vol. I, p. 428.) Bottari was librarian to Cardinal Neri Corsini, and he doubtlessly obtained his information from some member of the Corsini family. Between 1820 and 1830, a fire broke out in the villa, destroying such paintings as may have survived till that time. These meagre notices of the frescoes of the Spedaletto have lately received a notable addition in a remarkable document, found among the Public Archives at Milan, by Herr Müller-Walde. This document is, apparently, a report of some agent of Lodovico, Il Moro, giving a brief account of the chief painters then in Florence, with a view to their employment at Milan. (App. II, Doc. XXIV.) This report was, no doubt, inclosed in some letter to the Duke, from which it has been unfortunately separated: it is written in a fifteenth-century hand, on one side of a single sheet, and is without signature, date, or other indication. But here is the document, at length, done into English:

"Sandro di Botticelli, a most excellent painter, both on panel and wall; his works have a virile air, and are [executed] with the greatest judgment and perfect proportion.

"Filippino, the son of Fra Filippo, the best disciple of the aforesaid, and the son of the most singular master of his times; his works have a sweeter air, but not, I think, so much art.

"Il Perugino, a singular master, especially of wall-painting; his works have an angelical and very sweet air.

"Domenico di Grilandaio, a good master on panel, and still more on the wall; his works have a good air, and he is a man of expedition, and one who executes much work.

"All these aforesaid painters have given proof of their skill in the Chapel of Pope Sixtus, excepting Filippino; but all afterwards at the Spedaletto of Lorenzo, Il Magnifico; and it is hard to say who bears off the palm."

The explanation which Herr Müller-Walde has put upon this document will, certainly, not bear to be examined. This report was plainly written during the lifetime of the painters named in it; and, therefore, before the death of Domenico Ghirlandaio, in 1494. Indeed, Lorenzo de' Medici would seem to have been still living when it was written. Again, the fact that neither Verrocchio, Leonardo da Vinci, nor the Pollaiuoli, are mentioned in this report, points to it having been drawn up not earlier than 1485, at which time Verrocchio and Lorenzo di Credi were in Venice, Leonardo in Milan, and the Pollaiuoli at Rome. But it is also clear, I think, from this document that the frescoes in the Spedaletto were executed not long after the frescoes in the Sistine Chapel; and that this report was written while both works were still fresh in the public mind. The Sistine Chapel was consecrated, and its paintings thrown open to the public view, in August, 1483: the frescoes of the Spedaletto were executed, as I conjecture, c. 1484; and this report written c. 1485-6. Such a conjecture at least accords with what we know of the doings of the four painters in question, at this time.

Revue Archéologique, 1901, II, pp. 12-20

In the spring of 1901, I was enabled, by the kindness of Prince Tommaso Corsini, to make a careful examination of the Spedaletto. This villa, which now serves as the "fattoria" of the vast estates by which it is surrounded, is situated in the outskirts of Volterra, on a low hill, lying a short distance off the high road to Pontedera. It is a rectangular, brick building of two storeys, surrounding an open court. In the centre of one of the longer sides of the building, a low tower rises above the entrance to the villa: and in the centre of the other side, opposite to it, may still be traced the great tower, now truncated, which served for the defence of the place. In Giuseppe Zocchi's view of Cafaggiolo, another Medicean villa, which, like the Spedaletto, lay in a remote, unprotected part of the country, the same arrangement of a fortified gateway, and battlemented tower, may be seen represented in its original condition; as well as the moat, of which all trace has disappeared at the Spedaletto. An examination of the fabric shows that it was entirely gutted by the fire of 1820-30. The rooms on the ground floor, now partly vaulted, appear to have been originally covered by wooden ceilings, which, no doubt, greatly contributed to the ravages of the fire. Except in a few of the lower rooms, which are now turned to the purposes of the "fattoria," the whole of the internal plastering has been renewed. The loggia to which Bottari alludes, once opened into the courtyard, on the side opposite to the entrance gateway; but it is now inclosed. On removing the whitewash from the main wall of this loggia, near the entrance to the old staircase, I found small patches of the original "intonaco" retaining traces of red colour; and the rest of the surface of the plaster charred by fire. Here, no doubt, had been the fresco by Ghirlandaio which Vasari describes. To the left of the courtyard, on entering the villa by the gateway, was the great "sala," or hall, now divided into two rooms serving as offices of the "fattoria." There is a tradition, Prince Corsini tells me, that on one of the walls of this "sala," were the remains of a fresco, consisting of the lower part of some figures, which perished in the fire of 1820-30. This tradition is, in all probability, a true one; for in the villa of Poggia a Caiano, which like the Spedaletto was built by Lorenzo, Il Magnifico, the loggia and the great "sala" were the portions of the building to be decorated with frescoes. The loss of the frescoes of the Spedaletto are much to be deplored; for they appear to have

G. Zocchi, Vedute delle Ville della Toscana, Firenze, 1744, Pl. 36.

formed a series of profane stories which, although less monumental in character than the stories of the Old and New Testaments, in the Sistine Chapel, approached them in artistic interest.

The report of the agent of the Duke of Milan possesses even greater value as a piece of contemporary criticism upon the painters named in it, than as a record of their frescoes at Rome and Volterra. Botticelli is placed first on the list; and in spite of the agent's protest that it is impossible to say which of the four painters bears off the palm, the rest of his report amounts to an admission that Botticelli was held to be the first painter then living at Florence. Of his strange, bizarre conception of things, of the peculiar sentiment which runs through his work, a sentiment as some writers have thought "of ineffable melancholy," this reporter has nothing to say: he notes only in Botticelli's work the "aria virile," that virile air, his "optima ragione et integra proportione," the great judgment and fine sense of proportion shown in his works. The former is an expression which the modern critic would have used in characterizing the manner of Andrea da Castagno, or Antonio Pollaiuoli; the latter that of Domenico Ghirlandaio or Leonardo da Vinci. For us, Botticelli is a visionary painter, who sees and depicts more than meets the outward eye. May not, then, the secret of his greatness lie in the fact that our modern view of him, and the view of his contemporaries, are, in their measure, and from their several standpoints, equally true? Of Filippino, the agent reports that in comparison with his master, Botticelli, his works have a sweeter air, but not so much art. Perugino he especially extols as a painter of fresco, and characterizes his manner as "angelica et molto dolce": and Ghirlandaio he characterizes as the able master, skilled alike in the painting of walls and panels, a "man of expedition," of infinite business, who, as Vasari tells us, boasted that no one, no matter how trifling his wants, left his workshop unsatisfied. In laying stress upon the business capacities of Ghirlandaio, the agent probably had in his mind what had reached him concerning Leonardo da Vinci, whose brooding and delays may well have occasioned the Duke of Milan to seek out another painter at Florence, who would carry out with greater expedition the numerous works which he desired to have executed. The criticisms of the Duke's agent, according to the usage of his age, are brief and trite; but the more deeply the student of Florentine art becomes versed in his subject, the more, I think, while elaborating or refining upon the agent's sentences, will he come to endorse his judgments.

Vasari, ed. Sansoni, III, 270.

The picture by Botticelli which approaches most nearly in manner to the frescoes of the Sistine Chapel, is the altarpiece which he painted for the high altar of the church of San Barnaba, in Florence. Francesco Albertini mentions this painting in his "Memoriale": "In sancto Barnaba e una tauola grande per mano di Sandro Bocticelli." Another notice of the painting is preserved in Antonio Petrei's epitome of the "Libro di Antonio Billi": "in s[to] bernaba una tauola di n*os*tra Don*n*a et s[ta] catherina;" and the Anonimo Gaddiano records that it formed the picture of the high altar: "E disua mano i*n*sanb*er*naba latauola dell' altare maggiore di n*os*tra don*n*a et s[ta] caterina." Vasari merely says that Botticelli executed a picture for the nuns of San Barnaba: "Lauorò nelle conuertite vna tauola a quelle monache, & a quelle di San Barnabà, similmente vn' altra." The church of San Barnaba, which still remains in the quarter of San Giovanni, at the crossway where the Via Panicale runs into the Via Guelfa, was built

l.c., ed. 1510, fol. 4, recto.

App. II, Doc. I, fol. 49, tergo.

App. II, Doc. II, fol. 83, tergo.

Vasari, ed. 1550, I, 492.

by the Florentine Republic, to commemorate the victory won by the Guelfs of Florence over the Ghibellines of Arezzo, on the feast of St. Barnabas, 1289, at Campaldino, in the Casentino. According to a tradition, which went long unquestioned, Dante himself fought on the side of the victorious Florentines; and there are passages in the "Divina Commedia" which lend colour to the story. The church, begun in 1322, was in 1335 committed to the care of the "Consoli" of the "Arte de' Medici e degli Speziali," in accordance with the usage by which the charges of maintaining the principal churches of the city were laid upon one or another of the "Arti Maggiori." On the façade, above the door of the church, is a relief in glazed terra cotta, a work of the early part of the sixteenth century, bearing the arms of the "Arte degli Speziali," a figure of the Virgin and Child in a red field, and the inscription, SVB GVBERNATIONEM ARTIS AROMATARIORVM. The church with the monastery, which had been built adjoining it, were granted in the year 1350, by the "Consoli" of the "Arte degli Speziali," to certain Augustine canons of Santa Maria Maddelena of Castelfranco di Sotto, who continued in the possession of them until 1506. In 1522, the house was granted to the Carmelite nuns, for whom Vasari erroneously asserts that Botticelli's picture was painted. These good nuns circulated the legend that a stranger of venerable appearance sought the prioress one day, and told her to request the church of San Barnaba. She did so, and her petition was granted her. When the nuns took possession of their new house, the prioress immediately recognized in the figure of St. Barnabas, in Botticelli's picture over the high altar, the unknown stranger who had told her to ask for the convent. And so it was believed, concludes the pious confessor of the nuns who relates the miracle, "that St. Barnabas himself had called the Sacred Virgins to the service of his church." The altarpiece appears to have remained over the altar, in its original state, until the beginning of the eighteenth century, when the nuns resolved to decorate their church with ornaments in stucco, and a new ceiling of carved wood, which was finished in the year 1717. The principal panel of Botticelli's altarpiece was then placed in the head of the choir, behind the high altar; but, relates Giuseppe Richa, "the panel was very low and long," and in order to bring it into better proportion with the architecture of the choir, "it has been enlarged by Agostino Veracini, who has so well imitated the ancient manner, that all seems to be by one hand." To our eyes, alas! the additions and retouches of Veracini are only too apparent. But these were not the only mischances which the altarpiece underwent at this time: the original frame was destroyed; and the painted panels having been removed from the "gradino," in course of time three of these little pictures disappeared. At the suppression of the monasteries, under the French dominion, in 1808, the principal panel, and the four remaining "predella" pictures were removed to the gallery of the Florentine Academy, where they are still preserved.

G. Richa, Chiese Fior., VII, 55-6.

Id., VII, 58 and 60.

Id., VII, 62-3.

Id., VII, 65.

The statement of the "Anonimo Gaddiano" that this picture was painted for the high altar of the church, is borne out by the notices which Giuseppe Richa has preserved. The tribune, or "capella maggiore," belonged to the Florentine Republic, as founders and patrons of the church: and Stefano Rosselli records in his "Sepoltuario" that the lily of the Republic was carved in stone, above the arch of the tribune. Botticelli's picture was, therefore, doubtlessly painted at the instance of the "Consoli" of the "Arte de' Medici e degli Speziali," the official wardens of the church.

Cod. Magliabechiano, XXVI, 24, fol. 1332, recto.

THE VIRGIN AND CHILD WITH SAINTS AND ANGELS—THE ALTAR-PIECE OF SAN BARNABA *Gallery of the Academy, Florence*

The principal panel of the altarpiece, No. 85 in the Florentine Academy, is still disfigured by the additions of Veracini, which have been removed in the illustration accompanying this volume. The line marking the top of the original painting may be seen running above the two "tondi," on either side of the curtains of the baldaquin, in the lunette of the arched recess. The lowest row of the marble slabs of the pavement have, also, been added by Veracini. In its original condition, the panel was somewhat broader than taller, and measured 8 ft. 4 in. in height, by 8 ft. 10 in. in width. The picture represents the Virgin seated with the Child, upon a raised and richly-carved, marble throne. On the right hand of the Virgin, in the place of honour, stands St. Barnabas, the patron of the church: he holds in his left hand a laurel-branch, to symbolize the victory which he brought to the Florentines, at Campaldino. According to the legend, the issue of the battle had been announced to the Priors of Florence by the saint himself, in the very hour of victory; although the messengers from the Florentine army did not arrive until the following day. Next, on the left of the Virgin, following the hieratic order of precedence, stands St. John the Baptist, the patron saint of the Florentine Republic. Third in degree, beside St. Barnabas, stands St. Augustine, the patron saint of the canons who at that time had the charge of the church and monastery. The saint is represented in the act of writing in a book, habited in a white mitre and a cope adorned with richly embroidered apparel, which he wears over the habit of an Augustinian canon. On the other side of the picture, somewhat behind the Baptist, stands St. Ignatius, vested in a cope and mitre, and holding a heart in his right hand. Lastly, on the extreme right of the picture, beside St. Augustine, stands St. Catherine of Alexandria, with the wheel of her martyrdom beside her: and on the opposite side of the picture, St. Michael the Archangel, in complete armour, holding a drawn sword in his right hand, and the world, with the trail of the serpent upon it, on his left. On either side of the Virgin, two angels are standing upon the raised pace of the throne: the foremost angel to the left of the Virgin holds up the crown of thorns, and the angel to her right, the nails of the crucifixion; while the others draw aside the purple and ermine curtains of the baldaquin. In the two circular reliefs, which are partially seen behind these curtains, set in the wall of the arched recess, are carved two kneeling figures, representing St. Gabriel delivering the angelic salutation to the Virgin.

Inlaid among the ornament carved on the steps of the throne, on which the Virgin is seated, is a marble table, inscribed with the first line of the last Canto of the "Paradiso" of Dante:

VERGINE MADRE FIGLIA DELTVO FIGLIO.

Long before Botticelli inscribed this verse on his picture, the invocation to the Virgin of which it is the opening line, had so possessed the imagination of our own poet, Chaucer, that he turned it into English, in one of the "Canterbury Tales." It occurs in "The Secounde Nonnes Tale":

"Thou mayde and moder, doughter of thi sone, l.c., v. 36-49.
Thow welle of mercy, synful soules cure,
In whom that God of bountes chees to wone;
Thou humble and heyh over every creature,
Thow nobeledst so ferforth oure nature,

That no disdeyn the maker had of kynde
His sone in blood and fleissh to clothe and wynde.

Withinne the cloyster of thi blisful sydes,
Took mannes schap the eternal love and pees,
That of the trine compas lord and guyde is,
Whom erthe, and see, and heven out of relees
Ay herien; and thou, virgine wemmeles,
Bar of thy body, and dwellest mayden pure,
The creatour of every creature."

The allusion which Botticelli here makes to this passage of the "Paradiso," affords a clue, as I think, to the true interpretation of the sentiment which he endeavoured to express in the figure of the Virgin, in this picture, and still more in such pictures as the two famous "tondi" in the Uffizi; in contradistinction to the interpretation of their sentiment which certain modern writers have attempted. But of this, when I come to discuss the latter paintings.

Well might the early commentators speak of this altarpiece as "una tauola di nostra donna et s^ta^ caterina"; for the figure of St. Catherine, notwithstanding its indifferent condition, still remains the most splendid passage in the picture. Nowhere has Botticelli portrayed the magisterial beauty, the heavy, fruit-like grace, of gravid women, with a more singular sentiment and power, than in this figure. The heads both of St. Catherine, and St. Barnabas, again reveal the influence of Andrea da Castagno which marks the earlier fresco of St. Augustine, in the church of Ognissanti. In the emaciated figure of St. John, Botticelli has recurred to that Giottesque conception of the Baptist to which Donatello has given supreme expression, in the marble statue now in the Museum of the Bargello, at Florence. In comparison to the figure of St. John, in the painting, that of St. Michael seems, perhaps, too mild and effeminate for the angel "of celestial armies prince"; but the original character of the head, it must be remembered, has almost disappeared under the mechanical touches of the restorer. The heads of the two bishops recall, both in character and execution, the heads of Moses, in the fresco of the "Destruction of Korah and his Company," in the Sistine Chapel; and the figures of the angels, with the long oval form of the heads, closely resemble the angels in the fresco of the "Temptation of Christ." Indeed, this altarpiece approaches more nearly in manner to the frescoes of the Sistine Chapel, than any other painting by Botticelli which has survived to our time. I must not pass over the beauty of invention and draughtsmanship which still distinguishes the figures of the Virgin and Child; nor the felicity of the device by which the angels who hold up the symbols of the Passion, or draw back the curtains of the baldaquin, are introduced into the picture in order to weave into an entire and rhythmical composition, the figures prescribed by the usages of the Church, in spite of their formal, and merely symbolical, arrangement.

This picture is, unfortunately, in a very indifferent condition. The original effect of its elaborate composition is still spoiled by the additions of Veracini, which destroy the proportions and relation of the various elements of its design. Still more deplorable are the restorations and repainting which the panel has undergone, probably at the time when it was enlarged. The green robe of the St. Catherine has been in great part repainted; the original colour may be seen where the lawn scarf falls over the dress. The embroideries on the cope of the St. Augustine, and the green robe of the St. Barnabas, have been coarsely retouched; the head of the St. John has been gone over; and the lights and reflections on the armour of the St. Michael have been heightened in a way that destroys the mass of the figure. The figures of the Virgin and Child and the angels to the left of the picture, are better preserved; indeed, from these passages we are able to form some idea of the original excellence of the rest of the painting. The heads, arms, and hands of the angels to the right have, on the other hand, been much repainted: in short, there are but few passages in the picture which remain in their original condition. In colouring, this altarpiece is the most brilliant and gothic of all Botticelli's larger paintings. The dominant colours are those of gold and purple, tempered by the green draperies of the St. Catherine, the azure robe of the Virgin, the cool armour of the Archangel, and the gray of the stonework in which the mosaics and marbles of the background are set. But the beauty of all this colouring has suffered as much at the hands of the restorer, as the draughtsmanship.

The "gradino" of the picture appears to have originally contained seven "predella" panels, of which the central one was painted with a Pietà, and the rest with stories from the legends of the saints, who are represented in the principal panel of the altarpiece. Of these seven panels, the first, reckoning from the left, which was painted with a story from the legend of St. Catherine of Alexandria, the third with a story from that of St. Barnabas, and the seventh with a story from the legend of St. Michael the Archangel, are now wanting. Of the remaining panels, the second, No. 162, which was originally placed below the figure of St. Augustine, is taken from a legend of mediæval origin which was in great vogue in Italy, during the fifteenth century. It is to be met with in the writings of more than one hagiographer of the time; in the "Catalogus Sanctorum," for example, compiled by Petrus de Natalibus: but let me tell it in the naïve English of William Caxton's version of the "Golden Legend": "I wylle sette here in one myracle, whiche I haue sene paynted on an aulter of saynt Austyn at the blacke Freres at Andwerpe; how be it, I fynde hit not in the legende myn exampler, neyther in Englysshe, Frensshe, ne in latyn. It was soo that this gloryous Doctor made and compyled many volummes as a fore is sayd; among whome he made a book of the Trynyte, in whiche he studyed, and mused sore in his mynde; soo ferforthe, that on a tyme as he wente by the see syde in Auffryke studyeng on the Trynyte, he fonde by the see syde a lytel childe, whyche hadde made a lytel pytte in the sonde, and in his honde a lytel spone. And wyth the spone he tooke oute Water of the large See, and poured hit in to the pytte: And whanne saynt augustyn behelde hym, he merueyled, and demaunded him, What he dyde. And he answerd and sayde, I wylle lade oute, and brynge alle this water of this See in to thys pytte. What sayd he, hit is Impossyble; How may hit be done, sythe the See is soo greete and large, and thy pytte and spone so lytylle: yes forsothe sayd he, I shalle lyghtlyer and sonner drawe alle the Water of the See, and brynge hit in to this pytte, than thow shalt brynge the mysterye of the Trynyte and his dyuynyte in to thy lytel vnderstandynge, as to the regard therof. For the mysterye of the Trynyte is greter and larger to the com-

l.c., ed. Venice, 1493, Lib. VII, Cap. 128.

W. Caxton, The Golden Legende, ed. 1483, fol. cclxxvi, tergo.

paryson of thy witte and brayne, than is this grete See vnto this lytel pytte. And therwyth the chylde vanysshed awey." According to other versions of the legend it was not on the shore of Africa, but of Italy, at Cività Vecchia, that this vision was seen by St. Augustine. In the picture, the boy is kneeling by the little pit which he has scooped out in the sand, while the saint in a mitre and a purple cope, which he wears over the habit of an Augustine canon, stoops to question him.

Bollandus, Acta Sanctorum, ed. 1863. XL, 357.

The fourth and central panel, No. 157, is painted with a Pietà, a three-quarter length figure of the dead Christ, set within the tomb, with the hands outspread: in the distance, seen beyond the branches of some trees, is a hilly and watered landscape. On the ledge of the tomb are the nails and the sponge; and in the landscape, in tiny figures, Christ bearing the Cross, is led away to Golgotha by a company of soldiers.

The fifth panel, No. 161, represents Salome hastening out of the prison, with the head of St. John the Baptist in a charger. Her yellow hair is bound by a fillet of pearls; and her dress of leaf-green is relieved against the clear red of a castellated brick wall, beyond which is seen a break of landscape.

The story represented in the sixth panel, No. 158, is taken, not from the legend of St. Ambrose, as the authorities of the gallery would have us believe, but from the legend of St. Ignatius, Bishop of Antioch. The dead body of the saint, vested in a cope and mitre, is laid out upon a bier, which is covered by a striped cloth, on the far side of which stand two men who are cutting open the heart, which they have taken out of the body. The figures are relieved against a dark background. The legend which this little picture illustrates, is to be found, amongst other places, in the "Catalogus Sanctorum," compiled by Petrus de Natalibus, Bishop of Aquileia. According to this version, St. Ignatius, "during the many torments to which he was subjected at the hands of the Emperor Trajan, never ceased from calling upon the name of Christ; and when his torturers asked why he repeated it so often, he replied, that he might have that name written upon his heart, and, therefore, could not cease from calling upon Christ. After his death, certain curious persons who had heard this, wishing to find out the truth of it, plucked his heart from out his body, and cutting it open, found written across it, in letters of gold, the name of Jesus Christ." The same legend is repeated in one of the Florentine Miracle Plays, the "Rappresentatione di sancto Ignatio, Vescouo & Martyre," which has come down to us in more than one edition, of which the earliest was printed at Florence, at the end of the fifteenth century. The chief part of the play is taken up with a representation of the martyrdom of St. Ignatius. After he has been subjected to various torments, the emperor orders the saint to be cast to the lions, but in the words of stage directions, "Elioni gli corrono adosso & solamente lo affogano." St. Ignatius having at last thus met with his death, the play proceeds:

l.c., ed. Venice, 1493, Lib. III, Cap. 63.

> "El caualiere abirri dice: [At public executions in Florence, in the fifteenth century, the "cavaliere" always accompanied the "birri," or bailiffs, who had charge of the criminal.]
> Costui ha ilnome di iesu i*n*uocato;
> ueggiam se come edisse elha nel cuore:
> fate che sia subito sparato,
> chio uo chiarirmi & far chiaro ilsignore.

Vn birro al caualiere risponde:
  Io uegho bene che tu sarai impazzato,
  eseneridera lo imperadore,
  che lhabbi facto p*er* hauer suo credito:
  scripto uitrouerrai; mirami il fegato.
El caualiere al birra risponde:
  Questo no*n* nuoce.
El birro:
  Et anche non gioua,
  ma solo io lo faro per contentarti:
  presto de facti sua uedrai la proua;
  stare a uedere chio nefaro due parti.
Vnaltro dice alprimo birro mentre che lo spara:
  Credi trouarui qualche cosa nuoua;
  douerrei del polmon nel ceffo darti.
El caualiere albirro dice:
  Bada costui: & non midar piu noia,
  che loffitio farai, che ha fare el boia.
El birro caua fuori elcuore & uedeui scripto p*er* tucto ilnome
  di Giesu tagliandolo dice:
  Questo mipare uno stupente segno;
  ue scripto qui Giesu, come ciha decto:
  natura o arte o nostro humano i*n*gegno
  non potre partorire simile effecto.
  costui ha far ribellar tucto ilregno,
  & alla nuoua fe farlo suggecto.
  uo che allo imp*er*adore siporti & mostri
  che oggi spacciati sono q*ue*sti dei nostri."

These four "predella" panels vary slightly in size: Nos. 157 and 161 measure 6 in. in height by 14¼ in. in length; and Nos. 158 and 162, 6 in. in height by 13¾ in. in length. The panels on which they are painted are somewhat larger than the actual pictures. Unlike the principal panel of the altarpiece, they are not only in an excellent state of preservation, but, in the fine quality of their workmanship, equal to anything of the kind by Botticelli, which has come down to us. These little pictures show that Botticelli was able to work with the same spontaneity and sureness of hand with the brush, as with the pen. The directness and delicacy with which in the little Pietà, the finest, perhaps, in point of execution of all these "predella" panels, the blonde flesh of the Christ is painted against the blonder sky, and the trees and distant hills, rendered, as in the landscape in the "Adoration of the Magi," No. 1286, in the Gallery of the Uffizi, wholly by their tone and mass, suggest certain qualities of painting that we are apt exclusively to associate with the achievements of modern art. Scarcely less admirable than this "Pietà" is the "Vision of St. Augustine:" the relief of the richly wrought figures against the bare shore and waveless sea, recalls, in its way, the fresco in the Sistine Chapel, of "Moses in the land of Midian."

In the absence of any definite record of the date at which this altarpiece was painted, it is, in my opinion, to be ascribed on internal evidence, to the period immediately succeeding Botticelli's return to Florence, after painting in the Sistine Chapel, and therefore to the years 1482-3.

A number of school pictures have come down to us, whose origin is to be traced to this altarpiece. A decorative and well-preserved version of the figure of the Virgin, at half length, with the Child, before a niche of coloured marbles, which was once in the gallery of the Palazzo Panciatichi-Ximenes, at Florence, is now in the collection of Mr. Robert Benson, of London. Like a similar version of the Virgin and Child in the Bardi altarpiece, this panel was probably executed in the workshop of Botticelli, and from the cartoon for the altarpiece; the colouring and the background alone being varied. It differs from its original only in the quality of its line and colour. Another, but greatly inferior version of the same group, a circular-headed panel, in which the Virgin is represented standing at three-quarter length, with the Child, before a semicircular recess in a pierced screen, the lines of which have been borrowed from the throne in the altarpiece from San Barnaba, is in the collection of Lord Battersea, at London. A circular-headed panel of the Virgin and Child, in which the figures are more freely varied from the original, than in that which I have just described, and a landscape substituted for the architectural background, is in the Jarves Collection, No. 74, at Yale College, New Haven, U.S.A. A fourth version, a small panel of the Virgin at full length, enthroned with the Child, the figures of which had been freely imitated from the altarpiece of San Barnaba, was lately in the collection of Sir Thomas Gibson Carmichael. This panel, which was somewhat feeble in execution, and of little individual character, was inscribed with the first two verses of the last canto of the "Paradiso" of Dante.

Directly inspired by the principal panel of the altarpiece, once in the church of San Barnaba, is a large altarpiece in the right aisle of the church of San Giovanni, at Montelupo, near Florence, representing the Virgin and Child enthroned with St. Laurence, St. John the Evangelist, St. Sebastian, and St. Roch. Not only is the general arrangement of the picture, and the design of the architectural background, but the figure of the Virgin, and still more that of the Child, have been directly imitated from the altarpiece from San Barnaba. The figure of St. John the Evangelist, who is writing in a book, has been suggested by that of St. Augustine; and the head of St. Sebastian has been copied from the head of St. Catherine in the original. By the same hand as the picture at Montelupo, is another altarpiece, which has lately been hung in the Gallery of the Uffizi, No. 3438, representing the Virgin and Child enthroned, and surrounded by the patron saints of the Medici: the figures of St. Laurence, in these two paintings, are especially similar. Unlike the picture at Montelupo, this altarpiece is in a very indifferent state of preservation, having been transferred to canvas, and much repainted. The figure of the Baptist in this picture is likewise reminiscent of the same figure in the altarpiece of San Barnaba.

Besides these pictures, there is a series of half-length figures of Christ as the "Salvator Mundi," whose origin is, perhaps, to be traced to the altarpiece of San Barnaba. Of these panels, the finest and most original is in the Morelli Collection, No. 29, in the Academy at Bergamo, a picture which Morelli himself ascribed to Botticelli; but for once I find myself in agreement with Dr. Ulmann and the German critics, who dismiss it as a work of the school. In its forms and colouring, as in the method of its execution, however, the picture so nearly resembles the genuine works of Botticelli, that it is only to be distinguished from them in the quality of

I. Lermolieff, Die Galerie Borghese, ed. 1890, p. 111.

H. Ulmann, S. Botticelli, p. 139, note 3.

its draughtsmanship. The faulty drawing of the eyes, the feeble design of the hands and draperies, the want of due construction in the figure generally, unquestionably betray the skilful, but superficial, imitator. I suspect that the cartoon for the head of the Baptist, in the altarpiece of San Barnaba, was used for the head of the "Christ" at Bergamo; so closely does the drawing of the features in both pictures resemble one another: but although the panel in the Morelli Collection probably came from Botticelli's workshop, the hands and accessory details could scarcely have been designed by him. The resemblance of the left hand of this "Salvator Mundi," to the right hand of the angel who holds up the crown of thorns in the altarpiece of San Barnaba, seems to bear out my theory of the origin of the Bergamo panel. A similar picture of a somewhat later date, in which the head has been reversed, and the crown of thorns placed in the right hand, which in the picture at Bergamo is raised in benediction, was lately in the possession of Mr. George Donaldson, at London. This panel, which in its forms and colouring far less nearly resembles Botticelli's manner than the panel at Bergamo, must be regarded as the work of some imitator, rather than of one of his immediate disciples. A copy of the panel at London, in which the little figures, and the view beyond the loggia, in the background, are omitted, is in the Library at Christ Church, Oxford, No. 14, where it bears the name of Andrea da Castagno. It appears to be the work of some Florentine painter, working at the beginning of the sixteenth century, whose manner stands in little, or no, relation with that of Botticelli. But so little individual character have these various copies and imitations, that it seems impossible for the student to do more than trace their design to its origin, and to note how such a panel as the "Salvator Mundi" at Bergamo, closely resembles the genuine works of Botticelli in all its superficial aspects, and how such a panel as that at Christ Church, Oxford, is to be connected with his school only by the analogy of its subject.

One other picture remains to be discussed in relation with the altarpiece once in the church of San Barnaba, a "tondo" in the Corsini Gallery, at Florence, No. 167. This picture, Prince Tommaso Corsini tells me, was one of three large "tondi," which came into the possession of the Corsini family, towards the end of the seventeenth century, from the Medicean Villa of Careggi, which had been leased to them. The fine, early "tondo" by Filippino Lippi was one of these pictures; and the third, an inferior work by some nameless, Florentine painter, which also remains in the gallery. The "tondo" in question represents at three-quarter length, the Virgin and Child surrounded by six angels. The Child is not seated, as in the altarpiece of San Barnaba, but stands astride, on his mother's knees, as he turns towards her. In the background of the picture, two of the angels, on either side of the Virgin, hold up, over her head, a crown stuck with little branches of lily, olive, and palm; while with the other hand, they draw back the embroidered curtains of a baldaquin. Somewhat in front of them, two of the angels, on the left of the picture, exhibit the spear and the sponge; and the other two angels, on the right, the crown of thorns and the nails. Unfortunately, this picture is so much repainted (if, indeed, it be not an old copy of some original now lost), that it is no longer possible to speak of its execution. The figures want their proper relief and "keeping," and the colouring is crude and opaque; yet the general design remains, closely recalling in its motive, as I have shown, certain passages in the altarpiece of San Barnaba. I cannot think with Morelli that it was painted from a cartoon by Botticelli's own hand: I rather regard it as an adaptation from the altarpiece, done in his workshop, and probably from a sketch by him. The figures, which are well designed to fill the space of the picture, are conceived more nearly in the spirit of Botticelli, than the majority of the numerous school-pictures of the kind; yet there are certain exaggerations of the painter's manner in some of the forms and attitudes, that could only be ascribed to an imitator.

The picture, which, more than any other painting by Botticelli, has in our own days gone to fix the popular notion of him as an artist, is the celebrated "tondo" of the "Magnificat," in the Gallery of the Uffizi, No. 1267bis; a work closely allied in style with the altarpiece of San Barnaba. This "tondo" was bought for the gallery, from a certain Ottavio Magherini, in 1784. Of its previous history, nothing appears to be known; but the commentators of Vasari have sought to identify it with a "tondo" which was once in the church of San Francesco, otherwise called San Salvatore al Monte, without the Porta San Miniato, at Florence. Vasari, in the first edition of the "Lives," relates that Botticelli executed "in San Francesco, beyond the Porta San Miniato, a 'tondo' of a Madonna with some angels as large as life, which was held to be a very beautiful work"; in the second edition, Vasari inserted after this notice, a long anecdote of a jest which Botticelli played upon a disciple of his, called Biagio, who had made a copy of the picture. In the course of the anecdote, Vasari speaks of "the eight heads of the angels," who were around the Virgin in this picture. There is more than one early copy of the "tondo" of the "Magnificat"; but no circular picture containing eight angels, by Botticelli's own hand, has come down to us. The only other notice of this "tondo," besides that of Vasari, occurs in the "Bellezze di Fiorenza," by Francesco Bocchi, published in 1591. "In the church of San Francesco al Monte," says that writer, "in a chapel on the right hand, is to be seen a very beautiful 'tondo' by the hand of Sandro Botticelli, in which is painted a Madonna with the Child in her lap, and around her are angels who appear to be singing with much grace: this picture is much esteemed by the artificers." After that time, the fate of the painting is lost in obscurity. The present church of San Salvatore del Mondo e San Francesco, to give its full dedication, in which Francesco Bocchi saw this "tondo" in 1591, was begun from the designs of Il Cronaca, about the year 1489. Whether Botticelli painted the picture for this new church, or whether it had been executed for the earlier church, which was destroyed by the subsidence of the hill-side on which it was built, there is no evidence to show. It is, however, a very doubtful point whether Vasari's allusion to the "eight heads of the angels," thrown off, as it was, in the course of a garrulous story, is to be understood in a literal sense. On the other hand, Vasari was speaking of a picture perfectly well known in Florence, where he was writing. The angels in the "tondo" of the "Magnificat," moreover, are not singing as Francesco Bocchi describes them. The only "tondo" of the Virgin and Child, which has come down to us, containing eight angels who are singing, is in the Raczinsky collection, No. 9, in the Nationalgalerie, at Berlin. Although this "tondo" may have come from Botticelli's workshop, it was certainly not executed by his own hand. On the whole, then, such evidence as we have, does not go to bear out the

Vasari, ed. Sansoni, III, 329.

Id., ed. 1550, I, 495.

Id., ed. 1568, I, 473.

l.c., p. 126.

L. Landucci, Diario, p. 58.

THE VIRGIN AND CHILD WITH FIVE ANGELS—THE TONDO OF THE MAGNIFICAT *Uffizi Gallery, Florence*

conjecture of the commentators of Vasari, that the "tondo" of the "Magnificat," was the picture once in the church of San Francesco.

This famous "tondo" represents the Virgin seated with the Child in her lap: she turns slightly to the left, as she dips a pen in the ink-horn, which is proffered her by one of two boy angels, who hold up before her a book in which she has inscribed in Gothic characters, the opening words of her exaltation: Magnificat a*nim*a mea d*omi*nu*m* [et exs]ultauit sp*iritu*s m[eus in Deo] Luke,
salutari m[eo. Quia respexit] humilita[tem ancille s]ue ecce eni[m ex hoc I, 46-49.
beatam] me dice*n*t om*n*[es generationes;] Quia [fecit mihi &c.] On the preceding page, which is almost covered by her hand, may be read some
disjointed words of the song of Zacharias: Ad f[aciendam miseri- Luke,
cordiam &c.]; and lower down on the page: Iusiu[randum, quod iurauit I, 72-79.
ad Abraham] patre[m nostrum, daturum se nobis: ut] sine [timore, de manu inimicorum nostrorum liberati, serviamus illi, i]n s*anct*i[tate et iustitia coram ipso,] omni[bus diebus nostris.] Et tu[, puer, &c.] Here the legend grows chaotic; but the words "preibis" and "umbra mortis" may still be made out. The Holy Child lays his right hand on the right arm of the Virgin, as if to guide her hand in the writing, and his left on the bitten pomegranate, the emblem of the Fall, which she holds in the other hand. Above the two angels, with the book and the ink-horn, on the left, is a third angel who clasps them by the shoulders, as he bends over them. On either side of the picture, behind this group of figures, are two other angels who hold a starry crown above the head of the Virgin, and above
the crown a radiant orb of light: "lo raggio dell' alta luce, che da sè è Paradiso,
vera." In the background through a circular window opening, corre- XXXIII,
sponding with the circumference of the picture, is seen a distant stretch of 53-54.
landscape with a winding river.

This panel, unfortunately, is in a very bad state of preservation: the greater part of its surface has been flayed by over-cleaning, and has afterward been freely retouched. The head of the Virgin and the figure of the Child have been so entirely gone over, and stippled up, that their original outlines have in great part been destroyed and their modelling distorted. In retouching the hand of the Virgin which rests on the book, the lavish restorer has added a "blob" of colour which, at first sight, might be taken for the tip of a sixth finger. Most of the other figures have suffered in greater or lesser degree: for instance, the profile of the angel on the left holding the ink-horn, has been forced by dark touches in the background, which throw the head out of tone with the rest of the picture. The best preserved passage is the figure of the angel on the right, behind the Virgin; and from this, it is still possible to form some notion of the original beauty of the execution of the whole. The colour, also, has lost much of that clarity and pureness of quality which distinguishes the genuine works of Botticelli from those of his imitators. In the course of these restorations the "aria virile" of Botticelli's draughtsmanship has been lost, and the forms have been sweetened and "prettified"; a misfortune which, no doubt, has contributed not a little to the extraordinary popularity of the picture. Indeed, in its present condition, it is possible, perhaps, to understand how to an unpractised eye, the picture has seemed to furnish evidence in support of the attribution of not a few of those circular school-pictures, "into which the attendant angels depress their heads so naïvely," to the master himself. The composition and design of the picture remain, however, among the more exquisite, if not among the greater, of Botticelli's achievements. The art with which the figures are composed within the difficult space of the "tondo," the beauty of such passages as the head of the Virgin, especially in the design of the hair seen beneath the thrice-folded veil of lawn, and falling among the parti-coloured scarf knotted about her neck, and above all its high-wrought, exotic, sentiment, render it for us, the work most typical of that aspect of Botticelli's genius which determined the character of the school of his imitators in Florence. I have for convenience discussed the picture in this place, for although this "tondo" closely recalls in the general character of the forms, and especially in the drawing of the Child, the folds of the draperies and the landscape, the altarpiece of San Barnaba, it is nevertheless somewhat earlier in character than that work, and may well have been executed immediately before Botticelli's journey to Rome, in 1481.

W. H. Pater, The Renaissance, ed. 1873, p. 44.

It was Mr. Pater who first suggested that Vasari's story, whether true or false, of how Botticelli perpetuated in the altarpiece which he painted for Matteo Palmieri, the heresy held by his patron, that the human race is "an incarnation of those angels who, in the revolt of Lucifer, were neither for God nor for his enemies," "interprets much of the peculiar sentiment with which he infuses his profane and sacred persons, comely, and in a certain sense like angels, but with a sense of displacement or loss about them—the wistfulness of exiles conscious of a passion and energy greater than any known issue of them explains, which runs through all his varied work with a sentiment of ineffable melancholy." And so, refining upon this idea, that writer adds, that for Botticelli the Madonna also, "though she holds in her hands the 'Desire of all Nations,' is one of those who are neither for God nor for his enemies; and her choice is on her face." "Her trouble is in the very caress of the mysterious child, whose gaze is always far from her." "Once, indeed, he guides her hand to transcribe in a book the words of her exaltation, the *Ave*, and the *Magnificat*, and the *Gaude Maria*, and the young angels, glad to rouse her for a moment from her dejection, are eager to hold the inkhorn and support the book; but the pen almost drops from the hand, and the high cold words have no meaning for her." It may seem a little late, at this hour, to take this exquisite, personal revery as so much matter-of-fact criticism; yet, in a sense, as criticism it was put forth, and as criticism it has gone to determine, more than any other single utterance, the interpretation which is currently put upon the sentiment of Botticelli's paintings. We now know beyond question, that the altarpiece which embodied the heretical fancies of Matteo Palmieri, was the work of another painter, who, beyond the fact that he was a Florentine and a contemporary, occurs in no sort of relation to Botticelli. Too little mindful of the outward forms and observances of religion, too deeply enamoured of that old Pagan world of the senses, Botticelli may well have been, during no small a part of his life; but to read such fancies into the work of the painter who was called to Rome, by the Pope himself, within a few years of the scandal which followed upon the exposure of Matteo Palmieri's heresies,—a painter against whom the only semblance of unorthodoxy that could, on any evidence, be urged, is that his religious pictures are too deeply coloured by the indelible influence of Dante, can scarcely serve to elucidate his real meaning. As I have said, the key to the true interpretation of the sentiment with which Botticelli informs his conception of the Virgin, is perhaps to be found in the verse from the "Paradiso," which he inscribed on the steps of her throne in the altarpiece of San Barnaba. Following upon that clue, one might attempt to indicate the actual sentiment, if not the precise subject, of the "Madonna of the Magnificat," by that passage in the "Divine Comedy," in which Dante describes his vision of the Virgin:

"Io vidi sovra lei tanta allegrezza
Piover, portata nelle menti sante
Create a trasvolar per quella altezza,
Che quantunque io avea visto davante,
Di tanta ammirazion non mi sospese,
Nè mi mostrò di Dio tanto sembiante.
E quell' amor, che primo lì discese,
Cantando *Ave Maria, gratia plena*,
Dinanzi a lei le sue ali distese.
Rispose alla divina cantilena,
Da tutte parti, la beata Corte,
Sì ch' ogni vista sen fe più serena."

Paradiso, XXXII, 88-99.

In striving to express aspirations and joys of the spirit as transcendental as these, by actual, physical shapes and forms, it is no wonder that Botticelli should have lent to them, consciously or unconsciously, something of the melancholy and lassitude which follows upon great passion. But even in this, he was not so unorthodox as some might suppose: for have not the whole body of the theologians by common consent put into the mouth of Holy Church herself, the cry of the Shunammite, "Fulcite me floribus, stipate me malis, quia amore langueo"?

Two school-copies of this "tondo" exist: one, coarse and crude in quality, is in the Gallery of the Louvre, No. 183; the other, a somewhat better picture, in the Palazzo Alessandri, at Florence. In both, the angel to the left, holding the crown over the Virgin's head, is omitted, besides other minor variations, such as the omission of the diaper patterns on some of the draperies.

To the "tondo" of the "Magnificat" must also be traced the motive of several school-works by various hands, and of varying quality. In a "tondo" formerly in the Palazzo Canigiani, at Florence, and now in the Academy at Vienna, No. 1133, the figures of the Virgin and the two angels by her side recall in their general arrangement, and in relation to the space of the panel, the figure of the Virgin and the two angels holding the book in the "tondo" of the "Magnificat." But here the resemblance ceases, and the other parts of the design are either varied, or omitted. Another "tondo," a somewhat later and more mannered school-work, in the Ducal collection at Saxe-Meiningen, recalls in its composition the picture at Vienna: the attitude of the Virgin is preserved in a general way, in its relation to the space of the picture, the figure of the Child who stands astride on his mother's knees is reversed, and a figure of the Baptist substituted for the two angels.

Besides these works by immediate disciples of Botticelli, there are two "tondi," the work of some sixteenth-century imitators of Botticelli; the one in the possession of the Marchese Fabio Chigi, at Siena, recalling the "tondo" in the Academy at Vienna; the other in the possession of M. de la Rozière, at Paris, recalling the panel at Meiningen: but they possess little character or interest.

A small picture on panel of this period, No. 19 in the Sala Dorata, of the Museo Poldi-Pezzoli, at Milan, may be noticed here, on account of the similarity of its motive with that of the "Madonna of the Magnificat"; although of a somewhat later time. It represents the Virgin at three-quarter length, with the Child in her lap, turned to the left, and seated before a stone plinth, on which lies a book of offices, resting on a cushion. The Virgin rests her right hand upon the open volume, as if expounding its mysteries, and with the left she holds the Child, who has placed both hands on hers, and is looking upward at her over his shoulder. Around his left wrist hangs the crown of thorns, and in his hand are the nails. At the Virgin's side, a majolica bowl, filled with cherries, rests on a pile of books; and behind her, in the background to the right, through an open window, is seen a break of landscape. The picture, as Morelli has remarked, is "a genuine, though unfortunately much restored," work. The head of the Virgin has been so much repainted that it has almost entirely lost its original character: the dark, opaque blue of the Virgin's robe, a colour not to be found in the genuine pictures of Botticelli, further marks the extensive nature of the restorations to which this painting has been subjected. The figure of the Child, and the hands of the Virgin, are, however, in a far better state of preservation; and in these passages may still be seen all the vigour and distinction of Botticelli's draughtsmanship. Such things, together with the sentiment and the design, remain to attest the original beauty of the painting.

I. Lermolieff, Die Galerie Borghese, ed 1890, p. 111.

A drawing, an allegorical figure of Abundance, which stands apart by itself among the extant drawings of the earlier Florentine masters, can with still greater certainty be ascribed to the years immediately succeeding Botticelli's return from Rome, in 1482. Unlike the great mass of Florentine drawings which have come down to us, it is not merely a sketch, or study, for some fresco or tempera-painting; but was evidently intended to exist for its own sake: the portion of it which has been completed, having been carried to the highest degree of finish. It was formerly in the possession of Samuel Rogers, the poet; and when his collection was dispersed by Messrs. Christie, on 28th April, 1856, and the following days, the drawing was thus described in the catalogue for the eighth day's sale: "Verrocchio. Lot 923. A female, with a cornucopia, leading a child —washed with red, on white. Fine." It went (such was the estimation in which the earlier drawings of the Florentine school were then held), for the small sum of £6, and was bought by Mr. Morris Moore, the enthusiastic collector who sold the little picture of Apollo and Marsyas, by Perugino, to the Louvre, on the condition that it should always be called a Raphael. Afterwards, this drawing of "Abundance" passed successively into the collections of Sir Charles Robinson, and Mr. John Malcolm of Poltalloch. In 1877-8, it was exhibited by Mr. Malcolm at the Winter Exhibition of Drawings by the Old Masters held in London, at the Grosvenor Gallery, No. 846; and again at a similar exhibition held in May and June, 1879, at the Ecole des Beaux Arts, at Paris, No. 21. In 1895, it was acquired with the rest of the Malcolm Collection, by the Trustees of the British Museum, and is now in the Print Room. The drawing has been mounted on the back of what appears to be a portion of one of Vasari's mounts. Whether or no this mount originally belonged to the drawing, is a question

ABUNDANCE *From the drawing in the British Museum*

which cannot now be decided. It is, however, by no means improbable that the drawing was in Vasari's collection; for he expressly states that he possessed in his Book of Drawings, several excellent sheets by Sandro: "e noi nel nostro libro n'habbiamo alcuni [disegni], che son fatti con molta pratica, e giudizio." Vasari, ed. 1568, I, 474.

Botticelli has represented the virtue of Abundance in this drawing, by the figure of a woman clad in translucent draperies. She is seen almost in full face, as she steps forward, bearing in her right hand a cornucopia filled with fruits, which a naked "amorino" by her side helps her to support, and leading with her left another, half-clad "amorino" with a bunch of grapes; behind whom are two other naked "putti" with fruit. The cornucopia and the naked "putto," as well as a fifth "putto" but partially indicated, on the left margin of the sheet, have been sketched in black chalk; while the rest of the drawing is elaborately finished in pen and wash. The beauty of the draughtsmanship, the subtlety of the line by which the form and movement of the naked body of the woman is expressed beneath the fluttering folds of the drapery, the fantastic invention of the dress, the girdled breasts, the sleeves twice caught back by the knotted ribbons, the strange attire of the hair, the bizarre character of the head, lend to this drawing something of the same inexplicable fascination which the figure of Flora in the painting of the "Spring," possesses for the lover of Botticelli's art: and this, too, in spite of the truth with which Botticelli has adhered in the figure, to the angular, Tuscan, type, and such lapses in the drawing, as the undue length of the left arm.

The folds of the draperies, so unlike in their forms to the Filippesque folds in the earlier pictures of Botticelli, suggest that this drawing was inspired by some antique statue of the Abundance, one of the many such which Botticelli may well have seen, during his stay at Rome. In its execution, this drawing affords a characteristic instance of the elaborate method which Botticelli ordinarily employed in his studies and sketches. The composition was first sketched in, on the white paper, in this case with black chalk, but more commonly with a lead style: the design thus determined, some colour of a blonde vermilion appears to have been next rubbed into the paper, to form a ground for the portions to be proceeded with. The design was then finally drawn in with the pen, with perfect decision, but with great freedom and lightness of hand; the modelling was next added by means of a bistre wash; the shadows being afterwards hatched over with the pen from right to left, and the lights heightened with white. The drawing measures 12½ in. in height, by 10¼ in. in width. With the exception of a few retouches in white on the hair and feet of the Abundance, and on two of the "putti" to the right, this drawing is in an admirable state of preservation.

In the Musée Condé, at Chantilly, is a large painting executed in tempera, on canvas, which both in subject and treatment recalls the drawing in the Malcolm Collection. This painting represents a woman in flying draperies carrying a large basket on her head filled with grapes, pears, apples, and other fruits, and with two naked "putti" by her side: it is doubtlessly intended for an allegorical representation of "Autumn." The general attitude of the principal figure has, however, been copied from the figure of the woman bearing a bundle of faggots on her head, in the fresco of the "Temptation," in the Sistine Chapel at Rome; but the head is seen more in full face, and with the left hand she is dragging along a drunken "amorino," with a string of bells round his neck, and a pipe in his hand. In these points, as well as in the character of the draperies, the picture at Chantilly recalls the Malcolm drawing. The other "amorino," on the left of the picture, has been directly copied from the "putto" starting at a snake which creeps out of the grapes he is carrying, in the Sistine fresco. Coarse in execution, and florid in its forms and details, this picture is probably the work of some disciple of Botticelli, at the time he was working at Rome. By the same hand as the picture at Chantilly, is the large "tondo" of the Virgin and Child enthroned, with St. John and six angels, in the Borghese Gallery at Rome, No. 348, as may be seen in certain mannerisms of draughtsmanship; especially in such passages as the head of the drunken "putto" in the picture at Chantilly, and the head of the Christ in the "tondo." Somewhat crude in colour, and very mannered in drawing, this "tondo" may have been suggested by some picture or sketch by Botticelli; but it certainly cannot have been executed from a cartoon by the master's own hand, as Morelli suggested; for its composition is far too diffuse, the attitudes of the figures too lifeless, and their masses too ill-balanced, to bear out such a supposition.

I. Lermolieff, Die Galerie Borghese, ed. 1890, p. 105.

To the time immediately succeeding Botticelli's return from Rome, belongs, also, the "portrait of a young man," No. 626 in the National Gallery, London. This fine head was formerly in the collection of Lord Northwick, at Thirlestane House, Cheltenham, where it passed as a portrait of Masaccio, by himself; and as such it was exhibited at the Art Treasures Exhibition, held at Manchester in 1857, No. 51. At the sale of the Northwick Collection, at Thirlestane House, in 1859, the picture was bought for the National Gallery, Lot 1127, for £108 3*s*. Dr. J. P. Richter, in his "Italian Art in the National Gallery," published in 1883, first pointed out that the portrait was by Botticelli: but it is only within the last ten, or twelve, years, that the name of its real author has been substituted for the name of Masaccio. It is painted on a panel, measuring 14 in. in height, by 11 in. in width, and represents the head and shoulders of a young man, with a "mazzo" of reddish brown hair, seen in full face, against a dark background. He wears a red "biretta," or cap, and a brown tunic edged with fur, and tied at the throat with a lace. The plain, work-a-day dress, the frank, disingenuous air and Tuscan head of the youth, suggest that it may be a portrait of some "discepolo."

l.c., p. 24.

With the exception of the early and much damaged head of one of the Medici, in the Gallery of the Uffizi, No. 1154, this is the only portrait on panel by Botticelli's hand which has come down to us; and admirable as are some of the heads in the Sistine frescoes, we possess no finer example of his art as a portrait-painter. In its direct and unaffected endeavour to present those outward lineaments which reveal character and temperament, no less than in the simplicity of its means, this admirable head is comparable to the portraits of the great northern masters. Those who think that bizarre traits of invention, an exotic sentiment or a strain of profound melancholy, are invariable qualities of Botticelli's manner, would do well to take this, one of the finest Florentine portraits of the fifteenth century, as the touchstone of what Botticelli was able to achieve in the region of purely humanistic art.

The earliest paintings designed, if not executed, by Botticelli, after his return to Florence in 1482, to which a date can be assigned with any certainty, are a series of furniture panels, with stories from the "Decameron."

PORTRAIT OF A YOUNG MAN *National Gallery, London*

Among the passages which Vasari inserted into the life of Botticelli, in the second edition, is one where he speaks of four pictures of little figures, in Casa Pucci, illustrating Boccaccio's novel of Nastagio degli Onesti: "in casa Pucci fece di figure piccole la nouella del Boccaccio, di Nastagio degl' Honesti, in quattro quadri di pittura molto vaga, e bella." These pictures remained in the possession of the Pucci family, in their palace in the Via de' Pucci, until 1868, when they were sold "for a hundred thousand francs [about £4,000] to an English gentleman." This was Mr. Alexander Barker, of London, whose fine collection of early Italian pictures included, amongst other things, the "Mars and Venus" now in the National Gallery. At the first sale of the Barker collection, which took place at Christie's, during the lifetime of the owner, on 6th and 8th June, 1874, these four pictures were bought in, since they did not reach the price which Mr. Barker put upon them. The first of the series, Lot 96, "Lady pursued by the knight and his dogs"; the second, Lot 97, "The knight throwing the lady's heart to the dogs"; were bought in for £525 apiece; the third, Lot 92, "The Feast in the Pineta," for £997 10*s.*; and the fourth, Lot 93, "The Marriage Feast," for £682 10*s.*, making a total of £2,730. When the remainder of the Barker collection was again put up at Christie's, on the 19th and 20th June, 1879, after the owner's death, these pictures fetched the following prices: Lot 504, "The Banquet in the Pineta," £441; Lot 505, "The Marriage Feast," £294; Lot 506, "Scene in the Pineta," £168; Lot 507, "Scene in the Pineta," £183 15*s.*; making a total of £1,086 15*s.* The sale catalogue does not distinguish between the subjects of the last two lots.

Vasari, ed. 1568, I, 471.

Id., ed. Sansoni, III, 314, note.

All the four pictures shortly afterwards passed into the collection of Mr. Frederick R. Leyland, of London, by whom they were exhibited in 1880, at the Eleventh Exhibition of Old Masters at Burlington House, Nos. 213-3 and 253-4. After Mr. Leyland's death, they were again put up at Christie's, with the rest of his collection, on 28th May, 1892, and the four pictures were sold, Lot 93, for £1,365. They were bought by M. Aynard, Député du Rhône, it is said, for the public gallery of Lyons; but the money not being forthcoming, or the pictures not liked, three of the panels were sold by him to M. G. Spiridon, of Paris, and the remaining panel, the last of the series, representing the "Marriage Feast," to Mr. George Donaldson, by whom it was exhibited at the Exhibition of Early Italian Art, at the New Gallery, in 1893-4, No. 156. It is now in the collection of Mr. Vernon Watney.

The novel of the "Decameron" of Boccaccio, which these pictures illustrate, is the eighth of the fifth day, related by Philomena, under the rule of Fiammetta. I will attempt to turn into English the passages from which Botticelli derived the subject of these paintings. "In Ravenna, a most ancient city of Romagna," begins the novel, "dwelt formerly many persons of noble and gentle family, among whom was a youth called Nastagio degli Onesti, who by the deaths of his father and an uncle of his, had been left rich beyond computation. He, as young men are apt to do, being unmarried, fell in love with a daughter of Messer Paolo Traversari, a young girl of far nobler birth than his own, hoping by his service to bring her to love him: but although his endeavours were most lavish, fine, and laudable, they not only gained him nothing, but rather appeared hurtful to him, so cruel, hard, and unrelenting did his lady-love show herself to him; but whether out of pride of her singular beauty, or the nobility of her birth, so haughty and disdainful did she become, that neither he, nor anything which pleased him, was pleasing to her." "And so," continues the novel after a little, "the young man persevering beyond all moderation, both in his love and his expenses, it seemed to his friends and relatives that he was in danger of consuming both himself and his substance; they, therefore, many times prayed and counselled him to leave Ravenna, and live abroad for a time, that by so doing he might lessen both love and its costs. Of this advice Nastagio often made light, but being, however, urged by them, and no longer able to say no, he consented to do so; and having caused great preparations to be made, as if he were about to set out for France, or Spain, or some other distant country, he mounted his horse, and accompanied by many of his friends, left Ravenna and went to a place some three miles beyond the city, called Chiassi: and having ordered pavilions and tents to be pitched there, he told those who had accompanied him, that there he intended to stay, and that they might return to Ravenna. When Nastagio had pitched his camp there, he began to lead the finest and most magnificent life that ever was led; inviting now these, now those, friends to sup or dine, as he had been used to do. Now it happened about the beginning of May, the season being a very fine one, that he fell thinking of his cruel lady, and having ordered all his family to leave him by himself, that he might the better be able to meditate at his pleasure, he wandered on, lost in thought, far into the Pine Forest. It had already passed the fifth hour of the day, and he had gone a good half mile into the Pine Forest, without thinking of eating, or any other thing, when suddenly he seemed to hear the loud cries and groans of a woman. His sweet thoughts being thus interrupted, he raised his eyes to see who it might be; when marvelling to find himself far in the Pine Forest, and looking before him, he saw coming out of a thicket full of bushes and briars, and running towards the place where he was, a most beautiful girl, naked, dishevelled, and torn all over by the bushes and briars, weeping and crying aloud for mercy; and at either side of her, he saw two very large and fierce mastiffs, which, running hard after her, savagely bit her as often as they overtook her: and behind her, he saw riding on a black courser, a gloomy knight of a very angry countenance, with a rapier in his hand, who with fearful and shameful words threatened her with death. The sight filled Nastagio with astonishment and fear, until pity for the unfortunate lady awoke in him the desire to set her free, if he could; but finding himself without arms, he ran to take the branch of a tree to serve for a truncheon, and began to oppose and beat off the dogs and the knight."

It is at this point in the novel, that Botticelli has paused to make the design for the first panel of the series. He has laid the scene of it in the famous "Pineta," of which some portions still remain beyond the church of Sant' Apollinare in Classe, along the shore of the Adriatic. In the middle distance, on the left, Nastagio is seen talking with his servants, in front of the sumptuous pavilions which he has caused to be pitched in the midst of the pine-forest. In the foreground, on the same side of the picture, he is again seen wandering through the wood, with his hands clasped before him, plunged in thought. He is dressed in hose and tunic, with his "cappuccio," the cap and scarf worn by Florentine citizens in the fifteenth century, thrown over his shoulder. On the other side of the picture, the lady, naked, with the two mastiffs fastening on her flanks, and followed by the knight in a richly wrought suit of armour, who rides a white courser and brandishes a naked sword in his right hand, flies with outstretched hands towards Nastagio, who has armed himself with a branch, which he has torn from a tree, and with which he attempts to beat off the dogs. In the distance is seen, between the pine-trees, an estuary flowing out to the sea, and laden with ships; and, on either side, some distant hills enclosing the bay.

"But the knight," continues the novel, "when he saw this, cried out to him from afar, 'Nastagio, do not oppose yourself: let the dogs and me do what this wicked woman deserves.' So saying, the hounds, seizing the young woman by the flanks, stayed her in her flight; and the knight having caught them up, dismounted from his horse. At this, Nastagio, drawing near, said, 'I know not who you may be, that you know me thus: but this I tell you, that it is great cowardice in an armed knight to seek to kill a naked woman, and to set dogs at her, as if she were a wild beast: I, certainly, will defend her in so far as I am able.' Then the knight answered, 'Nastagio, I was of the same city as you, and you were still a little child when I, who was called Messer Guido degli Anastagi, was far more enamoured of this woman, than you now are of the daughter of Il Traversari: but through her disdain and cruelty, such was my heavy fate, that one day, like a desperate man, I killed myself with this rapier which you see in my hand, for which I am doomed to eternal punishment. Not long after, this woman, who rejoiced beyond measure at my death, died also; and for her sin of cruelty, and the delight which she took in my torments, she not repenting of it, since she did not think that she had done wrong on that score, but rather deserved well, was likewise condemned to the pains of hell; where, as soon as she had descended, it was decreed as a punishment for her and me, that she should fly before me, and that I, who once so greatly loved her, should follow her, not as a lover, but as a mortal enemy. And as many times as I overtake her, I kill her with this rapier with which I killed myself; and I cut her open through the back, and that hard and cold heart into which neither love nor pity were ever able to enter, together with the other entrails, (as you shall see full soon,) I pluck from her body, and throw to these dogs to eat. Nor does a great space of time go by before she (such is the sentence and power of God!) rises up, as if she had not been dead, and begins anew her dolorous flight, and the dogs and I follow her: and it comes to pass that on every Friday, at this hour, I overtake her here; and here I kill her, as you shall see. But think not that we may cease upon other days, for I overtake her in other places where she imagined, or wrought, her malice against me: and having become, as you see, her enemy who was her lover, it is decreed that I should follow her in this manner for as many years, as she exercised months of cruelty towards me. Leave me then to carry out the sentence of divine justice, nor seek to oppose what you are unable to prevent.' At this Nastagio drew back in fear and astonishment, and the knight, like a rabid dog, throwing the woman upon her knees, while the two mastiffs held her down, ran her, with all his might, through the body. She fell at the blow with her face to the earth, still weeping and crying aloud; and the knight having taken a knife, and opened her body in the reins, and plucking out the heart and the other entrails, threw them to the two mastiffs, who immediately devoured them like starving beasts. After a little, as if none of these things had happened, the young woman suddenly rose to her feet, and began to fly towards the sea, with the dogs at her heels still biting and tearing her; and the knight having taken his rapier, remounted his horse and began to follow her: and in a short time they were so removed from sight, that Nastagio was no longer able to see them."

In the second panel of the series, Botticelli has represented, in the foreground of the picture, the lady stretched out with her face to the earth, while the knight, who is standing over her, cuts open her body in the reins. On the left, Nastagio turns away with a gesture of horror; and on the right, the two mastiffs devour the heart and the entrails, while the white courser of the knight stands tied to a tree behind them. In the centre of the picture, in the middle distance, is seen the young woman, who has risen to her feet, and is pursued anew by the knight and his dogs. These stories take place, as in the former picture, in the midst of the pine-forest; but the landscape which is seen between the pine-trees is varied: the expanse of water is less enclosed by the surrounding hills, and on the left is a walled town, with a bridge over an arm of the sea. In the foreground of the picture, among the pine-trees on the left, are two fawns drinking at a fountain.

At this sight, runs the novel, "Nastagio stood a great while betwixt pity and fear; but after a little he bethought him, that this thing might be turned greatly to his advantage, since it happened every Friday: to which end, having marked the spot, he returned to his servants, and afterwards, when it seemed fit to him, sent for some of his kinspeople and friends, and said to them: 'You have long urged me that I should cease from loving my disdainful lady, and put a limit to my expenses; this I am ready to do, provided you obtain me a favour, which is, that on Friday next, you bring it to pass that Messer Paolo Traversari, his wife and daughter, and all the women of their family, and any others whom you please, come here to dine with me. Why I wish this, you shall then see.' The request seemed to them a very small matter, and having returned to Ravenna, when the time came, they invited all those whom Nastagio desired, although it proved a hard business to bring along the young woman beloved by him; but in the end she went along with the rest. Nastagio had caused magnificent preparations to be made for a feast, and the tables to be placed beneath the pines, around the very spot, where he had seen the murder of the cruel lady; and the men and women having been set in their places at table, he so ordered it that the young woman beloved by him was seated immediately opposite to the spot, where the deed was used to take place. As soon as the last course was come, all began to hear the desperate cry of the hunted lady; whereupon everyone marvelling greatly, and asking what it was, and no one being able to tell, they all rose up, and looking to see what it might be, perceived the unhappy lady and the knight and the dogs; nor was it long before they were all in the very midst of the guests. A great noise was made by the dogs and the knight; and several persons sprang forward in order to help the young woman: but the knight speaking to them as he had spoken to Nastagio, not only caused them to draw back, but filled them all with fear and astonishment. Then doing the same deed which he had done on the former occasion, all the ladies who were present, (many of whom had been kinspeople of the unhappy lady and the knight, and remembered his love and death,) wept as bitterly as if that which they had seen, had happened to themselves. When the deed had been brought to an end, and the lady and the knight had gone away, it set those who had witnessed it, on many and various arguments: but none had been so greatly terrified as the young lady beloved by Nastagio, who had seen and heard everything distinctly, and knew that these things touched her more nearly than any other person, as she called to mind the cruelty which she had always used towards Nastagio; so that she seemed already to flee before him incensed with anger, with the mastiffs at her heels; and such was her terror, lest this should ever happen to her, that, her hatred of him having been changed into love, she sent that very evening a trusty chamber-woman to him, who entreated him in her name to come and see her, for that she was ready to fulfil his desires."

The third panel represents the feast which Nastagio gave to Paolo Traversari and his wife and daughter in the Pineta. In a clearing in the forest, two long tables have been set at right angles to one another: on the far side of the one running along the centre of the picture are seated seven men; and at the other, which is seen in perspective on the left of the painting, are seated six women. Behind the two benches on which the guests are seated, rises a "spalliera," or back-board, covered with a tapestry of diaper work: and along the top of the "spalliera" runs a wreath of cones and pine-branches; above which are set, at intervals, three shields of arms, surrounded by garlands, similarly contrived. The shield placed above the centre of the "spalliera," behind the women, is blazoned with the arms of Pucci: argent, a Moor's head couped proper, and banded argent; the band charged with three cross-taus sable. The second shield above the centre of the longer "spalliera," behind the men, is blazoned with the red "palle" in the gold field of the Medici; the central "palla" bearing the three golden fleurs-de-lys of France which had been granted them in 1465, by Louis XI. The third shield, which is placed above the end of the same "spalliera," on the right, is blazoned with the arms of Pucci, as before, impaling Bini: azure, a chevron between two roses in chief, and six mounts surmounting one another, 1, 2, and 3, in base, or.

The last course of the feast has come, the tables being set with dishes of fruit, sweetmeats, and wafers, when the guests rise to their feet as the hunted lady flees into their midst, and the two mastiffs seize her by either flank, while the knight follows hard on his white courser, brandishing his sword. In their dismay, the ladies have overturned the table before them, and the dishes are thrown to the ground. Nastagio, who has risen from a chair set at the angle between the two tables, holds out both hands in the endeavour to reassure his guests, and at the same time fixes his eyes on the daughter of Paolo Traversari. One of the youths at the table on the right, has seized a tabor to serve as a weapon to beat off the dogs. Another tabor is hanging from the trunk of a tree, above the "spalliera"; and on the table before him is a pipe and a lute. In the middle distance, on the extreme right of the panel, Nastagio is again represented talking to the chamber-woman, who has been sent to him by the daughter of Paolo Traversari: in the distance, an arm of the sea, girt by a rocky shore, with a turretted castle by the water's edge, on the left, is seen beyond the trunks of the pine-trees.

Nastagio replied to the waiting-woman who had been sent to him by the daughter of Traversari, that he only desired of her mistress what was consistent with her honour, which was to make her his wife. And so, concludes the novel, "on the Sunday following, Nastagio married the lady:

and their nuptials having been duly celebrated, he long lived happily with her."

In the fourth and last painting of the series, Botticelli has represented the marriage feast of Nastagio degli Onesti with the daughter of Paolo Traversari; and the picture which he gives of it is, in all its details, an idealistic representation of one of the great Florentine marriage feasts of the time. Let me illustrate my meaning. In the "Zibaldone quaresimale," (a miscellany which at once fulfilled the functions of a commonplace book, a diary, and the fly-leaves of the family Bible in England,) compiled by Giovanni Rucellai, the builder of the Palazzo Rucellai, and the façade of the church of Santa Maria Novella, in Florence, the writer has left a long account of the feast which he made on the occasion of the marriage of his son, Bernardo, with Nannina, the daughter of Piero de' Medici, Il Gottoso, on 8th June, 1466. This feast, Giovanni tells us, was held in front of the Palazzo Rucellai, "in su uno palchetto," on a stage or raised platform, which filled all the Piazza and the Loggia of the Rucellai, and the portion of the Via della Vigna before the façade of their palace. This "palchetto," adds the writer, was constructed upon a triangular plan, "con bellissimo apparato di panni d'arazzi pancali e spalliera, e con un cielo di sopra per difesa del sole di panni turchini, con essi adornato per tutto il detto cielo con ghirlande, coperto di verzura e con rose nel mezzo delle ghirlande, con festoni di verzura dattorno, con scudi la metà coll' arme de' Medici e la metà coll' arme de' Rucellai, e con più altri adornamenti; e massimamente una credenziera fornita d'arienti lavorati molta ricca; la quale cosa fu tenuto il più bello e più gentile parato che si sia mai fatto a festa di nozze."

C. Marcotti, Un Mercante Fior., p. 82.

In Botticelli's picture, the feast, likewise, takes place in the open air; but instead of the canopy, or "cielo" of blue cloths, the guests are shielded from the sun by a stately loggia of Florentine architecture: on more ordinary occasions than that which Giovanni Rucellai describes, the marriage-feasts were celebrated in the loggia attached to the palaces of the great Florentine families. The loggia of the picture is seen in the perspective of its length, and encloses two walks which extend between three rows of five piers, supporting semicircular arches. These arcades are, in their turn, connected with one another by three sets of cross arches. The guests are seated at two, long, narrow tables, extending the entire length of the loggia: the women at the left side of the table on the left, and the men at the right side of the opposite table. Behind each of the benches on which these figures are seated, is a "spalliera," or back-board, hung with cloths of arras, "panni d'arazzi pancali," which are placed against the lateral piers of the loggia. Above the capitals of the three foremost piers of the loggia, facing the spectator, are three shields or "scudi," of which the one on the right is blazoned with the arms of the Pucci; and that on the left, to use the phrase of the "Zibaldone," is blazoned "la metà coll' arme de' Pucci, e la metà coll' arme de' Bini," or, as we should say, with Pucci impaling Bini; while the central shield is blazoned with the arms of the Medici. All three shields are surrounded by garlands of green leaves, "ghirlande di verzura"; and before the central pier is placed a sideboard, covered with richly wrought plate, the "credenza fornita d'arienti lavorati molta ricca," of Giovanni Rucellai's description. In the link-holders attached to each of the foremost piers, are placed branches of olive, the symbol of peaceful prosperity: among the gifts at the Rucellai marriage

Id., p. 87

was "uno magnifico ulivo in su un carro." Eleven men, in the dress of Florentine citizens, are seated at the table on the right, facing seven or eight women who are seated on the opposite table. The bridegroom is seated by himself, in a wrought metal chair, at the women's table opposite the bride, to whom he offers a bowl of wine: she wears the same dress as in the third panel of the series.

The last course of the banquet is being brought to table; the linen table-cloths are strewn with roses and other flowers; and before each guest is laid a two-pronged fork, and a "tazza," or bowl, for the wine, "trebbiano" or "vermiglio." To the extreme left of the picture, four pages in hose and tunic, bring in various dishes; of which the first is filled with cakes, or "berlingozzi," the second with rolled wafers, "cialdoni," and the rest with various fruits. On the other side, four other pages bring in other dishes, the first of which contains cakes, the other three "zuccherini," or sweetmeats of various kinds. Behind the loggia rises a triumphal arch, ornamented with Corinthian columns, bas-reliefs and statues, and imitated from the antique Roman arches; and beyond, in the distance, is an open landscape with a river, and the spires of a distant town.

The arms which Botticelli has introduced into the third and last panels of the series, show that these pictures must have been painted to celebrate the marriage of one of the Pucci with a lady of the Bini family. The commentators of the Florentine edition of Vasari, published by Le Monnier, in 1846, put forth the conjecture that they were painted to celebrate the marriage of Pierfrancesco di Giovanni Bini, with Lucrezia di Francesco di Giovanni Pucci, in 1487. This, however, must be an error, for, according to an elementary law of Italian, as of English, heraldry, when the arms of a husband and wife are impaled, the arms of the husband are invariably blazoned on the dexter side of the shield, and those of the wife on the sinister side. That the bridegroom was a Pucci, and not a Bini, is further shown by the single shield of the Pucci which occurs in both panels. On the contrary, these pictures were, no doubt, painted to celebrate the marriage of Giannozzo Pucci, with his second wife, Lucrezia, the daughter of Piero di Giovanni Bini, in 1483. Giannozzo was thrice married: his first wife, Smeralda, had died in 1482, and his father, Antonio, in 1484. For Antonio Pucci, the Pollaiuoli painted, c. 1475, the large altar-piece of the "Martyrdom of St. Sebastian," now in our National Gallery, No. 292, for his family chapel, beside the atrium of the Santissima Annunziata in Florence: for Antonio, also, Botticelli probably painted the tondo of the "Adoration of the Magi," to which Vasari alludes. The arms of the Medici were doubtlessly introduced into these pictures, in compliment to the chief citizen of the Florentine Republic; for the family of the Pucci, as Jacopo Nardi records, had always been "molto affezionata e devota alla grandezza de' Medici." In 1494, when Piero di Lorenzo de' Medici was turned out of Florence, Giannozzo Pucci was detained on suspicion of account of his partiality to the Medici; and three years later, he was taken in a conspiracy to restore Piero de' Medici, and beheaded along with Lorenzo Tornabuoni, (whose marriage Botticelli had also celebrated by his paintings,) Bernardo del Nero and others, on the 17th August, 1497.

l.c., V, 114, note.

P. Litta, Famiglie celebri Italiane, Disp. 158, Tav. V.

L. Landucci, Diario, pp. 155-156.

These four paintings, as Messrs. Crowe and Cavalcaselle have noted, are not well preserved, and have been here and there retouched with colour. The panel, which in their opinion has suffered most, is the last of the series,

l.c., ed. Le Monnier, VI, 249.

representing the Marriage Feast. Each of them measures about 32 in. in height, by 55 in. in width: they probably formed the panels of the "spalliera," or panelled back, of a "lettuccio," or bench, fixed against a wall. All the four panels were certainly designed by Botticelli himself; but their execution appears to have been almost entirely carried out by assistants, and not, perhaps, in every case from a cartoon by the master. At least three different hands are to be detected in these pictures. In the first panel, the figures of the hunted lady with the dogs and the knight on horseback are less firmly drawn than the two figures of Nastagio in the foreground: the former figures, though more thoroughly Botticellesque in form, are weaker in character, and appear to have suffered more from retouching. The execution of the second panel, which is probably by the same hand, is more nearly in Botticelli's manner, especially the figure of the knight as he bends over the prostrate lady: the drawing, moreover, is firmer throughout than that of the first panel. I suspect that Botticelli himself directed the execution of these two panels. In design, they are admirable: the sense of decoration with which the dark pine-trees are silhouetted against the clear sky and delicate distance, and the felicity with which the figures are introduced among the pine-trunks, render them among the finest of Botticelli's inventions of this kind.

In the execution of the third panel, the Feast in the Pineta, the most able, but in some respects the least interesting, of the series, is unquestionably to be traced the hand of the assistant who painted the "Massacre of the Innocents," in the background of the altar-piece by Domenico Ghirlandaio, dated 1488, in the chapel of the Spedale degli Innocenti, at Florence, and the "predella" panels which formerly belonged to it, and which are now in the gallery of the hospital, Nos. 63 to 70. The hand of this assistant is clearly to be seen in the squat, rounded forms of the naked lady in the foreground, and the waiting-woman who is talking to Nastagio in the middle distance on the right. The peculiar character which he gives to his heads (the over-emphasis in the drawing of the lower eyelid, and the short, squab form of the nose, being among their more obvious characteristics), enables the hand of this assistant to be easily recognized. If Botticelli really gave the cartoon for this panel, we have here a remarkable instance of the free way in which an assistant, not of the master's school, was allowed to treat the design of his employer who had been temporarily obliged to avail himself of his assistance, through stress of work. It appears from the original agreements for Ghirlandaio's altar-piece of the Innocenti, which are preserved among the archives of the Hospital, and which were published at Florence in 1902, by Signor Gaetano Bruscoli, in a pamphlet entitled, "L'Adorazione dei Magi: Tavola di Domenico Ghirlandaio nella chiesa dello Spedale degl' Innocenti," that the name of this assistant was Bartolommeo di Giovanni. But I shall discuss this painter and his works, at length, when I come to speak of the disciples of Botticelli.

In design, the fourth and last panel of the series is, perhaps, the most splendid; but in execution it is certainly the feeblest of the series. The painting has suffered much from retouching, as Messrs. Crowe and Cavalcaselle have remarked, but this does not disguise the fact that the painter was so feeble a draughtsman as to be unable to diminish properly a group of figures seen in perspective. For instance, the head of the woman who is seated on the far side of the bride, is nearly half as large again as the head of the bride. Indeed, the drawing of the figures throughout is of the feeblest. The execution of the rest of the picture, especially of the architecture, is more satisfactory, and must have closely followed Botticelli's drawing. Nothing could be more spacious and splendid, in design and arrangement, than the architecture of the Loggia; the design of which recalls the ruined basilica in the background of the "tondo" of the "Adoration of the Magi," in the National Gallery, at London, No. 1033. The execution of this panel is, in my opinion, by the same hand as the large panel of the recumbent Venus surrounded by Amorini, in the Louvre, No. 1,299.

In the collection of the Marchesi Torrigiani, in their palace in the Piazza Mozzi, at Florence, is a furniture-panel painted with the story of the lady hunted by the knight and the mastiffs in the Pineta; and among the "cassoni" panels lately belonging to Lord Ashburnham, at London, was another panel of the "Feast in the Pineta." Both pictures have been attributed to Botticelli, and both would seem to have belonged to the same series, illustrating the novel of Nastagio. In its composition, the panel from Lord Ashburnham's Collection follows, in a general way, the painting of the same subject in the series executed for the Pucci; but in its details it is freely varied. In style, it recalls rather the manner of Francesco Botticini, and the school of Cosimo Rosselli, than that of Sandro Botticelli. At first sight, this panel would seem to be earlier in point of date, than the panel which came from Botticelli's workshop; but the resemblance between the two pictures is such, that one is forced to conclude that the picture from the Ashburnham Collection is a free version by some belated painter, who was certainly not one of Botticelli's disciples, of the panel executed in his workshop for the Pucci. A more careful examination of the panel in the Torrigiani Collection than I have been able to make, would probably establish similar conclusions in regard to that picture.

In 1484, as I have already shown, Botticelli appears to have been at work on the frescoes, now destroyed, of the Spedaletto, near Volterra, for Lorenzo, Il Magnifico; the following year, between the months of February and August, 1485, he was engaged in painting an altar-piece for the chapel of the Bardi, in the Basilica of Santo Spirito, at Florence. Although the proposal to rebuild the Gothic church of Santo Spirito had been mooted as early as 1433, and a design had been given by Filippo Brunelleschi, some years before his death, the first column of the new basilica was not erected until 1454. Even then, the work proceeded slowly; and it was not until the destruction of the old church by fire, in March, 1470-1, that any great effort was made to complete the building according to Brunelleschi's design. Giuseppe Richa, in his notices of the Florentine churches, quoting what was, perhaps, a contemporary document, says that office was first said in the new church, in 1481: and Lucca Landucci records in his "Diary" that during the month of April, 1482, "the cupola of Santo Spirito was finished, and sermons were preached there under it." The altar-piece in the last of the four chapels, in the head of the left transept, belonging to the family of the Corbinelli, a work of the school of Cosimo Rosselli, bears the date 1482: and a large number of the altars in the transepts and the choir of the church appear to have been furnished with altar-pieces and painted altar-frontals, which in many instances they still retain, not long after the completion of the cupola. Signor Igino Supino, the keeper of the Museum of the Bargello at Florence, has

G. Richa, Notizie, IX, 14.

L. Landucci, Diario, p. 41.

recently discovered among the private archives of Count Francesco Guicciardini, an account-book of Giovanni d'Agnolo de' Bardi, containing entries of the payments made by him for this altar-piece and its frame.

App. II, Doc. XXV.

The book itself, which is lettered B, contains the accounts of Giovanni, in double entry, from 1484 till 1487. The first payment, which occurs at fol. 35, recto, is entered thus: "Monday, 7th February [1484-5], for the Chapel of Santo Spirito, 24 fiorini, 8 soldi, 5 danari a oro larghi, for 23 fiorini, 10 soldi, larghi d'oro in oro, paid to Giuliano da San Gallo, wood-worker, who received it in cash; and this sum is for the carving of the frame of the painting on panel made by Sandro del Botticello." The second payment is entered at fol. 39 tergo, thus: "Wednesday, 3rd August [1485], for the chapel of Santo Spirito, 78 fiorini, 15 soldi, a oro larghi, for 75 fiorini [larghi], d'oro in oro, paid to Sandro del Botticello in cash, of which 2 fiorini are for ultramarine (azzuro), and 38 fiorini for the gold and the gilding of the altar-piece (mettitura della tavola), and 35 fiorini for his painting (pel suo pennello)." The "fiorino largo d'oro," and the "fiorino largo d'oro in oro," were properly the same coin: but the debtor of the "fiorino largo d'oro in oro" was held "*ex conventione*" to pay the money in specie; whereas the debtor of the "fiorino largo d'oro" was free to pay its current equivalent in other and less sterling money; hence the higher rate of exchange.

I. Orsini, Monete Fiorentine, p. xxiii.

The sum paid to Giuliano da San Gallo probably included the entire cost of the frame and the panel for the picture: the 38 florins paid for the gold and "mettitura della tavola," included the costly item of the gilding of the frame. In spite of the expression "fatta" used in the first entry, it would seem that the painting, though already begun in February, 1484-5, was chiefly executed in the interval between the dates of these two entries; and for that reason Botticelli received payment six months after Giuliano da San Gallo.

App. II, Doc. I, fol 49, tergo.

App. II, Doc. II, fol. 85, recto.

Id., fol. 83, tergo.

Vasari, ed. 1550, I, 491.

Both Antonio Billi, and the Anonimo Gaddiano, speak of the altar-piece which Botticelli painted for the chapel of the Bardi, in the basilica of Santo Spirito: the former, according to the version of the "Codice Petrei," merely records the picture in the briefest way, "Vna tauola in sto spirito di sto *giouan*ni"; the latter speaks of it at greater length, as an altar-piece containing figures of the Madonna and St. John the Baptist, "In sto spirito e disua mano nella capella de Bardj latauola dell altare dove edipinto vna n*ost*ra donna et v*n*o sa*n* giova*nn*j batta." Elsewhere, the Anonimo Gaddiano interpolates in a later hand, among his notices of Botticelli, a second reference to the picture, taken apparently from the "Libro di Billi," "Vna tauola in sto sp*iri*to dig*iouan*nj deb*ar*dj." Besides these, Vasari in the first edition of the "Lives" states that Botticelli "painted in Santo Spirito at Florence, in the chapel of the Bardi, a picture on panel which is worked with diligence and admirably finished; in it are some olive and palm which are executed 'con sommo amore.'" The chapel of the Bardi is the last, on the left hand, of the four chapels in the head of the church of Santo Spirito, behind the high altar: the arms of the Bardi; or, a bend of fusils gules, within a bordure componée argent and azure; may still be seen above the arch of the chapel. When Giovanni Cinelli published his edition of the

l. c., p. 144.

Vasari, ed. Le Monnier, V, 111, note.

"Bellezze di Firenze," in 1677 Botticelli's altar-piece had already been removed, in order to make way for the painting by Jacopo Vignali, who died in 1664, of the "Communion of the Blessed Chiara of Montefalco," which is still to be seen above the altar of the chapel. According to the Florentine commentators of Vasari, Botticelli's picture was removed to

THE VIRGIN AND CHILD WITH ST. JOHN THE EVANGELIST AND THE BAPTIST
THE ALTAR-PIECE OF SANTO SPIRITO *Berlin Gallery*

the house of the patrons of the chapel, where it remained until 1825, when it was sold to Fedele Acciaj, a picture-dealer of Florence: in 1829, it was acquired by Baron Rumohr for the Royal Museum at Berlin, where it is still preserved, No. 106. Whether the altar-piece, like the private papers of Giovanni de' Bardi, descended to the Guicciardini, I do not know; but more than one member of that house contracted a marriage with a lady of the Bardi family.

P. Litta, Famiglie Celebri Italiane, Vol. III, Fam. Guicciardini, Tav. III.

The carved frame of Giuliano da San Gallo has long since disappeared; and with it the paintings which, in all probability, once decorated the "gradino." The panel at Berlin represents the Virgin and Child enthroned, with St. John the Baptist, the patron-saint of Florence, standing on their right, and St. John the Evangelist, the patron-saint of the founder of the chapel, on their left. The Child lies in the lap of the Virgin, who raises him somewhat, as he puts out his hands to take her breast, which she bares with her right hand. The Baptist, portrayed in the same maugre character in which Botticelli had painted him in the altar-piece from the church of San Barnaba, calls the attention of the spectator to the Holy Child, by a gesture of the right hand: in the left, he holds a reed-cross to which is attached a little scroll inscribed, "ECCE AGNVS DEI QVI TOLLIS PECHATA MV[N]DI"; and at his feet lies a baptismal laver. St. John the Evangelist is represented holding a book and a pen, in allusion to the divine behest recorded in the opening chapter of the Apocalypse, "write in a book"; behind him is seen the head of the eagle. The low, screen-like structure of white marble, on which the Virgin is seated, extends across the whole space of the picture, and consists of three semicircular recesses between projecting elbow-pieces, resembling a series of choir-stalls. Before the central recess in which the figure of the Virgin is placed, is a pace, or step, of white marble, the face of which, like the faces of the elbow-pieces, is richly carved with a frieze-like ornament. Behind the central recess, and above the figure of the Virgin, rises an arbour-like niche of plaited palm-branches, such as are still carried in procession, in Italy, on Palm Sunday: and in the head of the niche is set a small, plaited cross of palms. Behind the recess to the left, and above the figure of the Baptist, rises a similar niche of cypress; and behind the niche on the right, behind and above St. John the Divine, another of ilex. On each of the four arms, or elbow-pieces, of the marble screen, is placed a shallow bowl, filled with red and white roses, about which are intertwined narrow scrolls bearing the legend,

QVASI PLANTAZIO ROSE IN IERICHO

This legend is to be read, almost in its entirety, on the scroll immediately to the right of the Virgin, and partially on the others. In the midst of each of these bowls of roses is placed a copper vase, chased with arabesques, and fantistically bound about with branches of olives. Around the necks of these vases are wound other scrolls, bearing the legend,

QVASI OLIVA SPEZIOSA IN CHANPIS

variously spelt on the scroll immediately to the Virgin's left,

QVASI OLIVA ISPEZIOSA IN CAM[P]IS

This variation in spelling seems to be due to restorations. In the two vases on either side of the Virgin, are two wands of lilies which rise above her head, between the niches, or arbours: and round about their stalks are twined other scrolls bearing legends. On the scroll to the Virgin's right may be read the words,

SIC VT LILIVM

and on that to the Virgin's left, a few letters of the remaining words of the legend,

I[N] CA[MP]IS

In the other two vases at either side of the picture, are placed branches of citron or lemon; and on the scroll about the branch to the right, may be read the words,

[Q]VAS[I] CEDRVS E[XALTATA SVM IN LIBANO]

Some letters of the last two words may be made out on the scroll round the branch to the left, thus:

IN LIB[AN]O

Botticelli, it will be noted, mistook the Latin "cedrus," a cedar, for the Italian "cedro," a citron or lemon. In the head of the niche, or arbour, of plaited palm-branches, above the figure of the Virgin, runs a scroll bearing a legend partially erased, but still to be deciphered,

QVASI [P]ALMA [EXALT]ATA [S]VM I[N CA]DES

Across the head of the niche of cypress, above the figure of the Baptist, runs another scroll bearing the legend,

QVASI [CVPR]ES[SV]M [*sic*] IN MONTE SION

Lastly, across the head of the third niche of ilex, above the figure of St. John the Evangelist, runs a scroll bearing the legend of which only a few letters can now be deciphered,

QVAS[I] PLAT[A]NVS [EXALTATA SVM IVXTA AQVAM IN PLATEIS]

In the fifteenth century, the plane-tree, Platanus Orientalis, is said to have been unknown in Tuscany: this would explain why Botticelli used another tree instead of the plane, but not why he chose the ilex.

The symbolism of all this imagery, as elaborate in its allusion as a canzone of Dante, "a truth concealed under a beautiful untruth," is, with one exception, taken from the rendering in the Vulgate of a passage in the 14th chapter of the Book of Ecclesiasticus, the Wisdom of Jesus the son of Sirach, in which Wisdom praises herself: "I came out of the mouth of the Most High. . . . And I took root in an honourable people, even in the portion of the Lord's inheritance. I was exalted like a cedar in Libanus, and as a cypress tree upon Mount Sion. I was exalted like a palm tree in Cades, and as a rose plant in Jericho, as a fair olive in the fields, and grew up as a plane tree near to the water by the way-sides." In the painting, all this imagery is used figuratively of the Holy Child, the incarnation of the Heavenly Wisdom. Immediately below the pace of the throne, before the Virgin's feet, resting against a covered vessel, is a "pax," painted with a little figure of Christ crucified: "We preach Christ crucified, unto the Jews a stumbling-block, and unto the Greeks foolishness; but unto them which are called, both Jews and Greeks, Christ the power of God, and the wisdom of God."

Ecclesiasticus, XXIV, 3, 12-14.

1 Corinthians, I, 23-24.

Admirable and inventive as are the accessory devices and ornaments by which Botticelli here, as in the altar-piece of San Barnaba, has sought to weave the formal, detached figures into an entire composition, symbolically as well as pictorially complete, this painting nevertheless remains an altar-piece painted in obedience to ecclesiastical usages; and as such it can never possess for us moderns quite the same charm and interest, as a work in which the master was free to choose his own subject and decide upon its treatment: yet, notwithstanding, it is one of the most splendid works of Botticelli, and of all his large altar-pieces, not only the best preserved, but the finest in the quality, and the most equal in the excellence, of its workmanship. Especially admirable is the figure of the Child, which for beauty of line and fleshiness of modelling, is unsurpassed by anything which we have by Botticelli; and the mystical flowers and leafy niches, drawn, as Vasari says, "con sommo amore," are of a naturalism as exquisite, as their symbolism is elaborate. The head of the Evangelist with its mane-like hair and beard, recalls the figure of Moses in the Sistine frescoes; and in the figure of the Baptist, Botticelli repeats, but with greater severity and beauty of draughtsmanship, that traditional conception of the patron saint of Florence which he had painted in the altar-piece of San Barnaba. In colour, the picture is warm, clear and luminous: against the deep, subdued greens and gilded lights of the foliage in the background, the azure of the Virgin's robe is contrasted with the brilliant, golden purple of her dress, the colder and grayer purple of the robe of the Evangelist, and the bricky purple of the Baptist's robe; the silvery flesh of the Virgin and the Child with the ruddy flesh of the saints. On comparing this picture with the earlier frescoes of the Sistine Chapel, and the still earlier painting of the "Spring," we find in it a further accent in the mannerisms of its draughtsmanship, a more nervous and emphatic delineation of the forms. In the course of the seven years which had elapsed since Botticelli painted the latter picture, his art had rapidly attained to that full ripeness of manner, beyond which any further development must, in the nature of things, tend towards a deterioration.

The panel on which the picture is painted, measures 6 ft. 1 in. in height, and 5 ft. 11 in. in breadth. There are unmistakable traces that the painting was worked from a full-size cartoon: the ornament on the pace at the Virgin's feet has been pricked with a point on to the "gesso ground"; and the outline of the covered vessel behind the little crucifixion, has been traced with a style on the ground, while it was still fresh, and afterwards enlarged on the right side. Many of the citron and olive leaves are painted with an "impasto" unusual in tempera pictures of the fifteenth century. Gilding has been freely used in the ornaments of the Virgin's robe, in the vases on the arms of the throne, and in the lights of the foliage; especially in the palm, cypress, and ilex leaves of the niches. The picture having suffered somewhat from unskilful cleaning, this surface gilding has been damaged in many places. At an early period, probably towards the close of the sixteenth, or the beginning of the seventeenth century, when the picture was cleaned, the legends on the scrolls among the flowers and foliage, were repainted in larger, coarser letters, and the spelling modernized. Thus, the original E in the word MONTE on the scroll in the head of the niche behind the Baptist, may be seen side by side with the E of the repainted inscription. The upper part of the left margin of the panel, varying in breadth from some 2½ inches to an inch, has also been damaged and coarsely restored. With the exception of these blemishes and some other local retouches of little importance, this panel is well preserved: indeed, as I have said, of all the large altar-pieces by Botticelli, it is beyond comparison in the finest state of preservation.

An admirable copy, which undoubtedly came from Botticelli's workshop, of the upper part of the Virgin's figure and the Child, is in the collection of Mr. Alexander Mann, of Glasgow. The background of this copy differs from the altar-piece, and in place of the arbour of plaited palm-branches is a landscape, seen through an arched opening, in front of which the Virgin is seated; but both figures closely follow the original at Berlin, except in the folds of the veil of the Virgin's head. Indeed, these figures have every appearance of having been painted from the original cartoon; and it is only in the quality of the execution, that the fine judge of these things will detect the hand of an assistant, who has lost much of the subtile drawing and fleshy modelling of the original. This panel, which is painted in tempera, is unvarnished, and in an unusually fine state of preservation. It is probably by the same hand as a half-length figure of the "Salvator Mundi" in the Morelli Collection, No. 29, in the Academy at Bergamo.

In the Gallery of the Uffizi, Frame 57, No. 193, is a drawing of a seated figure of St. Jerome, in the habit of a Cardinal, holding a pen and book, drawn in silver-point on a faded, red ground, and heightened with white. It measures 9¾ inches in height and 5 inches in width. It is the only genuine drawing in silver-point by Botticelli which has come down to us; and it shows that Botticelli did not work with the same expressiveness with the style, as with the pen. Not only do the head and hands of this St. Jerome recall those of St. John the Evangelist in the picture at Berlin, but the folds of the drapery which fall over the knees of the Cardinal closely resemble those in the corresponding passage in the figure of the Virgin: indeed, it is evident from the marked similarity of their style, that the drawing and painting are of the same period.

Closely recalling the altar-piece of the Bardi, in the quality and accent of its draughtsmanship, is a panel of "Mars and Venus," in the National Gallery, at London, No. 915. This picture was acquired in Florence, by Mr. Alexander Barker; and at the first sale of his collection, by Messrs. Christie, on 6th and 8th June, 1874, was bought for the National Gallery, Lot 88, for £1,050. The panel on which it is painted, measures 2 feet 3½ inches in height, and 5 feet 8 inches in length. These unusual proportions would seem to show that this picture could not have formed part of a "cassone," or coffer; but was probably executed for the panel of a bed, or couch, or some such piece of furniture,—"per vano di lettucci, letti," to use Vasari's phrase.

Within a wood of myrtle, on the left of the picture, the Goddess Venus, robed, as in the painting of the "Spring," in a long white dress, braided with narrow fillets of golden embroidery, reclines at length on the green sward, with her right arm resting on a purple cushion. On the other side of the picture opposite to her, lies the God Mars, asleep and naked. In a hollow branch of the tree, against which the God has propped his head, a swarm of hornets have made their nest: upon such pillows do the lovers of Venus take their rest. Through the corselet on which he rests his left arm, has crept a young satyr with sprouting horns: and behind the figures of the God and Goddess, two other baby-satyrs, one of whom has put on the God's helmet backwards, are trying to shoulder his tilting lance; while

MARS AND VENUS *National Gallery, London*

a fourth attempts to arouse him by blowing through a shell into his ear. In the background, through a break in the myrtle trees, is seen a distant landscape.

Dr. J. P. Richter, in his "Lectures on the National Gallery," has, to the further confusion of the subject, expressed the opinion that this picture is intended to represent not Mars and Venus, but Giuliano de' Medici and La Bella Simonetta, and that its interpretation must be looked for in the "Stanze" of Poliziano. I have already discussed the myth which has grown up within the present century, concerning the portraits of Simonetta which Botticelli is supposed to have painted, and have shown that the whole legend rests upon a mere suppositon, unsupported by any direct evidence. Upon the death of Simonetta in 1476, Poliziano had laid aside his "Stanze" unfinished; and at the time at which this picture was painted, c. 1485, Botticelli could no longer have had any reason for celebrating the loves of Giuliano and his mistress. More than this, the heads in this picture are surely no portraits. On the other hand, the amours of Mars and Venus was one of those commonplaces of mythology, which are constantly found recurring in the art and literature of Florence at this time. In the museum at South Kensington is a relief in "gesso," [1859, No. 5887,] somewhat earlier in date than Botticelli's picture, representing Venus lying naked on one side, and Mars asleep on the other, surrounded by "Amorini"; a "diamante," or ring of the Medici, an impress of Cosimo, Il Vecchio, forming the frame of the composition. The arrangement and attitudes of the figures of the God and Goddess closely recall Botticelli's painting; but in spirit and treatment they are very different. It would seem, then, that we here have evidence of some version of this subject, current at the time in the Florentine "botteghe," according to which Mars is represented sleeping while Venus wakes; a conception which remains unexplained by the verses of Lorenzo, Il Magnifico, on the "Amori di Venere e Marte," and such other contemporary allusions to the antique myth, as are known to me.

l.c., p. 54.

Except for some slight, local restorations of little moment, this panel is in a fine state of preservation. Intended merely as a furniture-panel, its actual execution has not been carried as far as that of the Bardi altar-piece; but that reservation allowed, it must be admitted that the "Mars and Venus" is but little inferior in quality to that fine work. The drawing of the "amorini," for example, admirable as they are in conception, have not the same beauty and subtlety of line as the figure of the Holy Child in the altar-piece. In point of execution, the Venus is, perhaps, the finest passage in the painting: the design of the hands and the folds of the white dress as it falls over the recumbent figure, shows the art of Botticelli in one of its fortunate moments. The Pollaiuolesque drawing of the figure of Mars serves to mark how little Botticelli's manner had changed in the rendering of the nude, since the time when he worked as the assistant of Antonio Pollaiuoli.

Two school-works have come down to us which seem to have been suggested by this panel of "Mars and Venus"; one in the National Gallery at London, No. 916, and the other in the Louvre, No. 1,299. Both represent Venus lying draped, in a meadow, with three "amorini," who are throwing roses at her; and in both the figure of Venus appears to have been taken in a general way from the "Mars and Venus." The name of Jacopo del Sellaio has been suggested as the author of the version in the National Gallery; but the picture seems to me to be the work of some immediate disciple of Botticelli. The version in the Louvre is by the same hand, if I mistake not, as the "Marriage Feast of Nastagio degli Onesti," in the collection of Mr. Watney, and the "Virgin and Child," belonging to Lord Battersea, at London.

C. Conti, "Découverte de deux Fresques de Sandro Botticelli." C. Ephrussi, "Les deux Fresques du Musée du Louvre attribuées à Sandro Botticelli." App. II, Doc. XXVI, fol. 380, recto. Vasari, ed. Sansoni, III, 269.

During the month of September, 1873, some wall-paintings to which none of the early commentators had left any allusion, were discovered at Florence, in a villa in the Chiasso Macerelli, a suburban road leading from a crossway near Ponte a Rifredi, to San Pietro a Careggi and the famous villa of the Medici. It is to this road that Lorenzo, Il Magnifico, alludes in the opening verses of his "Beoni," as the way by which he returned from his villa to the city, "per la via ch' entra alla Porta Faentia." The villa in which the frescoes were discovered, then the property of Dott. Petronio Lemmi, dates back, in its origin at least, to the fourteenth century. In 1469, it was acquired by purchase from the Gagliani, by the noble family of the Tornabuoni; and it is described in the "Denunzia" returned by Giovambattista di Francesco Tornabuoni, in 1480, as "a 'podere' or farm, in the Parish and Piviere of Santo Stefano in Pane, at a place called Chiasso a Mascierelli, with a house for the owner and farm servants, bounded on the first side by the road, on the second, by the property of Lorenzo de' Medici; on the third, by the property of Tommaso Lotheri." The property remained in the possession of the Tornabuoni until 1541, when, having successively passed through a number of hands, it finally came into the possession of the Lemmi in 1824. For Giovanni Tornabuoni, the elder, whose sister Lucrezia became the wife of Piero de' Medici, Il Gottoso, and the mother of Lorenzo, Il Magnifico, Domenico Ghirlandaio painted the choir of the church of Santa Maria Novella. These famous frescoes were begun in the year 1485 and finished in 1490; and Vasari, after describing them at length, adds that "for the same Giovanni Tornabuoni [Ghirlandaio] painted at the Chasso Maccherelli [*i.e.*, Chiasso Macerelli], his villa not far distant from the city, a chapel on the torrent of the Terzolle, which is to-day half ruined through its nearness to the stream." Of this chapel, which must have stood at some little distance from the villa, since the stream of the Terzolle is not upon the same side of the road as the house, there were still some traces remaining in 1832. The villa is a quadrangular building of two stories surrounding a courtyard, with a projecting wing, containing an open loggia at the south-west angle; and the east side of the house abuts on a bye road which leads up from the Chiasso Macerelli in the direction of Montughi. The frescoes were discovered on the upper floor of the villa, on the side towards Fiesole and the north-east, in a room which originally measured, before a portion was partitioned off to form a passage-way, 29 ft. 2½ in. in length, by 17 ft. 2½ in. in breadth. At that time, I believe, it was used as one of the kitchen offices. The room was lighted by two small windows in the two longer walls of the room; one of them looking north-east, the other south-west, into the courtyard; and it was entered from the adjoining rooms on the other two sides. Some traces of painting having been observed under the whitewash, with which the room was covered, the owner took steps to have them laid bare. It soon became evident that, at one time, the whole of the room had been decorated with paintings; but only on two of the walls were any considerable remains to be found. On the exterior wall towards the north-east, the two paintings were uncovered which, as subsequent research has shown, represent Lorenzo, the son of Giovanni Tornabuoni, in the circle of the

Seven Liberal Arts, and his young wife, Giovanna, with Venus and the Three Graces. These paintings were afterwards removed and sold to the Louvre. On the opposite wall, to the right of the window looking into the courtyard, were found the remains of another painting by the same hand, consisting of the figure of an old man in the scarlet habit of a Gonfalonier, with his right arm round a girl, who is beside him. The head of the girl is much damaged, and that of the man entirely effaced. These figures are seen at three-quarter length, standing behind the parapet of a loggia, over which is thrown a red carpet, decorated with an oriental pattern in white. The top of this parapet is nearly 4 ft. from the floor of the room. Beside the figures is a rosebush; and in the background is a river winding between some hills, and laden with boats; and a number of little figures on the banks, touched in with great mastery of hand. This ruined painting measured 6 ft. 3 in. in height, and 4 ft. 3½ in. in breadth. It is probable that it may have represented Giovanni Tornabuoni, who was "Gonfaloniere di Giustitia" in 1482, and his young daughter; and that the room originally contained the portraits of all his family. The fragment in question was left in situ, when the other paintings were cut from the walls.

The two paintings now in the Louvre were separated from one another by the window in the north wall, and were inclosed by pilasters decorated with arabesques on either side, and by a plinth below, as if seen through the openings of a loggia: of these painted ornaments some portions have been preserved. The deplorable condition of these paintings is in a great measure due to the fact that they were laid in "a fresco," and largely finished "a secco"; and that much of the superficial painting in tempera has perished, or come away with the whitewash, leaving the under-painting stripped. Nor was this the only cause that contributed to their present condition. At one time, owing to the rain having been allowed to make its way through the roof, it became necessary to remove the original wooden ceiling, with its beams and corbels; and in so doing the upper part of the paintings on the walls appear to have been greatly damaged. Moreover, during the vicissitudes which the room had undergone in the course of four centuries, large patches of the "intonaco" have been destroyed, which are now filled with plain plaster. Messrs. Cavalcaselle and Crowe, who saw the paintings before they were cut out of the wall of the villa, and sold to the Louvre in 1882, state that they had not only lost greatly in effect by their removal from their original position, but that actual surface of the paintings had also suffered much in the process.

Cavalcaselle and Crowe, ed. Le Monnier, VI, 262.

The portraits of Lorenzo Tornabuoni and his wife Giovanna, in these frescoes, are to be recognized from two medals, attributed to Niccolò Fiorentino, which were struck to commemorate their marriage in 1486. The medal of Lorenzo bears on the obverse, his head in profile with the legend: LAVRENTIVS . TORNABONVS . IO . FI . : and on the reverse a figure of Mercury. Lorenzo was born on 10th August, 1468, and his education was directed by Poliziano, the tutor of his cousin, Pierino de' Medici. More than one letter of Poliziano's bears evidence of the care and affection which he had for the nephew of his patron. In the dedication of his latin poem, entitled "Ambra, in poetae Homeri enarratione pronuntiata," the third of the "Sylvae," Poliziano, who inscribes the poem to Lorenzo Tornabuoni, speaks of his study of Homer, "nam et Homeri studiosus es quasique noster consectaneus"; and adds that he dedicates the poem to him, "ut sit amoris

A. Poliziano, Prose Volgari, etc., ed. Del Lungo, p. 333.

nostri monimentum, sit incitamentum tibi ad studia literarum, praesertimque graecarum: in quibus tamen ita tantum processisti, ut videare ad summum brevi, si modo perrexeris, evasurus." The dedication is dated from Florence, "pridie nonas Novembres MCCCCLXXXV", the year before Lorenzo's marriage. The medal of his wife, Giovanna, likewise contains her head in profile on the obverse, with the legend, IOANNA . ALBIZA . VXOR . LAVRENTII . DETORNABONIS; and on the reverse, on some copies, the three naked Graces, copied from the antique, and inscribed, CASTITAS, PVLCHRITVDO, AMOR. Giovanna, the daughter of Maso degli Albizzi, "a lady of singular beauty," says Scipione Ammirato, in his unfinished work, "Delle Famiglie Nobili Fiorentine," "was married in the year 1486, on 15th June, to Lorenzo Tornabuoni." Their marriage was arranged by Lorenzo, Il Magnifico, himself, adds Ammirato, who goes on to describe the splendour of their nuptials. If we may believe all that their contemporaries have left in praise of them, Lorenzo and Giovanna were "the exampled pair and mirror of their kind." "Ma è vero che l'estremo del riso è occupato dal pianto," as her historian reflects: and the marriage, begun amid such auspicious circumstances, was destined to end with the greatest measure of unhappiness. Giovanna died in the second year of her marriage while giving birth to her second child, as we learn from the epitaph which Poliziano composed for her tomb:

J. Friedlaender, Die Italienischen Schaumünzen, pl. XXVIII, No. 13.

l.c., ed. 1615, p. 42.

"Stirpe fui, forma, natoque, opibusque, viroque
Felix, ingenio, moribus atque animo.
Sed cum alter partus jam nuptae ageretur et annus,
Heu! nondum nata cum sobole interii.
Tristius ut caderem, tantum mihi Parca bonorum
Ostendit potius perfida quam tribuit."

A. Poliziano, Prose Volgari, etc., ed. Del Lungo, p. 154.

In 1488, the year of Giovanna's death, Domenico Ghirlandaio painted the beautiful portrait of her, which for many years was exhibited at the National Gallery, and afterwards sold to M. Rodolphe Kann, of Paris. It represents Giovanna at half-length, in profile to the left: in the background is a cartellino inscribed:

ARS VTINAM MORES ANIMVMQVE EFFINGERE POSSES,
PVLCHRIOR IN TERRIS NVLLA TABELLA FORET. MCCCCLXXXVIII.

The fate of her husband was yet more tragic; his family had, since the marriage of Lucrezia Tornabuoni with Piero, Il Gottoso, been great supporters of the Medici; and in 1497, Lorenzo Tornabuoni with Gianozzo Pucci (whose marriage Botticelli also commemorated in a series of paintings) and three other noble Florentines, were arrested by the faction of Savonarola, on a charge of conspiring to restore Piero di Lorenzo de' Medici. They were condemned to death, and executed on the night of 17th August, 1497, as Lucca Landucci records in his "Diary," adding with a touch of emotion, to which that good diarist rarely gives way, "che non fu sanza lacrime di me, quando vidi passare a' Tornaquinci, in una bara, quel giovanetto Lorenzo, inanzi dì poco."

L. Landucci, Diario, p. 156.

Besides the portraits which I have mentioned, Domenico Ghirlandaio painted both Lorenzo and Giovanna in the frescoes of the choir of Santa Maria Novella; Lorenzo, in the story of "St. Joachim driven out of the Temple"; and Giovanna in the story of the "Visitation."

Of the two wall-paintings, now on the staircase of the Louvre, that

LORENZO TORNABUONI AND THE LIBERAL ARTS *Louvre, Paris*

representing Lorenzo Tornabuoni with the Seven Liberal Arts, No. 1298, originally filled the wall to the right of the window in Villa Lemmi. The Seven Liberal Arts formed the Trivium and Quadrivium of mediæval studies: Grammar, Dialectic, Rhetoric, the Trivium; and Arithmetic, Music, Geometry, and Astrology, the Quadrivium. The course in Arts at our Universities, is the modern equivalent to these studies. Burchiello, the barber-poet, who flourished at Florence, in the age of Cosimo di Medici, has celebrated in one of his sonnets, these arts and their virtues:

"Septe son larti liberali: & prima
Grammatica dellaltre e uia & porta;
Loyca laseconda, per cui scorta
Iluero dal falso si cognosce & 'lima;
Rectorica laterza, che per rima
Parlando improsa luditor conforta;
Arismetrica laquarta, la uia torta
Per numeri diriga a uera stima;
Et laquinta si e Geometria,
che ogni cosa con ragion misura;
Musica e lasexta melodia,
che suona & canta con gran dirictura;
La septima si e Astrologia
chel ciel qua giu cimostra per figura:
Soprogni creatura
Sarebbe chi sapesse ciaschuna arte;
Ma contento sipuo chi nesa parte.

Burchiello, Sonetti, ed. 1514, sig. L recto.

Unlike the designer of the Liberal Arts on the North Italian engraved "Tarocchi Cards," Botticelli gives his figures the same symbols as the figures of the Arts and Sciences in the fresco of the "Triumph of St. Thomas Aquinas," on the left wall of the Spanish Chapel, or Chapter House, of Santa Maria Novella.

Lorenzo Tornabuoni is represented in this painting with long hair, and wearing a red biretta and a long plain Florentine dress, shot with red in the shadows. A young woman leads him by the right hand towards a group of women, who are seated in a round, in the clearing of a wood. Raised above the rest, who sit upon the ground, is a figure more magisterial than the others, dressed in an ample robe of blue, lined with fur. But let me illustrate these allegorical figures by a writer of the twelfth century, who comes to my hand, Alain de L'Isle, Bishop of Auxerre. He thus describes them in his Latin poem, entitled, "Cyclopaediae Anticlaudiani, seu de Officio Viri Boni":

"Cautae, prudentes, pulchrae, similesque puellae
Septem, quae vultum sub septem vultibus unum
Reddunt, quas facias, genus, aestas, forma, potestas
Una tenet, tenet una fides, tenet una voluntas,
Assistunt Phronesi, Phronesis decreta sequuntur."

ed. T. Wright, Dist. II, Cap. VI, v. 16.

In the fresco, Phronesis (whom Alain de L'Isle feigns to be the charioteer of the car of Wisdom,) holds in her left hand a bow, and raises her right hand, as she addresses Lorenzo. In the fresco in the Spanish Chapel, Philosophy holds an arrow in one hand, and a bow in the other.

The figure of the woman who is leading Lorenzo into the circle of the

Arts, is clad in a red cloak, which she wears over a long, ungirdled white robe. She carries no symbol to distinguish her; but the figure doubtless is intended to personify Grammar, which, as Burchiello says, "of all the other arts, is the way and the gate." In the paintings of the Spanish Chapel, two boys are represented kneeling before the figure of Grammar, who is about to unlock the door of a narrow portal, which is beside her.

Of the three figures who are sitting on the right hand of Phronesis, the outermost is Rhetoric, in a dress of green, with dishevelled hair, holding an open scroll in her right hand. The scroll which the figure of Rhetoric in the Spanish Chapel holds, is inscribed, "Mulceo dum loquor varios induta colores." Next to her is Dialectic, or Logic, in a yellow dress with the sleeves slit and laced; and with her hair confined by a kerchief which falls over her shoulders. In her right hand she holds what appears to be a rod; but which is probably the wand of a flowering branch, such as the figure of Logic in the Spanish Chapel holds: in the left she holds a scorpion.

ed. T. Wright, Dist. III, Cap. I, v. 25.

"Dextra manus florum donatur honore, sinistram
Scorpius accendens caudae mucrone minatur."

The third figure, next to Phronesis, in a robe of grape-purple lined with blue, represents Arithmetic; she holds in her left hand a table inscribed with Pythagorean figures:

Id., Dist. III, Cap. IV, v. 17.

"Mensam Pythagorae, quae menti pabula donat,
Delicias animi sapiens, non corporis escas,
Sustinet una manus."

On the left hand of Phronesis, and seated next to her, is Geometry in a green dress, with her hair fantastically plaited after the elaborate fashion in which the Botticelli delights. She carries over her left shoulder a large square.

Next to Geometry, in a hooded dress of yellow and grape-purple, is Astrology, who holds an Armillary sphere in front of her:

Id., Dist. IV, Cap. I, v. 11.

"Implet sphaera manum."

The last of the three figures seated on the left of Phronesis, represents Music. She is in a blue dress, her red cloak having fallen about her waist, and her back is turned toward the spectator, as she blows with her left hand, the bellows of a small portative organ, and touches the keys with her right. In this symbol of the portative organ, as in the square which Geometry carries, Botticelli follows the paintings in the Spanish Chapel, rather than the descriptions of Alain de l'Isle.

The lower portions of the figures of Astrology and Music have been destroyed, as well as the lower part of the figure of Lorenzo with a "putto" at his side, of which only the head remains. M. Ephrussi states that the body of this "putto" and a shield which he held, have disappeared since 1873. The shield was probably blazoned with the arms of the Tornabuoni. In the background of the picture is a thick wood, prefiguring, perhaps, the "selva oscura" of the natural world. This foliage, like the foreground of the picture, having been entirely finished "a secco," little more than the under-painting in fresco now remains. The fragment in the Louvre, which includes a part of the painted pilaster on the right, and of the plinth below,

GIOVANNA TORNABUONI WITH VENUS AND THE GRACES *Louvre, Paris*

measures 7 feet 10 inches in height, by 8 feet 10¾ inches in length. On the pedestal of the pilaster, to the right, may be seen the traces of a shield bearing the arms of the Albizzi; sable, two annulets concentric or; which seems to form the first sketch for a part of the design which was afterwards altered.

In the second wall-painting now in the Louvre, No. 1297, Giovanna is represented almost as in Ghirlandaio's fresco, standing in profile to the left, in a long, plain dress of purple velvet, made in the fashion of the time, with cut sleeves, and embroidered with pearls on the bodice. Round her neck is a string of pearls, from which hangs a jewel at her throat; and a white kerchief covers her head. She stands on the right of the picture, with both hands extended, holding a linen cloth, into which Venus, who steps towards her, is about to drop a handful of flowers, (according to the Florentine commentators,) of which only the rough outlines sketched upon the "intonaco," now remain. This motive, in which the whole meaning of the painting centres, contains, perhaps, some allusion which is yet to be elucidated. The figure of Venus is draped, as in the picture of the "Spring," but of a form more girlish and virginal. Her hair is plaited, and she wears a long, white dress, embroidered at the neck, about which is thrown a robe of a rosy red colour, flowered with gold. She is followed by the Graces in dresses of yellow and white and green and grape-purple, who tread with naked feet over the flowery sward. Beside the figure of Giovanna, is a winged "putto" bearing a shield, now nearly destroyed, which was probably blazoned with the arms of the Albizzi. The scene is laid within a walled garden: the grass, which was originally elaborated, painted with flowers "a secco," is so perished that little remains except the dark green of the under-painting; the figures are relieved against what appears to be the wall of the garden, and on the left of the picture is a sun-dial, or fountain, and some flowers. A portion of the head of Venus, her left leg and the legs of the Grace beside her, have been destroyed. The fragment in the Louvre, which includes part of the pilaster on the right side, measures 6 feet 11¼ inches in height, and 9 feet 4¼ inches in length. According to Signor Conti, a portion of this fresco beyond the fountain had been destroyed by the construction of the passage-way and partition wall, mentioned above. It originally filled the wall to the left of the window.

In spite of their damaged condition, these wall-paintings still rank among the rarest and most charming of Botticelli's inventions; and, like the "Spring" and the "Birth of Venus," more nearly in the spirit of Greek art, than anything which Florentine Painting had as yet produced. "Reanimate Greek," Ruskin has called Botticelli: certainly in the blytheness and incomparable fusion of the ideal with the naturalistic, which characterize these wall-paintings, there is no little measure of justification for the phrase. The figures of Lucrezia Tornabuoni with Venus and the Graces, are among the gayest and most living of all the creatures that move in the world of Botticelli's imagination, with nothing of that sense of "loss or displacement" about them, which has been thought an invariable colour of his mood. In these delightful figures, we seem rather to meet again, in statelier and more solemn guise, those sweet, wholesome Tuscan girls, who still live in the "Fiammetta" of Boccaccio, or the catches of Franco Sacchetti's, which Rossetti has done into English.

Gayer and more characteristic in colour, than the paintings of Botticelli in true fresco, they recall his finest drawings in the spontaneity of their execution, and the expressive beauty of their line. In the composition of the painting of "Lorenzo Tornabuoni with the Liberal Arts," may be noted the disposition of the two groups of the three figures of the Arts, placed opposite to, and balancing, one another; an arrangement which again occurs in the little picture of the "Last Communion of St. Jerome," and with greater elaboration in the "Calumny of Apelles."

On the back of a sheet of architectural drawings by the hand of Giuliano da San Gallo, among the unexhibited drawings in the Uffizi, Catagoria II, No. 1567A, is a study in pen and ink, washed with bistre, and heightened with white, of the figure of the Grace on the extreme left of Botticelli's wall-painting of "Lucrezia Tornabuoni, with Venus and the Graces." Of Giuliano da San Gallo as a figure draughtsman, I shall speak at length when I come to discuss the imitators of Botticelli. The drawing in question is the only trace which we have, of any influence which these wall-paintings may have exercised over Sandro's contemporaries.

The story of that incomparable painting, the "Birth of Venus," has already been told, by the way, in the foregoing account of the no less famous picture of the "Spring." Like the "Spring," it was painted, but at a later time, for the decoration of Castello, the villa of Lorenzo and Giovanni, the sons of Pierfrancesco de' Medici: and no doubt it was one

App. II, Doc. II, fol. 85, recto.

of the pictures by Botticelli, which the "Anonimo Gaddiano" mentions as being at Castello, at the time that the Villa was in the possession of Giovanni delle Bande Nere, between 1503 and 1526. The earliest direct

Vasari, ed. 1550, I, 492.

allusion to this painting occurs in the first edition of the "Lives" of Vasari, who says that there were at Castello two paintings of Venus; one representing "the birth of Venus, and those airs and winds that bring her

App. II, Doc. XVI.

to land with the Loves." In the inventory, which I have already cited, of the household goods and furniture which were at Castello in 1598, the picture is described as "one large painting on canvas, antique, in which is painted a Venus above a shell, with other figures, in a gilt frame": it then hung in the "Chamber of the Grand Duke, on the ground floor." It is

App. II, Doc. XVII, fol. 1, tergo.

again described in similar terms in another inventory of the household goods in the Villa of Castello, taken in the year 1638. The picture remained at Castello until 1815, when it was brought to the Gallery of the Uffizi, where it is still preserved, No. 39. Unlike the picture of the "Spring," it is painted on canvas: it measures 5 feet $6\frac{3}{4}$ inches in height by 9 feet $\frac{1}{4}$ inch in length. The two strips of canvas on which it is painted, have been sewn together in the direction of the length of the picture. But to come to a description of the painting.

The Goddess, amid a shower of roses, stands naked in the little bark of the shell, in the attitude of the Medicean Venus. On the left of the picture, two winged zephyrs "blow hard across the gray water, moving forward the dainty-lipped shell on which she sails; the sea 'showing his teeth' on thin lines of foam, and sucking in one by one the falling roses, each severe in outline, plucked off short at the stalk, but embrowned a little, as Botticelli's roses always are." On the other side, a nymph in an ample dress of white, powdered with sprigs of corn-cockle, having a wreath of myrtle about the neck, and girdled about the waist with rose-branches, steps forward on the shore, ready to cast a purple cloak, sprinkled with knots of daisies, about the naked goddess, as soon as she shall step to land. The orange trees are in flower; and along the water's edge, the distant shore juts out into little promontories in the clear morning air.

The subject of the Birth of Venus, it has been argued, but with more

THE BIRTH OF VENUS *Uffizi Gallery, Florence*

reason than in the case of the "Spring," was taken from the "Stanze" of Poliziano, begun in celebration of the joust of Giuliano de' Medici. A passage of the first book of the "Stanze," written in imitation of the description of the gates of the Temple of Phœbus, in the sixth book of the Æneid, describes the doors of the Palace of Venus storied with the feuds and Loves of the gods:

"Mille et mille colori formon le porte
Di gemme, et di si uiui intagli chiare,
Che tutte altre opre sarien roze et morte,
Da far di se natura uergognare." Ed. 1494, Lib. I, St. 97.

In one is cut the unhappy lot of ancient Cælius, in others the stories of Vulcan, Jupiter and Europa, Bacchus and Ariadne; and among the rest, the birth of Venus, which is described in the following verses:

"Nel tempestoso Egeo in grembo a Tethi, Lib. I, St. 99-103.
Siuede il fusto genitale accolto
Sotto diuerso uolger di pianeti
Errar per londe in biancha schiuma auolto;
E dentro nata in acti uaghi et lieti,
Vna donzella non con human uolto,
Da zephiri lasciui spinta a proda,
Gir soura un Nichio; et par chel ciel ne goda.

"Vera la schiuma, et uero el mar, diresti,
Et uero il nichio, et uer soffiar di uenti:
La dea negliochi folgorar, uedresti,
E il ciel riderle atorno et glielementi:
Lhore priemer larena in bianche uesti;
Laura in cresparle ecrini distesi e lenti:
Non una non diuersa esser lor faccia,
Come par che a sorelle ben confaccia.

"Giurar potresti che dellonde uscissi
La Dea premendo colla dextra il crino,
Collaltra il dolce pomo ricoprissi:
Et stampata dal pie sacro et diuino,
Dherba et di fiori larena si uestissi:
Poi con sembiante lieto et peregrino,
Dalle tre nymphe in grembo fussi accolta,
E di stellato uestimento inuolta.

"Questa con ambe man le tien sospesa
Sopra lumide trecce una ghirlanda
Doro et di gemme orientali accesa:
Questa una perla alli orechi accomanda:
Laltra al bel pecto e bianchi homeri intesa
Par che richi monili intorno spanda,
De qua soleano cerchiar lor proprie gole
Quando nel ciel guidauono le carole.

" Indi paion leuate in uer le ſpere
Seder sopra una nuuola dargento:
Laer tremante ti parria uedere
Nel duro saxo, et tutto il ciel contento;
Tutti li Dei di sua bilta godere
Et del felice lecto hauer talento;
Ciascun sembrar nel uolto marauiglia,
Con fronte crespa, e rileuate ciglia."

It would seem that in this description of the birth of Venus, Poliziano intended to describe the lost painting of Venus Anodyomene, by Apelles. In a letter written in 1494, nearly twenty years after the "Stanze" had been begun and discarded, Poliziano sent to Antonio Urcèo Codro, at Bologna, some specimens "taken at chance," of a little book of Greek epigrams, which he had lately composed. "Read first, then," he says, "what I have composed in imitation of not a few ancient writers upon the Venus of Apelles which our Pliny calls Anadyomene, and worthily described," he says, "in certain Greek verses, by which it may still be illustrated." In the epigram that follows, the attitude of the Venus in the painting is thus described:

A. Politianus, Opera, ed. 1519, fol. 46, tergo.

Καὶ τᾷ μὲν ῥαθάμιγγας ἁλιβρέκτοιο καράνου
Δεξιτερᾷ θλίβεν, καὶ κελάρυζεν ἀφρός,
. . . . ἁδέ γε λαιᾷ
Ἔσκεπε τὰν ἅβαν τὰν ἔθ' ὑποβρύχιον, . . .

or in the Latin version of Jacques Toussain:

" Et manu quidem guttas mari perfusi capitis
Dextera stringebat, & resonabat spuma
. . . at laeva
Tegebat pubem adhuc demersam," . . .

The Greek verses "tot antiquorum," from which this epigram was imitated, were doubtlessly the five epigrams by Antipater Sidonius, Archias, Democritus, Julianus Aegyptius, and Leonidas, which are to be found in the fourth Book of the Greek Anthology of Maximus Planudes, printed for the first time at Florence, in 1494. These and other ancient allusions to the painting of Apelles, with one exception occasioned, apparently, by the exigences of the scansion of the verse, are in complete agreement in describing the figure of Venus as wringing the ooze out of her hair with her hands; the word being used in the plural. In no instance is any mention made of one hand "tegens pubem," as Poliziano has it. Indeed, it is scarcely probable that this Venus was in such an attitude, since it is generally supposed that the lower part of the figure was still in the water. All the existing works of art which appear to be derived from the painting of Apelles, show both hands wringing out the hair. On the other hand, there is a type of statue which represents Venus with the legs draped, and the hands practically in the attitude of the Medicean Venus; the one screening her bosom with her hair, and the other covering the pubes. Copies of this statue were certainly existing early in the Middle Age; so that Poliziano may well have been acquainted with a marble, or other copy of this type, and so have been led into the error of supposing it to be the Venus Anadyomene of Apelles. Again it is clear Poliziano had this type of statue more exclusively in his mind in the "Stanze," where he describes Venus "premendo colla dextra il crino," than in the Epigram, where, partly following the Epigrammatists of the Greek Anthology, he makes her wringing out her hair with her right hand. Botticelli represents his Venus pressing her right hand against her breast, while with the left she gathers about her the tresses of her hair, to hide her nakedness. His choice of this attitude may be explained in two ways; either by supposing that the type of statue in question, commonly passed in Florence, in the fifteenth century, as the Venus Anadyomene of Apelles, and that Botticelli was familiar with it, as he probably was with the type of the Medicean Venus; or that the painter took the subject of his picture from the "Stanze" of Poliziano. The latter explanation is by far the more probable; for although Botticelli departs from Poliziano's description in certain minor particulars, it is evident that he had the passage in mind, while designing more things in the picture than the attitude of the principal figure. In all that part of its design in which the damsel "of more than human countenance" is driven to shore by the breath of the wanton zephyrs, while the heavens laugh around her as she goes forward on the shell, the painter has followed the poet; but in place of the three nymphs who in the poem cover the goddess with a garment sprinkled with stars, as she steps to shore, Botticelli, for the greater simplicity of his design, introduces but a single figure. It would seem, then, that Botticelli invented the picture, with Poliziano's verses before him, interpreting this passage as he conceived its meaning, or modifying that as the nature of his design seemed to demand.

The poet recovers the story as a scholar, from out the vestiges of the vanished Greek world, relying on the felicity of a phrase, or the beauty with which he turns a familiar image, for the effect of his verses: the painter, ever careful of that tradition of naturalism which, for him, is an inseparable part of his art, seeks to refashion the legend out of his vision of the sensuous world around him, of what is "here and now." In place of the "stormy Aegean," Botticelli paints the water which has given birth to this damsel of more than human mould, as he may have seen it on his way to Rome, at Trasimeno, or Bolsena. The low, grassy dunes run down to the edge of the water which breaks under the light winds, into little waves among the bulrushes at the shore, only to stretch away at the horizon, serene and motionless as the sky above it. In the nude figure of the Venus Botticelli is careful to preserve the expressive, rather than beautiful, Tuscan type as he found it at Florence; scrupulously noting the long oval of the head, set on the lithe neck and drooping shoulders; the body big in structure and proportions, though angular in form, and heavy at the articulations of the joints; the arms large, the breasts little and rounded, the hands plebeian with thick joints and broad, square nails. Even the abundant golden hair, which at first sight might appear a piece of pedantry borrowed from the antique, is found to be an actual Florentine trait.

"Se poi si tira su le bionde trecce
Decco la donna di sette bellezze"

ends one of the Florentine "Rispetti" on the seven beauties which a woman ought to possess. Yet all these lineaments and characters, literally copied from the actual type around him, become in this figure of Venus transfigured by the sentiment of which they are themselves the expression.

Clad in the proper robes of the gods, this "donzella" wears her garments of nakedness like some cloistral habit; and comes on with a high, ineffable blytheness, which savours rather of the circles of Paradise, than of the heights of Olympus.

The colour, "cadaverous, or at least cold," which Pater noticed in the picture, is partly due to the fact that the medium, the glair and yolk of egg, with which the pigments were tempered, has much deteriorated in consequence of the canvas on which the picture is painted, not having afforded it the same projection as a panel, and partly because the painting has not been varnished, which is a great preservative against the action of the atmosphere, and particularly against damp, from which it appears to have suffered. Otherwise it is well preserved, although it is not in the untouched condition of the "Spring"; but it appears to have suffered rather from over-cleaning, than from repainting. Its surface has, however, been retouched in places; and a number of these retouches have darkened with time; but the worst damage has befallen the right arm of the Venus, which has been partially gone over, and much of the beauty of its outline destroyed. The left margin of the picture, especially about the feet of the Winds, has become discoloured, apparently through damp.

Unmistakable traits of form and manner are not wanting to show, that this picture of the "Birth of Venus" was executed some years subsequently to the "Spring." The tilt of the nude figure of Venus, used here to express a sense of forward motion, the greater mannerism in the drawing of the heads and the cast of the draperies, the character of the landscape, the severe, almost formal, design of the orange trees, the convention employed to represent the grass in the foreground, a convention peculiarly characteristic of many of Botticelli's last pictures, and the free use of gold in heightening the lights, especially the elaborate hatching on the purple cloak held by the nymph, all tend to show that this picture was executed at a somewhat later date than the Bardi altarpiece, now at Berlin. In manner, this painting approaches nearest to the two wall paintings in the Louvre, which came from the Villa Lemmi, and which are known to have been executed shortly after the month of June, 1486.

In point of execution, the whole of this painting is not, perhaps, of equal excellence. I seem to detect the hand of an assistant in some of the draperies, especially in the white dress of the nymph which, however admirable in design, and in the manner in which it expresses the movement of the figure, and heightens the mass of the limbs, is, nevertheless, a little mechanical in many of the details of its folds. This is not the only instance in one of Botticelli's principal works, of a passage which obviously lacks the fine drawing, and perfectly realized intention, of the cartoon from which it was painted. The figure of Venus, however, possesses all the most subtile and rhythmical qualities of Botticelli's line. In the exquisite art by which the masses of her hair, caught by the breath of the Winds, are portrayed with a sense of hieratic voluptuousness, "sicut purpura regis," Botticelli forestalls something of Leonardo's power of giving definite expression to the fleeting shapes of such mutable things, as clouds or waves. Scarcely less admirable is the design of the interlocked figures of the Zephyrs, and the rendering of the swift movement by which they come forward.

But if in execution the picture is less equal than some of the other paintings by Botticelli, in conception it is, perhaps, among the greatest of his works. As a piece of imagination, this picture must always rank among the supreme creations of Italian painting in the fifteenth century. Unlike not a few of Botticelli's great inventions, it presents a single and entire action: and the ingenuous, but dramatic, treatment of its theme serves to lift it above the level of mere allegory, the strain of which still colours the "Spring" and the "Calumny of Apelles." The avoidance of everything extraneous to the action of the picture, lends to it some more actual quality of antique simplicity, than its author was, perhaps, consciously striving to recover. Nowhere does Botticelli so completely break away from the usages of that school of mediaeval painting, from which he derived his art; nowhere, as in this painting of the "Birth of Venus," does he so nearly anticipate the temper of our modern tradition of historical and dramatic painting, which began to be formulated in Italy during the sixteenth century, in the attempt to recur to the spirit of classic art.

An old copy on canvas of the figure of Venus against a dark background, is in the Museum at Berlin, No. 1124. This copy, which is coarse in drawing and crude in colouring, presents some variations from the original in the design of the hair, and in the addition of the two plaits, which fall over the shoulders. A large part of the falling hair on the right side of the figure, may be seen painted out, under the dark background. Two similar paintings of a Venus, on panel, were formerly in the collection of the Rev. Walter Davenport Bromley, which was dispersed in 1863. One of them is described by Dr. Waagen in his "Treasures of Art in Great Britain," as a "whole-length figure of Venus, only lightly draped with a blue garment, a somewhat slighter repetition of the picture in the Berlin Museum, with a few alterations": the other, also a whole-length figure, holding a garland of roses, came from the Palazzo Ferroni, in Florence. In the new Florentine edition of their "History of Painting in Italy," Messrs. Cavalcaselle and Crowe ascribe both these panels to the school of Botticelli. One, if not both, of them afterwards passed into the collection of Lord Ashburton, and probably perished in the fire at Bath House, London. According to Antonio Petrei's version of the "Libro di Billi," Botticelli painted "many naked women, which were more beautiful than anything else which he did." The "Anonimo Gaddiano," also, states that Botticelli painted "many, most beautiful naked women"; and Vasari, in the first edition of the "Lives," records "that throughout the city, in divers houses," were "many naked women," by his hand. All such paintings by the master himself have long since been lost, or destroyed. The "Venus" with the garland of roses, once in the Davenport Bromley collection, may well have been a school version of some lost original by Botticelli; and the naked "Venus" against a dark background, by Lorenzo di Credi, now in the Uffizi, No. 3452, probably owed its suggestion to one or another of these pictures. Their early disappearance must largely be attributed to the work of fanaticism. "Figure ignude," "figures and portraits of beautiful women, the work of the first painters and sculptors of the time," were among "the vain things of great price," which went to heap up Savonarola's Bonfire of Vanities: and those paintings of the nude by Botticelli, which may have survived this outbreak of Puritanism, could have fared little better in the later times of the Catholic Reaction, when such pictures of the "antichi moderni" were no longer held in esteem as works of art.

l.c., III, p. 374.

l.c., ed. Le Monnier, VI, 301.

App. II, Doc. I, fol. 49, tergo.

App. II, Doc. II, fol. 85, recto.

Vasari, ed. 1550, I, 492.

Signor Milanesi, citing some document, which in spite of a repeated search, I have been unable to trace, states in his notes to the last Florentine edition of Vasari, that in 1487, Botticelli painted a circular picture for the audience chamber of the "Magistrato de' Massai della Camera": "nel 1487 dipinse un tondo per la Sala dell' Udienza del Magistrato de' Massai della Camera." The omission of any reference to the subject of this picture, or to the price paid for it, would seem to show that Signor Milanesi was not acquainted with the document in its original form; but had drawn his information from some such source as the "Spogli" of the Senator Carlo Strozzi, or some later antiquary. The "Magistrato de' Massai della Camera," according to Benedetto Varchi in his Florentine Histories, was a Magistracy of two citizens, who took account of all judicial sentences; with authority to compound them, or reduce their penalties, as they might deem reasonable: besides this, they had the care of all public records of a certain date. This Magistracy, which was abolished in 1533, had its court, or "Sala dell' Udienza," in the Palazzo Vecchio.

Vasari, ed. Sansoni, III, 322, note.

l.c., Lib. XIV, Cap. X.

Among the pictures of the Grand Ducal collection at Florence, is a circular panel by Botticelli, which is not only a work of the time in question, but which, also, may well have come from one of the offices of the Republic. This is the famous "tondo," called the "Madonna of the Pomegranate," in the Uffizi, No. 1289, which was brought to the Gallery in December, 1780, from the Guardaroba of the Palazzo Pitti. In the seventeenth century, it had already formed part of the collection of Cardinal Leopoldo de' Medici; and it is thus described in the inventory of his effects, dated 14th November, 1675: "a picture on panel, round, $2\frac{1}{3}$ braccia in diameter, wherein is painted Our Lady seated with the Child in her arms, and with six angels at rather more than half-length, one of whom holds in his hand a lily, by the hand of Botticelli, with a frame carved, and in part gilded, with a blue ground." The painting still retains its original carved and gilded frame; the principal member of which is decorated with a diaper of fleurs-de-lys, on a blue ground; a device that might be taken to show that it had been executed for some office of the Republic.

Vasari, ed. Sansoni, III, 329.

App. II, Doc. XXVII. fol. 77, tergo.

This picture is painted on a panel measuring four feet eight inches in diameter. Unlike the "tondo of the Magnificat," it has almost escaped the hands of the restorer, and remains in a fine state of preservation. The retouches, which may be detected on its surface, are local and unimportant; and the coat of dirt, which obscures the original brilliancy of its colouring, is a proof of its condition. It represents the Virgin at three-quarter length, seated almost in full face, in the centre of the panel, and holding the Child, who raises his right hand in the act of benediction, and lays the other on a pomegranate, the symbol of the Fall, which his mother is holding. Encircling the Virgin, are six winged figures of angels; three upon either side. The two outer figures, which are seen to the knee, bear lily-wands; and the stole on the breast of the angel on the left, bears the legend thrice repeated, AVE GRAZIA PLENA. They lean upon a rope of roses, which is suspended from behind the Virgin. Each of the angels next to them holds an open book; and from above, a halo of light is shed upon Mary.

Both by reason of its better preservation, and of the more exquisite qualities of its design and draughtsmanship, this "tondo" must be accounted a far rarer work of art, than the more popular painting of the "Madonna of the Magnificat." The motive of its composition, the circle of figures around the Virgin seen in perspective within the circle of the panel, is a device as remarkable for its originality, as for its simplicity and beauty. Nor is the picture less admirable in execution. Of the rhythmical, yet virile, quality

THE VIRGIN AND CHILD WITH SIX ANGELS—THE TONDO OF THE POMEGRANATE *Uffizi Gallery, Florence*

of Botticelli's line, expressive at once of subtile movement and delicate structure of form, no more fortunate example is to be found. In colour, the painting is still golden and luminous, in spite of its somewhat darkened condition. The smalt azure of the Virgin's mantle, repeated in the paler blue of the skyey background, is contrasted with the warm purple of her dress, the deeper reds of the roses and the golden purple of the dress of the angel on the right; which last is counterbalanced in its turn, by the golden yellow and white draperies of the angel, on the opposite side of the picture. In its original state, the picture must have possessed something of that actual quality of sunlight in the golden, luminous glow of its colouring, which still lingers for us in the "Calumny of Apelles," and in some of the other small panels of the master.

In this "tondo," perhaps, more than in any other work of the kind, Botticelli gives expression to that idea of the Madonna, the peculiar sentiment of which was afterwards seized upon and exaggerated by his disciples. Unlike the works of his followers, the sentiment in this picture, as in every genuine work of Botticelli, proceeds naturally out of his conception of the subject. To interpret this sentiment aright, we must understand his theme as he conceived it; a theme which, for him at least, would have admitted of no fantastical, or unreal, interpretation or treatment. If some colour of Dante, as I have sought to show, is to be traced in certain of Botticelli's earlier paintings of the Madonna, this painting, in its attempt to express by precise visual images of the world around us, the most transcendent and ineffable vision of heavenly things, is surely among the most Dantesque of his designs. Although the picture is not in any sense an illustration of this, or that, passage of the "Divina Commedia," the images of the poet may help us to interpret and understand the intention of the painter, as, perhaps, nothing else is able to do. It is, then, in a very definite, and even orthodox, sense, (if Dante be orthodox,) that Botticelli seeks to express by the forms and features of the human creature, the face "ch' a Cristo più s'assomiglia": and, like the poet, he allows the sensuous images of his imagination to inform and prefigure his intellectual conception of the Court of Heaven:

Ciò ch' io vedeva, mi sembrava un riso
Dell' universo: perchè mia ebbrezza
Entrava per l'udire e per lo viso.
O gioia! o ineffabile allegrezza!
O vita intera d'amore e di pace!
O senza brama sicura ricchezza!

Paradiso, xxvii. 4-9.

A good school-version of this "tondo," in a fine state of preservation, is in the collection of Mr. Julius Wernher, of London. Two of the six angels in the original have been omitted in this copy, and the colouring of the two pictures presents many differences. Indeed, there can be little doubt that this version was executed from Botticelli's cartoon, and not from the finished picture. Another copy of the figures of the Virgin and Child, painted on a circular-headed panel, against some architecture on the left, with a landscape beyond on the right, a feeble work of no individual character, was among the pictures of the late Mr. J. F. Leyland, of London, whose collection was dispersed in 1892.

Of a somewhat later date than the "tondo" of 1487, as I conjecture, is the painting of "Pallas and the Centaur," now in the Palazzo Pitti, at

Florence. But before I proceed to discuss this picture, I must point out that it is a wholly different work from the lost painting of Pallas, which, according to Vasari, Botticelli executed for Lorenzo, Il Magnifico. "In Casa Medici, for Lorenzo the elder," records Vasari in the first edition of the "Lives," Botticelli "executed many works, and chiefly a Pallas, above an impress of branches, which put forth fire; and this he painted as large as life." It seems that this device of "vna Pallade su vna impresa di bronconi, che buttavano fuoco," was borne by Giuliano de' Medici, the brother of Lorenzo. A contemporary account of the "Giostra," or Tourney, in which Giuliano, the knight of "La bella Simonetta," bore off the prize, in 1475, contains a particular description of all the trappings, shields, impresses, and other "tilting furniture" of the combatants, who entered the lists on that famous occasion. According to this account, in the equipage of Giuliano was a man-at-arms on horseback, who "bore a great staff painted blue, from which hung a standard of Alexandrine taffety, jagged and fringed about; and in the upper part of this standard was a sun, and in the middle a great figure in the likeness of Pallas, habited in a tunic of fine gold, which reached to the knees; and under the tunic was a white vestment shaded with finely ground gold, and a pair of buskins on her legs. And the feet of this figure rested upon two flames of fire; and from the said flames went forth other flames, which consumed certain branches of olive that were in the standard, from the middle downwards; and from the middle upwards were branches without fire. She had upon her head a burnished morion of antique form; and her locks, which were all inwove, fluttered to the wind. This same Pallas held in her right hand a tilting-lance, and in her left hand the shield of the Medusa. And near to this figure, was a field adorned with flowers of various colours, and from it rose the stump of an olive, to the trunk of which was bound, by a golden cord, a God of Love, with his hands behind him. And at his feet lay his bow, quiver, and broken arrows. There was set upon the trunk of the olive, to which was bound the God of Love, a legend of golden letters, in the French tongue, which read, LASANS PAR: and the aforesaid Pallas fixedly looked towards the sun, which was above her."

Vasari, ed. 1550, I. 492.

G. Poggi, La Giostra Medicea del 1475, e la 'Pallade' del Botticelli. App. II, Doc. XXVIII, fol. 122, tergo.

It would appear from another contemporary document, that this standard was painted by Andrea Verrocchio; for in an account rendered by the painter's heirs to Lorenzo, Il Magnifico, of various works, which Andrea had executed for the Medici, occurs the item: "Per dipintura d'uno stendardo ch*on* 1° spiritello per la Giostra di Giuliano." The design of this lost work of Verrocchio has, perhaps, in part come down to us. One of the panels of a richly intarsiated door, in the Ducal palace at Urbino, is inlaid with a figure of Pallas, which closely recalls the foregoing description of Giuliano's standard. This door, which bears the date 1505, is apparently of Florentine manufacture. The figure of Pallas habited in a tunic, worn over an underskirt, with a morion on her head and buskins on her feet, holds in her right hand a tilting-lance, and in her left a shield bearing the head of Medusa. Below the feet of the figure is a cluster of flames. There is much in the conception of this figure, in the form of the morion, and other ornaments, and in the design of the draperies, which recalls the manner of Verrocchio. Certainly, the original from which it was taken, must have been designed at least a score of years before the date of the execution of the door. Again, this figure of Pallas is looking up, in all probability, at the sun, which in the standard was above the goddess, but which is

C. de Fabriczy, Andrea del Verrocchio ai servigi dei Medici.

omitted in the intarsia panel. Altogether then, we may not unreasonably hazard the conjecture, that the design of the panel may be a version of a part of Verrocchio's standard, redrawn to satisfy the requirements of the intarsia-worker.

Such an allegory of Pallas appears to have been the subject of the decorative painting recorded by Vasari, which Botticelli executed for Casa Medici. In the inventory of the goods of Lorenzo, Il Magnifico, taken at the time of his death in 1492, an ancient copy of which is preserved among the Florentine Archives, are enumerated only two works by Botticelli, among the contents of the palace in the Via Larga, now known as the Palazzo Riccardi. One of these was the tester of a bed; the other, which hung "in the chamber of Piero," is thus described: "Vno panno in uno intauolato messo d'*or*° alto br*accia* 4 *in* circha & la*rgho* br*accia* 2 entro vj una fighura di pa[llade . . .] et co*n* 1° schudo dand*/*sse & vna lancia darcho di mano di sand*r*° dibotticello *fiorinj* 10." (App. II, Doc. XXIX, fol. 32, tergo.) The copyist having failed to read certain words in the original draft, has left a blank space in his transcript, which I have in part attempted to supply. But it is by no means certain that the remainder of the passage has been correctly copied. It has been conjectured that the contracted word "dand*/*sse" is to be read "dand*re*sse," a corrupted form of "d' arnese": but the expression "scudo d' arnese" is as little intelligible as "lancia d'arco." Dr. Warburg has suggested that for "dand*/*sse" should be read "dimedusa": indeed, the only solution of the question would seem to be, that the copyist has failed to read a passage which ran in the original, "et con 1° schudo dimedusa & vna lancia dagiostra." If these emendations are correct, the passage would run in English: "A canvas in a gilt frame, 8 feet in height, or thereabouts, and 4 in breadth, in which is painted a figure of Pa[llas . . .] and with a shield of Medusa and a tilting lance by the hand of Sandro di Botticello, [appraised at] 10 florins."

This painting of Pallas was probably among the furniture, pictures, and other works of art collected by Lorenzo, Il Magnifico, which were sold by auction at Or San Michele, in August, 1495, after the flight of Piero de' Medici. (L. Landucci, Diario, p. 114.) Whether it was among the remnant of the collection which was recovered by Giuliano di Lorenzo de' Medici in 1512, and whether Vasari himself saw it in their palace in the Via Larga, or whether he merely described the picture from hearsay, there is nothing to show. (A. Lapini, Diario, p. 85.) All that is to be learnt of it with certainty, is that it has long since disappeared. It is true that in the inventory of the contents of the Palazzo de' Medici, in the Via Larga, taken in 1598, there is an entry of "1 great picture on canvas, in a gilt frame, in which is painted the goddess Pallas." (App. II, Doc. XVI.) But nothing is recorded which would serve to identify this picture with the lost painting by Botticelli.

The conclusion, then, to be drawn from such notices of this Pallas as we possess, is, that it was an early work executed by Botticelli for, or in compliment to, Giuliano de' Medici, and, therefore, executed before the date of his murder in 1478. The room of the Palazzo Medici, in which the picture hung in 1492, was at that time the bed-chamber of Piero, the son of Lorenzo, Il Magnifico. It is not improbable, that it may previously have been the chamber of Giuliano de' Medici, and that the five tilting helmets which it contained, and which are described in the inventory as "doni di giostra," may have been among the prizes of that famous knight of tourney, especially as one of these helmets bore for its crest a figure of Minerva:

though, as we learn from the letters of Poliziano, Piero himself engaged and excelled in such soldierly sports. I may add, for the sake of distinction, that the impress of the "rami d' ulivo e fiamme di fuoco," with which the trappings of Giuliano's equipage were powdered, probably suggested to Poliziano that other device of the "tronconi verdi incaualciati, iquali mostrauano fiamme e vampi di fuoco intrinseco," which he invented for the young Piero de' Medici; an impress which is as different in its form from the device of Giuliano, as it is in its allusion.

P. Giovio "Dialogo dell'Imprese Militari et Amorose," ed. 1574, p. 49.

Let us now turn to the painting of "Pallas and the Centaur." In the spring of 1895, Mr. William Spence, an English amateur, long resident at Florence, called attention to a large painting, evidently by Botticelli, which was then hanging unnoticed in a corridor of the royal apartments in the Palazzo Pitti. The picture represents an allegorical figure of a woman, with a shield at her back, holding a halberd in her left hand, and with the other plucking a centaur by the hair of the head. Her dress is powdered with interlaced rings set with diamond points; an impress first used by Cosimo de' Medici, and afterwards by other members of his family, including Lorenzo, Il Magnifico. This figure closely recalls a figure of Pallas in an early tapestry at Paris, the drawing for which, the work of some immediate follower of Botticelli, is preserved in the Uffizi. The painting was immediately declared by the Italian connoisseurs to be the lost "Pallas," which Botticelli painted for Lorenzo, Il Magnifico. Subsequent research, however, has shown this conjecture to be mistaken: we now know that the canvas in the Palazzo Pitti was originally painted for Lorenzo, and Giovanni, di Pierfrancesco de' Medici, and hung in their palace in the Via Larga, on the site of which now stand the more modern portions of the Palazzo Riccardi. In an inventory made in 1516 for the division of their property between their heirs, Pierfrancesco, the son of Lorenzo and the father of Lorenzino, and Giovanni delle Bande Nere, the son of Giovanni, among the contents of the "second bed-chamber above the great chamber on the ground floor," in the palace in the Via Larga, was:

App. II, Doc. XXX, No. 24, fol. 2, recto.

"jª figura conuna minerva ejº Centaurº."

In what appears to be the first draught of the same inventory, which is bound up with it in the same volume, the picture is more particularly described as "jª Figura conuna minerva e ce*n*tauro i*n* tela e asse drito": that is, "a figure-piece with a Minerva and Centaur, on canvas, and boarded at the back." The picture appears to have fallen to the share of Giovanni delle Bande Nere, and to have been removed to the Villa of Castello, which also became his property. In an inventory, already cited, of all the household goods which were at Castello, in the year 1598, it is thus described: "1 large picture antique, on canvas, wherein is painted a woman and a centaur, in a gilt frame": and again, at greater length, in the later Inventory of the year 1638, already alluded to: "A picture on panel [in error for canvas,] 4 braccia high and 3 braccia wide, in a frame of poplar stained in imitation of walnut, filleted and flourished with gold, in which is painted a woman, as large as life, who takes a Centaur by the hair with the right hand, and holds in the left a halberd [pillo d'arme in asta]."

Id., No. 40, fol. 1, recto.

App. II, Doc. XVI.

App. II, Doc. XVII, fol. 1, tergo.

At a later time, probably when the "Spring" and the "Birth of Venus" were taken to the Uffizi, in 1815, this painting of "Pallas and the Centaur" was hung in the gallery of the Palazzo Pitti. An engraving of it by F. Spagnoli, after a drawing by A. Frassinetti, appeared in the fourth volume of a work entitled: "La Galleria Pitti illustrata," published by Luigi

PALLAS AND THE CENTAUR *Pitti Palace, Florence*

Bardi at Florence, in 1837-42. The plate bore the title "Allegoria," and the painting was duly ascribed to Botticelli. The picture was still in the Pitti Gallery, in 1853; but shortly before the marriage of the Archduke Ferdinand of Lorraine, in 1856, it was found necessary to increase the Royal Apartments on the first floor of the Palace, by reducing the twenty rooms of the Pitti Gallery to fourteen. The pictures in the rooms, which were then given over to use of the Archducal family, were placed in a hall on the right of the entrance to the palace, where they remained many years. But in 1861, on the representation of the Director, the Marchese Paolo Ferroni, that these pictures formed part of the "Galleria Palatina," which had become the property of the State, they were handed over to him, and again exhibited in one of the rooms of the Pitti Gallery. A few pictures, however, which had been placed in other parts of the palace, were overlooked when this transfer was effected; and among them was this painting of the "Pallas," which was hung in a dark room used as a passage, on the second floor of the palace, where it remained unnoticed and neglected, until attention was drawn to its real nature, in 1895. It is now exhibited in one of the rooms of the Royal Apartments.

E. Ridolfi, La Pallade di Sandro Botticelli.

Like the "Birth of Venus," the "Pallas" is painted in tempera, on canvas. It measures 6 feet 9 inches in height, by 4 feet 10 inches in breadth; and these dimensions with the addition of $5\frac{1}{2}$ inches on every side for the frame, exactly correspond to the measurements of the picture given in the old inventories, namely, 4 braccia in height by 3 braccia in width. The surface of the picture has suffered not so much from repainting, as from an attempt to retouch the numberless cracks and flaws, which have been caused by the unequal resistance of the hard tempera and the yielding canvas. This process of retouching has, unfortunately, been carried farther in one or two passages of the painting. The head of the Pallas has especially suffered in this way: the outlines have been gone over, and the modelling of the face has been so spoiled by stippling, that little of the original beauty and virility of its drawing now remains. But with these exceptions, the painting is fairly well preserved.

The figure of Pallas is habited in a white dress, powdered, as I have said, with the rings of the Medici, either singly, or interlaced in groups of three or four: and the neck of the dress is edged with a series of interlaced rings. About the breasts and arms of the figure, are slender, trailing branches of olive, curiously entwined through other rings; and an ample robe of a deep, but clear, leaf-green is thrown over her right shoulder, and falls about her loins. Her head is garlanded with olive, her hair is dishevelled, and on her forehead is a jewel set with a large diamond. Another such diamond is set in the haft of the halberd, of elaborately wrought steel, which she holds in her left hand. With her right hand, the goddess plucks by the hair of the head a Centaur, hirsute and bearded, as in Dante, and "armed with arrows." In his right hand, he carries a bow, and about his body is slung a quiver. On the left of the picture, behind the figure of the Centaur, rises a cliff-like mass of gray rock, beyond which, in the distant landscape, shut in by gently rising hills, lies a vast sheet of still water intended, perhaps, for some arm of the sea, for a great ship is seen floating upon it.

The deep leaf-green of the robe, which the figure of Pallas wears over her white dress, forms the principal mass of local colour in the picture, and the dominant note of a colour scheme in which greens, grays and blues predominate; the gray greens of the olive branches, which serve to unite the masses of the green robe, the warmer green of the foreground, the gray rock behind the Centaur, and the pale sky and blue distance. These cool colours are in their turn contrasted with the dusky flank and brown flesh-tints of the Centaur, by the side of which the flesh-tints of the Pallas appear wan and silvery. Warmer, or more primary, colours occur only in the actual gold used in the interlaced rings and other ornaments of the dress of the "Pallas," in the golden yellow of her buskins, and the vermillion of the strap of the quiver, and in the handle of the bow, which the Centaur carries. Such a choice and arrangement of colours form a scheme very unlike those of the altar-pieces of San Barnaba or Santo Spirito; although the principles, on which it is composed, are already to be found underlying the colour-scheme of the "Spring." The figure of the Centaur is conceived with admirable force and truth of character; and the largeness of its relief against the mass of rock in the background, and the beauty and naturalism of its draughtsmanship, might seem to warrant the conclusion, that it had been painted at the height of Botticelli's career, shortly before, or after, the journey to Rome. But the forward tilt of the figure of Pallas, the fluid line of her draperies, and the austere character of the landscape, all point to the picture having been executed at a considerably later date. The stretch of still water in the background, enclosed by bare shores, forestalls the land-scape in the altarpiece painted for the church of San Marco, a picture which appears to have been completed c. 1490. Again, the convention of the grass in the foreground is one, which we have already noted in the foreground of "The Birth of Venus," and which is again found in more than one painting of a later date. Other such points of resemblance might be noted; but it is in the general character of the picture, and in the precise accent of its line, rather than in such minor traits, that the date of its execution appears. Painted subsequently to "The Birth of Venus" and the tondo of 1487, yet before the altarpiece of San Marco, I would ascribe it, approximately to the year 1488. Few of Botticelli's works possess such large qualities of design, as this painting of "Pallas and the Centaur"; in none, perhaps, does he so nearly anticipate the "grand manner" of the sixteenth century as in this painting. Had he always drawn with the same force and beauty of design as he has drawn this figure of the Centaur, the legend could scarcely have arisen that Ghirlandaio was the greater draughtsman.

I may add here, in regard to the meaning of the impress of the "diamante," which Cosimo de' Medici first bore in the form of three such rings interlaced, that Paolo Giovio, in his "Dialogo dell' Imprese Militari et Amorose," has left a memorable instance of how soon the significance of such things is apt to be forgotten. "The three 'diamanti,' which you see carved in the chamber where I sleep and study," say Giovio, "were borne by the great Cosimo; but to tell you the truth, although I have searched with every diligence, I have never been able to find out precisely what they are intended to signify; and Pope Clement, who in the days of his early fortune slept in the same chamber, always remained in doubt touching their meaning."

l.c., ed. 1574, p. 47.

Although no allusion occurs in Greek, or Roman, art or literature, so far as I am aware, which might explain or account for this conception of Pallas with a Centaur, Botticelli, notwithstanding, appears to have taken the motive of the goddess plucking the Centaur by the hair of the head, from the antique. On the frieze of the loggia which forms the background of Botticelli's panel of the "Calumny of Apelles," in the Uffizi, No. 1182, immediately above the figure of Midas, the painter has represented a woman dragging along by the hair of the head a centaur, who is bound and ridden by a Cupid; a composition which must have been taken directly from some work of ancient art. But if the pictorial motive of the composition is to be traced to such a suggestion, the allegory underlying it is clearly of another kind. When the painting was first discovered in 1895, Signor Ridolfi, the late director of the Uffizi, expressed the opinion, in one of the Florentine papers, that the picture contained an allusion to the statesmanship of Lorenzo de' Medici, who "having overcome the spirit of disorder and violence personified in the Centaur, secured for the people a time of peace and prosperity." Certainly, to a Florentine of the fifteenth century, and a lover of Dante like Botticelli, the Centaur was above all things the emblem of rapine and violence: in the seventh circle of hell they keep watch over the fosse of boiling blood,

> "in la qual bolle
> Mal che per violenza in altrui noccia."

Inferno, XII, 47-8.

Signor Ridolfi, however, went on to assert that "there was ample reason to believe that Botticelli painted the picture in March, 1480, when Lorenzo, on his return from Naples, was received with great rejoicings on account of the triumph which he had achieved in having induced the King of Naples to leave the league against the Florentines and become their ally." But to such an argument, there is more than one objection. The league, which Lorenzo formed with the King of Naples, served to effect a greater balance of power between the two factions, and to support the Florentines in their struggle against the Pope, rather than diminish the ardour with which the war was being prosecuted; and though the invasion of the Turks brought about a secession of hostilities, in the beginning of the year 1481; so long as Sixtus IV. remained on the papal throne, Italy was torn by intestine wars. If we are to look for any such meaning in the painting, we must surely turn to a later period in the life of Lorenzo, to the time of his alliance with Pope Innocent VIII., for its application. "From the end of the war against Sarzana," in 1487, as Machiavelli puts it, "until the year 1492, in which Lorenzo died, the Florentines lived in great felicity." Lorenzo formed his alliance with Innocent VIII. during the first half of the year 1487; and not only contrived to install himself as the chief adviser of the Pope, but succeeded in keeping the rival powers of Italy at peace so long as he lived. At such a time the "Pallas and the Centaur" might well have been painted, in compliment to Lorenzo, to whose genius Italy owed the repression of the rapine and lawlessness, which constantly attended the petty warfare by which the country had been overrun. But perhaps the allusion was less elaborate, and the picture while celebrating the genius of the goddess and the giver of all those good arts by which our original nature is tamed and brought to civility, was intended as a compliment to the Medici, who had not only borne her image in their standards, but who had ever fostered her cult by their munificent patronage of the arts.

But to come to the tapestry, which is in the possession of the Comte de Baudreüil, and the drawing for it, which is in the Gallery of the Uffizi. This tapestry represents Pallas almost in the attitude of the painting, in the Palazzo Pitti, but without the green robe. She holds in her right hand, the helmet, "powerful to make men invisible," which Pluto gave to Perseus,

E. Müntz, Histoire de l'Art pendant la Renaissance, Vol. I, front.

when Pallas sent him to kill the Medusa: and in her left, instead of the lance of the painting, the goddess holds an olive branch. Suspended from the trunk of a tree to the left of the goddess, is the shield, or "aegis," of Minerva bearing the head of Medusa: and on a label above it are inscribed the verses:

EX CAPITE . ETHEREI . NATA . SVM . IOVIS . ALMA MINERVA
MORTALES . CVNCTIS . ARTIBVS . ERVDIENS

Above the figure of Pallas, is suspended a shield, surmounted by a mitre and crozier, and bearing the arms: quarterly; first and fourth, on a barry of four, azure and argent, three hearts gules ensigned with three coronets argent; second and third, ermine, on a fess azure four fleurs-de-lys argent. From a holly tree on the left of the figure are suspended a Roman sword and corselet, and below them is a label inscribed, SVB SOLE SVB VMBRA VIRENS. This motto is repeated once on the upper border, and twice on the right border, of the tapestry: a crowned heart being placed between each repetition of the motto.

The coat in the first and fourth quarters of this shield is that of the French family of de Baudreüil; and it is probable, as Dr. Warburg has pointed out to me, that the shield may be that of Guy de Baudreüil, or Bandereul, who was Abbot of the Benedictine monastery of St. Peter's, Corbigny, in Le Morvan, a district formerly belonging to the Duchies of Burgundy and Nivernais. His name is the thirty-fifth in the "Series Decanorum seu Abbatum" of the Monastery, as given in the "Gallia Christiana" of Sainte-Marthe: and it is there stated, that he is called "antiquus abbas," in a certain "computus" of the year 1530, which is subscribed by his nephew, Jacques de Baudreüil, or Bandereul, who succeeded him as Abbot, and to whom he appears to have transferred the abbey in consideration of a pension. Whether or no this conjecture is borne out by the coat in the second and third quarters of this shield, I have had no opportunity of ascertaining; and I must leave it to some French antiquary to discover whose arms they may be.

l.c., Vol. IV, col. 478.

The cartoon from which this tapestry was woven, could not well have been executed before 1490, or later than the opening years of the sixteenth century. The tapestry itself, which seems to have been intended to serve as a "portière" or door-curtain, is probably of Flemish manufacture; but the cartoon, like that of the "Adam and Eve" which Leonardo designed "per una portiera, che si aveva a fare in Fiandra d'oro e di seta tessuta," was doubtlessly made in Florence, and probably in Botticelli's own workshop.

Vasari, ed. Sansoni, IV, 22.

The sheet in the Uffizi, Frame 52, No. 201, which must doubtlessly have served as the drawing from which this cartoon was made, contains a study for the figure of Pallas holding a helmet, which has been partially cut away, in her right hand, and an olive wand in her left. The figure is placed in the same attitude as the figure in the tapestry, and is similarly draped. It has been first sketched with black chalk, on a rubbed, red ground, and afterwards put in with the pen, and heightened with white. The sheet itself has been square for enlargement. The head and left shoulder show a "pentimento," having been redrawn on that side, thereby giving due breadth to the shoulders. This drawing has been inscribed "sandro botticello," in a sixteenth century hand, and at first sight might almost be mistaken for a genuine drawing by the master. But when we come to examine this figure, we find that, although it contains most of Botticelli's mannerisms, it possesses little of his beauty of structure, or mastery of design. Its draughtsman has especially lost himself in the folds of the draperies, which are confused and meaningless: and the timid use of hatching in the shadows, and the trick of rendering the minor folds by a multiplicity of little fluted cavities, clearly distinguish his work from that of his master. By the same hand is a drawing of a seated figure of "Faith" in the Malcolm Collection, and perhaps another sheet, which I shall discuss together, in their place. The figure of Pallas in the drawing would seem to have been suggested by the figure of the goddess in the painting of "Pallas and the Centaur"; for although the action of the arms and hands is wholly different, and the one figure is more turned away from the spectator than the other, both in the attitude of the rest of the body, and many of the chief lines of the draperies, in the drawing, appear to have been copied from the picture. Indeed, it would seem as if Botticelli did little more than supervise the execution of the cartoon for the tapestry. The lost "Pallas," painted for Giuliano de' Medici, or Lorenzo, Il Magnifico, was probably a wholly different composition: and it is possible that Botticelli himself may have preserved for us a reminiscence of it in the little figure of "Pallas," which he painted among the reliefs on the base of the Throne, in the picture of the "Calumny of Apelles," in the Uffizi. There the goddess is represented in long flowing robes, with a tilting lance in one hand, and the head of Medusa in the other.

Vasari alone, among the early commentators, speaks of an altar-piece of the "Annunciation," which Botticelli painted for a chapel in the church of the Cestello, at Florence: "Ne' monaci di Cestello a vna cappella fece vna tauola d'una Annunziata." His statement, however, is borne out by documentary evidence. In the seventeenth century, a certain Don Ignazio Signorini, a monk of the Badia di Settimo, a famous Cistercian Abbey on the banks of the Arno, below Florence, compiled "from various fragments of many ancient writings," then preserved among the archives of his house, certain "Memorie del Monasterio di Settimo," which are cited by Signor Milanesi in writing his notes to Vasari. Interspersed among these "Memorials" are many notices relating to the Cestello, a cell of great antiquity in the Borgo Pinti, at Florence, which had been granted to the monks of the Badia a Settimo, in the fourteenth century. "In 1480," records Signorini, "the church of the Cestello, threatening ruin from sheer antiquity, the Monks took thought to obtain the wherewithal to rebuild it; and since the Monastery did not possess the means for the whole of that expense, they endeavoured to seek out friends and lovers of the convent, who would contribute to the fabric." A sum of 300 florins having been collected for the work, the "Cappella Maggiore" was begun on the 26th March, 1480: whereupon "many other citizens undertook to build each one his own chapel, as may be seen in the 'Libro de' Benefattori'; and in a few years the building was brought to perfection." The "Libro de' Benefattori" to which Signorini here alludes, and from which he draws the notices of the lateral chapels which follow in his manuscript, is still preserved among the archives of the Cestello.

Vasari, ed. 1550, I, 492.

App. II, Doc. XXXI, fol. 56, recto.

This document is the original book of "Ricordi," begun in 1480, in which Don Antonio, one of the monks of the Cestello, who was entrusted with the duty of collecting and disbursing the various sums of money needed for the rebuilding of the church, recorded from time to time, as he states on the first page of the manuscript, "all the principal benefactors of the monastery of Santa Maria Magdalena of the order of Cestello," who

App. II, Doc. XXXII, fol. 1, recto.

contributed to this pious work, "and especially the founders of the chapels of the said church, and others who adorned the said church and monastery." In 1483, the "Cappella Maggiore" was finished, and the body of the church roofed in: and in 1488, the work of completing the lateral chapels of the nave was going forward. "On the 19th March, 1488[-9]," runs one of the entries in this "Libro de' Benefattori," "Benedetto di Ser Giovanni Guardi caused a chapel to be built and founded in the Cestello of Florence, the second on the right hand on entering the church; and it is called the chapel of the Annunciation: and he spent at my hands, that is to say, through me, Don Antonio, in building the said chapel, fifty ducats, namely with the glass of the window; and moreover, he spent on the altarpiece of the said chapel, which was by the hand of Sandro Botticello, thirty ducats. And we are obliged to pray to God for him and for his ancestors as benefactors of our monastery: other particulars till now, there are none." In a later entry, Don Antonio records that "on 26th June, 1490, Fra Benedetto Pagagnotti, Bishop of Vasione, and suffragan of Florence, consecrated the altar of Benedetto Guardi," and granted certain yearly indulgences. He also adds, that the founder gave an altar-cloth of white damask, and a pair of iron candlesticks, for the use of the chapel, on two subsequent occasions. From these entries, then, it would appear that the building of the chapel of the Guardi was begun in March 1488-9, and finished and consecrated on 26th June, 1490; and that, therefore, the altar-piece of the "Annunciation" was painted in the interval between these two dates.

Id., fol. 7, recto.

In 1628, Pope Urban VIII, having two nieces among the Carmelite nuns of Santa Maria degli Angeli, forced the monks of the Cestello to exchange their house, which was "one of the larger and more commodious in Florence," for that of the nuns in Borgo San Frediano. The relics of Santa Maria Maddelena de' Pazzi, whose cult was then much in fashion, having been translated to the Cestello, the church was re-dedicated to that saint; and the former church of the nuns in Borgo San Frediano was, henceforth, called the new Cestello. Although the nave and choir of the old Cestello were renewed by the nuns, in the taste of the time; the lateral chapels and their altar-pieces, with the exception of the chapel of the Nasi, were allowed to remain undisturbed. Both Stefano Rosselli, in his "Sepoltuario Fiorentino," compiled in 1657, and Giovanni Cinelli in his edition of the "Bellezze di Firenze," published in 1677, allude to the "Annunciation" by Botticelli, in the chapel of the Guardi: and as late as 1754, Giuseppe Richa records that the picture was still over the altar of the chapel. The silence of subsequent writers in regard to this altar-piece, seems to show that it was removed from the church not long after Giuseppe Richa wrote his "Notizie delle chiese Fiorentine." The church of Santa Maria Maddelena de' Pazzi remains, so far as its fabric is concerned, much in the condition to which it was reduced by the nuns, in the seventeenth century. The chapel of the Guardi is the second chapel to the right, on entering the church from the beautiful cloister of Giuliano da San Gallo. In the head of the vault is yet to be seen among the modern "stucchi" with which the chapel is covered, the greyhound rampant of the Guardi; and on the floor is an inscription stating that in 1778, the chapel which had already been rededicated to St. Raphael, the Archangel, passed, at the death of the last of the Paganelli, into other hands. It would seem then, that the "Annunciation" by Botticelli was removed between the years 1754 and 1778, when the present paintings by Piattoli and the ornaments in stucco were put up,

G. Richa, Chiese Fior., I, 311.

Cod. Magliabechiano, XXVI, 22, fol. 457, tergo.

G. Cinelli, l.c., p. 487.

G. Richa, Chiese Fior., I, 322.

THE ANNUNCIATION *Uffizi Gallery, Florence*

and the altar re-dedicated to St. Raphael. Had the "Annunciation" remained in the church at the time of the Napoleonic Dominion of Florence, the picture would doubtless have been taken to Paris, along with the other fine altar-pieces of the church, which are still in the Louvre. For long, this altar-piece was thought to be lost. Federigo Fantozzi, in his "Nuova Guida di Firenze," sought to identify it with an old copy of the miraculous fresco of the Santissima Annunziata, still to be seen in the fifth chapel to the right, on entering the church of Santa Maria Maddelena de' Pazzi. The absurdity of this attribution was pointed out by the commentators of the Florentine edition of Vasari, begun in 1846, who nevertheless fell into the error of supposing that its frame, which bears the date, MDXIII, was the original frame of the lost "Annunciation" of Botticelli. At length, in 1872, it was discovered "in a little chapel in the middle of a 'campo,' or field, which had formerly belonged to the nuns of Santa Maria Maddelena de' Pazzi," and taken to the Gallery of the Uffizi, where it bears the number, 1316.

l.c., ed. 1844, p. 293.

Vasari, ed. Le Monnier, V, 114, note.

Vasari, ed. Sansoni, III, 314, note.

This altar-piece still retains its original frame, ornamented on either side with pilasters, which support an entablature and rest upon a "gradino." The panels of the pilasters, and the frieze of the entablature, are painted with arabesques in gold, upon a blue ground: and the "gradino" is painted in imitation of five marble panels. Of these, the oblong panel in the centre is broken by a little "Pietà," a three-quarter figure of the Dead Christ displayed within the tomb, on the front of which hangs the Sudarium. This figure recalls the panel in the Florentine Academy, No. 157, which once formed the central panel of the "gradino" of the altar-piece, and in the church of San Barnaba. The oblong panel to the left is inscribed with gold letters on a blue ground:

SPIRITVS . SANTVS . SVPERVENIET . INTE
ET . VIRTVS . ALTISSIMI . OBVMBRABIT . TIBI

and the panel to the left, in similar fashion:

ECCE . ANCILLA . DOMINI . FIAT
MICHI . SECVNDVM . VERBVM . TVVM

Below each of the pilasters, at either end of the gradino, within a smaller, square panel, is a shield bearing the arms of the donor. Stefano Rosselli, with that vagueness which characterizes the terms of Italian heraldry, blazons the arms of the guardi thus: "Campo, sopra d'arg. sotto rosso, cane nero con collare d'oro." Such, with a slight variation, is the blazon of the shield to the left, which in terms of English heraldry, is, "Party per bend argent and gules, a greyhound rampant sable, collared gules." In the shield to the right, however, the field is sable, and the greyhound proper; variations which are probably due to the caprice of the painter.

The picture itself, which is painted on a panel measuring 4 feet 9¾ inches in height, by 5 feet ½ inch in breadth, remains unvarnished and in a fine state of preservation. The Virgin is represented as not yet quite risen from the desk, at which she has been praying, as she turns towards the angel who has just descended, his raiment still caught by the air as he kneels to her on one knee, and with an eager gesture stretches forth the right hand with the consolatory words, "Ne timeas Maria." An open book lies upon the lectern, which is partially seen on the extreme right of the picture; and behind the figure of the Angel, through a doorway which opens upon a terraced garden, is a distant landscape with a town beside a river. The motive of the composition is to be traced back to the tabernacle of Donatello, in Santa Croce; but here Botticelli appears rather to have had in his mind, the altar-piece by Fra Filippo Lippi, in the church of San Lorenzo, at Florence. Certainly, the attitude of the Virgin, and the way in which the figure and the lectern are introduced into the design, are reminiscent of Fra Filippo's painting; the figure of the angel, however, differs from that picture, and is conceived more entirely in the vein of Botticelli. Its motive and attitude are found repeated in the little "Annunciation," in the predella of the altar-piece from San Marco, now in the Florentine Academy, No. 47.

When first seen as a whole, without regard to the details of its execution, the general effect of this picture is certainly impressive. Admirable in the simplicity both of its conception and treatment, the masses of the figures are well contrived and disposed; and their movements finely expressive of "the passion of their minds," the mingled awe and fear of the Virgin, and the solemn eagerness of the angel to deliver his high message, though not without some first word of consolation. But regarded more closely, the picture is found to be coarse and mannered in draughtsmanship, the hands and heads are lifeless in spite of the vivacity of the attitudes; and the draperies are notional and arbitrary in their folds, especially in those passages where they fall about the feet of the figures. The colouring of the picture, again, possesses nothing of that luminous, translucent quality which distinguishes Botticelli's colour: the cold purple of the angel's robe, the crude brick-red of the tiling on the floor, the chill, heavy gray of the wall behind the figures, do not recall the genuine works of the painter. Yet this is the picture which undoubtedly came to the Cestello in 1490, from the "bottega" of Botticelli, as the master's own work. The fact is significant; for this altar-piece could have been, by no means, the only school-picture which passed in Botticelli's day as the work of his own hand.

I. Lermolieff, Die Galerie Borghese, 1890, p. 107.

Morelli, who first remarked the indifferent execution of this picture, expressed the opinion that it was probably done from a sketch by the master. The mass, disposition and movement of the figures, however, so greatly surpasses the elaboration of the design, in all the details of the extremities and draperies, that I suspect Botticelli may have had some share in the preliminary stages of the cartoon; although his hand is certainly not to be traced in any of its details.

By the same hand apparently as this "Annunciation," is a panel of "The Virgin and Child" in the National Gallery, No. 782, a version of a design by Botticelli, of which the panel at Dresden, No. 8, is, perhaps, the original. Like the altar-piece of the Cestello, this panel is hard in execution and crude in colour; and the head of the Virgin and the character of the landscape in the two pictures closely recall one another.

Another painting of the "Annunciation," a fresco, far more characteristic than the altar-piece of the Cestello, of the original manner in which Botticelli treated a traditional subject of this kind, may be discussed here, since its condition is such that it is difficult to determine with any great certainty the date at which it was executed. This fresco, or rather such vestiges of it as remain, fill two lunettes on the right wall of the atrium before the church of the suppressed monastery of San Martino, now the "Instituto de' Minorenni Corrigendi," in the Via della Scala, at Florence.

The buildings of this monastery had been originally erected in 1313 by Cione di Lapo de' Pollini, as a hospital, under the control of the Spedale di Santa Maria della Scala, at Siena, from which it took its name. I have already related how, in this hospital, which stood but a short distance from the houses of Botticelli's family, an incredible number of persons died of the plague in 1479. In its original state, the fresco of the "Annunciation" decorated the loggia of this hospital. The monastery of San Martino a Mugnone having been razed to the ground, in common with all the buildings in the immediate neighbourhood of the walls of Florence, at the time of the siege, in 1529, the nuns were allowed to take refuge in the Spedale della Scala; and in 1531 the building was given to them for their convent upon certain conditions; one of which was, that they should not remove any arms, paintings or inscription, either in the church or hospital. These conditions long proved an obstacle to the desire on the part of the nuns to rebuild the church; and it was not till 1623 that a compromise was arrived at, which enabled them to realize their intention.

G. Richa, Chiese Fior., III, 327-8.

Id., III, 335-341.

The following year, in the course of these works, the loggia of the hospital, at the angle of the Via della Scala and the Via Polverosa, was inclosed in order to form an atrium in front of the church; and above it, opening into the church, was built a gallery, from which the nuns might hear mass. The construction of this gallery necessitated the rebuilding of the vault of the loggia; and entailed considerable damage to the paintings in question. The margins and ends of the lunettes appear to have been hacked away at this time; and the frescoes themselves, which had no doubt suffered from exposure to the air, considerably repainted. The latter process was probably repeated at a subsequent date.

In the lunette to the right, the Virgin is seen kneeling upon a carpet spread upon the floor of her chamber; and through an open doorway on the left, is her bed in the adjoining room. In the lunette to the left, the angel Gabriel is represented as yet descending, his hands folded on his breast, and his ample skirts caught back by the ruffled air, as he is still borne upon it by his own lightness. In the background on the right, is part of a pilaster, with some ornament in "grisaille" on the shaft. The figures of the Virgin and the Angel, which are turned towards one another, are placed on the extreme right and left of the composition, so as to leave the whole extent of the bare chamber unbroken between them; a device in which lies not a little of the beauty and originality of the design. The lunette containing the figure of the Virgin, has been so completely repainted, that little can now be made out beyond the general lines of its design. The other lunette is in a far better state of preservation. The attitude of the tall, slant figure of the angel, bent a little at the knee and hip, with the feet placed straightly together, is one which occurs many times in the drawings for the "Dante" at Berlin; in the angel, for instance, who bears the name of "Sandro di Mariano," in the design of the "Angelic Hierarchies," which forms the illustration to Canto XXVIII. of the "Paradiso." Again, the fluted folds of the draperies recall the figures of the Winds in the "Birth of Venus." Deplorable as the condition of this figure is, its general design remains intact, and some traces of the original beauty of its line and modelling are yet to be seen in the draperies; for which reason, although it is extremely difficult to form any real judgment of a painting in such a condition, I cannot forbear hazarding the conjecture, that in this fresco we may possess the remains of a genuine and truly admirable work by Botticelli. Certainly, the design is by him: none of his disciples could have invented so original and impressive a composition, or one so profoundly touched by the peculiar sentiment, which distinguishes Botticelli's finest works. I may add that Messrs. Cavalcaselle and Crowe notice this fresco among the works of Filippino Lippi, whose manner it seemed to recall to them.

Cavalcaselle and Crowe, ed. Le Monnier, VII, 99.

Following a usage which had long obtained in Florence, of placing the fabrics of the principal churches of the city in the charge of one or another of the Florentine guilds; on the 5th August, 1427, by a decree of the Republic, the church of San Marco was committed to the care of the Silk-Weavers' guild, the Università di Por Santa Maria, or Arte della Seta, as it was afterwards called. At what time, it does not appear, but it could scarcely have been long after the date of this decree, the Orefici, or Goldsmiths, who formed a branch of the Arte della Seta, founded in the church of San Marco a chapel dedicated to St. Eligius, their patron saint, popularly known in Florence as San Lò, and in England as St. Loy. At this chapel was suspended a banner bearing the arms of the Arte della Seta, on 25th April, the festival of St. Mark, when the members of the guild came with torches, to make a yearly offering of wax in the church. This chapel is stated in a "ricordo," written c. 1525, to have been "molto antiquata" at the time of its renewal, towards the end of the fifteenth century. In this same "ricordo," which is found in a Repertory kept by the monks of San Marco of the masses and other offices, which they were under obligation to perform, are set forth the following circumstances attending the reconstruction and endowment of this altar: "a certain provision having been made by the Arte [della Seta] in the year 1488, or some more exact time, with the full authority of its members, and an office of conservators appointed, it was decreed, that out of gratitude for the officiation of the said chapel which the friars perform, and for the said office, [a yearly office for the dead, which they were required to celebrate on 1st December, the feast of St. Elegius,] that the guild should pay us every year by way of alms, lire 40 piccioli; and it is their pleasure that the said alms be confirmed every five years, by the consuls for the time being: and in this manner is it always observed. And the said guild, in addition to this, made the altarpiece on which they spent 100 gold ducats, and the grate and the plastering of the chapel, which they maintain at their proper charges." Now although it is not directly stated in this "ricordo," for what purpose the provision was voted, and the office of conservators instituted by the guild in 1488, there can be little doubt from the context, that the reconstruction and custody of the chapel were the objects in view. This interpretation is borne out by the minute of a resolution preserved in one of the books of the Arte della Seta. On 29th April, 1490, the Consuls and Counsellors of the guild, after having approved of various provisions regarding the "sensali," or brokers of the guild, and their periodical "agguaglio" or settlement of accounts, resolved that "whereas the members of the Arte [della Seta] are patrons, and have the care and custody of the church of San Marco, and possess also a chapel there, certain monies having been set aside to build and adorn it, which in part has been done, and inasmuch as the friars of the said church, of a truth do diligently say mass there, and continually exercise themselves for the health of souls, and especially of their benefactors," etc., "it is resolved and ordained that for the next five years, out of the total yield of the imposts on the periodical settlements of the said

F. L. Del Migliore, Firenze Illustrata, I, 210.

App. II, Doc. XXXIII.

App. II, Doc. XXXIV, fol. 304, tergo.

brokers, which shall be levied every year during the month of August, the 'proveditore' set apart lire 40 piccioli per lira e soldo, and afterwards send every year, during the month of October, beginning in October next following, the said lire 40 for alms, to the said friars, and that they be required to perform every year an office for the dead, for the souls of the benefactors of the said guild, upon its feast-day, and that the Consuls for the time being have power to terminate it, &c." From this it would appear that the alms of lire 40 for the office of the dead, was not voted until some two years after the provision had been made for the renewal of the chapel; and that in April, 1490, the work of building and adorning it was still proceeding. But the guild would scarcely have ordered the payment of this alms to be begun in October, 1490, unless it had been anticipated that the chapel would have been sufficiently advanced at that time, to admit of the altar being consecrated, and office said at it. On the other hand, the consecration of the chapel would not necessarily imply that the altar-piece was finished and in place. On the evidence of these indications, we must conclude, then, that the commission for this altar-piece was given not earlier than 1488; and that the picture was finished not earlier than 1490, and probably in that year.

It is to this altar-piece that Vasari alludes in his life of Botticelli, where he says that "the Arte of Porta Santa Maria commissioned that master to paint in San Marco a Coronation of Our Lady, on panel, with a choir of angels, which was admirably designed and executed by him." Vasari, however, is not the earliest commentator to speak of this picture: Francesco Albertini, who wrote in 1510, mentions in his "Memoriale," among other works of art in San Marco, "la tauola . . . di Sa*n*dro." In the version of the "Libro di Billi" made by Antonio Petri, is recorded the precise position of this altar-piece, at the end of the church, beside the great door on the left: "Vna tauola ins[to] marcho allato alla porta d*e*lla chiesa amano sinistra"; and the Anonimo Gaddiano repeats this notice with slight variation: "Nella chiesa defratj di sa*n* marcho e disua mano vna gra*n* tauola allato allaporta della chiesa."

Vasari, ed. 1550, I, 492.

l.c., fol 4, tergo.

App. II, Doc. I, fol. 49, tergo.

App. II, Doc. II, fol. 83, recto.

For nearly a century, the yearly alms of lire 40 appears to have been confirmed from time to time, by the Consuls of the Arte della Seta: the last occasion which is recorded, was in 1575, when it was renewed for five years. In 1580, a scheme was put in hand to reduce the lateral altars of the church of San Marco, to a common form and order, according to a design which had been prepared by John of Bologna. This work was gradually proceeding for some years after that date. It may be that the Arte della Seta did not care to be at the expense of renewing their chapel in the new taste: but for whatever reason it was, they relinquished their rights in the altar, and its renovation was carried out by others. On the margin of the "ricordo" cited above, is written in a later hand: "The obligation is ended, because the chapel is given to the Brandolini." Before the altar, which now stands on the site of the chapel of the Arte della Seta, beside the great doorway to the left, on entering the church of San Marco, is an inscription stating that the altar was erected in its present form in 1596, by Vincenzio and Alessandro Brandolini. At that time, no doubt, Botticelli's painting was removed to make way for the picture of the "Transfiguration" by Giovanni Battista Paggi, which is now above this altar. When Stefano Rosselli compiled his "Sepoltuario Fiorentino" in 1657, Botticelli's altar-piece was hanging in the Chapter House of the monastery; and the oldest fathers

G. Richa, Chiese fior., VII, 136.

Cod. Magliabechiano, XXVI, 23, fol. 1160, tergo.

then living in the convent, were unable to remember, precisely, over which of the altars of the church it had originally been placed. In the Chapter House, it was again seen by Giovanni Cinelli, in 1677, and by Ferdinando Leopoldo del Migliore, in 1684; and there it appears to have remained until the time of the suppression of the monastery, in 1808, when the principal panel and the "gradino" were taken to the gallery of the Florentine Academy, where they are still preserved, Nos. 73 and 74.

G. Cinelli, Bellezze di Firenze, ed. 1677, p. 16.

F. L. del Migliore, Firenze Illustrata, I, 220.

When Stefano Rosselli saw this altar-piece in the Chapter House of San Marco, in 1657, there were to be seen "at the foot," the arms of the Arte di Por Santa Maria; namely, "campo bianco con una porta rossa." These arms were, no doubt, painted at either end of the "gradino," on the frame which is now lost. It is, moreover, stated in the "ricordo" cited above, that these arms were repeated, together with those of the Orefici, namely, "campo rosso con una coppa d'oro," on the vault of the chapel.

Cod. Magliabechiano, XXVI, 23, fol. 1160, tergo.

The principal painting of this altar-piece, No. 73, is a large, circular-headed panel which measures 12 feet 4 inches in height, and 8 feet in breadth. The form and dimensions of this panel show, that it could not have belonged to a detached altar-piece of the common type, framed with lateral pilasters and entablature above, like the altar-pieces of San Barnaba and Santo Spirito, in their original state. The minute of 1490, in the books of the Arte della Seta, speaks of the "building" of the chapel, and the "ricordo" of c. 1525 alludes to the "testudine," or vault, which was above the altar. From these indications, taken in conjunction with the shape and dimensions of this panel, there can be little doubt that in its general form, this chapel must have resembled those vaulted, or domed, chapels resting upon four columns, which were frequently placed at the end of the church, beside the great doorway. An instance of this kind which still exists, is the chapel of the Capponi in Santa Felicità, designed by Brunelleschi; another, which has disappeared, was the chapel of the Maringhi, in Sant' Ambrogio. In both cases, the circular-headed panel of the altar-piece entirely filled one of the arches of the vault, which abutted against the wall of the church. And of such a form, no doubt, was the chapel for which Botticelli painted the altar-piece in question.

But to return to the painting itself. In the upper part, seated on the right, is God the Father in a triple tiara, who raises his right hand in benediction, and with the left places a crown on the head of the Virgin, who sits opposite to him with her hands crossed on her breast. Behind these figures is a triple glory of vermilion and azure seraphim; and encircling all, "a choir of angels," dancing in a round, with their hands interlocked; while other angels on either side scatter lapfuls of roses. In the lower part of the picture, are four whole-length figures of saints, standing in a landscape. The figure on the extreme left of the panel, is St. John the Evangelist. He holds up an unwritten book in his right hand, and raises the left as he looks towards heaven in response to the voice: "Quod vides, scribe in libro." He is here represented as the patron of the "setaioli," or silk-mercers, and his statue by Baccio da Montelupo stands in the niche of the Arte di Por Santa Maria, on the exterior of Or San Michele. On the extreme right is St. Eligius, the patron of the "Orefici," or goldsmiths, habited in the processional vestments of a bishop. Between these two saints are two other figures; that on the left, representing St. Augustine, and that on the right, St. Jerome. St. Augustine, who is writing in a book, is vested in a jewelled mitre, and a cope which he wears over the rochet of

THE CORONATION OF THE VIRGIN—THE ALTAR-PIECE OF SAN MARCO
Gallery of the Academy, Florence

an Augustine canon. St. Jerome is dressed in the scarlet hat and robes of a cardinal: he holds a book in his left hand; and raises his right hand to his breast, as he looks upward at the beatific vision of God and the Virgin.

To this vision in the upper part of the picture, our eyes also are irresistibly drawn; but not to the same actors in the heavenly scene. Like his master, Fra Filippo Lippi, in the fresco at Spoleto, Botticelli fashions his principal figures in accordance to their traditional representation. Like Fra Filippo, too, he gives a circular form to the glory which encircles them; and borrows the motive of the angels scattering roses, by which Fra Filippo, along with other such devices, sought to give greater pictorial significance to his painting, than the traditional groups of singing angels admitted of. But here Botticelli, with that power of invention, which sets him among the most imaginative of the Florentines, easily surpasses his master; and by a device as felicitous as ingenious, transmutes Fra Filippo's somewhat confused composition into one of the greatest simplicity and beauty. Taking the verse of the Psalmist, "Laudent nomen ejus in choro," in its literal signification, Botticelli introduces the round of dancing figures, in place of the traditional groups of singing angels; and by the the rhythmic movements of the dancers, invokes in the imagination the measured sound of the choir, now unseen, with a power of suggestion which was not possible in the case of the earlier, singing or playing figures. Fra Angelico, perhaps, in his dance of the Blessed Spirits in Paradise, has expressed in painting the holy gaiety of the Court of Heaven with greater spirituality; but even he has not rendered with so keen a sense of exhilaration, the ecstatic movement of the heavenly dance, as Botticelli has done in these figures. The device of the circle within the circle,—of the upright wheels of the seraphim seen within the receding round of the dancing angels, like the lines of an orrery, —is not less exquisite in idea, than the individual figures which compose the circle are in design. The figures of the four saints below, severely conceived and largely drawn, possess a certain rugged, Giottesque accent which sets them in sharp contrast to the delicate beauty of the boyish figures above: and the bleak character of the landscape in which the saints are standing, is opposed in the same abrupt manner to the floor of heaven, "impurpled with celestial roses."

These divergent notes in the conception of the picture have their counterpart in its execution. A careful examination of the panel shows that, although the whole of it was certainly painted from a full-size cartoon by the master's own hand, the execution of every part is not of an equal excellence. The figures of the Virgin and God the Father lack the vitality, which distinguishes the figures of the angels around them. The line here is often perfunctory; the modelling little expressive: and in many passages, such as the head of the Virgin and the folds of her draperies, it is not difficult to detect the hand of the assistant, who has not thoroughly understood the essential significance of the cartoon from which he was working. The figures of the dancing angels, on the contrary, are drawn with incomparable vivacity. The bellying draperies, which cling about, and lend mass to the lithe, boyish figures, seem informed by the very melody to which they are moving; and the design of the heads and interlocked hands possesses all that beauty of form and sentiment, which is peculiar to the master. Especially lovely is the motive of the angel, who looks upward at God the Father and the Virgin, through the halo of golden rays which issue from their midst. Lastly, the figures of the saints below, though greatly inferior in draughtsmanship to the two saints in the Bardi altar-piece, exhibit all the forms of Botticelli's manner.

As in his other great altar-pieces, Sandro here partially reverts to that use of ultramarine and purple and gold, which tradition had prescribed for such ceremonial paintings; and the gold background of the upper part of the panel serves to emphasize the other Giottesque traits, which I have already remarked in its design. But what is most noticeable in the colouring of the picture is, that the blue and bluish-grays, which are freely employed, are opaque and want their proper quality of colour. Such prominent masses in the composition as the blue of the Virgin's mantle, or the paler blue of the cope of St. Eligius, do not possess that clear and luminous intensity of hue which invariably distinguishes the genuine works of the master from those of his imitators, no less than the quality of his line. Even the variegated coats of the angels, of saffron and red, purple and blue, grape-purple and white, or grape-purple and green, and the like, though of more beauty and quality of colour than the rest of the picture, lack the golden tone of Botticelli's finest work. The panel may have lost something from over-cleaning; but this opacity of pigment cannot be accounted for by its condition, since with the exception of numerous local retouches, which are easily to be distinguished from the original tempera, it has escaped any appreciable repainting. Indeed, the deficient quality of its colouring, as of its draughtsmanship, can only be explained by the very considerable assistance which Botticelli must have had in its execution. The justness of this conclusion becomes still more evident, when we examine the stories which formed the "predella" of this altar-piece.

These stories, five in number, are painted on a single panel, measuring 7½ inches in height by 8 feet 8¾ inches in length, and divided from one another by four, feigned balusters. The central story of the "Annunciation" has reference to the "Coronation of the Virgin," in the upper part of the picture; and the two stories on either side of this "Annunciation," illustrate the legends of the four saints in the lower part, each being placed below the figure to which it refers. But to take them in their order, from left to right. The first on the left, is a story of "St. John writing the Book of the Revelations in the Island of Patmos." The saint, in a robe of blue and purple, is seated on a rock by the seashore; he is turned towards the right, and intently records his vision in a book. Behind him rises a rocky crag, and before him stretches the sea. The second story is of "St. Augustine in his Study." The saint, who is vested in a green cope over a white rochet, is seated in full-face at a table, with an open book before him, and a pen and ink-horn at his side. As he pauses in his reading, he lays his right hand on his breast, with the gesture of the earlier figure of the saint in the church of Ognissanti. Behind him, against the wall of the room in which he is seated, is a cupboard filled with books. The third story is that of the "Annunciation." On the right, within her chamber, is seated the Virgin, with a book on her knees, in a blue mantle lined with green, which she wears over a purple dress. She lays her right hand on her bosom, as the angel, in a dress of blue and saffron with a lily-wand in his left hand, hastens to deliver his salutation, stretching out his right hand as he kneels on one knee to her, an attitude which recalls the angel in the altar-piece painted for the Cestello. Between the two figures, through an open doorway, is seen a distant landscape. The fourth story is of "St. Jerome in the Wilderness." The saint, half-clad in a purple robe, which he gathers about him with his left hand, kneels, turned towards a crucifix, which is bound to a young sapling, on the left of the composition. In his right hand he holds a stone, with which he has been striking his breast; an open book is by his side, and on the rocky cliff which rises behind him, hangs his cardinal's hat. In the background, on either side of the cliff-like crag, which rises behind the saint, is a distant landscape with stretches of water and town-capped hills. The fifth and last story is taken from the Legend of St. Eligius. This story, which according to an old hagiographer, was commonly painted above the doorways of blacksmiths' shops in Italy, savours, as he says, rather of devotion than truth. It does not occur in the life of St. Eligius written by St. Ouen; and, like the vision of St. Augustine of the child by the seashore, was probably of Italian origin. I have been unable to find it in any early "Legendario"; and so must content myself with telling the story, as best I can, by aid of the picture itself and such modern versions of the legend as are known to me.

Vita Prodigiosa di S. Eligio, Pisa, 1767, p. 69.

The devil, bent upon the temptation of the saint, came to his shop one day in the guise of a beautiful woman, bringing him a horse to be shod which, being possessed of an evil spirit, was so restive that it was not to be held in. The saint, however, nothing daunted, resorted to the simple expedient of cutting off its hoof, and having shod it, of miraculously uniting the severed pastern to the leg of the horse, to the confusion of the devil. In Botticelli's painting the saint, in the dress of a blacksmith, stands on the left of the composition, before his forge, shoeing the severed hoof. On the other side of the composition is the white horse whose pastern the saint has cut off, turned towards the left, and held by a boy in red hose and a scarlet cloak. Between the boy and the forge, turned towards the forge, is the devil in the guise of a woman in a dark green dress, with sprouting horns on her forehead, holding up a bundle of rods before her face.

Botticelli has borrowed the composition of this story from the relief by Nanni di Banco, below the statue of St. Eligius, in the niche of the Arte dei Manescalchi, on the west side of Or San Michele. Only in two particulars does he vary his composition from the original, turning the figure of the saint more in full face, and reversing that of the boy who holds the horse, in order to adapt the design to its place at the end of the "gradino." It is to be observed, that while the figures in the other stories, being in a sitting or kneeling posture, are at full length, these alone are seen at three-quarter length, as in the marble relief.

As in the case of the panels, which formed part of the "gradino" of the altar-piece of San Barnaba, we have here a series of stories which are entirely and indubitably the work of Botticelli's own hand. Admirable alike in design and colour, this "predella" is painted with the greatest freedom, and is preserved in an almost untouched state. Such a work, now that the date of its execution has been ascertained with tolerable certainty, must constitute for the student an artistic document of no little value in the criticism of this period of the master's career. Especially noble is the design of the "St. Augustine in his Study." Botticelli afterwards returned to this subject in a little panel now preserved in the Uffizi; but he did not again succeed in portraying the figure of the great prelate and doctor of the church with the same vigour and profound sentiment of pietistic learning. Admirable, too, in their expression of character, are the figures of St. Jerome and the Evangelist. Although somewhat obscured by dirt and varnish, this "predella" still retains its luminous depth of colour, a quality which is heightened not a little by the use of gold in the hatched high lights; and the clear, smalt blues and golden purples are very unlike those of the principal panel. The precise note of these colours, and of the saffron of the angel's robe, is peculiarly characteristic of Botticelli's colouring at this time, as we have seen in studying the "tondo" of 1487. Nor must we overlook the admirable keeping of the local masses, the deficiency of which is one of the chief defects of the principal panel.

In connection with this altar-piece may be studied a drawing by Botticelli of the Baptist, which is among the most important of the few extant drawings by him for pictures. The sheet in question, which is preserved in the Gallery of the Uffizi, Frame 55, No. 188, is executed in pen and bistre wash on a rubbed red ground, the lights being elaborately hatched in white. It represents the Baptist standing at full length, and turned somewhat towards the left. The right hand is slightly extended, as if holding a reed-cross, and in the left, with which the saint gathers together the mantle which he wears over his tunic of camel's hair, is a scroll, inscribed ECE AGNVS DEI. Those Giottesque traits, which I remarked in the altar-piece, and particularly in the figures of the four saints, re-occur in this drawing with greater emphasis: the forms of the nude are here more rugged, the folds of the drapery more linear and mannered. And yet the characters of the vigorous head and bony, uncouth hands, with the exaggerated form of the first finger, have their counterpart in this "predella," although the painting is probably of an earlier date than the drawing. But with all its mannerisms, how logical is the construction of this figure of the Baptist, how solid is the modelling, how large the relief. And these precisely are the qualities which the followers of Botticelli overlooked in their anxiety to imitate the exterior idiosyncrasies of his form and line.

A picture to which it is difficult to assign a date with precision, but which is certainly of this period, and probably executed not long after the altar-piece of San Marco, is a small panel of little, entire figures, formerly in the collection of the Marchese Gino Capponi, where it was attributed to Andrea da Castagno: it is now in the possession of his heirs, the Marchesi Farinola, in the Palazzo Capponi, at Florence. Morelli first pointed out that it was an original piece by Botticelli, and not, as Dr. Bode had pronounced it to be, a copy of a little panel in the Palazzo Balbi, at Genoa, which he ascribed to Filippino Lippi. The panel at Genoa, on the contrary, and another version of the same subject in the collection of Sir William Abdy, at Paris, are apparently contemporary copies of the original at Florence. The existence of two old copies shows that the picture was held in great repute at the time: and it is probable that this is the painting to which the Anonimo Gaddiano alludes. Botticelli, he says, "made very many little works which were most beautiful, and among the rest, a St. Jerome, a singular work." The "Last Communion of St. Jerome" is a subject which has been treated by the masters of various schools, both early and late. In the collection of Lorenzo, Il Magnifico, was a picture of "San Girol^mo^ quando s[i]chommunicha"; and other famous renderings of a later date, are the altar-pieces by Agostino Carracci, now in the Academy, at Bologna, and by Domenichino, in the gallery of the Vatican. The subject is derived from a legendary history of St. Jerome of mediæval origin, which was translated from the Latin into Italian, in the fifteenth century, and acquired a great popularity, running through a number of printed editions. The earliest

F. Fantozzi, Guida di Firenze, ed. 1844, p. 399.

I. Lermolieff, Die Galerie Borghese, ed. 1890, p. 146, note.

App. II, Doc. II, fol. 85, recto.

App. II, Doc. XXIX, fol. 6, recto.

Hain, Nos. 8637 and 8638.

THE LAST COMMUNION OF ST. JEROME *Collection of the Marchesi Farinola, Florence*

editions known to me which bear a date, were printed at Venice and Messina in 1473; the earliest edition printed at Florence is dated 1490. Beyond the Alps, the original Latin version was printed at Paris and Delft. The Florentine edition, which according to the usage of the time is without a title-page, begins thus: "Incomincia il Deuoto Tra*n*sito del Glorioso Sancto Hieronymo, Ridocto in lingua Fiore*n*tina"; and the colophon adds that it was printed "in Firenze per Ser Fra*n*cescho Bonacorsi a contemplatione delle diuote persone: Nelanno della salute. M. CCCC. LXXXX. Adi. XIII. di febraio." The tract opens with a brief life of the saint, which is followed by an apocryphal letter of the Blessed Eusebius bearing the title: "Incomincia la epistola del Beato Eusebio: laquale mando albeato Damasio uescouo di portue*n*se: & a Theodonio Senatore di Roma deltransito del beatissimo Sancto Hieronymo co*n*fessore et doctore excellentissimo." It is in the course of this letter that the account of the last communion of St. Jerome occurs, from which Botticelli has taken the subject of his picture. The rest of the book contains other apocryphal letters from St. Augustine, Bishop of Hippo, to the St. Cyril, Bishop of Jerusalem, and of St. Cyril to St. Augustine, relating certain visions which they and others had of St. Jerome, at the time of his death, with an account of his miracles, and some pieces in praise of his sanctity. From these letters, Signorelli took the subjects of three of the stories of a "predella," now in the collection of Dr. Ludwig Mond, at London.

Id., No. 8647.

l.c., sig. a viij, tergo.

The earlier chapters of the "Letter of the Blessed Eusebius," from which Botticelli has taken the subject of his picture, relate how St. Jerome, feeling his end to be near, made various exhortations and admonitions, which are set down at length, to those about him; how he took leave of his disciples, and how he ordered his tomb. These things being ended, the legend goes on to relate, that "one of the monks brought him the most holy body of our Lord Jesus Christ; and as soon as the man of God saw it, he immediately, with our aid, cast himself down with his face to the earth; and crying out as loudly as he was able, with a great lamentation, began to say: 'Lord, what am I, that thou shouldest enter into my house; what desert have I, a sinner? Truly, my Lord, I am not worthy. Am I better than my fathers of the Old Testament? To Moses, thou wouldest not show thyself for so long as the twinkling of an eye; wherefore now dost thou so humble thyself, that thou deignest to come to a sinner; and not only wouldst thou eat with him, but thou biddest him to eat of thee.' And as soon as the priest who held the eucharist came near to him, the glorious man, with our aid, raised himself on his knees, and lifted his head, and with many tears and sighs, beating his breast many times, he said: 'Thou art my God and my Lord, who suffered Death and the Passion for me, and none other!'" and so fell to making a plenary confession of his faith with many prayers, which are set down at length in the "Epistle of the Blessed Eusebius." And when the saint had made an end of these words, he "received the most holy body of Christ, and cast himself again upon the ground, with his hands crossed upon his breast, singing the canticle of Simeon, the prophet, 'Nunc dimittis servum tuum,' etc. And when he had finished, all those who were present, suddenly saw in the place where he lay, so divine a light to shine, that if all the beams of the sun had presently shone forth, they could not so greatly have dazzled them; insomuch that by no means were they able to look at the

l.c., Cap. VII-XVIII, sig. b iij, tergo, to e viij, tergo.

Id., Cap. XXI, sig. f vj, recto.

glorious man as he rose up towards the East. This light continuing for a space of time, certain of those who stood around, saw there companies of angels passing away on every side, in the likeness of flames. Others did not see the angels, but heard a voice from heaven which said: 'Come, my beloved, this is the time that thou receivest the reward of thy labour, which for love of me bravely hast thou borne.' Some there were that neither saw the angels, nor heard the voice, but heard only the voice of the blessed Jerome, who said, when that other voice was ended, 'Behold, I come to Thee merciful Jesus! Receive Thou me whom Thou hast redeemed with thy precious Blood!' Then, having made an end of speaking, that most holy spirit, like a star radiant with every virtue, left his body, ascending to the glorious realm of heaven."

Such is the legend from which Botticelli has taken the subject of his painting, rejecting the merely supernatural element, for the human interest of the story. The scene is laid in a cell of green, wattled reeds. On the right of the picture, the dying saint, who has just risen from his bed, his hands clasped in prayer, kneels with the help of two young monks in brown habits, who hold the linen cloth before him. The holy man puts forth to the uttermost, the lees of life which remain in him, in order once more to partake of the body of Christ, as the priest who is vested in a chasuble of clear purple with azure apparel, and attended by two acolytes bearing lighted candles, bends towards him and places the consecrated wafer between his lips. Behind the figures is seen the bed of the saint, with its sheepskin coverlet: above the head of the bed, against the green wall of the cell, hangs a crucifix surrounded by palms and olive-branches, and on one side a cardinal's hat. Seen through a window in each of the lateral walls of the cell, and again above the gable of the wattled roof, is one of those cloudless and luminous skies, which seem to bring a touch of actual sunlight into Botticelli's paintings.

To express that smallness of the body in relation to the head, which is characteristic of very aged persons, Botticelli has unduly exaggerated the head of the St. Jerome; and this, perhaps, is the one defect in a picture, which otherwise must be placed among the finest of his smaller works. In character, however, the head as well as the hands of the saint are admirable; and there is a touch of Dantesque power in the art, by which the whole interest of the scene is centred in the struggle between the spiritual aspiration, and the physical weakness, of the saint. The luminous, translucent quality of its colouring is especially lovely: the clear, delicate purple of the priest's chasuble, its azure apparel and dark green lining, occur with jewel-like brillance against the white habit of St. Jerome, the white cloth which is held up before him, the grayish-brown habits of the monks and the surplices of the acolytes; while the green palms and wattled walls of the cell, and the breaks of azure sky, appear the cooler in contrast to the touch of scarlet in the cardinal's hat forming the background of the picture. The symmetrical disposition of the two groups of triple figures, counterposed to one another, is an arrangement which forms the central motive of two of Botticelli's later compositions, the wall-painting of "Lorenzo Tornabuoni and the Liberal Arts," in the Louvre, No. 1298, and the painting of the "Calumny of Apelles," in the Uffizi, No. 1182. The panel on which this little picture is painted, measures 12¾ in. in height, by 9½ in. in breadth; and the painting itself is in an excellent state of preservation, having been carefully cleaned by Signor Cavenaghi of Milan, a few years ago, who then skilfully repaired a crack, which ran down the centre of the panel.

The façade of the cathedral church of Santa Maria del Fiore, begun by Francesco Talenti and Giovanni di Lapo Ghini in 1357, had, in the course of a century and a half, been covered with marble, and enriched with reliefs and statues, to about a third of its total height. Francesco Albertini, in his "Memoriale," declares this unfinished façade to have been "without order or proportion"; and a drawing of it, made in the sixteenth century, and still preserved in the Museum of the "Opera" of Santa Maria del Fiore, No. 131, shows that it had been put together at the hands of successive architects and sculptors, with little continuity of design, or unity of effect. About this time a project was mooted, (chiefly at the instance of Lorenzo, Il Magnifico, according to Francesco Albertini,) to remove this unfinished work, and to erect a new façade according to a good design. In the minutes of the deliberations of the "Operai," or wardens of the works, of Santa Maria del Fiore, preserved among the archives of the "Opera," it is recorded that on the 12th February, 1489-90, many of the chief citizens of Florence having represented to the Consuls of the Arte della Lana, to whom was committed the maintenance of the fabric of the cathedral, that it was greatly to the reproach of the city that the façade should remain in that unfinished condition, "sine aliqua ratione aut iure architecture," leave was given to the "Operai" to move in the matter. A later minute in the same volume records that designs, or models, for the proposed façade having meanwhile been obtained from eleven artists, among whom were Giuliano Maiano, lately dead, Benedetto da Maiano, Cecco di Giorgio, the Sienese, Filippino Lippi and Antonio Pollaiuoli; on 5th January, 1490-1, the "Operai" called together the Consuls of the Arte della Lana, a number of representative citizens and forty of the principal artists, both architects, sculptors, painters, goldsmiths, workers in wood and others, who are called in the minute "architecti"; meaning, I suppose, that they were persons of acknowledged skill in the theory, if not in the practice, of architecture. Among the painters present were Lorenzo di Credi, Domenico Ghirlandaio, Cosimo Rosselli, Perugino, "Sander Botticelli" (the original is in Latin), and Alessio Baldovinetti; but Luca Signorelli, Il Graffione and eight of the other "architecti" summoned to attend, were absent. These persons having assembled in the loggia of the "Opera," and having viewed the drawings and models which were displayed there, Carlo de' Benci, the first speaker, (a canon of the cathedral and an architect of some repute, who had himself submitted a model,) proposed that the decision should be left in the hands of Lorenzo, Il Magnifico. Four of the principal citizens, who then rose in succession, were of the opinion that the decision should be deferred to another time, since the matter demanded more mature consideration. Whereupon Lorenzo himself rose, and, after complimenting the artists who had submitted the various drawings and models, moved that, inasmuch as the work which they were discussing would be of an enduring nature, it demanded a more careful examination, and therefore it was fitting that their decision should be deferred. The meeting was accordingly postponed, and the archives of the "Opera" do not record that any further steps were then taken in the matter. There can be little doubt that as the project had been set on foot by Lorenzo, so it was interrupted by his death, in 1492. The unfinished façade was not removed till 1586; and the project to erect a new one was only realized in our own time.

App. II, Doc. XXXV.

A A

An acquaintance with the theory of architecture was a customary and necessary part of the equipment of every Florentine painter in the fifteenth century; so that a man pre-eminent as a painter, was naturally regarded as a judge of architecture, at least in the matter of its design. The beauty of the architectural inventions, which Botticelli introduces into the backgrounds of his paintings, however, shows that he had studied such things with more than ordinary care and judgment; and it is significant that on the occasion in question, both his master, Antonio Pollaiuoli, and his disciple, Filippino Lippi, should submit designs as practical architects for so important a work as the façade of Santa Maria del Fiore.

In this connection may be cited the testimony, which a disciple of Piero della Francesca and a fellow-student of Leonardo da Vinci, in their mathematical studies, bears to Botticelli's skill in perspective. Luca Paccioli, in the introduction to his "Summa de Arithmetica, Geometria, Proportione & Proportionalita," printed at Venice in 1494, mentions among the many artists of renown who at that time, in the various cities of Italy, were skilled in this art, at Florence, Botticelli, Fillippino and Domenico Ghirlandaio: "Florentie Alexander buticelli Philippinus & Dominicus grilandaio." "Qui omnes," adds the writer by way of formal compliment, "opera sua libela & circino proportionando mirabiliter perficiunt: ad eo vt non humana sed divina oculis appareant, nec hijs aliud q*uam* sola anima deesse videtur."

l.c., fol. 3, tergo.

The following year, 1491, Botticelli was himself commissioned by the "Operai" of Santa Maria del Fiore, to decorate, in company with Domenico and David Ghirlandaio, and Gherardo, the miniaturist, and his partners, Bartolommeo and Monte di Giovanni, the vault of the chapel of San Zenobio, in mosaic. It is the last occasion on which he and Domenico Ghirlandaio are found working together. In the volume already cited, containing the minutes of the Deliberations of the "Operai," from 1486 to 1491, is the following entry: "On the eighteenth day of May, 1491, Antonio Paganelli and Tommaso Minerbetti, the 'Operai' or Wardens of the Works of Santa Maria del Fiore in the city of Florence, together with the Overseers of the Ordinances of the said Guild [*i.e.* the Arte della Lana,] that is to say, Ruggiero di Niccolo de' Corbinelli, Francesco di Antonio di Taddeo, and Lorenzo di Piero di Cosimo de' Medici etc., deliberated, and deliberating, gave out on contract to Domenico and David, brothers and sons of Tommaso di Currado del Ghirlandaio, citizens and painters of Florence, in that place then present, for the one part, and to Sandro di Mariano Botticello, painter, and Gherardo di Giovanni, miniaturist, and his partners, also there present for the other half part, to be executed for the said Office of Works, in mosaic in the chapel of San Zenobio, situated in the said church of Santa Maria del Fiore in Florence, two parts out of four of the vault or ceiling of the said chapel, namely two of the four spiculiform compartments [spiculos] of the chapel aforesaid, and to each one of the said parties, one of the said compartments with its figures; at such a price and according to such times, modes and forms, as shall seem proper to the Wardens present, or for the time being, of the said Works, notwithstanding etc."

App. II, Doc. XXXVI, fol. 49, tergo.

A Florentine diarist of the time, Tribaldo de' Rossi, has recorded in his "Ricordanze," that this chapel of San Zenobio "was begun to be storied in mosaic by two master-painters," in the month of August, 1491: "Richordo, chome d'Aghosto nel 1491, si chominciò a istoriare di musaicho la chapela

Delizie degli Eruditi Toscani, XXIII, 272.

di San Zanobi di Santa Maria del Fiore da due maestri dipintori." The books of the "Opera" of Santa Maria del Fiore, moreover, contain the following entries of payments made by the "Operai," in connection with the work:

"25th August, 1491, to Sandro di Mariano del Botticello on account of the mosaics to be executed in the chapel of San Zenobio, fiorini -,—lire 20, soldi 4. (App. II, Doc. XXXVI, fol. 138, tergo, and fol. 139, tergo.)

"23rd December, 1491, to Domenico and David di Tommaso del Grillandaio, masters of mosaic, on account of their labour in executing the mosaic in the chapel of San Zenobio, fiorini 70,—lire 89, soldi 18.

" to Sandro di Mariano, Gherardo and Monte, masters of mosaic, on the said account, ut supra, fiorini 47,—lire— soldi 15.

"30th June, 1492, to Domenico and David di Tommaso, masters of mosaic, on account of the work which is being executed in the chapel of San Zenobio, fiorini 21,—lire— soldi 10. (App. II, Doc. XXXVII, fol. 66, recto, and fol. 68, tergo.)

" to Gherardo and Monte, masters of mosaic, on account of the work which is being executed in the chapel of San Zenobio, fiorini 2,—lire -, soldi 10.

"18th December, 1492, to Gherardo and Monte di Giovanni and Sandro di Mariano, masters of mosaic on account of the mosaic executed in the chapel of San Zenobio. fiorini 31,—lire 35, soldi 11."

According to these entries, Botticelli, Gherardo and Monte, received between August 25th, 1491 and December 18th, 1492, a total amount of more than 89 fiorini, (reckoning lire 6 and soldi 10 to a fiorino), and Domenico and David Ghirlandaio, nearly 105 fiorini. Now at a rough calculation, each of the four compartments of the vault contains more than thirty square braccia, which at 6 fiorini the square braccio, (the price allowed for the work when it was resumed in 1510,) gives a total of about 180 fiorini. It would appear, therefore, that at the time that these entries cease, in December, 1492, the work must have been far from complete, having probably been brought to a standstill by the death of Lorenzo, Il Magnifico, in April, 1492. A year later, however, these mosaics were resumed by the order of Piero de' Medici, and the decoration of a third compartment was put in hand. In a later volume of the Deliberations of the "Operai," from 1491 to 1498, is a minute to the effect that, on December 31st, 1493, the Wardens "gave out on contract to Gherardo and Monte, brothers, and sons of the late Giovanni, miniaturists, citizens of Florence, etc., to be executed in mosaic, one spiculiform compartment [spiculum] of the four which are in the principal chapel, namely that of San Zenobio, in the said church; to wit, the one which is, in vulgar parlance, *lungo l'arco dinanzi*, [beside the arch in front], in such a manner and form, and with such a figure, in stucco, and at such a price, and within such time and times, as shall be declared from time to time, by the Magnificent Pietro, the son of the late Lorenzo de' Medici, to whom they had remitted all the aforesaid matters." (Vasari, ed. Le Monnier VI., 340.) The work of filling this third compartment with mosaic was actually begun; for it appears from the books of the "Opera," that on the 12th of March, 1493-4, the Wardens resolved "that Domenico di Gregorio and Mariotto della Volpaia, and their workmen, be held to be removed from their office, if in the course of the present day, they shall not have adjusted the scaffold for the mosaic, so that Gherardo and Monte may be able to work there:" and a few days later, on the 20th of March, the sum of ten fiorini larghi was paid to Gherardo and Monte, on account of (App. II, Doc. XXXVII, fol. 21, recto and tergo.)

these mosaics. The books of the "Opera" contain no further evidence of the progress of the work at this time; it was probably interrupted by the flight of Piero de' Medici, in November, 1494.

From that time until 1504, an interval of ten years, nothing appears to have been done. Meanwhile Domenico Ghirlandaio had died on January 11th, 1493-4, and Gherardo in the earlier part of the year 1497. At length, on the 23rd December, 1504, the Consuls of the Arte della Lana, and the "Operai" of the Cathedral, "having regard to the consultation and discourse which on many and many occasions had taken place (so runs the minute of the Deliberation), concerning the finishing of the mosaics in the chapel of San Zenobio, long since begun," resolved to commission Monte, the brother of Gherardo, and David, the brother of Domenico Ghirlandaio, to execute, in competition, "two busts, or heads, in mosaic"; and to entrust the completion of the chapel to whoever should prove himself the better master. On the 30th of June, 1505, the two heads in mosaic were submitted to "Pietro Perugino, Lorenzo di Credi, Giovanni delle Corniole, and other painters," who judged Monte "to have depicted and worked the better."

Vasari, ed. Sansoni, III, 277, note, and 252.

Vasari, ed. Le Monnier, VI, 340.

On 30th June, 1505, the "Operai" resolved that in the event of the commission to finish the mosaics in the Chapel of San Zenobio having been given to Monte within three months' time, that he should retain as his own, his trial-piece of the head in mosaic, and that he should not be able to demand anything of the "Opera" on that account; but that, in the event of the commission to finish the chapel not having been given to him within the stipulated time, he should receive 100 fiorini, and the head should remain the property of the "Opera." The three months having expired, and the commission not having been given to Monte, he was paid the money, and the head was retained by the "Opera." Nevertheless, the mosaics of the chapel were still proceeded with; and the books of the "Opera" record payments made to Monte on that account, in 1508 and 1509. At length, on 27th June, 1510, the "Operai," having regard "to the ornament to the Chapel of San Zenobio, which had long since been begun to be set with mosaic in the four spiculiform compartments of the vault of the said chapel, by the hand of Monte and Gherardo," resolved to give to Monte, although absent, "the said four compartments of the vault of the said chapel to be wrought and set with mosaic, in the best manner, at the rate of six gold fiorini the square braccio." In spite of this formal commission, there is no evidence that any considerable progress was made with the work; and the death of Monte, which took place c. 1527, must finally have put an end to any chance that remained of completing these mosaics. The fact that all four compartments of the vault were given to Monte to set with mosaic, in 1510, would show that at that time none of the three compartments which had been begun, were as yet finished. I may add that the trial-piece of the head of San Zenobio, which Monte executed for the competition of 1505, is still preserved in the Museum of the "Opera" of Santa Maria del Fiore, No. 74.

Vasari, ed. Sansoni, III, 251.

Vasari, ed. Le Monnier, VI, 342.

Neither Vasari, nor the earlier commentators, make any allusion to the share which Botticelli had in the execution of these mosaics; although they speak of the part which Domenico Ghirlandaio and Gherardo took in them. Vasari states, in the life of Ghirlandaio, that, by reason of the death of Lorenzo, Il Magnifico, "the Chapel of San Zenobi, which was begun to be decorated in mosaic by Domenico, in company with Gherardo the miniaturist, remained unfinished." Again, speaking of the encouragement which Lorenzo extended to the revival of the art of working in mosaic, which took place

Vasari, ed. 1550, I, 487.

in Florence during the latter part of the fifteenth century, and especially of his patronage of Gherardo, Vasari says, that Lorenzo "caused him, in company with Domenico Ghirlandaio, to obtain from the 'Operai' of Santa Maria del Fiore, the commission of the chapels in the head and arms of the church; wherefore, as a beginning, he caused that of the Sacrament, where is the body of San Zenobio, to be given to him." Adding in the second edition of the "Lives," that Gherardo "would have executed with Domenico most admirable things, if death had not interposed itself; as one is able to judge from the beginning of that chapel which has remained imperfect." Another piece of evidence that these unfinished mosaics were still to be seen in the Cathedral, towards the end of the sixteenth century, occurs in a list compiled by Antonio Petrei, c. 1565-70, of the works of art then to be seen in the churches and public buildings of Florence, in which "Il musaico dela cap*pel*[la] di S[to] Zanobi," ascribed to Dominico Ghirlandaio, is set down among the notable things in Santa Maria del Fiore. A century later, these mosaics were no longer visible; a circumstance which led Ferdinando Leopoldo Del Migliore, in his "Firenze Illustrata," published in 1684, to assert that they had been in the "sotteraneo," or crypt, then known as the Chapel of San Zenobio, which is immediately below the chapel known in Vasari's time as the Chapel of the Sacrament, in the head of the Cathedral behind the high altar. Del Migliore was, no doubt, led astray by Vasari's expression, "doue è il corpo di S. Zanobi"; the body of the saint up to the year 1685, having been buried in the "sotteraneo," or lower chapel. But that Del Migliore is in error, is placed beyond all doubt by the statement contained in the minute of 31st December, 1493, that one of the compartments of the vault to be decorated in mosaic, was "lungo l'arco dinanzi"; an expression that can only apply to the upper chapel. To add to the confusion, Giuseppe Richa, in his notices of the Florentine churches, repeats Del Migliore's mistake.

Id., I, 489.

Vasari, ed. 1568, I, 454.

App. II, Doc. I, fol. 53, tergo.

l.c., p. 26.

G. Richa, Chiese Flor., VI, 168.

In order to indicate more clearly the part which Botticelli took in this work, I will endeavour to point out certain traits in the character of Gherardo as an artist, whose relation with Botticelli has hitherto been overlooked. Some notion of the esteem in which Gherardo was held in his day, is to be gathered from the fact that Vasari has written the life of this variously gifted artist, who painted both in fresco and in miniature, who worked in mosaic, and who was also an accomplished musician, and for some time organist of the Church of Sant' Egidio in Florence. Gherardo was born in the year 1445, the son of a stone-carver, Giovanni di Miniato, surnamed Fora. The few works in fresco by him, which have survived, are either in very indifferent condition, or have been entirely repainted; but like the many fine miniatures by his hand, and especially the larger ones of his later period, which have come down to us, they show him to have been one of the few imitators of Botticelli, who were able to appreciate some quality of his master's genius, apart from his outward and obvious mannerisms. Of his work as a painter I shall speak when I come to discuss the disciples of Botticelli: for the moment, I propose only to turn to one of the more famous codices illuminated by his hand, the Missal which he decorated with thirty-four storiated miniatures, besides smaller initial letters, for the Hospital of Santa Maria Nuova in Florence. This sumptuously beautiful volume, unfortunately robbed of its chief miniature at the Canon of the Mass, is now preserved in the Museum of the Bargello. Its miniatures, and especially some of the larger ones, reveal various and complex influences;

Vasari, ed. Sansoni, III, 237.

Id., III, 248.

they show the influence of Flemish, or at least northern, miniature-painting in their elaborate technique; and they show even more plainly the influence of Botticelli. Many of the smaller ones, on the other hand, betray the influence of Alesso Baldovinetti. This influence is so direct and unmistakable, that one cannot but conclude that at one period of his career, Gherardo must have studied under Alesso. According to Milanesi, Gherardo executed this Missal for the Church of Sant' Egidio, between the years 1474 and 1487. I suspect that the miniatures in which the influence of Alesso is most plainly discernible, may be among those which Gherardo first executed; and that those which are more Botticellesque in manner, may belong to the later time, when the volume was brought to a completion. Certainly, the large miniature at the beginning of the Psalter, which Gherardo executed for Matthias Corvinus, King of Hungary, shortly before the death of that monarch in 1490, and which is now in the Laurentian Library, shows the influence of Botticelli in a more direct and unmistakable fashion, than any of the earlier miniatures in the Missal. Here, then, we may possess a clue to the source of Gherardo's knowledge and practice of mosaic. When, in 1483, Baldovinetti received the commission to restore the mosaics in the Tribune of the Baptistery at Florence, the "Operai" declared that "he alone in all the realm and jurisdiction of Florence then understood that art." Whether or no we may believe Vasari's story, "that Alesso laboured much to find out the true method of working in mosaic, but that nothing ever turned out as he wished till a German, who was going on a pilgrimage to Rome, taught him the secret;" we can hardly doubt, that to Alesso was due the revival of this art in Florence during the latter part of the fifteenth century. David Ghirlandaio, also, like Gherardo, must have acquired the method of working in mosaic from Baldovinetti. Vasari says that Alesso taught the art to Domenico Ghirlandaio; it would seem rather that, though Domenico undoubtedly designed cartoons for mosaics, the execution of them was largely, if not entirely, carried out by his brother David. Indeed, Vasari, elsewhere, expressly speaks of the workshop which David had at Montaione, in the Valdelsa, for this purpose; and a further proof of this is afforded by the mosaic over the door into the atrium of the Annunziata at Florence, which is known to have been worked by David in 1490, apparently from his own cartoon. When the commission for the chapel of San Zenobio was given to Domenico and David Ghirlandaio, in 1491, they had already restored the mosaic on the old façade of the Cathedral in 1487, and had executed in 1490 that of the "Annunciation," which still remains over one of the side doors of the Cathedral, towards the Via de' Servi.

Vasari, ed. Sansoni, III, 248.

G. Richa, Chiese Fior., V, xxxv.

Vasari, ed. Sansoni, II, 596.

Id., II, 597.

Id., VI, 534.

Id. VI, 540, note.

Id. III, 280 and 274.

But to come to a conclusion. It is clear, I think, that Botticelli's share of the mosaics in the chapel of San Zenobio, like that of Domenico Ghirlandaio, was limited to giving a cartoon for one of the two compartments of the vault, to be executed in the one case by Gherardo, in the other by David. This conjecture, so far as Botticelli is concerned, is borne out by the fact that when, in 1493, the mosaics on the third compartment of the vault were given to Gherardo and Monte to execute, we no longer hear of Botticelli working in conjunction with them. Indeed, at the time when Vasari wrote, in 1550, all recollection of Botticelli's share in the work had been lost; and in the passage quoted above, the work is attributed to Domenico Ghirlandaio and Gherardo. Again, in the second edition of the "Lives," Vasari adds that Gherardo "made a great cartoon for some large figures of the Evangelists which he had to execute in mosaic, in the chapel of San Zenobio." It is possible, of course, that the cartoon for the third compartment of the vault, which was given to Gherardo and Monte in 1493, was designed by Gherardo himself. Be this as it may, we have no reason to doubt Vasari's statement, that the subjects of these mosaics were certain "large figures of the Evangelists." A vault of the same form as the vault of the chapel of San Zenobio, quadrangular in plan, and divided by simple, intersecting ribs, into four compartments, may be seen in the Cappella Maggiore of the Cathedral at Prato, painted by Fra Filippo, with four large figures of the Evangelists; and a second vault of the same common type, painted by Ghirlandaio himself, with figures of the Evangelists, similarly arranged, is to be seen in the Cappella Maggiore of Santa Maria Novella. That the mosaics of the four Evangelists upon the vault of the chapel of San Zenobio, recalled these frescoes, in their general arrangement, may be reasonably conjectured: but more than that, it is no longer possible to say, since no trace of these mosaics is now to be seen in the chapel.

Vasari, ed. 1568, I, 454.

On the 8th April, 1492, Lorenzo, Il Magnifico, died at his villa at Careggi. The signs and portents, which foretold his death, show with what apprehension the issue was anticipated; and the catastrophe proved, in the event, a turning point not only in the career of Botticelli, but also in the history of Florentine Art. "Fortune, the adversary of genius," says Vasari, "deprived the artists of that time of their best hope and support, through the death of Lorenzo." The private undertakings which he had carried on in a truly princely fashion, and the innumerable public works which his munificence had promoted, were alike interrupted: and after his death, Botticelli does not appear to have again received any important commission of a public nature. Vasari says that Sandro "was held in great regard" by the Magnifico, and that, "so long as Lorenzo lived, he always assisted him." Through the good offices, or at the instance, of Lorenzo, Botticelli had received the commission to execute the effigies of the Pazzi conspirators on the Bargello, in 1478, and the mosaics for the chapel of San Zenobio in 1491. At Lorenzo's villa of the Spedaletto, near Volterra, Botticelli painted, soon after his return from Rome, a series of frescoes; and "in Casa Medici," in the Via Larga, as Vasari records, "he executed many things for Lorenzo the elder; of which the most important ('massimamente' is the phrase used by Vasari), was the Pallas above an impress of branches," a painting which may have been executed, as I have shown, before the death of Giuliano, in 1478. The other works appear to have been of a decorative nature, and one of them is described in the inventory of Lorenzo's goods, taken at the time of his death; though the entry has hitherto been overlooked: "In the antechamber of Piero," which adjoined the room in which the "Pallas" hung, was "a bedstead of a rustic form, four braccia long, with predelle round about it of walnut and inlaid with intarsia, and bed-posts and mattress," appraised at one florin; and "a 'sopracielo,' or tester, for the said bed of the said antechamber, painted with a Fortune by the hand of Sandro di Botticello." From this, we may form some idea of what the other works executed by Botticelli in Casa Medici, may have been. Certainly, such deductions as may be drawn from the Inventory in question, seem to bear out what Vasari implies; that these remaining works were of minor importance to the "Pallas," and probably of a decorative nature. From the workshop of Botticelli, must have come a large number of furniture-panels and other works of the same kind. The

Id., ed. 1550, I, 495.

App. II, Doc. XXIX, fol. 48, recto.

"Mars and Venus" of the National Gallery probably formed, as I have said, the panel in the head of a bed; the four panels painted for the Pucci, seem to have ornamented the "spalliera" of a "lettuccio," or settle; and other paintings which remain to be discussed, were doubtlessly painted for the decoration of wall-panelling, or furniture. It is idle to conjecture further what these works, executed for Lorenzo, may have been; and, in common with all the other paintings done at the instance of the Magnifico, they have long since been lost, or destroyed. With the death of Lorenzo, Il Magnifico, to use Botticelli's own phrase, began "the troubles of Italy." Piero de' Medici, who succeeded his father as the chief citizen of the Florentine Republic, and the real, if not the nominal, head of the State, was a headstrong, arrogant youth of twenty-one, "cattivo di tutti e vizi," as a contemporary writer declares, with none of his father's genius for leading and governing men. The death of Lorenzo was followed by that of Innocent VIII, on July 25th, 1492, by the subsequent election of Roderigo Borgia to the Papacy, as Alexander VI, and by the death of Ferrante, King of Naples, in January, 1494. The death of Ferrante gave Charles VIII. of France the occasion which he sought of asserting his pretensions, as the heir of René, Duke of Anjou and King of Jerusalem, to the throne of Naples. Having formed a league with Lodovico Sforza, Charles prepared to march into Italy; whereupon Piero de' Medici threw over the French Alliance, and joined the Pope and the King of Naples. But the alliance of Florence with France was not, however, so easily to be set aside: for no small part of the mercantile interests of the Florentines depended upon a good understanding between the two countries. Lorenzo had always been keenly alive to the importance of amicable relations with France; and the fleurs-de-lys of the French King which he bore on his shield, were a sign to the world of the success with which his family had fostered those relations. When Piero refused to abandon the league with Naples, Charles VIII. banished the Florentine merchants from his kingdom, and so struck a blow at one of the material interests of Florence. Lorenzo di Pierfrancesco de' Medici, and his brother Giovanni, who had long regarded with jealousy the growing power of the elder branch of the family, found in the embarrassments of Piero, an opportunity to prosecute their ambitions. Lorenzo had been one of the envoys sent to the court of France to congratulate Charles VIII. upon his accession: and the two brothers did not scruple to use their influence in that quarter, in order to further their own interests.

Delizie degli Eruditi Toscani, XXIII, 291-4. L. Landucci, Diario, p. 67.

On the 24th April, 1494, Lorenzo and Giovanni were cited to appear before the Otto di Prattica. According to the more probable account, they were called upon to answer the accusation, that they had been plotting with the King of France against their cousin, Piero. The two brothers were committed to the Bargello, and examined, but without the formality of torture. Some days later they were ordered to be confined, Lorenzo at his villa of Castello, and Giovanni at Caffagiolo. In the following September, Charles VIII. crossed the Alps, and was joined by Lodovico Sforza; a few weeks later, Lorenzo and Giovanni escaped to the King at Vigevano, near Milan. On the 14th of November, five days after Piero de' Medici had fled from Florence, Lorenzo di Pierfrancesco de' Medici, and his brother Giovanni, with a number of other outlaws, who had been banished by the Medici, and among the rest the Neroni, who had been exiled by Piero, Il Gottoso, in 1466, and those who had fled the city on account of the Pazzi conspiracy in 1478, entered the city; a general amnesty having been

L. Landucci, Diario, p. 79.

Delizie degli Eruditi Toscani, XXI, 80.

granted to them by the Signoria. At the same time, the effigies painted by Andrea da Castagno, of those who had been declared rebels in 1434, and the effigies of the Pazzi conspirators, which Botticelli had painted on the front of the Bargello, were effaced by the order of the Signoria. Three days later, Charles VIII. made his entry into Florence. Lorenzo and his brother now joined the faction of Piero Capponi and the popular party, as a stepping-stone to their real design. They sought, like Lorenzo, Il Magnifico, to insinuate themselves into the chief power of the state by advocating the cause of the people, under the guise of private citizens; and in order to give colour to these pretensions, did not scruple to have recourse to the most extravagant expedients. No sooner had they returned to the city, than they caused, says Jacopo Nardi, "the [Medicean] arms of the 'palle' to be removed from the fronts of their houses, and the proper arms of the people, to wit, a red cross in a white field, to be put up in the place of them; and so abandoning the surname of Medici, they caused themselves by public decree, as singular lovers of liberty, to be called 'Popolani.'" After Charles VIII. had retired from Florence, a new Balia, or council of twenty, with the title of Accoppiatori, were created by Parliament, with the control of the public purse, and power to appoint all new magistrates. And although Lorenzo di Pierfrancesco de' Medici was younger by some years than the prescribed age, he was nevertheless appointed one of the twenty Accoppiatori: "and this was done," says a contemporary writer, "in order to give him extraordinary reputation, and so to make him head of the new state, for in that mutation the head alone was changed, and not the mode of government."

J. Nardi, Istorie Fior., ed. 1858, I, 35.

Id., I, 36.

F. de' Nerli, Commentari, ed. 1728, p. 64.

During the next few years immediately succeeding to these events, Lorenzo di Pierfrancesco is found in intercourse with some of the most eminent Florentine artists of the day. Vasari only once alludes to Lorenzo as a patron of the arts; namely, in the life of Michelagnolo, where he says that that master "made for Lorenzo di Pierfrancesco de' Medici, in marble, a little St. John." But it would seem also that Lorenzo, perhaps in conjunction with his brother, Giovanni, gave the commission to Filippino Lippi for the painting of the "Adoration of the Magi," which was once over the high altar of the church of San Donato a Scopeto, a monastery which formerly stood in the suburbs of Florence, on one of the slopes of Bellosguardo. This monastery, like many others, was pulled down at the time of the siege, in 1529, on account of its vicinity to the walls of Florence; and the altar-piece is now in the Gallery of the Uffizi, No. 1268. The back of the panel is inscribed: FILIPPVS ME PINSIT FLORENTINVS ADDI 29 DI MARZO 1496. That this picture was painted at the instance of Lorenzo, may be surmised from the portraits of himself, his father and his brother, which it contains. Filippino, according to Vasari, portrayed in it "Pier Francesco de' Medici the elder, son of Lorenzo di Bicci, in the figure of an astrologer, who holds a quadrant in his hand, and likewise Giovanni, father of the Signor Giovanni de' Medici, and another Pier Francesco, brother of that Signor Giovanni, and other notable persons." This statement of Vasari's is borne out by the fact, that the portrait of Pierfrancesco, the son of Lorenzo di Giovanni di Bicci, No. 6, among the portraits of the Medici, painted by Cristofano dell' Altissimo, for Cosimo I. de' Medici, which now hang in the corridor running from the Uffizi to the Palazzo Pitti, was copied from the figure of the magus with an astrolabe in his hand, who kneels in the foreground of the picture, on the left. The figure of the magus

Vasari, ed. Sansoni, VII, 147.

Vasari, ed. Sansoni, III, 473.

on the left, who takes the crown from off his head as he turns to kneel to the divine child, is a portrait of Giovanni di Pierfrancesco; and this again is shown by the fact that the portrait of Giovanni by Cristofano dell'Altissimo, No. 4 of the same series, has been taken from the head of this magus. The miniatures of Pierfrancesco and his son, Giovanni, ascribed to Bronzino, in the Uffizi, Frame 3364, have in turn been severally taken from the same heads in Filippino's altar-piece. The portrait-figure with the long hair who stands beside Giovanni, and hands to him the jewelled cup, which he is about to present to the child, is, no doubt, that to which Vasari alludes as a portrait of "un' altro Pier Francesco di esso Signor Giovanni fratello." But Vasari must here intend Lorenzo di Pierfrancesco, a mistake which he elsewhere makes, since Giovanni di Pierfrancesco had but one brother; and the only other member of the family of that name, was Pierfrancesco di Lorenzo di Pierfrancesco, who was not born until 1486. This head of the magus then, so far as I am aware, is the only portrait we have of the patron, who gave to Botticelli the commission for four of his greatest works, the "Spring," the "Birth of Venus," the "Pallas," and the illustrations to Dante.

Vasari, ed. Sansoni, VII, 147.

After Michelagnolo returned to Florence from Bologna, in the earlier part of the year 1495, "he made," as Vasari relates, "for Lorenzo di Pierfrancesco de' Medici, a little St. John in marble, and afterwards began to carve from another block of marble a sleeping Cupid of the size of life." Both statues must now be accounted among the lost works of Michelagnolo; at least, the marble figure at Berlin cannot be identified with the St. John. As to the Cupid, both Vasari and Condivi relate its history at length: but the latter probably had his version of the matter from Michelagnolo himself. Certainly his account is the more circumstantial and to our present purpose.

A. Condivi, Vita di Michelagnolo, ed. 1553, p. 10.

"Lorenzo di Pier Francesco de' Medici," writes Condivi, "having seen the Cupid, and judging it to be an admirable work, said to him, 'If you were to treat it so that it appeared to have been buried in the earth, I would send it to Rome, and it would pass for an antique, and you would sell it at a far better price.' Michelagnolo hearing that, immediately treated it in such a manner, that it appeared to have been made many ages ago; he being a man to whom no mode of skill was unknown. The figure having been sent to Rome in this condition, the Cardinal of San Giorgio bought it as an antique, for two hundred ducats; nevertheless the person [one Baldassarre del Milanese], who received that sum of money, wrote to Florence that thirty ducats were due to Michelagnolo, since that was the amount he had received for the Cupid, deceiving at the same time both Lorenzo di Pier Francesco and Michelagnolo. But meanwhile, it having come to the ears of the Cardinal that the Cupid had been made in Florence, he, disdaining to be cheated, sent one of his gentlemen thither, who, pretending to look for a sculptor to execute certain works in Rome, was directed, after going to some others, to the house of Michelagnolo"; and finding the young man, he asked him, in the course of their conversation, whether he had executed any piece of sculpture. "When Michelagnolo replied yes, and among other things, a Cupid of such a size and in such an attitude, the gentleman learned what he wished to know; and having related to Michelagnolo how the matter had gone, he promised him that if he would go with him to Rome, he would cause the rest of the money to be paid to him, and get him employment with his patron, whom he knew would gladly accept his service.

Michelagnolo, therefore, partly through disdain at having been defrauded, and partly in order to see Rome, which had been so cried up by the gentleman as the greatest field in the world for anyone to show his talent, went along with him and lodged in his house near the palace of the Cardinal, who having in the meantime been advised by letters how the matter stood, caused the man who had sold the statue to him as an antique, to be called to account; and having received back his money, gave up the figure to him, which afterwards falling, I know not in what manner, into the hands of the Duke Valentino, was given to the Marchioness of Mantua, and by her was sent to Mantua, where it is still to be seen in the house of those princes." This "Cupid" appears to have been bought by Charles I. of England with the rest of the Mantuan collection. A "child" by Michelagnolo Buonarrotti is enumerated in a letter of Daniel Nys, the king's agent, among the marbles which he had bought for Charles, and which were shipped to England in 1632.

W. N. Sainsbury, "Original Papers relating to Rubens," pp. 337-339.

On arriving at Rome, Michelagnolo addressed to Lorenzo di Pierfrancesco the following letter, which is still preserved among the private papers of the Medici, at Florence:

App. II, Doc. XXXVIII.

"Yħs

"On the 2nd day of July, 1496,

"Magnificent Lorenzo, etc. This is only to advise you that on Saturday last we arrived in safety, and immediately went to visit the Cardinal of San Giorgio, and I presented to him your letter. I think he received me willingly, and desired that I should forthwith go to see certain figures, about which I was occupied all that day; and, therefore, that day I did not present your other letters. On the Sunday following, the Cardinal came to the Casa Nuova and inquired for me. I went to him, and he asked what I thought of the things which I had seen. In reply, I told him what I thought; and certainly I think there are many fine things [among them]. Then the Cardinal asked me if I had judgement enough to execute some work of beauty. I replied that I could not make such great things, but that he should see what I could do. We have bought a piece of marble for a figure as large as life, and on Monday next I shall begin work. Since then, on Monday last, I presented your other letters to Pagolo Rucellai, who gave me the money I was in need of, and likewise those for the Cavalcanti. Afterwards I gave the letter to Baldassarre [del Milanese,] and demanded the figure of the child [or Cupid] of him, and said that I would give him back his money. He answered me very roughly, and said that he would first break it into a hundred pieces; that as for the child, he had bought it and it was his; and that he had letters to show that he had satisfied the person who had sent it to him, and he was under no apprehension that he should be obliged to give it up; and much he complained of you, saying that you had slandered him. And some of our Florentines have sought to bring us to an agreement, but they have availed nothing. Now I rely on bringing it about by the help of the Cardinal, for so I am advised by Baldassarre Balducci: of what follows you shall be informed. That is all. I have nothing more to tell you by this letter, and so I recommend myself to you. God keep you from evil.

"Michelagnolo in Rome."

On the back of the sheet on which this letter is written is the direction, "Sandro di bottjcello infirenze."

The fragment of evidence, slight as it may seem, which is contained in the endorsement of this letter, is of no little value in the elucidation of Botticelli's career, during the last decade of the fifteenth century. It is evident, for reasons which will appear, that a letter dispatched from Rome to Lorenzo di Pierfrancesco de' Medici at this time, was extremely liable to be intercepted by his political opponents at Florence. Since the contents of this letter are wholly addressed to Lorenzo, it is evident that Michelagnolo had arranged to forward it under cover to Botticelli, with a view to prevent any such miscarriage; and we must, therefore, conclude that when the letter was written, Sandro was in the entire confidence of his patron. At that time, Lorenzo and his brother, Giovanni, had already entered into antagonism with Savonarola and the Piagnoni, or Frateschi, as his partisans were called; just as at an earlier time they had come into antagonism with their cousin, Piero de' Medici, in their intrigues to get the chief power of the state into their hands. The friar was then at the height of his struggle with Rome. At the beginning of November, 1495, Pope Alexander VI. had issued a brief forbidding Savonarola to preach under pain of excommunication; but at the urgent entreaty of the Signoria, the prohibition was withdrawn, and in February, 1495-6, Savonarola returned to preach in the Duomo. From that time until his excommunication by the Pope, on 12th May, 1497, the name and authority of Savonarola were increasingly in the ascendant.

It would seem that the aim of Lorenzo, and Giovanni, di Pierfrancesco was to put themselves at the head of a third party, which on the one hand was to overthrow the power of the Piagnoni, and, on the other, to prevent the return of Piero de' Medici. Various were the rumours current as to the manner in which they were to effect their purpose. Savonarola himself believed, or affected to believe, that Lorenzo was plotting to become tyrant of Florence with the aid of the Duke of Milan. According to the version of the process against Savonarola, printed by the Signoria, in April, 1498, the friar said, or is reported to have said: "As to the tyrant whom, as I declared in the pulpit, [Sermon xxx on the Book of Job,] the following day, [2nd April, 1495,] those who were hunting down our fortunes wished to create, I say that I said it to give spirit to my followers who appeared indifferent, in order that I might keep them (not that I had any conjecture in the matter), and also to instil fear into the opposite party, lest they should revolt. And, in short, it was because I always had the notion that the Duke of Milan wished to make Lorenzo di Pierfrancesco [de' Medici] tyrant, and not that I had any certain knowledge of it; for I have always held Lorenzo in good account, and for a worthy man." Pietro Parenti, moreover, in his unpublished "Florentine Histories," states that Savonarola used his suspicions of Lorenzo to stir up the people against him; adding, that at the time of the disorders in the spring of 1498, Lorenzo, in order to avoid the odium of the charge which the Frateschi brought against him, of wishing to make himself tyrant, with the help of the Duke of Milan, left Florence, and went into Flanders where, as he gave out, his affairs took him. According to other writers, he went to Lyons on the pretence of fulfilling a vow. Of his withdrawal from Florence, we have a more particular account in a letter written by Paolo Somenzi, "orator" of the Duke of Milan, to the Florentines, on 29th June, 1497, in the course of which the writer states that "some three months ago, Lorenzino de' Medici began to remove the furniture of his house [in the Via Larga, at Florence], and afterwards sent

P. Villari, Storia di Savonarola, ed. 1888, II, xxx.

Cod. Magliabechiano, XXV, 305, fol. 50, tergo, and fol. 58, recto.

P. Villari, Storia di Savonarola, ed. 1888, II, clxix.

his son [Pierfrancesco] to Forlì, and now he himself has departed with all his family, and is gone to live in the Mugello:" "no one well knows the reason why he has taken this resolve, excepting that many say that he sought to make himself great, or in other words, the head of the city, as was Piero, and that in consequence of the thing having being discovered, his life was at hazard, and that it is for this reason he left the city."

Another circumstance which lent colour to these rumours, was the marriage which Giovanni di Pierfrancesco contracted at this time with the "Madonna of Imola," the famous Caterina Sforza, a natural daughter of Gian Galeazzo Maria, Duke of Milan. That this alliance was entered upon with a view of furthering the political intrigues of Lorenzo and his brother can scarcely be doubted; but such schemes were suddenly cut short by the death of Giovanni, which took place on 14th October, 1498, though not before he had seen accomplished the downfall of Savonarola. Simone Filipepi, the younger brother of Botticelli, believed that the ruin of the friar was in great part due to the machinations of Giovanni. In the course of his "Chronicle," of which I shall presently speak at length, Simone alludes to Giovanni as the "head" of the "company of the Compagnacci," a band of free livers, whose object was the persecution and overthrow of Savonarola and the Frateschi. In one place, he states that the assault made on San Marco by the Compagnacci, with Doffo Spini at their head, on the night of 8th April, 1498, when Savonarola was seized, was undertaken "at the instance of Giovanni di Pier Francesco de' Medici." In another, he asserts that towards the close of his career, Savonarola went in fear of his life, "by reason of the conspiracy which had been formed against him some time before in Imola and Forlì, by the contrivance of Giovanni di Pier Francesco de' Medici, and which afterwards in Florence was brought to bear fruit."

P. Villari and E. Casanova, Scelta di Prediche e Scritti di Savonarola, p. 467.

Id., p. 484.

It is difficult to think that Botticelli, holding, as he certainly did at a later period, the opinions of his brother, Simone, could have continued on the terms of trust and intimacy with Lorenzo di Pierfrancesco de' Medici, which he enjoyed at the date of Michelagnolo's letter in July, 1496. For a time, at least, the good relations between the master and his patron appear to have remained unchanged, since Sandro executed for Lorenzo some paintings, apparently of a decorative nature, in July, 1497. On the other hand, there are indications that the painter did not openly embrace the cause of Savonarola, until after the execution of the friar, on 23rd May, 1498. To the discussion of this question I shall presently return: what I wish here to point out is, that with the retirement of Lorenzo beyond the Alps, during the second half of the year 1497, his patronage of Botticelli appears to have come to an end. When the course of events at Florence permitted of Lorenzo's return, towards the latter part of the following year, Botticelli had openly thrown in his lot with the Piagnoni, and his workshop had become a notorious meeting-place of the men who were in keenest opposition to the political pretensions of his former patron. From that time until the death of Lorenzo, on 20th May, 1503, there is no vestige of evidence, direct or indirect, that Sandro again enjoyed the patronage of the man to whose munificence we owe a series of his most admirable and most famous works.

If these conclusions be correct, they are of no little value as an aid in determining the date of one of the last of Sandro's masterpieces, and in accounting for the unfinished state in which it has come down to us. The codex of Dante which Botticelli began to decorate with miniatures for

Lorenzo di Pierfrancesco de' Medici, had been entirely lost sight of, when in 1854 Dr. G. F. Waagen first drew attention in his "Treasures of Art [l.c., III, 307.] in Great Britain," to a volume which he had seen some three years before, among the manuscripts in the collection of the Duke of Hamilton, at Hamilton Palace near Glasgow. This volume Dr. Waagen describes as a codex of the "Divina Commedia," in "large folio, of the second half of the fifteenth century, containing indubitably the richest illustrations existing of this great poem, each page having a picture; all, however, with the exception of one page, consisting of drawings with the pen. Various hands of various artistic skill are discernible; that of Sandro Botticelli is very obvious: . . . while many of the drawings at the early part of the work are very interesting and spirited, the larger figures in the latter part are the finest and most original with which this poem has ever been illustrated."

[Vasari, ed. Sansoni, III, 317, note.] The notice which the "Anonimo Gaddiano" has preserved of the codex illustrated by Botticelli, was unknown until Milanesi first quoted it in the notes to the third volume of his edition of Vasari, which appeared [App. II, Doc. II, fol. 84, recto.] in 1878. The "Anonimo" records that Botticelli "painted and worked with stories a Dante on vellum, for Lorenzo di Pierfrancesco de' Medici, which was held to be a marvellous thing." Milanesi was unaware of the existence of the volume in the Hamilton Palace collection: for in spite of Dr. Waagen's notice, it appears to have attracted little attention, and to have been seen by few persons. At Berlin, however, the volume was not lost sight of; and when, in 1882, it was offered for sale by auction at Messrs. Sotheby's, along with the other manuscripts in the Duke of Hamilton's library, Dr. Lippmann, acting on behalf of the Prussian government, came over to London, stopped the sale and purchased the entire collection, in order to secure it. Thus an unrivalled monument of Italian art was allowed to leave this country, before any effort had been made to acquire it for the nation, and, indeed, before the directors of our museums had realized its importance. It was not, as Dr. Lippmann tells us, until the volume passed into the Berlin Museum in 1882, "that the drawings became widely known, or that Botticelli was finally recognized as their sole author." The volume, as it came to Berlin, consisted of eighty-eight sheets of vellum, "bound together in boards, apparently in the eighteenth century, when the book was also furnished with an index by one Claudio Molini, an Italian bookseller in Paris"; of the eighty-eight sheets of vellum, of which the series consists, eighty-five are illustrated. They are now mounted separately, so that both sides of the sheets may be seen.

Not long after the volume had been acquired by the Prussian Government, eight drawings in the Vatican Library were recognized by M. Josef Strzygowski, as having once formed part of the series at Berlin. These eight drawings, executed on seven sheets of vellum, are bound up in a [Bibl. Vaticano, Codici della Regina di Svezia, No. 1896, fol. 97-103.] volume of miscellaneous pieces which had once formed part of the library of Queen Christina of Sweden. After her death at Rome, in 1689, her books, or the chief part of them, were acquired by Pope Alexander VIII, and placed in the library of the Vatican, where they are still preserved. The drawings in question were well known to students of Dante, having [l.c., Vol. II, p. 174.] been described by M. Colomb de Batines in his "Bibliografia Dantesca"; but until 1886, their real authorship was not suspected.

The leaves on which this "Dante" is executed, are formed of fine goat-skin parchment, averaging 12½ inches in height, and 18½ inches in width. The drawings themselves are somewhat smaller than the leaves on which they are executed, the more finished of the miniatures, namely, that to Canto XVIII of the "Inferno," measuring nearly 12 inches in height, by 17½ inches in width. They are drawn on the smooth, or "flesh side," of the sheet: on the rougher, or "hair side," is written a canto of the poem, in six columns, in that late black-letter character, which was in vogue at Florence during the latter part of the fifteenth century. The drawings and text are so arranged that, when the book was open, the illustration occupied the page on the left hand of the reader, facing the text of the canto which it illustrates. Preceding the illustration to the first canto of the "Inferno," is an introductory chart of Hell: both drawings are on the same sheet; the chart being on the recto, and the illustration to Canto I, on the tergo. This sheet is in the Vatican; as are also the drawings to Cantos IX, X, XII, XIII, XV and XVI of the "Inferno." The sheets containing the illustrations to Cantos II, III, IV, V, VI, VII, XI and XIV of the "Inferno" are wanting. The drawings at Berlin begin with the illustration for Canto VIII of the "Inferno," and continue with the drawing for Canto XVII in an unbroken series, to that for Canto XXX of the "Paradiso." In addition to the illustration to Canto XXXIV of the "Inferno," which was intended to face the text, there is a large representation of Lucifer, which is drawn on two sheets of parchment joined together. The page on which the illustration for Canto XXXI of the "Paradiso" was intended to have been drawn, is left blank; and the unfinished drawing for Canto XXXII is the last of the series.

The drawings were first sketched in with a metal style, probably made of an alloy of lead and silver; and the design having thus been determined, was afterwards drawn in with the pen, in ink. Besides many passages which are carried no farther than the preliminary stage, two of the drawings, namely those for Canto XXX of the "Inferno" and Canto VIII of the "Purgatorio," remain merely sketched in with the style. In others, again, the design has been wholly, or partially, erased; as in the case of the illustrations to Cantos XIX, XXI and XXXII of the "Paradiso." In many of the drawings for this portion of the "Commedia," the figures of Beatrice and Dante are drawn in with the pen, although the rest of the design is not even indicated. The drawings for Cantos IX to XX of the "Paradiso" have been left in this condition. On the other hand, four of the sheets, namely the introductory Chart of Hell, and the illustrations for Cantos X, XV and XVIII of the "Inferno" have been begun in colour; and in two instances, the colouring has been carried to a considerable degree of forwardness. From the method and character of their colouring, there can be little doubt, as I shall show, that the painter intended to adorn the whole of the volume with a series of finished miniatures in colour.

Already in the earlier part of the fourteenth century, the fashion had grown into use, both at Florence and in other parts of Italy, of freely illustrating manuscript copies of the "Divina Commedia." In the more richly-decorated manuscripts, each canto of the poem is embellished with a drawing, which is more commonly placed at the beginning of the particular canto to which it refers. Indeed, the edition of the "Commedia" printed at Florence, in 1481, with the commentaries of Cristoforo Landino, was an attempt to produce an illustrated copy of the poem, upon the plan of the manuscripts, by means of the printing press. The task of illustrating the entire "Commedia" in this fashion was so arduous a one, that only in a very few instances has the work been brought to completion, and even then the series is rarely the production of a single hand. Dr. Ludwig Volkmann, who has learnedly investigated the whole subject of the illustration of the "Commedia," in his "Iconografia Dantesca," describes nearly a score of manuscripts in which the attempt to profusely illustrate the poem has been carried to a certain degree of advancement. These illustrations are either executed in true miniature, or drawn with the pen, and occasionally washed with colour. The earliest manuscript to which a date can be assigned, is the Palatine codex, No. 313, preserved in the Biblioteca Nazionale at Florence. This codex, which artistically is one of the most important, was written previously to the year 1333. The manuscript which contains the greatest number of illustrations in true miniature, is the Egerton manuscript, No. 943, in the British Museum. This manuscript, which was executed about the middle of the fourteenth century, contains at least one miniature to each of the hundred cantos of their poem: the volume, however, possesses greater interest for the student of iconography, than for the connoisseur. But these, and other manuscripts, are described at length in Dr. Volkmann's admirable work. The codex which Botticelli undertook to illustrate for Lorenzo di Pierfrancesco de' Medici, was begun on a more comprehensive and elaborate scale, than any of the manuscripts which have come down to us; not even excepting the sumptuously ornate volume executed for the Duke Federigo of Montefeltro, which is now preserved in the Vatican Library. In the codex begun by Botticelli, the plan of devoting every other page of a folio volume to a single, elaborately finished miniature, appears to have been employed for the first and only time.

l.c., ed. London, 1899, p. 40, etc.

Cod. Urbinati, No. 365.

In the earlier manuscripts, each miniature represents, for the most part, but a single episode, illustrative of the principal theme of the canto to which it refers. Occasionally, however, more than one episode is represented in the same miniature; the figures of Dante and the chief actors in the poem, being repeated in each episode, in accordance with the tradition of Giottesque painting. With the course of time, there appears to have been a tendency to represent more and more incidents in each miniature. It is this traditional mode of illustrating the "Divina Commedia" which Botticelli takes up and elaborates, increasing the number of episodes in each design in accordance with the rapidity of the action of the poem. In the prints to the edition of 1481, there are rarely less than two episodes; whereas a large number of the drawings for the "Inferno," at Berlin and Rome, contain five or six, and a few as many as seven, or even eight, incidents.

The letter addressed by Dante to his patron, Can Grande, whether authentic or apocryphal, sets forth what, in the view of his time, was the grand characteristic of the poem which led its author to call his work a Comedy. After giving a definition of the terms, Comedy and Tragedy, the writer of this letter observes that Tragedy "speaks in a style elate and sublime, and at the beginning is admirable and quiet, at the end or exit fetid and horrible"; whereas "Comedy begins with the asperity of a subject, and ends prosperously, and speaks in a remiss and humble style." Hence, he argues, it is easy to see "why the present work is called a Comedy"; for "if we consider the style of speech, that style is remiss and humble, being the vulgar speech, in which even the women talk with one another." Here, surely, we have a clue to the temper in which the early commentators and illustrators of the "Commedia" approached the poem. Like the woman who saw on Dante's face, the marks of his journey through hell, they discuss and illustrate the poem, as they might the account of some traveller who had returned from exploring an unknown land. This attitude is especially observable in the discussion of the "Hell." Vasari records that Filippo Brunelleschi "gave much study to the questions of Dante, which were admirably well understood by him, concerning the sites and the measures." These studies of Brunelleschi were continued by his friend, Antonio Manetti, after whose death, Girolamo Benivieni composed, partly from his papers and partly from the discourse which he had had with him, those "Dialogues concerning the site, form and measures of the Hell of Dante," which were printed for the first time at Florence in 1506. That Antonio Manetti was intimate with Botticelli's family, is shown by a piece of evidence, which I shall presently adduce; and thus, no doubt, he was the friend of Sandro, as he had been the friend of Paolo Uccello (who painted his own head with that of Manetti and Brunelleschi in one piece), and of Antonio Pollaiuoli, in whose will he is named executor. Antonio Manetti was born on 6th July, 1423, and died on 26th May, 1496. He bore several offices under the Republic; was skilled in mathematics and architecture, and a great student of Dante. Bernardo del Nero dedicated his translation of the "De Monarchia" of Dante, to him; and among the Magliabechian manuscripts, Cl. VII, No. 10, in the Biblioteca Nazionale, at Florence, is a copy of the "Commedia" written in Manetti's own hand, in 1462. Recent research, I may add, has shown that Manetti was the transcriber, rather than the author, of the novel of "Il Grasso, legnaiuolo," and the "Life of Brunelleschi."

Vasari, ed. Sansoni, II, 333.

A. Chiappelli, "Pagine d'antica arte fiorentina," p. 159.

From the studies of such men as Antonio Manetti, Cristoforo Landino and Girolamo Benivieni, Botticelli doubtless derived no little assistance in designing his illustrations to Dante. Certainly, he approached the "Commedia" in the literal and scrupulous spirit in which these commentators had discussed it. For him, the poem is a piece of human experience, described in the language of vulgar parlance; and he illustrates it accordingly, in the terms of common nature. Rarely does Botticelli show anything of that grand elevation of style which, in Dante's view, was proper to the delineation of Tragedy, and which was first associated with the poem in the frescoes of Luca Signorelli. The copy of Dante which Michelagnolo illustrated is unfortunately lost; but there can be little doubt that he treated the "Commedia" in the elate and sublime style, in which he treated the incident of Charon in the fresco of the "Last Judgement." Since that time, all the more considerable illustrations of the poem have been conceived in an heroic or ideal vein, such as Dante himself was careful to dissociate from his "Commedia." The designs of Blake and Flaxman are the most notable instances of illustrations conceived in this vein; and, perhaps, it is the only one in which the poem could be adequately treated, in our modern view of its theme, so indelible has been the influence of Michelagnolo.

But it was not merely in regard to such general considerations, that Botticelli accepted the traditional view of the "Commedia." It is true that the miniatures contained in the earlier codices, show so little conformity of type in the visual images evoked by the poem, that at first sight tradition would seem to have had but a small part in shaping them. We must remember, however, that these miniatures were produced in the most

diverse parts of Italy; whereas it was at Florence that the systematic study of Dante was chiefly undertaken, and the visual imagery suggested by the poem became, in the course of time, determined and fixed; in the same way as what we may call the topography of the "Inferno." For our immediate purpose, therefore, we need concern ourselves only with those miniatures which are clearly of Florentine origin. Dr. Lippmann has remarked how some of the early miniatures, and notably those in the codex at Altona, recall in their general conception the designs of Botticelli. One of the most remarkable instances of this kind has hitherto escaped notice. Prefixed to the first canto of the "Inferno" in the Palatine codex, No. 313, preserved in the Biblioteca Nazionale, at Florence, is a miniature which has been cut from another manuscript, and which appears to be of a somewhat later date, than the volume into which it has been pasted. This miniature, in so far as its general conception and arrangement are concerned, contains all the elements of Botticelli's design for the same canto. On the left of the miniature, Dante is seen emerging from the wood; in the centre, he is about to ascend the hill, which rises on the right of the design, as the leopard, the lion and the wolf descend towards him. Again, below, on the right, Dante, after he has turned back, meets with Virgil; and above in the heavens is the sun. This probably was by no means the only instance in which Botticelli, while illustrating the "Inferno," made use of a traditional composition, as he habitually would have done in treating some religious subject, such as an "Annunciation" or a "Pietà." A work of another nature enables us to appreciate more than any manuscript, perhaps, the extent to which Sandro was indebted to tradition for the imagery of his designs: I allude to the fresco of the "Inferno," in the older chapel of the Strozzi, in the church of Santa Maria Novella, at Florence. This painting, which Botticelli must certainly have
Vasari, ed. Le Monnier, I, xxiii. seen and known, is ascribed by Lorenzo Ghiberti in his second commentary to Nardo, the brother of Andrea Orcagna. It was, therefore, the work of a man who might have seen Dante in the flesh, and is among the earliest illustrations of the "Divina Commedia." If we make due allowance for the differences of style, which must necessarily exist between a Giottesque painter, like Nardo, and a master of the latter part of the fifteenth century, like Sandro, we cannot but remark, in so far as the visualized imagery is concerned, the close similarity of conception which is everywhere to be found between this fresco and the designs of Botticelli. But I shall hereafter have occasion to note their resemblance to one another: so with this, I will now examine categorically the drawings at Berlin and Rome, as well as the cuts in the edition of 1481.

The first drawing of the series is the chart of Hell, which exhibits with great minuteness its "site, form and measures"; the exact determination of which had greatly preoccupied the early commentators. It was
Vasari, ed. Sansoni, III, 463. such a representation of Hell with all its circles and chasms, that Raggio, the broker, whom Filippino painted in the Brancacci Chapel, standing beside his friend, Sandro, carved in miniature on a shell. According to the conception of Dante, Hell is a vast funnel-shaped cavity, extending to the centre of our world, and vaulted over by the crust of the earth's surface. Immediately above its lowest circle stands the holy Jerusalem, in the middle of the mediaeval world. This vast, dim, circular cavern gradually grows smaller, as it descends in a series of precipitous, cliff-like ledges of rock, which form a number of horizontal and circular stages,

constituting the nine circles of the "Inferno." In the drawing, which exhibits this cone-shaped cavity in a vertical section, not only are these circles shown with the eighteen subdivisions of the last three, but the various punishments which are severally exacted in them, are represented by minute figures of the souls in torment. Above, in the left hand corner, Virgil and Dante are seen passing through the gate of Hell into "the dark plain," which forms a kind of ante-region to the great river Acheron, and the circles of the cavern. Owing to the scale on which the drawing is executed, the ninth and lowest circle is so minute in size that Botticelli has redrawn it on a larger scale, in order to show more clearly its four subdivisions, as seen from above, with Lucifer in the last of them. The rocky sides of the cavern are tinted in brown and yellow, against which the tiny figures of the sinners are seen in pallid relief, as in the design for Canto XVIII of the "Inferno," hereafter to be described. The drawing, which is enclosed in a border of gold leaf, has suffered much from use: the colour has flaked way in many places, and the surface has been damaged by friction.

INFERNO. Canto I.—On the left of the drawing Dante, lost in contemplation with his hands clasped before him, wanders through the "dark wood," represented by oaks and pine trees. On the right of this figure of Dante, two other figures appear to have been erased. The upper one probably represented the poet emerging from the wood at the foot of the hill, which rose up where the valley ended. The lower figure, of which only the outline of the head and one of the feet can be made out, appears to have represented the poet seated on the ground, with his face covered with his cloak, "full of sleep," after he had left the true way. In the centre of the composition, the leopard "with the spotted skin" impedes his way up the hill. Again, on the right, Dante starts in terror at the lion, who comes upon him "with head erect and furious hunger." Lastly, on the extreme right of the drawing, the she-wolf springs out upon the poet, who, as he turns to rush down the hill in terror, is stopped by Virgil in the garb of a mediaeval magus. The animals are the semi-heraldic creatures of the gothic bestiaries.

Dante, "Inferno," translated by J. A. Carlyle.

The print of 1481 resembles the drawing in its general conception and arrangement, but the figure of Dante is only thrice represented in it. On the right, where the poet wanders through the wood, the action of the figure closely recalls the drawing. The same action occurs in the figure of Nastagio degli Onesti, in the first of the four furniture-panels painted for the Pucci. In the centre of the print, Dante is again seen emerging from the wood, as the leopard and the lion advance towards him. Lastly, on the right of the print, the poet flies from the she-wolf as Virgil comes towards him. Across the upper part, both of the print and the drawing, fall "the rays of the planet which leads men straight on every road."

Canto II.—The drawings for this and the six following cantos are wanting. On the left of the print of 1481, Dante unburdens himself to Virgil of his misgivings: "Look if there be worth in me sufficient, before thou trust me to the arduous passage." Virgil replies by relating how a lady, "fair and blessed," had come down from heaven to bid him aid Dante "with his ornate speech, and with what is necessary for his escape." Botticelli seeks to convey this by representing in the centre of the print, Virgil showing to Dante a vision of Beatrice, which appears in the sky. This is a significant instance of how naïvely Botticelli followed the mediaeval convention, whose scope was to overcome the limitations of painting, by ignoring the chronological sequence of events, and to lend to a picture the copiousness and vivid character of a narrative, by representing successive actions as if they were occurring simultaneously. In the distance on the right, cut in the side of a rocky hill, is the gate of Hell, inscribed over the portal PER ME, the opening words of the next canto.

CANTO III.—On the left of the print of 1481, Dante and Virgil approach the gate of Hell, whose portal is inscribed with the three opening lines of the canto, of which little more than the first words, PER ME ƧI VA, are seen repeated. In the centre, having passed the portal, Virgil points out to Dante the long train of those "who lived without blame and without praise." They follow the ensign which "whirling ran so quickly, that it seemed to scorn all pause." Botticelli represents this banner borne by a devil, although there is nothing in the text to warrant this. One of the foremost spirits of the train wears a mitre, and is perhaps intended for "the shadow of him who through cowardice made the great refusal." To the right of the print, on the bank of the stream, Acheron, Virgil and Dante parley with "Charon the demon, with eyes of glowing coal," seated in his craft. Botticelli, like the painter of the fresco in Santa Maria Novella, represents Charon as the mediaeval devil, half man, half beast, with bat-like wings. In front of the group of Virgil and Dante, the latter is again represented fallen on the bank of the stream, "like one who is seized with sleep," in terror, as "the dusky champaign trembled," and "the tearful ground gave out wind and flashed with a crimson light."

In a few copies of the "Dante" of 1481 is a second version, in reverse, of this illustration to Canto III. The incidents represented are the same, and their arrangement is similar; but the whole design has been redrawn, and the plates engraved by another and inferior hand. Such differences of detail as the company of the spirits, who wheel round as they follow the ensign, or the souls which cling to the sides of Charon's boat, show that these variations can scarcely be due to the engraver; while the existence of a second plate would seem to point to dissatisfaction with what had been done, on the part of their designer, or the printer of the volume.

CANTO IV.—In the upper part of the print of 1481, Dante is represented waking "on the brink of the dolorous Valley of the Abyss, which gathers thunder of endless wailings." On the left, Dante and Virgil descend into the "blind world." As they go their way, the latter points out the "four great shadows," who approach them from the other side; Homer with a "great sword in hand," Horace, Ovid and Lucan. The whole of the foreground of the composition is taken up by the "noble castle, seven times circled with lofty walls, defended round by a fair rivulet," which the poets now enter. Unlike the painter of the fresco in Santa Maria Novella, Botticelli represents these walls of a circular form, each with its entrance gateway. Before the outermost gate, burns the "fire which conquered a hemisphere of the darkness." Within the circle of the seven walls in "a meadow of fresh verdure," Dante and Virgil are seen talking to a knight in complete steel, intended, no doubt, for "Caesar armed": the group on the right seems to represent Aristotle "sitting amid a philosophic family."

CANTO V.—The poets now enter the second circle, or proper commencement of Hell. On the left of the print of 1481, they approach Minos, "who sits horrific and grins; examines the crime upon the entrance;

judges," and "with his tail makes as many circles round himself," as the number of circles the spirit will have to descend. On the other side of the print, Dante and Virgil pause in their passage through the "place void of all light, which bellows like a sea in a tempest," to speak with Paolo and Francesca, who hover above them, locked in one another's arms. In the centre of the composition, the souls of the carnal sinners are driven hither and thither by the blast. The incident of Dante fainting with pity at the story of Francesca, is passed over in the illustration as one of secondary importance to the great plan and structure of the poem.

CANTO VI.—Dante awakes from his swoon to find himself transported into the third circle, where the sin of gluttony is punished. In the print of 1481, the shadows of the gluttonous, whom the perpetual rain of "great hailstones" subdues, lie scattered on the ground. On the left, Virgil stoops down to take up earth, and with full fists cast it into the ravening gullets of Cerberus, who at the approach of the poets, pauses as he rends piecemeal the spirits. Behind Virgil, Dante stands in terror. "Cerberus, a monster fierce and strange, with three throats," is represented here, as in the fresco of Santa Maria Novella, in the form of a devil with "clawed hands" and bat's wings; his middle head half human, half bestial, the side ones those of a dog. On the right, Dante and Virgil are again seen talking to Ciacco, the Florentine, who raises himself on one knee.

CANTO VII.—The poets now prepare to descend to the fourth circle, when they encounter "Plutus, the great enemy." On the right, in the print of 1481, Virgil followed by Dante, is seen to approach Plutus. At the mention of the name of Michael the Archangel, the monster falls to the ground, "as sails swelled by the wind, fall entangled when the mast breaks." The poets now enter the fourth circle, where the Prodigal and Avaricious are punished by rolling great weights against one another, "by force of chest." On the left of the print, Dante and Virgil are seen discoursing of the shadows, who are represented rolling their loads against one another in opposing files. Dante inquires, "whether all those tonsured on our left were of the clergy." Below, in the foreground of the print, are seen the heads of the two poets as they descend to the fifth circle, where, in the marsh of Styx, are punished the Wrathful and the Gloomy-sluggish. The description of the marsh occurs in the latter portion of this canto, but Botticelli introduces these incidents into the illustration to the next canto.

CANTO VIII.—The drawing for this canto is the first of the series preserved at Berlin. Like the greater number of the drawings, it is marked below with the number of the canto in arabic numerals. On the right, the poets are seen descending through a rocky gorge, on the far bank of the marsh Styx, into the fifth circle. Immediately in front of this group, they are again represented looking up at a battlemented tower, through a window of which a devil holds out two lighted torches: "long before we reached the foot of the high tower, our eyes went upwards to its summit because of two flamelets that we saw put there, and another from afar give signal back." The answering beacon is represented by two other torches placed on the top of the tower, which forms the entrance gateway to the city of Dis, in the foreground. The marsh Styx lies between the two towers. By the side of the tower on the far bank, Virgil, followed by Dante, steps into the bark of Phlegyas. Beside the boat are seen the souls of those whom anger has overcome "like swine in the mire." Halfway across the marsh, the bark of Phlegyas is again represented. Virgil thrusts off the spirit of Filippo Argenti as he clings with both hands to the side of the boat; and again, seated in the stern, he puts his arms round Dante's neck, and kisses his face, in approbation of his loathing of the foul spirit. In the lower left-hand corner of the drawing, the bark of Phlegyas is moored to the opposite shore, and the poets having alighted, Virgil is seen to parley with the fallen spirits, who keep the gate of the city of Dis. On the left, he is again represented returning to Dante with "his eyes upon the ground, and his eyebrows shorn of all boldness," saying with sighs, "Who hath denied me the doleful houses?" Above these figures, Phlegyas is seen recrossing the marsh.

The print of 1481 bears little pictorial resemblance to the drawing, although similar to it in its general conception and choice of incidents. Botticelli introduces a third tower into this design, from which the answering beacon of the two torches is given. The poets are four times represented in this print: as they descend the gorge; as they enter the bark of Phlegyas; as Virgil thrusts Filippo Argenti from the side of the boat while crossing the marsh; and again, on the near bank, as Virgil returns to Dante, after being refused entrance at the gate.

Canto IX.—In the drawing which is preserved at the Vatican, the gateway of the city of Dis again rises in the midst of the foreground. On the extreme left, Virgil and Dante discourse of their failure to enter the city. Close by they are again represented looking up at the tower above the gateway. Virgil points out to Dante above the battlements, the three hellish Furies "who had the limbs and attitude of women, and were girt with greenest hydras:" "This is Megaera on the left hand; she that weeps upon the right is Alecto; Tesiphone is in the middle." At the sight of Dante they cry, "Let Medusa come, that we may change him into stone." Behind them, a devil holds up the head of the Gorgon; and below, in a third group, Virgil is seen covering the eyes of Dante with his hands lest he should see her. Suddenly there is heard "a crash of fearful sound, at which both the shores trembled." In the background of the drawing, the messenger of Heaven passes "the Stygian ferry with soles unwet," while the struggling spirits in the marsh run all asunder, "as frogs before their enemy the serpent." Below, the angel is again represented at the gate, which he has opened with a wand. A crowd of devils look out from its open portal; and near by, Dante is seen kneeling by the side of Virgil, who has made a sign to him to bow down before the angel. The poets now pass the gate without resistance, and enter a spacious plain full of sepulchres, each with its lid upraised, giving forth flames. Dante asks, "What are these people who, buried within those chests, make themselves heard by their painful sighs?" Virgil replies, "These are the archheretics with their followers of every sect." The poets are again seen as they pass on between the tombs and the battlemented wall of the city.

The print of 1481 bears small resemblance to the drawing. Three towers are here represented, as in the engraving for the previous canto. The marsh of Styx flows between the two furthest ones, and the wall of the city of Dis extends along the foreground. On the right, without the wall, an infernal fury, with dug-like breasts, girt about the middle with a dragon, displays the head of the Gorgon in the shield of Minerva; a curious interpretation of Dante which was, perhaps, not unassociated in Botticelli's mind with his conception of Pallas. On the other side of the composition,

Virgil covers with his hand Dante's eyes, lest he should see the Medusa. In the background the angel hastens over the marsh, and again on the extreme right of the print, he is seen through the gateway of the city of Dis, which opens at the touch of his wand. At his approach, the devils herd together on either side of the gate, while on the tower above are seen the three furies.

CANTO X.—In the drawing at the Vatican, the scene is again laid in the plain of the burning sepulchres. The poets, having entered by the gate which is represented on the right of the sheet, with its doors open and a herd of devils on either side, proceed "by a narrow path between the tombs and the city wall," which extends across the background of the composition. On the left, in a second group, Virgil is seen laying his right hand on Dante's shoulder, and pointing with his left to the tomb from which Farinata degli Uberti rises up: "And the bold and ready hands of my guide pushed me among the sepultures to him, saying: 'Let thy words be numbered.'" Below, Dante is again represented talking with Farinata, who rises "from the girdle up," among the flames in the open tomb. Bewildered at the hard sayings of Farinata, he returns to Virgil; and as the poets continue on their way by the city wall, the latter bids him remember what he has heard against himself, adding, as he raises his finger, "When thou shalt stand before the sweet ray of her whose bright eye seeth all, from her shalt thou know the journey of thy life." The poets, leaving the wall, now turn to the left hand, "by a path striking into a valley," which even up there annoys them with its fetor. As they come forward, on the left of the drawing, Dante covers his nose and mouth with his hand. They approach the lid of a great sarcophagus bearing the inscription, ANASTASIO PAPA GVARDO, the allusion to which first occurs in the following canto. In this drawing, the long habits of Dante and Virgil, some nine figures in all, have been coloured in tempera; the rest of the drawing being left in outline. The colours used for the dresses are the same as those employed in the drawing for Canto XVIII of the Inferno, hereafter to be described.

The print of 1481 offers little resemblance to the drawing, except in its general conception and arrangement. Three incidents are represented; that of the poets entering the city of Dis, of Dante talking with Farinata, and of Virgil and Dante approaching the tomb of Pope Anastasius, which is inscribed PAPANAƧTAƧIO GVARDO.

CANTO XI.—The drawing is wanting. In the background of the print of 1481 are seen the burning sepulchres, with the city-wall beyond; and in the foreground "the high bank formed of large broken stones," which divides the sixth from the seventh circle. On the right of the print, the poets are seated among the stones, under the lid of the sarcophagus of Pope Anastasius, which bears the same legend as in the last drawing. Virgil now discourses to Dante of the nature of the three circles which they have yet to visit.

CANTO XII.—The poets now descend to the seventh circle, by a cleft which had been rent in the rocky precipice, when Christ died upon the Cross. In the upper, right-hand corner of the drawing, at the Vatican, they find prone, at the top of the broken cleft, the Minotaur; half man, half bull. At the mention of Theseus, Duke of Athens, he springs up in blind fury, "as a bull that breaks loose in the moment when he has received the fatal stroke, and cannot go, but plunges hither and thither."

At this Virgil cries, "Run to the passage: whilst he is in fury it is good that thou descend"; and Dante is represented a second time, hastening ahead down the rocky cleft. Below, the poets are again seen approaching the "river of blood," "in which boils every one who by violence injures others." Between the river and the precipice are the troops of centaurs, "running one behind the other, armed with arrows, as they were wont on earth to go, in hunting." "Around the fosse they go by thousands, piercing with their arrows whatever spirit wrenches itself out of the blood further than its guilt has allotted for it." Three of the band come forth with bows and javelins; and Virgil with outstretched hand, names them to Dante, as they stand there in the centre of the composition. He, who draws the bow at them, is Nessus; the second, "who is looking down upon his breast, is the great Chiron"; the third is Pholus. The poets pass on to the brink of the fosse, accompanied by the centaur, Nessus, who names to them many of the tyrants and murderers within the river, as they go along the bank. At length, they come to where "the blood grew shallow, until it covered the feet only"; and they are again represented as having crossed the fosse and about to enter the wood of the self-murderers, which is indicated on the lower margin of the drawing, as the circle of the burning sepulchres is on the upper margin. Lastly, Nessus is seen re-crossing the ford.

The print of 1481 shows considerable variation from the drawing, and the arrangement of the incidents represented in it, is again in reverse. On the left, the poets encounter the Minotaur. On the other side, they are accosted by the three centaurs, a group which closely recalls the drawing. On the extreme right, Dante is seen seated on the back of Nessus, with Virgil at his side, after having crossed the ford. It is to be observed that in the print, Botticelli represents the centaurs hunting upon both banks of the fosse: in the drawing, however, following the text, they are represented only on the far bank, under the rocky precipice. It was this print that Walter Pater had in mind when he wrote, that Botticelli, "forgetful of the actual circumstances of their appearance," had "gone off with delight on the thought of the centaurs themselves, bright small creatures of the woodland, with arch, baby faces and mignon forms, drawing tiny bows." But, although the naïvety with which the engraver has unconsciously translated Botticelli's design into stamp, more than justifies this charming, whimsical criticism; the drawing, which was unknown to Pater, fails to bear it out. The figures of the Minotaur, now lying upon the ground, and now plunging in blind fury at the gibe of Virgil, are designed with an energy and truth of character, that are worthy of the antique conception of the monster; and Antonio Pollaiuoli himself could scarcely have expressed the monstrous form and bestial spirit of the creature with greater vigour, or a keener sense of actuality.

CANTO XIII.—In the upper, right-hand corner of the drawing in the Vatican, Nessus is about to recross the ford, as the poets enter the wood of the self-murderers, which lies in the second round of the seventh circle. The allusion is to the opening lines of the canto: "Nessus had not yet reached the other side, when we moved into a wood, which by no path was marked. Not green the foliage, but of a colour dusky; not smooth the branches, but gnarled and warped." In the invention of the shapes of the trees which form the wood, the painter again gives rein to his imagination. Unlike those in the fresco of Santa Maria Novella, which are of a common

Giottesque, decorative type, Botticelli conceives the dismal wood as a tangled network of lopped and stunted thorns, with sparse, holly-like leaves. The harpies who make their nests there, are represented, as Dante describes them, with human heads, clawed feet, and "the large belly feathered": but their wide wings are those of the dragon of the mediaeval bestiaries, and they end "foul in many a scaly fold," in accordance with the antique conception of them; although there is no such allusion in the text. On the left of the composition, the poets are again seen in their passage through the wood. Dante talks with the soul of Pietro delle Vigne, who is imprisoned in the great thorn, which the poet has unwittingly rended. The shade of the chancellor is represented by a human face, which appears from among the branches. In the middle of the composition, the two naked spirits of Lano, the Sienese, and Jacomo da Sant' Andrea, flee through the wood, pursued by the black hell-hounds. Lano turns to one side, and takes refuge under a tree, as the dogs come up with him. Jacomo is twice represented below: the second time squatting under the bush, which imprisons the soul of the Florentine, while the dogs thrust their teeth into his back, in order to rend him in pieces. In front of the tree, Dante is again seen, gathering up the broken leaves and branches, as Virgil stands with a gesture of amazement. The allusion, however, is to the opening lines of the following canto: "The love of my native place constraining me, I gathered up the scattered leaves, and gave them back to him who was already hoarse." The fosse of blood and the region of the burning sand are severally represented on the upper and lower margins of the drawing.

The print of 1481 shows much the same choice and arrangement of the incidents represented, but in reverse. The return of Nessus over the ford, and the flight of the two spirits are omitted; Lano and Jacomo being represented once only, as they crouch under the trees. The individual groups in the print, however, bear small pictorial resemblance to those in the drawing.

Canto XIV.—The drawing is wanting. The scene of the print of 1481 is laid in the third round of the seventh circle, where "over the great sand, falling slowly, rained dilated flakes of fire." Here are punished those who have done violence against God, against Nature, and against Nature and Art. On the right, the poets are seen coming out of the dismal wood, which forms the background of the print; on the left, they come "to where there gushes forth from the wood" the little rivulet of blood, by which Phlegethon flows down into Cocytus. Dante, pointing to the crowned figure which lies unmoved amid the flames, inquires "who is that great spirit, who seems to care not for the fire?" Virgil replies, that it is Capaneus, "one of the seven kings, who laid siege to Thebes"; he who "held, and seems to hold, God in defiance."

Canto XV.—The poets proceed across the region of the burning sand, by one of the rocky dams, which form the banks of the rivulet of blood. In this and in the next design, which are preserved at the Vatican, the scene is apparently drawn in sharp perspective, as if the intention were to represent the region of the burning sand in the form of a steep, shelving bank, or incline: and, indeed, such a form appears to be indicated in the introductory chart to the "Inferno." Such a conception of the region might be thought to follow from the passage in Canto XIV, which describes how the rivulet of blood "ran down across the sand." Over the burning waste, as we look down upon it, are scattered the naked forms of the spirits, some "lying supine upon the ground, some sitting all crouched up, and others roaming incessantly." On the left, as Dante descends by the dam, followed by Virgil, whose figure is only partially seen, a spirit, who plucks him by the skirt of his robe, is recognized by him as his teacher, Ser Brunetto Latini. Below, Dante is again seen talking with Ser Brunetto, Virgil standing by; and in the lower corner, the poet is represented a third time, continuing his discourse with the spirit. The sharp perspective of this design gives it a certain map-like character. The painter began to colour this sheet in tempera, but has done little more than to lay in the background, model the forms of the spirits in umber and terra-verde, and partially colour two of the figures of Dante. The falling tongues of flames, which were to have been added in body-colour, are but partly indicated. The colours used for the dress of Dante are those employed in the drawing for Canto XVIII of the "Inferno."

The print of 1481 recalls the drawing only in its general conception and arrangement. Dante, however, is represented only once, talking with the spirit of Ser Brunetto, while Virgil stands by.

Canto XVI.—Continuing their way down the steep dam of the rivulet, the poets encounter the shades of Guido Guerra, Tegghiaio Aldobrandi and Jacopo Rusticucci: "all the three make of themselves a wheel," holding one another's hands, as Virgil and Dante talk with them. Below, at the bidding of his guide, Dante unloosens the cord with which he was girt, and with which he "thought some time to catch the leopard of the painted skin." For a third time the poets are seen, as Virgil throws the cord into the abyss, which they now reach, near to where the rivulet falls into Malebolge. At this, the monster, Geryon, rises from the abyss; his head being indicated on the lower margin of the sheet. This drawing is more satisfactory as a composition than the preceding one, owing to the circle of the Usurers, first mentioned in the following canto, being introduced under a rocky ledge, which serves to break the monotony of the background.

Again, the design of the print of 1481 differs considerably from the drawing. The two poets are seen talking to the three spirits in the centre of the composition; and again on the right, Virgil casts the cord into the abyss, from which the head of Geryon appears, as Dante raises his hands with a gesture of astonishment.

Canto XVII.—With the drawing for this canto, the designs preserved at Berlin continue in an unbroken series, to Canto XXX of the "Paradiso." On the right of the drawing, the poets are seen about to descend from the dam to the level brink of the abyss "which closes the great sand with stone." Virgil with outstretched hand, bids Dante behold the savage beast "that pollutes the whole world." The figure of Geryon is depicted in accordance with Dante's description: "His face was the face of a just man, so mild an aspect had it outwardly; and the rest was all a reptile's body. He had two paws, hairy to the armpits; the neck, and the breast, and both the flanks, were painted with knots and circlets"; the tail ended "in the venomed fork" of a scorpion. The poets are again seen in the centre of the composition, on the brink of the abyss, with Geryon before them, who at the bidding of Virgil has come ashore, resting his fore-quarters on the rocky ledge, but "draws not his tail upon the bank." Dante now proceeds alone, along the margin of the burning sand, "on the utmost limit of that seventh circle," where among the falling flames are seated the souls of the Usurers. From the neck of each hangs a pouch, left blank in the drawing, "and thereon it seems their eye is feasting." Dante is twice represented, the second time talking with two spirits, doubtless intended for those whose pouches, according to the text, bore the arms of the Gianfigliazzi and the Ubbriachi. Dante now returns, and finds his guide "already mounted on the haunch of the dreadful animal." Virgil bids him get up in front; whereat Dante trembles all over, "as one who has the shivering of the quartan." Having placed himself on the huge shoulders, Virgil clasps him with his arms. Geryon is now thrice represented with the poets on his back, as he sets out from his station backwards, like a bark, and wheeling round, slowly descends the abyss in great circles. The figure of Geryon in this drawing is the most impressive of all Botticelli's devils. Unlike the painter of the fresco in Santa Maria Novella, Sandro scrupulously follows Dante's description, and makes the monster go wingless, treading the air with his paws.

The print of 1481 resembles the drawing in its general conception; but contains only three incidents. On the right, Dante is seen talking with the souls of the Usurers. The pouches of two of them are blazoned; one with the goose of the Ubbriachi, the other with the lion rampant of the Gianfigliazzi. In the centre of the composition, Dante returns to find Virgil already mounted upon Geryon, who is here represented crowned. As in the drawing, Dante folds his arms upon his breast, with a gesture of fear and trembling. Below, the heads of the monster and the two poets are seen as the former descends the abyss.

Canto XVIII.—The poets now enter the eighth circle, formed by the shelving sides of Malebolge, with its ten successive fosses, or chasms. From the base of the high cliff surrounding the abyss into which they have just descended, great arch-like masses of rock bridge the fosses, and pass from embankment to embankment, "down to the well which truncates and collects them." In the upper, left-hand corner, Geryon relieved of his load, bounds off, "like an arrow from the string." As Virgil turns to the left, followed by Dante, they pause to regard the naked spirits of the Panders and Seducers, who are perpetually driven forward in two circles, which rotate in opposite directions, by "horned demons with large scourges." Again, on the right, Virgil stands still, while Dante goes back a little; having recognized one of the spirits, Venedico Caccianimico, who in vain "thought to hide himself, lowering his face." The poets now turn to the right, over the neck of rock which spans the first fosse, or chasm. "From the ancient bridge," they stop to view the train of spirits, who move towards them, on the inner side of the chasm, as Virgil points out to Dante the great soul of Jason. They now come "to where the narrow pathway crosses the second bank, and makes of it a buttress for another arch." In the drawing, Dante covers his face with his hand, at the foul sight and smell which now accost him. This is one of the few instances in which Botticelli exceeds the strict letter of the text. Not until they mount to the ridge of the next arch, are the poets able to see the bottom of the second chasm, in which the souls of the Flatterers are condemned to wallow in excrement. Dante recognizes the spirit of Alessio Interminei of Lucca, who stands up in the filth, beating his pate. Again, in the lower right-hand corner of the drawing, the poets are seen for the sixth time, as they descend to the third chasm.

As this, with the exception of the chart of the "Inferno," is the most finished of the four sheets begun in colour, I shall describe it with some particularity. Apart from the figure of Geryon, and a passage on the right, the whole design is elaborately coloured in a thin, glue-tempera, worked like a miniature. Throughout the drawing, the figure of Dante is habited in a purple robe, over a grass-green under-dress, with a white collar and vermilion biretta: that of Virgil, in a grape-purple robe over an ultramarine under-dress, with a tippet of ermine, and the tall, purple bonnet bordered with ermine, of an eastern magus. These colours appear very clear and brilliant against the dull colouring of the rest of the drawing; the brown rocks, the brown-black pool, the tawny bronze hue of the demons and the bleached forms of the spirits. The shadows of these figures are lightly hatched with umber and terra-verde, and the lights formed by leaving the vellum. Both the colours employed, and the method of working them, are those of a miniature-painter of the time. Neither is the pigment used with that freedom which we find in Botticelli's panel-pictures, nor does the colour-scheme recall that of any of his smaller paintings. The modelling of the forms, however, is executed so nearly in the manner and spirit of the outlines, that it is difficult to think that this colouring is not by Botticelli's own hand. To this question, however, I shall presently return.

The print of 1481 bears small resemblance to the drawing. Undue importance is given to the figure of Geryon as he ascends in the middle distance, after the poets have dismounted. Dante and Virgil are thrice represented: on the first bank talking with the spirit of Venedico Caccianimico; on the bridge over the first chasm, as they regard the spirit of Jason; and again on the second bridge, speaking with the soul of Alessio Interminei. The drawing is a far more adequate illustration of the canto, than the engraving.

Canto XIX.—The poets ascend the third bridge over the chasm of the Simonists; the chasm of the Flatterers being still seen in the distance. From the crown of the arch where the poets are standing, they behold "the livid stone, on the sides and on the bottom, full of holes, all of one breadth": "from the mouth of each, emerges a sinner's feet and legs, up to the calf," and "of all both the soles were on fire." Dante inquires "Who is that who writhes himself, quivering more than all his fellows?" Virgil answers: "If thou wilt have me carry thee down there, by that lower bank, thou shalt learn from him about himself and about his wrongs." The poets are now thrice represented: as they reach "the fourth bulwark," at the foot of the bridge; as Virgil carries Dante down from the bank into the chasm; and as they stand upon "the perforated and narrow bottom," talking with the spirit of Pope Nicholas III. Dante stands with both his hands uplifted, as he rebukes the spirit of him who was "clothed with the great mantle." In a fifth group, Virgil and Dante are partially seen as they reascend the side of the chasm: "with both arms he took me, and, when he had me quite upon his breast, remounted by the path where he had descended."

The print of 1481 is the last of the series which has come down to us. Except in the choice of the incidents represented, it bears little resemblance to the drawing. In this instance, the composition is not in reverse. Virgil and Dante are represented in four different groups: as they stand conversing on the crown of the arch; as they descend into the chasm; as they discourse with the spirit of Pope Nicholas III; and as Virgil, with Dante in his arms, remounts by the path by which they descended. The second and fourth of these groups, which differ greatly from the corresponding groups in the drawing, occur on the right of the bridge; whereas in the drawing they are placed on the left.

CANTO XX.—From the summit of the arch which spans the fourth chasm, Dante, "leaning on one of the rocks of the hard cliff," sees through the circular valley, "a people coming silent and weeping, at the pace which the Litanies make in this world": each one appeared "wondrously distorted, from the chin to the commencement of the chest, so that the face was turned towards the loins; and they had to come backward, for to look before them was denied." These are the Diviners, Augers and Sorcerers, who sought to look into the future, which belongs to God alone. Virgil points out to Dante various spirits: Amphiaräus, Tiresias, Aruns, Manto, Eurypylus, Michael Scott and the rest. But "Cain and the thorns already holds the confine of both hemispheres": the moon is setting, and it is time to go. Again the poets are seen about to cross the bridge over the next chasm.

CANTO XXI.—In the upper right-hand corner of the drawing, the poets are represented going "from bridge to bridge, with other talk," unrecorded in the Comedy. "As in the arsenal of the Venetians boils the clammy pitch, to caulk their damaged ships," so in the fifth chasm boils "by art divine a dense pitch," in which are immersed the Barrators. While Dante is gazing intently into the chasm, from the crown of the arch that spans it, Virgil draws him sharply back from where he is standing, bidding him have care. Dante turns round to see what he must shun, and perceives "a black demon come running up the cliff," with "wings outspread and light of foot." His shoulders are laden with the haunches of a sinner, "one of Santa Zita's elders," the chief magistrates of Lucca: "and of each foot he held the sinews grasped." Again the demon is seen hurling the spirit into the chasm; and a third time, as he turns and wheels "along the flinty cliff," while the soul falls headlong into the pitch. As the spirit of the barrator comes up again writhing, the demons who lurk under the cover of the bridge, cry: "Here the Sacred Face besteads not," and thrust him under with their hooks.

Below, Dante is again seen cowering down behind a jagg of the rock, while Virgil goes forward to parley with Malacoda, the spokesman of the demons who have been hiding under the bridge. When Virgil tells him that he comes secure against all their weapons, "for it is willed in Heaven that I show another this savage way," Malacoda lets fall his hook. Virgil now tells Dante that he may securely return; and the poet is a third time represented, with his hand crossed on his breast, approaching Virgil and the demons. Malacoda informs the poets that "to go farther by this cliff will not be possible; for the sixth arch is all in fragments at the bottom"; but if they will proceed along the chasm, "near at hand is another cliff which forms a path." With this, he offers to send ten of his fellows, with Barbariccia at their head, to guide the poets "to the other crag, which all unbroken goes across the dens." The incident of Virgil and Dante setting out under the guidance of the demons, is shown on the right of the drawing:

> "Per l'argine sinistro volta dienno;
>   Ma prima avea ciascun la lingua stretta
> Coi denti, verso lor duca per cenno,
>   Ed egli avea del cul fatto trombetta."

CANTO XXII.—Virgil and Dante now proceed along the inner edge of the fifth chasm of the boiling pitch, escorted by the ten demons. On the left of the drawing, the poets are seen following the demons; Dante intent on observing "every habit of the chasm, and of the people that were burning in it." "As at the edge of the water of a ditch, the frogs stand only with their muzzles out, so that they hide their feet and other bulk; thus stood on every hand the sinners." At the approach of Barbariccia, they instantly retire beneath the seething pitch. One, however, tarrying longer than the others, is hooked by Graffiacane, who hauls him up by his pitchy locks, like an otter. The demons are about to flay the wretched spirit, when Dante asks Virgil to learn, if he can, "who is that piteous wight, fallen into the hand of his adversaries." The spirit, in reply to Virgil, confesses that he practised barratry, in the service of King Thibault of Navarre. In the drawing, the soul of the barrator is seen still hanging by the hair, as Graffiacane lands him with his hook. Again, he is seen lying on the bank, as the demons who gather round him, try to catch at him with their hooks: on the left, Virgil and Dante draw near to speak with him. The subsequent altercation of the demons, and the ruse by which the spirit of the Navarrese escapes from their clutches, is indicated by the figure of the barrator on the edge of the bank, in the act of leaping into the pitch: "the Navarrese chose well his time; planted his soles upon the ground, and in an instant leapt and from their purpose freed himself." The subsequent incidents of this canto are passed over in the drawing. In the upper part of the design, the spirits of the fourth chasm are seen in the distance.

CANTO XXIII.—"Silent, apart and without escort, we went on, the one before and the other after; as the Minor Friars go their way." In the upper left-hand corner of the drawing, Virgil, followed by Dante, proceeds with measured steps: both are meditating on what they have seen in the chasm of the burning pitch. Suddenly Dante is aware that the Malebranche are after them. Virgil seeks to reassure his companion, but before he has done speaking, the demons come on, with wings extended, as if in will to seize them: whereat Virgil suddenly takes Dante, "as a mother . . . who takes her child and flies, and caring more for him than for herself, pauses not so long as even to cast a shift about her. And down from the ridge of the hard bank, supine he gave himself to the pendent rock, which dams up one side of the other chasm." This incident is represented in the upper part of the drawing. Virgil, with Dante in his arms, hastens over the arch which spans the next chasm, pursued by the demons, who angrily threaten the poets with their hooks. Below, Virgil and Dante are again seen, entering the sixth chasm of the Hypocrites. Here they find "a painted people, who were going round with steps exceeding slow, weeping, and in their look tired and overcome. They had cloaks on, with deep hoods before their eyes, made in the shape that they make for the monks in Cologne. Outward they are gilded, so that it dazzles; but within all is of lead." One of the Hypocrites, who hears the Tuscan speech of Dante, calls after him, and in answer to his question, tells the poet that he was of the Frati Godenti of Bologna, and by name Catalano. As Dante is about to reply to him, his eyes fall on "one, cross-fixed in the ground with three stakes." The friar tells him that this is Caiaphas, and that in like fashion his father-in-law, Annas, "is racked in this ditch, and the others of that council, which was a seed of evil for the Jews."

In these last three drawings, Botticelli gives a free rein to his imagination in portraying the mediaeval devil, as it was known to him in Giottesque art, and upon the stage of the Florentine "Sacre Rappresentazioni," or miracle plays. Although he treats these monstrous incubi, compounded, as he conceives them, of man, beast, bird and reptile, with genuine invention both as to form and character, it is difficult for us to feel the sense of illusion in regard to them, which we do in the case of the other images, human or divine, with which he peoples the triple region of the "Commedia." But the time had come when it was no longer possible to take such a phantasm of the mediaeval mind literally; and Michelagnolo, who on the one hand, transmutes it by his genius into the sublime figure of his Charon, on the other, uses it as the principal motive of those grotesque masks, which were to play so genial a part in the decoration of Florentine architecture, during the sixteenth century.

Canto XXIV.—The poets now reach the shattered bridge, which leads to the seventh chasm of the Thieves. "My guide turned to me with that sweet aspect which I saw before at the foot of the mountain. He opened his arms after having chosen some plan within himself, first looking well at the ruin, and took hold of me. And as one who works, and calculates, always seeming to provide beforehand; so lifting me up towards the top of one big block, he looked out another splinter, saying, 'Now clamber over that, but try first if it will carry thee.' . . . We, however, came at length to the point from which the last stone breaks off. The breath was so exhausted from my lungs when I was up, that I could no farther; nay, seated me at my first arrival." On the right and left of the upper part of the drawing, is seen in the distance the chasm of the Hypocrites. In the middle, Virgil is twice represented helping Dante up from ledge to ledge of the broken rock; a third time Dante is seen seated on the crest of the ruin, as Virgil remonstrates with him: "Now it behoves thee thus to free thyself from sloth, for on sitting down or under coverlet, men come not into fame." Again, the poets are partially seen, as they make their way up the side of the next rugged bridge, which was "greatly steeper than the former": and yet a fifth time, as they gain "the ridge of the arch which crosses there." Below they are twice depicted, descending into the chasm from the eighth bank. Within the chasm Dante now sees "a fearful throng of serpents." "Let Libya boast no longer with its sand; for though it engenders Chelydri, Jaculi and Pareae, and Cenchres with Amphisbaena, plagues so numerous or so dire it never showed." The allusion is to Lucan, as Landino notes in his commentaries; adding, that among the various kinds of serpents which inhabit the Libyan desert, are the Pareae, "which march on the tail, the rest of the body being raised from the ground," and the Amphisbaena, which have "two heads, one where it ought naturally to be, and the other at the tail." Botticelli represents both these creatures in this and the following drawing. The poem continues: "Amid this cruel and most dismal swarm were people running, naked and terrified. . . . They had their hands tied behind them with serpents. . . . And lo! at one who was near our shore, sprang up a serpent, which transfixed him there where the neck is bound upon the shoulders. Neither 'O' nor 'I' was ever written so quickly as he took fire, and burnt, and dropt down, all changed to ashes. And after he was thus dissolved upon the ground the ashes reunited, and of themselves at once resumed the former shape." This incident is represented in the centre of the composition: a dragon seizes the sinner by the shoulder and is about to devour him, as the fire kindles at his feet. Again, for the eighth time, Virgil and Dante are seen talking with the sinner after his ashes have re-united. In reply to Virgil, he tells the poet that he is Vanni Fucci, who robbed the sacristy of San Jacopo, at Pistoia, of its goodly furniture. On the left of the sheet, a six-footed dragon springs upon another sinner, in allusion to an episode which occurs in the next canto.

CANTO XXV.—The scene is similar to that of the last drawing: the chasm of the Hypocrites still appearing in the distance. Virgil and Dante are twice represented at half length, as they proceed through the chasm. Firstly, as they gaze at Vanni Fucci who, as he ends the angry prophecy with which the last canto closes, raises his hands with both the figs, shouting, "Take them, God, for at thee I aim them!" And again, as "a serpent with six feet," which Botticelli represents as a dragon, darts up in front of the spirit of Agnello Brunelleschi and fastens itself upon him: "with its middle feet it clasped his belly, with the anterior it seized his arms, then fixed its teeth in both his cheeks; the hinder feet it stretched along his thighs, and put its tail between the two, and bent it upwards on his loins behind." The transformation of the sinner described in the poem is passed over in the drawing, as likewise are the subsequent metamorphoses of men into serpents, and serpents into men. On the right of the sheet, however, is represented an incident, which occurs in the poem, before the latter transformations. After Vanni Fucci had fled away, Dante sees a Centaur "full of rage, come crying: 'Where is, where is the surly one?' Maremma, I do believe, has not so many snakes as he had on his haunch, to where our human form begins. Over his shoulders, behind the head, a dragon lay with outstretched wings, and it sets on fire every one he meets. My master said: 'That is Cacus, who, beneath the rock of Mount Aventine, full often made a lake of blood:'" adding, that he goes here, and not with his brethren, along the river of blood, "because of the cunning theft he made of the great herd that lay near him." Botticelli represents the Centaur bearing the dragon on his head, like the crest of one of those "elmi da parata," or ceremonial helms, of which an example is preserved in the Museum of the Bargello at Florence.

CANTO XXVI.—The poets depart from the seventh chasm, by the bourns by which they had descended. Virgil remounts and draws Dante up, and as they pursue their way "among the jaggs and branches of the cliff, the foot without the hand sped not." In the upper part of the drawing, Virgil and Dante are twice represented; as they climb up out of the chasm of the Thieves, and again as they reach the further bank of the eighth chasm, wherein are punished the Evil Counsellors. Dante now sees within the fosse innumerable flames, which gleam like fireflies on a summer's evening, when the moon is hidden. "I stood upon the bridge, having risen so to look, that, if I had not caught a rock, I should have fallen down without being pushed. And the guide who saw me thus attent, said: 'Within those fires are the spirits: each swathes himself with that which burns him.'" Virgil points out the flames in which Ulysses and Diomed are tortured, and the poets question them. In the drawing, Virgil and Dante are represented standing on the crown of the arch which spans the chasm, looking at the flames in the fosse below. Dante leans against the rock which has prevented his fall; and out of the flame in which the spirits of Ulysses and Diomed are imprisoned, "two in one fire," appear two human faces.

CANTO XXVII.—"The flame was now erect and quiet, having ceased to speak, and now went away from us with license of the sweet poet; when another, that came behind it, made us turn our eyes to its top, for a confused sound that issued therefrom." Virgil and Dante now speak with the spirit of Count Guido da Montefeltro; and their discourse fills the remainder of the canto. In the drawing, the foregoing scene is repeated. Virgil and Dante are seen still standing on the arch; on either side of which, in the fosse below, are the flames in which the spirits of the Evil Counsellors are burning. Several of the flames have human faces, though only one spirit is made to speak in the course of the canto. This design is, perhaps, the feeblest and emptiest of the whole series.

CANTO XXVIII.—The closing lines of the previous canto relate how the poets pass on to the arch that spans the ninth chasm, in which are punished the Sowers of Scandal and Schism: "Who, even with words set free, could ever fully tell, by oft relating, the blood and the wounds that I now saw?" In the drawing, the poets are seen standing on the crown of the arch on the right, as they look down into the fosse in which are the mangled forms of the spirits, and among them on the left, a devil who slashes at one of them with a two-handed sword. Dante now sees Mahomet, "ripped from the chin down": he is represented in the upper part of the drawing, with his entrails hanging between his legs. On the right of this figure goes Ali, his nephew, "cleft in the face from chin to forelock." Immediately below the arch stands Pier da Medicina, "his throat pierced, and nose cut off up to the eyebrows," and with but a single ear. He lays his hand upon the jaw of one of his companions, the Roman Curius, and opens his mouth, saying, "this outcast quenched the doubt in Caesar, affirming that to men prepared delay is always hurtful." Below this group, the Ghibelline, Mosca de' Lamberti, is seen with both hands cut off, raising the stumps, so that the "blood defiles his face." Again, on the left of Pier da Medicina, Bertran de Born, the troubadour, who carries his severed head in his hand like a lantern, lifts it up as he approaches the foot of the bridge, to bring its words nearer to the poets, who look down on him from the arch.

CANTO XXIX.—In the drawing, the chasm of the Sowers of Scandal and Schism is seen in the distance, with Virgil and Dante talking together on the bridge; while in the fosse below, Bertran de Born still holds up his head to them. Near by, Dante's kinsman, Geri del Bello, is seen to point at the poet, and "vehemently threaten with his finger": but Dante does not perceive him, so intent is he "upon him who once held Altaforte." The poets now come to the arch over the tenth chasm, in which the Falsifiers of every sort are punished: "When we were above the last cloister of Malebolge, so that its lay-brethren could appear to our view, lamentations pierced me, manifold, which had their arrows barbed with pity; whereat I covered my ears with my hands." In the drawing, as the poets pass over the bridge, Dante stops his ears. They now descend "on the last bank of the long cliff, again to the left hand." As they look at, and listen to, the sick, who could not raise their bodies, Dante sees "two leaning on each other, (as pan is leant on pan to warm,) from head to foot spotted with scabs." Each of them "plied thick the clawing of his nails upon himself, for the great fury of their itch which has no other succour." When Virgil declares, "I am one, who with this living man descend from steep to steep, and mean to show him Hell," they spring asunder, and each turns trembling to Dante. This is the incident represented on the right of the sheet. In answer to the poets, they tell them that they are the spirits of Griffolino of Arezzo, and Capocchio, the Florentine. The two figures which are running, as one fastens its teeth into the back of the other, can hardly be intended to represent the shades of Gianni Schicchi and ancient Myrrha, first alluded to in the next canto, as Dr. Lippmann has suggested: though the motive of these figures was, no doubt, suggested by that incident.

CANTO XXX.—Virgil and Dante pursue their way through the tenth chasm. The drawing for this canto is only lightly, and partially, sketched with the style. The surface of the vellum shows signs of abrasion; and there are other indications that an earlier design has been erased. The figures of Virgil and Dante are twice indicated: standing together on the edge of the fosse, with their backs turned to the spectator, in the centre of the sheet; and again in somewhat smaller figures, but in much the same attitude, immediately below the former ones. The two who approach them running, on the right, are probably intended for the "two shadows, pale and naked," of Gianni Schicchi and ancient Myrrha, "which ran biting in the manner that a hungry swine does, when he is thrust out from his sty." Again, on the right, the shade of Gianni Schicchi has seized upon Capocchio "and fixed its tusks on his neck-joint, so that, dragging him, it made the solid bottom claw his belly." Immediately above the poets, swollen with dropsy, is Adamo da Brescia, "shapen like a lute, if he had only had his groin cut short at the part where man is forked." On the left of the sheet is indicated the bridge over the fosse, by which the poets have come. This unfinished sheet affords an admirable example of the way in which Botticelli first sketched in his inventions with the style. The beauty and rhythm of line with which he rapidly suggests naturalistic form and movement, afford most significant evidence of his power as a draughtsman.

CANTO XXXI.—The poets now cross the bank dividing the last chasm of Malebolge from the ninth circle, which forms the central and lowest pit of hell. As they go their way in silence, Dante hears "a high horn sound so loudly that it would have made any thunder weak." Looking up, he sees in the darkness what he imagines to be the lofty towers of a town. Virgil tells him that "they are not towers, but giants," who stand "in the well around its bank, from the navel downwards all of them." In the drawing, the pit of the ninth circle fills the foreground; and the giants, who are naked and six in number, are ranged at intervals around the well of the circle, looking outward like the watch-towers of a castle. In the upper left-hand corner, the poets are seen descending the bank as they discourse of "the horrible giants, whom Jove from heaven still threatens with his thunders." Below, in a second group, they are seen approaching one of these huge creatures, who shouts unintelligible words at them: "This is Nimrod, through whose ill device one language is not still used in the world." Virgil now speaks "towards him: 'Stupid soul! keep to thy horn; and vent thyself with that: . . . search on thy neck, and thou wilt find the belt that holds it tied.'" In the drawing, the figure is represented blowing a horn held by a chain which is passed round his neck. As the poets proceed, "turning to the left," they find another giant, "far more fierce and large": "he had his right arm pinioned down behind, and the other before, with a chain which held him clasped from the neck downwards, and on the uncovered part went round to the fifth turn." Virgil, in a third group, points him out to Dante: he is Ephialtes, who "willep to try his power against high Jove." As the poets proceed on their way, Dante desires to see "the immense Briareus": Virgil answers him, "Thou shalt see Antaeus near at hand, who speaks and is unfettered, who will put us into the bottom of all guilt. He whom thou desirest to see, is far beyond, and is tied and shaped like this one, save that he seems in aspect more ferocious." In the drawing, Virgil is seen turning round to answer Dante, in a fourth group, on the right of the figure of Ephialtes; Briareus is represented below, at half length, bound with a chain, in the centre of the composition. Between these figures on the right of the sheet, Antaeus, unchained, is represented bending down as he places Virgil with Dante in his arms, "gently on the deep, which swallows Lucifer with Judas." The figures of the giants in this drawing are very Pollaiuolesque in form, and show that in the treatment of the nude, the manner of Botticelli had undergone little change since the time when, in January, 1473-4, he finished the painting of St. Sebastian for the church of Santa Maria Maggiore.

Canto XXXII.—"When we were down in the dark pit, under the giants' feet, much lower, and I still was gazing at the high wall, I heard a voice say to me: 'Look how thou passest: take care that with thy soles thou tread not on the heads of the weary, wretched brothers.' Whereat I turned myself, and saw before my feet a lake, which through frost had the semblance of glass and not of water. . . . And as the frog, to croak, sits with his muzzle out of the water, . . . so, livid, up to where the hue of shame appears, the doleful shades were in the ice, sounding with their teeth like storks." Botticelli represents this incident by a device which he again employs in the illustrations to Cantos X and XXIX of the "Purgatorio," and Canto III of the "Paradiso." Virgil and Dante are seen standing by the wall of the pit, on the outermost ring of the ninth circle, inscribed in the painter's hand, "chaina." Dante is represented with his right hand raised, screening his eyes, as he looks up at the giants, whose feet are seen resting on a ledge of the pit, in the upper part of the drawing; and again, on the same figure, the head and right hand are drawn a second time, in order to represent the sudden movement of the poet, as he looks down in astonishment, at the wretched souls imprisoned in the ice. At Dante's feet are seen "two so pressed against each other, that they had the hair of their heads intermixed"; they are Napoleone and Alessandro, the sons of Count Alberto. There is nothing in the drawing to show which are the other spirits mentioned in this canto. The poets now go "towards the middle," into the second ring, which is inscribed "antenora." In a second group, Dante is seen bending down with the hair of one of the spirits, whose face he had violently struck with his foot, coiled in his hand; this is Bocca degli Abbati, whose treachery largely contributed to the defeat of the Guelphs at Montaperti. Again, in the foreground, Virgil and Dante are seen bending over "two frozen in one hole so closely, that the one head was a cap to the other; and as bread is chewed for hunger, so the uppermost put his teeth into the other, there where the brain joins with the nape." They are Count Ugolino della Gherardesca and the Archbishop of Pisa, Ruggieri degli Ubaldini, whose story is told in the next canto. Dante, I may add, describes the spirits of this ninth circle as lying ice-bound up to the jowl in the frozen marsh; but Botticelli, who in this and the following drawing, disregarding the strict letter of the text, represents the whole of their forms as they lie in the lake, and makes no attempt to show what part of their bodies rises above the surface of the ice. It is only in the lowest ring of the Giudecca that "the souls were wholly covered, and shone through the ice like straw in glass."

CANTO XXXIII.—All the four rings, or divisions, of the ninth circle are shown in the drawing, and are severally inscribed by the painter, "chaina giudecha," "antenora," "tolemea," "giudecha." In the centre of the composition, Virgil and Dante are seen in the ring of Antenora, as they listen to the story of Ugolino della Gherardesca: "from the fell repast that sinner raised his mouth, wiping it upon the hair of the head he had laid waste behind." The poets now go forward into the third ring, or Ptolomaea, "where the frost ruggedly inwraps another people, not bent forwards, but all reversed." Below, in the centre of the sheet, Virgil and Dante are again seen talking with the friar, Alberigo de' Manfredi, who has gone down "quick into Hell."

CANTO XXXIV.—There are two illustrations to this last canto. In the first, Dis, "the emperor of the dolorous realm," is seen at half-length, as he stands forth "from mid breast out of the ice." He is represented as Dante describes him, with "three faces on his head"; "the one in front," the other two "that were adjoined to this, above the very middle of each shoulder." Under each are "two mighty wings," fashioned like those of a bat. In every mouth he champs a sinner with his teeth; in the middle mouth is Judas Iscariot, "who has his head within, and outside plies his legs"; of the other two "who have their heads beneath," that on the left is Brutus, and the other on the right, Cassius. "'But night is reascending, and now we must depart, for we have seen the whole.' As he desired, I clasped his neck: and he took opportunity of time and place; and when the wings were opened far, applied him to the shaggy sides, and then from shag to shag, descended down between the tangled hair and frozen crusts." Dante is represented clasping the shoulders of Virgil as he descends the side of Dis, "from shag to shag," to the centre of the universe. The drawing is unfinished; the lower portion of the figure of Dis, and his left wing, being merely sketched in with the style.

The second illustration is twice the size of the other designs, being drawn on two sheets of vellum fastened together. It represents the figure of Dis at whole length, his body being covered with shags of hair, and his feet clawed. A circle drawn in the middle of the sheet, and cutting the figure of Dis in two places, marks the division of the innermost rings of the ninth circle, as indicated by the inscription, "tolomea giudecha." The progress of the poets is shown by a series of eight groups. In the first, as Virgil bids Dante look in front of him, the latter shrinks back behind his guide on account of the wind, which he now feels. As they proceed Virgil shows to Dante, the "creature which was once so fair." In the third and fourth groups, Dante is seen clasping Virgil by the neck as he descends by the shaggy side of Dis. When they come "to where the thigh revolves just on the swelling of the haunch," Virgil turns his head where he had had his feet before, and grapples on the hair as one who mounts. In the sixth group, the poets issue forth through an opening of the rock. In the next, Dante is seated on the edge of the rock, and looks up, thinking to see Lucifer as he had left him, and sees him "with his legs turned upwards." Virgil stands over him, resolving him of his perplexity. In the eighth and last group, which is merely sketched in with the style, the poets ascend "by that hidden road, to return into the bright world."

PURGATORIO. CANTO I.—The drawing which is inscribed below with the opening words of the canto, "1 perchore[r] miglioraqua," contains a bird's-eye view of Purgatory: this view, like the diagram prefixed to the Inferno, was intended to serve as a kind of introductory chart to the whole canticle. Botticelli represents the island, on which the mountain of Purgatory rises, of a circular form. According to Dante, the mountain reaches to the heaven of the moon, the first of the celestial spheres. It rises at the antipodes of Jerusalem, and its bulk is equal and opposite to the cavity of Hell. The lower part of the mountain forms a kind of ante-region, in which atonement is made for delay in repentance. Purgatory proper consists of seven circular terraces, connected by steep stairways; and in these circles are severally purged the seven deadly sins: Pride, Envy, Anger, Sloth, Avarice, Gluttony, Lust. On the summit of the mountain is the Earthly Paradise, formerly the Garden of Eden. The mount of Purgatory being of a much less complicated form than the cavity of Hell, the ingenuity of the commentators was naturally exercised in a far minor degree about the one, than the other. The earliest representation of Purgatory known to me, occurs in the background of the painting which was executed in 1465, by Domenico di Michelino, from the design of Alesso Baldovinetti, and which is still in the cathedral at Florence. Here the painter represents the lower portion of the mountain, which forms a sort of ante-region to Purgatory proper, by a single terrace; giving great prominence to the gateway, with the angel seated before it, by which entrance is gained to the first of the seven circles. Botticelli, on the contrary, represents in his drawing, all the lower part of the mount with great elaboration. He shows the gap in the hillside, and the narrow way leading to "the uppermost edge of the high bank," with the hollow in which lie the souls of the kings and princes who have delayed their repentance, and above all, the overhanging cliff up which Dante is carried in a trance by the golden eagle. The upper part of the mountain, encircled by its seven terraces, and crowned by the Earthly Paradise, is represented much as it is seen in Alesso's design, except that Botticelli makes no attempt to indicate the souls which people it.

J. Gaye, "Carteggio inedito," II, vi.

In the centre of the drawing, Virgil and Dante are seen in little figures, crossing the "lonely plain" after emerging from the cleft at the foot of the mountain behind them: "the sweet hue of oriental sapphire, which was deepening on the serene face of the sky, pure even to the first sphere, renewed delight to mine eyes, as soon as I issued forth from the dead air which had saddened me both eyes and heart." Dante now sees "an old man, alone, and in appearance worthy of so great reverence, that greater no son owes to father; he wore his beard long, and mingled with white hair, like unto his locks." He demands of the poets: "Who are ye that against the blind river have fled the eternal prison?" "My leader then lay hold of me, and with words and with signs made reverent my knees and brow." On the right of the drawing, in larger figures, Dante is seen kneeling down before the venerable guardian of the place, the younger Cato of Utica, while Virgil stands by his side. The figure of Cato is drawn with the pen; but those of the poets are merely sketched in with the style. Cato bids Virgil "see that thou gird this man with a smooth rush, and lave his face, so that thou mayest wash away all stain from it." Cato having done speaking, the poets recross the plain: "when we came to where the dew strives with the sun, and through being in a place where under the light breeze it rises little, my Master gently placed both hands outspread upon the short grass; wherefore I, who was aware of his purpose, raised towards him my tearful cheeks; there he made manifest in me that colour which Hell concealed." Below, in a third group, Virgil kneels down to gather the dew, as Dante, with his hands crossed on his breast, bends towards him. "We then approached the desert shore" which "bears rushes above the soft mud, where the wave beats on it": "there he girt me as another willed." In the drawing, on the left of the last group, Virgil binds Dante round the waist with a girdle of rushes. In the distance, on the left margin of the sheet, a bark slightly sketched with the style, crosses the sound: below, it is again represented as it nears the shore, and a troop of naked spirits hurry from out it. This incident, however, forms the opening episode of the next canto.

CANTO II.—The drawing, which is inscribed below, "2 gia era ilsole alorezonte," is unfinished. "We were yet beside the sea, . . . and lo! as at the approach of morning, Mars burns red through the thick vapours, down in the west above the ocean floor, such a light . . . appeared to me coming over the sea so swiftly that no flight could equal its movement. . . . My Master as yet spake not a word, until the first white gleams were seen to be wings; then when he well recognized the helmsman, he cried: 'Bend, bend thy knees; behold the angel of God: fold thy hands. . . . See how he disdains human means, so that he wants not oar, nor other sail than his own wings, between shores so distant.' . . . On the poop stood the heavenly steersman, . . . and more than a hundred spirits sat therein. . . . Then he made to them the sign of Holy Cross; whereat they all cast themselves upon the shore, and he departed as swiftly as he had come." Below in the centre of the drawing, Dante kneels down, as Virgil by his side bids him do reverence to the angel. On the left, the bark has touched the shore; and as the angel, who is seated in the poop, makes the sign of the Cross, its freight of souls hasten to land. Above, in the distance, the ship with the angel alone at the helm, is seen returning across the sound. The spirits now ask the poets to direct them to the mount. When they perceive that Dante breathes and is alive, they gather round him. "I saw one of them come forward to embrace me with so great emotion, that it moved me to do the like. O shadows empty, save in the appearance! Thrice behind it I crossed my hands, and as often I brought them to my breast." The spirit is that:

"Of his Casella, whom he wooed to sing,
Met in the milder shades of Purgatory."

In the centre of the drawing, the musician at the head of a troop of souls, comes forward to embrace Dante, as Virgil stands by his side. At the request of the poet, he sings one of Dante's "canzoni." "We were all fixed and intent on his notes; and behold! the old man, reverent, crying: 'What is this, laggard spirits? What indifference, what halt is this? Haste to the mount to strip you of the slough, which suffers not God to be manifest to you!'" At this, the spirits "leave the song and go towards the mountain, as a man who goes and knows not to what place he may come. Nor was our own departure the less hasty." In the drawing, above the group of Dante and Casella embracing, Cato is represented chiding a troop of spirits who hurry towards the mount, on the right of the sheet. This group of spirits, with both the ships and the figure of the angel in the distance, are only sketched in with the style; as are, also, some slight indications of the rocky background, on the right.

CANTO III.—The drawing is inscribed below, with the opening words of the canto: "3 auegnia chelasubitana fugha." "The sun, which shone red behind us, was broken in front of me, according to the figure in which his rays were checked by me. I turned aside in fear of having been abandoned, when I saw that before myself alone the earth was darkened." On the left of the drawing, as the poets make their way across the plain, Dante is seen to turn in fear, when he perceives only his own shadow, and not that of Virgil. Behind them in the heavens, is the sun; near the shore is the troop of spirits from whom they have parted; and in the distance, the angel steers back his bark across the sound. When the poets reach the foot of the mountain, they find the rock too steep for ascent. "'Now who knows on which hand the hill-side slopes down,' said my Master, staying his steps, 'so that he may be able to climb who goes without wings?'" As Virgil stands "examining the fashion of the way," Dante sees coming towards them, "on the left hand, a company of souls who moved their feet towards us, and yet appeared not to do so, so slowly they came. 'Lift up,' said I to my Master, 'thine eyes. Behold here is some one who will give us counsel, if thou mayest not have it of thyself.' Then he looked at them, and with a frank countenance replied: 'Let us go thither, for they come slowly.'" When the spirits beheld the poets approaching, "they all drew close to the hard crags of the lofty bank, and stood fast and close, as he who is in doubt pauses to look." Upon Virgil inquiring "where the mountain slopes so that it may be possible to go upwards," the spirits come forward, "as sheep issue from the fold." "When those in front saw the light on the ground broken on my right side, so that the shadow fell from me to the rock, they stayed and drew themselves back a little, and all the others that came after, not knowing the reason, did the like." In the drawing, the poets are thrice represented: as they stand at the foot of the mountain perplexed by its steepness; as they turn aside towards the troop of approaching spirits, on the right; and as Virgil asks of them the way, and the foremost of them start back, when they perceive the shadow which the body of Dante casts. The deviation from the strict letter of the text in representing the poets turning to the right, instead of to the left, is the first of a series of similar lapses on the part of Botticelli, hereafter to be noticed. The concluding episode of the canto, in which Dante converses with the spirit of Manfred, is passed over in the drawing.

CANTO IV.—The drawing is inscribed below with the opening words of the canto: "4 quando perdilectan[ze]." "Full fifty degrees had the sun climbed, and I had not perceived it, when we came to a place where those spirits with one voice cried to us; 'Here is your quest!' Many a time the villager hedges up with a forkful of thorns an opening larger, . . . than was the gap by which my leader mounted, and I after him, we two alone, when the troop parted from us. . . . We were going up through the cloven rock, and on either side its face pressed upon us, and the ground beneath needed both feet and hands. . . . I was weary, when I began: 'O, sweet father, turn thee and behold how I remain behind alone, if thou stay not.' 'My son,' said he, 'draw thyself as far as there,' pointing me out a terrace a little above us, which on that side encircles all the hill. His words so spurred me on, that I forced myself, clambering behind him, until I had the circuit under my feet." In the drawing, on the left, Virgil, followed by Dante, is seen about to enter the cleft in the rock, to which the troop of spirits direct them. Above, the poets are twice represented on their way through the narrow gorge; and a fourth time, as they are seated upon the first terrace, which encircles the mount. Virgil now explains to Dante the course of the sun, and why in this hemisphere they "were smitten by him on the left." When he had done speaking, the poets hear a voice: "at the sound of it each of us turned, and we saw on the left a great stone. . . . We drew thither, and there were persons who rested in the shade behind the rock, as a man settles himself to rest through listlessness. And one of them who seemed to me weary, was sitting and embracing his knees, holding his face down low between them." Dante approaches him, and recognizes the spirit of Belacqua. This episode is shown in the upper part of the drawing, on the right, where the poets are seen approaching a troop of spirits, who sit crouching in a cleft of the rock.

CANTO V.—The drawing is inscribed below, with the opening words of the canto: "5 iera gia daquelonbre parttito." "I had already parted from those shades, and was following the footsteps of my leader, when behind me, pointing the finger, one of them cried: 'Look how it seems that the ray of the sun shines not on the left of him who is lowermost, and as a living man he seems to carry himself.' I turned back my eyes at the sound of these words, and saw them gaze in astonishment at me, even me, and the light that was broken." Below, on the left of the drawing, one of a troop of spirits who sit crouching under the rock, points with his finger at Dante, who has just passed them. As he goes on his way, he turns towards Virgil, who reproves him for giving heed to them. "And meanwhile across the hillside came people a little in front of us, saying '*Miserere*' verse by verse. When they perceived that I gave no place by reason of my body, to the passage of the rays, they changed their chant into an 'O' long and hoarse; and two of them in guise of messengers ran to meet us, and ask of us: 'Make us acquainted with your condition.' And my Master: 'Ye can go your way, and take back word to them that sent you, that the body of this man is very flesh.' . . . Never saw I burning vapours cleave the serene sky in the early night, nor august clouds as the sun is setting, so quickly, but that they returned upward in less time, and having arrived there, wheeled round to us, with the others, like a troop which runs without rein." In the drawing, above and somewhat to the right of the last episode, Virgil is represented a second time, speaking with two naked spirits who have come forward, "in the guise of messengers": on the right, the two spirits are again seen hastening back to their troop, and they in their turn wheel round to Virgil and Dante, who are again represented on the left. The poets now talk with the spirits, among whom are Jacopo del Cassero, Buonconte da Montefeltro, and La Pia . The groups of figures illustrating these incidents are arranged diagonally across the page, from left to right. Above and below are seen other groups of naked spirits, for the most part seated on the rock.

CANTO VI.—The drawing is inscribed below, with the opening words of the canto: "6 quando siparte elgiuocho delazara." "When the game of hazard breaks up, he who loses remains dolefully recalling the throws, and learns by his grief; with the other, all the folk go their way; one goes in front, and one catches him from behind, and another on one side brings himself to his remembrance. . . . Such was I in that dense crowd, turning, now here, now there, my face to them, and promising, I freed myself from them." In the lower left-hand corner of the drawing, Dante is seen surrounded by a crowd of spirits, among whom are Federigo Novello, Count Orso and Pierre de la Brosse. They importune him to remember them in his prayers: Virgil stands by, with a gesture of astonishment, and other spirits draw near, in a long file from the right. Some of the latter figures are but slightly sketched in with the style. The poem continues: "When I was free from all those shades, . . . I began, 'Methinks thou expressly deniest, O my light, in a certain passage, that prayer may bend the decree of Heaven, and this people pray only for that. Would, then, their hope be vain, or is thy saying not rightly manifest to me?'" Virgil answers him, touching the efficacy of prayer for those in Purgatory. In the drawing, above and somewhat to the right of the last episode, Dante is seen earnestly discoursing with Virgil, as they make their way up the rugged mountain. Virgil having told Dante that Beatrice will resolve him of his doubt, when they shall reach the summit of the mountain, adds: "But see there a soul which, placed all alone, looks solitary towards us: it will point out to us the speediest way. . . . Then Virgil drew near to it, praying that it would show us the easiest ascent; and it answered not his question, but inquired of us concerning our country and our life. And the sweet Leader began: 'Mantua—' And the shade all hermit-like, rapt in itself, sprang towards him from the place where before it was standing, saying: 'O Mantuan, I am Sordello of thy land.' And the one embraced the other." This meeting with Sordello, which forms the subject of the remainder of the canto, is represented in the drawing, by a group of figures slightly sketched in with the style, above and again somewhat to the right of the last episode. The naked spirit of Sordello springs forward about to clasp Virgil who, like Dante, raises both his hands in amazement. Immediately to the left of Sordello, two or three other figures are slightly sketched in; and again, on the right of the sheet, three spirits are indicated, sitting upon the rock. Some portions of these unfinished passages appear to have been put in in ink, and afterwards erased.

CANTO VII.—The drawing is inscribed below, with the first line of the canto: "7 poscia chelachoglenze oneste eliete." Virgil, in reply to Sordello, now declares who he is: "As he who suddenly sees a thing before him, whereat he so wonders that he believes and believes not, saying, 'It is, it is not'; such seemed he, and then he bent his brow and humbly turned again towards him, and embraced him where the inferior takes hold." In the lower left-hand corner of the sheet, the spirit of Sordello is seen reverently kneeling before Virgil, as he clasps him round the waist; for Botticelli interprets the text with Landino, in the sense of "sotto le braccia," or as other early commentators have it, "ove 'l nutrir." Presently Virgil asks the Mantuan to show them, how they may "come most quickly to the place, where Purgatory has its proper beginning." Sordello answers: "As far as I can go, I put myself at thy side as guide. But see how the day is already declining, and to go upwards in the night is not possible; therefore it is good to think about some convenient resting-place. Here are spirits on the right, apart; if thou give me thy consent, I will lead thee to them, and not without delight will they become known to thee.' 'How is that?' it was answered, 'he who would wish to ascend by night, would he be hindered by others, or would it be that he could not?' And the good Sordello drew his finger along the ground, saying: 'Look, even this line thou wouldst not pass after the sun is gone down; not, however, that aught else than the darkness of night would give hindrance in going upward: that, through lack of power, perplexes the will.'" In the drawing, this incident is represented by a second group of Dante and Virgil with Sordello, who bends down in front of them, as he draws a line with his finger on the ground. The poets, led by Sordello, now make their way to a hollow in the hillside: "There I saw souls sit singing '*Salve Regina*' on the green and on the flowers, who by reason of the valley did not appear from without. 'Before the little sun which remains, sinks to rest,' began the Mantuan, who had led us aside, 'desire not that I guide you among them. From this ledge you will better discern the acts and countenances of each and all, than were you received among them in the hollow below.'" In the drawing, Sordello and the poets are twice represented on the upper portion of the sheet, as the former points out, one by one, the souls of the kings and princes who had put off repentance by reason of their cares of state. Within the hollow, upwards of a score of figures are shown in the drawing, but only three have been finished in ink, and of the rest, many are but vaguely indicated with the style. In their present condition, there is little or nothing in these figures to connect them with the persons named in the poem. In the foreground, sketched with the style, a crowned spirit is represented talking with another who wears the papal tiara; but there is no allusion to any pope in this canto.

CANTO VIII.—This drawing is in a very unfinished state, having been but partially sketched in with the style. It is inscribed below with the opening line of the canto: "8 era gia lora che uolge eldisio." Dante now fixes his gaze on one of the souls who has risen up: "it joined and lifted both its palms, fixing its eyes toward the east, as it were saying to God, 'Aught else I heed not.'" This figure is slightly sketched in on the lower part of the sheet, to the left. Another naked figure immediately behind it, perhaps relates to the same incident. The poem continues: "I saw come forth on high, and descend below, two angels with two flaming swords, broke short and deprived of their points. Green as little leaves just born were their raiments, which they drew after them, beaten and blown about by their green wings. . . . 'Both come from the bosom of Mary,' said Sordello, 'to guard the valley, because of the serpent which will straightway appear.' . . . And Sordello again: 'Let us go down forthwith among the mighty shades, and we will speak to them; very pleasing will it be to them to see you.'" In the upper part of the sheet, on the left, the flying figure of one of the angels is seen descending; and above, on the right, and again in smaller figures in the centre of the sheet, Dante and Virgil, preceded by Sordello, are seen descending into the hollow. The episode of the meeting with Nino de' Visconti and Corrado Malaspina, which follows, is passed over in the drawing. As they were speaking, Sordello drew Virgil aside, saying: "'See there our adversary,' and pointed his finger that he might look that way. On that side, where the little valley has no rampart, was a snake, perchance that same which gave to Eve the bitter food. Through the grass and flowers came the evil worm. . . . I saw not, and therefore I cannot tell, how the celestial falcons moved; but right well I saw both the one and the other, after they had descended. Hearing the green wings cleave the air, the serpent fled, and the angels turned upward to their posts, flying back abreast." In the lower part of the sheet, in the centre, Sordello is seen calling Virgil's attention to the snake, which approaches on the right. Above, on the same side of the design, are seen the figures of two angels: one but partially sketched in; the other, at full length, brandishing as he descends, his pointless sword at the snake, which is indicated a second time. The two nude figures of Sordello in this drawing are sketched with great mastery and expressiveness. Few of the precursors of Leonardo anticipated in so large a degree, his power of improvising with the pen, as did Botticelli.

CANTO IX—The drawing is inscribed below, with the opening line of the canto: "9 laconchubina dititane anticho." "The concubine of ancient Tithonus was already growing white on the gallery of the east, . . . when I, who had in me some part of Adam's nature, overcome by sleep, lay down on the grass, where already all five of us were sitting. . . . In a dream, I seemed to see hovering in the heavens an eagle with feathers of gold, with its wings outspread and making ready to swoop. . . . Then methought that, after wheeling a little, terrible as a thunderbolt it descended, and snatched me upwards as far as the fiery sphere. There it seemed that it and I burned, and the imagined fire so scorched me, that my sleep was needs broken." In the lower left-hand corner of the drawing, Dante is represented lying prone and asleep, with Virgil, Sordello, Nino and Corrado seated near him, on the grass. Immediately above this group, the eagle is seen carrying aloft the sleeping poet in his talons, as Virgil floats upward at their side. Again, in the upper part of the drawing, Dante is represented a third time, lying asleep upon the ledge of the rock which surrounds Purgatory proper; as the eagle who has just released him from his hold, hovers over him, about to take flight. "Alone beside me was my Comforter. . . . 'Have no fear,' said my Master, 'reassure thyself, for we are at a good point; hold not back, but put forth all thy strength. Thou art now arrived at Purgatory; see there the gallery which encloses it round; see the entry there where appears a break' . . . We drew near, and came to such a place, that there, where before had seemed to me a breach, like a crack which parts a wall, I saw a gate, and below it three steps leading to it, of divers colours, and a warder who as yet spake no word. And as I opened more and more mine eyes, I saw that he sat upon the topmost step, . . . and held a naked sword in his hand. . . . Up by the three steps, with a good will my Leader led me, saying: 'Ask humbly that he unfasten the lock.' Devoutly I threw myself at the holy feet; I prayed that out of mercy he would open to me; but first upon my breast three times I smote myself. Seven P's upon my forehead he described with the point of the sword, and he said, 'See that thou wash these wounds when thou art within.'" Immediately to the right of the sleeping figure of Dante, on the circling ledge of the rock, the poet is again represented with Virgil at his side, who points the way towards the gate of Purgatory. On the right, the poets are once more represented before the gate; and again for the fifth time, Dante is seen humbly kneeling in supplication at the feet of the angel, who is seated before the gateway, holding in his right hand the sword with which he marks the seven P's on Dante's forehead, and in his left the two keys of gold and silver. The three steps above which he is seated, are but partially indicated in the drawing. Immediately behind the angel, the figures of the poets, slightly sketched in with the style, are seen entering by the open door. This is in allusion to the concluding lines of the canto which relate how the angel unlocked the gate with the two keys: "then he pushed the door of the sacred portal, saying: 'Enter; but

I would have you know that he who looks back, returns.'" This sheet is an especially admirable piece of pen-work; and the figure of the angel extremely noble.

CANTO X.—From this point, each drawing is inscribed only with the arabic numeral of the canto which it illustrates. "After we were within the threshold of the gate, ... we mounted up through a riven crag, which kept moving to the one side and the other, like a wave that falls back and draws near. . . . But when above we stood free and on the open, where the mount is set back, I being weary, and both uncertain of our way, we halted above on the level, which was more lonely than roads through desert places. . . . Thereon we had not as yet put forward our feet, when all around I perceived the bank which, being upright, lacked means of ascent, to be of white marble, and so adorned with carvings, that not only Polycletus, but Nature herself, would there be put to shame." Below, in the centre of the drawing, is the head of the gateway through which the poet entered. Immediately on the left, Virgil and Dante are seen making their way up through the zigzag passage in the rock, to the level of the first, or lowest, circle of Purgatory. Here the poets are thrice represented, as they view the marble reliefs with which the precipitous face of the rock is carved. On the left, they are standing before the sculptured figures of St. Gabriel delivering the divine salutation to the Virgin: "One would have sworn that he was saying '*Ave,*' because there was imaged she who turned the key to open the supreme love: and she bore impressed upon her action this legend, '*Ecce ancilla Dei,*' as aptly as a figure is made by a seal on wax." The kneeling figures of the Virgin and the angel recall the "predella" of the altar-piece, once in the church at San Marco, and now in the Academy, at Florence, No. 49. The background is left blank. "'Fix not thy mind on one place alone,' said the sweet Master, who had me on that side where mankind has the heart; wherefore I turned my face, and saw behind Mary, on that side where was he who urged me, another story set upon the rock." To indicate this sudden movement, Botticelli has drawn the upper portion of Dante's figure a second time, bending forward in front of Virgil: a device which he has elsewhere employed in the illustrations to Canto XXXII of the "Inferno," Canto XXIX of the "Purgatorio," and Canto III of the "Paradiso." The poem continues: "Wherefore I passed across Virgil and took myself near, so that it might be displayed to mine eyes. There in the very marble was carved the car and the oxen drawing the sacred ark, whereby men fear an office not entrusted to them. Before it appeared a throng of people. . . . There, girt up, before the blessed vessel, went dancing the lowly Psalmist. . . . Opposite, figured at a window of a great palace, Michal was looking on, as a woman despiteful and sad." The drawing here is unfinished. David, high-girt and playing on a psaltery, goes before; followed by two dancing figures, one with a timbrel and the other with a horn. On the left is the ark set on the new car, and drawn by a yoke of oxen. Elaborating upon the passing allusion in the poem, Botticelli has represented the oxen grown restive, and Uzzah lying dead by the side of the car, having been smitten by God for his error in putting forth his hand to steady the ark. In the background is the "great palace," with the figure of Michal faintly indicated at one of the upper windows. The palace, which is of an architecture of very Roman proportions, as well as the ark and the body of the car, are merely sketched in with the style; and many figures are obviously wanting to complete

II Samuel, cap. VI.

the composition. Dante now moves on to observe the third relief: "There was storied the high glory of the Roman princedom, whose worth moved Gregory to his great victory; I tell of Trajan, the emperor; and a poor widow was at his bridle, in an attitude of tears and of grief. About him appeared the trampling and the throng of horsemen, and the golden eagles over him swayed visibly to the wind. The poor creature among all these seemed to be saying: 'Sire, avenge me for my son, who is dead, whereby I grieve at heart.' And he in answer to her: 'Wait now until I return.' And she, as one in whom grief is urgent: 'My Lord, if thou return not?' And he: 'Whoso shall be in my stead, will do it for thee.' And she: 'What will another's good deed be to thee, if thy own thou puttest out of mind?' Wherefore he: 'Now comfort thyself, for it needs be that I do my duty before I move. Justice wills it, and pity holds me back.'"

The whole sheet is most imaginative and beautiful: but this last story, which is elaborately drawn in with the pen, is one of the most extraordinary pieces of invention to be found in this series of drawings. The widow stands beside her son, lying dead on the ground, as she supplicates the emperor, who has turned back to listen to her petition; while his troop of horsemen stream onward through a great Roman arch, which is seen on the right. "Fu copioso di figure nelle storie," Vasari remarks of Sandro: and here in the space of a few inches, he renders with greatest beauty and intricacy of design, the movement and confusion of a vast troop of men-at-arms, the trampling of their horses, and the glitter and sway of their arms and banners. Indeed, Botticelli here produces with simpler means, and in a larger manner, not a little of the effect which Altdorfer afterwards produced in his famous "Battle of Arbela," in the Munich Gallery. The design of the horses, especially that which Trajan rides, is admirable in its movement and vivacity. The attitude of the page on the left, I may add, recalls that of the Mercury in the painting of the "Spring," and certain figures in some of the early "Adorations."

"While I was delighting myself with gazing on the images, . . . 'Behold here,' murmured the Poet, 'many people; but they make few steps. These will put us in the way to the lofty stairs.' . . . As, to support solar or roof, is often seen for corbel, a figure joining the knees and breast, . . . thus fashioned saw I these, when I scanned them well. True it is, that they were more or less drawn together, according as they had more or less on their backs; and he who showed most patience in his gestures, weeping seemed to say: 'I can no more.'" These are they who have sinned through pride, each bearing on his back a heavy burden. Two of them are represented on the left of the drawing, approaching the last and fourth group of Dante and Virgil, who look toward, and discourse of, them.

Canto XI.—This canto opens with the paraphrase of the Lord's Prayer, which the souls recite as they go their way. Virgil now asks the spirits to show them, "on which hand is the shortest way towards the stair." "It was not manifest from whom came the words which they uttered in reply to those, which he whom I was following had spoken; but it was said: 'Come to the right along the bank with us, and ye shall find the pass which is possible for a living man to ascend.'" The spirit who has spoken, adds that he is Omberto, the son of Guglielmo Aldobrandesco. "Listening, I bowed down my face, and one of them (not he who was speaking) twisted himself beneath the weight which encumbers him; and saw me, and knew me, and called me, holding with difficulty his eyes fixed on me, who all bowed, was going with them. 'Oh,' said I to him, 'art thou not Oderisi, the honour of Gubbio, and the honour of that art which in Paris is called illuminating?'" Oderisi now replies to Dante, and in the course of his speech makes the famous allusion to Cimabue and Giotto. The drawing is unfinished. Virgil and Dante are thrice represented in it: the first time on the right, as they approach the spirit of those who sinned through pride; again in the centre of the sheet, as Virgil inquires the way of Omberto; and a third time on the left, as Dante stoops down to talk with Oderisi. The figures of the poets, and of some six or seven of the souls, are drawn in ink; two other spirits are indicated with the style on the right: but all the upper part of the sheet has been left blank. In this drawing, Botticelli again falls into error of representing the poets going from the right to the left, instead of from the left to the right, as the shade of Omberto directs them. The same mistake occurs in the following nine designs to Cantos XII-XIX.

Canto XII.—Virgil bids Dante to give over speaking with Oderisi, and pass on: "Both of us were already showing how light of foot we were, when he said to me: 'Cast thine eyes downward; it will be to thy good, for solace of thy way, to behold the bed of thy footsteps.' As, in order that their memory may endure, the tombs underground bear portrayed above those buried therein, that which they once were, . . . so saw I there figured, but of better semblance according to the workmanship, as much of the rock as projects forth for roadway from the mountain. I saw him who was created more noble than any other creature, falling like lightning down from heaven on one side: I saw Briareus, pierced by the celestial dart, lying weighed to the earth by the chill of death, on the other. I saw Thymbraeus, I saw Pallas and Mars yet in arms, around their father, looking at the scattered limbs of the giants. I saw Nimrod at the foot of his mighty work, as though bewildered. . . . O Niobe, with what sorrowing eyes saw I thee portrayed upon the roadway, amid seven and seven of thy children slain! O Saul, how on thine own sword thou didst appear dead in Gilboa! . . . The hard pavement, moreover, . . . showed how the Assyrians fled in rout after Holofernes was dead. . . . I saw Troy in ashes and in pits." In the drawing, on the right, Dante and Virgil are seen looking down at the figures on the pavement, as they approach a representation of Satan, lying prone, in the guise of a hairy monster, with bat's wings and clawed hands, fallen "as lightning from heaven." Immediately above, lies Briareus, stricken by the bolt; and on the left, gazing on the scattered limbs of the giants, stand Jupiter, Apollo and Mars, armed in the manner of Roman knights, with Pallas, who is portrayed much as Botticelli must have portrayed her in the lost painting executed for Giuliano de' Medici, holding a tilting lance and a shield bearing the head of Medusa. In the centre of the sheet, near the last group, is seen the fall of the tower of Babel, with Nimrod standing in bewilderment at the base. The allusion here is to the mediaeval tradition, that the tower of Babel was the work of Nimrod. Landino who relates the legend, adds that, according "to the sentence of the sybil, all men once spoke the same tongue, and they all built a very lofty tower, thinking thereby to ascend to heaven; but the gods destroyed the tower by winds, and made a division of language, giving to each man his own." On the left of the last story, Niobe is represented with three of her children lying dead around her; the rest of the group being unfinished. Near by is sketched the figure of Saul fallen upon his sword; on the left of the sheet is the city of Troy laid waste; and on the opposite side, above the figure of Briareus, is the host of the Assyrians in flight. The last three are drawn only with the style. From the simile with which Dante introduces his description of this figured pavement, it is evident that he had in his mind those sepulchral slabs, either incised, or carved in very low relief, with the effigy of the person commemorated; examples of which dating from Dante's time are rare, though a great number of somewhat later date still form a large part of the pavement of the church of Santa Croce at Florence. Botticelli, however, who never loses sight of the explanatory purpose of these drawings, makes no attempt to represent them foreshortened on the surface of the pavement, as they would properly have appeared; but draws them on the same plane as the figures of Dante and Virgil, from which he distinguishes them merely by representing them on a smaller scale. The same device is employed in the cut illustrating this canto, in the edition of the "Divina Commedia," printed at Venice in 1564.

Virgil now speaks: "'Raise upright thy head; there is no longer time to go bending thus. See, there is an angel who is preparing to meet us. . . . Adorn with reverence thine actions and thy countenance, so that it may delight him to send us up on high.' . . . To us came the beauteous creature, arrayed in white. . . . He opened his arms, and then he opened his wings, saying, 'Come: here are the steps at hand, and easily henceforth does one ascend.' . . . He led us where the rock was cut; there he beat his wings over my forehead: then he promised me a safe journey. . . . We were already mounting up by the holy stairs, and I seemed to myself far more light than I had seemed before on the level; wherefore I: 'Master, say what heavy thing has been lifted from me, that I scarce feel any fatigue in journeying?' He answered: "When the P's which still remain on thy forehead, wellnigh effaced shall be, as one has been, wholly obliterated, thy feet will be so overcome by thy good will, that not only will they feel no weariness, but it will be a delight to them to be urged upwards.'" In the drawing on the right, Virgil bids Dante to behold the angel who stands, with arms and wings outstretched, at the foot of the stairs on the left. In the midst, between these figures, the angel is a second time represented, spreading his arms and wings about Dante, as Virgil stands by. Again, at the foot of the stairs, the angel beats his wings about Dante's forehead; in these last two incidents, Botticelli represents the figures of Dante and the angel embracing in the ceremonial attitude used at the Pax. Lastly, higher up the stairs in the left-hand corner of the sheet, the poets are seen for the fifth time. Virgil, in answer to Dante's question, explains how the angel has removed one of the P's from his forehead, at which the poet, to assure himself, raises his hand to his forehead. Below, by the side of the steps, are seen two of the souls of the proud, bearing their burdens, in allusion to the previous canto.

Canto XIII.—The poets now gain "the head of the stair, where a second time the mount is cut back." Here in the second circle of Purgatory, is purged the sin of Envy. "'If here we await someone of whom to ask the road,' the Poet was saying, 'I fear that perchance our choice may bring too great delay.' Then he directed his eyes fixedly to the sun; he made of his right side the centre of his movement, and turned the left part of himself. . . . As much as is reckoned here for a mile, so far had we already gone in a short time, through the eagerness of our will.

And flying towards us were heard, though unseen, spirits speaking courteous bidding to the table of love. The first voice that passed in its flight said in loud tone, '*Vinum non habent*,' and went repeating it behind us. And before it had wholly gone out of hearing in the distance another passed, crying, 'I am Orestes,' and also did not stay. 'O, father,' said I, 'what voices are these?' And as I asked, lo, a third, saying, 'Love them from whom ye have suffered evil.' And the good Master: 'This circle doth scourge the sin of envy, and therefore are the cords of the whip wielded by love. . . . But fix thine eyes intently through the air, and thou shalt see people sitting in front of us, and each one is seated along the cliff.' Then I looked before me, and saw shades with cloaks not different to the colour of the rock. . . . When I had arrived so near to them that their attitudes came clearly to me, . . . they appeared to me covered with coarse hair-cloth, and one was supporting another with the shoulder, and all were supported by the bank: . . . in all of them a thread of iron pierces the eyelid and stitches it, just as is done to a wild hawk, because it rests not quiet." In the drawing, on the right, the poets are seen at the head of the stairs, which they have just ascended; and Virgil is represented a second time, turning round and looking up at the sun, for guidance on the way.

In the centre of the sheet, Dante in an attitude of great beauty and expressiveness, looks up in astonishment, with both hands raised above his head, on hearing the voices of the invisible spirits. Near by, the poets are represented for a third time, as Virgil points out to Dante the souls of the envious, who sit ranged along the bank; and again, on the left of the sheet, as they approach the spirits, who are likened in the poem to blind men, begging by the pardons at the church-doors. The last but one of the spirits on the left, is represented "raising its chin upward in fashion of one who is blind." This is Sapia, a lady of Siena, with whom the poets now speak.

CANTO XIV.—"'Who is this that circles our mountain before that death have given him release?' . . . 'I know not who he may be; but I know that he is not alone.' . . . Thus two spirits, leaning the one against the other, were talking of me there, on the right hand; then they held their faces upraised to speak to me, and one said: 'O soul, that imprisoned yet in the body, goest thy way towards heaven, for charity console us, and tell us whence thou comest, and who thou art.'" In the drawing on the right, Virgil stands by, while Dante talks with the two spirits, who declare themselves to be Guido del Duca and Rinier da Calboli. Having done speaking the poets pass on: "We knew that those dear souls heard us go, therefore by their silence they made us confident of the road. After we were alone, as we went forward, a voice which came towards us, seemed like a bolt when it cleaves the air, saying: 'Whosoever finds me, shall slay me;' and it fled, like thunder which melts away, if suddenly it rive the cloud. When our hearing had truce from it, lo, another with so loud a crash, that it was like to a peal of thunder which quickly follows after: 'I am Aglauros, that became a stone.'" In the centre of the drawing, Dante and Virgil are again seen hastening on their way; and on the left side of the sheet, having come to a part of the circle where they are alone, they look upwards with gestures of amazement, on hearing the voices of Cain and Aglauros.

CANTO XV.—"The mount had been so circled by us, that we were already going straight towards the sunset; when I felt the splendour weigh down my brow far more than before. . . . Wherefore I raised my hands above my eyebrows, and made myself a shade against the sun, which takes away the excess of vision. . . . 'What is that, sweet father, from which I cannot screen my face so much as may avail me,' said I, 'and which seems to be moving toward us?' 'Marvel not if the family of Heaven still dazzle thee,' he answered me; 'it is a messenger who comes to bid man ascend.' . . . When we came to the blessed angel, he said in a glad voice: 'Enter here,' to a stair far less steep than the others. We were mounting, having already departed thence, and '*Beati misericordes*' was chanted behind us, and 'Rejoice thou that overcomest!'" In the drawing on the right, Dante is seen shielding his eyes from the dazzling light which, as Virgil explains to him, proceeds from the heavenly messenger who comes to bid them mount. Nearer to the centre of the sheet, the poets are seen approaching the angel who stands at the foot of the stairs; and again, for the third time, as they ascend the steps. The souls of the envious are ranged in pairs against the bank, on either side of the stairs. In the upper part of the sheet on the left, are other figures of Dante and Virgil, sketched with the style. This group, which from the pen outline of the rock passing through the figures, appears to have been rejected, has reference to the passage beginning: "My Master and I were both going upward alone, and I was thinking as I went, to gain profit from his words." On the other side of the stair, drawn with the pen, is the figure of Dante lying prone in a trance upon the rock, in allusion to the vision, which forms the subject of the concluding portion of this canto: "I saw that I was come upon the next gallery, [*i.e.*, of the third circle,] so that my wandering eyes made me silent. There I seemed to be suddenly drawn into an ecstatic vision." This drawing is one of the least concentrated and inspired of the illustrations to the "Purgatorio."

CANTO XVI.—The poets continue their way through the third circle. "The darkness of hell and of a night bereft of every planet . . . made not to my sight so thick a veil, as that smoke which there covered us, . . . for it suffered not the eye to stay open; wherefore my tried and faithful escort moved beside me and offered me his shoulder. . . . I heard voices, and each one seemed to pray for peace and for mercy, to the Lamb of God who takes away sins. . . . 'Are those spirits, Master, which I hear?' said I. And he said to me: 'Thou apprehendest truly, and they go untying the knot of anger.' 'Now who art thou who cleavest our smoke, and talkest of us, as if thou didst still measure time by calends?' Thus by a voice was it spoken. Wherefore my Master said: 'Answer, and ask if from hence one goes upward.'" Dante invites the spirit, who declares himself to be Marco Lombardo, to follow him; and as they go, the poet propounds certain questions touching free will. In the drawing on the right, Dante is seen holding Virgil's robe and following him, "as a blind man goes behind his guide in order not to stray." In the centre of the sheet, Virgil and Dante are again represented turning round at the voice of Marco Lombardo, who is represented as one of a company of naked spirits, with their hands clasped in adoration: and again on the left, Virgil is seen for the third time, followed by Dante, who turns round as the spirit of Marco takes farewell of him: "'God be with you, for further I may not come with you. Behold the light, which shines through the smoke, already grows brighter; the angel is there, and I must needs depart before I be seen of him.' Thus he turned, and longer would not hear me."

CANTO XVII.—As the poets go their way, they gradually issue from the cloud of smoke, and again behold the sun, which is already setting. Making his own footsteps equal to those of his guide, Dante now falls into "a deep fantasy," in which he sees famous examples of wrath and its punishment. "As sleep is broken, when on a sudden a new day strikes on the closed eyelids, . . . so mine imagination fell down as soon as a light smote my face, greater far than that to which we are used. I turned myself to see where I was, when a voice said: 'Here is the ascent. This is the divine spirit who, without prayer, points us out the way to go on high, and conceals itself in its own light. . . . Let us endeavour to ascend before it grows dark, for after it will not be possible until the day return.' So spake my Leader, and I and he turned our steps to a stair; and as soon as I was at the first step, I felt, as it were, one move his wing near me, and fan me in the face and say: '*Beati pacifici*, who are without evil wrath.'" In the drawing, on the right, Dante, wrapt in deep fantasy, pursues his journey with Virgil at his side. In the centre of the sheet, he holds up both his hands to screen his eyes from the dazzling light of the angel, who stands at the foot of the stairs leading to the next circle, and points out the way. On the left are seen two of the souls of the Wrathful; and above, at the head of the stairs, Dante and Virgil are represented, for a third time, discoursing, after they have gained the fourth circle, where the sin of Sloth is purged. This last group is in allusion to the concluding episode of the canto, where Virgil in reply to Dante, explains that love is the root of all sin, no less than of all virtue. This drawing is one of the least inspired of the series.

Canto XVIII.—Virgil continues to discourse of love, and afterwards of free will and the origin of morality. "That gentle shade through whom Pietola is more renowned than the city of Mantua, had layed aside the burthen of my load: wherefore I, who had gathered his reasoning upon my questions, clear and plain, was standing like a man who, drowsy, wanders. But this drowsiness was taken from me suddenly by a people who, behind our shoulders, were already coming towards us. . . . Quickly were they upon us, for all that mighty crowd was moving at a run, and two foremost shouted as they wept: 'Mary fled in haste to the mountains, and Caesar, to subdue Ilerda, stung Marseilles, and then hurried into Spain.' 'O people, in whom keen fervour now haply atones for the negligence and delay committed by you through lukewarmness in right-doing, tell us where the opening is near.' These words spake my Leader." In the drawing, on the right, the poets are seen conversing on their way: in the centre of the sheet, as Virgil makes an end of speaking, and Dante stands "drowsy" in meditation, they are overtaken by the crowd of spirits who come running, weeping and crying out like a rout of Baccanals. Again, on the left, the poets are seen for the third time, as Virgil asks the spirits to show them the way.

Canto XIX.—"In the hour when the diurnal heat, overcome by earth, or at times by Saturn, can no more warm the cold of the moon . . . came to me in a dream a woman stuttering, with eyes a-squint, crooked legs, deformed hands and sallow of hue. . . . 'I am,' she sang, 'I am a sweet Siren, who charms aside the mariners in mid-sea; so full of pleasure am I to hear. I turned Ulysses from his road, wandering to my song.'" The dream proceeds and Dante awakens: "I turned my eyes and the good Virgil said: '. . . Rise and come. Let us find the opening by which thou mayst enter.' . . . Following him, I was bearing my brow as one who, having it burthened with thought, makes of himself a half-arch of a bridge, when I heard: 'Come, here is the passage,' spoken in a manner sweet and benign, such as is not heard in this mortal life. With outspread wings, which seemed like those of a swan, he who thus spake to us, turned us upward between the two walls of the hard rock. Then he moved his feathers and fanned us, declaring that they, *qui lugent*, are blessed, for they shall possess their souls lords of consolation." In the drawing, on the right, Dante, lying on the ground, is seen awakening from his dream and looking up at Virgil. In the centre of the drawing, the angel is seen standing at the foot of the stairs as he points the way to Virgil, who approaches, followed by Dante bowed, like a "half-arch," in meditation. Behind the angel the poets are again seen ascending the steps to the fifth circle, where the sin of avarice and prodigality is expiated.

"When I stood unconfined in the fifth circle, I saw throughout it people who wept as they all lay on the earth, face downwards. '*Adhaesit pavimento anima mea*,' I heard them say, with sighs so deep that their words were hardly to be understood." Virgil having asked of them the way, one of the spirits answers: "'If ye come secure from lying prone, and wish to find the way most speedily, let your right hands be ever on the outside.' . . . When I was able to act in accordance with my thought, I stood over that creature, whose words erewhile had caused me to take note of him, saying: 'Spirit, in whom weeping ripens that without which man is not able to turn to God, delay a while for me thy greater care. Tell me who thou wast, and why ye have your backs turned upwards.' . . . And he to me: 'Wherefore Heaven turns our back towards itself thou shalt know, but first, *scias quod ego fui successor Petri*.'" Pope Adrian V, for of such the spirit is, now talks with Dante: "I had knelt down, and would have spoken, but as I began, and he perceived by hearing only my reverence, 'What reason,' said he, 'has thus bowed thee down?' And I to him: 'While I stood upright my conscience pricked me because of your dignity.' 'Straighten thy legs and rise up, brother,' he replied; 'err not. A fellow-servant I am with thee and with the others unto one Power. . . . Now go thy way; I desire not that thou tarry longer, for thy stay impedes my weeping, wherewith I ripen that of which thou hast spoken.'" In the drawing, the souls of the avaricious and prodigal are seen lying prone, with their hands and feet bound. Before one of the spirits, who wears a mitre on his head, Dante and Virgil pause on their way. Immediately before the standing figure of Dante, the poet is represented a second time, kneeling, to indicate the sudden act of reverence which he makes to Pope Adrian on discovering his high dignity; and again, on the right, the poets are seen departing on their way, in obedience to the pope's behest: "Go thy way now." Following the directions which the spirits have given them, Dante and Virgil proceed with their right hands "ever on the outside." On gaining the fifth circle, the poets are rightly represented going from the left to the right, in accordance with the various indications scattered through the poem.

Canto XX.—"We were going with slow steps and rare, and I intent on the shades which I heard piteously weeping and bewailing, when by chance I heard one cry 'Sweet Mary' in front of us, . . . 'so poor wast thou, as may be seen by that hostelry, where thou didst lay down thy holy burden.' . . . These words were so pleasing to me, that I passed on to have knowledge of that spirit from whom they seemed to come. . . . 'O soul that speakest so well,' I said, 'tell me who thou wast, and wherefore thou alone renewest these worthy praises?' . . . And he: 'I will tell thee. . . . I was root of the evil tree which so overshadows every Christian land, that good fruit is rarely plucked therefrom. . . . On earth I was called Hugh Capet, and of me were sprung the Philips and the Lewises, by whom of late France has been ruled.'" In the drawing on the left, Dante and Virgil are seen slowly making their way over the spirits, which strew the floor of the rock. Nearer to the centre the poets pause on their way, as Dante bends down to converse with the spirit of Hugh Capet, who looks up at him. "We were already parted from him, and were endeavouring to pass over the road as quickly as was permitted to our power, when I felt the mount quake as a thing about to fall; whereat a chill seized me, such as is wont to take him who goes to his death. . . . Then arose on every side a cry, such that my Master turned himself towards me, saying: 'Fear not whilst I guide thee.' '*Gloria in excelsis Deo,*' all were saying, by what I gathered from those who were near, whence it was possible to distinguish the cry. We stood motionless and in suspense, like the shepherds who first heard that chaunt, until the quaking ceased and the cry was finished. Then we resumed our holy journey, looking at the shades which lay upon the earth, already returned to their wonted lament." In the drawing on the right, the poets are represented for the third time, as they stand motionless in suspense, at the trembling of the mountain,—Dante with his hands folded across his breast: and again, near the margin of the sheet, as they resume their way, and look down at the spirits.

Canto XXI.—As the poets hasten on their way, a shade overtakes them: "it was coming behind us, gazing on the multitude at its feet; nor were we aware of it, so it spake first, saying: 'My brethren, God give you peace.' We turned suddenly, and Virgil made him the salutation which became his; then he began: 'May the righteous court which banishes me into eternal exile, place thee in peace among the blessed council!' 'How?' said he, (and we were going stoutly the while,) 'if ye be shades that God on high accounts not worthy, who has escorted you thus far up his ladder?'" Virgil answers: "If thou regardest the marks which this man beareth, . . . thou wilt right well perceive that it is meet he should reign with the just, . . . wherefore I was drawn forth from the ample throat of Hell to show him the way"; and in turn asks the spirit why the mountain had a little before shook so violently. The spirit, having replied to Virgil, adds in answer to his further question as to who he was: "On earth men still call me Statius; I sang of Thebes and afterwards of the great Achilles. . . . Seed to my ardour were the sparks of the divine flame that kindled me, and at which more than a thousand have been fired; I speak of the Aeneid, which was mother and nurse to me in poetry. . . . And to have lived on earth when Virgil lived, I would gladly add a year more than I owe to obtain my going forth from exile." "The words caused Virgil to turn to me with a countenance which in its silence said, 'Be silent.'" When Statius asks Dante why he smiled, Virgil bids him tell the poet what he desires to know. "Wherefore I: 'Perchance thou dost marvel, ancient spirit, at the smile which I gave; but I will that greater wonder take thee. He who guides mine eyes on high, is that Virgil from whom thou didst gather power to sing of men and gods. If thou didst suppose that there was other cause for my smile, give it over for untrue, and believe it to have been those words which thou spakest of him.' Already he was bending down to embrace my Teacher's feet; but he said to him: 'Brother, forbear, for thou art a shade, and a shade thou seest.' And he rising: 'Now canst thou understand the measure of the love which kindleth me towards thee, when I forget our emptiness, treating the shadows like a solid thing.'" In the drawing, Dante, Virgil and Statius are thrice represented, making their way over the spirits which lie scattered on the ground. On the left, Statius salutes the poets as he overtakes them from behind. In the centre of the sheet, all three are standing still as Statius throws up both hands, apparently in wonder and perplexity at seeing Dante smile; though the allusion here is not very evident. Again, on the right, Statius kneels and attempts to embrace Virgil, who stoops down to restrain him, as Dante stands over them with his hands raised in astonishment. Both in this and the following drawings, Statius is represented wearing one of those scrolled, Pollaiuolesque hats, which frequently occur in Botticelli's earlier works.

Canto XXII.—The drawing is inscribed below with the opening words of the canto: "gia eralan[gel] 22." "Already was the angel left behind us, . . . who had directed our steps to the sixth circle. . . . And I lighter than through the other entries, was going forward in such wise that without any labour I followed on high the swift spirits; when Virgil began: 'Love, kindled by virtue, ever kindles other love.'" Statius now relates, in answer to Virgil, how he turned from sin, and how his conversion was brought about through reading certain passages of his poems: "Through thee I became a poet, through thee a Christian." "Both the poets were already silent, intent anew on looking round, freed from the ascent and the walls. . . . When my Leader: 'I think that it behoves us to turn our right shoulders to the outer edge, circling the mount as we are wont to do.' Thus usage was our guide. . . . They journeyed on in front, and I by myself behind; and I listened to their discourse, which gave me understanding in poetry. But soon the sweet converse was broken by a tree which we found in the midst of our path, with apples pleasant and good to smell. And as a fir-tree grows less by degrees upward, from branch to branch, so that grows downward. . . . On the side upon which our road was shut in, there fell from the lofty rock a clear stream, and diffused itself over the leaves. The two poets drew near the tree, and a voice from within the leaves cried, 'Of this food ye shall have dearth.'" The voice then cites certain famous examples of temperance, with which the canto closes. In the drawing, Virgil and Statius are represented on the right, discoursing together as they mount the stairs, followed by Dante. Higher up on the same side of the sheet they are seen a second time, having gained the level of the sixth circle, where the sin of Gluttony is expiated: the two Latin poets go on before, followed by Dante. Botticelli again represents them turning to the left, instead of to the right; a point on which the text is very explicit. The same error occurs in the following five designs to Cantos XXIII—XXVII. On the left of the sheet, they are seen a third time, looking up at the tree which they come upon in the midst of their path, growing downwards, with the clear stream falling through its branches. Botticelli represents this mystical tree in the likeness of a fir-tree, whereas in the text its general form alone is described as diminishing "come abete." In the succeeding drawings, Sandro portrays it in accordance with Dante's description, "laden with apples." In this sheet, the figures and the tree are touched in with the pen, while the rest of the design is merely sketched with the style.

CANTO XXIII.—"Whilst I was peering with mine eyes through the green branches, . . . my more than father said to me: 'Come now, my son, for the time which is allotted to us must be more usefully apportioned.' I turned my face, and not less quickly my step, towards the sages who were talking in such sort that they rendered the journey of no labour to me. And lo, I heard one weep and sing '*Labia mea Domine*,' in a fashion that begat both joy and grief. 'O, sweet Father, what is that which I hear?' began I, and he: 'Shades, perchance, that come loosening the knot of their debt.' As pilgrims deep in thought, when overtaking by the way people unknown to them, turn towards them, but stay not; so behind us, but moving more quickly, came a company of souls silent and devout, and passed on, as they gazed on us in wonder. Each was dark and hollow of eye, pallid of face, and so wasted that the skin took form from the bone. I was already wondering what thus famishes them; . . . and lo! from the hollow of its head a shade turned its eyes on me, and gazed fixedly; then it cried aloud, 'What grace is this vouchsafed me?' Never should I have recognized him by his countenance, but in his voice was manifest to me that which was subdued in his aspect. This spark rekindled in me all my memory of the altered features, and I beheld again the face of Forese." The discourse of Dante with his wife's kinsman fills the rest of the canto. In the drawing, on the right, Dante is seen looking up into the branches of the mystical tree, which is here represented in accordance with its description in the poem. Somewhat nearer to the centre of the sheet, Dante is again represented in the act of following Virgil and Statius, as the company of the emaciated spirits overtakes them. On the left of the sheet, Dante is seen a third time, talking with the shade of Forese. Virgil and Statius go before, and the throng of wasted spirits accompanies the poets. All the figures are represented going at a quick pace, in allusion to the opening lines of the following canto. It is remarkable how Pollaiuolesque in manner Botticelli's drawing of the nude here becomes, in the attempt to render the accentuated forms of the emaciated spirits.

CANTO XXIV.—"Neither talking made our journeying, nor the journey our talking, more slow; but still, as we discoursed, we were going stoutly." Dante continues to converse with Forese, who points out to him Pope Martin IV and many others: the poet also speaks with Bonagiunta da Lucca. "As the man who is weary of running lets his comrades go before, and thus paces on until the panting of his chest is abated, so Forese let the holy flock pass on, and came behind with me, saying: 'When shall it be that I see thee again?'" Forese now leaves Dante, who remains with Virgil and Statius. "When he was gone so far in front of us that my eyes went in pursuit of him, as my mind of his words, there appeared to me the laden and lusty branches of another apple tree. . . . I saw people beneath it raise their hands and cry, I know not what, towards the leaves, like children who beg for something, eager and unsatisfied, and he of whom they beg responds not, but to make their own wish the keener, holds their desire on high and hides it not." The poets now hear a voice from the tree, citing instances of Gluttony. "Full a thousand paces and more we went onward, each meditating, without a word. 'Why go ye thus in thought, ye solitary three?' a voice suddenly said. . . . I raised my head to behold who it was, and never was seen in a furnace, glass or metal so glowing and ruddy, as I beheld one who was saying: 'If it please you to mount upward, here you needs must turn.'" In the drawing, on the right, the spirit of Forese falls back from his company, as he inquires of Dante when he shall see him again. In front of them, Virgil and Statius pause as they look up at the second mystical tree, which is seen in the centre of the sheet, with the wasted spirits below it, who raise their hands towards the branches and cry out for the fruit like children. Below, in front of the tree, Virgil and Dante are again represented listening, with gestures of wonderment, to the voice which comes from its branches. Again, on the left, the angel who is to guide the poets to the next circle, appears to Dante, who is standing alone. The background of the drawing, on the left of the sheet, is only slightly sketched in with the style.

CANTO XXV.—"As does the man who stays not, but goes his way, whatever may betide him, if the spur of necessity goad him, thus entered we through the passage, one before another taking the stair, which through its narrowness uncouples those who mount." In the drawing on the right, the poets are seen entering in single file, the narrow passage in the rock leading to the stairs to the seventh circle. Statius goes first and Dante last; his figure alone of the three being touched in with the pen. Although their "going was quick," the poets converse on the way, and Statius takes occasion of a question of Dante's, to explain the nature of the soul. "By this time we were come to the last circuit, and had turned to the right hand, and were intent on other care. Here the bank flashes forth flame, and the cornice breathes a blast upwards, which blows it back and keeps it away from the level. Wherefore it behoved us to go one by one, on the open side; and on this hand I feared the fire, and on that I feared to fall downwards. My Leader kept saying: 'Throughout this place one must needs keep a strict curb on the eyes, because for a little one could go astray.' '*Summae Deus clementiae*' in the bosom of the great heat I heard them chanting, which made me not less eager to turn. And I saw spirits going through the flame, wherefore I looked at them and at my steps, apportioning my view from time to time." Dante now hears the spirits recall famous instances of chastity. In the drawing, the three poets resume their journey, having gained the level of the seventh circle. Virgil, pointing to the fire, warns Dante to "keep a strict curb on the eyes." Again, on the left of the sheet, the three poets are seen for the third time as they proceed on their journey.

CANTO XXVI.—"While we thus were going along the brink, one before another, and the good Master kept saying, 'Take heed; profit thyself by my warning,' I by my shadow made the flame appear more ruddy. . . . This was the occasion which led the spirits to speak of me, and they began to say among themselves: 'That one seems not an unreal body. . . . Tell us how it is that thou makest of thyself a partition to the Sun, as if thou wert not yet entered within the net of death.' So spake one of them to me, and I should already have declared myself, had I not been intent on another new thing which then appeared, for through the midst of the burning way came a throng with their faces opposite to these last, which made me pause in wonderment. There I behold on every side, each shade make ready and kiss one with another, without stopping, content with a brief greeting . . . and those same who had before intreated me, drew near to me again, intent on listening." Dante now speaks with them and inquires: "'Who are ye, and what is that crowd which goes its way behind your backs?'" One of the spirits replies: "'I am Guido Guinicelli, and already I purge myself through not having put off my repentance to the last.' As, under the bitter sentence of Lycurgus, became the two sons at seeing again their mother, so became I, but not to so great a height do I rise, when I hear him name himself the father of me, and of others my betters, who ever used sweet and graceful rhymes of love." Guido asks: "'What is the reason that thou showest in thy speech and in thy look that thou holdest me dear.' And I to him: 'Your sweet writings which, so long as the modern use shall last, will make their very ink precious.' 'O brother,' said he, 'he whom I distinguish for thee with my finger' (and he pointed to a spirit in front) 'was a better craftsman in the mother speech.' . . . Then . . . he disappeared through the fire, as a fish through the water when it goes to the bottom. I went forward a little to him who was pointed out to me, and said that for his name my desire was preparing a gracious place." The spirit replies in the Provençal dialect, and declares himself the poet, Arnald Daniel. In the drawing, on the right, Statius goes on in front, as Virgil, with his finger raised, tells Dante to profit by his warning. In the centre of the sheet Dante is again seen talking with the spirit of Guido Guinicelli; and for a third time, on the left, as he steps forward to speak with Arnald Daniel, while Virgil and Statius come on behind. The episode of the spirits meeting and embracing one another, is shown in the drawing to the previous canto.

CANTO XXVII.—"The day was departing, when the glad angel of God appeared to us. Without the flame was he standing on the bank, and singing '*Beati mundo corde*,' in a voice far more living than ours. Afterwards he said to us, when we were nigh him: 'Further ye may not go, holy spirits, unless the fire first bite you; enter into it, and to the chant beyond be ye not deaf': so that when I heard it, I became as one who is put into the grave." Virgil seeks to reassure Dante, telling him that "here may be torment, but not death." "When he saw me yet stand firm and stiff, troubled a little he said: 'Behold now, my son, between Beatrice and thee is this wall.' . . . My stubbornness having yielded, I turned to my wise Leader, hearing the name which ever flourishes in my mind; . . . at which he smiled, as one does at a child that is won by an apple. Then he entered the fire in front of me, praying Statius that he would come behind, who for a long way had hitherto separated us. When I was within, I would have flung myself into boiling glass to cool me. . . . A voice which was singing on the other side, guided us; and we, intent only upon it, came forth there where the ascent began. . . . The way mounted straight through the rock, towards such a quarter that I took away in front of me the rays of the sun, which was already low. . . . As the herdsman, who lodges out of doors, passes the night in quiet beside his flock, watching that a wild beast scatter it not, such were we then all three; I like the goat and they like shepherds: . . . so ruminating and so gazing on them, sleep took me." In a dream, Dante now beholds a vision of Rachael and Leah. At dawn the poets awake and resume their journey until the whole stair is passed. "On the topmost step, Virgil fixed his eyes on me and said: . . . 'Thou art come to a part where of myself I can no longer have discernment. I have drawn thee hither with wit and with art, henceforth take thine own pleasure for guide. . . . Free, upright and whole is thy own judgement, and it were a fault not to act in accordance to its prompting; wherefore thee over thyself I crown and mitre.'"

In the drawing, in the lower right-hand corner, the angel is seen appearing to the poets on the edge of the flaming circuit, as he bids them enter the fire. Statius goes in front, and behind him Virgil exhorts Dante, who stands with his hands clasped before him and his head bowed, "to put away all fear." On the left, the poets are seen a second time within the flames: Virgil who goes first, comforts Dante by "discoursing the while of Beatrice," and Statius follows after. On the farther bank stands the angel, who points to the stairs, and chants: "*Venite, benedicti Patris mei.*" Again, on the left, Statius, Virgil and Dante are seen ascending the last stair which leads to the wood of the Earthly Paradise. On the level at the top of the stairs, the three poets are for the fourth time represented, resting upon the ground: Dante lies prone in sleep, while Virgil and Statius sit with their heads propped upon their hands. Botticelli here departs somewhat from the text, in which the poets are described as resting during the course of their ascent, and before they gain the summit; each making his "bed of a step." In the upper part of the drawing, on the left, they are seen for a fifth time, as Virgil places a garland on the head of Dante, while Statius stands by. Behind them, along the upper margin of the sheet, are indicated the trees of the mystical wood. In this and the two previous designs, the form and movement of the flames are rendered with great rhythm and beauty of line, and compose a most lovely pattern with nude forms of the spirits, as they hasten in opposite directions through the fire. The drawing to Canto XXVI is especially fortunate as a piece of lineal invention.

Canto XXVIII.—The Poets now leave the bank, and enter "the divine forest, thick and living," of the Earthly Paradise. "Already my slow steps had carried me so far within the ancient wood, that I could no longer see where I entered it, and lo! a stream prevented me going further. . . . I stood still with my feet, but with mine eyes I passed beyond the rivulet, in order to gaze upon the great variety of the fresh foliage; and there appeared to me . . . a lady all alone, who went along singing, and gathering flower from flower wherewith all her way was painted. 'Ah, fair lady,' . . . said I to her, 'may it please thee to draw near toward this stream, so that I may be able to hear what thou singest.' . . . She turned towards me over the red and yellow flowers, . . . drawing herself so near that the sweet sound came to me with its meaning. As soon as she came to where the grass is bathed by the waves of the fair stream, she did me the grace of raising her eyes." The lady, whom Beatrice afterwards calls Matilda, now speaks with Dante, and discourses of the nature of the place, and of the stream which runs through it, and which on the one hand is called Lethe, and on the other Eunoe. In the drawing, on the left, the three poets are represented entering the forest; Statius and Dante, who go in front, look up among the branches; while Virgil, who stands behind them, casts his eyes downward. On the other side of the drawing, Matilda is seen among the trees, gathering flowers. In the centre of the sheet, Dante is again seen standing on the near bank of the stream, which runs through the wood, as he discourses with Matilda, who is represented for a second time on the farther bank. Behind Dante stand Virgil and Statius. The trees in the background are only in part touched in with pen. This simple and exquisitely idyllic design occurs in striking contrast to the splendid and imaginative series of drawings which now follows.

Canto XXIX.—The drawing is inscribed below: "chantand° 29." "Singing as a lady enamoured, she went on, ending with the words, '*Beati, quorum tecta sunt peccata.*' . . . Then she moved against the stream, going along the bank, and I abreast of her. . . . There were not a hundred paces between hers and mine, when the banks gave a turn equally in such sort, that I again faced the east. Nor had we thus gone long on our way, when the lady turned wholly towards me, saying: 'My brother, look and listen.' And lo, a brightness suddenly flashed from all sides through the great forest. . . . While I was going along, . . . the air became in front of us like a burning fire under the green branches. . . . A little farther on, the long interval which was still between us and them, made counterfeit in appearance seven trees of gold; but when I was so near them that the common object which deceives the senses, lost not through distance any one of its features, that faculty which gleans argument for the reason, perceived that they were candlesticks. . . . I turned round, full of admiration, to the good Virgil; and he replied with a look not less full of astonishment. . . . Then saw I people robed in white, follow nigh, as if after their leaders. . . . When on my bank I had reached such a point that only the river separated me, . . . I saw the flames go forward, leaving behind them the air painted, and they had the semblance of pencils drawn along, so that above them the air remained marked by seven lists. . . . Under so fair a sky as I describe, four and twenty elders, two by two, came crowned with lilies: . . . after them followed four living creatures, each crowned with green leaves. Everyone was pinioned with six wings, the feathers full of eyes. . . . To describe their form I scatter rhymes no more; . . . but read Ezekiel, for he depicts them as he saw them come from the cold quarter, with wind, with cloud and with fire. . . . The space between these four, contained a triumphal car on two wheels, which came drawn by the neck of a griffon; and he stretched on high both his wings, between the midmost, and the three and three lists, so that to none did he hurt, by cleaving it. On high they rose, so that they passed out of sight. His members, so far as he was a bird, were of gold, and the rest were white mingled with vermilion. . . . Three ladies came dancing in a round by the right wheel; the one so red that scarcely would she have been seen within the fire, the second was as if the flesh and the bone had been made of emerald, the third appeared as snow newly fallen. . . . On the left, four made holiday, clad in purple. . . . After all the afore-mentioned group, I saw two aged men unlike in raiment, but like in feature, both dignified and grave. The one showed himself one of the familiars of that great Hippocrates, whom nature made for the creatures which she holds most dear. The other showed the contrary care, with a sword bright and sharp, such that on this side of the stream it made me fear. Afterwards I saw four of humble mien; and behind all, an old man who came alone sleeping, with his countenance undimmed. And these seven were habited as the former throng; but they had not a garland of lilies round their heads, but rather of roses and other purple flowers."

In the drawing, in the lower left-hand corner, Matilda is seen on the far side of the stream, and Dante abreast of her on the near side, followed by Virgil and Statius, as they all proceed along the banks. On the right margin of the sheet, where the stream turns with a circular sweep "towards the east," Dante is again seen standing on the near bank between Virgil and Statius, and Matilda on the other side of the rivulet. The head and left arm and hand of Dante are drawn a second time, to indicate his sudden movement, as he turns to Virgil, "full of admiration" at the sight of the approaching throng. Within the curve of the stream, and filling the greater part of the sheet, the heavenly pageant advances in the contrary direction to that which the poets and Matilda have taken. Foremost come the seven angels abreast, bearing the seven golden candlesticks, whose flames trail behind them in seven lists, "all in those colours of which the sun makes his bow." Behind the angel, in a double file, come the twenty-four elders, representing the books of the Old Testament. In order to express their symbolical meaning, Botticelli portrays them holding up open books above their heads: he omits, however, to show them "crowned with lilies." After them comes the griffon, drawing the car. Near the right wheel, dancing in a round, are the three Theological Virtues; and in like manner, near the left wheel, the four Cardinal Virtues. The car itself is but slightly indicated with the style: and of the "four creatures," symbolizing the Evangelists, which advanced at the four corners of it, only two are shown; namely, the eagle at the front right-hand corner, which is touched with the pen, and the lion at the back right-hand corner, merely sketched with the style. Of the figures following the car, which are also unfinished, St. Peter and St. Paul, followed by the four Doctors of the church, alone are indicated. All this latter part of the pageant, however, is fully shown in the next design.

Canto XXX.—"When the car was opposite to me, the sound of thunder was heard, and all those worthy people seemed to have their further going forbidden, halting there with the first ensigns." Thus the previous canto ends, and the present one begins: "When the septentrion of the first heaven . . . stood fixed, the truthful people, who before had come between the griffon and it, turned towards the car, as if to their place; and one of them . . . cried thrice: '*Veni sponsa de Libano*,' and all the others after him. . . . Upon the divine chariot uprose a hundred, *ad vocem tanti senis*, ministers and messengers of life eternal. All were saying, '*Benedictus qui venis*' and '*Manibus o date lilia plenis*,' scattering flowers above and around. . . . Within a cloud of flowers which was rising from angelic hands, . . . wreathed with olive, over a white veil, a lady appeared to me, clad in the colours of living flame, under a green mantle. . . . I turned to the left . . . to say to Virgil: 'Less than a dram of blood is left in me that trembleth not; I recognize the tokens of the ancient flame.' But Virgil had left us bereft of himself." Beatrice now calls on Dante by name, and recounts to those around her, how he had fallen away from the promise of his youth, and how she had caused him to make this journey for his salvation.

In the drawing, the pageant has moved on along the curving bank of the stream, and the car has arrived opposite to where Dante is standing, as in the previous drawing. On the left are seen the twenty-four elders, and behind them the seven angels bearing the seven golden candlesticks: all have come to a halt, and stand facing the car. In the centre of the sheet is the griffon, his wings rising up out of sight, on either side of the midmost of the seven lists which trail from the golden candlesticks; a piece of symbolism which is more clearly shown in the next design. At the four corners of the car stand the "four living creatures"; the eagle, the angel, the ox and the bull; symbolizing the four evangelists. Within the car is seated Beatrice, wreathed with olive, and holding an olive branch in her right hand. She turns to Dante, who stands on the opposite bank with Statius on his right; Virgil having departed. On the other side of the stream stands Matilda. Dante casts down his eyes, as Beatrice recounts his errors. Upon the car stand three angels, and round about it are five other angels, all scattering flowers. Near the right wheel, dancing in a round, are the three Theological Virtues; and near the left wheel, the four Cardinal Virtues. Following the car come St. Luke and St. Paul, the latter bearing a sword: and behind them follow the "four of humble mien," doubtless intended for St. James, St. Peter, St. John, and St. Jude, as most commentators, including Landino, hold; but "some," observes Vellutelli, "have understood by these 'four of humble mien,' the four doctors of the church." Of this opinion was Botticelli, who has here represented them as such. St. Ambrose is habited as a bishop, St. Gregory the Great as a pope, St. Jerome as a cardinal, and St. Augustine as a bishop: all carry open books. On their right, "the old man sleeping," symbolizes St. John as the writer of the Apocalypse. These last seven figures properly represent the books of the New Testament. Neither these figures, nor the symbolical figures of the four evangelists, wear garlands, as set forth in the poem.

Canto XXXI. Beatrice continues to reprove Dante, who now makes confession of his fault. "Then, when my heart had restored to me the sense of outward things, over me I saw the lady, whom I had found alone, and she was saying: 'Hold me! hold me!' She had brought me into the river up to the neck, and drawing me behind her, was passing over the water as light as a shuttle. When I was near the blessed shore, '*Asperges me*,' I heard so sweetly that I cannot recall it to mind, much less can I write it. The beautiful lady opened her arms, clasped my head, and plunged me under, where it behoved that I swallowed the water; then she drew me forth, and bathed, led me within the dance of the four fair ones, and each covered me with her arms. 'Here are we nymphs, and in the heavens we are stars; ere Beatrice descended to the world, we were ordained to her for her handmaidens. We will lead thee to her eyes, but in the joyous light that is within, will the three beyond, who look more deeply, make keen thine own.' Thus singing they began; and afterwards they led me with them to the breast of the griffon, where was Beatrice turned towards us."

In the drawing, the holy pageant is seen going its way, as the twenty-four elders move out of the picture, on the left. The angels who, in the foregoing design, stand upon or around the car, scattering flowers, are here omitted: and St. Peter and St. Paul are severally represented carrying the keys and a sword, in addition to an open book. In the lower, right-hand corner of the sheet, Dante, with Statius at his side, is seen looking at the holy pageant beyond the stream. Immediately in front of these figures, Dante is again represented, up to his middle in the stream, as he catches at the skirts of Matilda who, with Statius, passes over the water "light as a shuttle." Again, on the left, Matilda is seen bending down, as she takes Dante's head in both her hands, in order to immerse him in the river. Beyond the stream, near the left wheel of the car, Dante is portrayed for a fourth time, kneeling down within the circle of the Cardinal Virtues, as they dance around him: and yet again, after they have led him with them "to the breast of the griffon," followed by Matilda and Statius. The three Theological Virtues are also shown a second time, near the griffon.

Canto XXXII.—The procession passes on "through the high wood," followed by Dante, Statius and Matilda, at "the wheel that made its orbit with the lesser arc." In the drawing, the holy pageant is seen in the upper left-hand portion of the sheet, "returning with the sun," from left to right, after having made the circuit of the wood. For the sake, apparently, of greater simplicity, the angels bearing the seven golden candlesticks and the twenty-four elders are here omitted, though the seven lists that stream from the candlesticks are represented along the upper margin of the sheet. In the hurry of invention, Botticelli has counterchanged the positions of the eagle and the bull, and has drawn St. Augustine and St. Ambrose in the papal, instead of the episcopal, habit. Below, on the left side of the sheet, Dante, Statius and Matilda are twice represented as they follow the holy pageant.

After a space Beatrice alights from the car: "I heard all murmur 'Adam'; then they circled round a tree despoiled of blossoms and other foliage on every branch. Its top, which spreads the wider the higher it ascends, would be marvelled at for height by the Indians in their forests." Then the griffon, "turning to the pole which he had drawn, dragged it to the foot of the widowed branch, and left the pole of the car bound to it. . . . Disclosing a colour less than of roses and more than of violets, the tree was renewed which before had had its branches so bare." Dante now falls into a deep slumber, but confesses himself unable to describe how he fell asleep: "Wherefore I pass on to when I awoke, and I say that a shining light tore from me the veil of sleep, and one was calling: 'Arise! what doest thou?' . . . So came I to myself, and saw that pious Lady, who before had been the guide of my steps along the river, standing over me; and all in doubt I said: 'Where is Beatrice?' whereat she: 'Behold her underneath the new foliage, sitting at its root. Behold the company that encircles her; the others go their way on high after the griffon.' . . . She was sitting alone on the uncorrupted earth, as guardian left there of the wain, which I saw the biform creature bind. The seven nymphs in a circle, with those lights in their hands which are secure from Aquilo and Auster, made of themselves a cloister about her." Beatrice bids Dante: "Keep now thine eyes on the car, and what thou seest, when thou art returned yonder, see that thou write:" and the poet tells how he saw "the bird of Jove swoop down through the tree, rending the bark, as well as the blossoms and the new leaves; and he smote the car with all his force, whereat it reeled as a ship in a tempest. . . . Afterwards I saw come into the hollow of the triumphal chariot a vixen, which from all good food seemed to be fasting. . . . Next from thence, whence it had before come, I saw the eagle descend into the ark of the car, and leave it covered with its own feathers. . . . Then it seemed to me that the earth was opened between both the wheels, and I saw a dragon come forth, who fixed his tail up through the car; and, as a wasp that draweth back its sting, drawing to himself the malignant tail, he tore off part of the bottom and went his way wandering about. That which remained . . . was covered again with feathers. . . . Transformed thus, the holy engine put forth heads through its parts, three over the pole and one at each corner. The first were horned like an ox, but the four had a single horn on the forehead. . . . Seated above it there appeared to me a shameless harlot, with eyes quick to glance around. And as though she should not be taken from him, I saw straightly beside her a giant, and they kissed together awhile."

In the drawing, below in the central part, Dante is seen, on one knee, raising himself from his sleep at the sound of the voice: "Arise! what doest thou?" On the upper margin the elders ascend into heaven, after the griffon. Again, on the right, Dante is seen for a fourth time, approaching, in company with Matilda and Statius, the tree to which the car has been bound by the griffon. At the foot of the tree sits Beatrice, surrounded by the seven nymphs, the Theological and Cardinal Virtues, seated in a round, with the seven candlesticks in their hands. Above in the tree, the Roman eagle is represented swooping down among the branches and despoiling the new foliage; and below, a second time, descending into the car which is seen transformed. The car itself is covered with feathers; three horned heads have appeared over the pole, and one at every corner. In the forepart of the car is the vixen; beside the right wheel the dragon goes his way, wandering about; and seated within the car are the harlot and giant, toying with one another. In this drawing, the trees of the holy wood, omitted in the three previous designs, are here and there indicated. The incident with which the canto closes, of the giant chasing the harlot through the wood, is passed over in the drawing.

CANTO XXXIII.—"'*Deus, venerunt gentes,*' weeping, the ladies began alternately, now three, now four, a sweet psalmody; and Beatrice, sighing and pitiful, listened to them in such sort that little more beside the cross was Mary changed. But after the other maidens gave place for her to speak, risen upright on her feet, she replied, being in hue like fire: '*Modicum et non videbitis me, et iterum,* my beloved sisters, *modicum et vos videbitis me.*' Then she placed them all the seven before her, and beckoning only, she caused me and the lady and the sage who remained, to follow after her." In the drawing, on the left, Beatrice is seated on the ground, with the seven Virtues around her, and before her stand Dante, Statius and Matilda. The car, and the tree to which it was bound, are not shown in this drawing, and the seven candlesticks held by the Virtues are also omitted. In the centre of the sheet Beatrice is again seen, making her way across the holy wood, preceded by the seven Virtues and followed by Dante, Statius and Matilda. As they go, Beatrice discourses to Dante, and interpreting the vision which he has just seen, ends with a prophecy, "obscure as Themis and Sphinx." At length, the seven Virtues halt before a spring, from which flow two streams, Lethe and Eunoe. Beatrice now turns to Matilda: "'Behold Eunoe which there springs forth: lead him to it, and as thou art wont, revive his fainting virtue.' Like a gentle spirit that makes not excuse, but has its will of the will of another, as soon as it is outwardly declared by a sign, so the fair lady, after I had been taken by her, moved forward, and courteously said to Statius: 'Come with him!' If I had, reader, longer space for writing, I should sing, though in part, the sweet draught which never would have sated me." In the drawing, the stream Eunoe is represented skirting the holy wood in a wide circle; and on the right of the sheet, Matilda is seen for the last time, immersing Dante in the waters of the mystical river, while Statius stands by on the inner bank.

Such is the subject-matter of these drawings in illustration to the last six cantos of the "Purgatorio." Regarded as a whole, they form a divine allegory comparable, within its limits, to the profane allegory of the "Spring." Perhaps no portion of the "Divina Commedia" lends itself in the same degree to illustration, from the point of view of a Florentine draughtsman of the fifteenth century, as do these cantos: for Botticelli, at least, they afforded an occasion to produce a series of inventions which, viewed as illustration, stand out from the rest of these drawings by reason of the sumptuous beauty of their design, apart from the imagination, sentiment and expressiveness, which unfailingly characterize them. The holy pageant itself, like the "Trionfi" of the cassone-painters, was evidently associated in the mind of Sandro with those public processions which were annually held in Florence on certain festivals, and which Vasari describes in the life of Il

Cecca. But Botticelli, it has been said, was a "visionary painter"; and the outward, spectacular elements in these drawings become expressive of the spirit and of things spiritual, in a way that the cassone-painters little anticipated.

PARADISO, CANTO I.—The drawing recalls the concluding verse of the "Purgatorio": "Pure and made ready to mount up to the stars." Again the scene is laid in the "divine forest" that crowns the mount of Purgatory; and within its circle of tall, slender trees which rise up against the clear, mid-day sky, Dante and Beatrice begin their heavenward journey. The allusion is to the passage in which the poet describes how, when he saw Beatrice turn and gaze upon the sun, "from her action, poured through the eyes into my imagination, mine was made, and I fixed mine eyes on the sun beyond our wont." So consumed is he by "the inborn and perpetual thirst for the Kingdom of God," that it is not until Beatrice presently tells him, "Thou art not upon earth as thou believest; but a thunderbolt falling from its proper site never sped as thou dost, who art returning to it," that he perceives that he is being swiftly borne to heaven. Botticelli represents Beatrice and Dante lost in contemplation of "the eternal wheels," as they ascend into the circle of the first heaven. Beatrice, who is greater in stature than Dante, holds a wand in her right hand, and places her left on the arm of the poet. The feet of the figures are placed straightly together, an attitude peculiarly characteristic of Botticelli's flying figures.

That element of vision which is one of the chief characteristics of the designs to the concluding cantos of the "Purgatorio," is characteristic of this drawing in a still more heightened degree. The most lovely and spiritual of all these designs, it is the one which most nearly satisfies the requirements of our modern notion of what such illustrations should be. This, perhaps, is largely due to the fact that the expression of the sentiment suggested by the action forms so large a part of the subject-matter of the design, and the elucidation of the action itself so small a one, that for the moment we forget the exegetical purpose of the draughtsman. Certainly, Botticelli has represented the ascent of Beatrice and Dante into heaven, as they rise up from the pale circle of slender trees which symbolize the holy wood of Purgatory, with a sense of mystery and spiritual yearning which is unapproached in the whole course of Florentine art. From this point, these designs become more subjective in conception and treatment, as the poem grows more metaphysical in character; and when the earth begins to recede and the horizon enlarge before the poet and his guide, the scene of the heavens, as well, for the most part, as the spirits which inhabit there, are represented by mere signs and symbols. Rarely is more than one incident now introduced into each design; and in the greater number of the drawings, the only human figures portrayed are those of Dante and Beatrice. In all this, Botticelli follows the tradition of the earlier illustrators of the "Divina Commedia"; as a glance at such a manuscript as the Palatine Codex, No. 313, preserved in the Biblioteca Nazionale, at Florence, will suffice to show. Moreover, in many of the ensuing drawings, which represent Dante and Beatrice discoursing together, as they proceed through the spheres, even the symbols denoting the scene and incident are wanting; so that there is nothing, excepting the action and gestures of the figures, to indicate what passage of the text is intended to be illustrated.

CANTO II.—In answer to Dante's inquiry, "What are the murky signs in this body which below on earth make some tell tales of Cain?" Beatrice shows that they proceed not from dense and rare, as Dante wrongly conceives, but from other causes which she explains to him. Dante is represented looking up at the figure of the universe, on the left of the drawing, as Beatrice thus concludes her discourse: "The motion and virtue of the holy wheels must needs proceed from the blessed movers; as the craft of the hammer from the smith. And the heaven which so many lights make beautiful, from the profound mind that revolves it, takes the image, and makes of it a seal. And as the soul within your dust is diffused through different members, and conformed to divers faculties, so the Intelligence unfoldeth its goodness multiplied through the stars, revolving itself upon its unity. Diverse virtue maketh diverse alloy with the precious body which it quickens, and with which it is bound, as life in you. By reason of the glad nature whence it springs, the mingled virtue shines through the body as joy through the living pupil. From this, not from dense and rare, comes that which appears different between light and light: this is the formal principle which produces, in conformity with its goodness, the dull and the clear."

In the drawing, Beatrice and Dante are seen standing within the heaven of the moon, represented by a circle. As she discourses, Beatrice turns towards a figure of the heavens, on the left of the sheet. In this figure, the earth is inscribed "tera"; the spheres of the air and fire, "aria" and "fuocho"; and the heavens of the moon, Mercury, Venus, the sun, Mars, Jupiter, Saturn, the fixed stars and the Primum Mobile, are severally indicated by their symbols. The figure was, no doubt, partly intended as a chart to explain the nature and position of the various spheres through which Dante now passes; just as the figure of Purgatory is introduced into the background of the drawing for the first canto of the "Purgatorio." The drawing is apparently unfinished, the symbols being wanting which should denote the heaven in which Beatrice and Dante stand. The group of Beatrice and Dante is admirable in gesture and expression.

Canto III.—The drawing for this canto is one of great beauty: it represents certain spirits of those who on earth had taken vows which, through no fault of their own, they had failed to keep, appearing to Beatrice and Dante in the heaven of the moon.

"As through glasses transparent and polished, or through waters clear and tranquil, yet not so deep that the bottom be lost to sight, the images of our faces return so weak, that a pearl on a white forehead comes not less faintly to our eyes; in such wise saw I many faces ready to speak; so that I ran into the contrary error to that which kindled love between the man and the fountain. As soon as I was aware of them, judging them to be mirrored images, I turned my eyes to see of whom they were, and saw naught, and turned them back straight on the light of my sweet guide, who, smiling, glowed with her sacred eyes." To express this sudden action on the part of the poet, Botticelli employs a device which he has already used in the illustrations to Canto XXXII. of the "Inferno," and Cantos X. and XXIX. of the "Purgatorio." Beatrice and Dante are standing within the heaven of the moon, turned towards the left. As Beatrice discourses of the spirits, she extends her right hand and lays her left on the shoulder of the poet, who stands with both hands raised in astonishment. Above the figure of Dante, Botticelli has drawn the head and shoulder of the poet a second time, in the act of turning back, and looking up towards the right, in the expectation of seeing the spirits, whose reflection he imagines that he has been looking upon. Beatrice tells Dante that they are "true substances" which he beholds, and bids him talk with them. Dante now speaks with the spirit of Piccarda de' Donati.

CANTO IV.—Beatrice continues to discourse with Dante in the heaven of the moon. Only nine of the spirits are now seen on the left of the drawing; the concluding lines of the last canto tell how Piccarda, having done speaking, "vanished as does a heavy body through deep water." Beatrice divines that Dante has fallen into doubt concerning two questions which she proceeds to resolve for him. In the drawing, as she is seen discoursing, Dante, with both hands upraised, gazes into her face with love and amazement, in allusion to the concluding lines of the canto: "Beatrice gazed upon me with eyes filled with the sparks of love, and so divine, that, my powers overcome, I turned away and with downcast eyes, became as one lost." The draperies of Beatrice are somewhat confused, but the action of the figure is very spirited. The little figures on the left, however, are not inferior to those in the previous drawing.

CANTO V.—Beatrice, still discoursing to Dante in the heaven of the moon, resolves him how, with no other service, can a broken vow be repaid, since "the freedom of the will" is "the greatest gift which God of his bounty made in creating." The drawing shows Beatrice poised in air, with her feet set straightly together, as she discourses with great animation to Dante, who stands before her with one hand upraised. Of all the single groups of Beatrice and Dante, this is, perhaps, the grandest and most expressive: the action and the flying draperies of the figure of Beatrice are designed with the greatest beauty and vivacity, and set in admirable contrast to the simplicity and repose of the figure of Dante. The care with which the former figure was designed, appears from the manner in which it was drawn and redrawn with the style, before it was finally touched in with the pen. The circle is merely indicated with the style, and the symbols are wanting.

CANTO VI.—In the concluding verses of the previous canto, the poet tells how Beatrice, as she finished speaking, "turned round all full of desire to that quarter where the world is most living. Her silence and her change of countenance imposed silence on my eager intellect, which already was proposing new questions. And as an arrow that strikes the mark before the bowstring be still, so sped we into the second realm. . . . As in a stew, which is still and clear, the fish draw near to that which comes from without, in such sort that they deem it their food, so did I see more than a thousand splendours draw towards us, and from each was heard, 'Behold one who will increase our loves.'" One of the spirits speaks to Dante, who enquires of him his name and why he inhabits this sphere of heaven. The reply of the Emperor Justinian (for of such the spirit is) fills the whole of Canto VI. The drawing appears to have reference to the passage quoted above from Canto V. It represents Beatrice and Dante ascending into the heaven of Mercury, which is inhabited by the souls of those who sought honour in active life. The spirits are symbolized by tongues of flame powdered over the field of the sphere. Again Dante gazes into Beatrice's face as she ascends with her eyes fixed on the eternal wheels. The figures, admirable in their movement, are rendered with the greatest vivacity and rhythm of line.

CANTO VII.—After the spirit of Justinian has departed, Dante, moved by what he has heard, falls into doubt touching certain questions concerning the Redemption. Beatrice resolves him of this and other matters. In the drawing, Beatrice and Dante are seen standing and discoursing together, in the heaven of Mercury which, as in the last drawing, is represented by a sphere powdered with tongues of flame, arranged in concentric circles. The figures face one another; Beatrice raising her right hand as she discourses.

CANTO VIII.—Beatrice and Dante now ascend to the third heaven of Venus: "I was not aware of my ascent to it, but of being therein my Lady gave me assurance enough, since I saw her become more beautiful. And as a spark is seen in a flame, and as a voice is distinguished in a voice, when one is stayed and the other goes and returns, so saw I in that light other lamps move in a circle more and less swiftly, according to the measure, I believe, of their eternal vision." These "lights divine" approach Beatrice and Dante, "leaving the wheel first began by the Seraphim on high." One of them addresses the poet, and in reply to his question, "Say who ye are," declares itself the spirit of him on whose brow gleamed "the crown of that land which the Danube waters after it leaves its German banks," Charles Martel. In the drawing, Beatrice and Dante are seen standing in the heaven of Venus, turned towards the left. Beatrice points to the flame in which the spirit of Charles Martel approaches them, and Dante raises both his hands as he listens to his discourse. The spirits are symbolized by tongues of flame, arranged in concentric circles over some two-thirds of the field of the sphere, and above the heads of Dante and Beatrice.

CANTO IX.—Dante, in the earlier verses of this canto, relates how, after the spirit of Charles Martel had done speaking, "another of those splendours came towards me, and by outwardly brightening signified its wish to please me. The eyes of Beatrice, which were fixed upon me as before, made me assured of her dear assent to my desire." In reply to Dante, the soul of Cunizza, the sister of Ezzelino, speaks from out the flame. In the drawing, Beatrice and Dante are represented standing within the sphere of Venus. Both figures are turned to the left, with the right hand raised: Dante regards some object before him, which is not indicated in the drawing, as Beatrice fixes her gaze upon him. A number of concentric circles, lightly drawn within the sphere, show that Botticelli intended to powder its field with tongues of flame, symbolizing the spirits, as in the previous sheet. The right foot of Dante has been erased and redrawn, and a slight change made in the drapery of the figure.

CANTO X.—Beatrice and Dante ascend into the heaven of the sun, "the greatest minister of nature, that stamps the world with the worth of heaven." Again Dante is unconscious of his ascent. "How shining that needs must be of itself which was within the sun, where I entered, being apparent not by colour but by light; though I should call upon wit and art and use, I could not tell it so that it could ever be imagined." In the drawing, Beatrice and Dante are represented within the sphere of the sun, turned to the right. Beatrice uplifts her right hand on high as she gazes upon Dante, who shields his eyes with his right hand as he looks upward. Botticelli probably intended to introduce some symbolical figures in the upper part of the sheet, to complete the design, in allusion to the verses which follow: "I saw many living and victorious splendours make of us a centre and of themselves a crown."

CANTO XI.—To what passage of the text this drawing has reference is not very evident. The greater part of the canto is taken up by the discourse of St. Thomas Aquinas touching the life of St. Francis and his own successors in the Order of St. Dominic. In the drawing, Beatrice and Dante are represented standing in the sphere of the sun: Beatrice extends her right hand as she looks towards the spectator, while Dante places his hand on his breast as he looks before him. It is probable that they are listening to the speech of St. Thomas, and that Botticelli intended to introduce other figures into the design, which would have made clear the allusion to the text. The right hand of Beatrice has been twice sketched in different actions with the style, before it was finally touched in with the pen.

Canto XII.—Again the drawing is unfinished, so that its connection with the text can only be surmised. The opening verses of the canto relate how, after St. Thomas had done speaking, "the holy mill-wheel began to revolve, and in its circling had not turned wholly round, ere a second enclosed it with a circle, and gathered motion to motion and song to song. . . . After that the dance and the great and high festival both of the song, and likewise of flaming light with light, joyous and gentle, had become still, . . . from the heart of one of the new lights came a voice which made me seem, as I turned to where it was, the needle to the star." The spirit of St. Bonaventura now speaks, and his discourse fills the rest of the canto.

It is to these opening verses that the drawing probably has reference. The figures of Beatrice and Dante, turned to the right, are represented standing within the sphere of the sun. Beatrice, with a gesture of her right hand, gazes on Dante, who shields his eyes as he looks before him. The action of this group is one of great beauty. Within the circle of the sphere some five or six concentric circles have been drawn in with the style, to serve as an indication for the arrangement of the flames, or other figures, which were to have symbolized the spirits and their wheel-like movements.

Canto XIII.—Again the drawing is unfinished, and the allusion uncertain. Probably the design has reference to the elaborate figure with which the canto opens, of the twenty-four stars which revolve in two concentric circles, and encircle in a "two-fold dance" the place where Dante and Beatrice are standing. Beatrice and Dante are again represented, turned to the left, in the sphere of the sun. Beatrice looks towards the poet as Dante gazes upwards, with a gesture of the right hand. A number of concentric circles are again indicated with the style, within the circle of the sphere.

Canto XIV.—St. Thomas having made an end, the spirit of Solomon speaks, after which Beatrice and Dante ascend to the fifth heaven of Mars: "And behold, round about, a lustre of equal brightness arose over that which was there, like to an horizon that grows bright again. . . . I seemed to begin to see there new substances, and that they made a circle without the other two circumferences . . . and I saw myself alone with my Lady translated to a more lofty salvation. Well did I perceive that I was lifted more on high through the fiery laughter of the star, which seemed to me ruddier than its wont." In the drawing, Beatrice and Dante are twice represented; below, at half length, as they rise into the sphere of Mars, and again at full length as they stand within the circle of its sphere. In both groups, Dante is represented looking upwards with a gesture of amazement: in the latter, Beatrice turns towards him with her right hand upraised. The allusion is, probably, to the vision of the Cross, which the poet now sees: "As distinct with lesser and greater lights, the galaxy gleams white between the poles of the world, so that it makes very sages to doubt; thus constellated in the depths of Mars, those rays made the venerable sign, which the junctures of quadrants make in a round. Here my memory outdoes my wit, since that Cross so flashed forth Christ, that I know not how to find a worthy similitude." Botticelli, no doubt, intended to add a figure symbolical of this vision.

CANTO XV.—Beatrice and Dante tarry in the heaven of Mars. The earlier verses of the canto relate how, like a meteor in the sky at night, "from the horn which stretches to the right at the foot of that cross, ran a star of the constellation which shines there; nor did the gem depart from its riband, but coursed on by the radial band; so that it seemed like fire behind alabaster. . . . '*O sanguis meus, O superinfusa gratia Dei, sicut tibi, cui bis unquam coeli janua reclusa?*' So spake that light; wherefore I gave heed to it: then I turned back my gaze to my Lady, and on this side and on that was astounded; for within her eyes was burning such a smile, that I thought I had touched with mine the depth of my grace and of my Paradise." The spirit of his ancestor, Cacciaguida, now speaks with Dante out of the star. It is to this passage that the drawing, probably, has reference. Beatrice and Dante, turned towards the right, are seen standing within the circle of the sphere. Beatrice, motioning with her hand to some object before them, turns towards Dante, who starts back with a gesture of astonishment. Botticelli, no doubt, intended to add some figure symbolizing the star out of which the spirit of Cacciaguida speaks. The figure of Dante is of an unusual beauty of gesture and expression. This group appears to have been erased and redesigned.

CANTO XVI.—Cacciaguida having done speaking, with the close of the last canto, Dante now resumes the conversation. "With the 'ye' that Rome first suffered, wherein her family little perseveres, began again my words. Wherefore Beatrice, who was a little apart, smiling, seemed like her who coughed at the first fault written of Guinivere. I began: 'Ye are my father.'" In the drawing, Dante stands in the lower part of the sphere, with his hand on his breast, as if about to speak; while Beatrice is placed on the left, somewhat above him and "a little apart, smiling" upon him. Again the figure symbolizing the spirit of Cacciaguida is wanting. The hair of Beatrice appears to have been erased.

CANTO XVII.—In answer to Dante's question as to "what sort of fortune is drawing near" for him, Cacciaguida foretells the poet's exile and subsequent wanderings. In the drawing, Dante is represented standing with his hands folded upon his breast and his head bowed, as if listening in grief to the prophecy of his ancestor: Beatrice stands near the poet, on the left, regarding him. Perhaps, the allusion is to the opening lines of the next canto: "Already was that blessed mirror rejoicing by himself in his own word, and I was tasting mine, tempering the sweet with the bitter; and that Lady who was leading me to God said, 'Change thy thoughts; think that I am near to him who disburthens every wrong.'" The figures of Beatrice and Dante as originally sketched, show considerable variation from those afterwards put in with the pen. The other figures are wanting.

CANTO XVIII.—The spirit of Cacciaguida again speaks; after which Beatrice and Dante ascend to the sixth heaven of Jupiter. The poet now sees the spirits of the just form certain words: "within the lights, holy creatures sang as they were flying, and formed now a D, now an I, now an L by their figures. . . . They displayed themselves then in five times seven vowels and consonants; and I noted the parts as they appeared uttered to me. '*Diligite justitiam*' were the first verb and noun of all the painting; '*Qui judicatis terram*' were last." After this there appeared to arise "more than a thousand lights, and mount up, one much and another little, according as the sun, which kindles them, allotted them; and each resting in its place, I saw that studded fire represent the head and neck of an eagle." In the drawing, Beatrice and Dante are twice represented: below, they are seen at half-length, as they ascend into the sphere of Jupiter; and again, at whole-length, as they stand in the midst of its circle. In the latter group, Dante who is on the right, starts back with a fine gesture of amazement, while Beatrice stands in the middle of the sphere, regarding him with an air of great sweetness and nobility. The vision, whether of the letters, or of the eagle, is wanting. Below, on the margin of the sheet, partially cut away, are inscribed the opening words of the canto, thus: "18 gia sighodeua so[lo]."

Canto XIX.—The speech of the eagle concerning divine justice and unjust rulers, fills the whole of this canto. The drawing is in a very unfinished condition. It represents Beatrice and Dante standing together within the sphere of Jupiter; probably listening to the discourse of the eagle. These figures have been sketched with the style, partially touched in with the pen, and afterwards for the most part erased.

Canto XX.—The flaming eagle again speaks, showing who are the five spirits who make him "a circle for eyelid," and how it comes to pass that the souls of certain gentiles are among them. In the drawing, Beatrice and Dante are again seen standing within the sphere of Jupiter. Beatrice looks towards Dante and makes a motion with her right hand to some object before them, at which the poet is looking with astonishment. The vision of the eagle, which is apparently the object of their attention, is again wanting. On the lower margin of the sheet are written the opening words of the canto: "Quando choluj 20."

Canto XXI.—Beatrice and Dante now ascend into the seventh heaven of Saturn. "Already were mine eyes fixed again on the countenance of my Lady . . . and she smiled not, but began again to me: 'If I should smile, thou wouldst become what Semele was when she was turned to ashes; for my beauty, which is kindled the more by the steps of the eternal palace, as thou hast seen, so much the more one ascends, were it not tempered, so shines, that at its brightness thy mortal power would be as a leaf which a thunderbolt brasts. We have been lifted up to the seventh splendour, which beneath the breast of the burning Lion now shines down, mingled with his might. . . . Within the crystal which, as it circles the world, bears the name of its illustrious leader, under whom all evil lay dead, of the colour of gold which a ray shines through, I saw a ladder raised so far on high that my sight followed it not. I saw, also, descending by its steps so many splendours, that I thought every light which appears in the heaven, thence had been scattered. And as by their natural habit the daws together, at the break of day, bestir themselves to warm their chilled feathers; then some go away without returning; others turn back to whence they started; and others, wheeling, make a sojourn; such method, it seemed to me, was there in that sparkling which gathered together so soon as it smote upon a certain step."

In the drawing, Beatrice and Dante are seen standing within the sphere of Saturn, at the foot of the ladder which, as it ascends, is intersected by the circumference of the sphere. Beatrice, pointing upwards with her left hand, turns with a grave countenance to Dante, and discourses with him as he looks upward in astonishment. The souls of those that have lived the contemplative life, are represented as diminutive, winged angels which fly hither and thither, like daws at daybreak. Botticelli had originally represented Beatrice and Dante a second time in figures of a smaller size, climbing the ladder; but as this incident occurs in the next canto, and forms the subject of the drawing which follows, he has erased these figures: their design, however, may still be made out. Slightly sketched with the style on the upper part of the drawing, above the circle of the sphere, is a part of the zodiac, symbolizing the eighth heaven of the fixed stars, to which the ladder ascends.

Canto XXII.—St. Peter Damian having done speaking, Dante beholds "more little flames descend from step to step and wheel around"; and when they had halted, they "gave a cry of so high sound that it would not be possible here to find its like." With these words the foregoing canto ends; Canto XXII begins: "Overcome with amazement, I turned me to my guide, as a child who always runs back thither where he has most trust; and she, as a mother who succours forthwith her pale and panting boy with her voice, which is used to well dispose him, said to me: 'Knowest thou not that thou art in heaven? . . . How the song would have transformed thee, and I by my smiling, thou art able now to think, since the shout has so greatly moved thee." In the drawing, Dante is represented running towards Beatrice, like a child, as she throws her arms around him to succour him. The rapid movement of these figures is very characteristic of Botticelli's later manner. They stand upon the sphere of Saturn, which is represented by the upper part of a circle. Behind them Jacob's ladder rises into the heaven of the fixed stars, represented by a second circle which intersects the first. On the ladder Beatrice and Dante are again seen, in smaller figures, ascending into the eighth heaven. After St. Benedict, whose discourse fills the earlier portion of this canto, had done speaking and had drawn back to his company, "his company drew together; then like a whirlwind, it was all gathered upon high. The sweet Lady urged me after them with a sign alone, up over that ladder, so did her virtue overcome my nature. Nor ever here below, where by nature we mount and fall, was motion so swift that it would equal my flight." On the upper margin of the drawing, a part of the zodiac is indicated with the style. On the left of the sheet is the sign of the Crab; on the right that of the Scales.

Canto XXIII.—Dante and Beatrice enter the eighth heaven in "the sign which follows the Bull." On the lower part of margin of the drawing is sketched with the style a part of the zodiac, with the signs of the Crab, the Twins and the Bull. The present canto opens with a description of the eighth heaven: "I saw, above thousands of lamps, a sun which kindled them all and each, as ours does the supernal shows of things; and through the living light appeared the shining substance so bright upon mine eyes, that they endured it not." Presently Beatrice bids Dante look up: "'Here is the rose, wherein the Divine Word was made flesh; here are the lilies, to whose odour the good way was taken.'"

In the drawing, Beatrice and Dante stand together within the circle of the sphere: Beatrice points on high as she turns to Dante, who looks upwards, with both hands raised in astonishment. Above them is the figure of a burning sun with a human countenance, symbolizing Christ, around whom circle, on orbits concentric with the sphere in which Beatrice and Dante are standing, tongues of flame symbolizing "the battalions of the triumph of Christ." Again, immediately above the heads of Beatrice and Dante is a single great flame, surrounded by a circle of twelve smaller flames, symbolizing the spirits of the Virgin and the Apostles, the rose and the lilies of the passage cited above.

CANTO XXIV.—At the conclusion of the foregoing canto, the spirit of the Virgin mounts on high to Christ, while the saints remain. Beatrice having called upon the "company elect to the great supper of the blessed Lamb," to give heed to Dante's "boundless desire, and shower upon him somewhat, . . . those joyful souls made themselves spheres upon fixed poles, flaming mightily like unto comets. And as wheels in the framing of clocks revolve, in such sort that the first, to him who gives heed, seems to be still, and the last to fly, so did those carols dancing variously, swift and slow, make me appraise their riches. From that one which I noted of chiefest beauty, I saw issue a fire so blissful that it knew none there of greater brightness; and three times around Beatrice did it turn with a song so divine, that my imagination repeats it not to me." The spirit of St. Peter now speaks and examines Dante concerning Faith. In this, as in the previous drawing, a burning sun with a human countenance is represented in the upper part of the design, surrounded by tongues of flames symbolizing the spirits of the saints, which move around the sun on a series of concentric orbits. Below, Beatrice and Dante are seen standing side by side, upon the sphere of the seventh heaven. As they look upwards, Beatrice, with her left hand on Dante's shoulder, touches his elbow with her right hand, as if bidding him give heed to the spirit of St. Peter which hovers immediately above them, and is indicated by the word "piero."

CANTO XXV.—Beatrice and Dante tarry in the eighth heaven; and the spirit of St. James questions Dante concerning Hope. The saint having done speaking, "'*sperent in te*' was heard above us, to which all the choirs responded; then among them a light brightened, so that if the Crab contained such a crystal, the winter would have a month of a single day." The great flame is the spirit of St. John. "'This is he who lay upon the breast of our Pelican, and this is he who from upon the cross was elected to the great office.' Thus spake my Lady; nor for all that did she remove her eyes from their intent, after her words more than before. As he who gazes and makes himself ready to see the sun eclipsed a while, and through looking is deprived of sight, so became I at this last fire, until it was said to me: 'Wherefore dost thou dazzle thyself to behold a thing which here hath no place?'"

In the drawing, the burning sun encircled by the tongues of flame, is again represented in the upper part of the design, while below Beatrice and Dante are seen standing upon the sphere of the seventh heaven. Immediately above the head of Dante are three tongues of flame severally inscribed "piero," "giouani" and "jachopo." Beatrice with her right hand uplifted as she speaks, gazes steadfastly at the spirit of St. John, while Dante looks up at the flame, with both hands raised in wonderment.

CANTO XXVI.—St. John now examines Dante concerning Love. Dante having replied, "a most sweet song resounded through the heaven, and my Lady cried with the others: 'Holy, holy, holy!' . . . From mine eyes did Beatrice chase every mote with the ray of hers which shone out for more than a thousand miles; wherefore saw I afterwards better than before, and as one astounded I inquired concerning a fourth light," the spirit of Adam. It is to this incident that the drawing appears to have reference. The burning sun, encircled with tongues of flame, fills the upper part of the design, as before. Below, Beatrice with her right hand uplifted, turns to Dante, who covers his eyes with his right hand. Above the head of Dante are four tongues of flame inscribed, "piero," "giouani," "iachopo" and "adamo."

CANTO XXVII.—The first part of the canto, in which St. Peter rebukes the bishops of Rome before all the court of Paradise, is passed over in the drawing. After the blessed spirits have ascended, Beatrice bids Dante cast down his eyes, and see how he has revolved. "Since that hour when I had first looked, I saw that I had moved through all the arc which the first Clime makes from the middle to the end, so that I saw on that side, by Cadiz, the vain path of Ulysses, and on this, near by, the shore on which Europa became a sweet burden. And further had the site of this little floor been disclosed to me; but the sun had proceeded beneath my feet, and had gone its way a sign and more." In the drawing, Beatrice and Dante are seen standing upon the floor of the eighth heaven, as they look down upon the spheres through which they have passed. "And though nature or art in the flesh of man, or in her pictures, has made baits to take the eyes, in order to possess the mind, all united would appear nothing to the divine pleasure which shone out upon me, when I turned to her laughing countenance. And the virtue which the look bestowed on me, rapt me from the fair nest of Leda, and bore me into the swiftest heaven." In the drawing, Beatrice and Dante are represented a second time, as they ascend into the ninth heaven, or Primum Mobile, which, being nearest to God, moves the fastest. Beatrice lays her left hand on Dante's shoulder, and with the right motions him upwards. The strange, cloud-like form in the background of the drawing, may have a reference to the image which Dante employs in the description of the ascent of the spirits, after St. Peter has done speaking: "As our air falls down in flakes of frozen vapours, when the horn of the heavenly goat is in contact with the sun. Thus saw I the ether become adorned, and float on high in flakes of the triumphant vapours which had made their sojourn there with us."

CANTO XXVIII.—"As I turned about . . . I saw a point from which radiated a light so keen, that the eye which it drowns, must needs close itself, by reason of its great sharpness, . . . around the point, a circle of fire was whirling so swiftly that it would have outdone that motion which most quickly encircles the world; and this was girt around by another, and that by a third, and the third after by the fourth, the fourth by the fifth, and the fifth by the sixth. Beyond followed the seventh, already so outspread in breadth, that the messenger of Juno entire would be too narrow to contain it. So the eighth and the ninth; and each one moved more slowly according as it was further removed in number from the first." Beatrice now explains to Dante the order and nature of the angelic hierarchy. In the drawing, Beatrice and Dante are seen standing on the floor of the ninth heaven; the poet looks upwards with his hands raised in wonderment, as his guide, with her right hand uplifted, discourses to him. The whole of the background of the drawing is filled with a representation of the Trinity encircled by the nine orders of angels. On the right margin of the sheet, Botticelli has written their names, now partially cut away, in this order: "trinit[a]," represented by a diminutive circle; "cherub[ini]," "serafi[ni]," by two circles of winged heads; "tron[i]," represented by angels holding tabors; "domin[azioni]," by angels with pennons bearing a cross; "uirtut[i]," by angels with shields blazoned with a cross, recalling the red cross on a white ground of the shield of the people of Florence; "podest[adi]," by angels with orb and sceptre; "princ[ipati]," by angels wearing a stole, crossed on the breast; "arch[angeli]," by angels with scrolls; "an[geli]," by angels holding tablets. The little circle representing the Trinity, the orders of the Cherubim and Seraphim, and part of the order of the Thrones, are merely sketched with the style; the rest of the design is elaborately touched in with the pen. On the tablet, which the fourth angel on the left is holding, Botticelli has inscribed his name, "sandr°/dima/rian/o"; not by way of signature, as it would seem, but as an expression of the hope that his own spirit might ultimately find salvation among the least of the angels. This elaborate drawing is one of the skyiest of Botticelli's inventions. Despite the number and ornate character of the figures with which the field of the design is powdered, its effect as a whole remains as large and simple as a sky fretted with light, fleecy clouds at sundown.

Canto XXIX.—Dante tarries in the ninth heaven, while Beatrice expounds to him certain questions concerning the nature of the angels. In the drawing, Beatrice is seen in the foreground, as she discourses to Dante, who stands by her side. They form one of the noblest and most dramatic of the many fine groups, which occur in these drawings for the "Paradiso."

In the background are seen the last five of the nine circles of the angelic hierarchy. The larger portion of the last three circles is touched in with the pen; the remainder being merely sketched with the style. The details of the figures are the same as in the foregoing design; but by spacing the angels more widely apart, Botticelli has varied their effect, as a background to the principal figures of Beatrice and Dante.

Canto XXX.—Beatrice and Dante ascend to the highest or empyrean heaven. A living light now shines around Dante, which deprives him of sight. Presently he is aware that he is rising above his own virtue: "And I was rekindled with fresh vision, so that no light is so pure but my eyes would have resisted it. And I saw a light in the form of a river, shining with effulgence, between the two banks which were painted with a wondrous spring. From such stream issued living sparks which on every side settled on the flowers, like rubies which gold encircles. Then, as if drunken with the odours, they plunged themselves again in the wondrous gulf; and if one entered, another would issue forth." In the drawing, Dante and Beatrice are represented flying upwards, above the river of light. The living sparks which issue from the stream, are represented by tiny winged genii, rayed with light, which now settle like bees upon the flowers by the banks of the stream, and now plunge into the stream. The flame-like character of these flowers strangely recalls some of the borders, with which William Blake has decorated certain pages of his "Prophetic Books." The genii and flowers on the right bank of the stream are merely sketched in with the style.

Canto XXXI.—Dante now describes, "how in form of a white rose was displayed to me the holy militia, which in his own blood Christ espoused."

This image is employed throughout the last three cantos of the poem. The page intended for the illustration to the present canto has been left blank.

Canto XXXII.—This canto contains a further description of the company of the saints. The drawing has been left in a very unfinished state. The step-like degrees in the form of a rose, on which the saints are seated, are roughly indicated with the style. On the summit three diminutive figures are drawn in ink. That on the right represents the Virgin seated, in allusion to St. Bernard's behest to Dante: "Scan the circles, even to the most remote, until thou seest the queen sitting, to whom this kingdom is subject and devoted." The figure seated on the left of the Virgin can hardly be intended for Christ, as Dr. Lippmann has suggested. According to the poem, Adam, "the Father through whose rash taste the human race tastes so much bitterness," was placed on the Virgin's left. Nor can the flying angel on the right of these seated figures be intended for the Archangel Gabriel; but rather one of the company of angels who are indicated with the style, as they hover above the figure of the Virgin: "with wings outstretched, I saw more than a thousand angels keeping festival, each distinct both in effulgence and in office."

Canto XXXIII.—The page intended for the illustration to this canto has been left blank.

A work of art can only be appreciated at its proper value from the standpoint of its author; and in criticising a work of ancient art, we are apt by ignoring its author's point of view, to demand something which lay without his design, and to pass over much that is admirable in what he has given us. If we approach Botticelli's designs in the expectation of finding illustrations in our modern acceptation of the term, we shall have to confess with a recent critic that, "as illustrations, these drawings will to most people prove disappointing," since they fail "to give them to a heightened degree, feelings of the kind and quality that they have had in reading Dante." But Botticelli did not attempt to illustrate the "Divina Commedia" in the sense in which Blake and Flaxman endeavoured to illustrate it, by representing in a single incident, the pictorially significant moment in the action of a canto which might best suggest, not only that action, but also the thoughts and emotions associated with it. When Vasari, alluding to Landino's edition of 1481, says that Botticelli "commentated a part of Dante and figured the "Inferno," he touches upon the essential aim of Botticelli in making these designs. The greater number of the miniatures in the earlier manuscripts of the "Commedia" contain but a single incident, and were evidently intended to serve as a kind of pictorial rubric, or indication of the chief contents of the cantos to which they severally refer. As time went on, the tendency was to increase the number of incidents represented in each miniature; and Botticelli, in adopting and amplifying this mode of illustration, sought to give an elaborate representation of the entire action of the poem. Where the action is rapid, as in the "Inferno," a series of incidents (in some instances as many as seven or eight) are successively represented on the same sheet; where the action gives place to the metaphysical disquisitions of the actors, as in the "Paradiso," a single incident often suffices to serve the purpose of the draughtsman.

These illustrations, then, were intended to form a pictorial commentary of the entire action of the "Divina Commedia," and, viewed as such, they must appear to every student of Dante to far surpass every attempt of the kind, whether as a work of art, or as a pictorial interpretation of the poem. But before I discuss these drawings as a piece of invention and draughtsmanship, let me add what remains to be said of their iconographic character. From the point of view of the scholarship of his time, there is little in these illustrations which could have appeared inadequate or mistaken. To such men as Cristoforo Landino, or Girolamo Benivieni, they must have seemed a sufficient commentary upon the most abstruse of poems, and, as the "Anonimo Gaddiano" characterizes it, a "marvellous" work of art. Yet Botticelli might have exclaimed with Leonardo: "I am no man of letters." An anecdote preserved by Vasari, shows in what light the painter's study of Dante was regarded by his neighbours and fellow-craftsmen. "It is said," [Vasari, ed. 1550, I, 495.] so runs the story in the first edition of the "Lives," "that Sandro himself once accused in jest before the Otto, a friend of his of heresy; and he, having appeared, demanded who had accused him, and of what; and when he was told that it was Sandro, who had declared that he held the opinion of the Epicureans, that the soul dies with the body, he replied and said: 'It is true that I hold this opinion of his soul, which is brute, and he, indeed, is a heretic; since without letters he comments upon Dante, and takes his name in vain.'" In the second edition, Vasari lends a greater air of probability to [Id., ed. 1568, I, 474.] the anecdote, by stating that the accusation was made before the priest of their parish. But the story becomes intelligible, in the spirit at least, if not in the letter, when we realize what were the capacities of the average Florentine craftsman for such an undertaking. How crude, for example, not only in execution, but in conception, are the miniatures in the Egerton manuscript, No. 943, which iconographically is among the most important of the early codices. Botticelli's drawings, on the contrary, show an acquaintance with the poem, which would have been remarkable in any scholar of his day; an acquaintance so intimate that we might apply to him the phrase which Vasari uses of Michelagnolo, "il suo famigliarissimo Dante." Indeed, the instinct for scholarship which these designs reveal in one who by education was no man of letters, is perhaps as extraordinary a testimony to Botticelli's genius and intellect, as any trait to be found in his works. If the task of illustrating the "Divina Commedia," even according to the primitive scheme of the early manuscripts, was so arduous a one, that in few codices have the miniatures been brought to anything like completion; how much greater was the labour necessary to carry through a series of illustrations, on the scale on which Botticelli began these designs. Vasari, no doubt, preserves a real tradition of the "botteghe," when he states that over the study and illustration of Dante, Sandro "consumed much time, [Id., ed. 1550, I, 494.] whereby the neglect of his work was the cause of infinite disorders in his life"; and we cannot wonder that such a view of his studies should have obtained among men, who were concerned with little beyond professional skill and success.

As to the relation which the cuts in the edition of 1481, bear to the drawings executed for Lorenzo di Pierfrancesco de' Medici, one thing is beyond question; that the former are no mere engraver's version of the latter. From internal evidence I conclude that Botticelli, not long after the death of Lorenzo, Il Magnifico, resumed the scheme on which he had long been meditating, of designing a complete pictorial commentary on Dante; and that he began by redrawing and varying, on a larger and more elaborate scale, the subjects which he had already designed for the edition of 1481.

The colouring of the leaf at Berlin, and the other three in the Vatican, presents a question of no little difficulty. I have remarked that neither the pigments, nor the handling, recall the paintings on panel by Botticelli of this period; yet the forms and modelling are so nearly in his manner, that it is difficult to think that Sandro had not at least a share in their colouring. It is likely enough, from what we know of the methods of the Florentine painters of the fifteenth century, that in a work of this magnitude, and of this special character, Botticelli might have availed himself of the assistance of some professional miniaturist. The only craftsmen, so far as they are known to us by their works, who could have worked so nearly in Botticelli's manner, as the colouring of these leaves assuredly is, were Gherardo and his brother, Monte. Sumptuous and extraordinary as the finished manuscript would doubtless have been, it is impossible to regret that the illuminating of these outlines was never carried farther. In their present state, they remain the capital work of one of the greatest and most exquisite masters of line; had they been finished in colour, they must have sunk to the lower level of the miniaturist's art.

It has been conjectured that Botticelli was dissatisfied with his attempts to colour these drawings, and finally decided to leave the pen outlines without further addition. But what evidence is there of any such determination? The outlines themselves are far from having been brought to completion; over forty of these designs are in a more or less unfinished state, and two of them are not even begun. The condition in which the leaves have come down to us, does not at all answer to the idea, which obtained at the end of the fifteenth century, of a fine and costly manuscript; indeed, there can be little doubt that the whole volume was intended to be highly finished in miniature. For some reason or another, the work was interrupted and never afterwards resumed. This interruption took place, if I mistake not, about the time of Lorenzo di Pierfrancesco de' Medici's flight from Florence, in 1497. When Lorenzo returned, after the death of Savonarola, Botticelli had become the associate and avowed partisan of men who were in keenest opposition to the political intrigues of Lorenzo; and as I have already pointed out, there is no evidence, direct or indirect, that Sandro was again employed by his former patron. From the internal evidence of the drawings themselves, it is difficult to think that any of them would have been executed at a date subsequent to the execution of Savonarola. The earliest of them were probably begun not long after the death of Lorenzo, Il Magnifico, in 1492, and the latest before the close of the year 1497.

It is impossible, perhaps, to understand the essential character of Botticelli's art, its beauties and idiosyncrasies, its limitations and defects, without an exhaustive study of these illustrations to Dante; for like every great Florentine painter, Botticelli was before all things preoccupied with design; and in these illustrations is exemplified the whole range of his art as a draughtsman. Here he impresses us more vividly than elsewhere with the originality of his invention, the variety and dramatic expressiveness of his attitudes and gestures, and still more with that gift of "vision" which sharply distinguishes him from the naturalists; the power of rendering the outward and visible expressive of the unseen, so that more is intended than meets the eye. Again, these drawings show, even more clearly than the paintings, in how large a degree the secret of his art lies in his unique gift of linear expression. For Botticelli, pure line was a form of draughtsmanship as capable of suggesting relief, as of rendering contour. Indeed, it would almost seem that his mental images were conceived in terms of line, so naturally are the movements and gestures of his figures expressed by it. In short, these drawings are the production of a great improviser with the pen, and the master of a line unrivalled in its rhythm and expressiveness. With such a line, figure and background are woven into web after web of lovely and intricate imagery, the most harmonious in movement, the most vivacious in expression, and become transmuted by that peculiar sentiment which runs through all that he did; and with this inscrutable sentiment, which seems to proceed now from a sensuous conception of divine things, now from a visionary apprehension of physical loveliness, Botticelli succeeds in imparting a sense of uncommon beauty to forms which in themselves are not always beautiful.

I have shown how the visual imagery suggested by the "Divina Commedia" had become fixed by tradition in Botticelli's time, and how all the apparatus for the illustration of the poem was, in its essential elements, ready to his hand. This is especially obvious in the designs to the "Inferno"; for not only their conception and treatment, but in some instances even their composition, have been suggested by, or founded upon, earlier paintings or miniatures. These and other such traditional considerations necessary to the expository purpose of these designs, as the number of figures and incidents in each drawing, their disposition and scale, the remote "bird's-eye" point of sight from which they are seen, all tended to hinder Botticelli's invention, and restrict him to the immediate exigences of his task. Again, of all the canzoni, the "Inferno" lends itself the least to illustration: indeed, we may doubt whether even Michelagnolo could have portrayed the punishments of the Giudecca, with the dignity and effect with which Dante has described them. Moreover, for us, the punishments of Hell when no longer transfigured by Dante's art, have lost their actuality, and have become merely gruesome and revolting; just as the mediaeval devil, which figures so largely in Botticelli's designs, has lost its terror, and has become merely grotesque.

Apart from the qualities of his draughtsmanship, we must confess that in these illustrations to the "Inferno," Botticelli did not always succeed beyond his precursors. His Satan, for instance, is a mere repetition of the traditional image of the fiend; and Nardo Orcagna has portrayed the region of the flaming tombs with far greater impressiveness, than Botticelli has done in his design to Canto X. On the other hand, his figure of the Minotaur plunging in blind fury is admirable in character and energy; his Geryon a gorgeous monster, "vermillion-spotted, golden, green and blue." And yet, only here and there, does the dry, expository matter of these drawings become completely fused and transmuted by his imagination; as in the illustration to Canto XIII, where, by a stroke of real invention, Botticelli represents the Wood of the Self-Murderers of a horrid and unearthly growth, and weaves into a web of exquisitely nervous and intricate line, the figures of the naked souls as they flee in terror from the hell-hounds, through the thorny thicket. Again, in some of the later drawings, the exegetical purpose of the artist is too little tempered by invention; and Botticelli seems to have been conscious that the dominant note of these cantos was pitched beyond the compass of his own art.

As we turn over the illustrations to the "Purgatorio," it soon becomes evident that Botticelli is here working with greater effect, and that his imagination is less fettered by tradition, than in the illustrations to the

"Inferno." The reason of this is to be found in the fact that not only do the early codices contain far fewer designs for the "Purgatorio" than for the "Inferno," but the theme of Purgatory was a much less popular one with the early painters, than the theme of Hell: while of all the canzoni, the "Purgatorio" offers the greatest field for the illustrator. Again, in the majority of these designs, the long, frieze-like arrangement of the figures, suggested by the successive terraces of the mount, lends itself far more readily to effective composition, than the scattered, chart-like disposition of the figures, which we repeatedly find in the illustrations to the "Inferno." And so among "the milder shades of Purgatory," the imagination of Botticelli moves more easily than in the circles of Hell; and almost every one of these sheets is either admirable as a whole, or contains some truly admirable form or motive: things noble in conception, as the figure of the angel seated before the gate of Purgatory, in the drawing to Canto IX; or sumptuous and prodigal of invention, as the story of Trajan and the widow, in that to Canto X; or expressive of a sudden and overwhelming emotion, as the grand and agitated figure of Dante in the design to Canto XIII. As an instance of the felicity with which Botticelli is able to weave his inventions into a lovely tissue of swift, sensitive line, may be especially cited the design to Canto XXVI, in which the articulate movement of the figures among the rush and swirl of the flames, is rendered with the utmost rhythm, vivacity and freedom of hand. Regarded merely as illustration, the drawings for the last six cantos are, perhaps, the finest of the whole series. The first of these, representing the meeting of the poets with Matilda in the wood of the Earthly Paradise, is redolent of those forest glades and flowery places in which Fra Filippo delighted; and its tender, pastoral mood serves to emphasize the decorative richness and hieractic beauty of the four designs, illustrating the heavenly pageant, which follow it. In its outward presentment, the pageant recalls, as I have said, the "Trionfi" of the cassone-painters; but unlike the panels of the cassone-painters, the allegorical character of its theme is transfigured by that ray of apocalyptic vision, which asserts itself more and more in the last works of Botticelli.

This exaltation of mood runs through all the designs to the "Paradiso." Exquisite as is the opening drawing of the series, its inscrutable sentiment of spiritual aspiration, which for us forms so large a part of its pictorial content, was not entirely intentional on the part of the artist; I mean, that much which now appeals to us in this design, is of the nature of an accidental quality, beautiful, it is true, but beautiful in the sense of some accidental quality of colour imparted by time. It is, however, in the score or so of designs which follows it, that Botticelli attains to the finest and most serious reaches of his art. In these, he attempts to figure the whole of the subtle matter of the "Paradiso" by a series of groups of Beatrice and Dante, as they discourse on their upward journey through the spheres of Heaven. In the bulk of these drawings, as we have seen, the accessory portions of the design were evidently intended to have been of a purely symbolical character, and only in a few instances are other figures introduced, than those of the poet and his guide. Thus, the mere apparatus of the illustrator was reduced to a minimum, and the artist forced to rely entirely upon the attitudes and gestures of his figures to tell his story. With what singular success Botticelli has accomplished this difficult task, is shown in the beauty, variety and expressiveness, of the postures and

THE VIRGIN AND CHILD, WITH THREE ANGELS *Ambrosiana, Milan*

movements of these figures, in the endless invention and felicitous management of their draperies, and in the diversity of vivid and lofty emotions which animate them. Such things are among the most difficult achievements of art, and only the greatest masters succeed in them to admiration. Again, the beauty with which Botticelli has drawn the angelic hierarchies, only makes us regret the more, that the last illustrations to the "Paradiso," representing the mystical rose of God and his saints, were never carried out. The small beginnings of one of them, which has come down to us, shows from its scale, that in elaborate and sumptuous design, it was to have surpassed the rest.

Such is the character of this unique series of illustrations to Dante; a series equally singular, whether considered as a work of art, or as a pictorial commentary on the "Divina Commedia." Certainly, no other body of early designs has come down to us, which at all approaches these drawings in the elaboration and completeness with which the entire scene and action of the poem is set forth and figured. With the help of these drawings, we are enabled to realize more nearly than by any other means, the actual images which arose in Dante's mind as he was writing; and so correct that modernity of sentiment and interpretation which is apt to distort our perception of a poem, whose imagery is more vividly and deliberately visualized, than that of any other piece of literature, ancient or modern. But this, after all, is but another way of remarking how much the art of Botticelli had in common with the art of the Giottesque painters.

I now propose to discuss, on account of their relation to these illustrations to Dante, certain paintings on panel, which, upon internal evidence, appear to have been executed during the interval between the death of Lorenzo, Il Magnifico, in 1492, and the execution of Savonarola, in 1498. Of these, the earliest in manner is the little "tondo" of the Virgin and Child with three angels, in the gallery of the Ambrosiana, at Milan, No. 72. The one early notice, which might possibly refer to this painting, is the passage in the second edition of the "Lives," in which Vasari says: "Of great beauty, also, is a small 'tondo' by his hand, which is to be seen in the chamber of the Prior of the Angeli, at Florence, of little figures, but full of grace, and executed with admirable care and thought." No other notice of the "tondo" here recorded, has come down to us. The Camaldoline monastery of Santa Maria degli Angioli, in the Via degli Alfani, at Florence, was suppressed in 1808; and the works of art which it contained, have long since been dispersed.

Vasari, ed. 1568, I, 474.

The picture in the Ambrosiana is painted on a panel which measures $25\frac{3}{4}$ inches in diameter; and is in an admirable state of preservation. The scene in which the action of the picture is laid, was evidently suggested by one of those embanked gardens of the many villas which look out over the Arno, from the hillsides around Florence. On the right of the picture, under the curtains of a sumptuous pavilion, the Virgin kneels before the Child, who is upheld by an angel, on the left. As he attempts, with baby steps, to approach his mother, she extends her right hand to him, and with her left presses her breast, from which milk prills forth towards him, as from one of those little Roman bronzes of naked Venus. On the right and left of the picture, behind this central group, are two other figures of angels, who turn away from the Virgin as they draw apart the curtains of the pavilion, which fall upon the dwarf-wall and stone seat enclosing the garden. On the seat lies the Virgin's Book of Hours; and in the distance, seen through the curtains of the pavilion, beyond the dwarf-wall, is a landscape, evidently suggested by the reaches of the Arno. Below, in the foreground, is a vase of lilies. This exquisite little "tondo" is touched in with that extraordinary freedom of hand which distinguishes all the genuine works of the master at this period. The forms of the angels, and particularly the folds of their fluttering draperies, closely recall not a few figures in the illustrations to Dante. In colour, it is among the loveliest of Botticelli's smaller paintings. The mantle which the Virgin wears over her purple dress, is of that clear, smalt azure which is peculiarly characteristic of the master. The angel who supports the Child, is clad in pearly grape-gray skirts over an under-dress of pale green, the angel on the left of the composition, in a pale saffron dress with pale red sleeves, and the angel on the opposite side, in a white dress with blue sleeves. The pavilion is crowned with a wreath of foliage, and the curtains are of purple bordered with pearls and gold. The use which Botticelli here makes of the Giottesque motive of the angels drawing back the curtains of the pavilion, is as original as it is beautiful; and the almost symmetrical disposition of the simple elements of this composition lends to it great dignity and decorative effect. Less sensuous in feeling than the "tondo" of the "Magnificat," this little picture already anticipates that hieratic sense of the beauty of earthly things, tempered by a serener and more spiritual mood, which is characteristic of the last works of Botticelli. Indeed, the clear, tranquil light which pervades the landscape in this painting, is the counterpart of the seraphic gaiety of the angels who attend the holy Child and his mother.

Vasari, ed. 1550, I, 496.

Vasari alone of all the early commentators alludes to the famous painting by Botticelli of the "Calumny of Apelles." "Of nearly the same dimensions," he writes in the first edition of the "Lives," "as [the 'Adoration of the Magi,' formerly in the church of Santa Maria Novella,] is to be seen to-day, by his hand, in the possession of Fabio Segni, a painting on panel of the 'Calumny of Apelles,' wherein Sandro has divinely imitated the conceit of that ancient painter; and he made a gift of it to Antonio Segni, his very good friend. And this panel is so beautiful, that both on account of the invention of Apelles, and the painting of Sandro, it has been honoured by this epigram:

"Indicio quemquam ne falso lædere tentent
Terrarum Reges, parua Tabella monet.
Huic similem Aegypti Regi donauit Apelles:
Rex fuit, & dignus munere, munus eo."

Id., ed. 1568, I, 475.

In the second edition, Vasari adds that this epigram, from the pen of Messer Fabio, had been inscribed by him below the picture. At an early period, (perhaps already in the seventeenth century,) the picture passed into the Grand Ducal Collection, and is still preserved in the gallery of the Uffizi, No. 1,182.

S. Salvini, Fasti dell' Accademia Fior., pp. 92-98.

This Antonio Segni was of the family of the Segna Guidi, of the Gonfalone Lion Nero, in the quarter of Santa Croce; a family who bore no relationship to that from which Bernardo Segni, the historian, was descended. Between 1447 and 1492, various members of the Segna Guidi enjoyed the office of the Priorate on seven different occasions, and among them, in 1460, Neri d' Antonio, the father of Botticelli's patron. It appears from a "Denunzia" returned in January or February, 1480-1, that this

THE CALUMNY OF APELLES *Uffizi Gallery, Florence*

Antonio (his father being dead) was then living with his mother, Monna Nanna, in a house in the parish of San Romeo, or Remigio as it is now called, at Florence. From indications afforded by other "Denunzie," it would appear that this house was situated between the present Via de' Neri and the Piazza d'Arno. In addition to this property, they also possessed a small farmstead in the parish and "piviere" of San Giusto. Antonio states that he is twenty-one years of age, and adds: "I do not keep a shop, but I repair at times to the bank of the Bartolini." The gross assessment of his property is returned at some 460 florins. With this modest patrimony, Antonio would seem to have afterwards attained to wealth. According to Vasari, he was not only the friend and patron of Botticelli, but also of Leonardo da Vinci: "ad Antonio Segni, suo amicissimo," says Vasari in his life of the latter master, "fece in su un foglio un Nettuno." The drawing of Neptune, in the library at Windsor, was probably the study for the finished design which he made for Antonio; and if this is so, it must have been executed after Leonardo's return to Florence in 1500. What we are able to learn, then, of the age and circumstances of Antonio Segni, lends colour to my conjecture, based on the internal evidence of the picture, that the "Calumny of Apelles" was painted c. 1494. Antonio married Francesca, the daughter of Bartolo Corsi, by whom, in 1502, he had Fabio, the writer of the Latin epigrams which Vasari inserted into the first edition of the "Lives." Of this Fabio, who was a great lover of arts and letters, and especially skilled in the composition of Latin poetry, there is an account in the "Fasti Consolari dell' Accademia Fiorentina," of Salvino Salvini.

App. II, Doc. XXXIX, fol. 17, recto.

Vasari, ed. Sansoni, IV, 25.

It has been commonly assumed that Botticelli derived the suggestion of his painting from the treatise "De Pictura," of Leon Battista Alberti, who quotes in it, almost word for word, the description which Lucian gives in his tractate "De Calumnia," of the picture painted by Apelles for Ptolemy Philopater, king of Egypt; yet indications are not wanting to show that Botticelli was acquainted with the original of Lucian, or at least with a translation of it. The works of Lucian had been brought to Italy early in the fifteenth century, by Aurispa and Filelfo; and at Florence they were first printed in 1496. But before turning to Lucian, let me quote the passage in the original Latin of the "De Pictura," in which Alberti alludes to the painting of Apelles. It occurs in the third book, where he speaks of the various arts of which painters should have some knowledge: "Proxime no*n* ab re erit, si Poetis & Rhetorib*us* delectabu*ntur*. Nam hj q*ui*dem multa cu*m* pictor*e* habent ornamen*t*a co*m*munja, neq*ue* par*um* illj q*ui*dem multar*um* rer*um* notitja copiosi literatj ad historiæ compositjone*m* pulchre co*n*struenda*m* iuuabu*nt*, que o*mn*is laus præsertjm i*n* inue*nt*jone co*n*sistit. Atq*ue* ea q*ui*dem ha*n*c habent ujm, ut etia*m* sola inue*nt*jo sine pictura delectet. Laudat*ur* jlla calumniæ descriptjo, qua*m* ab apelle, picta*m* refert lucjanus. Eam q*ui*dem enarrar*e* mjnime ab instituto alienu*m* e*ss*e ce*n*seo, q*u*o pictores admonea*ntur* eiusmodj inue*nt*ionib*us* fabricandis aduigilar*e* oporter*e*. Erat aut*em* uir unus cuj aures inge*nt*es extaba*nt*, quem circa duæ a*d*staba*nt* mulieres inscitja & suspitjo: parte alia ipsa calu*m*nia a*d*ductat cuj forma mulierculæ speciosæ, s*ed* quæ ipso uultu nimis callere astu uidebatur; manu sinistra face*m* accensa*m* [tenens], altera uero manu p*er* capillos tradens adolescentem q*ui* manus ad celum tendit: duxq*ue* huius e*st* uir q*ui*da*m* pallore obsitus deformis trucj aspectu que*m* merito co*m*pares ijs, quos in acie longus labor co*n*fecerit. Hunc e*ss*e

l.c., MS. Riccardiano, No. 767, fol. 85, recto.

L L

ljuore*m* merito dixer*e*; su*n*t & alia duæ calu*m*niæ comites mulieres ornamenta dominæ co*m*ponentes, jnsidiæ & fraus: post has pulla & sordidjssima ueste op*er*ta sese dilania*n*s, adest penitentja: p*ro*xime seque*n*te pudica & uerecu*n*da ueritate. Quæ plane histor*ia*, et si du*m* recitat*ur* a*ni*m*o*s tenet, q*uan*tu*m* censes eam gr*ati*æ et amœnitatis ex ipsa pictura industria pictoris exhibuisse?"

Doubtless, to this allusion of Alberti's were due the many attempts which were made in Italy, during the latter half of the fifteenth, and the earlier part of the sixteenth century, to restore from Lucian's description, the lost composition of Apelles. In the inventory of the goods of Lorenzo, Il Magnifico, taken at the time of his death in 1492, are enumerated four stained cloths, one of which was painted "colla storia della Calumnia." This notice suffices to show that Botticelli was not the first painter of the fifteenth century to attempt the reconstruction of Apelles' painting. A miniature in one of the Hamilton manuscripts, No. 416, now at Berlin, and a famous drawing by Mantegna, in the British Museum, are among the earlier attempts of the kind. Mantegna's design was engraved by Girolamo Mocetto, and the British Museum possesses a sketch of it by Rembrandt. Somewhat later in date are the paintings by Francia Bigio in the Pitti Gallery, No. 427, and by some unknown hand, in the gallery at Nimes; and the drawing attributed to Raphael in the Louvre, No. 1616. Of these, and yet later attempts to restore the composition of Apelles, a full account will be found in Richard Förster's study, "Die Verleumdung des Apelles in der Renaissance," which is printed in the Prussian "Jahrbuch." But let us now turn to our author.

App. II, Doc. XXIX, fol. 56, recto.

l.c., Vol. VIII, p. 29.

"Apelles, the Ephesian," says Lucian, "was unjustly accused of bearing a part in the conspiracy which Theodotus had formed against Ptolemy [Philopater, king of Egypt], at Tyre, though he had never been at Tyre, or knew anything of Theodotus, any more than he was a commander under Ptolemy, and had the care of Phoenicia entrusted to him. One Antiphilus, a rival artist, who envied him, both for the excellency of his painting, and the esteem in which he was held by the king, had, it seems, informed Ptolemy that he was privy to the transaction, that a person had seen him at supper with Theodotus at Phoenice, and in close conference with him during the whole entertainment, and that, in short, the defection of Tyre, and the taking of Pelusium, were both owing to the counsel and assistance of Apelles. Ptolemy, a man in other respects not overwise, and nursed up from his infancy by that adulation which is generally bestowed on tyrants, was so worked upon by this improbable and absurd calumny, that, never considering with himself that the accuser was one of his rivals, or how impossible it was for a poor painter to support such a conspiracy, especially one whom he had so highly favoured and preferred to all of his profession, and without even so much as enquiring whether Apelles had ever been at Tyre, grew so exasperated, as to fill the whole palace with complaints of his ingratitude, calling him a traitor and conspirator; insomuch that if one of those who were taken up at the same time, struck with compassion for Apelles, and detesting the impudent falsehood of Antiphilus, had not declared that he had no concern in it, he would, probably, have lost his head, and paid himself the price of Tyrian perjury and falsehood. Ptolemy is said so severely to have repented of his credulity, as to make Apelles a present of a hundred talents, and to have given Antiphilus to him as a slave. Apelles, who long bore in mind the danger he had been

Lucian, trans. by T. Francklin, II, 364.

in, revenged the calumny against him by a picture which I shall here describe to you.

"On the right-hand side sits a man with ears almost as large as Midas's, stretching forth his hand towards the figure of Calumny, who appears at a distance coming up to him; he is attended by two women, who, I imagine, represent Ignorance and Suspicion. From the other side approaches Calumny, in the form of a woman, to the last degree beautiful, but seeming warm and inflamed, as full of anger and resentment, bearing a lighted torch in her left hand, and with her right, dragging by the hair of his head, a young man, who lifts up his eyes to heaven, as calling the gods to witness his innocence. Before her stands a pale, ugly figure, with sharp eyes, and emaciated, like a man worn down by disease, which we easily perceive is meant for Envy; and behind are two women, who seem to be employed in dressing, adorning and assisting her; one of whom, as my interpreter informed me, was Treachery, and the other Deceit: at some distance, in the back part of the picture, stood a woman, in a mourning habit, all torn and ragged, which, we were told, represented Penitence; as she turned her eyes back, she blushed and wept at the sight of Truth, who was approaching towards her. In this manner did Apelles express the danger he had escaped from."

Unlike Mantegna, Botticelli represents, on the right of the composition, the judge, or prince, "with ears almost as large as Midas's, stretching out his hand towards the figure of Calumny," in accordance with Lucian's description. His allusions to Midas and the gesture of the prince have both been omitted by Alberti. Ignorance and Suspicion are represented, with Dantesque literalness, seizing the prince by his ass's ears, as they whisper their delusions and misgivings to him. In designing the group of figures which approach the throne, Botticelli, however, would seem to have had in mind Alberti's description. Calumny, the central figure of the group, is represented as a woman most beautiful to look upon, but in countenance callous beyond measure through cunning; not as Lucian describes her, full of anger and resentment. She holds a lighted torch in her left hand; and with the right, drags after her by the hair, a young man almost naked, who raises his clasped hands towards heaven. Envy, a man pale, and loathsome, as if worn by disease, is "the guide of Calumny," and leads her by the wrist towards the throne of the prince; and attendant upon Calumny, tricking her hair and adorning her with flowers, come Treachery and Deceit. Lastly, on the left of the composition, clad in sable raiment, squalid and torn, stands Remorse, sorrowfully regarding the naked Truth who, with her hand upraised to heaven, testifies to the innocence of the victim.

In the arrangement of these figures, Botticelli recurs to a device which he has elsewhere employed in the fresco of "Lorenzo Tornabuoni and the Liberal Arts," now in the Louvre, No. 1298, and in the little panel of the "Last Communion of St. Jerome," in the possession of the Marchese Farinola, at Florence. The figures of the prince with Ignorance and Suspicion, and those of Calumny, Treachery and Deceit, are arranged in two triple groups, which are counterposed to one another; but their disposition is less formal than in the panel at Florence. The action of the figures is marked by that feverish energy of movement, which is peculiarly characteristic of the last period of Botticelli's art, and which here becomes in the highest degree expressive of the passions which animate them. That malady of the soul which was presently to overtake the painter, is already foreshadowed.

The scene of this allegory is laid in a court, or hall, enclosed by arcades of an elaborate architecture, decorated with an almost Gothic profusion of ornament. On the far side, parallel to the picture-plane, a series of three arches open on to a great expanse of still water and serene sky: and on the right, behind the tribune of the prince, two other arches are shown in perspective. The coupled piers of these arcades are richly ornamented with niches containing statues; and the friezes and the double bases of the piers, as well as the sunk panels on the soffits of the arches and on the pace of the tribune, are sculptured with figures in relief. The subjects of these reliefs have been taken indifferently from sacred and profane story, in a way that recalls the choice of subjects on the pavement described in Canto XII of the "Purgatorio."

In the niche of the pier immediately behind the seated figure of the prince, is a statue of Judith with a sword in her right hand, and the head of Holofernes at her feet. In the frieze above this figure, Judith is again represented standing at the entrance of Holofernes' tent, while her serving-maid places the head in the "bag of meat": and in the relief below the niche, the two women are seen returning to Bethulia; a theme which forms the subject of Sandro's early painting in the Uffizi. The niche of the pier in the centre of the picture is ornamented with a figure of St. George, standing astride in an attitude which recalls the statue by Donatello, originally executed for one of the niches of Or San Michele; and still more the fresco of Pippo Spano by Andrea da Castagno, now in the Museum of Sant' Appollonia at Florence. In the central panel of the soffit of the arch, on the left of this pier, is a relief of St. George on horseback, slaying the dragon. The niche on the face of the next pier, to the left, contains a statue of David with the head of Goliath at his feet, which is perhaps reminiscent of the marble David by Donatello, now in the Bargello at Florence. In the relief which is partially seen below the niche, David is standing astride the headless body of the Goliath. Again, the statue in the niche on the right, next to that containing the statue of Judith, represents a man dressed in Florentine habit, with "mazzocchio" and "lucco," and evidently intended for some worthy famous in Tuscan story. The figure holding a sword, on the farther pier of the arch to the left, is perhaps intended for St. Paul; but the rest of these statues lack any distinguishing symbol by which they might be identified: some of them are habited as prophets, others armed as warriors.

As for the other reliefs, the subjects of many of them have been directly taken from antique mythology. The upper panel of the base immediately to the left of the figure of "Truth," represents Apollo and Daphne, and shows how the god "catched at love, and filled his arms with bays." That immediately to the left of this last, portrays Hercules hurling Lichas, whom he has seized by the feet, into the sea. The frieze above these two stories, probably represents Hercules capturing the horses of Diomedes; and that relief above the statue of David, a baby-satyr leading a man towards a woman, who lies on the ground and leans with her right elbow on a cushion; while another little satyr, who stands behind her, lifts up her mantle. The attitude of the woman recalls the figure of the goddess in the painting of "Mars and Venus," in the National Gallery, and, perhaps, the same theme is the subject of this frieze. One of the lower reliefs on the base to the right of the figure of "Remorse," is carved with a "Judgment of Paris"; the Trojan shepherd is seated on the right, and the three goddesses stand before him on the left. In the panel at the spring of the central arch on the left, Mutius Scaevola is seen in the act of stabbing the secretary of Porsenna, at the door of his tent; and in the relief next to this, the Roman knight holds his hand in the flame of the altar, before the king, who is represented seated, in the third panel on the right. The central panel on the soffit of the arch to the right, may, perhaps, represent the "Fall of the Titans"; and the relief on the frieze at the angle of the hall, to the right, the story of Prometheus. The little panel on the pace of the throne, to the right, is carved with a figure of Pallas leaning on a tilting lance, and holding the head of Medusa in her left hand; a motive to which I have already alluded in my account of the lost painting of Pallas, which was executed for the Medici: the panel on the left of this, may possibly represent the story of Jupiter and Antiope.

Although the themes of these reliefs have been taken from antique mythology, the designs in which Botticelli has set them forth, do not appear to have been suggested by any remains of antique art. On the other hand, the motives of some of the remaining reliefs which are of a purely decorative character, were evidently taken from such a source. The two recumbent river gods holding cornucopiae, and resting on vases which discharge water, on the soffit of the arch to the right, and the lion ridden by a cupid on the frieze above the statue of St. George, are of this kind. Very Roman in character, again, is the relief on the soffit of the arch to the right, representing a pyramid surmounted by a statue of a god, which two persons below appear to be venerating; and so are the figures of a maenad with a timbrel, on the base below the St. George, and a cupid with a mask on one of the bases to the left. A delightful piece of invention is the frieze above the figure of the prince: it represents a centaur ridden by a cupid, and led by a woman who has seized him by the hair of the head; while another cupid, on the right, breaks his bow. The central motive of this composition recalls at once the famous statue of the centaur ridden by a cupid in the Louvre. Of a not less genial fancy is the relief of a centaur and his family, on the pace of the throne. Here, however, Botticelli attempts to reconstruct a painting by Zeuxis, which Lucian has described in one of his tractates. Except in one or two minor particulars, he scrupulously follows his author, with whom he was evidently familiar; but here is Lucian's account of the picture: "The female centaur is lying down on a smooth turf; that part which represents a mare is stretched on the ground, with the hind feet extended backwards; the fore feet not reaching out as if she laid on her side, but one of them as kneeling, with the hoof bent under, the other raised up and trampling on the grass, like a horse prepared to leap: she holds one of the young ones in her arms, and suckles it like a child at her woman's breast; and the other at her dugs like a colt. In the upper part of the picture is seen a male centaur, as watching from a place of observation, supposed to be the father; he is behind, and is seen only to the horse part of the figure, and appears smiling, showing a lion's cub, which he lifts up as if to frighten the young ones in sport." In Botticelli's relief, the male centaur is entirely seen, approaching the female; the young ones are represented as satyrs, and a third young satyr, playing with an animal, is introduced into the lower right-hand corner of the composition. Another relief which likewise owes its suggestion to a literary

Lucian, Zeuxis, § 3.

source, is the story of Trajan and the Widow, sculptured on the base to the extreme left of the panel. Botticelli has elsewhere handled this theme with extraordinary beauty and elaboration, in the illustration to Canto XII of the "Purgatorio." Here the composition consists only of three figures: the emperor on horseback, the widow and the dead body of her son who lies at her feet. Again, in the three panels at the spring of the arch on the left, Botticelli reverts to another theme which he has elsewhere handled: namely, Boccaccio's story of Nastagio degli Onesti, which formed the subject of the panels executed for the marriage of Giannozzo Pucci with Lucrezia Bini, in 1483. In the panel on the left, Messer Guido degli Anastagi is represented on horseback, followed by his hounds, as he pursues the naked lady, who is seen in the central panel, flying from him in terror. Beside the lady stands Nastagio, who has armed himself with the branch of a tree, in order to defend her. And in the panel on the right, Messer Guido, who has dismounted from his horse, is represented in the act of cutting the heart out of the lady, who lies prone before him.

All these statues and reliefs are coloured in imitation of bronze, gilt and set in the warm, gray stone-work of the arcades. They are kept, however, very blonde in tone, and the lights are heightened with gold. In thus representing them, Botticelli had in mind a good tradition of Florentine art: for all the great architectural bronzes of Florence, such as the gates of the Baptistery, were originally gilt in imitation of the antique. Against this blonde, architectural background, with its breaks of yet blonder sky and water, the colouring of the figures occurs with a jewel-like richness and intensity. The central figure of Calumny is clad in a white dress with grape-purple sleeves, and an outer robe of smalt azure, extremely clear and brilliant. The figure of Deceit, partially seen behind her, is dressed in a leaf-green; and that of Treachery on the left, who adorns her with red roses, wears a purple dress and saffron robe. These colours are contrasted with the brown and black of the torn raiment of Envy, and the gray and black of the figure of Remorse. The prince wears a dress of a golden leaf-green of a peculiar intensity, under a robe of deep purple of the colour of "spilt wine"; and the figures either side of him are habited in blue and purple, and in green and grape-purple. The lights of these green draperies are elaborately hatched with gold. For sheer beauty and translucent clarity of pigment, this painting is unsurpassed in the whole course of Florentine Art. The light lies in these colours, as in a gem; and some ray of actual sunshine seems to linger in the golden atmosphere in which the scene is bathed.

That tendency which I have elsewhere remarked in Botticelli, to render his figures more and more vivacious in movement and expressive in action, is carried to its height in this painting; and both action and movement here become agitated and even feverish. The restless search after expression which produced this trait, has everywhere left its mark on the picture. It is to be seen in the nervous and accentuated drawing of the figures, especially in the joints and extremities; as well as in those strange contrasts of mood and colour, which constantly occur in Botticelli's work, but which here seem to have been used with definite intention. The contrast of the unruly and insistent rout which throng this sumptuous hall, with the serene calm of the cloudless sky and untroubled waters which lie beyond, and of the stormy passions which impel the actors in this scene, with the clear sunlight in which it is bathed, are employed here with such strange and

ST. AUGUSTINE IN HIS CELL *Uffizi Gallery, Florence*

inscrutable effect, that they appear to be an integral part of the painter's conception of the allegory; as though he intended to symbolize by them something of the contradictions of "this unintelligible world." Indeed, so far is the search after expression carried in this painting, that the figurative and generalized character which is proper to an allegory, is almost lost in the individuality with which its figures, and the passions which actuate them, are represented.

The manner in which Vasari speaks of this masterpiece, associating it with the altar-piece once in the church of Santa Maria Novella, and adding that he thought it "bella quanto possa essere," shows in what estimation he held it. Nor has his judgment been reversed by modern criticism. Although the picture exhibits all the mannerisms of the last period of Botticelli's art, in power of invention and execution, the painter's hand here has lost nothing of its cunning. Especially characteristic of the period at which it was painted, are the accentuated drawing of the figure, the agitated forms of the draperies which bear the closest resemblance to many of the figures in the illustrations to Dante, the peculiar leaf-green and smalt azure, the fastidious technique and the hatching of the lights with gold. From these and other such indications, I conclude that the "Calumny of Apelles" was painted c. 1494. Except for a few local retouches on the breast of the figure of Truth and elsewhere, the painting is in an excellent state of preservation: indeed, the fine condition of the gold-hatching, which is especially liable to suffer at the hands of the restorer, is the best evidence of its condition.

Vasari, ed. 1568, II, 475.

Of somewhat later date than the "Calumny of Apelles," is the little painting in the Uffizi, No. 1179, of "St. Augustine in his Cell," which recalls both in conception and manner, the story of the same saint in the "gradino" of the altar-piece once in the church of San Marco, and now in the Academy of Florence, No. 47. Vasari alludes to this little panel in his life of Fra Filippo Lippi, as a work by that master: "In the possession of Bernardo Vecchietti, a Florentine gentleman, and a greater vertuoso and more worthy a man than I know how to say, is a little picture by the hand of the same master of a Saint Augustine at his studies, which is most beautiful." In the eighteenth century, the painting had passed into the possession of Ignatius Hugford, an Englishman, who acquired some reputation at Florence, in his day, as a painter; and by him it was lent to an exhibition of ancient works of art, which were brought together in the second cloister of the Annunziata, by the Florentine Academicians of Design, in 1767. It is described in the catalogue of the exhibition as "un S. Agostino che scrive, di Fra Filippo Lippi." After the death of Ignatius Hugford, the picture was acquired in 1779 for the Gallery of the Uffizi, where it continued to bear the name of the Fra Filippo, till Morelli first drew attention to its true authorship, in 1877.

Id., ed. Sansoni, II, 625.

"Il Trionfo delle Bell'Arti renduto gloriosissimo," etc., p. 8.

I. Lermolieff, Die Galerie Borghese, ed. 1890, p. 44.

I suspect, however, that Vasari's attribution of this panel to Fra Filippo was merely a slip of the pen; and that it still bore the name of Botticelli, when that writer saw it in the possession of Bernardo Vecchietti, who was not only an ardent collector and the patron of John of Bologna in his youth, but a fine connoisseur. Raffaello Borghini, in his "Riposo," has left a long account of the works of art which Bernardo had brought together in his villa, on the hills near Vacciano, without the Porta San Niccolò. The title of his book was suggested to Borghini by the name of this villa, and there, among such notable things as fragments of the "Cartoon of Pisa," which l.c., ed. 1584, p. 13. have since disappeared, he mentions "del Botticello vn bellissimo quadro di pittura"; but of a picture by Fra Filippo, he says nothing.

This little painting is executed on a panel which measures 15 inches in height, and 10⅝ inches in width. It represents St. Augustine seated at a table in a vaulted cell, in the act of writing in a book, which he raises somewhat with his left hand. He is vested in a purple cope bordered with blue, which he wears over the black habit of an Augustine canon. On the table before him are an inkstand and another open book, and at his feet some fragments of papers lie scattered on the floor. Across the arch opening into the cell, at the level of the impost mouldings, is a rod supporting a curtain, which has been partly drawn and fastened to the pier on the left. Behind the head of the saint, in the lunette formed by the semicircular vault of the cell, is a relief of the Virgin and Child within a wreath of foliage; and in the spandrels above the arch of the cell, are two heads in relief, also set in garlands, and evidently reminiscent of antique ornament. In the lateral wall of the cell on the right is a doorway, and on the left a recess filled with books.

The story of St. Augustine in the "predella" of the altar-piece of San Marco, possesses a largeness of design and a certain elevation and nobility of sentiment, which are wanting in the little panel in the Uffizi. Yet, if the latter is in comparison somewhat dryly conceived, it is distinguished by a beauty of workmanship which exhibits Botticelli's skill as a craftsman at its height. The vestments and aureole of the saint are hatched in the lights with gold, as elaborately as some miniature by Gherardo; and the golden purple and clear smalt blue of the saint's cope, seen in contrast with the black habit lit with gold, the warm leaf-green curtain lined with pale red, the clear blue-gray of the architecture and the bluer gray of the panels of the vault, possess a gem-like depth and clarity of colour. Indeed, this beauty of pigment coupled with the beauty of the workmanship, give to this little painting something of the exquisite and sumptuous quality of a piece of fine jeweller's work. The head and hands of the saint are drawn with that nervousness, which already distinguishes the "Calumny of Apelles"; but the folds of the draperies are designed in a smaller and more broken manner, and betray a more tremulous character, than the draperies in that picture.

The same hesitative and tremulous drawing of the draperies, and the same fastidious workmanship, are to be found in a little picture, or perhaps fragment of a picture, which has passed within the last few years into the collection of Hernn Richard von Kaufmann at Berlin, who acquired it at London, from the late Mr. Buttery, the well-known restorer. This little panel, which measures 13¾ inches in height, and 7½ inches in width, represents Judith coming forth from the tent of Holofernes, with the head of the captain of the Assyrians in her left hand, and a sword in her right. She is seen at full length, in three-quarter face to the left, as she turns to look at the head, which she holds up before her. She is clad in a dress of grape-gray, laced over a skirt of clear purple, the lights of which are elaborately hatched with gold. Over all, falling about her shoulders, she wears a yellow robe, which is seen against the red curtains of the tent behind her. Both the character of the folds, and the elaborate fashion in which the lights of the draperies are hatched with gold, closely recall the little panel of "St. Augustine" in the Uffizi. Only in this panel, the line is more tremulous and mannered, and the nervousness of the forms betrays

JUDITH WITH THE HEAD OF HOLOFERNES
Collection of Professor Richard von Kaufmann, Berlin

that sense of effort which comes of a consciousness of failing power. These traits, and the greater frequency of such faults of drawing, as the disproportion between the head of Holofernes and that of the Judith, point to this fragment having been executed subsequently to the panel of "St. Augustine in his cell."

To this period, I would attribute a little picture of the Virgin and Child with St. John, in the collection of Mr. J. P. Heseltine, of London. It was formerly in the collection of Mr. Graham Charles Somerwell; and at the sale of his pictures, at Messrs. Christie's, on 23rd April, 1887, Lot 149, it was bought by Mr. Heseltine for £504, and was afterwards shown by him, in 1894, at the 25th Exhibition of Old Masters at Burlington House, No. 169. It is painted on a panel, which measures 18 inches in height, and 14½ inches in breadth. It represents the Virgin on the right of the picture, seated on a parapet which runs across the foreground. She holds the Child with both hands, on her left knee, and bends forward a little towards the young St. John, who is seen on the left of the picture, in profile, as he kneels with clasped hands before the holy Child. In the background, above the parapet, on the left, is seen a distant landscape, with rocks and trees in the middle distance, and a winding river beyond. This picture is of no little value in affording us an insight into the methods of Botticelli's workshop. The general character and composition of the figures of the Virgin and Child are thoroughly Botticellesque; and the Virgin's head, which is more carefully worked than the rest of the picture, is of the type of the Virgin in the "tondo" of the Ambrosiana. But the figure of the Child, and still more that of the Baptist, are too feeble in drawing and modelling to be ascribed to Botticelli himself. Moreover, the colouring of the panel, though deep and golden in tone, lacks the translucent quality of the master's own painting, and the landscape is of another character than his. On looking, however, more carefully into the picture, we see that Botticelli, with that inimitable freedom and sureness of hand which characterizes his slightest sketch, has touched in the frieze of nudes and horses, with which the parapet is decorated. On the right of the figure of St. John, a horse ridden by a naked man brandishing a sword is represented leaping over another nude figure; and on the left of the Baptist, are the back of another nude horseman and portions of two standing figures. This frieze is painted in grisaille, and the lights are heightened with gold, in a manner that closely resembles the painting of the reliefs in the "Calumny of Apelles." The vitality and expressiveness of these figures only serve to emphasize the inferiority of the rest of the picture; yet notwithstanding it is among the best of the school-pictures, both as regards composition and colour. The difficulty of working in gold "a mordente," no doubt led Botticelli to touch in this frieze himself, since the assistant who executed this panel lacked the requisite skill: but this circumstance shows that the picture was not only executed in Sandro's workshop, but under his supervision, and probably from a drawing by the master.

By the hand of the same assistant is a "tondo" which lately passed from the collection of the Duca di Brindisi, at Florence, into that of Mrs. J. L. Gardner, of Boston, U.S.A. On the left of this "tondo," the Virgin kneels in adoration of the Child, whom St. Joseph, as he stoops down with outstretched hands, is about to place on the ground before her. Behind the Virgin, two shepherds approach, one of them carrying a black ewe round his neck; and in the distance, beyond the ruined piers of the

M M

building in which the stall has been erected, is seen a landscape with a river and wooded heights. The figure of the Virgin is very Botticellesque in manner; but the draperies of St. Joseph, and still more the figures of the two shepherds, are of another character, and show that the painter of this "tondo" must have learned his art under some master of the naturalistic school. That this picture is by the same hand as the panel in Mr. Heseltine's collection, is chiefly to be seen in the figure of the Virgin and in the landscape. The latter, especially, lacks the freedom of the master's own hand; and the forms of the trees and hills are wholly unlike those which occur in such authentic paintings of this period, as the "tondo" of the Ambrosiana. Although brilliant and decorative in colour, the pigments want the translucency and depth of the genuine painting of the master; and the figure of St. Joseph, effective and original in motive as it is, was more probably suggested by some work of Botticelli's, than taken directly from a design by him. Indeed, the whole picture has the character of an independent school-work, in which all the lighter and more attractive qualities of Sandro's art are imitated and exaggerated.

App. II, Doc. XL, fol. 160, recto, fol. 229, recto and fol. 239, recto.

P. Villari and E. Casanova, Scelta di Prediche e Scritti di Savonarola, p. 459.

App. II, Doc. XLI, fol. 97, recto.

Meanwhile, in the interval which had elapsed since the return of the "Denunzia" of 1480-1, many changes had been brought about in Botticelli's family. His father, Mariano, the tanner, had died, and was buried in Ognissanti on 20th February, 1481-2, while Sandro was away at Rome, working on the frescoes of the Sistine Chapel. On the 5th February, 1492-3, Monna Nera, the wife of Sandro's eldest brother, Giovanni, was laid to her rest in the same church; and a few weeks later, on the 30th March, 1493, she was followed to the grave by her husband, "Giouannj dimariano, vochato botticello," as he is named in the "Libri de' Morti" of Florence; leaving their eldest son, Benincasa, the head of the family. Towards the latter part of the year 1493, or the beginning of 1494, Sandro's third brother, Simone, returned from Naples, where already, in 1457, he had gone as a boy; and came to live with the painter and the rest of his family, at Florence, in the houses in the Via Nuova, which they had occupied since 1468. Simone was still at Naples, in 1493, in the service of a Florentine merchant, as he himself records in his Chronicle: but he had returned to Florence, certainly before March, 1495, and probably before April, 1494; in which month Sandro purchased some property in the suburbs of the city, a transaction in which Simone appears to have had an interest. The property was acquired on a tenure known in Florentine law as "conductio ad livellum"; that is to say (in terms of its nearest English equivalent), it was held at a yearly fee-farm rent, and was secured to the purchaser, his brothers and their heirs male. The conveyance of this property is preserved in a protocol of the notary, Ser Giovanni da Romena, in the State Archives at Florence. This instrument sets forth how, on the 19th April, 1494, in the parish of Santa Maria in Campo, in Florence, and in the presence of two witnesses, Don Bernardo della Volta, hospitaller and rector of the Hospital of Santa Maria Nuova in Florence, by virtue of his office "gave and conceded at a perpetual due, or fee-farm rent, to Sandro, son of the late Mariano di Vanni di Amideo de' Filipepi, singular painter and citizen of Florence, of the parish of Santa Lucia d'Ognissanti, in Florence, present and accepting on behalf of himself and Antonio and Simone, his brothers and the sons of the said late Mariano, and for the sons of the late Giovanni di Mariano, his brother, and for the sons of the said Sandro, Antonio and Simone, and of the sons of the said

THE VIRGIN AND CHILD WITH ST. JOHN *Collection of J. P. Heseltine, Esq.*

Giovanni, grandsons of the brother of the said Sandro, and for the sons and male descendants legitimate and natural of everyone of them in the male line in perpetuity &c. a farm with a house for the owner, and with tilled, vine-, olive- and fruit-bearing lands, situated in the parish of San Sepolcro in the Commune of Florence, near and without the gate of San Frediano at Florence, bounded on the first side by the road-way, on the second by the property of Pierfilippo de' Pandolfini, on the third by that of Jacopo de' Cavalieri, and on the fourth by that formerly belonging to Friars of Monte Oliveto [&c.], for the price of the beneficial ownership of the said farm, of 155 fiorini larghi d'oro of good money, at the costs of the said contractor, and for the yearly rent-charge, or due, of one pair of capons, and with the exceptions and reservations below written [&c.]." Here follow the conditions customary in such conveyances, to be observed by the purchaser and the vendor. A note on the margin of this document shows that after the death of Sandro, the hospital acknowledged the right of his brother, Simone, to the property: and although it is not so stated in this instrument, it would appear from the "Portata," or return to the officials of the new tax, called the "Decima," which Sandro and Simone jointly made of their property in 1495, that the purchase had been made jointly by the two brothers.

The volume in which this "Portata" is preserved, is dated 1498, the year in which the tax appears to have been actually levied; but the greater number of the "Portate" in the same volume bear endorsements showing that they were returned in March, April or May, 1495; and Luca Landucci records in his Diary, that on the 18th March, 1494-5, "it was ordered that the writings of the tax of the Decima, which is to be placed on real property, be returned before the end of March." There can be little doubt, then, that the "Portata" in question was actually drawn up between the months of March and May of that year. The "Decima" was levied on real estate only, and was so called because all such property was taxed to a tenth of its value: consequently these "Portate" do not contain the valuable particulars of the family and movable property, which are found in the earlier "Denunzie."

l.c., p. 101.

S. Ammirato, Istorie Fior., ed. 1641, III, 206.

In their "Portata," "Alessandro and Simone, sons of Mariano di Vanni Filipepi," state that they live in the house of Benincasa and Lorenzo Filipepi, their nephews. It appears from the "Portata" of Benincasa and Lorenzo, returned the same year, that this was the house in the Via Nuova which Giovanni, their father, had bought, and in which Botticelli had lived with his family since 1468. Sandro and Simone proceed to state that they are possessed of "a gentleman's house, situated in the parish of San Sepolcro, beyond the Porta San Frediano, with twelve 'staiora,' [a measure of land equal to rather more than half an acre,] or thereabouts, of old vineyard, and part planted with 'posticci,' [or trees to serve for vine props,] and fruit trees, which we bought at the price of 156 fiorini larghi di grossi, 'a reda maschulina,' [that is, to be held on a peppercorn rent, and to revert to the vendors in the event of failure of male issue,] from Santa Maria Nuova, the deed drawn up by Ser Giovanni di Marco da Romena, notary of the said hospital, on the 19th day of April, 1494; bounded on the first and second sides by the property of Pierfilippo Pandolfini; and on the third side by that of Jacopo del Cavaliere and his brother, hosiers; and on the fourth side by 'Le Cave,' that is to say, the property of the Friars of Monte Oliveto, and other boundaries. Lorenzo da Sansepolcro farms the

App. II, Doc. XLII, fol. 75, recto.

App. II, Doc. XLIV, fol. 178, recto.

said vineyard, and lives in the said house at our charges." They add that the property yields four barrels of wine and two "stai," or bushels, of figs and other fruit, a year, and that they have to pay a "livello," or fine, of a pair of capons every year to the Hospital of Santa Maria Nuova. The property was assessed at 2 fiorini, 17 soldi, and 5 danari; and Sandro and Simone were taxed in a sum of 4 soldi, 4 danari.

G. Carocci, Dintorni di Firenze, p. 197.

G. Richa, Chiese Fior., X, 321-4.

The name of San Sepolcro is still given to all that part of the hills of Bellosguardo adjacent to the parish church of San Vito, which, until 1719, retained its ancient dedication to San Sepolcro. In early times, the hill was in the possession of the Knight Templars, who had a house in Florence near the Ponte Vecchio; and already in the twelfth century, an oratory dedicated to San Sepolcro had been erected on this part of the hills of Bellosguardo. Upon the suppression of the Knight Templars, in 1311, the hill was granted to the Knights of St. John of Jerusalem. It would seem that the property of Sandro and Simone was bounded on the first and second sides by the "podere" of the Villa Nuti, anciently called "Le Lune"; a fine, fifteenth-century house, attributed to Il Cronaca, which in 1498 was in the possession of Pierfilippo Pandolfini, and which, in 1504, passed to the Antinori. It is now owned by Mr. Spencer Stanhope, the painter. The property of Jacopo del Cavaliere and his brother, which according to this "Portata" formed the boundary of Sandro and Simone's property on the third side, was doubtlessly the present Villa Chiocchini, which adjoins the Villa Nuti, on the Via di San Vito, leading from the Prato dello Strozzino to the Via Pisana in the direction of Monticelli. In 1490, the villa in question was in the possession of a certain Filippo di Domenico, hosier, and this person and the Filippo di Domenico del Cavaliere, hosier, with whom (as I shall show) Sandro afterwards came to words, if not to blows, in 1497, are doubtlessly the same person as the brother of Jacopo del Cavaliere: both brothers are called hosiers, in the "Portata."

G. Carocci, Dintorni di Firenze, p. 198.

It would appear, then, from these indications, that the villa of Sandro and Simone was situated on the right-hand side of the Via di Monte Oliveto, a road leading from the Via Pisana, a little without the Porta San Frediano, up past the entrance of the monastery of Monte Oliveto, to the church of San Vito and the Prato dello Strozzino. The house still stands midway between the "villino" near the second gateway of the monastery of Monte Oliveto and the Villa Nuti; and its "podere" is bounded towards the south by the "podere" of the Villa Nuti, and on the side away from the roadway by the "podere" of the Villa Chiocchini. The "villino" near the second gateway of the monastery, was probably the property called "Le Cave" in the "Portata"; but of this conjecture I have no evidence.

The villa, which once belonged to Sandro and Simone, is one of those characteristic accumulations of buildings, half mansion, half farmhouse, which lie thickly scattered over the hills around Florence. The central tower, which rises above the rest of the building, had probably been built a couple of centuries at least, when the property came into the possession of the painter and his brother. The house is delightfully situated on the slope of the hill of Bellosguardo, in a garden of olive trees, and looks out over the lower valley of the Arno, towards the distant Pisan hills and the crests of the Carrara mountains. After the death of Simone, who survived his brother Sandro for some years, the property seems to have reverted to the hospital of Santa Maria Nuova; and a note at the foot of this "Portata," in the hand of some official of the Decima, shows that in 1525 it had passed into the possession of the Antinori, who at that time owned the Villa Nuti. The "Portata" of Sandro and Simone, I should add, is not in the writing of the painter, as Johan Gaye has stated; but is in the same hand as the "Portata" of Benincasa and Lorenzo Filipepi, which is preserved in the same volume. The hand is, probably, that of Benincasa, who as head of the family might well have drafted these returns. It appears from the "Portata" of Benincasa and Lorenzo, that in 1495 they still possessed the seven parcels of land in the parish of Santa Maria a Peretola, which their family had owned since 1469. It also appears, from a note on the margin of this return, that the house in the Via Nuova, in which they were living with Sandro and Simone at this time, had in 1532 descended to Giovanni, the son of Benincasa. From a third "Portata" in the same volume, we learn that Sandro's second brother, Antonio, was living in the adjoining house in the Via Nuova which their father, Mariano, had rented as early as 1480, from the Prior of San Paolo. Antonio states that he is an "attore," or agent, at the "Magistrato dei Pupilli," or Court of Wards, that he has no other calling, and is old. The office of the "Magistrato de' Pupilli" was at that time in the building which is now occupied by the Compagnia della Misericordia, facing the campanile of the cathedral. Of his family Antonio gives no account, since the nature of the "Decima" did not call for it. I have not succeeded in ascertaining whether his wife, Bartolommea, was still alive; but his daughter, Lisabetta, was probably married, and his two sons, Mariano, the painter, and Bartolomeo, may have been living with him, though the latter was much away from Florence. But of both these sons there is more to tell in the sequel.

J. Gaye, Carteggio Inedito, I, 343.

App. II, Doc. XLIII, fol. 81, recto.

These documents go far to disprove the statement which Vasari interpolated in the second edition of the "Lives," that Botticelli was so obstinately affected towards Savonarola, that "becoming a Piagnone, [as the followers of the friar were then called,] he neglected his work, whereby in the end he found himself old and poor to a degree, that had not Lorenzo de' Medici, while he lived, assisted him, and afterwards had not his friends and many men of wealth had a care for his genius, he would almost have died of hunger." The more measured account which Vasari gives in the first edition of the "Lives," is far nearer in accordance with the contents of these documents, than the version which I have quoted. There, Vasari merely states that Sandro "growing old and unmindful, was brought to a very sorry condition"; adding, that "he is said to have gained much, but to have squandered all through recklessness, without any advantage to himself." That Botticelli might have been a comparatively rich man, whereas in 1495, as his "Portata" shows, he was a comparatively poor one, is evident enough. It was not until 1494 that he was possessed of any landed property, the staple security of wealth at that time; and even then, he only acquired what to all purposes, was only a partial and life interest in a small estate, which cost but 155 fiorini larghi. On the other hand, it is incredible that Sandro could have come to actual want, so long as he and his brother continued, as they did to the time of their deaths, in the possession of this property; or his family, with whom he appears to have lived to the end, remained in the condition in which we find them at this period.

Vasari, ed. 1568, I, 473.

Vasari, ed. 1550, I, 495.

Simone, the brother of Botticelli, is mentioned as a zealous partisan of Savonarola, and a writer of a chronicle of the times in which the friar flourished, in certain passages of the "Giornate" of Ser Lorenzo Violi, first quoted by Professor Villari in the appendix to his life of the friar. This Lorenzo Violi, a devoted follower of Savonarola, took down all his later sermons in cypher as they were preached; and in his "Giornate" he has left an account of Fra Girolamo and his teaching, cast into the form of a dialogue. This work, which he composed towards the close of his life, (he died about the year 1544, at the age of eighty,) remained unfinished, and has come down to us in a single manuscript, preserved in the Biblioteca Nazionale, at Florence. In one passage, after relating a certain incident which took place in the workshop of Botticelli, Lorenzo Violi adds, that "Simone, the brother of the said painter, being also present there, made a record of it in his Chronicle; that is to say, in a book of his in which Simone described all the notable things of those times." This book, he goes on to state, was "bound in parchment" and formed "a kind of short chronicle of the things occurring in those times in Italy; and I have seen the book and read it." Elsewhere in the "Giornate," Lorenzo Violi remarks in support of some assertion, that he had read it "in quella cronica del Botticello, a carte 436," etc. Another follower of Savonarola, Fra Benedetto da Firenze, likewise alludes to the "Chronicle" of Simone Filipepi, in his "Vulnera Diligentis," which remains in manuscript.

P. Villari, Storia di Savonarola, ed. 1861, II, cxci, etc.

Id., II, xxv, note 1.

App. II., Doc. XLVI, fol. 41, tergo.

The "Chronicle" of Simone was long thought to be lost, until a copious series of excerpts from it was discovered in a volume of miscellaneous pieces, relating to Savonarola, among the Archives of the Vatican, and printed at length by Professor Villari and Signor Casanova, at the end of their "Scelta di Prediche e Scritti di Fra Girolamo Savonarola," published at Florence, in 1898. The "Chronicle," in the form in which it has come down to us, consists of a series of notices arranged in two sections, both of which begin with an account of the preaching of Savonarola at Florence, in 1489, and end with the death of Pope Alexander VI, in 1503. The first part, although it bears the title "Alcune Memorie notabili di fra Girolamo Savonarola," is, in fact, as Ser Lorenzo Violi describes it, "a short chronicle of the things occurring in those times in Italy"; and records chiefly the invasion of Charles VIII, the intrigues of Alexander VI, and the campaigns of Cesare Borgia; the notices which relate to Savonarola being comparatively few in number. The second part, which is entitled, "Nota di alcuni particolari pertinenti al Padre fra Girolamo Savonarola da Ferrara ecc," is composed, on the contrary, almost entirely of notices relating to Savonarola and his followers, for the most part gathered out of the personal experiences of the writer, who has set them down, apparently as they occurred to him, without strict regard to their order of time. From internal evidence, this chronicle appears to have been written *c.* 1503. In one passage, in the first part, Simone refers to the election of Piero Soderini as Perpetual Gonfalonier, an event which took place on 22nd September, 1502. Later on, in the second part, Simone records an event on the day on which it happened, namely 9th April, 1503. Again, in one of the last notices of the second part, the writer alludes to Lodovico Sforza, as "now a prisoner in France." Lodovico was captured by Louis XII, on 10th April, 1500, and died a prisoner, in 1510. Finally, the first part closes with a notice of the death of Alexander VI, an event which occurred on 18th August, 1503.

l.c., pp. 453-518.

Id., p. 471.

Id., p. 498.

Id., p. 510.

Id. p. 474.

Simone, as I have shown, appears to have returned from Naples shortly before the invasion of Italy by Charles VIII. In the presence of the French king at Florence, Savonarola found the opportunity, or necessity, of first taking part in the public affairs of the State: thus, Simone became an actual spectator of the entire political career of the friar. The "Chronicle" shows that its writer was not only a devout follower of Savonarola's religious teaching, but a zealous supporter of his policy in temporal matters. An intimate of the Convent of San Marco, Simone appears to have regularly attended the religious functions in which Savonarola took a part, and to have been present at those turbulent scenes which preceded his arrest and execution. But long before he came under the influence of the friar, Simone appears to have been of a credulous and superstitious cast of mind. In a volume of miscellaneous pieces in the handwriting of Antonio Manetti, the mathematician and student of Dante, of whom I have already given some account, is the following "ricordo," which throws no little light on the character of Simone:

"Herewith I will copy out a head of a letter which Simone di Mariano Botticelli wrote from Rome, to Giovanni, his brother, at Florence, on the 17th day of August, 1482: Yesterday our Lord sent a letter to the Monsignor of Novara to read, which Messer Marchionne, a merchant of Germany, a man worthy of belief, and well known here at Court, wrote to him; and it relates how in Bohemia, spirits have appeared in human form, and they summon persons to be present in a wood within three days, as if before one who is their chief; and whoever goes not, dies at the end of three days, and they that go thither, return afterwards, and are unable to recount anything, like those who have lost their memory. And these spirits summon not persons unless they be heretics, of which there are many here. This seems to me a great miracle, if it be true. I also have seen the letter, and I know it to be by the hand of Messer Marchionne, a man of credit and affairs, and he has, moreover, from eight to ten thousand ducats in receipts. Bonciano Costi knows him, and so do many merchants who are here: and soon it will happen this way." How characteristic a trait is the tender of Messer Marchionne's worldly success, as evidence of his veracity in spiritual matters! The vein of superstition which colours this childish fable, runs through the "Chronicle": there, for instance, Simone never tires of telling how all who withstood the friar, or contributed to his downfall, came to some untimely, or violent, end.

App. II, Doc. XLVII.

On the other hand, he appears to have been not only a man of real piety, but also a lover of books, and a student of Dante; traits which go far to explain the intimate terms on which he seems to have lived with his brother. In the Biblioteca Nazionale, at Florence, is a manuscript which once belonged to Simone, of an anonymous commentary, dedicated to Benedetto Manetti, on the canzone of Dante, beginning: "Tre donne intorno al cor mi son venute." This volume bears on the tergo of the fly-leaf, the inscription:

+yhs 1495

N° xxxj°
q*ue*sto e dj Simone dj Mariano filipepj
i dio bono fine faccj dj Luj.

The manuscript was formerly in the Strozzi Library, where it bore the number 572: it now bears the press-mark, Classe VII, Codice 1152. The first leaf of the text is ornamented with some damaged miniatures, and the volume still retains its original, blind-tooled binding. The number which the book bore in the library of Simone, "Nº xxxjº.," shows that he possessed a considerable collection for those times.

In the absence of all direct evidence as to the attitude which Sandro assumed towards Savonarola and his teaching, during the lifetime of the friar, the "Chronicle" of Simone becomes especially valuable, not only because it shows how ardent and active a supporter its writer was of Fra Girolamo, during the last stormy years of his ministry, but, also, because it affords many negative indications that, up to that time, Botticelli had not openly thrown in his lot with the Piagnoni. In one respect, the ascendency of Savonarola cannot have failed to influence his art: and, indeed, all the last works of Sandro bear ample proof of it. I allude to Savonarola's fiery condemnation of the fashions in ecclesiastical painting then in vogue, and his endeavour to inculcate a purely religious form of art, both in the churches and the houses of the citizens. A single passage from one of his sermons must suffice to illustrate the tenets of the friar. In one place, in the Lenten course upon Amos, delivered in 1495, he exclaims: "Look, what customs has Florence; in what manner the Florentine women give in marriage their daughters! They bring them forth on show, and deck them out so that they appear as nymphs; and first of all they bring them to Santa Liperata. These are your idols which you have placed in my temple! The images of your gods are the images and similitudes of the figures, which you cause to be painted in the churches; and then the young men go saying of this and that figure, this is the Magdalene, and that is Saint John. For you cause the figures to be painted in the churches, in the similitude of this or of that woman, which is most wrongly done, and in great contempt of the things of God. You, painters, do ill; albeit, if you knew the scandal which comes of it, and that which I know, you would not paint them. You set up all the vanities in the churches. Do you believe that the Virgin Mary went dressed in this manner, as you paint her? I tell you that she went simply dressed and veiled, like a poor woman who is pained if her face be seen: and thus, Saint Elizabeth went simply dressed. You would do a great, good work to destroy these figures that are thus dishonestly painted, for you make the Virgin Mary appear dressed as a harlot; and naught is heeded, unless it redound to your own honour."

Prediche di Frate Hieronymo da Ferrara, ed. Firenze, 1496, sig. li, tergo.

To appreciate the significance and effect of this invective, one need but contrast the frescoes completed in the year 1490, by Domenico Ghirlandaio on the walls of the choir of Santa Maria Novella, with the early paintings of Fra Bartolommeo. In the former, a greater prominence is frequently given to the portrait-figures, which are everywhere introduced into these frescoes, attired in the most sumptuous fashions of the time, than to the actors in the sacred stories which ostensibly form their subjects. In the works of Fra Bartolommeo, on the contrary, the absence of all such portraiture and costume-painting, constitutes one of the essential elements of his grand and generalized manner; and the influence which he exercised over such painters as Raffaello and Andrea del Sarto, show how far-reaching were the puritanical tenets of the friar. If Savonarola did not succeed in removing from the churches such paintings as he disapproved of, he, at least, succeeded in inducing his followers to destroy a vast number of portraits and other profane pictures which adorned their houses. For Savonarola, the representation of the nude was in itself an immodest and reprehensible thing. Vasari, in his life of Fra Bartolommeo, relates how the friar, "crying out every day in the pulpit, that lascivious pictures and music and amorous books often lead the thoughts to evil actions, was persuaded that it was not right to have in a house, where there are young girls, painted figures of naked men and women. Wherefore the people being fired by his words, during the following Carnival, when it was the custom of the city to make bonfires of logs and other wood, in the public squares, and on the evening of Shrove Tuesday to burn them amid amorous dances, in which a man and a woman, taking each other by the hand, turned round and round, singing certain ballads, Fra Girolamo brought it about, that on that day so great a number of paintings and sculptures of the nude, many by the hands of excellent masters, together with books, lutes and song-books, were brought to that place, [and burnt,] that the loss was very great, and especially to Painting; for thither Baccio brought all the drawings which he had made from the nude, and Lorenzo di Credi also followed his example, and many others who had the name of Piagnoni." Had Botticelli been of the number, it is not likely that the circumstance would have escaped tradition: yet that does not lessen the probability, that some of his paintings may have perished in the holocaust.

Vasari, ed. Sansoni, IV, 128.

The Burning of the Vanities, as these bonfires were called, took place on two several occasions. The first was on Shrove Tuesday, 1496-7, when, according to an account preserved in the "Life of Savonarola," which is generally attributed to Fra Pacifico Burlamacchi, a pyramidal wooden structure nearly sixty feet in height, having eight faces with fifteen degrees, or steps, on each face, was erected in the middle of the Piazza della Signoria, and filled with faggots. On the degrees, or steps, were piled the "vanities," which the children had collected from every part of the city. "On the first step were foreign hangings of great price, but full of immodest figures; above these, on the second step, were a great number of figures and portraits of beautiful women, Florentine and others, made by the hands of the most excellent artists, painters, and sculptors." On the other steps were heaped chess-boards, playing cards, musical instruments, and books of music; false hair, perfumes, mirrors, and the like; books of the poets, both in Latin and the vulgar tongue; copies of the "Morgante Maggiore," "Boccaccio," "Petrarch," and so forth. "There were many things," adds the writer, "of great price, as pictures and sculptures, chess-boards of ivory and alabaster, in such sort that a Venetian merchant offered twenty thousand scudi for them; which thing being known, an effigy was made of him and placed on the top of the pile, in a chair, as the prince of those vanities."

Ed. Milano, 1847, pp. 120-126.

On the Shrove Tuesday of the following year, 1497-8, another structure, similar to the first, but of greater dimensions, was erected in the Piazza; and the "vanities" collected by the children were more numerous and of far greater value, than those which had been burnt the year before. Amongst other things, says our writer, were "some sculptured heads of beautiful women of past times, as the beautiful Bencina, Lena Morella, the beautiful Bina, Maria de' Lenzi, and others, carved in marble by the ablest sculptors; and there was a certain copy of 'Petrarch,' so adorned with gold and miniatures that it was valued at fifty scudi." Luca Landucci, moreover, mentions among the "many things of great price, valued at thousands of florins," and burnt on this occasion, were "figure ignude." The supposition that among such figures were paintings by Botticelli, would go to account for the early disappearance of similar works by him. The

N N

App. II, Doc. I, fol. 49, tergo. epitomist of the "Libro di Antonio Billi" records how Sandro painted "piu femmine igniude belle piu ch*e* alchuno altro," many naked women, which were more beautiful than anything else of his: and the Anonimo App. II, Doc. II, fol. 85, recto. Gaddiano speaks of "piu fe*m*mine gnude bellissime." These writers would seem, however, to repeat here some tradition, rather than allude to any Vasari, ed. 1550, I, 492. picture which they had seen. Vasari, again, states that Botticelli painted very many pictures of naked women for divers houses throughout the city: "per la città, in diverse case fece . . . femmine ignude assai"; yet he was able to point only to the paintings at Castello, of the "Spring" and the "Birth of Venus," the only two works of the kind by the master's own hand, which have come down to us.

Let us now turn to such passages in the "Chronicle" of Simone, as may serve to illustrate the part which he and his brother played, during the final struggle of Savonarola with the Papal authority. The breve of L. Landucci, Diario, p. 152. Alexander VI., promulgating the sentence of excommunication upon Savonarola, was published in five of the principal churches of Florence, on the 18th June, 1497; and the friar immediately sought to defend his position in an "Epistola contro la scomunica surrettizia." The effect of the Papal breve was to give the ascendency, for the moment, to the "Arrabbiati," as the infuriated opponents of the friar were termed. The races of Barbary horses, which had been suppressed at the instance of Savonarola, were renewed; and the city seemed to have returned to the liberty which it had enjoyed in the days of Lorenzo, Il Magnifico. Mean- P. Villari and E. Casanova, Scelta di Prediche e Scritti di Savonarola, pp. 512-518. while the Frateschi had not abandoned their cause for lost. A petition signed by all the friars of the convent of San Marco was sent to the Pope, setting forth the life and doctrine of their prior, and praying the successor of St. Peter to remove the disabilities of excommunication. This petition was accompanied by another, signed by 363 citizens of Florence. Among the names appended to the second petition, is that of Simone di Mariano Filipepi, who has inserted a copy of both documents in his "Chronicle."

For the moment the attention alike of the followers and detractors of Fra Girolamo was engaged by the discovery that five of the foremost citizens of Florence, including Lorenzo Tornabuoni and Gianozzo Pucci, whose marriages Botticelli had celebrated in his paintings, had conspired to restore Piero di Lorenzo de' Medici to the chief citizenship of the state. L Landucci, Diario, pp. 155-157. This discovery, and the revulsion of popular feeling which it brought about, led to the summary execution of the conspirators on 17th August, 1497, and placed the Frateschi once more in the ascendency. Meanwhile Savonarola had withdrawn himself into the seclusion of his cell, and was devoting himself entirely to the accomplishment of his great work, "Il Trionfo della Croce," which was to be at once a complete exposition of his teaching, and an apology for the course of action which he was premeditating. The work appeared in Latin, towards the close of the year 1497, under the title "De veritate fidei in dominicae Crucis triumphum," and its publication was immediately followed by a popular paraphrase in Vasari, ed. 1550, I, 494. the vulgar tongue. Vasari records that Botticelli "put into stamp the triumph of the Faith of Fra Girolamo Savonarola of Ferrara." None of the cuts in the extant editions of this work, is to be identified with any such print from a design by Botticelli. It is probable, therefore, that the print to which Vasari alludes, was an independent sheet, the subject of which was suggested by the principal theme of Savonarola's book; or it may have celebrated the triumph of the Faith in the death of the friar.

However this may be, its disappearance is, no doubt, to be ascribed to the popularity which it enjoyed.

On 2nd February, 1497-8, Savonarola returned to preach, in spite of the Papal prohibition, contending always "that the excommunication was neither valid nor binding." The second Burning of the Vanities, which took place on the following Shrove Tuesday, was quickly followed by what proved to be the turning point in Savonarola's career. A Franciscan, called Fra Francesco da Puglia, in a course of Lenten sermons given in Santa Croce, had attacked Savonarola with unusual violence. He was answered by one of the monks of San Marco, Fra Domenico da Pescia, who, having formulated the doctrine of Savonarola, proposed to the Franciscan that they should submit the truth of their tenets to the ordeal by fire. Simone, after recounting in his "Chronicle" the circumstances of this challenge, goes on to relate "how (as I, Simone di Mariano Filipepi, learned not long after from Doffo Spini, then head of the company of the Compagnacci, so called, which consisted of three hundred of the most vicious youths of the city,) the design of the other party was not indeed to bring about the Trial by Fire, but to use the occasion to have Fra Girolamo and his followers, who were about 150 persons, all holy and god-fearing men, cut to pieces by the aforesaid youths. And this same Doffo said that, when the priors and the other officers of the Republic withdrew, he had the sign given him from the palace to carry out what had been planned; but he, as it pleased God, had not the will to do it." "I was present," adds the writer, "at that spectacle; therefore I will relate so much of it as I saw, and know to be the truth." Simone then gives a long account of the procession of Savonarola and his friars from San Marco, and of all that happened in the Piazza della Signoria, on 7th April, 1498, adding a second time, "I was present at everything, and saw and took cognizance of these things." Simone also declares that the plot to kill Savonarola and his friars, which Doffo Spini failed to carry out, had been planned by Giovanni di Pierfrancesco de' Medici, with the connivance of his wife, Caterina Sforza, Lady of Imola and Forlì, and Ludovico Sforza, Duke of Milan.

L. Landucci, Diario, p. 162.

P. Villari and E. Casanova, Scelta di Prediche e Scritti di Savonarola, pp. 481-483.

Id., p. 484.

The day following the Trial by Fire, being Palm Sunday, Savonarola preached at San Marco, and Fra Mariano Ughi, one of the friars of San Marco, was appointed to preach in the Cathedral. "Fra Mariano," says Simone, "going by the Via del Cocomero, as upon other festivals, to preach after vespers in the Duomo, a great multitude of men and women who were in San Marco, followed him, in order to hear his sermon. And when he had arrived near the church, the Compagnacci, with a great number of the common sort of the people, began to throw stones at them, and taking their arms in their hands, drove back the preacher with those who were behind; so that he was forced to retire to San Marco, amid the howls and shrieks of those who were with him. And I, the writer, was present at all this." Simone then goes on to relate how the mob, having followed the Fra Mariano back to the convent, set up such a tumult in the Piazza, that the monks were obliged to shut the doors of the church; and how, after nightfall, the rabble set fire to the doors of the convent; and how, finally, Savonarola was taken with Fra Domenico and Fra Silvestro, and brought prisoners to the Palazzo della Signoria.

Id., p. 487.

"I have omitted to tell," Simone presently adds, "how, on the night that the Compagnacci attacked the Convent of San Marco, not content with the capture of the three friars, they robbed the place and almost

Id., p. 498.

put it to sack, carrying away large quantities of wine and oil and whatever they could lay their hands on. I, having retired within the house during those days when Fra Girolamo was taken, in order to avoid the bad blood, there came to me one Baccio di Boccalino, a general broker, but chiefly a dealer in cast clothing, and with him was Lotto Lotti, of the same calling, who two-thirds of the day used to be drunk, and whose real business was lending money at usury, to thieves and whores on pawn; and this Lotto, having come to me in my room, laid hold of a scimitar in order to deal me a blow, saying: 'Ah, traitor, you are one of those who, with Fra Girolamo, caused Bernardo del Nero, my uncle, to be beheaded.' I immediately replied as best I could, in the face of that onslaught, and said to him, 'Lotto, I was never one of those, nor have I ever had any thought of such a thing, nor do I know what you say: you are in error and are wrongly informed about me, and have mistaken me for some one else;' and so did I work upon him with fair words, that I caused him to put back his arms, though not before he had uttered many insulting words to me: but God and right reason were my help, so that I escaped."

J. Nardi, Istorie Fior., ed. 1858, I, 126.

L. Landucci, Diario, p. 174.

The arrest of Savonarola and the two friars was followed by their examination under torture by those in power, in the hope of extorting evidence to strengthen their indictment. "Many of the citizens and the common sort of the people," records Jacopo Nardi, "were summoned and taken, some of whom were several times examined and others put to the torture by the Otto, to see if they could discover whether there had been any accord, or conspiracy, between the citizens and the sectaries of the friar, that they might so much the more charge and defame the said friar and his followers; so that many citizens left the city through fear." According to Landucci, these arrests were made on the 23rd April, fifteen days after the arrest of Savonarola. A few days later, a number of citizens were condemned to pay various fines, and on 1st May all were released except "the three poor friars."

P. Villari and E. Casanova, Scelta di Prediche e Scritti di Savonarola, p. 493.

"At the time when Fra Girolamo was taken," says Simone, "many worthy men had to fly from Florence, taking refuge at some villa in the country, or at Bologna, or at Siena, or elsewhere, in order not to be persecuted by those who were in power, and who were nearly all enemies of the doctrine of that said father. And I, Simone di Mariano de' Filipepi, went then to Bologna, where I found many others of our party: of those that remained, every day some were taken and tortured, and declared incapable of holding office." It is significant that Sandro is never once mentioned in the "Chronicle," as having been present at any of the events which preceded the death of Savonarola, and that Simone alone of all their family should have been forced to fly from Florence, at the time of the friar's arrest in 1498. That Sandro was able to remain in the city, shows that up to that time he had not become the avowed and active supporter of Savonarola's faction, which Simone had been. Still more significant is the fact that the name of Sandro is not found, like that of Simone, among the signatories to the petition on behalf of Savonarola, which the Piagnoni presented to Pope Alexander VI. in 1497. On the other hand, I have shown that Botticelli enjoyed the confidence of Lorenzo di Pierfrancesco de' Medici, the untiring opponent of the friar, as late as July, 1496, and that he was still in his employment in July, 1497. The flight of Lorenzo from Florence in the course of the latter year, and the absence of all evidence that Botticelli was again employed by him, seem to point to the fact that a rupture occurred between Lorenzo and the painter about this time, as a consequence of Sandro's avowed attachment to the party of Savonarola, and his hatred of the share which Lorenzo was held by the followers of Fra Girolamo to have had in what they regarded as his martyrdom. This conclusion is materially strengthened by two other circumstances: the bitter animosity displayed by Simone in his "Chronicle" towards Lorenzo, and the fact that after the death of the friar, Botticelli's workshop became a notorious meeting-place of the Piagnoni. Like Michelagnolo, Sandro no doubt had been deeply impressed by the personality and teaching of Savonarola, but all such evidence as we possess, goes to show that the painter did not openly throw in his lot with the Piagnoni, until after the death of the friar; and perhaps the active part which Simone had taken in furthering the cause of Fra Girolamo, contributed not a little to the tradition which Vasari has preserved, that Botticelli "fu molto partigiano a quella setta." Vasari, ed. 1550, I, 495.

Let us now turn to enquire what may be learned about Botticelli, during this troubled time. At the time when the letter, which I have quoted, was addressed by Michelagnolo to Lorenzo di Pierfrancesco de' Medici, under cover to Botticelli, in July, 1496, the painter was engaged on a painting of San Francesco in the new dormitory of the monastery of Monticelli, which then stood beyond the Porta a San Piero Gattolino, a gate of Florence, now called the Porta Romana. This monastery, a house of Franciscan nuns, called Le Romite, had been founded during the lifetime of San Francesco by the saint himself, at a place beyond the Porta San Frediano, which still bears the name of Monticelli. After the death of the Beata Chiara degli Ubaldini, the first abbess, the community was removed by her nephew, the Cardinal Ottaviano, to a house beyond the Porta Romana. Giuseppe Richa, describing the position of this second house, says that it was "situated on the rising ground which divides the Strada Romana [the present Via Senese] from the Stradone, [an avenue of cypresses,] which leads to Poggio Imperiale, distant rather more than the shot of an arquebuse from the fountain which Madama Maddalena of Austria, grand-duchess of Tuscany, caused to be made at the beginning of the Stradone." Some scanty remains of the fountain may still be seen near the four statues of the philosophers, which stand at the beginning of the Strada del Poggio Imperiale. At a later time, this house was destined to become "the sweet cloister" of Piccarda de' Donati, who in Paradise reminds Dante how he had known her upon earth, and how, as a girl, she had vainly sought refuge here from the world.

G. Richa, Chiese Fior., II, 176, &c.

Id. II, 182.

Paradiso, III, 43, &c.

The entries in the ledgers of the convent, of the payments made to Botticelli on account of the painting, which he executed there, form the only record of it which has come down to us. It appears from these books of account, which are now preserved among the Florentine Archives, that the new dormitory of Monticelli was in the course of building, during the latter part of the year 1494; and that in 1496, Botticelli was commissioned to paint a "St. Francis," doubtlessly in fresco, for the sum of twenty gold florins, which he received in its equivalent of lire 132. This money was paid to the painter in five several amounts, the first of which was made on 14th June, and the last on the 19th August, 1496, apparently upon the completion of the fresco. One of the payments was made in cash, to Botticelli himself, and the others were made to an assistant. In two instances the name of the assistant is given: "iac° di franc°, suo carçone."

App. II, Doc. XLVIII, c. 173.

Of this Jacopo di Francesco, I shall speak when I come to discuss the disciples of Botticelli.

Cod. Magliabechiano, XXVI, 22, fol. 422, tergo.

The nuns of Monticelli continued to live in their house beyond the Porta Romana, until the year 1529, when, as Stefano Rosselli records in his "Sepoltuario Fiorentino," the city of Florence being at war with Pope Clement VII, and expecting the siege which followed, the nuns were commanded by those who then had the government of the city, to leave their house, and retire within the walls; and on the 21st September, 1529, the fabric of the monastery, the value of which was estimated at 80,000 ducats, was by the command of the Signoria razed to the ground, lest, from its proximity to the walls of the city, it might afford cover to the enemy. If, as there is every reason to think, the "St. Francis" of Botticelli was painted in fresco, it must have perished in the general destruction of the building. In 1531, the site of a "Lazzeretto" within the city, near the Porta alla Croce, was granted to the nuns of Monticelli, and here they had their house until the time of its suppression in 1808, when its fabric, and that of the adjoining convent of Montedomini, were by a decree of Napoleon, turned into a "Casa di Lavoro."

App. II, Doc. XLIX

The following year, Botticelli executed some paintings, probably of a decorative nature, at the Villa of Castello, for his old patron, Lorenzo di Pierfrancesco de' Medici. The document recording this work is preserved among the miscellaneous papers of the Medici, in the State Archives at Florence. It is written upon a half-sheet of paper, and runs thus:

"Certificate is given by me, Basino, on behalf of Sandro Botjcello, for fifty-seven days-work which he has [due to him] here with three painters, at 14 soldi the day; and one [painter] for sixteen days' work at 10 soldi, and I give him wine; and one journeyman at 7 soldi the day who has [due to him] eighteen days' work. Do you now make [the account]. On the 3rd day of July, 1497.

"Basino at Castello."

Below, the recipient of the certificate has cast up the various items thus:

[57 days' work, at 14 soldi the day,]	"*lire*	39	18	0
[16 days' work, at 10 soldi the day,]		8	0	0
[18 days' work, at 7 soldi the day,]		6	6	0
	lire	54	4	0"

This certificate is endorsed:

"To the worthy master Lionado Strozi, in Florence."

Lionardo Strozzi appears to have been the factotum of Lorenzo and Giovanni di Pierfrancesco de' Medici: and on the completion of the paintings at Castello, Botticelli, no doubt, brought back with him to Florence this certificate under the hand of Basino, evidently the "Maestro di Casa," or agent, in charge of the villa, and received from Lionardo the amount due to him and his assistants for the work. The smallness of the sum received for these paintings, equal to a little more than 8 fiorini larghi d'oro, the brief time in which they were executed, some three weeks at the outside, and the number of assistants employed on them, all point to the conclusion that they could not have formed a work of great importance. They have, probably, been long since destroyed in the course of the many alterations and embellishments which the Villa of Castello has undergone, since the time of Botticelli. This is the last recorded occasion, on which the painter is known to have had dealings with Lorenzo di Pierfrancesco de' Medici.

A contemporary chronicler records, that when on the 2nd of February, 1497-8, Savonarola returned, in defiance of the Papal excommunication, to preach in the Cathedral church of Santa Maria del Fiore, it was "to the great joy and satisfaction of his followers, notwithstanding the opposition of the priests, friars and preachers, and of the affected laymen; so that according to the diversity of opinion and inclination, no few disputes and quarrels were bred in the city." In the midst of these disorders, the figure of Botticelli passes for a moment across the pages of this uncertain history. In the protocol of the notary, Ser Giovanni Carsidoni, for the years 1491-1500, preserved among the State Archives at Florence, is a "promissio de non offendendo," or, as we should say, a surety for the keeping of the peace, which sets forth how, on the 18th February, 1497-8, in the presence of two witnesses, "Antonio di Migliore Guidotti, citizen of Florence, promised to me, the notary below named, [Ser Giovanni Carsidoni,] that Sandro di Mariano, alias di Botticello, should not offend in word, or deed, &c., Filippo di Domenico del Cavaliere, hosier, and in the event that the same do offend him in word, or deed, to pay &c., in lieu of punishment &c., 50 gold florins, half to the office of the Otto &c., and half to the party affronted, &c." This instrument, which is concluded with the customary obligations, is followed by another of the same date, and in the same form, which sets forth how Domenico di Antonio di Domenico, of Borgo San Lorenzo, a town in the Mugello, became surety in a similar amount for Filippo di Domenico di Bartolommeo del Cavaliere, that he, on his part, should not offend in word, or deed, Sandro di Mariano di Botticello.

J. Nardi, Istorie Fior. ed. 1858, I, 111.

App. II, Doc. L, fol. 215, tergo.

Filippo di Domenico del Cavaliere, hosier, and his brother, Jacopo, were, as I have shown, the owners of a property which adjoined that of Sandro and Simone, at Bellosguardo. This "promissio de non offendendo" unfortunately tells us nothing of the nature of the quarrel, which arose between the painter and his neighbour; and so we are left to conjecture whether it arose out of some dispute in conjunction with their properties at Bellosguardo, or whether it was bred of that "diversity of opinion and inclination," touching Savonarola's defiance of the Papal authority, which, as Jacopo Nardi records, occasioned no few disputes and quarrels in the city at this time. Some colour is given to the latter conjecture by the fact that the protocol, which contains the two instruments in question, also contains a great number of similar instruments, the majority of which were executed during the stormy years when the fortunes of Savonarola were in the balance. On the other hand, the incident recalls one of the three anecdotes which Vasari tells in the second edition of the "Lives," regarding Botticelli's love of jesting. "There once came to live next door to Sandro," he relates, "a cloth-weaver, who put up fully eight looms: and these, when they were at work, what with the noise of the treadles and the clatter of the frames, not only deafened poor Sandro, but caused the whole house to shake, which was not more stoutly built than it need have been; so that between one and the other, he could neither work, nor stay in the house. And having many times besought his neighbour to remedy this annoyance, since he had replied that in his own house he would, and could, do that

Vasari, ed. 1568, I, 473.

which best pleased him, Sandro, growing angry, poised on the top of his wall, which was higher than that of his neighbour, and not very stable, a huge stone of more than a cartload, which, whenever the wall shook a little, seemed about to fall and demolish the roof and floors and cloth and looms of his neighbour: and he, alarmed at this danger, hastened to Sandro, who answered him in the very same words, that in his own house he could, and would, do that which pleased him: so that, not being able to arrive at any other conclusion, he was obliged to agree to reasonable terms, and become a good neighbour to Sandro." Now, as far as we can learn from the "Denunzie" which Botticelli, or his family, returned at various times to the officials of the taxes, (and the series is a fairly complete one,) the painter had at no time for his neighbour in the Via Nuova, a "tessitore di drappi," or cloth-weaver. Is Vasari's anecdote, then, authentic, or merely one of the many good stories of the "botteghe," which had been handed down in his time, and which may have had its origin in this dispute of Sandro's with his neighbour, the "calzaiuolo," or weaver of hose?

There is yet another matter to be remarked in connection with this "promissio de non offendendo." Antonio di Migliore Guidotti, who gave surety for Botticelli, appears to have been one of the young men who, like Antonio Segni, gathered around the painter towards the end of his life, and who probably were of the number of that "accademia di scioperati," who frequented his workshop after the death of Savonarola. This Antonio was the grandson of the Antonio di Migliore Guidotti, "maestro di legname" and architect, who is named at the end of the "Novella del Grasso Legnajuolo," among those who had heard the story told many times by Brunelleschi himself, and from whom the writer obtained its particulars. The younger Antonio Guidotti was born in 1472, and was, therefore, Botticelli's junior by some twenty-eight years. According to a "Portata" returned for the "Decima" of 1498, Monna Lisa, widow of Migliore di Antonio Guidotti, and daughter of Bernardo d'Antonio degli Alberti, and Antonio di Migliore Guidotti, her son, at that time rented a dwelling house in Florence, situated in the Via Larga, and owned a podere, in the parish of Santo Stefano in Pane, near Florence. The Via Larga, in which Antonio and his mother lived, opened into the Piazza di San Marco; and in the church of San Marco, the Guidotti had their burial-place. Antonio appears to have been an ardent follower of Savonarola, for his name occurs among those of the 363 Florentine citizens, who signed the letter addressed to Alexander VI. in 1497, praying him to revoke the sentence of excommunication against Savonarola.

A. Manetti, Operette Istoriche, p. 66.

App. II, Doc. LI, fol. 39, recto.

App. II, Doc. LII, fol. 70, recto.

P. Villari and E. Casanova, Scelta di Prediche e Scritti di Savonarola, p. 515.

On the 15th November, 1499, Botticelli matriculated as a painter in the "Arte dei Medici e degli Speziali," the Florentine guild of physicians and apothecaries, with whom were associated the painters, stationers, barbers, perfumers, hat-makers, glaziers, wax-chandlers, colourmen, rope-makers, sieve-makers, potters and other trades. His matriculation is entered in the register of the guild in the latin formula commonly employed for the purpose. Done into English, it would run thus: "Alexandro di Mariano di Botticello, [so the name stands translated in the index to the volume,] painter, wishing to be admitted to the grade of master in the said guild, and to be placed and inscribed in the register of the said guild, among the others registered in the said guild, etc., promised and swore, etc. He is under obligation to pay six fiorini di sugello."

App. II, Doc. LIII, fol. 38, recto.

The student will naturally inquire how it was that so eminent a painter as Botticelli, was not enrolled a member of his guild, until he had reached his fifty-fifth year. A glance at the history of the corporation in question may, perhaps, enable us to give a partial, if not a complete, answer to this question. It would appear from certain notarial documents published by Signor Milanesi in his "Nuovi Documenti per la Storia dell' Arte Toscana," that already in the thirteenth century, an "Arte dei Pittori" had existed as a separate guild, under the presidency of a rector. (l.c., pp. 13-15, Doc. 16, 19, 25, etc.) In the earlier part of the fourteenth century, a number of the lesser guilds appear to have been incorporated with the larger and more flourishing bodies; and in the course of the second decade of that century, the "Arte dei Pittori" was merged into the "Arte dei Medici e degli Speziali," which, at that time, was one of the twelve "Arti Maggiori." The extant registers of matriculation in this guild for the city and county of Florence, begin in 1297, and end abruptly in 1444. After a long interval, during which all trace of them has disappeared, the register for the city begins again on 8th January, 1490-1. From this time, until 16th March, 1494-5, the name of one obscure painter is alone to be found in this register. From the latter date, until 23rd July, 1496, there is again a break, during which the register does not appear to have been kept; and from the date of its recommencement, no painter is inscribed in it, until 1st September, 1499, on which day Pietro Perugino matriculated. On 20th September, and on 2nd November, next following, the names of two unimportant painters are entered; and on 15th of the latter month, those of Botticelli, Raffaello di Bartolommeo Capponi, painter, in the Garbo, and Francesco di Niccolò del Dolzemele, painter, who had his shop in the same street. From that time onward, the names of painters constantly occur in these registers. The registers for the county of Florence, begins again in 1470, with the "Libro Nero"; but the name of not a single painter is to be found in it, during the fifteenth century.

It is evident, then, that not only were these registers kept in a very lax fashion; but that, for some reason or another, from 8th January, 1490-1, until 1st September, 1499, with a single unimportant exception, the painters were not called upon, or did not trouble, to matriculate in the guild. This state of things, however, must have been going on during the greater part of the last half of the fifteenth century. Had the enactments of the guild which were in force during the fourteenth century, been still in full vigour at that time, Botticelli would, in the ordinary course, have matriculated c. 1465-70. With the ease and prosperity which Florence enjoyed under Cosimo, Piero and Lorenzo, de' Medici, many popular institutions appear to have been very laxly administered, or allowed to fall into disuse. We have seen into how parlous a state, the Campagnia di San Luca had been allowed to lapse, towards the end of the fifteenth century; and Luca Landucci records how the religious company of the apothecaries, which had almost passed out of mind, was renewed and reorganized in the year 1500. (L. Landucci, Diario Fior., p. 217.) The revival of the matriculations of the painters, which took place in 1499, may possibly be due to motives of policy, arising from the unstable nature of the government. Unless a Florentine citizen was enrolled in one of the guilds, or "Arti," he was entitled neither to vote in the parliaments of the people, nor to offer himself for election to any office of the Republic: and the necessity, under which the popular party found itself, to assert its rights at this critical period of Florentine history, may perhaps be traced the causes which led to the stricter observance of the ordinances of the guilds, and to the revival of the religious confraternities, which took place at this time.

Vasari, ed. 1550, I, 492.

Vasari, ed. Sansoni, IV, 141.

About the year of his matriculation in the "Arte dei Medici e degli Speziali," Botticelli appears to have executed a series of paintings for the decoration of a room in the Via dei Servi at Florence. Vasari records in the first edition of the "Lives," that "in the Via dei Servi, in the house of Giovanni Vespucci, which is now the property of Piero Salviati, [Botticelli] executed around a chamber, many pictures enclosed by ornaments of walnut, by way of frames and wainscots, with many figures most life-like and beautiful." Another chamber in the same house was decorated, probably about the same time, by Piero di Cosimo. In the life of that master, Vasari states that "he executed for Giovan Vespucci, who lived opposite to San Michele in the Via dei Servi, in a house which is now the property of Pier Salviati, some stories of bacchanals which are around a chamber; and in these he painted such strange fauns, satyrs, woodland creatures, striplings and bacchantes, that it is a marvel to see the diversity of the shepherd's pouches and garments, and the variety of the goat-like faces, done with a grace and an imitation most true to nature. And in one story, there is Silenus riding upon an ass, accompanied by a crowd of boys who keep him from falling, and give him wherewith to drink."

App. II, Doc. LIV, fol. 550, recto.

It would seem, however, that both Botticelli and Piero di Cosimo executed these paintings not for Giovanni Vespucci, but for his father, Messer Guidantonio, a famous Doctor of Laws in his day, and an inveterate opponent of Savonarola. Among other offices which he bore under the Republic, was that, on two occasions, of Gonfalonier of Florence. But I have already given some account of the Vespucci, in discussing the fresco of St. Augustine which Botticelli painted for another member of the same family, in the church of Ognissanti. It appears from a note appended to the "Portata alla Decima" which Messer Guidantonio returned in 1495, that he bought the house in the Via dei Servi, from the Arte del Cambio, on 5th March, 1498-9: it is probable, then, that the paintings of Botticelli and Piero di Cosimo were executed not long after the date of that purchase.

l.c., ed. 1584, pp. 351 and 377.

F. Baldinucci, Notizie de' Professori del Disegno, ed. 1767, Vol. XIII, p. 34.

Of the fate of these panels, nothing certainly is known. When Raffaello Borghini wrote "Il Riposo" in 1584, the house in the Via dei Servi had passed into the possession of Giovanni de' Bardi di Vernio; but that writer particularly adds, that the paintings of Piero were "held in esteem by Signor Giovanni"; both rooms with their decorations being then, apparently, intact. In the latter part of the seventeenth century, the house which had formerly belonged to the Vespucci, together with some of the adjoining buildings, were transformed by Lodovico Incontri, who had studied architecture under Giulio Parigi, into the present Palazzo Incontri. If these rooms had remained untouched until that time, they were, no doubt, then dismantled, and their paintings dispersed.

I. Lermolieff, Die Galerie Borghese, ed. 1890, p. 111.

Giovanni Morelli first suggested in his "Studies in the Borghese Gallery," that a furniture-panel painted with the story of Virginia Romana, in his own collection, "may have been one of those which, according to Vasari, Botticelli executed for Giovanni Vespucci"; since the painting in question, like those which Vasari describes, contains a great number of figures "vivissime e belle." This panel had been bought by Morelli from the gallery of the Monte di Pietà, at Rome, where it had been deposited as a pawn. In 1870, Morelli exhibited it in the "Esposizione Cristiana," held in the Terme Diocleziane, as a genuine work by Sandro Botticelli; and after the death of its owner, in 1891, it passed with the rest of his collection to the Accademia Carrara, at Bergamo, where it bears the number 25. The

THE STORY OF VIRGINIA *Morelli Collection, Bergamo. (From a photograph by D. Anderson, Rome)*

panel on which it is painted, measures $32\frac{1}{4}$ inches in height, and 65 inches in length. We commonly speak of such furniture-pieces as cassone-panels; but it is evident from its measurements that the painting in question is too large by much, to have formed the panel of a "cassone," or coffer. Such decorative pictures were used, as Vasari tells us, "per vani di lettucci, letti": that is, as panels for the heads of beds, or framed into a "spalliera" or wainscot, forming the back of a "lettuccio," or settle. In the latter part of the fifteenth century, these "spalliere" which had originally formed the backs of settles, were carried round the walls of a chamber, and united with the doors of cupboards sunk in the thickness of the wall, became wainscots in our modern sense of the word. For some such decorative purpose as this, the panel in the gallery at Bergamo was unquestionably intended. In the fifteenth century, the "letto," the "lettuccio" with its "spalliera," the "cassone" and the "colmo," or devotional picture, formed the chief articles of furniture in a Florentine bedroom.

The story of Virginia is set forth in this panel in a series of six groups, containing more than fifty figures. The scene is laid in a great basilica, viewed in the direction of its length, from a kind of ambulatory, enriched with lateral doorways and stories in relief. The architecture of this building appears to us, more Florentine in character than Roman, which Botticelli doubtless intended. The hall itself is supported on either side by a range of pilasters, decorated with arabesques, and ends within an apsidal recess of a semi-hexagonal plan, containing the tribune. As to the source from which Botticelli took this and other stories from Roman history, of which I shall have occasion to speak, there is little doubt that, like Giovanni Villani, he was acquainted with both Livy and Valerius Maximus: but in the pre-occupation which he shares with the latter writer, with the moral aspect of the legends, Sandro passes over many of the circumstances which Livy is careful to describe.

Livy, Lib. III, Cap. 44-50. Val. Maximus, Lib. VI, Cap. 1.

In the first group, on the left of the panel, Marcus Claudius the servant to Appius Claudius, on the pretext that she is his slave, seizes Virginia as she is going in the company of some women to see a public game, that was being held in Rome. The girl turns in terror to one of the four women who accompany her; while another attempts to restrain Marcus from accomplishing his purpose. On the right, a citizen approaches, and with a gesture of astonishment, inquires the cause. In a second group, within the body of the basilica, on the left, Marcus, followed by Virginia and the four women, points to the tribunal at the end of the hall, whither he leads her, in order to give an air of legality to the rape. The third group is arranged within the recess of the tribune, and appears to represent simultaneously various incidents which, according to Livy's version of the story, took place on two successive occasions. Appius Claudius, on whose orders Marcus has seized the damsel, presides as the principal judge, on a raised seat, in the centre of the tribune. Before him, on the left, stand Virginia, accompanied by three women, Marcus, and a Roman knight, probably intended for Icilius, to whom Virginia had been promised in marriage. Appius has delivered his sentence in favour of Marcus. The girl and the women stand weeping, with their faces buried in their hands; and Icilius reaches forward to restrain Marcus from seizing the damsel; while, on the right of the group, her father, Virginius, arrives unexpectedly from the camp at Algidus, and ascending the steps of the tribune, in an attitude of supplication, approaches the judge, who makes a gesture of impatience. Again, on the extreme right, Virginius is represented a second time, as he turns away, and covers his face with his hands, after Appius has refused to hear him.

Below, in a fourth group, in the body of the hall on the right, Virginius having seized his daughter by her long hair, is about to plunge the knife, (which, according to Livy, he snatches up from a butcher's stall in the market-place,) into her bosom; while the three women, in frantic attitudes of dismay, followed by Marcus, rush forward to prevent him. In a fifth group, on the extreme right of the panel, five women stand at the doorway of the ambulatory, as Virginius mounts his horse, in order to ride post to the camp of the Romans: on the left of this group, another knight leans on the saddle of a white horse. Lastly, in a sixth group, in the centre of the foreground, Botticelli with an equal disregard of place and time, represents Virginius, after he has joined the army, relating to the Roman soldiery all the circumstances of the outrage. A group of some ten mounted knights have drawn up their horses in a circle, while Virginius on the right, holding a naked sword in his right hand, and the dagger with which he killed his daughter in the left, conjures his comrades to join with him, in avenging her death.

Lastly, over each pediment of the two lateral doorways in the ambulatory, is a relief sculptured with a story taken apparently from Roman history. That on the right, may be intended for the story of Tarpeia; the host of Tatius being naively represented throwing their shields, as they pass, into a sarcophagus of marble.

Livy, Lib. I, Cap. 11. Val. Maximus, Lib. IX, Cap. 6.

Unfortunately, this panel has been much damaged by washing and retouching. The heads have especially suffered in this way: indeed, the head of Virginia in the fourth story is one of the few which, though rubbed, has escaped disfigurement. Many passages of the picture, such as the green draperies, the ornaments of the dresses and the stories in relief, were originally heightened with gold, of which few traces now remain: but here and there a figure, such as that of Virginia in the first story, or of the mounted soldier with his back turned, in the centre of the foreground, shows that in its original state, gilding was freely employed in this, as in other paintings of the same period.

As a piece of design, however, the picture is among the most admirable of the last works of Botticelli. Although the figures are designed with that vehemence of movement and gesture which characterizes the "Calumny of Apelles," the composition as a whole, is marked by a certain largeness and breadth of treatment, which is lacking in the earlier panel. This effect is due, in part, to the character of the architecture, which, without excessive ornateness, is admirable in light and shade, and in variety of surface; and in part to the architectonical arrangement of the figures in a series of groups, whose disposition and mass are strictly determined by the symmetrical and spacious order of the building. Scarcely another of Botticelli's minor works exemplifies as strikingly as this, his gift of historical painting. No longer content, like the earlier "cassone" painters, with merely illustrating the narrative, or symbolical aspect of the story, he seeks to represent its dramatic colour and significance. The first part of the legend, ending with the death of Virginia, is set forth in its fewest and most essential incidents. To these incidents succeeds the comparatively unimportant one of Virginius mounting his horse to ride post to the Roman army, in order that emphasis may be laid upon the event in which the story culminates, and to which is allotted the most prominent place in the composition. For it is, as I have said, with the moral and dramatic significance of his theme that Botticelli is chiefly preoccupied; and in introducing the angry figure of Virginius amid the surging mass of mounted warriors into the centre of the foreground, he forcibly suggests the retribution which shall presently overtake Appius and his fellows in misrule.

Another furniture-panel representing the story of Lucretia, is so similar to this panel of Virginia Romana in the method of its execution, and in the conception and treatment of its theme, that the two paintings may well have formed part of the same series of decorations; notwithstanding that they are of slightly different proportions and, by no means of an equal excellence of workmanship. The panel in question was formerly in the collection of the Earl of Ashburnham, and was shown by him at the Exhibition of Early Italian Art, held at the New Gallery in 1893-4, No. 160, as a work by Sandro Botticelli. Shortly afterwards, it passed into the collection of Mrs. J. L. Gardner, of Boston, U.S.A. The panel on which it is painted, measures 33½ inches in height, by 70 inches in length. Here, again, Botticelli is so preoccupied with the moral issue of the story, that he passes over many of those circumstances related by Livy, which for us have become an indissoluble part of the legend. The three incidents, in which the story is set forth in this panel, contain but one half the number of figures in the panel at Bergamo. As in that painting, they are arranged symmetrically, and in a perspective of architecture, which is here intended to represent the Roman Forum. The incident which Shakespeare employs with great effect in his poem, of Sextus Tarquinius, attended by a single companion, surprising Lucretia in her chamber, by night, is passed over, or rather modified, by Botticelli as being inconsistent with architectonical treatment of the story; and on the left of the panel, at the open doorway of a palace, Botticelli represents Tarquin seizing Lucretia by the robe, threatening her with a dagger which he holds in his right hand, unless she yield to his pleasure. Before the steps of the palace, stands a negro slave who has accompanied Tarquin, and holds his sword. On the right of the panel, in an open loggia corresponding to the palace, Lucretia, in the presence of Collatinus, her husband, Spurius Lucretius, her father, Publius Valerius and Lucius Junius Brutus, whom she has summoned to Rome, sinks to the ground, mortally wounded by her own hand, as they reach forward to prevent her fall. Between these two stories, filling the principal part of the picture, is a composition of some twenty figures, representing the dead body of Lucretia with the dagger in her breast, laid out on the plinth of a column, in the midst of the Forum. On an upper member of the base, before the shaft of the column, stands Brutus with a drawn sword, calling upon the Roman people to vengeance; while a number of armed knights with drawn swords, and other citizens, gather around the body.

Livy, Lib. I, Cap. 57-60. Val. Maximus, Lib. VI, Cap. 1.

Behind the column, which is surmounted by a statue of David with the head of Goliath at his feet, rises a triumphal arch, of the Corinthian order, ornamented with reliefs and statues. The design of its architecture has been imitated from the Arch of Constantine at Rome, which Botticelli had before introduced into the fresco of "Korah and his company," in the Sistine chapel: but in its details and ornaments, the painter has freely followed his own invention. The relief over the central archway, representing the captives and spoils of a Roman triumph, has obviously been imitated from some antique original. That above the main entablature on the left, is carved with the story of Marcus Curtius leaping into the fiery gulf, which

[Livy, Lib. VII, Cap. 6. Val. Maximus, Lib. V, Cap. 6.] opened in the midst of the Forum. Marcus mounted upon his horse, in the centre of the composition, is about to leap into the crevasse which gives forth flame, in the foreground on the left: behind the figure of Marcus, stands a crowd of Romans in various attitudes of astonishment and dismay. The corresponding relief, on the right of the arch, apparently represents Achilles dragging the body of Hector round the walls of Troy. The Grecian hero, mounted on a horse at full gallop, drags along in the foreground, the body of his enemy, by a rope tied round his neck: in the background is seen the camp of the Greeks. Many are the sources from which Botticelli may have been acquainted with the story of the Trojan wars: Giovanni [G. Villani, Croniche Fior., Lib. I, Cap. XIV.] Villani, speaking of the destruction of Troy, says that "Omero poeta, e Virgilio, e Ovidio, e Dario, e più altri savi (chi gli vorrà cercare) ne fecero compiutamente menzione in versi e in prosa."

The two lower reliefs, immediately above the lateral archways, represent [Livy, Lib. II, Cap. 12. Val. Maximus, Lib. III, Cap. 3.] the story of Mutius Scaevola. That on the left represents the Roman knight stabbing the secretary of Porsenna, in error for the king, at the entrance to his tent: that on right, represents the fortitude of Mutius Scaevola. On one side of the composition, Porsenna is seated before a circular altar, attended by his courtiers, and on the other, Mutius, who holds his hand in the flame of the altar, as he grasps a naked sword. The relief over the arch of the loggia on the right of the panel, represents the story of Horatius Cocles. On the right, the Roman knight keeps at bay [Livy, Lib. II, Cap. 10. Val. Maximus, Lib. III, Cap. 2.] the cohort of Porsenna, while the Romans on the far bank of the Tiber destroy the last remnant of the Pons Sublicius. Again, in the foreground on the left, Horatius is seen a second time, as he plunges with his horse into the river, to rejoin his comrades. Of the two reliefs over the entrance of the palace, on the left of the panel, the upper one represents a flight of horsemen, and appears to be of a purely decorative nature; while the lower one sets forth the story of Judith, a theme of which Botticelli never tires. On the left, Judith and her maid are seen putting the head of Holofernes into the bag of meat, before the door of his tent; and on the right, the two women approach the walls of Bethulia, Judith carrying the sword, and the maid the bag on her head, as in the little panel in the Uffizi, No. 1156.

This panel is in a better state than that in the Morelli collection, but it is far inferior to it in design and execution. The treatment of the composition as a whole, and particularly of the architecture, lacks that breadth of effect which distinguishes the painting at Bergamo. The diversity of character in the heads, and the unfailing care and refinement with which every figure in that panel is designed, are no longer distinctive traits of this. The forms are blunter, and the execution is more summary: indeed, in one or two passages of the picture, and notably in the figure of the Moor, which is partially seen on the left of the panel, so little of Botticelli's manner is to be traced, that it is evident he must have had considerable assistance in its execution. The golden tone of the panel is largely due to the coat of varnish, which obscures the original brilliancy of its colouring. And although such traits as the full warm green of Lucretia's robe, and the heightening of the lights of the draperies with gold, are undoubtedly characteristic of Botticelli; the reddish tint used in much of the architecture recalls an earlier manner than his, and suggests another hand.

In this place it will be convenient to notice a picture which is now lost, but which must have been executed during the last years of the fif-

THE STORY OF LUCREZIA *Collection of Mrs. J. L. Gardner, Boston, U.S.A. (From a photograph by H. Dixon and Son)*

teenth century if, as I conjecture, two early copies of it are still in existence. Vasari states in one of the notices interpolated into the second edition of the "Lives," that by the hand of Sandro, "in Santa Maria Maggiore at Florence, is a 'Pietà' of little figures, beside the chapel of the Panciatichi, a thing of great beauty." This is the only early notice of the picture which has come down to us. For the same church, Botticelli had executed in January, 1473-4, the panel of St. Sebastian, now in the Museum at Berlin, No. 1128. The chapel of the Panciatichi still remains in its original position, in the first bay of the right aisle, on entering the building. Stefano Rosselli, records in his "Sepoltuario Fiorentino," compiled in the year 1657, how the chapel which anciently was enclosed "by a grill of iron," had, at that time, recently "been reduced to a more modern form, and the grill taken away." At the present day, few of the original features of the chapel are to be seen, with the exception of the arms of the Panciatichi above the arch of the nave-arcade, which opens into the chapel, the square pier and respond of Gothic architecture supporting the arch, and below in the pavement, the sepulchral slab of Bartolommeo Panciatichi with an inscription stating that he founded and endowed the chapel in 1430. When Giuseppe Richa published the third volume of his "Notizie istoriche delle Chiese Fiorentine," in 1755, the "Pietà" of Sandro Botticelli hung in the Sacristy. Since that time, every trace of the picture has disappeared: it was probably sold at the time of the suppression of the monastery attached to the church, in 1808.

Vasari, ed. 1568, I, 471.

Cod. Magliabechiano, XXVI, 23, fol. 921, tergo.

l.c., III, 281.

The majority of recent writers upon Botticelli, following an opinion put forward by Signor Milanesi in his edition of Vasari, have sought to identify the painting once in Santa Maria Maggiore, with a large "Pietà" attributed to Botticelli, in the gallery at Munich, No. 1010. But if the indications given by Vasari, of the "Pietà" are to be taken literally, that painting was neither an altar-piece, nor a work of considerable dimensions: it was a picture, he is careful to state, of little figures, and it hung beside the altar. The panel at Munich, however, does not answer to this account, for it is clearly an altar-piece, and the figures which it contains, are upwards of four feet in height. Moreover, although it may well have been executed in Botticelli's workshop, and even from drawings by him, it is clearly not a work by his own hand, as Morelli considered it. Somewhat diffuse and disjointed in its composition, it lacks the dramatic unity of the genuine works of the master. The forms and relief are more naturalistic in treatment, than those which he employed at this period, and neither the colour, nor the execution, recall his hand. Mr. Berenson, in ascribing the execution of this panel to Raffaellino del Garbo, has expressed what is, perhaps, a suggestive personal conviction, rather than a demonstrable proposition in connoisseurship. In the Museo Poldi Pezzoli, at Milan, is another "Pietà," No. 552, of smaller dimensions than the one at Munich, and of an upright form. It is painted on a panel which measures 3 feet 6¼ inches in height, and 2 feet 4 inches in width. Although coarse and mannered in drawing, and crude in colour, this picture, in its faults, as in its technique, is clearly the work of some immediate disciple of Botticelli. The dead body of Christ lies in the lap of the Virgin, who is seated, facing the spectators, in the centre of the picture. One of the Maries who stands on the left of the Virgin, supports the head of Jesus: on the other side of the composition, the weeping Magdalen kneels and embraces his feet; while the third Mary, who stands behind the latter figure, covers her face with

Vasari, ed. Sansoni, III, 312, note.

B. Berenson, The Drawings of the Florentine Painters, I, 84.

her robe. The Virgin, who has fainted, sinks back and is supported by St. John, who stands behind her: and in the background, before the entrance to the sepulchre, St. Joseph of Arimathea is seen looking towards heaven, and holding up the crown of thorns and the nails of the crucifixion. This work in the simple, yet interwoven design of the figures, in its rhythm of line and movement, in its dramatic presentation of grief and abandonment and in its intense expression of religious sentiment, exhibits a series of traits so intimately characteristic of Botticelli, that it is difficult to think that the composition in its original form, whether as a cartoon, or a finished painting, was not the production of his own hand. Another early copy on panel of this "Pietà," dating from the early part of the sixteenth century, was lately sold with the Bourgeois collection, at Cologne. This version, which differed from the panel at Milan only in some minor details, was no longer executed in the technique of the master. The existence of such a copy, however, would point to some well-known original. It is difficult to think that Vasari would have mistaken the panel at Milan for a genuine work by Botticelli. It is probable, therefore, that we possess two early versions of some lost "Pietà" by the master, a work whose popularity may have been largely due to its having been placed in some public building at Florence: and these circumstances, together with the small size and upright form of the picture may, perhaps, warrant the conjecture that this original was no other than the "Pietà" which Vasari saw in Santa Maria Maggiore, hanging "beside the chapel of the Panciatichi." The custom of suspending votive pictures against the columns of the churches, appear to have been a common one in Florence, in the fourteenth and fifteenth centuries: and like the painting of St. Sebastian, which was once in the same church "in vna colonna," this "Pietà," to judge from its size and form, may well have hung against the quadrangular pier, or respond, at the entrance to the chapel.

Vasari, ed. 1550, I, 494.

Allusion has already been made to that passage in the first edition of the "Lives," in which Vasari records that, beside the cuts in illustration to Dante, Botticelli "put into stamp the triumph of the Faith of Fra Girolamo Savonarola of Ferrara"; and it has been shown that this print probably existed as an independent sheet, and not as an illustration to a lost edition of the "Trionfo della Croce" of Fra Girolamo, as some have thought. Whether the subject of this engraving was suggested by the theme of Savonarola's book, or whether Botticelli sought to celebrate in it, the triumph of the Faith in the death of the friar, as I have suggested, it was executed, in all probability, about the time of Savonarola's execution, in 1498, and belonged to a group of prints engraved in what is known as the "broad manner," in order to distinguish them from that earlier group of engravings in the "fine manner," which has already been discussed, and of which the cuts in illustration to Dante, and the "Triumph of Bacchus" are among the most remarkable examples. Of the extant engravings in the "broad manner," unquestionably the most remarkable is the large print on two sheets of the "Assumption of the Virgin," which was clearly done from a drawing by Botticelli; although, as in the earlier group of prints in the "fine manner," the engraver has varied many of the details. The impression of this engraving preserved in the print room of the British Museum, measures 0,82 cm. in height and 0,56 cm. in width, exclusive of the margin: and another fine impression is in the gallery of the Uffizi. In the upper part of the print, the Virgin is represented enthroned in the heavens, in the midst of a choir of angels. At her feet are three half-length figures of angels, winged like seraphs, and bearing in their hands branches of palm, olive and rose. Right and left of the two cherubim which form the arms of the throne on which the Virgin is seated, are two figures of angels which are turned outwards, and bear branches of olive, lily and rose. Such imagery was of the time: in a contemporary "Laude" to the Virgin occurs the verse: "Rose, gigli & viole esco*n* deluiso uostro." Above and behind the figure of the Madonna, is a group of seven kneeling figures of angels with lily-wands, who sing from a scroll which they are holding. This group, and the figures below, are so arranged as to form a kind of "mandorla" or glory, around the figure of the Virgin. On either side of this group in the upper corners of the composition, are two other groups of flying angels, with musical instruments. The figures on the left, bear severally a lute, psaltery and two trumpets; those on the right, a rebec, a double pipe, a timbril and a trumpet. Below, in the centre of the sheet, is the empty tomb of the Virgin, round which stand, or kneel, eleven of the apostles. The twelfth apostle, St. Thomas, is seen in the central part of the composition, upon a hill which rises on the left of the picture, kneeling at the feet of the Virgin, who is in the act of giving him her girdle, a famous relic still venerated at Prato. Lastly, in the distance, between a break in the hills, is a view of Rome, in which the column of Trajan, the Pantheon, Nero's tower, the Colosseum, and perhaps the Basilica of Constantine, among other buildings, may be recognized.

The original design, whether drawing or painting, from which this engraving was taken, must have been among the grandest and most vigorous works of this last period of Botticelli's art. The large and rugged treatment of the figures of the apostles, their strange, mane-like hair and beards, their fervent and agitated gestures and attitudes, lend to this part of the design, a forcible and primitive character, which recalls, though largely, perhaps, in an accidental fashion, the grand and impressive art of Andrea da Castagno. Not less vigorous in conception, but of greater beauty of form and movement, is the figure of the Virgin; and the motive and arrangement of the angels who form a "mandorla" around her, are among the most lovely and imaginative of the many inventions of the kind which Botticelli has left us. The lateral groups of angels playing upon musical instruments, are less well designed, though many of the attitudes closely recall Botticelli's manner. But in these figures, as in the details of the landscape, the hand of the engraver is doubtless to be detected in that process of free translation into black and white, which is characteristic of the earliest Florentine engravings. In this composition, Botticelli not only reverts to one of the traditional compositions of Giottesque art, but he treats it with a vigour and ruggedness of expression, which in itself is essentially Giottesque. That this trait is not an exceptional or accidental one, is shown by the many schoolworks of the period, which are frankly variations in Botticelli's manner, upon similar, traditional themes of Giottesque art; and by the persistent recurrence of this energetic and rugged character in the last works of the master.

A drawing which may have served as a preliminary study for this "Assumption," is preserved in the "Libro Resta," in the Ambrosian Library, at Milan. It represents St. Thomas kneeling, almost in the attitude of the figure in this engraving; but with certain differences in the arrangement of the draperies, and especially of the mantle, which in the drawing is thrown round the figure, and over the left shoulder. This study, which appears to be of a somewhat earlier date than the furniture-panels painted with the stories of Lucretia and Virginia, is drawn with the pen on a rubbed, red ground, and washed with bistre, and heightened with white. Admirable in action, and in the rendering of the profoundly religious sentiment of which that action is expressive, this study enables us, perhaps, to form an adequate notion of the quality of the finished composition in its original form.

In the gallery at Parma, is a painting of an "Assumption," Sala III, No. 56, by some follower of Filippino Lippi. The Virgin, who is enthroned in a "mandorla" of seraphim, is giving her girdle to St. Thomas, who kneels below her, in front of the empty tomb; and on either side of the apostle, stand St. Benedict and St. Michael the archangel. The figures of the Virgin and St. Thomas have been imitated (the latter in reverse) from this engraving of the "Assumption," or perhaps from its lost original; and that of St. Michael from the figure of the archangel in the altar-piece of San Barnaba, now in the academy at Florence, No. 85. The painter of this feeble school-work has, however, taken little more than the attitudes of Botticelli's figures, which he has draped in his own fashion.

The essential difference between the earlier prints in the "fine manner," and those in the "broad manner," lies in the various practice of the craftsmen who engraved them. The former group is clearly the production of men who habitually worked in "niello," whereas the latter group reveal the hand of a craftsman who employed the burin solely for the purpose of producing prints. Hence, not only is this "Assumption," (like the rest of the engravings in the "broad manner,") more effective in treatment and more economical in method, than the earlier group of prints; but the forms and relief are rendered with a freedom and power of expression which anticipates the maturer art of Il Robetta and his contemporaries. Again, this "Assumption," unlike the earlier group of prints, so closely recalls in its forms the manner of Botticelli at this period, that it can hardly be doubted that the engraver of this plate had at one time worked directly under the master.

Engraved in the "broad manner," is a set of twelve prints of the Sibyls, [Bartsch, vol. xiii, pp. 92-95, Nos. 9-20,] copied in part from the set of plates of the same figures, engraved in the "fine manner," [Bartsch, vol. xiii, pp. 172-175, Nos. 25-36,] which I have already described. In the case of the five prints which in the original series possess a distinctly Pollaiuolesque character, the figures are either copied without material alteration, or are else redrawn in such a manner as to give to them unmistakably a Botticellesque character: but in the case of the remaining prints, the figures, which in the original series had been taken either from the "Master E. S.," or from some other northern source, have been entirely redesigned in the manner of Botticelli. This character is very evident in the scheme of the draperies.

There is also a set of twenty-four plates in the "broad manner" of the Prophets, [Bartsch, vol. xiii, pp. 169-172, Nos. 1-24,] copied in great part from plates of the same figures, engraved in the "fine manner," [Bartsch, vol. XIII, pp. 165-167, Nos. 1-24,] already described. Only in a few instances have the original designs been redrawn, and the Botticellesque character of these copies is not so pronounced as in those of the Sibyls. Yet there is an evident attempt on the part of the engraver to modify the

German elements of their design, as in the figures of Amos and Ezechiel; and to omit the Finiguerresque profusion of ornament, as in the plate of Samuel. In the print of Jacob, Jeremiah and Elisha, we find a Botticellesque hat substituted for the Finiguerresque head-dress of the original plate. These copies, or versions, in the "broad manner" go to bear out my contention, that the engraver of this group of prints must have worked under Botticelli, at some time or another. Indeed, these copies might, with far more reason, have been ascribed to him, than the earlier sets of plates in the "fine manner," which for so long were associated with his name.

There is yet another plate engraved in the "broad manner," which was unmistakably done from a design by some follower of Botticelli, probably the engraver of the plate. This print which was formerly attributed to Giovanni Antonio da Brescia, [Passavant, vol. V, p. 108, No. 33,] represents the Virgin enthroned with the Child seated on a cushion, which is placed on her left knee. He holds a pomegranate in his left hand, and raises the other in the act of benediction. On the right of the Virgin, stands St. Helena holding the cross; and on the left of the Virgin, St. Michael the archangel, clad in armour, holding an orb and sword. Beneath the figure of the Virgin is the inscription: LACTA · MARIA · FILIVM · TVVM · CREATO/REM · TVV*M* · LACTA · PANEM · CELI · LACTA · / PRETIVM · MVNDI · PREBE · LAMBEN/TI · MAMILLAM · VT · IPSE · P*RE*BEAT · PER · CVTIENTI · MAXILLAM ·/ Beneath the figure of St. Helena is inscribed: QVAM · VIDES · HELENAM · AMPLECTI · / EST · X̂PIANOR*VM* · SPES · ROMANOR*VM* · VICTO*R*IA ·/ CECOR*VM* · DVX · / CONVERSOR*VM* · VIA · CLAVDOR*VM* · BACVL*VM* · PAV/P*ER*V*M* · CO*N*SOLATIO · ARBOR · REFECTIONIS ·/ And beneath the figure of St. Michael: PRINCEPS · GLORIOSISIME ·/ MICHAEL · NOSTRI · HIC · ETVBI/*QVE* · SEMPER · PRECARE · PRO/NOBIS · FILIVM · DEI ·/ The figures, and especially the draperies, are very Botticellesque in manner. In the general character and arrangement of the figures, and in the design of the throne, which is decorated with carved balusters, and set in a screen, behind which some trees rise against the sky, this print closely recalls the altar-pieces by a follower of Botticelli, in the church of Montelupo and in the gallery of the Uffizi, No. 3438.

Before passing on to discuss the one painting by Botticelli which bears a date, and the last of his extant works of which the time of its execution is to be ascertained with any degree of certainty, let us turn back to an incident in the life of the painter which occurred a few days before the date of his matriculation in the "Arte dei Medici e degli Speziali;" since it casts a significant ray of light upon the circumstances in which Sandro was living and working, at the time when he painted this picture. To this incident, as I have already remarked, allusion is made by Lorenzo Violi, in his "Giornate," as having been recorded by Simone Filipepi, in his "Chronicle." (App. II, Doc. XLVI, fol. 41, tergo.) Speaking of the Trial by Fire, and of the part which Doffo Spini, the leader of the Compagnacci played on that occasion, Lorenzo relates towards the end of his third Dialogue, how this Doffo Spini "used to frequent the workshop of a painter called Sandro di Botticello, a man well known in the city, on account of his being one of the most excellent painters that there were at that time: and in his workshop was constantly an Academe of Idlers, [un Accademia di Scioperati,] among whom was the aforesaid Doffo. And there, discoursing many times of the death of Fra Girolamo, Doffo said that it was never their intention to cause the Franciscan friar to enter the flames, and that they assured him of this: but it sufficed them to use him in such sort, that by delaying the matter, they might accomplish their design to put an end to this business of the friar, and make away with him. Whence it was that Doffo discoursing many times in the said workshop of Sandro, Simone, the brother of the painter, who was also present there, recorded it in his 'Chronicle.'" The passage in the "Chronicle" of Simone, to which Lorenzo Violi here alludes, runs thus in the copy preserved in the Vatican: "I will here below copy out a record which I made on the 2nd November, 1499. Alessandro di Mariano Filipepi, my brother, one of the good painters which our city has had in these times, related in my presence, being at home, by the fire, about the third hour of the night, [*i.e.*, about eight o'clock in the evening,] how on that day, in his workshop, in the house of Sandro, he had been discoursing with Doffo Spini, about the case of Fra Girolamo. And in effect, upon Sandro questioning him, (because he knew that the said Doffo had been one of the chief persons who had always been chosen to examine him,) that he should tell him the plain truth as to what faults they found in Fra Girolamo, by which he deserved to die so infamous a death; whereat Doffo then replied to him: 'Sandro, have I to tell you the truth? Not only did we never find in him mortal sin; but, moreover, neither was venial sin found in him.' Then Sandro said to him: 'Wherefore did you cause him to die in so infamous a fashion?' He replied: 'Not I, but Benozzo Federighi was the cause of it. And if this prophet and his companions had not been put to death, and had they been sent back to San Marco, the people would have put us to sack, and we should all have been cut to pieces. The matter had so far gone forward, that thus we determined for our safety, that they should die.' Then they fell to speak of other matters, which there is no need to repeat."

App. II, Doc. LV.

The statement which Simone here makes by the way, that his brother's workshop was "in the house of Sandro," is confirmed indirectly by the "Denunzie" of Mariano, and that of Botticelli himself. The usual custom of the painters in the fifteenth century was to rent their shop in the central part of Florence, and to have their dwelling-house in some more remote, and less frequented, quarter of the city. Had Botticelli rented such a shop away from his house, it would certainly have been returned in those "Denunzie"; but since no such declaration occurs in them, we are led to conclude that from 1468, when Mariano was already in possession of the house in the Via Nuova, until the end of the painter's life, Sandro had his workshop "in the house," as Simone states. That "Accademia di Scioperati," that gathering of idle, disoccupied persons of which Lorenzo Violi speaks, had probably frequented Sandro's workshop in the Via Nuova, long before Simone had come to live with his brother in 1494, and the questions of Savonarola became there an all-absorbing theme of conversation. Vasari tells how Sandro was a "very witty person and full of jovial conceits," and how "in his workshop, jests and pleasantries were continually being made"; recording various instances of these "burle," which, though trite and banal as they may now appear to us, are typically Florentine in their humour. But with the coming of Simone and the ascendency of Savonarola, a change passed over the character of these gatherings; and the workshop of Sandro gradually became a notorious meeting-place of the partisans of the friar. The "Chronicle" of Simone reveals how ardent a follower of Fra Girolamo, and how constant an attendant at San Marco, was its writer, especially after the death of the friar. The great thesis of his book is to show that Savonarola spoke "as a

Vasari, ed. 1550, I, 495.

prophet and as one sent by God"; and he never tires of telling the most trivial anecdote that might show how all who acted in opposition or derogation to the friar came, like the children of Beth-el, to an untimely end. That Sandro largely, if not entirely, shared his brother's persuasions and preoccupations at the time of the anecdote of 1499, cannot be doubted. The earnestness with which he there interrogates Doffo Spini, and the ecstatic and mystical mood in which he paints the little picture, which we are about to discuss, can admit of no other conclusion. The avowal of such opinions was still fraught with as much danger, after the death of Savonarola, as it had previously been; for that event did not put an end to the civil disorders of the city; but the Florentines "continued in the same dissensions and were distraught by the same sects, as they had been during the lifetime of the friar." F. Nerli, Commentarj, ed. 1728, p. 81.

There is yet another anecdote in the "Chronicle" which I will cite in this place, since it shows how keenly Simone was aware of this danger, and also explains how Botticelli and his brother came to be the associate of the man who had been the leader of the Compagnacci, and one of the bitterest opponents of the friar. "This day, the 9th of April, 1503," runs the anecdote, "I, Simone di Mariano Filipepi, on coming out of the house, in order to go to Vespers at San Marco, was greeted by Doffo Spini, who was in company with Bartolommeo di Lorenzo Carducci. This Bartolommeo turned to me and said, that Fra Girolamo and the Piagnoni had ruined and undone the city. Whence between him and me fell many words which need not be written here, in order to avoid being tedious. But Doffo took up the argument and said, that he never had any intercourse with Fra Girolamo until he was put in prison; he [Doffo] being then one of the Otto who examined him; and that had he heard Fra Girolamo before that time, and been acquainted with him, as Simone here (turning to me) I should have been a greater partisan of his than Simone; because nothing except good was then seen of him until his death; but his case had gone forward in such sort, that it needs must have been done to him, as was done to Christ. He said other things which, perhaps, I shall write in this book, although they may not pass without danger: but in these days I find myself on the high sea, and it behoves me to steer well; trusting in God that my bark will reach the haven." But let us turn to the little painting in question. P. Villari and E. Casanova, Scelta di Prediche e Scritti di Savonarola, p. 498.

This picture was the first genuine work by Botticelli which found its way to England, perhaps the very first to leave Italy. It was acquired by William Young Ottley "from the Villa Aldobrandini," the famous palace, I take it, of that family on the Viminal, at Rome. The Aldobrandini, who were of an ancient Florentine stock, had their houses in that city on the Piazza Madonna, behind San Lorenzo; and the picture had probably been brought by them from Florence, in the time of Clement VIII. Ottley had collected at Rome, "about the end of 1798, or in the beginning of 1799, when the principal families were in the acutest stage of their misery," a number of important Italian pictures, by the masters then in vogue. These were offered for sale by Messrs. Christie in 1801. The "Nativity" by Botticelli, if acquired at that time, was not included in the sale; and I find it mentioned for the first time, in the catalogue of Ottley's second sale, which took place at Christie's on 25th May, 1811, when the picture, Lot 32, was bought in for £42. Ottley, who mistook the painting for the altar-piece, once in the church of Santa Maria Novella, and now in the Uffizi, No. 1286, appears W. Y. Ottley, Italian School of Design, p. 405.

G. F. Waagen, Art and Artists in England, II, 125-6.

to have conceived an admiration for the picture, which was altogether at variance with the taste of the time. When, in 1835 Dr. Waagen expressed his approbation of the fine collection of early Italian masters which Ottley had formed, the latter complained that "so long as he had been in England, no one had paid so much attention to them" as his visitor; and Dr. Waagen had certainly reason to observe, that "Mr. Ottley is one of the few persons who recognized the noble and rich intellectual treasures in these ancient works of art at a time when they were, in general, despised or forgotten." After Ottley's death, it was put up a second time at Christie's, with the remainder of his collection, on 4th March, 1837, Lot 75, when it was sold for the trifling sum of £25 4*s.* The painting afterwards passed into the collection of Mr. W. Fuller Maitland, of Stanstead House, Essex, and was exhibited by him, in 1857, at the Art Treasures Exhibition, at Manchester, No. 78; in 1871, at the second Exhibition of Old Masters at Burlington House, No 278; and more recently at the South Kensington Museum, where, as a boy, I first saw it. It was finally purchased for the National Gallery, in 1878, from Mr. Fuller Maitland, for £1,500, where it now bears the number 1034.

Luke ii, 1-20.

This "Nativity" is painted on a canvas which measures 3 feet 6½ inches in height, and 2 feet 5½ inches in width. It represents, with that spiritual fervour and ecstatic power of imagination, which are peculiarly characteristic of this last phase of Botticelli's art, the story of the Nativity and the Adoration of the Shepherds, as related in the Gospel according to St. Luke, but with a mystical and prophetic intention, which is obscurely set forth in a Greek inscription, arranged in three lines of uncial characters, on the upper margin of the panel. The first to decipher this inscription, and to indicate its probable meaning, was Mr. Sidney Colvin, in a letter which was printed in the "Academy" of 15th February, 1871. To his emendation of the few letters which have been erased by accidental injury in the original, and to his translation of the text, I have little to add; but in my attempt to comment upon it, I have endeavoured to interpret its meaning with that blunt literality which a Florentine of the fifteenth century would have employed in writing it. In the course of this inscription occurs the name of the painter; but neither here, nor in the drawing at Berlin, in illustration of Canto XXVIII of the "Paradiso," (the only two works of Botticelli which bear his name,) does it occur merely by way of signature.

This inscription runs thus in the original, the letters in brackets being wanting:

ΤΑΥΤΗΝ·ΓΡΑΦΗΝ ·ΕΝ ·ΤΩι ·ΤΕΛΕΙ ·ΤΟΥ ·ΧΣΣΣΣΣ ·ΕΤȢΣ ·ΕΝ ·ΤΑΙΣ·ΤΑΡ[ΑΧΑΙ]Σ·
ΤΗΣ · ΙΤΑΛΙΑΣ · ΑΛΕΞΑΝΔΡΟΣ · ΕΓΩ · ΕΝ · ΤΩι · ΜΕΤΑ · ΧΡΟΝΟΝ · ΗΜΙΧΡΟΝΩι ·
ΕΓΡΑΦΟΝ · ΠΑΡΑ · ΤΟ · ΕΝΔΕ/ΚΑΤΟΝ · ΤȢ · ΑΓΙȢ · ΙΩΑΝΝȢ · ΕΝ · ΤΩι ·
ΑΠΟΚΑΛΥΨΕΩΣ · Β͠ · ΟΥΑΙ · ΕΝ · ΤΗι · ΛΥΣΕΙ · ΤΩΝ · Γ · [Κ]ΑΙ · ΗΜΙΣΥ · ΕΤΩΝ ·
ΤȢ · ΔΙΑΒΟΛȢ · ΕΠΕΙΤΑ · ΔΕΣΜΟΘΗΣΕΤΑΙ · ΕΝ · ΤΩι · ΙΒ͠ · ΚΑΙ · /ΒΛΕΨΟΜΕΝ ·
ΠΑ[ΤΟΥΜΕ]ΝΟΝ · ΟΜΟΙΟΝ · ΤΗι · ΓΡΑΦΗι · ΤΑΥΤΗι./

In modern cursive Greek, accented and pointed, it would read thus:

Ταύτην γραφήν ἐν τῷ τέλει τοῦ χσσσσσ ἔτους ἐν ταῖς ταραχαῖς τῆς Ἰταλίας Ἀλέξανδρος ἐγώ ἐν τῷ μετὰ χρόνον ἡμιχρόνῳ ἔγραφον, παρὰ τὸ ἑνδέκατον τοῦ ἁγίου Ἰωάννου, ἐν τῷ

THE ADORATION OF THE SHEPHERDS *National Gallery, London*

Ἀποκαλύψεως δευτέρῳ [βωι] οὐαὶ, ἐν τῇ λύσει τῶν γ' καὶ ἥμισυ ἔτων τοῦ διάβολου. ἐπεῖτα δεσμωθήσεται (ἐν τῷ δωδεκάτῳ [ιβωι]) καὶ βλέψομεν πατούμενον ὅμοιον ταύτῃ τῇ γραφῇ.

Done literally into English, this inscription would seem to run:
"This picture, at the end of the year 1500, in the troubles of Italy, I, Alessandro, painted in the half-time after the time, at the time of the fulfilment of the 11th of St. John, in the second war of the Apocalypse, in the loosing of the devil for three and a half years: then he shall be chained according to the twelfth, and we shall see him trodden down as in this picture."

I will first endeavour to elucidate those passages in this inscription, of which the meaning is dubious, or obscure:

"At the end of the year 1500":—There can be little doubt that the year 1500 is intended by the numerals ΧΣΣΣΣΣ; yet it does not seem possible to explain them in any consistent manner. In the Greek numeration Χ is the symbol for 600, and Σ for 200: but Botticelli here seems to have used Χ for Χίλιος, a thousand, and Σ for the Latin C, the symbol for centum, a hundred. This odd inconsistency is the more puzzling, since later on in the inscription, Sandro rightly uses Γ as the Greek symbol for 3. Can it be that, after the inscrutable way of mystics, Botticelli sought to obscure the date? Be that as it may, there can be small doubt as to the year intended. According to the Florentine computation, the year 1500 ended on the 24th March, 1501, of the Roman Calendar.

"In the troubles of Italy":—By this expression is clearly intended the whole series of invasions, wars and disorders, which since the death of Lorenzo, Il Magnifico, had overwhelmed, and which in 1501 still disturbed the peace of Italy.

"In the half-time after the time":—We have here an evident allusion to the mystical period, "a time and times and half a time," mentioned in chap. xii, v. 14 of the Book of the Revelation of St. John. Botticelli, doubtless, had in his mind the "tempus et tempora et dimidium temporis" of the Vulgate, rather than the καιρὸς καὶ καιροὶ καὶ ἥμισυ καιροῦ of the Septuagint, which was probably unknown to him: hence the form of the phrase as it occurs in the inscription. This mystical period is, also, twice mentioned in the book of Daniel; in chap. vii, v. 25, and in chap. xii, v. 7. Botticelli, I think, following Savonarola, interpreted this mystical period to prefigure an actual period of three and a half years. The friar's sermons in exposition of the Apocalypse are, as I have said, unfortunately lost: but in the Biblioteca Nazionale at Florence, is a copy of the Vulgate, printed at Basle in 1491, the margins of which are covered with a gloss, written by him in minute characters. In this gloss, the passage in question is commentated thus: "*per tempus:* per unum annum. *& tempora:* per duos annos: *& dimidium temporis:* idest anni. et nota quod tempus christi & antechristi quantum ad proprias personas est trium annorum cum dimidio." App. II, Doc. LVI.

"At the time of the fulfilment of the 11th of St. John," in the second woe of the Apocalypse":—With the tribulations foretold in chap. xi of the Revelation of St. John, the second woe of the Apocalypse is brought to a conclusion.

"In the loosing of the Devil for three and a half years":—This period of misrule, which must clearly be understood to fall within the time of the second woe, and to form part of "the fulfilment of the 11th of St. John," can only be taken to refer to the "three days and a half," during which the dead bodies of the two witnesses shall be unburied in the street of the great city, as foretold in chap. xi, v. 8-9 of the Book of the Revelation. Botticelli probably identified this mystical period with the actual space of "forty and two months," or three and a half years, during which the Gentiles shall tread the holy city under foot, as foretold in v. 2 of the same chapter. Certainly, the three and a half years of the loosing of the Devil is to be identified with the mystical period of "a time and times and half a time," alluded to in the first part of the inscription.

In the light of these elucidations, the inscription may be paraphrased thus: "I, Sandro, painted this picture, at the end of the year 1500, [*i.e.* 24th March, 1501, c.s.,] during the troubles of Italy, in the half year after the first year of the three and a half years, of the loosing of the devil, in accordance with the fulfilment of the 11th chapter of St. John, in the second woe of the Apocalypse: then he shall be chained according to the 12th chapter, and we shall see him trodden down as in this picture."

That Botticelli is here applying the obscure prophecies of the Apocalypse to contemporary events, needs no demonstration; and it is equally evident that if we would elucidate his meaning, we must turn to the events themselves, rather than to the inscrutable symbolism and dark forebodings, "obscure as Themis and Sphinx," which bear the name of St. John. The chronicle of Simone Filipepi makes it abundantly clear what events Botticelli precisely intended by "the troubles of Italy," and why he associated these events with the certain prophecies of the Apocalypse. "Fra Girolamo," records Simone, "began to preach at Florence in the year 1489, as a prophet and as one sent by God, foretelling the scourge that should overtake all Italy, and exhorting everyone to repentance." "Ecce gladius Domini super terram cito et velociter," is a burden of which the friar never tires in his sermons. "I began," says Savonarola himself in his "Compendio delle Rivelazioni," "publicly to expound the Apocalypse to the people in our church of San Marco, on the 1st of August, 1489, which was a Sunday. And continuing to preach all that year in Florence, I repeatedly set forth three things to the people: the first was, that the Church should be renewed in those times; the second, that, previous to this renewal, God would visit all Italy with a great scourge; and the third, that these things would come to pass quickly." Simone Filipepi, speaking of these sermons, records that Fra Girolamo "used often to say in his sermons: I mistrust this peaceful time; it will pass away, and that quickly, and one will come from over the mountains, like Cyrus, who will trouble and put to confusion all Italy, and take the fortresses with the battlements. Of this, the wise-heads of the world then made jest, and especially Lorenzo de' Medici; and everyone put these sayings down to the simplicity of the friar. But all afterwards came true, in the year 1494, at the hands of the King of France, and not long after at the hands of the Duke Valentino, as is recorded in the histories."

P. Villari and E. Casanova, Scelta di Prediche e Scritti di Savonarola, p. 453.

l.c., p. 354.

l.c., p. 474.

"At the end of the year 1500," the Duke Valentino, as Caesar Borgia was popularly called in Florence, was at the height of his campaign in the Romagna. Simone, in the first part of his "Chronicle," relates all the circumstances of this cruel war: he tells how Cesare, having been created a cardinal, unfrocked himself in order to follow the fortunes of a soldier, how he engaged in the project to seize, by force of arms, the states in the Romagna which had once belonged to the Papacy, and how he murdered his brother, the Duke of Gandia, that he might be "the only

l. c., p. 468.

one to reign." "Nor," adds Simone, "did the Pope make any example of this new Cain, by reason of the love which he bore to him; but afterwards gave him to wife a kinswoman of the King of France. Whither, having gone in his galleys, with many followers and with vast pomp, as soon as he had concluded a treaty touching many matters, with the said king, he returned to the damage and ruin of Italy. And beginning with the Romagna, after he had joined himself to the French soldiery, he suddenly took, without fighting, Imola and Forlì. Then, after many battles, he captured Faenza; the lord of that place, who was a young man of a most beautiful presence, submitting himself to him. Whereat Valentino, after he had satisfied for some time his wicked and most shameful lusts upon his body, with great cruelty caused him to be strangled and thrown into the Tiber. Then he took Pesaro without fighting, and chased out its rightful lord; and he did the same thing at Rimini. And ranging thus throughout Italy, as if he were the new scourge, or rather the executioner, of God, he made his way towards Piombino in Tuscany, and took it without unsheathing his sword: and afterwards returning to Rome by sea, he narrowly escaped drowning. The year following, 1501, he came with his men into the territory of Florence, by the Val di Marina, and set himself down at Campi, between Florence and Prato, having with him the Signor Paolo Orsini, an infamous man and a bastard, like himself, and the Duke of Gravina and Vitellozzo Vitelli: and there they remained about 15 days with very great hurt; and they did damage to that State to the value of more than two hundred thousand ducats, which nearly all fell upon the peasants. But the design which they had, of bringing back Piero de' Medici, did not otherwise succeed."

The marriage of Cesare Borgia with Charlotte d'Albret was announced on 22nd May, 1499; and the following October, Louis XII captured Milan. Cesare began his campaign in the Romagna by taking Imola and Forlì, in January, 1499-1500. For the moment, his plan of aggression was interrupted by the return of Ludovico Sforza to Milan, in the course of the following month. In October, 1500, Cesare set out from Rome with an army of 10,000 men, and quickly possessed himself of Rimini and Pesaro: Faenza offered, however, a stouter resistance, and it did not capitulate till 20th April, 1501. A glance at the "Diario" of Luca Landucci shows with what feelings of alarm and loathing the progress of Cesare Borgia was watched in Florence, "at the end of the year 1500." When in May, 1501, Valentino and his men passed over into Tuscany, it seemed as though Sandro's worst apprehensions were to be fulfilled, and that Florence was to share the fate of many a town in the Romagna.

But here let us turn to inquire precisely what events, according to the expectation of the painter, were to come to pass "in fulfilment of the 11th of St. John." There can be little doubt, as Mr. Colvin first suggested, that "the two witnesses," who should "prophecy a thousand, two hundred and three score days, clothed in sackcloth," were understood by Botticelli to prefigure Savonarola and Fra Domenico da Pescia, who, as a preacher, bore a conspicuous part in the mission of the friar. Fra Silvestro, the other inmate of San Marco, who was executed with Savonarola, was altogether a subordinate figure, and was not distinguished as a preacher. The gloss written by Savonarola on this chapter, in the margins of his Bible, makes it abundantly clear in what sense he interpreted the passage in question. Against the passage, "diebus mille ducentis sexaginta," he

App. II, Doc. LVI.

writes: "dies hic nominat quia lucem predicant ueritatis"; and the verse, "If any man hurt them, fire proceedeth out of their mouth," etc., he annotates: "*ignis:* idest predicatio que eos ad ignem condemnabit." A religious enthusiast might have easily seen in the extraordinary ascendency of the friar, a fulfilment of such prophecies; and if, as seems probable, Botticelli understood the period of "a thousand, two hundred and three score days" in its literal sense of three and a half years, he might readily have reconciled the prophecy with the event; since the period which elapsed from the time when Savonarola first took a part in the public affairs of the city, (when on 5th November, 1494, he was appointed one of the five ambassadors of the Republic to treat with Charles VIII,) until the time of his execution on 23rd May, 1498, exceeded only by a few days the appointed term. But to pass on to the other circumstances of the prophecy. "The beast that ascendeth out of the bottomless pit," the antichrist, according to Savonarola's gloss, that was to make war against the two witnesses "after they shall have finished their testimony," and "overcome them and kill them," was probably understood by Botticelli to typify the whole of the powers, ecclesiastical and civil, by which Savonarola's death was accomplished, and his attempt to establish a theocratic government overthrown. The "three days and a half," during which the dead bodies of the two witnesses were to be unburied "in the street of the great city, which spiritually is called Sodom and Egypt," when "they that dwell upon the earth shall rejoice over them and make merry," (a prediction which would appear from Luca Landucci's "Diario," to have been very literally fulfilled,) was doubtless, I think, identified, in Botticelli's mind, with the "time and times and half a time" of the inscription, that is, with the three and a half years during which the devil was to be loosed. After this period of tribulation, so runs the inscription, "he shall be chained according to the twelfth, and we shall see him trodden down as in this picture." The allusion here to the 12th chapter of the Revelation of St. John, clearly has reference to verses 7-9: "And there was war in heaven: Michael and his angels fought against the dragon; and the dragon fought and his angels, and prevailed not; neither was their place found any more in heaven. And the great dragon was cast out, that old serpent, called the Devil and Satan, which deceiveth the whole world: he was cast out into the earth, and his angels were cast out with him."

In reading the records and writings of Savonarola's followers, the student cannot fail to be struck by the insistency with which they allude to, and the confidence with which they expected, the fulfilment of the friar's prediction that the church should be renewed, that previously to this renewal God would visit all Italy with a great scourge, "un gran flagello," and that these things would come to pass quickly. When Charles VIII crossed the Alps, and descended upon Italy, the followers of Savonarola saw in him the "flagello" predicted by their prophet. Time went on, yet the renewal of the Church which was to follow this time of tribulation, did not come to pass: the friar was excommunicated, arrested, and put to death; yet his prophecy was not fulfilled. Luca Landucci, who was present when the confession, which Savonarola was purported to have made under torture, was publicly read, relates how his soul was filled with grief, when he heard it. "I looked," he writes, "to have seen Florence a new Jerusalem, whence should issue the laws and the splendour and example of holy living, and to have seen the renewal of the Church, the

L. Landucci, Diario, p. 173

conversion of the infidel, and the consolation of the good; and I beheld the contrary things." When, after the execution of the friar, Cesare Borgia undertook his campaign in the Romagna, and in the Spring of 1501, threatened to cross the Appenines and ravage Tuscany, Botticelli appears to have foreseen in him the scourge which, according Savonarola's prediction, was to precede the renewal of the Church. Indeed, the words used by Simone, in the passage already quoted, which was written after the death of Alexander VI, when the danger had long passed away, admits of little doubt on the point. That "new Cain," he there writes of Cesare, went ranging through Italy, "quasi novo flagello, anzi boia di Dio." By the passage in the inscription, "in the loosing of the Devil for three and a half years, then he shall be chained according to the twelfth, and we shall see him trodden down as in this picture," Botticelli would appear to allude to the scourge that was to fall upon all Italy, and the subsequent renewal of the Church, which Savonarola had foretold. And in identifying this scourge and the subsequent renewal of the Church, with the events foretold in the 11th and 12th chapters of the book of Revelation, Sandro was probably repeating what Savonarola had set forth in his lost sermons on the Apocalypse.

But to come to the picture: under the thatched roof of the stall, which has been erected in the opening of a mass of rock, in the centre of the picture, the Virgin kneels turned towards the left, and adores the child who lies before her, on a cloth spread upon the earth, with a pack-saddle for a pillow. On the left of the child, St. Joseph is seated on the ground, with his head resting upon his hand. Behind these figures, within the opening of the rock, are seen the ox and the ass, feeding at a wattled manger. On the roof of the pent-house, kneel three angels, severally draped in white, green and red; the two outer figures hold branches of olive, and the one in the midst an open book, from which all are singing. Above the roof of the stall, and beneath a circular glory which opens in the heavens, dancing in a round, is a choir of twelve angels who likewise are draped alternately in white, green and red. As they clasp one another's hands, they hold twelve branches of olive, round each of which are twined two scrolls, bearing legends; and from the stem of every branch hangs a crown of gold, suspended by golden chains. On the uppermost of these two scrolls, the legend from St. Luke, chap. ii, v. 14, "Gloria in excelsis Deo," appears to have been repeated: but only in one instance, is the entire passage still to be made out; namely, on the branch held by the two angels in red and white, immediately above the angel in green who kneels on the roof of the pent-house. Here the legend runs: GLO/RIA · IN · E/CELSI/S · D/EO/. On the scroll immediately to the left of this, held by the same angel in red, and the next figure in green, are the letters, GLO...EL...DEO. On the next scroll to the left, the word GLORIA; and on one of the scrolls to the right, the word DEO. The lower scrolls are inscribed with passages of what appears to be a hymn to the Virgin: but of these legends, only a few disjointed words, or letters, can now be deciphered. On the five scrolls held by the more distant, and therefore the lower, line of figures, as they are seen in perspective, may be read the following disjointed words, or letters, from left to right, thus: on the first scroll, [RE]GINA · SO/LA ... PRA ...; on the second, REGINA · SOLA...; on the third, ...VD (?)...FECHVNDA...; on the fourth, ...V[I]RGINVM... On the fifth, SACRA/RIVM · I[N]/ BETHL[EHEM] (?).... On the next scroll, held by the figures at the turn of the circle, on the extreme right of the panel, is repeated the word [S]ACRAR[IVM]. The scrolls held by the upper line of figures, are yet more damaged than those below: on one of those in the centre of the picture, are the letters, ..OSA.. / ... VRIS · ADMIRÂD...; and on another to the left, ..SPE[R]AN... The letters within the brackets are my conjectural emendations. Some of these disjointed words, or fragments of words, recall such expression from St. Casimir's Hymn to the Blessed Virgin, as, "Semper munda et faecunda, Virgo tu puerpera," or, "Decus mundi, lux profundi, Domini Sacrarium." But in spite of repeated search, I have not succeeded in tracing their source.

On a patch of sward, among the rocks in the foreground of the picture, stand three young men, in long robes, crowned with olive, who carry olive branches and embrace three angels. These figures are arranged symmetrically in three groups; the men in each instance being turned towards the left, and the angels to the right. To each olive branch, is attached a scroll, on which the latter part of the verse from St. Luke, (the first portion of which is inscribed on the scrolls of the angels above,) is repeated: "In terra pax hominibus bonae voluntatis." On the scroll borne by the figure on the right, may be deciphered the words, [H]OMINIBV[S] · BONE · VOL[V]NTA[TIS]: and on that borne by the figure on the left, by little more than the letters, [HOMI]NIBVS. The inscription on the scroll borne by the central figure, is almost completely erased. Without the rustic pillar supporting the roof of the pent-house, on the right of the panel, kneel two shepherds, in hose and tunic, garlanded with olive; and beside them stands an angel who holds an olive branch in his hand, as he points to the Holy Child. Without the post, on the opposite side of the picture, kneel three men in long robes, also garlanded with olive; as another angel by their side, carrying an olive branch, bids them adore the Christ. Scrolls are attached to the branches which the angels carry; but their legends have been almost completely erased. It has been thought that these three kneeling figures are intended to represent the three magi; but there is nothing, except their number, to warrant such a conjecture. On the contrary, these figures resemble, in their outward appearance, those of the three young men whom the angels are embracing in the foreground of the picture. They are probably intended to symbolize the adoration of the faithful; just as the figures of the angels embracing the young men are intended to symbolize that peace on earth and good will towards men, that is to follow the new birth of Christ. Lastly, in the lower corners of the painting, two devils in mediaeval shape, are seen fleeing away discomforted. In the distance, behind the pent-house, and through the opening of the central mass of rock, is a thick wood of young trees.

In conclusion, then, there is little doubt that this painting is to be understood in a mystical sense, to symbolize that new birth of Christ, which in Botticelli's mind was identified with the renewal of the Church, foretold by Savonarola; when, according to the predictions of the friar, the splendour and example of holy living, the conversion of the unbeliever and the consolation of the good, should be brought to pass, and the devil "cast out as in this picture."

Such is the subject of this painting, the most spiritual, perhaps, and certainly one of the most lovely and imaginative of all Botticelli's works. With the exception of some of the illustrations to Dante, nothing of his which has come down to us, more completely justifies Walter Pater's allusion to him as a "visionary painter," than this canvas. It is characteristic of

Botticelli's genius, that in the central group, around which he has woven the highly imaginative and original motives of the other figures, he should have employed the traditional composition of the Virgin worshipping the Child, with St. Joseph by their side, known as a "Nativity:" and a further touch of archaism which is no less characteristic, and which, perhaps, was equally unconscious on his part, is to be noted in the somewhat larger scale on which the figures of this central portion of the picture are drawn.

The picture has suffered from abrasion and washing, rather than from extensive retouching. Many of the legends on the scrolls, as we have seen, have partially, or entirely, disappeared; and the gold used in heightening the lights of certain passages, has also suffered in this way. Moreover, as in all paintings of the fifteenth century executed on canvas, the colours have tended to darken; and this, no doubt, has contributed to that effect of evening light, rather than of dawn, which pervades the picture. Yet, if the painting lack something of that gem-like clarity of tint, which is characteristic of the finest panel-pictures of this period, it remains one of the most exquisite pieces of Botticelli's colouring. The figures of the dancing angels which are seen against the clear, morning sky, are alternately clad in white, pale purple and olive green: and the lower groups of the three singing angels and the three angels who embrace the shepherds, are also clad in the same colours. The lights of these green and purple draperies, the dress of the Virgin, which is likewise of that deep, golden olive-green peculiarly characteristic of Botticelli's colour at this period, and the thatch on the roof of the pent-house, are all hatched with gold. Again, in the draperies of the figures which embrace the angels, a red inclining to purple predominates; and the greens of the trees and foreground tend to a golden brown.

One other picture of this period is conceived in the same mystical and imaginative vein; and although much of its symbolism is obscure, and its precise allusion is no longer, perhaps, to be made out, there can be little doubt as to the drift of its meaning. Like the mystical "Nativity" in the National Gallery, it has for its theme the great burden of Savonarola's teaching, as summed up by Simone Filipepi in the passage at the beginning of his "Chronicle," where he says that Fra Girolamo preached "as a prophet and as one sent by God, foretelling the scourge that should come upon all Italy, and exhorting every one to repentance." In its outward manifestation, this picture recalls some of the visions, or "immaginazioni," as Savonarola himself termed them, which the friar describes in his famous Sermon on the Renovation of the Church, and in the "Compendio delle Rivelazioni." Although the execution of this picture can scarcely be ascribed to Botticelli's own hand, the whole conception of the piece is so nearly in his vein, that its design must assuredly be given to him; moreover, it reveals in so impressive a manner, the moral aspect of Sandro's thought and feeling at this period of his life, that I cannot refrain from discussing it in this place. This remarkable painting is now in the collection of M. Aynard, of Lyons, who obtained it some years ago, in Florence. It is painted on a fine, linen canvas, which measures $27\frac{1}{2}$ inches in height by $15\frac{3}{4}$ inches in width; and it is, unfortunately, in a very indifferent state of preservation.

Set in a rock on a green sward, in the foreground of the picture, rises the Cross, on which hangs the crucified Christ. At the foot, clasping the tree of the Cross, lies the prostrate figure of the Magdalene, here doubtless intended as the symbol of the penitent human soul. On the right of the Cross, stands an angel holding a rod in his right hand, and in his left some kind of animal, by one of its hind legs, perhaps intended for a fox, in allusion to the verse: "Capite nobis vulpes parvulas, quae demoliuntur vineas." In the upper part of the picture, on the left, is a little figure of God the Father, seated in a glory of Seraphim, and holding an open book. In the sky, a number of shields blazoned with the cross, are seen to fall from heaven, as if rained by the Almighty upon the earth. These shields, which are of the same form as those borne by the Dominations, in Botticelli's drawing of the Angelic Hierarchy in illustration to Canto XXVII of the "Paradiso," fall across the picture from left to right, towards a bank of angry clouds, in which are a number of devils, who hurl burning brands upon the earth. As the brands fall upon the earth, they ignite everything in a general conflagration, which is seen to approach the walls of Florence, represented in the distance, on the left of the canvas. The motive recalls the oft-repeated warning of Savonarola, "O Florentia, propter peccata tua advenient tibi adversa." On the right of the angel, flame is belched up from the earth, as if from the mouth of hell. The dome and campanile of the Cathedral, the Baptistery, Or San Michele and the Palazzo Vecchio, with some other churches and public buildings, may be recognized in the view of Florence surrounded by her walls. The falling shields, blazoned with the Cross, apparently symbolical of that power of divine wrath which urges the evil spirits to hurl the burning brands upon the earth, recall the vision described by Savonarola in the "Compendio delle Rivelazioni," of the "*Crux irae Dei,*" which he suddenly saw "trouble the heavens and drive clouds through the air, and cast winds and lightning and thunderbolts, and rain down hail, fires and swords, and kill a great multitude of people, so that few remained upon the earth."

Song of Solomon, ii, 15.

P. Villari and E. Casanova, Scelta di Prediche e Scritti di Savonarola, p. 366.

The picture has suffered extensively from scouring and retouching, so much so that it is now difficult to speak of the character of its execution, or even to determine the original forms of some of its details, such as the animal which the angel is holding up. The attitude and draperies of the angel closely recall similar passages in the mystical "Nativity," No. 1034, in the National Gallery, and the whole conception of the prostrate figure of the Magdalene is entirely conceived in Sandro's vein: indeed, at first sight this picture might seem to be an authentic, but damaged, work by his hand. The figure of the Christ, however, has so little of his manner, and betrays the hand of some far more naturalistic painter than was Botticelli at this period of his career, that it is difficult to ascribe the actual execution of the painting to the master himself. The present condition of the picture, no doubt, is largely due to its execution on canvas, rather than on panel. The figure of the Magdalene, and much of the foreground, have especially suffered from scouring; and some of the figures of the devils in the sky are to be made out with difficulty. One of them, who holds a sheaf of burning brands on his arm, as he hurls one of them down, is to be seen immediately to the right of the knees of the Christ; and two other devils are partially to be seen hurling the flaming torches, from the clouds on the right of the former figure.

Of this period of Botticelli's art are a number of school-pictures which will be discussed in their place; the subjects of which are taken from the great themes of religious painting. Although they unmistakably reveal the influence of Botticelli's manner at this time, few of them bear any trace of

THE MAGDALEN AT THE FOOT OF THE CROSS *Collection of M. Aynard, Lyons*

the imaginative and mystical spirit which distinguishes the two paintings which I have just discussed. On the contrary, they betray a tendency on the part of their authors, to revert not only to traditional compositions of Giottesque art, but even to modes of Giottesque expression.

Of the same period, also, is a drawing in the Gallery of the Uffizi, Frame 53, No. 209, for a "Nativity," which has been taken for a preliminary study for the picture in the National Gallery; but though the general conception and arrangement of the composition is much the same, the seated figure of St. Joseph, on the left, is in another attitude; and the draperies throughout are different in arrangement, and more mannered in design. Nor does the drawing appear to have been used for any one of the many school-pictures of the "Nativity," which have come down to us. It is drawn with the pen on a rubbed red ground, the lights being heightened with white. This sheet has suffered considerably from retouching and rough usage, and has been cut to an oval form, measuring $6\frac{1}{4}$ inches in height, by $10\frac{1}{4}$ inches in length. Indeed, the pen-work shows so little of that vivacity of touch which distinguishes the genuine drawings of the master, that its genuineness might have been called into dispute, had not the action and relief of the figures unmistakably betrayed his hand.

A brief, but significant, allusion to the repute which Botticelli enjoyed as a painter, and the circumstances in which he was working, in the autumn of 1502, occurs in a letter of a contemporary. It appears from the correspondence of Isabella d'Este, the wife of Giovanni Francesco Gonzaga, Marquis of Mantua, that already in the year 1500, that munificent patroness of the arts had endeavoured to obtain from Pietro Perugino, a painting for the decoration of her famous "Camerino," in the ducal palace of "La Corte Vecchia," at Mantua. Having failed at that time to satisfy her wish, on the 15th September, 1502, she addressed the following letter to Francesco Malatesta, her agent at Florence: "Francesco; since we desire to have in our 'Camerino' paintings of histories, by the excellent painters, who are at present in Italy, among whom Il Perusino is famous; our will is, that you go to him, using, if it seems good to you, the mediation of some friends of his, and find out if he would accept the undertaking to paint a picture of the history, or invention, that we shall give to him: and the figures should be small as, you know, are those which are already in the aforesaid 'Camerino'; and should he accept the undertaking, you are to write word of it. Learn what price he would ask, and whether he would begin the work quickly; that we may send him the measures of the picture, with our fantasy: and see that you reply with diligence." App. II, Doc. LVII.

Eight days later, on 23rd of the same month, Francesco Malatesta sent the following reply to the Marchioness: "My most illustrious lady, I have received what your ladyship has written to me, that I should make enquiry of Il Perusino, the famous painter, in order to accomplish your desire to have a painting by his hand. I find that he is at present working at Siena, and does not return for eight or ten days. As soon as he comes, I will speak with him; and use every diligence, that he may be willing to undertake to serve your Ladyship. True it is, that I have been given to understand that the man is of slow performance, and, so to speak, scarcely ever finishes a work which he begins; so great are his delays.

"Another famous painter has been spoken of to me, who also has been much belauded to me. He is called Philipo di Fra Philipino; and I have spoken with him, and he has told me that he will not be able to begin such a work for these six months, since he is occupied with other labours; but that, perhaps, after these are finished, he will be able to serve your Ladyship.

"Another, Alexandro Botechiella, has been much extolled to me, both as an excellent painter, and as a man who works willingly, and has no hindrances, as the aforesaid. I have spoken with him; and he says that he would undertake the work at once, and would serve your Ladyship with a good will. I have thought fit to give notice of all these to your Ladyship, in order that you may make a choice of the one who most shall please you, to whom I continually recommend myself."

Of Francesco Malatesta's proposal that the commission for the picture might, as an alternative, be given to Filippino Lippi or Botticelli, we hear no more. His next letter to the Marchioness informs her that Perugino is willing to undertake the work; and on the 19th January, 1503, a formal contract for the painting was drawn up, and duly executed. But Perugino proved to be all that Malatesta had reported of him; and after infinite delays on his part, and endless letters and misgivings on that of the Marchioness, the picture was finally sent to Mantua, in June, 1505. It represents the "Battle of Love and Chastity," and is now in the Louvre, No. 429, with two paintings by Andrea Mantegna, and the two by Lorenzo Costa, which once formed part of the decorations of the "Camerino."

According to the writer of this letter, then, notwithstanding the great reputation which Botticelli still enjoyed at Florence, and his willingness and ability to work, he had nothing of the press of business which embarrassed his disciple, Filippino, now grown to greater fame than his master. Many circumstances had contributed to bring about this want of employment on the part of Sandro. His conversion to the doctrine of Savonarola was not calculated to render his work more acceptable to those rich patrons, on whom the worldly success of a painter largely depended. Moreover, nearly all the great masters who had been his rivals at the height of his career, had passed away since the death of Verrocchio in 1488. Dominico Ghirlandaio, Gherardo, Piero and Antonio Pollaiuoli, Benozzo Gozzoli, and Alesso Baldovinetti, had died in rapid succession; and a new generation of painters was springing up, whose ideals in art were very different from his own. The few years of life still remaining to him, were to witness the birth of a series of masterpieces, which for centuries were to eclipse the fame and name both of himself and his contemporaries, and which in the less academic and more widely appreciative judgement of our own age, are still to be accounted the supreme accomplishment of modern art. But at the time in question, although all Italy was already growing aware of the transcendent greatness of the new school, it was still mindful of the work of those masters, who, but a decade or two ago, had been held to have rivalled the masters of antiquity. This attitude of mind is clearly shown in the writings of a contemporary, who, since he appears to have been a man of very ordinary critical acumen, doubtless reflects the current
l.c., ed. opinion of his day. Ugolino Verino, in his Latin poem, "De Illustratione
1790, I, 130. Urbis Florentiae," devotes many verses to the praise of the Florentines who had excelled in painting. This poem would appear to have been composed about the year 1503; for it contains an allusion to the election of Piero Soderini as "Gonfaloniere a vita," which took place on 20th September, 1502, and another to Filippino Lippi, who died on the 18th April, 1504, as being still alive and painting, at the time the poem was written. Ugolino

himself died in the following year. After a brief reference to Giotto as the restorer of the art, and to Gaddo Gaddi as the founder of an illustrious family, Ugolino goes on to speak of the painters who were then living, or who had lately died, at Florence. A foremost place is given to Filippino Lippi.

> "Spirantes tabulas tanta nunc arte Philippus
> Excolit, ut Cous rediisse putetur Apelles;
> Grajorum nullo inferior, nulloque Latino."

Ugolino has no sooner uttered this hyperbole, than he has misgivings as to its justness, for he adds:

> "Et forsan superat Leonardus Vincius omnes;
> Tollere de tabula dextram sed nescit, &, instar
> Protogenis, multis unam perficit annis."

Leonardo returned to Florence in the spring of 1500, after the fall of his patron, Lodovico, Il Moro. A year later, as we learn from a contemporary letter-writer, he had produced nothing since his arrival there, but "uno schizzo in uno cartone." This was the cartoon for the altar-piece of the Annunziata, of the "Virgin in the lap of St. Anna." Although it was but a sketch, yet, according to Vasari, "men and women, young and old, continued for two days together to flock, as if to a solemn festival, to the room where it was, in order to behold the marvels of Leonardo. When the master left Florence, in May or June, 1502, on his appointment as military architect to Cesare Borgia, the "intendenti" were already saying with Ugolino, "forsan superat omnes Leonardus." Already it was recognized in Florence that he had laid the beginnings of what Vasari calls the "modern" manner; and a new generation of painters was springing up, which was presently to find in the works of Botticelli and his contemporaries, "una certa maniera secca e cruda e tagliente," a certain dry and hard manner, and one wanting in gradation.

A. Luzio, I Precettori d'Isabella d'Este, p. 32.

Vasari, ed. Sansoni, IV, 38.

l.c., IV, 11 and 10.

But to return to the poem: after an allusion to Domenico Ghirlandaio and his brothers, of whom David alone then survived, Ugolino thus refers to Botticelli:

> "Nec Zeuxi inferior pictura Sander habetur,
> Ille licet volucres pictis deluserit uvis."

The allusion to Zeuxis and the birds is taken from Pliny, Lib. xxxv, Cap. 10; but Ugolino would seem to have had nothing more in view here than a rhetorical passage. The only other living painter to which this writer alludes, is Pietro Perugino. Michelagnolo is mentioned neither as a painter, nor as a sculptor. That these rhetorical passages of Ugolino contain little more than formal compliments, is evident from an earlier epigram by him, entitled: "De pictoribus et scultoribus florentinis, qui priscis grecis equiperari possint." This epigram is contained in a volume of his Latin verses which is preserved in the Laurentian Library at Florence; the volume itself appears to have been written between the years 1488 and 1491, but the poem in question was probably composed shortly before the earlier date. In this epigram, it is Leonardo that is compared to Zeuxis, while Botticelli is likened to Apelles. After an allusion

App. II, Doc. LVIII.

to Pietro Pollaiuoli as a painter, Ugolino draws a parallel between the following masters, ancient and modern:

> "Æquarjq*ue* sibi non indignetur apelles
> Sandrum: iam notu*m* est nomen ubiq*ue* svum: Sander pictor Apelles.
> Eracleota licet Zeusis bene pinxeris vuis Zeusis
> Haud tamen est Thuscus uincius arte minor: Leonardvs pictor.
> Nec te pictoris sobolem memorande phylippe Phylippus
> Prætercam: primu*m* dignus habere locvm." pictor optimus.

Even at that date, Filippino would appear to have stood higher in the popular estimation than Botticelli.

At the time that Ugolino was writing his poem, "De Illustratione Urbis Florentiae," Michelagnolo was still engaged upon the statue which was to establish his fame in Florence; for as yet no work of his had been executed for a public building. It is in connection with the choice of a site for this statue that we catch another hasty view of Sandro at this time.

J. Gaye, Carteggio inedito, II, 455-468. In 1464, the "Operai," or Wardens of the Works, of Santa Maria del Fiore, commissioned Agostino di Duccio to execute a figure of a prophet in marble, "a ghuisa di gughante," to be placed "in sunono degli sproni," on one of the pinnacles above the pilasters, or rather buttresses, which are placed at intervals along the flanks of the cathedral. These pilasters may be seen crowned with statues, in the representation of the cathedral on the right wall of the Cappella degli Spagnuoli, in Santa Maria Novella. Two such statues were actually executed in brick and stucco by Donatello. The great block of marble which had been prepared for this statue was, however, spoiled in the blocking out by Bartolommeo di Pietro, called Baccellino, a stonecutter of Settignano, and lay for many years discarded in the courtyard of the "Opera." At length, in 1501, the spoiled marble was given to Michelagnolo Buonarroti "to fashion, complete and finish to perfection"; and he, after working upon it for two years or more, at length produced the famous statue of "David," now in the Florentine Academy. The "Deliberations" of the Wardens of the Works record how the statue of the David being "almost finished," the Consuls of the "Arte della Lana," in whom the maintenance of the cathedral was officially vested, and the Wardens, desiring to agree upon "a convenient and fit site" for the statue, called together the chief masters then in Florence, not only architects, but sculptors, painters, goldsmiths and others, that they might give their opinions as to the choice of a site. These masters having assembled on the 25th January, 1503-4, in the residence of the Wardens of the Works, were invited by two of the Wardens to say where, in their opinion, the statue should be placed: and their replies were recorded among the Deliberations of the "Operai," "word for word, in the vulgar tongue, as they fell from their lips." The first speaker, Messer Francesco di Lorenzo Filarete, the Herald of the Signoria, a poet and an architect, proposed a choice of two sites for the statue; "the first where the Judith stands, the second in the midst of the court of the Palace, where the David is"; of the two, the speaker himself preferred the former one. The "Judith and Holofernes" of Donatello had been brought from the garden of the Palazzo Medici, in the Via Larga, in 1495, and placed at the end of the "ringhiera," beside the steps of the principal entrance of the Palazzo Signoria, to the left

App. II, Doc. LIX.

L. Landucci, Diario, pp. 118 and 121.

on entering the palace. Donatello's bronze may be seen on this site, in a copy of a contemporary painting of the "Burning of Savonarola," preserved in his cell at San Marco: the bronze "David" of Donatello was brought, at the same time, from the court of the Palazzo Medici, and placed in the court of the Palazzo Signoria, where is now the bronze "Putto with the Dolphin," by Andrea Verrocchio. Francesco Monciatto, "legnaiuolo," who spoke next, reminded his hearers that the statue was originally intended to be placed above one of the exterior pilasters, or pinnacles, around the church [of Santa Maria del Fiore], he did not know why it was no longer proposed to place it there; "but," he added, "it seems to me it would there be a great ornament to the church." Upon this Cosimo Rosselli, the painter, got up and proposed that the statue should be placed "by the steps of the church, on the right hand, with a basement at the corner of the said steps." The fourth speaker was Sandro di Botticello: "Cosimo," he said, "has said precisely where it seems to me it should stand, in order to be seen by the passers by, and with a Judith at the other corner; or in the Loggia de' Signori [*i.e.*, the Loggia de' Lanzi]; but for preference at the corner of the church, and there, I judge, it would stand well, and that is the better place for the fame [of the work]." Giuliano da San Gallo, the architect, although approving of the position by the steps of the cathedral, suggested that since the marble was soft and friable, the statue should be placed, for protection, in the middle arch of the Loggia, in such a way that it would be possible to pass around it, or against the wall in a niche. Messer Angelo di Lorenzo Manfidi, "the second Herald, the nephew of Messer Francesco, the first speaker," proposed that it should be placed in the arch of the Loggia next the Palace, that it might not interfere with the ceremonies of the Signory, and the other magistrates. Il Riccio, the goldsmith, Lorenzo della Volpaia, Biagio d'Antonio Tucci, the painter, Bernardo di Marco, the joiner, and Leonardo da Vinci, all favoured one or another of the sites within the Loggia. Filippino Lippi, the painter, was of opinion that the statue should be placed near the Palace, but that the precise site should be left to the choice of the sculptor. He was followed by Galieno, the embroiderer, who suggested that it should be placed on a plinth, "where the lion [or Marzocco] of the Piazza stands," at the other end of the "Ringhiera." David Ghirlandaio, who followed, was in favour of this last proposal, while Antonio da San Gallo, the architect, urged that the statue should be protected by the Loggia; and Michelagnolo, the goldsmith, the father of Baccio Bandinelli, that it should be placed either in the Loggia or in the Palace, in the Sala del Consiglio. The other speakers, among whom were Giovanni, "piffero," the father of Benvenuto Cellini, Giovanni delle Corniole, the gem-cutter, Piero di Cosimo, Pietro Perugino, Lorenzo di Credi, and Francesco Granacci, the painters, Attavante, the miniature painter, Andrea della Robbia, the sculptor, and Il Cronaca, the architect, some of whose replies, for greater brevity, were not taken down, favoured some one, some another, of the foregoing proposals: Piero di Cosimo being of the opinion that the choice of the exact site should be left to Michelagnolo himself. This was eventually done, and the sculptor decided to set up the "David" on the site then occupied by the "Judith" of Donatello; namely, on the steps of the Palazzo Vecchio, to the right on coming out of the palace, as Messer Francesco Filarete had proposed in the first instance.

In the following October, Michelagnolo began the cartoon of the

"War with Pisa," for the Sala del Consiglio Maggiore; and in less than a year, in August, 1505, it had been brought to a conclusion. In this work he entered into deliberate rivalry, as a painter, with Leonardo da Vinci, who had completed, in February, 1505, the cartoon of the "Battle of Anghiari," for the decoration of the same hall. "These two cartoons," says Benvenuto Cellini, "stood, one in the palace of the Medici, the other in the Sala del Papa; and so long as they remained entire, they were the school of the world." In these stupendous masterpieces, the rapid transition from the art of the fifteenth century to the art of the sixteenth century had been completely effected; and while a new generation of painters in Florence flocked to study the works which were to change the whole course and direction of art, Botticelli was reverting more and more, not only in method, but in design and sentiment, to that tradition of Giottesque painting, from which he had so largely derived his art.

Of the time of the execution of these cartoons, is yet another record of Botticelli in his quality as a painter. The "Libro Rosso," the account-book of the "Compagnia di San Luca," which I have already cited and described, contains a series of entries of the fees owing and paid by its members, during the years 1503, 1504 and 1505. According to the debit side of one of these entries, "Sandro dimariano divannj," owed the Confraternity, on the 17th October, 1503, 17 soldi 4 danari, "p*er*le pintature [*i.e.*, dipingiture] delanno auenire, . . . ad*anarj* 4 lasetimana"; that is, for the cost of the paintings with which the "place," or house, of the Confraternity was annually decorated on the feast-day of their patron saint. In the earlier entries of 1472, a similar fee is charged under the head "p*e*lla soue*n*zione deluogho earte." In later times, when the "Compagnia di San Luca" had been merged into the "Accademia delle Belle Arti," these paintings were executed by the students attached to the society, as an exhibition of their skill and abilities. On the 18th October, 1504, Sandro is debited with 7 soldi, "p*er*la festa," that is, the yearly contribution required of each member towards the expenses of the feast of Saint Luke; on 18th October, 1505, with 17 soldi 4 danari, "sono epi*n*tj delan*no*," that is, the cost of the annual paintings, as before; and on the same day, with 7 soldi, "p*er*la festa," as for the previous year. The credit side of the account shows that on the 18th October, 1504, "Sandro dimaria[no]" paid 17 soldi 4 danari, for the paintings of the year last past; and on 18th October, 1505, 1 lire 4 soldi 4 danari, "per gratje delsuo debito," that is, in composition of his debt to the Confraternity.

App. II, Doc. XI, fol. 122, tergo, and fol. 123, recto.

To this last period of Botticelli's art are to be ascribed three furniture panels, painted with stories from the legend of San Zenobio, one of the patron saints of Florence. Two of these panels passed, some years ago, from the palace of the Marchesi Rondinelli, in the Via della Stufa, at Florence, into the collection of Dr. Ludwig Mond, of London, by whom they were lent to the Exhibition of Old Masters, held at Burlington House, in 1894, Nos. 158 and 164. Each of them measures 2 feet 2 inches in height, and 4 feet 11 inches in length. The other panel was formerly in the Metzger Collection at Florence; it afterwards passed into the Von Quandt Collection at Dresden; and at the sale of that collection, in 1868, was purchased for the Dresden Gallery, where it now hangs among the Tuscan pictures, No. 9. It measures 2 feet 2 inches in height, and 5 feet 11$\frac{3}{4}$ inches in length. At first sight it would seem that the panel at Dresden could scarcely have belonged to the same series as those in the collection of Dr.

STORIES FROM THE LEGEND OF ST. ZENOBIO. I *Collection of Dr. Ludwig Mond*

Mond. Yet not only is the height of all the three panels the same, but one, if not both, of Dr. Mond's pictures appear to have been reduced in length. Moreover, the stories in the Dresden panel form the sequel to those in the other two panels, and complete the legend of the saint. It is a question, then, whether the former panel, although it might seem from certain differences of drawing and colouring to have been painted at a somewhat earlier period than the other two, may not have formed a part of the decorations of the same room; for these paintings, like those which Botticelli executed for the houses of the Pucci and the Vespucci, doubtless formed the panels of some "lettuccio," or "spalliera." The differences of colour, however, may largely, if not entirely be accounted for; since the two panels in the collection of Dr. Mond are in a singularly pure state, whereas that in the Gallery at Dresden is covered by a heavy coat of golden varnish, which has changed in a considerable degree the original effect of its colouring. The Legend of San Zenobio has come down to us in more than one early form. Three of these versions in Italian and one in Latin, together with the rhymed "Storia di San Zanobi" of Bernardo Giambullari, were collected and printed at Florence in 1863, under the title of "La Vita di San Zanobi scritta da più antichi quattro diversi autori," etc. The version of the legend, however, which I propose to quote in illustration of these panels, occurs in the "Summa Historialis," written in Latin by Sant' Antonino, Archbishop of Florence, and printed at Basle in 1491. l.c., Par. II, Tit. X, Cap. XII.

The first of the two panels in the collection of Dr. Mond, contains four stories of the conversion of the saint to Christianity, and of his consecration to the priesthood. "Lux mundi Zenobius," (for such are the ecstatic words of the pious Antonino,) was born in Florence of a noble family, it is said of the Girolami, in the reign of the Emperor Constantine the Great, A.D. 334. From his earliest years, he gave himself to letters and to the study of Philosophy; and in Grammar, Dialectic and Rhetoric, none was like to him in all Tuscany. "Having attained to the twentieth year of his age, his parents would have sought for him in marriage a beautiful and noble girl; but he, renouncing all carnal marriages, gave his soul, chastely virginal, in marriage through faith to Christ; humbly seeking, and devoutly receiving, baptism at the hands of Teodoro, Bishop of Florence."

In the first story, on the extreme left of the panel, Zenobio is seen rejecting the girl whom his father and mother have brought to him. This group of eight figures is represented standing in a street of Florentine architecture. On the left is the girl, with her hands crossed upon her breast; on the right Zenobio, in a long habit and peaked hat, is seen turning away from her; and between them stands his father, who points with his left hand to the girl, as he turns towards his son with a gesture of astonishment.

To the right of this story, filling some two-thirds of the whole space of the picture, is a church surrounded by an open loggia, supported by pilasters. The shafts of the pilasters are decorated with arabesque ornament in black, on a yellow ground. On the pace before this loggia on the left of the building, which is seen in perspective on that side, is another group of eight figures, representing the baptism of Zenobio. The young man, naked except for a linen cloth about his loins, kneels turned towards the right, as he bends in prayer over a portable font. On the other side of the font stands the bishop, Teodoro, who is habited in processional vestments, and administers the rite of baptism by pouring water, out of a laver, over his head. Round about stand the clergy, with acolytes bearing candlesticks.

"When his father and mother," continues the legend, "heard this, they were filled with rage, and went with a number of their kinsfolk to the Bishop, with opprobrious words and threats. But Zenobio being present, and the divine grace already wonderfully working in him, such sweetness of speech fell from his lips, that not only did his kinsmen forget their indignation, but having left the error of the Gentiles, they themselves received the Sacrament of Baptism." The third story, a composition of ten figures, representing the baptism of the mother of Zenobio, fills the first bay of the loggia, fronting the spectator, on the left. The arrangement of the principal figures in this group, is a repetition of those in the foregoing story. Sophia, for such was his mother's name, kneels stripped to the waist, on the left side of the font, while the Bishop stands on the right, in the act of baptizing her. Behind her kneel Zenobio and his father, surrounded by the clergy and acolytes, with candles, and right and left of the group stand two laymen.

And so, runs the story, "despising the vanity of this world, Zenobio, having been consecrated priest by the Bishop, gave himself wholly to divine things," and afterwards became a canon of the cathedral church of San Salvatore, and Archdeacon of Florence. And Pope Damaso, hearing from St. Ambroise of his great sanctity, sent for him to Rome, and soon after made him a cardinal-deacon and legate at Constantinople. "Meanwhile it came to pass that Teodoro, Bishop of Florence, having died, no little controversy and contention arose between the catholics and heretics, concerning the choice of his successor; by reason of which Damaso sent Zenobio to the city to quell the tumult. But when he drew near to Florence, the people came out to meet him on the highway, receiving him with great honour; and having accompanied him to the church, they all began with one accord to cry out, 'Be Zenobio our Bishop!' But he, knowing the burden of that office, by all means sought to refuse it; and having returned to the Pope, declared that he had been able to accomplish nothing. But the magistrates and the people sent a solemn embassy to Damaso, saying that they had all of one accord made choice of Zenobio, and would have no other; and they besought him with steadfast entreaties, that he would deign to allow him to become their bishop. At first, the Pope refused their request, grieving that the holy man should be separated from him; but at length, overcome by the importunity of their prayers, he gave ear to their desire, and created Zenobio bishop of Florence."

The fourth story of the consecration of Zenobio to the episcopate, at Rome, fills the last two bays of the loggia, on the right of the panel. Habited in a cope, the saint is seen in profile towards the right, as he kneels before the Pope, who is enthroned under a baldaquin, with two cardinals by his side. Behind the saint, a bishop in processional vestments bends forward, as he places the mitre on his head; and right and left of the officiating bishop stand two other bishops with books of offices, and two acolytes with candlesticks.

The second panel in the collection of Dr. Mond, contains three stories representing as many miracles of the saint; for not only, runs the legend, did he cast out devils, but he raised many from the dead. Now it happened that "there were five sons of a certain noble lady, a widow and a Gentile,

STORIES FROM THE LEGEND OF ST. ZENOBIO. II *Collection of Dr. Ludwig Mond*

who having arrived at man's estate, used often to vex their mother with abuse and insults, and even with blows. But one day, when they had cruelly beaten her, she, being greatly angered, cursed them in these words, that the devil might so take them, that being goaded to madness, they should devour their arms with their own teeth. Divine vengeance immediately pursued them; for being possessed of evil spirits, and goaded to madness, they began each one to gnaw his own arms. Their mother seeing this, with many tears, called aloud for help; and the neighbours having been summoned by her cries, bound them with shackles, lest they might harm themselves and others. Finally their mother, who had been hitherto a Gentile, had recourse to the holy man of God, unfolding the unhappy condition of her sons; and he, having prayed from morning till the third hour, at length freed them from the devils, and restored them to health; and after he had instructed them in the faith, he baptized them, together with their mother." According to the versions of the legend written by Biagio, the monk, and Fra Giovammaria Tolosani, the number of her sons was two; whereas Sant' Antonino speaks of five sons.

On the left of the picture, on the floor of a vaulted oratory, containing a crucifix, and open to the street on three sides, lie the two sons, with their hands bound at the wrists; at their feet kneels San Zenobio, who raises his right hand in the act of casting out the evil spirits of which they are possessed. As the saint makes the sign of the cross, two diminutive devils, with clawed feet and bat's wings, escape out of their mouths. By their side, kneels their mother, with her face buried in her hands; and around them stand a cross-bearer, and five clerks, one of whom points out the miracle to a layman. In the background, beyond the pilasters of the oratory, is seen a distant landscape with a winding river. But to proceed with the legend.

"Now as a certain noble lady of Gaul was going on a pilgrimage [to Rome,] 'ad limina Apostolorum,' carrying her only son with her, who had fallen ill through the fatigue of the journey, she, having heard of the fame of the saint, caused the child to be committed to his care, against her return. But the boy, growing sick unto death, ended his life on the second festival after Easter, at the very time when the blessed Zenobio was going in procession to the church of San Pier Maggiore. . . . The mother of the lad having reached Florence that very day, on her return from Rome, found that her son had departed to the Lord; but she, although broken in spirit, nevertheless supported by the greatness of her faith, caused the dead body of her son to be taken up, and with a crowd of people following and commiserating her, repaired to the place whither she heard the saint was gone. But she meeting him in the way, (for he had already left the church of San Piero, and was proceeding with his clergy through the street which is called after the Albizi,) laid down the dead body of her son at his feet, and full of tears, rending her garments and tearing her hair with grief, cried aloud, that her only son, whom she had entrusted to his care, had rendered up his spirit, never to return again to his own. Moved by her tears, the holy man of God, after he had offered up a prayer and made the sign of the cross over him, restored him to his mother, brought back from the dead. Whereupon all the clergy and people having given thanks unto God, she with unbounded joy, was confirmed more and more in the faith."

In this story, a composition of twelve figures, which fills the centre of the picture, the noble lady of Gaul is represented seated before the doorway of a Florentine palace, with the dead body of her son lying in her lap. With outstretched hands she bends over her son, with the most violent expressions of grief. Before her kneels San Zenobio, his right hand raised in the act of making the sign of the cross; and round about kneel, or stand, his cross-bearer and clerks; while two laymen, on the right, press forward to behold the miracle.

The third story is on the extreme right of the panel. "A certain blind man," runs the legend, "who used to beg alms at the door of the cathedral church, having heard the report of his miracles, came to him in the street, and with unquestioning faith, besought him to take pity upon him; and inasmuch as he was a Gentile, the blessed Zenobio inquired of him, whether, having received his sight, he would be willing to become a Christian; and he assenting, Zenobio prayed for him, and straightway he received his sight."

In the painting, the blind man is seen in profile, to the left, as he kneels before the saint, who touches his eyes with his right hand. Behind Zenobio stands his cross-bearer, with two clerks and two laymen. This panel appears to have been slightly reduced in length, having been cut at either end, to the damage of the first and third stories. In the background, on the right, a street of houses is seen through an archway. These architectural backgrounds are of great interest, as showing the appearance of a Florentine street at the beginning of the sixteenth century.

It is evident from the most cursory comparison of the mystical "Nativity," No. 1034, in the National Gallery, with these panels, that the idiosyncrasies of Botticelli's manner have here become more exaggerated and insistent; his line is more rythmical, but less structural; his forms less beautiful in themselves, though not less expressive. This exaggeration in the drawing is especially to be observed in the hands and feet, and in the long fluted folds of the draperies. Yet the painter has lost nothing of his power of dramatic design; and the profound spirit of religious devotion which transfigures the little painting of the "Nativity," is everywhere present in these panels. Again, his colouring has become more simple in the course of years; of the jewel-like quality of the colouring of the "Calumny of Apelles," there is here scarcely a trace. In the earlier stories of the first panel, Zenobio is habited in a purple robe, which is seen against the scarlet dresses of the women. In the later stories, the white surplices of the clerks and acolytes, worn over blue cassocks, with purple "birette," and seen against the gray of the architecture and the heavy, golden yellow of the pilasters, on which arabesques are traced in black, form the dominant colours of the picture. In the second panel, the frequent masses of white afforded by the surplices of the clergy, seen against the large gray spaces of the architecture, and contrasted with such vivid and simple tints as the purple cope of Zenobio and the blue cassocks of his clerks, form a colour scheme of an almost cloistral simplicity and ingenuousness. With what approval would Savonarola have regarded such a painting as this!

The panel in the gallery at Dresden contains four stories, of which the first three relate to the same miracle.

Zenobio, according to the account of Sant' Antonino, raised three children from the dead at various times; and among them "a boy, to wit, of five years, whom some infuriated oxen with a wain, rushing headlong against him, near the cathedral church which stands in the public street,

STORIES FROM THE LEGEND OF ST. ZENOBIO. III *Dresden Gallery. (From a photograph by R. Tamme, Dresden)*

crushed to death; and his mother, with many tears, wrapping him in a linen cloth, carried him to Eugenio, the deacon of the holy man, that he, bringing him to Zenobio, might beseech him to restore the child to life; which was brought to pass."

The scene of the first story is laid in the piazza, before the cathedral. On the left, the wheel of a cart, of which only the hinder part comes within the picture, is represented passing over the body of the child, who lies prone upon the ground. On the right, his mother, together with two men and a boy, run forward to his aid. In the background is a street of houses, leading to one of the city gates, beyond which is seen a river and some distant hills.

In the second story, the mother, in an agony of grief, ascends the steps of the cathedral, with her dead child in her arms, as the deacon, Eugenio, comes forward to take the body. On the left, a civilian approaches and raises his hand in alarm at the sight; and behind the group, three ecclesiastics are seen standing at a lateral doorway of the church.

The third story is represented to the right of the second story, on the pace of the inlaid marble steps, before the façade of the cathedral, which is decorated with pilasters and a frieze enriched with arabesques, and inlaid with marble panels. The deacon, Eugenio, comes forward from the church, with the child restored to life, who runs to embrace his mother, on the left, as she bends down to take him in her arms. Beside the mother, stand a man and a woman; and behind her, at the door of the church, three ecclesiastics. According to one of the longer and more circumstantial versions of the legend, Eugenio carried the body into the church of San Salvatore, at that time the cathedral of Florence, to San Zenobio, who bid the two deacons, Eugenio and Crescenzio, pray with him over the child, who was thus restored to life.

"At length," concludes the legend, "being full of days and holy works, and foreseeing that his death was at hand, Zenobio assembled the clergy and the people in the church, and made known his departure to them all, exhorting them to live in brotherly love and mutual peace; and he consoled their grief at his approaching end, with the hope of the succour which he would render to them, after he had ascended into heaven. Thence having returned to his house, sick unto death, he devoutly received the sacraments of the church; and in the midst of his clergy, and the singing of psalms, that most holy spirit, released from the body, entered the heavenly kingdom, in the ninetieth year of his age, in the time of Pope Innocent the first, namely, on the 25th May, 424." The last story represents the death of Zenobio. Within a chamber, on the right of the panel, the saint lies propped up in his bed, with a mitre on his head, and with his right hand raised in the act of exhorting his clergy and people, who are gathered around him, to live in brotherly love and mutual peace. Among these figures, some fifteen in number, who kneel with clasped hands around the "cassa" of the bed, on which a crucifix and four lighted tapers have been placed at the foot, are two bishops, vested in cope and mitre, on the near side. In the background, through the arches of an open loggia, is seen a distant landscape.

Although in its general conception and treatment, this panel closely recalls those in the collection of Dr. Mond, there are, nevertheless, certain differences of colour, and still more of drawing, to be observed in them. The panel at Dresden, as I have said, is covered by a coat of dark varnish, which has considerably changed the original effect of its pigments. This is especially observable in the yellow ground of the pilasters, on which the arabesques are traced in black with some touches of colour, in the gray of the architecture and in the darker gray of the foreground. This yellow and these grays which, in their original state, probably resembled the colours of similar passages in the panels at London, have acquired from the dark varnish, a heavy and somewhat hot tint, which is far from agreeable. From the same cause, the blue of the cassock which the deacon, Eugenio, wears in the second and third stories in the Dresden panels, has taken a greenish tint. Were the varnish removed, the colouring of this panel would, I think, closely resemble that of the panels at London, although a greater variety of pigment is employed. The figure of the mother of the boy, in each of the first three stories of the Dresden panel, is clad in a pale purple dress, white headcloth, and bluish green mantle; the boy in a warm green tunic, bluish green hose, and scarlet shoes; and the woman in the third story, who stands by the mother, wears a dark grape-purple mantle, scarlet dress, and white head-cloth. In the last story, one of the bishops is vested in a pale purple, and the other in a deep grape-purple cope; the saint is in a white shirt, the coverlet of the bed is of scarlet, and a characteristic deep, golden green occurs in the figures around the bed. Notwithstanding such differences, then, I cannot but think, that these panels originally formed part of one and the same series; although that at Dresden was probably executed at a somewhat earlier period, than those at London. The latter may even have been executed at so late a date in Sandro's life, as 1505.

Vasari, ed. 1550, I, 495.

The last memorials of Botticelli are few and brief. Vasari, in the first edition of the "Lives," records how Sandro, "finally, growing old and disabled, used to walk with two sticks; whereby no longer being able to work, infirm and decrepit, reduced to a most pitiable condition, he passed from this life, in the 78th year of his age, and was buried in Ogni Santi at Florence, in the year 1515." In the second edition, Vasari states more explicitly that Sandro walked with two sticks, "because he was unable to hold himself upright." It is extremely probable that Vasari may have had this account from someone who had seen Sandro going about Florence, during the last few years of his life; but even if this anecdote of the painter in his old age be a true one, we now know that he died neither in his 78th year, nor in 1515.

Vasari, ed. 1568, I, 474.

The date of Botticelli's death is recorded in two series of the Death-Registers of Florence. In the "Libri dei Morti," kept by the "Magistrato della Grascia," a magistracy that had the control of the markets, it is thus recorded: "✠ 1510, In May. Sandro di Bartolommeo, painter, buried in Ognissanti on the 17th day of the said month." So little acquainted with the name of the painter was the scribe who penned this entry, that he has written "di Bartolommeo," in error for "di Botticello." In the "Libri dei Morti" of the "Arte dei Medici e degli Speziali," the Guild of Physicians and Apothecaries, the painter's name is correctly given, thus: "May, 1510, Sandro di Botticello, painter, on the 17th day, buried in Ognissanti."

App. II, Doc. LX., 329, recto.

App. II, Doc. LXI., fol. 45, tergo.

The church of Ognissanti, on the "tramezzo" of which, in 1480, Botticello had painted the fresco of St. Augustine, was at that time attached to a monastery of the Umiliati; but afterwards passed into the possession of the Franciscans, in 1561. The painter was buried in a little cemetery known as the "Ortaccio," which adjoins the nave of the church. The greater part of this cemetery is now covered with chapels and other buildings, the gradual accumulations of the last three centuries. In its original state, it consisted of a plot of ground, bounded on the west side, (or what, for practical purposes, we may call west,) by the nave of the church; on the north, by the right transept; on the east, by the backs of the houses which opened on the opposite side of the Via Nuova, (now a part of the Via Porcellana,) to that on which Botticelli lived; and on the south, partly by some houses which opened on Borgo Ognissanti, and partly by a wall which divided the cemetery from the piazza in front of the church. In the middle of this cemetery stood the cross, which still remains walled into an angle of one of the buildings which cover its site; and in the angle formed by the junction of the nave and transept, stands the campanile of the church. The exterior walls of the nave, the campanile and the transept, were formerly covered with the monuments, chiefly "tasselli," or small, marble tablets, bearing their names and arms, of the families who had their burial places in this cemetery.

In 1657, the year in which Stefano Rosselli completed his "Sepoltuario Fiorentino," a work which remains in manuscript, a little chapel, which still exists, had already been erected in this churchyard, against the east face of the campanile, as well as a series of buildings against the wall of the nave. These buildings which extend from the campanile to the wall on the piazza, include the chapel of San Lino, built in 1597, which serves as a side-entrance to the church from the piazza, the oratory of the Third Order of St. Francis, and a small sacristy and room adjoining the campanile. Rosselli begins his account of the monuments remaining in this churchyard, by describing those which were still to be seen on the portions of the walls of the nave and campanile, which had been roofed in when this room was constructed. "Entering," he says, "by a little doorway which is beside the Campagnia di San Diego [meaning the Cappella di San Diego d' Alcalà, which still exists in the right transept of the church, the door in question being on the right of the altar,] one enters under the campanile." . . . "Having passed the campanile, one enters a room by which one goes up into the pulpit, and which was formerly a part of the cemetery." Among the monuments which Rosselli describes as then existing in this room, was the slab of the grandfather of Amerigo Vespucci, which was to be seen in its original position, until a few years ago, when it was removed into the nave. Rosselli presently proceeds to speak of the monuments "in the little chapel, which is between the campanile and the cemetery, and which one enters by a door opening into the church," on the left of the altar of San Diego d' Alcalà. This is the little Cappella del Crocifissino, which still exists between the campanile and the Cappella di San Pietro d' Alcantara in the right transept; the latter chapel having been erected in 1722, on a part of the churchyard. Up to this point, Rosselli's account tallies with the fabric of the church, as it at present exists. But, continues Rosselli, "having passed the door of this chapel, [that is, the Capella del Crocifissino,] there follows another, by which one enters into that part of the cemetery which still remains unbuilt upon, and in which exist arms and memorials of divers families, as follows. Entering by the said door, on the left hand, upon the wall, is seen a square tablet of marble," etc. (Here follows a description of three "tasselli.") "Having passed by the aforesaid, walking still towards the east, on the same wall," etc. (Here follows a description

Cod. Magliabechiano, XXVI, 23, fol. 848, tergo, etc.

Id., fol. 849, recto.

R. Razzòli, Chiesa d'Ognissanti, p. 72.

Cod. Magliabechiano, XXVI, 23, fol. 851, recto.

of two other "tasselli.") "Having passed the said arms, in the middle of this wall-face is seen a very ancient sepulchre, with an arch, and little vault above, wherein used formerly to be a cist, or saracophagus," etc. "Having passed the said sepulchre, in the direction of the corner, arms of stone on the same wall, now wholly effaced. Having passed the aforesaid arms and inscription, *Sepulcrum* Joannis Petri Lenzi," etc. "Having passed the tomb of the Lenzi, there follows a modern coat of arms in stone, with this inscription, Mariano Filip[e]pi, et Filioru*m*, 1510, Leone ramp*ant*e con seste." (In the margin of the manuscript is sketched a shield with a lion rampant, holding a pair of compasses in its paws.) "Having passed the foregoing, and almost in the corner, a coat of arms and inscription," etc.

Id., fol. 852, tergo.

Upon examining this part of the church as it at present exists, in the light of Rosselli's account, it becomes apparent that in his time, the door of which he speaks, leading into the then uncovered part of the cemetery, was in the south wall of the right transept, close to the door of the Cappella del Crocifissino; and that this wall, through which the present arch opening into the Cappella di San Pietro d'Alcantara, was broken in 1722, formed together with the south wall of the Cappella del Nome di Gesù, built by Simone Vespucci, at the head of the right transept, a continuous wall-face on the exterior, reaching from the Cappella del Crocifissino to the north-east corner of the churchyard. In the middle of this wall-face was the "ancient sepulchre, with an arched and vaulted recess above;" and between this tomb and the north-east corner of the churchyard, and, therefore, on the exterior of the south wall of the chapel of Simone Vespucci, was the "tassello" of Mariano Filipepi. It would seem that this "tassello" was still in existence in 1740. In the library of the present monastery of Ognissanti is preserved a "Sepoltuario" lettered "C," and inscribed on the vellum cover, "Libro delle Sepulture d*el*la Ch*ies*[a] di s. salv*ado*[re] in Borg'og*n*[i] s*an*ti." It bears the date "20 Mag[o], 1740;" and on fol. 110 occur the arms given by Rosselli, and the inscription, "Sepoltura della famiglia de Filipepi." In a later "Sepoltuario," dated 1772, which is preserved in the same library, no mention occurs of the monument. At that time it may have already disappeared; but even if it survived the eighteenth century, it must certainly have been plastered over, or made away with, in 1839, when a chapel was built against the exterior of the south wall of the Cappella del Nome di Gesù, extending the whole length of the wall, and a vault of brick constructed beneath the floor of this new chapel, as a burial place for Caroline Bonaparte, the wife of Joachine Murat, King of Naples. Perhaps the ashes of the painter were desecrated to make room for the sister of Napoleon.

R. Razzòli, Chiesa d'Ognissanti, p. 78.

I may add that a third "Sepoltuario" in the library of Ognissanti, dated 1656, lettered "B," and inscribed on the vellum wrapper, "Libro delle Sepulture d*e*lla Ch*ies*[a] di S. Salv*ado*[re] in Borg'og*n*[i] S*an*ti," records, under letter F, the grave of the Filipepi thus: "S. Di Mariano Filipepi 1510." This is the same date as that recorded by Rosselli; and it is to be noted that, although Mariano Filipepi had been buried here in February, 1481-2, and Giovanni, called Il Botticello, in March, 1493-4, the slab bore the date of Sandro's death, 1510. Some one, then, there had been, who was not willing that the painter's grave should be wholly forgotten.

It now remains for me to speak of certain paintings now lost, which, according to various notices, more or less authentic, appear to have been the work of Botticelli; and to give some account of his designs for embroideries and of his drawings. If any estimate is to be formed of the importance of a picture, from the frequency with which it is cited by the commentators, it would seem that in the altar-piece which Botticelli painted for the Augustine Nuns of Sant' Elizabetta delle Convertite, at Florence, we have lost a considerable work of art. This Monastery had been founded in the fourteenth century for the receipt of certain courtezans, who through the preaching of Fra Simone da Cascia, had been moved to follow the example of the Magdalene. The church of these nuns still remains in the quarter of Santo Spirito, at the crossway where the Via del Campuccio runs into that part of the Via de' Serragli, which was formerly the Via Santa Chiara. Although many writers allude to the altar-piece, which Botticelli executed for this church, none describes the subject of it. The Epitomist of the Codice Petrei enumerates among the pictures painted by Botticelli, "Vna tauola nelle conuertite." The Anonimo Gaddiano adds that the picture was painted for the High Altar, but leaves a blank space in which he intended to insert a description of it: "Et nella chiesa delle suore delle co*n*uertite Dipinse latauola dell' altare maggiore che e. . . ." Vasari merely records that Botticelli painted such a picture; "Lavorò nelle conuertite vna tauola a quelle monache": and Raffaello Borghini in his "Riposo," repeats Vasari's statement. Giovanni Cinelli in his edition of the "Bellezze di Firenze," published in 1677, again alludes to the panel, and speaks of it as "assai bella." This painting was probably removed from over the High Altar about 1624, when at a great expense, "ut aurum hostis castitatis custos fieret pudicitiae," (in the words of the dedicatory inscription,) the Grand Duchess Maria Maddalena modernized the church, and enlarged the convent, incorporating with it the house in which St. Phillip Neri was born. In 1730, Botticelli's painting "hung in the entrance to the convent," according to the annotator of the edition of Borghini's "Riposo," published in that year, at Florence. When Giuseppe Richa printed the ninth volume of his "Notizie delle Chiese Fiorentine" in 1761, the picture was hanging in the Sacristy; and it was still to be seen in the church in 1802, according to the writer of "Firenza antica e moderna illustrata." That is the last notice of it which I have found. The convent was suppressed in 1808, and put to secular uses in 1837: and the painting was no longer in the church when Luigi Biadi published his "Notizie sulle Antiche Fabbriche di Firenze non terminate," in 1824. The patron saints of the Convertite, which according to the traditional use, would have been represented in this altar-piece, were St. Elizabeth, St. Mary Magdalene, and St. Augustine.

G. Richa, Notizie delle Chiese Fior., ix, 90-94.

App. II, Doc. I, fol. 49, tergo.

App. II, Doc. II, fol. 83, tergo.

Vasari, ed. 1550, I, 492.

l.c., ed. 1584, p. 351.

l.c., p. 170.

l.c., p. 285.

l.c., vol. viii, pp. 120-121.

l.c. p. 180.

We learn from a "ricordo" and a set of accounts, preserved in one of the books of the monastery, that in 1491, the nuns began to erect a "cappella," or chapel of the High Altar, which appears to have formed an addition to their original church. According to the "ricordo," the accounts for this work, which was carried out under the direction of the architect, "Magistro Giovanni Scorbachia," were approved by the Prior of Santo Spirito, as visitor of the Convent, on 19th February, 1493-4; and they included monies expended "inaconcime della altare, cioè uno dossale, lapredella [&] una corona." The payments for these ornaments of the High Altar are entered in the accounts which follow. A sum of 9½ gold florins was given to "Francesco, painter," for the woodwork, gold-leaf and execution, of the "corona," or crown, which appears to have been suspended above the altar. The "dossale" and "predella" cost only 17 lire.

App. II, Doc. LXII., fol. lxiiij, recto, and fol. lxviiij, recto.

The latter, no doubt, was the "gradino" for the candlesticks. The "dossale," however, might have been either the altar-frontal, or a hanging used in place of an altar-piece: so that even these documents leave us in doubt, whether the commission for the altar-piece was given to Botticelli before, or, (what is more probable,) after, the erection of the new chapel. The same accounts contain an entry of 91 lire, paid on 25th December, 1494, "to Jacopo, painter, who painted the altars, namely of the Crucifix and the Virgin Mary." These, no doubt, were the two lateral altars of the church, above which were preserved two miraculous images; one a wooden crucifix, the other a picture called the "Madonna dell' Amore." Was this "Jacopo, dipintore," Botticelli's assistant, Jacopo di Francesco Filippi; or merely one of the several painters of that name, who were then living?

G. Richa, Chiese Fior., IX, 95.

The "Anonimo Gaddiano" speaks of another picture which Botticelli painted for the High Altar of one of the Florentine churches, namely San Piero Gattolini: "In sa*n* piero gattolinj la tauola dell' altare maggre che sono. . . ." The writer omits to describe the subject of this altar-piece, and we do not possess any other notice of the picture. M. de Fabriczy has suggested that San Piero Gattolini is a slip of the pen for "San Pier Maggiore": but the "Anonimo Gaddiano" appears to have been singularly well informed in all that related to Botticelli; and we have no evidence that the error of attributing the Palmieri altar-piece to him was current before the time of Vasari. San Piero Gattolini was one of the thirty-six ancient parish churches of Florence, and stood within the gate of the city which anciently bore its name, and which is now called the Porta Romana. There appears to be some uncertainty as to the exact site of this church. The canons to whose care, it had been committed, after the siege of Florence, were forced to surrender it in 1547, and the fabric was shortly afterwards pulled down, to make way for the new fortifications, which were erected by order of Duke Cosimo I, in 1552. The little church of Serumido was afterwards built to supply the place of San Piero Gattolini, but (as it would seem) upon a different site.

App. II, Doc. II, fol. 85, recto.

Cod. Magliabechiano, XXVI, 22, fol. 122, tergo.

G. Richa, Notizie delle Chiese Fior., X, 109.

Vasari, in the additional notices which he inserted into his account of Botticelli, in the second edition of the "Lives," speaks of three pictures which at that time were preserved in the Ducal Wardrobe, at Florence. "In the Guardaroba of the Signor Duke Cosimo," runs the passages in question, "are, by his hand, two most beautiful heads of women in profile: one of these is said to have been the 'innamorata' of Giuliano de' Medici, the brother of Lorenzo, and the other, Madonna Lucrezia de' Tornabuoni, the wife of the said Lorenzo. In the same place is, likewise, by the hand of Sandro, a Bacchus, who is raising a barrel with both hands to his mouth, which is a figure full of grace." Since none of these pictures is to be found enumerated in the Inventory of the goods of Lorenzo de' Medici, taken at the time of his death, in 1492, it is probable that they came into the possession of the Medici, after their return to Florence in 1529. Two of these pictures, are described in an Inventory of the Guardaroba, dated 25th October, 1553, which is preserved among the State Archives at Florence. The painting of Bacchus, which then hung in the first chamber of the Guardaroba segreta, in the Palazzo Vecchio, is thus entered: "A picture of Bacchus, on canvas, 3 braccia high, with its frame." In the same room was also kept the portrait of Lucrezia Tornabuoni, which is correctly described in the Inventory as the wife of Piero de' Medici, Il Gottoso, (and therefore the mother, and not the wife, of Lorenzo, as Vasari erroneously

Vasari, ed. 1568, I, 474.

App. II, Doc. LXIII, fol. 29, tergo.

states,) thus: "A picture wherein is painted Madonna Lucretia di Piero de' Medici, in a gilt frame." Monna Lucrezia died on 25th March, 1482; and so this portrait, if by Botticelli, was doubtless one of his earlier works. No entry in this Inventory appears, however, to refer to the other portrait mentioned by Vasari, of Giuliano's "innamorata," whom popular tradition, ever in quest of the romantic, has not hesitated to identify with "La Bella Simonetta." It would seem, then, that this second portrait was added to the Ducal Collection in the interval between 1553, when this Inventory was taken, and 1568, when the picture was seen by Vasari. Elsewhere, I have already touched upon the question, whether this was a portrait of "La Bella Simonetta," or, what is more probable, of the mother of Pope Clement VII.

Id., fol. 30, recto.

Of the two portraits, I can find no notices of a later date: but the "Bacchus" was still in the Grand Ducal Collection in the seventeenth century. In an Inventory of the Guardaroba of the Grand Duke Ferdinand II, begun on 16th September, 1637, it is thus described: "A picture on canvas, about 2½ braccia long, in which is painted a nude antique Bacchus, who is drinking out of a little barrel, and pisses into an earthern jar, in a common frame." The painting was then hanging in the Palazzo Vecchio, in the Sala dei Gigli, adjoining the Guardaroba. If the two measurements given in this and the foregoing Inventories are severally those of the height and width of the picture, this canvas of Bacchus measured some 5 feet 9 inches in height, and 4 feet 9 inches in breadth, including the frame. I suspect that this picture, like many other precious works of art, such as the Labours of Hercules by the Pollaiuoli, may have perished in the fire of 17th December, 1690, when twenty-seven rooms of the "Depositeria," in the Palazzo Vecchio, were destroyed, and damage done to the value of 840,000 lire.

App. II, Doc. LXIV, p. 173, tergo.

F. Fantozzi, Nuova Guida di Firenze, ed. 1844, p. 41.

Another lost painting, which Vasari ascribes to Botticelli, in one of those passages, which he inserted into the second edition of the "Lives," was an altar-piece once over the High Altar of the church of San Francesco, at Montevarchi, in the upper valley of the Arno: "In S. Francesco di Monte Varchi fece la tauola dell' altar' maggiore." Vasari, however, would seem to allude here to the church of San Lodovico, originally annexed to a convent of Franciscan friars, which was suppressed in 1809, when the church became the "Prepositura" of Sant' Andrea a Cennano. Of the altar-piece ascribed to Botticelli, I have been unable to discover any trace.

Vasari, ed. 1568, I, 474.

The writers upon Florentine Art, who came after Vasari, have preserved a few notices of paintings ascribed to Botticelli, which can no longer be identified. Raffaello Borghini, in his "Riposo," printed at Florence, in 1584, mentions among the works of Botticelli, a painting in the possession of Francesco Trosci, of "the Virgin, with the Child on the ground raised by an angel, near whom is the young St. John, in a beautiful landscape."

l.c., p. 352.

Francesco Bocchi, in his "Bellezze di Fiorenza," printed at Florence, in 1591, describes, among the works of art then in the house of Messer Baccio Valori, the so-called Palazzo dei Visacci, in the Borgo degli Albizzi, at Florence, "a very large 'tondo,' wherein is painted and finely coloured by the hand of Sandro Botticello, a Madonna who holds the Child in her arms. The Virgin has a noble air, and her son likewise; and two angels, who appear full of grace and gaiety, are of a truth most beautiful and rare. Two vases of roses, which appear to be of a wonderful freshness, give

l.c., p. 182.

pleasure to whoever admires them; and the colouring, which is beautiful throughout, renders this painting noble and excellent." This picture, no doubt, was the 'tondo' of the Virgin and Child, with angels, to which l.c., ed. 1767, IV, 62. Filippo Baldinucci alludes in his "Notizie de' Professori del disegno," first published in 1681: it had then passed into the possession of Cavaliere Alessandro Valori. Such particulars in the foregoing description as the large dimensions of this "tondo," and the two vases of roses, recall the "tondo" ascribed to Botticelli, in the Borghese Collection, at Rome: but Bocchi speaks only of two angels, whereas the Borghese picture contains six angels, besides the figure of the young St. John.

l.c., p. 306. Giovanni Cinelli, in his edition of the "Bellezze di Firenze," published in 1677, speaks of "a Nativity by Sandro," which was then in the house of the Cavaliere Vasari, among the works of art, which the author of the "Lives of the Painters" had collected. Such notices of Cinelli as that in Id., p. 146. which he ascribes to Sandro the "Annunciation" in the chapel of the Frescobaldi, in the church of Santo Spirito, or the altar-piece of the "Three Archangels," once in the chapel of Gino Capponi, in the same church, founded as they are upon some obvious misconception, need not detain us. The former altar-piece is now known to be the work of Piero del Donzello; the latter was doubtlessly executed by Francesco Botticini in the workshop of Verrocchio.

Other paintings, which for the most part can no longer be traced, are found ascribed to Botticelli in the Inventories preserved among the records App. II., Doc. LXV, fol. 154, recto, and fol. 153, tergo. of the Guardaroba at Florence. In an Inventory of the Guardaroba of the Palazzo del Casino, begun on 8th of March, 1587-8, is enumerated among the paintings in the gallery, "a picture on panel with a Nativity of our Lord with the Magi, said to be by the hand of Botticelli, about $1\frac{1}{4}$ braccia high, and $1\frac{3}{4}$ braccia wide, in a carved and gilt wooden frame." In the same Inventory, two little pictures, $\frac{1}{3}$ of a braccio high, and $\frac{3}{4}$ of a braccio wide, one of the Marriage, and the other of the Death, of the Virgin, are ascribed to Botticelli: but these, no doubt, are the two predella-panels by Fra Angelico, now in the Gallery of the Uffizi, Nos. 1178 and 1184. In the Inventory, cited above, of the Guardaroba of the Grand Duke Ferdinand App. II, Doc. LXIV, fol. 128, recto. II, begun on 16th September, 1637, two other pictures are ascribed to Botticelli, which then hung in the great Terrazzo opening on to the court-yard of the Palazzo Vecchio. One is described as "a picture on canvas, $1\frac{3}{4}$ braccia high, in which is painted in oil, by the hand of Botticelli, as it is believed, an armed soldier in the act of wounding a young man with a woman who holds him back, in a wooden frame." The other piece is described as: "A picture on canvas, in which is painted by the hand of Botticelli, a Galatea naked, with Zephyr and other figures, $1\frac{3}{4}$ braccia high, and $1\frac{1}{3}$ braccia wide, in a wooden frame." This last entry suggests some design in the vein of the "Birth of Venus."

But to come to the designs which Botticelli executed for embroideries. Among the notices which Vasari inserted into his account of Sandro in the second edition of the "Lives," is more than one allusion to works of this Vasari, ed. 1568, I, 474. character. "He was one of the first," Vasari states, "who found out the method of executing banners and other draperies, 'di commesso,' as it is called, in order that the colours may not destroy, but show on either side, the colour of the cloth. And by his hand, executed in this fashion, is the baldaquin of Or San Michele, full of figures of Our Lady, all various and beautiful: and it shows that this method of execution preserves the cloth better than do the mordants, which corrode and render it little durable: nevertheless a mordant, by reason of its small cost, is more in use at the present day, than the other method." And presently Vasari adds, that Sandro "was lavish of figures in his stories, as may be seen in the embroideries of the frieze of the cross, which the friars of Santa Maria Novella carry in procession, all executed from his design." This "lavoro di commesso" which, according to Vasari, came into use at Florence during the last half of the fifteenth century, in the manufacture of banners and other church-hangings, consisted in a kind of mosaic of pieces of cloth of various colours, applied to the surface of the hanging, and so shaped and fitted together, as to form figures and other ornaments: by which means the hanging retained its original colour, on the reverse; whereas, with the use of mordants, the actual fabric of the hanging was stained, and the mordant showed through on the other side.

F. Baldinucci, Vocabolario dell'Arte del Disegno, ed. 1681, p. 37.

No example of this "lavoro di commesso," executed from designs by Botticelli, is now known to be in existence. The baldaquin of Or San Michele and the embroideries of the cross of Santa Maria Novella have long disappeared; nor is anything known of their history. It is probable that Botticelli occupied himself with designs for embroideries, from the time when he was working as the assistant of Antonio and Piero Pollaiuoli, in 1470. During that very year, the famous embroideries for the apparel and orphreys of the chasuble, two dalmatics and cope, of brocade woven in a single piece, for the church of San Giovanni at Florence, were being executed from the designs of Antonio Pollaiuoli, by Paolo da Verona, Coppino di Giovanni da Malines, Piero di Piero da Verona, Niccolò di Jacopo, Francese, and Antonio di Giovanni da Firenze. There is but one extant piece of embroidery of which the design can be ascribed, with any certainty, to Botticelli: namely the shield-shaped "cappuccio," or hood, of a cope, embroidered with a coronation of the Virgin, which is preserved in the Museo Poldi-Pezzoli, at Milan, No. 155. In the centre of the upper part of the design, enthroned within a mandorla of seraphim, is a figure of Christ, inscribed $\overline{\text{XPO}}$, in the act of placing the crown on the head of the Virgin who kneels before him, in profile, somewhat to the left. On either side of this group, the winged figure of an angel draws apart the blue curtains of a baldaquin, which is suspended above the head of Christ. Below each of the two angels, is a kneeling figure of a saint with his hands raised in prayer, and clad, apparently, in a monastic habit. With the exception of the heads and aureoles, these two figures are in so damaged a condition, that it is no longer possible to determine with certainty the form, or colour, of their habits. Right and left, flanking this composition, are two candelabra set on triangular bases, and wreathed with fruits. Below the figure of Christ, in a garland of fruitage, which is held by two flying angels, is a shield emblazoned with the arms of Portugal: Argent, within a bordure, gules, charged with ten turrets, or, five inescutcheons, azure, 1, 3 and 1, each charged with five bezants, argent, 2, 1 and 2. This shield is surmounted by the coronet of a marquis, and below the garland are three seraphim. Enclosing the whole composition, is a corded and interlaced border nearly 2 inches in width, worked in gold cord. The entire work, including the border, measures rather more than 18 inches in breadth, and in height. The figures and other ornaments within the border are embroidered in variously coloured silks, whipped over fine gold cord laid parallel across the field of the design. The finer parts of the design, such

Vasari, ed. Sansoni, III, 299.

as the heads and hands, are alone worked solidly. This same method of work is employed in the embroideries of the famous vestments executed for the church of San Giovanni, and now preserved in the museum of the Opera del Duomo, at Florence; and the piece in question is scarcely inferior to them, in the beauty and fineness of its workmanship. The blue and purple dresses of Christ and the Virgin are still very pure and brilliant in colour. The upper angel on the right, is clad in a robe of shot purple, and that on the left, of shot saffron; while the two smaller figures of the angels below are draped in deep purple.

The shield of arms, surmounted, as it is, by the coronet of a marquis, would seem to justify the conclusion that this "cappuccio," or hood, originally formed part of a set of vestments, executed for the chapel of the Cardinal of Portugal, in the church of San Miniato al Monte, at Florence. The same shield and coronet are repeated many times in the coat-armour, "picta regum signa," which decorate the principal frieze of the chapel. James, Archbishop of Lisbon, and Cardinal of Sant' Eustachio, to whose memory this chapel was erected, was of the royal house of Portugal, and the nephew of Alfonso II. He died suddenly at Florence, in 1459, while going as Papal Legate to the Emperor. The chapel was begun soon after the death of the cardinal; but it appears from documents lately published by Signor Giglioli, in the "Revista d'Arte," that Alesso Baldovinetti did not finally finish and receive payment for the frescoes, which he executed in this chapel, until 1473. Costly vestments would be among the last gifts which the founders of such a chapel would bestow upon it; and consequently there is no historical difficulty, as a recent writer in the "Rassegna d'Arte" has suggested, in ascribing the design of this embroidery to Botticelli. Indeed, the figures, and especially those of Christ and the Virgin, are so unmistakably in his manner, that it could hardly be pretended that this design came from any other workshop than his. The two kneeling figures in this embroidery probably represented St. Benedict and St. Bernard, in the white habit of the Olivetani, who were in possession of the Monastery of San Miniato al Monte from 1373 to 1553. This composition, admirable alike in motive and in movement, displays all the characteristics of Botticelli's manner at the height of his career, after his return to Florence from working in the Sistine Chapel; it was probably executed not later than 1485.

l.c., anno 1906, p. 95.

l.c., anno 1903, pp. 184-186.

A design for the lower part of a similar "cappuccio," or hood, of a cope, has survived in a drawing, now at Darmstadt. This drawing, which in its entirety represented a "Descent of the Holy Spirit at Pentecost," I shall discuss among the drawings of Botticelli's school. It recalls the last period of Botticelli's art, and may have been executed at so late a period as 1505. Again, among the drawings in the Louvre, No. 424, is a composition of some nine figures, representing a miracle of a saint. It is executed in outline, apparently with a brush, on a piece of fine linen fabric, and it has all the appearance of a tracing executed by some embroiderer, from a drawing by Botticelli, or by one of his immediate followers. On the right of the composition stands an apostle, or saint, crowned with an aureole, and holding a bowl in his left hand, as he raises the right in the act of performing a miracle. On the other side of the composition, facing the saint, are the figures of two youths, kneeling upon one knee, with clasped hands, and the nearer one with closed eyes. In the midst of these figures, also kneeling upon one knee and turned towards the saint, is seen a royal, or noble, personage who holds, in his right hand, a mantle which envelops the figures of the two youths; his eyes are closed as if with emotion. Behind the two youths stands a man holding a tray, on which are placed two bowl-shaped vessels. On the right of this latter figure, in the background of the composition, are two men and two women, in attitudes of astonishment. I have not succeeded in tracing the legend from which this story is taken; but the miracle would seem to consist in raising to life, or restoring to sight, the two sons of a king, or noble. The tracing measures 10½ inches in height, and 9 inches in width. In the dramatic conception and crowded treatment of its composition, in the forms and in the expressive and agitated movements of the figures, this design recalls Botticelli's manner towards the close of the fifteenth century. More it is not possible to say; since in a tracing of this kind, all the quality of the original draughtsmanship is necessarily lost.

In the Museo Civico, at Orvieto, are preserved a chasuble and two dalmatics of purple brocade on a gold ground, the apparels of which are richly embroidered with figures of saints, and stories of the Virgin, Christ and the Apostles, designed in the manner of Botticelli. The stories on one of the dalmatics, particularly those of the "Resurrection" and the "Circumcision," closely recall in manner the tracing in the Louvre. This resemblance is especially apparent in those portions of the design where the embroidery having been worn away, has left bare the original tracing on the linen ground. In the Galleria degli Arazzi, at Florence, No. 819, is the superfrontal of an altar-cloth, embroidered with eighteen figures of the Virgin and Child, the twelve Apostles, (as it would seem,) the Baptist, a female saint and St. Michael and St. Raphael, enthroned within arched compartments, against a landscape background. The two figures of the archangels, at either end of the composition, bear shields blazoned with the arms of the Canigiani. The Botticellesque character of its design is clearly shown in the attitudes, and still more in the heads, of the figures. Again, in the Bardini Collection, at Florence, was lately another superfrontal of an altar-cloth, very similar in its general conception to that in the Galleria degli Arazzi. At either end of this superfrontal, a compartment, containing the seated figure of a female saint, had been added at a slightly later period. The design of these two compartments, unlike that of the rest of the embroidery, is markedly Botticellesque in character. In these vestments and superfrontals, the larger part of the design is executed in coloured silks, whipped over fine gold cord; the more delicate portions, however, such as the heads and hands, are worked solidly. In this, they resemble the hood of the cope in the Museo Poldi-Pezzoli; and, although less admirable in design and workmanship than that remarkable fragment, it can hardly be doubted that the drawings from which these embroideries were executed, came out of Sandro's workshop, or, at least, were the production of one, or another, of his immediate followers.

The conclusion to be drawn from Vasari's notices, that Botticelli gave much time to designs for embroideries, is borne out not only by the examples which I have described, but also by the influence which he exercised over the Florentine school of embroiderers, at the beginning of the sixteenth century. Vasari states in his life of Raffaellino del Garbo, that this master, in his declining years, was reduced "to execute for some nuns and other persons, who at that time embroidered many vestments and church hangings, designs in chiaroscuro and borders of saints and stories, at a miserable

Vasari, ed. Sansoni, IV, 239.

price." In accordance with this notice, a large number of drawings for embroidery, in pen and bistre-wash, heightened with white and, for the most part, pricked for pouncing, have been traditionally given to Raffaellino del Garbo. These designs are described by Mr. Berenson, in his work on "The Drawings of the Florentine Painters." Four of them, Nos. 31, 32, 33 and 36 in his Catalogue, are attributed by him to his "Alunno di Dominico," of whom I shall have occasion to speak hereafter. The rest he ascribes to "Raffaellino di Carli," properly Raffaello de' Carli, and are described by him among the drawings which he gives to that painter, Nos. 609-658. Even if I felt called upon to penetrate into the mystery of the three Raffaello's, this is not the place to attempt that adventurous task. Here, I must only touch upon a single aspect of this difficult question: namely, whether all the drawings which Mr. Berenson ascribes to "Raffaellino di Carli," are really by the same hand. In such a drawing as that of the "Vision of St. Bernard," in the British Museum, No. 640, in Mr. Berenson's Catalogue, the draperies are "heavy and flowing": the line is never angular, but suggests the fall of some unyielding woollen stuff. Moreover, the attitudes, the forms of the hand and ear, recall, as Mr. Berenson has remarked, the altar-piece still in the church of Santo Spirito at Florence, among other paintings which are certainly the work of Raffaello de' Carli. Whoever may have been the author of this drawing, it is unquestionably by the hand of some Florentine draughtsman, whose early manner has been entirely transformed by the Umbrian influence of Pietro Perugino. On the other hand, in such a drawing as the "Baptism of Christ," in the Beckerath Collection, now in the print-room at Berlin, No. 609 in Mr. Berenson's Catalogue, the folds are no longer flowing, but angular; and the scheme of the draperies is purely Botticellesque in character. The whole of the designs for embroidery which are ascribed in Mr. Berenson's Catalogue to Raffaello de' Carli, approach more or less nearly in character, either to this "Vision of St. Bernard," or to this "Baptism of Christ." Of the drawings in the Uffizi, which are markedly Botticellesque in manner, two are still ascribed to Sandro, namely, a "St. Jerome," Frame 51, No. 222F, and a "Baptist," Frame 55, No. 196, both at half-length; while a third drawing of "Christ in the midst of the Apostles," Frame 101, No. 211, is inscribed in a hand of the sixteenth century, "Sandro di Botticello." The authentic paintings of Raffaello de' Carli show him to have been one of Domenico Ghirlandaio's disciples, whose manner was afterwards transformed under the influence of Pietro Perugino. The draperies in these paintings never display the Botticellesque character of the draperies in certain of the drawings: and it is difficult to think that a painter, the work of whose mature years never reveals any direct reminiscence of Sandro's design, would entirely change his manner in so radical a point as the scheme of his draperies. But this question, after all, is largely extraneous to our enquiry. Here it is sufficient to note that all these designs for embroidery appear to have been inspired, in some degree or another, by Botticelli; while a few of them, and notably those I have specified, appear to have been directly imitated from his designs.

Vasari, ed. 1568, I, 474.

But to pass on: "Sandro," records Vasari, "drew uncommonly well; and so much so, that for long after his time, craftsmen endeavoured to obtain his drawings. And we have some of them in our book, which are executed with much facility and judgment." In the workshops of the painters, the great mass of Botticelli's drawings were doubtless destroyed;

first by use, and afterwards by neglect, as in the course of years the fashion in painting veered round to the "modern manner." Excepting the illustrations to "Dante," at Berlin and Rome, only eight drawings can now be ascribed with any certainty to Botticelli's own hand. Of these, the beautiful and elaborate drawing of "Abundance," in the Malcolm Collection, No. 11, in the British Museum, stands apart by itself; as it was evidently intended to serve as a finished design, and not as a study for some painting or other work, like the rest of his extant drawings. If the fragment of one of Vasari's mounts, on which this allegory of "Abundance" has been laid down, originally belonged to it, the drawing was one of those sheets by Botticelli which Vasari, as he tells us, possessed in his famous book of drawings. A sheet of studies in silver-point of a head, and three whole-length figures of young men, in the Louvre, No. 104, and a similar sheet of five, nude and draped, whole-length figures, lately in the collection of Herr von Beckerath, and now in the Print-room Museum at Berlin, both of which retain Vasari's mounts, and are ascribed by him to Botticelli, doubtless came from the same collection. These two sheets, however, which are apparently by the same hand, so far from being the work of Botticelli, are not even of his school, and must be ascribed to some follower of Filippino Lippi.

Of the five genuine drawings by Sandro, which are preserved in the Gallery of the Uffizi, I have already described the design in silver-point for a seated figure of "St. Jerome," Frame 51, No. 222[F]; the somewhat later and more forcible, if more rugged, study for a figure of the Baptist, Frame 55, No. 188; and the sadly damaged study for a "Nativity," Frame 53, No. 209, which belongs to the last period of Botticelli's art. The beautiful design for a lunette, of three flying figures of angels who sing from an open book, Frame 55, No. 187, is perhaps, one of the earlier, certainly one of the most exquisite, in point of invention, of these scattered studies. In motive, in beauty of line and sentiment, it is comparable to the dancing ring of angels in the great "Coronation" of San Marco, now in the Academy, at Florence, No. 47, or the group of singing angels above the pent-house in the "Adoration of the Shepherds," in the National Gallery, No. 1034. Like the greater number of the genuine drawings by Sandro, it is drawn with the pen on a rubbed, red ground, and washed and heightened with white. The remaining drawing executed in a similar technique, but on white paper, is the study for a whole-length figure of an angel, with the right hand uplifted, Frame 54, No. 202. Although it appears to be genuine, it is the least inspired, and the poorest in point of quality, of all the sheets that are to be ascribed to Sandro's own hand.

In the "Libro Resta," fol. 14, preserved in the Biblioteca Ambrosiana, at Milan, are two genuine studies of Botticelli: the one, a late drawing for a kneeling figure of St. Thomas, which I have already described; the other, a drawing which Sebastian Resta, who formed the collection, attributed to Filippino Lippi. The latter represents a whole-length, draped figure of "Fortitude," holding a mace in her right hand, and a shield blazoned with the head of Medusa, in her left. The figure stands upon a four-footed pedestal, of a form which suggests that the sketch may have been given as a design for a bronze. It is sketched in pen and ink, with great decision and lightness of touch. In spontaneity of invention and execution, it is comparable to the most fortunate passages in the illustrations to "Dante"; and is probably somewhat earlier in date than those drawings. The conjecture that this sketch may have been intended as a design for a bronze, is borne out, in a measure, by a "plaquette," of which there is an example in lead in the Museum at Berlin, and another in bronze in the collection of the writer. This "plaquette" which measures 0,076 cm. in height, represents the naked figure of a "Galatea," standing upon a dolphin, and holding a vase of fruits in her right hand, and in her left, which is uplifted, a scarf which is caught by the breeze above her head. In the catalogue of the Berlin Museum, No. 644, it is described as being in the manner of the Pollaiuoli: but not only do the type and attitude of the figure closely recall that of the central figure in the painting of the "Birth of Venus," No. 39, in the Uffizi; but the conception of the whole piece is so entirely in the manner of Botticelli, that there can be little doubt that it was suggested by some design of his.

But let us come to a conclusion. "One longs," wrote Pater, speaking of the artists of the Italian Renaissance, "to penetrate into the lives of the men who have given expression to so much power and sweetness; but it is part of the reserve, the austere dignity and simplicity of their existence, that their histories are for the most part lost, or told but briefly." If Botticelli's life is told but briefly, it may be, perhaps, that outwardly it was little eventful. Born in his father's house overlooking the little graveyard of the church of Ognissanti, he removed with his family, while yet a lad, to the house in the neighbouring Via Nuova, where he continued to live with his brothers and nephews, until he made his last remove to the same graveyard, which lies within a stone's throw of his birth-place and of the house where he had lived, worked and died. As a boy, he may have gone to Prato, to learn his art with Fra Filippo; as a young man, he went to Pisa, where he worked with little success, and in the prime of manhood, to Rome, where he worked with great applause. After that time, there is no record of any journey which again took him beyond Tuscan territory. He was never married; nor is his name once mentioned in relation with that of a woman. Indeed, the one anecdote of him which throws any light on the private life of the man, would show that it was part of his plan of life to abstain from marriage. The "Anonimo Gaddiano" relates: "that on one occasion, being pressed by Messer Tommaso Soderini to take a wife, he replied to him: I would have you know, that not many nights since, it happened to me, that I dreamed I had taken a wife, and I was so greatly troubled at the thought of it, that I awoke; and in order that I might not fall asleep a second time and dream it over again, I arose and wandered about all night, through Florence, like one distracted: by which Messer Tommaso knew that that was no soil wherein to plant a vineyard." Sandro's loves were inseparable from his art: "it is said," relates Vasari, "that he loved beyond the common, those whom he knew to be studious of the art." Of such a friendship, the portrait of some "discepolo," as it would seem, in the National Gallery, is, perhaps, a memorial.

J. Mesnil, Quelques Documents sur Botticelli, in the "Miscellanea d'Arte," anno 1903, p. 88.

App. II, Doc. II, fol. 83, recto.

Vasari, ed. 1568, I, 474.

In remaining throughout his life in the family house, Botticelli followed a common usage of the Florentines: but from the very beginning of his career as a master-painter, he appears, also, to have had his workshop in the same house, which was a thing unusual, especially in the case of a craftsman of repute. In this workshop was passed the greater part of his life, working and idling with his disciples and assistants: for Vasari has little to tell about Sandro that is not an anecdote of him at work, or at play. Like Brunelleschi, he was not only a great lover of Dante, but also a great lover of jesting. Long after the vogue which Botticelli enjoyed as a painter had passed away, many a quip of his was remembered in Florence. "He was a man much given to jesting, and very facetious; and in his day, his works were greatly esteemed": other than that, the "Anonimo Gaddiano" has not to record of his character. "Wiles and pleasantries were for ever going on in his workshop," says Vasari, "where he continually retained, to learn his art, an infinite number of youths, who were wont to play many tricks and practical jokes, one with another." Indeed, the only anecdotes of Sandro which have come down to us are stories of his jests and witty retorts. His jests, like the trick which he played upon his disciple, Biagio, who had copied a "tondo" of his, are after the pattern of the "burle," which form a chief part of the subject-matter of the early Florentine "novelle," and of which that of "Il Grasso, Legnaiuolo," the most profound and relentless of all practical jokes, becomes the typical instance. His wit is of that plain and direct kind, which to our sophisticated ears sounds merely trite and outspoken; but which, in the verses of Dante assumes a certain prophetic impressiveness, from the circumstances in which it is uttered. Of such a character is that retort of Sandro's, which the "Anonimo Gaddiano" has preserved: "and to one who in arguing with him, had oftentimes said to him, that he would he had a hundred tongues, he replied; you ask for more tongues, and you already have more by half than you have need of; ask for brains, my poor man, for you have none." To appreciate the attitude of such wit, we must transport ourselves to that primitive age, in which the "Novellino" was regarded as "Il Libro di bel parlar gentile." In the pages of Franco Sacchetti, we may find the true apology of Sandro's humour. At Florence, in the fifteenth century, a good jest was a thing even more memorable than a fine work of art. "You desire to know," begins the anonymous life appended to the "novella" of "Il Grasso, Legnaiuolo," "who was this Filippo, who made this jest of Il Grasso, which you so greatly admire": and the writer goes on to explain that the author of this jest was "a man of great intellect, and of talent and wit beyond the common." He was, in fact, Filippo Brunelleschi, the architect!

App. II, Doc. II, fol. 83, recto.

Vasari, ed. 1550, I, 495.

Vasari, ed. 1568, I, 473.

App. II, Doc. II, fol. 83, recto.

In such an age, (if not, indeed, at all times, and in all places,) a man of talent, witty, facetious and given to "living at chance," as Botticelli, could not avoid gathering about him a goodly number of kindred spirits. That "accademia di scioperati," who, as Ser Lorenzo Violi records a little contemptuously, frequented Sandro's workshop, during the last years of the century, used, doubtless, to gather in his "bottega," long before Simone Filipepi came to live with his brother, in 1494, and the "questions of Fra Girolamo" became the principal theme of their conversation. Scarcely a single "member" of that "accademia di scioperati," during this earlier time, could now be named with any certainty: but we may, perhaps, form some idea of its character, from the accounts which have come down to us, of similar brigades; of that "crew and company of divers worthy men both such as held public offices, and such as were masters of various arts and men of talent, as painters, goldsmiths, sculptors and woodworkers, and suchlike craftsmen," who used to meet in the house of Tommaso Pecori, and at one of whose meetings the notion of the jest of "Il Grasso" first occurred to Brunelleschi; or that more formal "brigata di galantuomini," who afterwards, in the sixteenth century, used to meet in the rooms of Giovan Francesco Rusticci, "than whom was never man more full of pleasantries

App. II, Doc. XLVI, fol. 41, tergo.

G. Milanesi, Operette Istor. di A. Manetti, p. 3.

Vasari, ed. Sansoni, VI, 609, etc.

and caprices." The doings of this brigade, known as the "Compagnia del Paiuolo," which stand recorded in the pages of Vasari, may, perhaps, go to explain how a man of Botticelli's sensibility, who had laboured much and gained much, came to "squander all through recklessness, without any profit to himself." Such gatherings appear to have been characteristic of the life of the Florentine craftsmen, throughout the fifteenth and sixteenth centuries.

As we study the portrait which Botticelli has left of himself, in the "Adoration of the Magi," once in Santa Maria Novella, we feel that he wished to be remembered as a man of great intellectual power, and with a great capacity for enjoying the sensuous aspect of life. The agent who,
App. II, Doc. XXIV. about the year 1485, sent to the Duke of Milan his report of the chief painters then working in Florence, says of Botticelli that his paintings were executed "cum optima ragione," with a degree of right judgment and understanding which he found in the work, neither of Filippino Lippi, Perugino, nor even of Domenico Ghirlandaio. Vasari, on the other hand, although he bestows on Sandro "great praise" for all those pictures which he executed "con amore," is all for insisting upon the moral deficiencies
Ed. 1550, I, 490. of the man. "Nature," he says in the first edition of the "Lives," "labours to give great talents to many, and then, on the other hand, put into them a spirit of recklessness; whence, by giving no thought to their latter days, they often adorn the spittal by their death, as in life they honoured the world by their works." And so he goes on to relate that, after Botticelli
Id., I, 494. had finished the frescoes in the Sistine Chapel, "he received from the Pope a good sum of money, which he all ran through and consumed out of hand, during his stay in Rome, by living at chance, as was his wont." Moreover, if Vasari has exaggerated the sorry condition to which Sandro was latterly reduced, we now know that in his last years, he was a comparatively poor man, whereas he might have been a comparatively rich man.

But Vasari and the Duke's agent were severally noting the opposite sides of Botticelli's character; and such apparent contradictions, such divergent, or as some may think, discordant notes, run through the whole of Sandro's life. For Botticelli was typically a Florentine; with the endless capacity of many another great Florentine master, both for work and play. On the other hand, there were certain considerations that went to prejudice Vasari's view of Sandro. Early in the sixteenth century, a large number of the inferior productions of Botticelli's workshop, already passed as the genuine work of his own hand. Vasari was too fine a critic not to distinguish between the good and the bad: but although he did not pause to inquire to what extent this inferior work was authentic, he gives Sandro unstinted praise for all those paintings executed by him, as he
Id., I, 496. puts it, "doue lo strigneua lo amore & la affezzione." Again, Vasari was a staunch partisan of the Medici, to whom, indeed, he owed all his success in life. It was but natural, then, that he should look askance upon Savonarola and his followers; and express his regret that Botticelli was
Id., I, 496. "given to the things by which, through hypocrisy, the beautiful considerations of art are rendered tedious."

Looking back at the technical development of Botticelli's art, we see him, in the earliest authenticated picture by his hand which has come down to us, (the "Fortitude," in the Gallery of the Uffizi, No. 1299, a painting which, as we now know, was executed for the "Sala Magna" of the Mercanzia, in 1470,) already, in a moment of reaction, breaking away from the limitations of the manner which he had acquired from Fra Filippo, and attempting with all the ardour of youth, to render the relief and movements of a figure, as they had been revealed to him in the work of Antonio Pollaiuoli. In the elaborate modelling of the head and in the fastidious design of the hands of this figure, there is something almost feverish in his effort to realize these new qualities of naturalistic painting. From that time onwards, he gradually conforms more and more to the tradition of naturalistic painting, of which Domenico Ghirlandaio was the chief exponent during the latter part of the fifteenth century. In the "Adoration of the Magi," once in the church of Santa Maria Novella, the work, in which this phase of Sandro's manner found its completest expression, his art becomes eminently ordered and reasonable. Mass, contour, relief and colour, are all equably managed in due relation to one another. At no other moment of his career does he again so bridle his individuality, and repress what is strange, or bizarre, in his nature, as in this painting. The lucidity of its conception, the choice and arrangement of its figures, their motives and attitudes, in short, the whole technical management of the piece, show the hand of a master who has recognized that "in Nature, there is no effect which is without reason." In this "Adoration," which must have been executed not later than 1477, Botticelli was working, as it would seem, in conscious rivalry with Domenico Ghirlandaio and the naturalists; but a phase of painting essentially scientific in its aim, could not suffice to engross him for long. Behind the measured, almost academic exterior of this picture, lies a vein of dramatic imagination and poetical feeling, which was destined to prevent him becoming a mere naturalist among naturalists. Passing beyond the limitations of this phase of his manner, he henceforth surrenders himself more and more to the true bent of his genius. In the picture of the "Spring," executed about this time, he first finds himself; and a rendering of contour, unrivalled in its rhythm and subtilty of line, first becomes a principal factor in the presentation of an unrivalled piece of pictorial invention. When, in 1478, he was called upon to paint the effigies of the Pazzi conspirators upon the face of the Dogana, the nature of the commission forced him to emulate the once famous effigies of the conspirators of 1427, which Andrea da Castagno, the greatest of the naturalistic masters of the fifteenth century, had painted on the tower of the Palazzo del Podestà. That this chance of circumstance markedly influenced his manner, cannot be doubted. From that time forward, an element of large, and often rugged, power enters into his design: and in the fresco of "St. Augustine," which he painted in 1480, upon the "tramezzo" of the church of Ognissanti, that "aria virile," which, for his contemporaries, was one of the admirable traits of his manner, is seen in its most imposing aspect.

The following year, Botticelli was called to Rome to paint in the Sistine Chapel. The great opportunity of his life came to him when his powers were at their fullest maturity; and he produced a series of frescoes which stand apart from his other works, by reason of their monumental character, their dramatic invention, and the occasion on which they were produced. If we would realize the full measure of his genius and technical achievement, we must study Botticelli in these frescoes: they constitute the central fact in the story of his art. From the time of his return to Florence, in 1482, until the death of Lorenzo, Il Magnifico, in 1492, his manner undergoes so little change, that any conjecture as to the order in which the undated paintings of this period were produced, becomes a matter of great difficulty. As I have shown, during this interval his forms tend to become more mannered, and his figures more energetic in movement; at the same time, a certain largeness and serenity enter into his design, which tend to counterbalance the restless character of his compositions.

After the death of Lorenzo, Il Magnifico and the flight of Piero de' Medici from Florence, a couple of years later, Botticelli does not appear to have again obtained any commission of public importance. For a time, as I have shown, he seems to have been chiefly engaged upon the designs for the "Dante" of Lorenzo di Pier Francesco de' Medici; and after that, to have been drawn more and more away from his art, by the "questions of Fra Girolamo." In the paintings of the earlier, naturalistic phase of his manner, great attention is paid to the modelling and relief of the figure; but already in the painting of the "Spring," and the frescoes of the Sistine Chapel, more relief and structure is expressed by the outlines of the figures than is rendered, or even suggested, by the modelling within those outlines. In the illustrations to the "Dante," no attempt is made to express relief by cross-hatching, or shading; and in the few genuine chamber-pictures of the last period of his career, the relief of the figures becomes wholly subordinated to the delineation of their form and movement.

Regarded in its technical aspect, the distinguishing trait of Sandro's art undoubtedly lies in the peculiar and intimate quality of his linear design. Botticelli has been called "a supreme master of the single line"; but a subtler criticism would, I think, prefer to say that among the moderns, he is an unique master of contour,—that he invariably uses his line, to express a definite contour, not only in the outline of the figure, but of some feature, hand, or fold within its mass, and always with a rhythm and beauty of intention which is unparalleled in Florentine art. Ruskin has called Botticelli a "reanimate Greek," and we may re-echo his phrase with a meaning of which he himself, perhaps, was not conscious. In his peculiar rendering of contour, Botticelli came nearer, at least in the technical part of painting, to the literal realization of the ideal of the Renaissance, that new birth of antique art, than any other master of his age. The more the student inquires into the origins of Italian art, the more he realizes that early Sienese and Florentine painting is derived, by direct descent, from the late classical schools of painting. Many periods of decadence and renaissance have come and gone, since the gods of antiquity yielded their place to the saints of the Christian Hierarchy; but the aims and limitations of painting, its technique and principles of design, have remained essentially unchanged. The finer qualities of the art often became lost in the mere tradition of its processes; but it remained a form of design founded essentially upon outline used to express the contours of masses. Pliny, speaking of the pre-eminence to which Parrhasius attained in the rendering of outline, observes: "This is the highest subtlety of the painter's art; since to depict bodies and the middle surfaces of things is indeed a matter of difficult achievement, yet one in which many have attained to fame; but to render the contours of bodies and enclose the extremities of painted masses, is rarely effected with success in the art: for the outline ought itself to pass around and so to end them, that it may give assurance of other parts behind itself, and even suggest those which it hides."

C. Plinius Secundus, Nat. Hist., Lib. XXXV, Cap. 10.

If the student would appreciate to what degree Botticelli realizes in his design, this ideal quality of the contour, let him compare such a painting as the school-version of the figures of the Virgin, at half-length, with the Child, now in the collection of Mr. Alexander Mann, at Glasgow, with the same figures by Botticelli's own hand, in the Bardi altar-piece, now in the Museum at Berlin, No. 106. Both paintings were, doubtless, executed from the same cartoon: yet in the school-version the outline remains little more than the edge of a silhouette; while in the original picture it appears, in Pliny's phrase, so to enclose the figures as to give assurance of the parts behind itself, and even to suggest what it hides. But the standpoint of Botticelli differs from that of the naturalistic masters; he does not seek, at least in his mature work, merely to render the relief and mechanism of the human figure. In his contours, Sandro unites two distinct qualities: the swift rhythmical line which he inherited through Fra Filippo Lippi and Don Lorenzo Monaco, from the early Sienese masters—a line in its origin largely calligraphic; and the nervous, expressive line of Antonio Pollaiuoli and the naturalists, a line essentially constructive in its function. In uniting these two diverse qualities, Botticelli had a very definite aim in view; for he does not set himself merely to render form, but always form in motion. For him, every attitude is a movement arrested at the most significant moment of its development; the moment at which it best expresses that passion of the mind by which it is impelled. He seeks, then, to express form in its most imaginative and interpretive manifestation; in short, precisely that aspect of it which we vainly look for in the posed, inert model.

And so with his design in general: his compositions, the choice and arrangement of his figures, are evolved out of what is essentially a dramatic conception of the theme proposed; and the motives of his figures are invariably determined by the part which they play in the dramatic action. The same fine sequence of ideas is to be traced in every passage of his design; the dramatic relation of the parts to the whole, of the minor to the major motives, is never overlooked. When, in deference to the fashion of his age, he introduces portrait-figures into his religious compositions, he does not allow them to outweigh, or disturb, the real subject of the picture, as Domenico Ghirlandaio is apt to do. The ostensible theme of a painting by Sandro never becomes a mere incident in what, in effect, is a group of portrait-figures, as in many of Domenico's frescoes in Santa Maria Novella. On the contrary, Botticelli elaborates from his subject, with an unfailingly dramatic purpose, that variety of motives and attitudes which called forth the admiration of Vasari. Even in a single portrait-figure, Sandro will introduce some dramatic intention into his design, as in the portrait of a young man displaying a medal of Cosimo de' Medici, in the Gallery of the Uffizi.

His, then, is above all things a form of expressive art: for in thus evolving a design out of the dramatic action suggested by its theme, Botticelli was following a first principle of expression in the art of painting, as it was practised by the naturalistic masters of the fifteenth century; a principle which is summed up by Leonardo da Vinci in the apophthegm: "That figure is most admirable which best expresses by its action the passions of its mind." In conceiving gesture and attitude as a movement arrested at the most significant moment of its development, Sandro carries this principle of expression, this most difficult function of "good painting," as Leonardo has it, to its utmost limit: for the representation of form in movement can only be rendered by mental images of a supremely imaginative order; and in seeking thus to interpret the thoughts and passions of the mind, the "outward shows of things" become, in Botticelli's design, expressive of the spirit in the highest degree. Contour, relief, colour, are all equally transfigured by his imagination; so that his figures, while appealing to us with a surprising sense of actuality and vital being, are entirely removed from nature, in any obvious, or photographic, view. It is in this sense that Botticelli is to be regarded as a visionary painter, "and in his visionariness," as Pater has said, "resembles Dante." Like Dante, he is visionary, in that, while seeing with the eye, he divines more than meets the eye, "at the first sight of life." But visionary as he is, there is no trace in him of the mystic who "shuts the eye," that he may see inwardly things "invisible to mortal sight." For him, vision is that alert, divinatory outlook upon the visible world which enables him to interpret the unseen by the seen, the motive by the action, the searchings of the heart by a glance of the eye, a gesture of the hand.

This preoccupation with a form of art essentially expressive in its nature, precluded that Botticelli should become a seeker after some absolute, idealistic type of beauty. Even the antique world served to stimulate, rather than deaden, his imagination; for the masterpieces of ancient art still lay buried, for the most part, under the débris of the ages, or were things of which he had heard the far report, rather than seen. As we look upon his Graces dancing in a round, or his Venus Anadyomene borne over the waters, we feel that in designing these figures, Botticelli had in his mind some passage, let us say, out of Horace, or the Greek Anthology, rather than some actual piece of antique sculpture, or painting. Unfettered by any traditional, or academic, criterion of beauty, Botticelli pursues his art of expression to its logical conclusion: for him, that is the most beautiful that is the most expressive, and so his figures taken directly from the Tuscan type around him—large of frame and angular of movement, with thickset joints and powerful hands—though rarely lovely in themselves, invariably possess a peculiar force and beauty of expression, by which what would otherwise be plebeian, or even commonplace, is endued with infinite distinction.

Consciously, or unconsciously, Sandro holds with the romanticists in opposition to the academicians, that "there is no excellent beauty that hath not some strangeness in the proportion." And yet the sense of the unusual, or rare, which colours all his invention, those bizarre traits, as Vasari puts it, with conspicuous fairness, from his own academic point of view—"quelle strauaganzie, che possono far' conoscere la perfezzione del suo magistèrio," never become, on the one hand, merely odd or unbalanced, as in much of the work of such later Florentines as Jacopo da Pontormo, or Il Rosso; nor allow him, on the other, to lapse into that "decorum," which certain English critics of the last century have noted with admiration in the work of Domenico Ghirlandaio.

Vasari, ed. 1550, I, 494.

This vein of caprice, always charming, inventive, unexpected, is inseparable from the peculiar sentiment which runs through all Botticelli's work, and which has been so variously interpreted; but, perhaps, a sentiment as intimately efflorescent of the human spirit as this, is capable of a various interpretation. The failure of his own followers to detach and imitate this sentiment is, perhaps, the best evidence of how directly and spontaneously this sentiment proceeded from the peculiar temperament and personality of the painter; and in attempting its discussion, we must not forget of how complex a nature was that temperament, that personality. The disciple of the painter who was, beyond any other master of his day, "gratioso et ornato molto et sopra modo artifitioso," Sandro himself had been born in an age newly arrived at a degree of refinement and delicacy which had been unknown in Italy since antique times,—the age of Lorenzo, Il Magnifico and Poliziano, of an amatorious poetry that did not hesitate to define love as "the desire of beauty," (beauty which is ever passing,) or take as the motto of its philosophy, "Carpe diem":

"Quant' è bella giovinezza,
Che si fugge tuttavia!
Chi vuol esser lieto, sia:
Di doman non c'è certezza."

Although Dante became the poet of his election, and although he turned from the delicate manner of Fra Filippo to the virile, or nervous, art of Andrea da Castagno, or Antonio Pollaiuoli, Sandro could not escape from the spirit of his time; and we need not wonder if we find running throughout the texture of some design of his, though virile or nervous as theirs, an inscrutable sense of wistfulness and regret, which has much in common with the poetry of Lorenzo, but which is altogether foreign to the art of the naturalistic painters.

Again, in the attempt to analyze this vein of sentiment, we may note how much of the ingenuous spirit of the earlier part of the fifteenth century, Botticelli had imbibed from his master, Fra Filippo. We see this especially in the way in which he reverts to almost Giottesque motives and modes of conception in his last pictures, which were executed at a time when the sophisticated, and often tired, painting of the sixteenth century was already being called into existence. We see it in the ingenuousness with which he approaches antique legend in his "profane" pictures; an ingenuousness which spared him any sense of contradiction between the ascetic, Christian world and the old pagan world of the senses, and which has enabled such designs to become for us, ingrained as we are with the Christian spirit, "a more direct inlet into the Greek temper, than the works of the Greeks themselves." Again, we may note how, with the same ingenuousness, he embraces the teaching of Savonarola, that very reaction against the "new learning," which was to render the naive, blithe paganism of his "Spring" and his "Birth of Venus," no longer a possible thing in art. Or we may note how, when under the influence of the friar at the very close of his life, he essays a theme "obscure as Themis or Sphinx," (for such, indeed, is the burden of the Greek inscription on the "Adoration of the Shepherds," in the National Gallery,) his imagination, led by the same ingenuous spirit, remains untainted by any trace of superstition, and the painting that is to prefigure this dark prophecy, is found to be a piece of visionary art as "young-eyed" as the most radiant of his early works.

In noting such traits as these, however, we are remarking only the obverse of the medal: let us glance for a moment at the reverse. Ruskin first alludes to Botticelli, (so far as I am aware,) in a letter written in 1870, but only to remark the "strange hardness and gloom," which pervades his work. That is how that "aria virile" of the master, which called forth the admiration of his contemporaries, occurred to a critic who, in reality, took as his criterion in all questions of painting, the refined and gentle art of the English landscape-painters, and the English Pre-Raphaelites. But if Ruskin's appreciation was, after all, as purely a personal one as that of Pater, who found running through all Sandro's varied work, "a sentiment of ineffable melancholy," there still remains in both their views, a certain element of truth. Pater, it is true, failed to distinguish between the sentimentality of the school-pictures, and the genuine sentiment of Botticelli's authentic works; or to perceive that the one stands in precisely the same relation to the other, as the craft of the imitator to the craft of the master. But under such purely personal, or occasional, misapprehensions, lies, as I have said, an element of real observation. Botticelli was typically a Florentine; and his art constantly reveals the ever-shifting colours of the Florentine temperament. If his paintings display the keen sense of expressive beauty, the bizarre imagination, the amatorious sweetness and tenderness of the age in which he lived, they display, also, much of the feeling which is more distinctively characteristic of an earlier age of Florentine art. If, like Dante, he can faint with love, he inherits, in common with the naturalistic painters, no small a portion of the virility, the energy, the directness, and at times the gloom, or even some tincture of the cruelty of the Florentine temperament; qualities which live for all time in the "Divina Commedia." Such divergent, or, as it may seem to us, discordant traits, were neither incompatible, nor contradictory, in a Florentine of the fifteenth century: they were the current obverse and reverse of the Florentine character.

In reviewing the characteristics of Botticelli's art, in thus passing discursively from its purely technical, to its purely subjective, aspect, I have endeavoured to bring the complex nature of his genius, its many facets, its manifold lights and half-lights, at least partially into evidence. From one point of view, Botticelli may be said to have reconciled, and put to new and more expressive uses, the various innovations which the Florentine painters, and more especially the naturalistic masters, had successively introduced into their craft, during the course of the fifteenth century. Certain tendencies in the art of his time were, however, entirely overlooked, or ignored, by Sandro: and in noting these limitations of his interests, we may, perhaps, obtain a yet clearer notion of Botticelli's figure as a painter, and of the unique place which he occupies in the development of Florentine art. In his last pictures, Sandro himself appears to have realized that he had carried his practice to its limits, and exhausted the resources of his manner. Without the discoveries of Leonardo and Michelagnolo, the art of painting could have reached no further stage of development. It is significant that Botticelli should have been least preoccupied in his work, with the very problems of the painter's art in which the pioneers of Leonardo and Michelagnolo in those discoveries, made their first essays. In the discovery of the nude as a form of psychic expression, Michelagnolo transmuted into a new and living mode of pictorial art, what in the hands of Antonio Pollaiuoli had been essentially a naturalistic delineation of the form and mechanism of the human frame, based upon the idea of its anatomy. Of this anatomical conception of the figure, Botticelli appears to have taken little or no account: there is no evidence in his design that he ever made dissections of the human body. In his discovery of chiaroscuro, Leonardo achieved an innovation even more original and far-reaching in its effects, than the discovery of Michelagnolo. Vasari, with his wonted acumen, calls Leonardo the founder of "that manner, which we will call the modern." In the works of Leonardo's predecessors, the chiaroscuro of a picture is considered only in its relation to each successive object in the picture. In the paintings of Leonardo, the various objects in the picture are, for the first time, considered in relation to their place in a given scheme of chiaroscuro. He is the first to formulate the principles of aerial perspective, and to render the effect of the third dimension in painting, with all the subtilty of light and shade which distance produces: thus, in a certain sense, Leonardo becomes the founder of all modern art. By employing a "certain obscurity of the shadows well understood," by which the contours were lost, or the masses fused, according as the scheme of its chiaroscuro, Leonardo avoided that "dry, hard and cutting manner" of his predecessors, which Vasari particularly censures in Botticelli. But Botticelli was interested in chiaroscuro only in so far as it served to render relief: his contours are never lost, his masses never fused. In the works of his earlier, naturalistic period, when such problems preoccupied him more than in after years, his pictures are invariably lit by a full, clear, right or left light; and the effect of distance is obtained, as much by the diminishing lines of the perspective, as by the light and shade. In the works of his last years, when he had ceased to be exercised by such considerations, his chiaroscuro becomes, in principle, that of a bas-relief. These archaistic tendencies, which run through all Botticelli's work, were among the chief causes of the oblivion to which his paintings had been assigned within a century of his death.

Vasari, ed. 1568, vol. ii, Proemio.

APPENDIX I.

THE LIFE OF SANDRO BOTTICELLI, BY GIORGIO VASARI, ACCORDING TO THE FIRST EDITION OF "LE VITE DE' PIU ECCELLENTI ARCHITETTI, PITTORI, ET SCULTORI ITALIANI," ETC., PUBLISHED AT FLORENCE IN 1550.

SANDRO BOTTICELLO PITTOR FIORENTINO.

Sforzasi la natura, a molti dare la virtù, & in contrario gli mette la trascurattaggine per Vol. I. p. 490.
rouescio: perche non pensando al fine della vita loro, ornano spesso lo spedale della lor morte
come con l'opre in vita onorarono il mondo. Questi nel colmo delle felicità loro sono de i beni
della fortuna troppo carichi; & ne' bisogni ne son tanto digiuni, che gli aiuti vmani da la
bestialità del lor poco gouerno talme*n*te si fuggono; che co'l fine della morte loro vituperano
tutto l'onore, & la gloria della propria vita. Onde non sarebbe poca prudenzia ad ogni virtuoso,
& particularme*n*/te a gli artefici nostri, quando la sorte gli concede i beni della fortuna, saluarne p. 491.
per la vecchiezza, & per gli incomodi vna parte; accio il bisogno, che ogni ora nasce, non lo
percuota: come stranamente percosse Sandro Botticello, che cosi si chiamò ordinariamente,
per la cagione che appresso vedremo. Costui fu figliuolo di Mariano Filipepi cittadino
Fiorentino; dal quale diligenteme*n*te alleuato & fatto instruire in tutte quelle cose che vsanza
è di insegnarsi a fanciulli in quella città, prima che e' si ponghino a le botteghe; ancora che
ageuolmente apprendesse tutto quello che è voleua; era nientedimanco inquieto sempre; ne
si contentaua di scuola alcuna, di leggere, di scriuere o di abbaco; di maniera che il padre infastidito di questo ceruello si strauagante, per disperato lo pose a lo orefice con vn' suo compare chiamato Botticello, assai competente maestro all' ora in quella arte. Era in quella età
vna dimestichezza grandissima, & quasi che vna continoua pratica tra gli orefici & i pittori;
per la quale Sandro che era desta persona, & si era volto tutto a'l disegno; inuaghitosi della
pittura, si dispose volgersi a quella. Per il che aprendo liberamente l'animo suo al padre, da
lui che conobbe la inchinazione di quel ceruello, fu condotto a Fra Filippo del Carmine eccellentissimo pittore all' ora, & acconciato seco a imparare come Sandro stesso desideraua.
Datosi dunque tutto a quella arte, sequitò & imitò si fattamente il Maestro suo, che Fra
Filippo gli pose amore: & insegnolli di maniera che e' perue*n*ne tosto ad vn grado, che
nessuno lo arebbe stimato. Dipinse essendo giouanetto nella mercatantia di Fiorenza vna
fortezza fra le tauole delle virtu, che Antonio, & Piero del Pollaiuolo lauorarono. In S.
Spirito di Fiorenza fece vna tauola alla cappella de' Bardi, laquale è con diligenza lauorata/ & p.492.
a buon fin condotta; doue sono alcune oliue, & palme lauorate con sommo amore. Lauorò
nelle conuertite vna tauola a quelle monache, & a quelle di San Barnabà, similmente vn' altra.
In Ogni Santi dipinse a fresco nel tramezzo alla porta, che va in coro per i Vespucci vn Santo
Agostino, nel quale cercando egli allora di passare tutti coloro, ch' al suo tempo dipinsero
molto s'affaticò, la quale opera riuscì lodatissima per auere egli dimostrato nella testa di quel
santo, quella profonda cogitazione, & acutissima sottigliezza che suole essere nelle persone
sensate, & astratte continouamente nella inuestigazione di cose altissime & molto difficili.
Per il che venuto in credito & in riputazione, dall' arte di Porta Santa Maria gli fu fatto fare in
San Marco vna incoronazione di Nostra do*n*na in vna tauola, & vn' coro d'angeli; laquale fu
molto ben disegnata & condotta da lui. In casa Medici a LORENZO vecchio lauorò molte
cose, & massimamente vna Pallade su vna impresa di bronconi, che buttauano fuoco, laquale
dipinse grande qua*n*to il viuo & ancora vn S. Sebastiano in Santa Maria maggior' di Fiore*n*za.
Per la citta in diuerse case fece tondi di sua mano, & femmine ignude assai, dellequali oggi
ancora a Castello, luogo del Duca COSIMO di Fiorenza, sono due quadri figurati, l'uno, Venere
che nasce, & quelle aure & venti, che la fanno venire in terra con gli amori: & cosi vn' altra
Venere, che le grazie la fioriscono dinotando la primavera; lequali da lui con grazia si
veggono espresse. Nella via de' Serui in casa Giouanni Vespucci oggi di Piero Saluiati, fece
intorno vna camera molti quadri chiusi da ornamenti di noce per ricignimento & spalliera, con
molte figure, & viuissime, & belle. Ne' monaci di Cestello a vna cappella fece vna tauola
d'una Annunziata. In San Pietro Maggio/re alla porta del fianco fece vna tauola per Matteo p. 493.
Palmieri con infinito numero di figure, la assunzione di Nostra donna con le zone de' cieli,
come son figurate, il Patriarchi, i Profeti, gli Apostoli, gli Euangelisti, i Martiri, i Confessori, i
Dottori, le Vergini, & le Gerarchie; disegno dato gli da Matteo, ch' era litterato. La quale
opra egli con maestria & finitissima diligenza dipinse. Euui ritratto appie Matteo inginocchioni, & la sua moglie ancora. Ma con tutto che questa opera sia bellissima, & che ella
douesse vincere la inuidia; furono però alcuni maliuoli & detrattori, che non potendo dannarla
in altro: dissero che & Matteo & Sandro grauemente vi aueuano peccato in Eresia: il che se
è vero o non vero, non se ne aspetta il giudizio a me: basta che le figure che Sandro vi fece
veramente sono da lodare, per la fatica che e' durò nel girare i cerchi de' Cieli & tramezare tra
figure & figure d'Angeli, & scorci, & vedute in diuersi modi diuersamente, & tutto condotto

con buono disegno. Fu allogato a Sandro in questo tempo vna tauoletta piccola di figure di
tre quarti di braccio l'vna; La quale fu posta in Santa Maria Nouella fra le due porte nella
facciata principale della chiesa nello entrare per la porta del mezo a sinistra: Et euui dentro
la adorazione de' Magi; Doue si vede tanto affetto nel primo vecchio; che baciando il piede
al nostro Signore, & struggendosi di tenerezza, benissimo dimostra auere conseguito la fine
del lunghissimo suo viaggio: Et la figura di questo Re, è il proprio ritratto di COSIMO vecchio
de' Medici: di quanti a' dì nostri se ne ritruouano il piu viuo & piu naturale. Il secondo, che
è GIVLIANO de' Medici Padre di PAPA CLEMENTE VII, si vede che intentissimo con l'animo
p. 494. diuotamente rende reuerenzia a quel putto, & gli assegna il presento suo./ Il terzo inginocchiato egli ancora, pare che adorandolo, gli renda grazie; & lo confessi il vero Messia.
Ne si può descriuere la bellezza che Sandro mostrò nelle teste che vi si veggono; le quali co*n*
diuerse attitudini son' girate, quale in faccia, quale in profilo, quale in mezo occhio, & qual
chinata, & in piu altre maniere; et diuersità d'arie di giouani, di vecchi; co*n* tutte quelle
strauaga*n*zie che possono far' conoscere la perfezzione del suo magistèrio. Auendo egli distinto
le corti di tre Rè, di maniera che e' si co*m*prende, quali siano i seruidori dell' vno, & quali dell'
altro. Opera certo mirabilissima; Et per colorito, per disegno, & per componimento, ridotta
si bella; che ogni artefice ne resta oggi marauigliato: Et all' ora gli arrecò in Fiorenza & fuori
tanta fama che Papa Sisto IIII. auendo fatto fabbricare la cappella in Palazzo di Roma; &
volendola dipignere, ordinò ch' egli ne diuenisse capo; onde in quella fece di sua mano le infrascritte storie, cio è qua*n*do CHRISTO è tentato dal diauolo: quando Mosè amazza lo Egizzio,
& che riceue bere da le figlie di Ietro Madianite: similmente quando sacrificando i figliuoli di
Aaron venne fuoco da cielo: & alcuni Santi Papi nelle nicchie di sopra alle storie. La onde
acquistato fra molti concorrenti che seco lauorarono, & Fiorentini, & di altre città, fama &
nome maggiore; ebbe da'l Papa buona somma di danari; i quali ad vn' tempo destrutti, &
consumati tutti nella stanza di Roma, per viuere a caso, come era il solito suo; & finita insieme
quella parte che egli era stata allogata, & scopertala, se ne tornò subitamente a Fiorenza.
Doue per essere persona sofistica, comentò vna parte di Dante: & figurò lo inferno, & lo mise
in Stampa; dietro al quale consumò di molto tempo, perilche non lauorando fu cagione di
p. 495. infiniti disordini alla vita sua. Mise in stampa ancora il/ trionfo della Fede di fra Girolamo
Sauonarola da Ferrara, & fu molto partigiano a quella setta. Il che fu causa, che abbandonando
il dipignere, & non auendo entrate da viuere precipitò in disordine grandissimo.

Perche ostinato alla setta di quella parte, faccendo continuamente il piagnone & deuiandosi
da'l lauoro, invecchiando, & dimenticando, si condusse in molto mal' essere. Aueua lauorato
molte cose in quel di Volterra & molte a LORENZO vecchio de' Medici, il quale mentre visse
sempre lo souuenne. E in San Francesco fuor della porta San Miniato, vn tondo con vna
Madonna, con Angeli grandi quanto il viuo, il quale fu tenuto cosa bellissima. Dicesi, che
Sandro era persona molto piaceuole & faceta, & sempre baie & piaceuolezze si faceuano in
bottega sua, doue continouamente tenne a imparare infiniti giouani, i quali molte giostre &
vccellamenti vsauano farsi lun laltro: & Sandro stesso accusò per burla vno amico suo di Eresia
a gli Otto, il quale comparendo domandò chi l'aueua accusato & di che, perche sendogli detto
che Sandro era stato, il quale diceua ch' ei teneua l'opinione degli Epicurei, che l'Anima
morisse col corpo, rispose, & disse, egli è vero che io ho questa opinione dell' anima sua, ch' è
bestia, & bene è egli Eretico; poi che senza lettere comenta Dante, & mentoua il suo nome in
vano. Dicesi, ancora che molto amaua quegli, che vedeua studiosi della arte: & dicono che
guadagnò molto; & tutto per trascurataggine senza alcun frutto mandò in mala parte. Fu da
Lorenzo vecchio molto amato, & da infiniti ingegni, & onorati Cittadini ancora. Ma finalmente, condottosi vecchio & disutile, camminaua per terra con due mazze, perilche no*n*
potendo piu far niente, infermo & decrepito, ridotto in miseria, passò di questa vita d'anni
p. 496. LXXVIII: & in/ Ogni Santi di Fiorenza fu sepolto, L'anno MDXV. Meritò veramente Sandro
gran' Lode in tutte le pitture che e' fece doue lo strigneua lo amore & la affezzione; Et
ancora che e' si fusse indiritto come si disse a le cose, che per la ipocresia si recano a noia le
bellissime considerazioni della arte; E' non resta però che le sue cose, non siano & belle &
molto lodate: Et massimamente la tauola de' Magi di Santa Maria Nouella. In su la grandezza della quale si vede oggi di suo appresso di Fabio Segni vna tauola dentroui la Calumnia
di Apelle: doue Sandro diuinamente imitò il Capriccio di quello antico Pittore; Et la donò
ad Antonio Segni, suo amicissimo. Et è si bella questa Tauola che & per la inuenzione di
Apelle, & per la pittura di Sandro, è ella stata onorata di questo Epigramma.

Indicio quemquam ne falso lædere tentent
Terrarum Reges parua Tabella monet.
Huic similem AEgypti Regi donauit Apelles.
Rex fuit, & dignus munere: munus eo.

THE LIFE OF SANDRO BOTTICELLI, BY GIORGIO VASARI, ACCORDING TO THE SECOND EDITION OF "LE VITE DE' PIU ECCELLENTI PITTORI, SCULTORI, E ACHITETTORI," ETC., PUBLISHED AT FLORENCE IN 1568.

VITA DI SANDRO BOTTICELLO PITTOR FIORENTINO. Vol. I, p. 470.

Ne' medesimi tempi del Mag. Lorenzo Vecchio de' Medici, che fu veramente, per le persone d' ingegno, vn secol d'oro, fiori ancora Alessando: chiamato a l' uso nostro Sa*n*dro, e detto di Botticello per la cagione che apresso vedremo. Costui fu figliuolo di Mariano Filipepi Cittadino Fiorentino; dalquale diligentemente alleuato, & fatto instruire in tutte quelle cose, che vsanza è di insegnarsi a fanciulli in quella età, prima che e' si ponghino a le botteghe; ancora che ageuolmente apprendesse tutto quello, che è voleua; era nientedimanco inquieto sempre; ne si contentaua di scuola alcuna, di leggere, di scriuere o di abbaco: di maniera, che il padre infastidito di questo ceruello si strauaga*n*te, per disperato lo pose a lo orefice con vn suo compare
chiamato Botticel/lo, assai competente maestro all' ora in quell' arte. Era in quella età vna p. 471.
dimestichezza grandissima, & quasi che vna continoua pratica tra gli orefici, & i pittori; per la quale Sandro, che era destra persona, e si era volto tutto al disegno; inuaghitosi della pittura, si dispose volgersi a quella. Perilche aprendo liberamente l'animo suo al padre, da lui, che conobbe la inchinazione di quel ceruello, fu condotto a fra Filippo del Carmine eccellentissimo pittore all' ora, & acconcio seco a imparare, come Sandro stesso desideraua. Datosi dunque tutto a quell' arte, sequitò & imitò, si fattamente il maestro suo, che fra Filippo gli pose amore: & insegnolli di maniera che e' peruenne tosto ad vn grado, che nessuno lo harebbe stimato. Dipinse essendo giouanetto nella mercatanzia di Fiorenza vna fortezza fra le tauole delle virtù, che Antonio, & Piero del Pollaiuolo lauorarono. In S. Spirito di Fiorenza fece vna tauola alla cappella de' Bardi; laquale è con diligenza lauorata, & a buon fin co*n*dotta; doue sono alcune oliue, & palme lauorate con sommo amore. Lauorò nelle conuertite vna tauola a quelle monache, & a quelle di S. Barnabà, similmente vn' altra. In Ogni Santi dipinse a fresco nel tramezzo alla porta, che va in coro per i Vespucci vn S. Agostino, nelquale cercando egli allora di passare tutti coloro, ch' al suo tempo dipinsero; ma particolarmente Domenico Ghirlandaio, che haueua fatto dall' altra banda vn S. Girolamo, molto s' affaticò; la qual opera riusci lodatissima per hauere egli dimostrato nella testa di quel Santo, quella profonda cogitazione, & acutissima sottigliezza che suole essere nelle persone sensate, & astratte continuamente nella inuestigazione di cose altissime, & molto difficili. Questa pittura come si è detto nella vita del Ghirlandaio, questo anno 1564 è stata mutata dal luogo suo, salua, & intera. Perilche venuto in credito, & in riputazione, dall' arte di Porta Santa Maria gli fu fatto fare in S. Marco vna in coronazione di N. Donna in vna tauola, & vn coro d' Angeli; la quale fu molto ben disegnata, & co*n*dotta da lui. In casa Medici a Lorenzo vecchio lauorò molte cose, & massimamente vna Pallade su vna impresa di bro*n*coni, che buttauano fuoco, laquale dipinse gra*n*de quanto il viuo, & ancora vn S. Sebastiano. [*sic*] In S. Maria Maggior di Fiorenza è vna Pietà con figure piccole allato cappella di Pa*n*ciatichi molto bella. Per la città in diuerse case fece tondi di sua mano, & femmine ignude assai, dellequali hoggi ancora a Castello, villa del Duca Cosimo sono due quadri figurati, l' uno Venere, che nasce, & quelle aure, & venti, che la fanno venire in terra con gli amori: & cosi vn' altra Venere, che le grazie la fioriscono, dinotando la primavera; le quali da lui con grazia si veggono espresse. Nella via de' Serui in casa Giouanni Vespucci, hoggi di Piero Saluiati, fece intorno a vna camera molti quadri chiusi da ornamenti di noce, per ricignimento, & spalliera, con molte figure, & viuissime, & belle. Similmente in casa Pucci fece di figure piccole la nouella del Boccaccio, di Nastagio degl' Honesti, i*n* quattro quadri di pittura molto vaga, e bella, & in vn tondo l' Epifania. Ne' monaci di Cestello a vna cappella fece vna tauola d'una Annunziata. In S. Pietro Maggiore alla porta del fianco fece una tauola per Matteo Palmieri con infinito numero di figure, cio è la assunzione di N. Donna con le zone de' cieli, come son figurate, i Patriarchi, i Profeti, gl'
Apostoli, gli Euangelisti, i Martiri, i Confessori, i Dottori, le Vergini, & le Gerarchie, e tutto col p. 472.
disegno da/togli da Matteo, ch' era litterato, e valent' huomo. Laquale opera egli co*n* maestria, & finitissima diligenza dipinse. Euui ritratto appie Matteo in ginocchioni, & la sua moglie ancora. Ma con tutto, che questa opera sia bellissima, e ch' ella douesse vincere la inuidia; furono però alcuni maliuoli, & detrattori, che non potendo dannarla in altro: dissero che, & Matteo, & Sandro grauamente vi haueuano peccato in Eresia: il che se è vero, o non vero, non se ne aspetta il giudizio a me, basta che le figure che Sandro vi fece, veramente sono da lodare, per la fatica che e' durò nel girare i cerchi de' Cieli, & tramezare tra figure & figure d'Angeli, & scorci, & vedute in diuersi modi diuersamente, & tutto condotto con buono disegno. Fu allogato a Sandro in questo te*m*po vna tauoletta piccola di figure di tre quarti di braccio l'una; Laquale fu posta in S. Maria Nouella fra le due porte, nella facciata principale della chiesa nell' entrare per la porta del mezo a sinistra: Et euui dentro la adorazione de' Magi; Doue si vede tanto affetto nel primo vecchio; che baciando il piede al N. Signore, & struggendosi di tenerezza, benissimo dimostra hauere co*n*seguita la fine del lunghissimo suo uiaggio. Et la figura di questo Re, è il proprio ritratto di Cosimo vecchio de' Medici: di quanti a' di nostri se ne ritruouano il piu viuo,

& piu naturale. Il secondo, che è Giuliano de' Medici padre di Papa Clemente VII. si vede che intentissimo con l'animo, diuotamente rende riuerenza a quel putto, & gli assegna il presente suo. Il terzo inginocchiato egli ancora, pare che adorandolo, gli renda grazie; & lo confessi il vero Messia, è Giouanni figliuolo di Cosimo. Ne si può descriuere la bellezza che Sandro mostrò nelle teste che vi si veggono; lequali con diuerse attitudini son girate, quale in faccia, quale in profilo, quale in mezo occhio, & qual chinata, & in piu altre maniere; et diuersità d'arie di giouanni; di vecchi; con tutte quelle strauaganzie che possono far conoscere la perfezzione del suo magisterio. Hauendo egli distinto le corti di tre Re, di maniera che e' si comprende, quali siano i seruidori dell' uno, & quali dell' altro. Opera certa mirabilissima; E per colorito, per disegno, e per componimento, ridotta si bella, che ogni Artefice ne resta hoggi marauigliato. Et all' ora gli arrecò in Fiorenza, & fuori tanta fama che Papa Sisto IIII. hauendo fatto fabricare la cappella in palazzo di Roma; & volendola dipignere, ordinò ch' egli ne diuenisse capo; onde in quella fece di sua mano le infrascritte storie, cioè quando Christo è tentato dal diauolo: quando Mosè amazza lo Egizzio, & che riceue bere da le figlie di Ietro Madianite. Similmente quando sacrificando i figliuoli di Aron venne fuoco da cielo: & alcuni Santi Papi nelle nicchie di sopra alle storie. La onde acquistato fra molti concorrenti che seco lauorarono, & Fiorentini, & di altre città, fama, & nome maggiore; hebbe da'l Papa buona somma di danari; i quale ad vn tempo destrutti, & consumati tutti nella stanza di Roma, per viuere a caso, come era il solito suo; & finita insieme quella parte, che egli era stata allogata, & scopertala, se ne tornò subitamente a Fiorenza. Doue per essere persona sofistica comentò vna parte di Dante: & figurò lo inferno, & lo mise in Stampa dietro alquale consumò di molto tempo, perilche non lauorando fu cagione di infiniti disordini alla vita sua. Mise in stampa ancora, molte cose sue di disegni che egli haueua fatti ma in cattiua
p. 473. maniera perche l' intaglio era mal fatto, on/de il meglio, che si vegga di sua mano è il triomfo della Fede, di fra Girolamo Sauonarola da Ferrara; della setta delquale fu inguisa partigiano, che cio fu causa, che egli abandonando il dipignere, e non hauendo entrate da viuere precipitò in disordine grandissimo. Percioche, essendo ostinato a quella parte, e facendo (come si chiamauano allora), il Piagnone si diuiò dal lauorare: Onde invltimo si trouo vecchio, e pouero di sorte, che se Lor. de' Medici mentre che visse, per loquale, oltre a molte altre cose, haueua assai lauorato allo Spedaletto in quel di Volterra, non l' hauesse souuenuto, & poi gl' amici, & molti huomini da bene stati affetionati alla sua virtù si sarebbe quasi morto di fame. E di mano di Sandro in S. Francesco fuor della porta a S. Miniato in vn tondo vna Madonna, con alcuni Angeli grandi quanto il viuo, il quale fu tenuto cosa bellissima. Fu Sandro persona molto piaceuole, a fece molte burle a i suoi discepoli, & amici, onde si racconta; che hauendo vn suo creato, che haueua nome Biagio fatto vn tondo simile al sopradetto appunto, per venderlo, che Sandro lo vendè sei fiorini d' oro a vn Cittadino; e che trouato Biagio gli disse: Io ho pur finalmente venduto questa tua pittura, però si vuole stassera appicarla in alto, perche hauerà miglior veduta, e dimattina andare a casa il detto Cittadino, e condurlo qua, accio la veggia a buon aria al luogo suo; poi ti annoueri i contanti. O quanto hauete ben fatto maestro mio, disse Biagio. E poi andato a bottega mise il tondo in luogo assai ben alto, e partissi. In tanto Sandro, e Iacopo, che era vn' altro suo discepolo, fecero di carta otto capuci a uso di cittadini, & con la cera bianca gl' accommodarono sopra le otto teste degl' Angeli, che in detto tondo erano intorno alla Madonna. Onde uenuta la mattina, eccoti Biagio, che ha seco il cittadino, che haueua compera la pittura, e sapeua la burla, & entrati in bottega alzando Biagio gl' occhi vide la sua Madonna non in mezzo a gl' Angeli, ma in mezzo alla Signoria di Firenze starsi a sedere fra que' capucci. Onde uolle cominciare a gridare, e scusarsi con colui, che l' haueua mercatata, ma vedendo, che taceua anzi lodaua la pittura se ne stette anch' esso. Finalmente andato Biagio col cittadino a casa hebbe il pagamento de' sei fiorini; secondo, che dal maestro era stata mercatata la pittura, e poi tornato a bottega, quando apunto Sandro, e Iacopo haueuano leuate i capucci di carta, vide i suoi Angeli, essere Angeli, e non cittadini in capuccio. Perche tutto stupeffato non sapeua, che si dire, pur finalmente riuolto a Sandro disse, Maestro mio, io non so se io mi sogno, o se gli è uero; questi Angeli quando io uenni qua haueuano i capucci rossi in capo, & hora non gli hanno, che vuol dir questo? Tu sei fuor di te Biagio, disse Sandro. Questi danari t' hanno fatto uscire del seminato: se cotesto fusse, credi tu che quel cittadino l' hauesse compero? Gli è vero, soggiunse Biagio, che non me n' ha detto nulla, tutta uia a me pareua strana cosa. Finalmente tutti gl' altri garzoni furono intorno a costui, e tanto dissono, che gli fecion credere, che fussino stati Capogiroli. Venne vna volta ad habitare allato a Sandro un tessidore di drappi, & rizzò ben otto telaia; iquali quando lauorauano, faceuano non solo col romore delle calcole, & ribattimento delle casse, assordare il pouero Sandro, ma tremare tutta la casa, che non era piu gagliarda di muraglia, che si bisognasse, donde fra per l' una cosa, & per l' altra non poteua
p. 474. lauorare o stare in casa. Et pregato piu volte il uicino che/ rimediasse a questo fastidio, poi che egli hebbe detto, che in casa sua voleua & poteua far quel che piu gli piaceua; Sandro sdegnato, in sul suo muro, che era piu alto di quel del vicino, & non molto gagliardo, pose in billico vna grossissima pietra, e di piu che di carrata, che pareua che ogni poco che'l muro si mouesse, fusse per cadere, & sfondare i tetti, & palchi, & tele, & telai del vicino; il quale impaurito di questo pericolo, e ricorrendo a Sandro, gli fu risposto con le medesime parole che in casa sua poteua, & uoleua far quelche gli piaceua, ne potendo cauarne altra conclusione, fu necessitato a uenir agli accordi ragioneuoli: & far a Sandro buona uicinanza. Raccontasi ancora, che Sandro accusò

per burla vn amico suo di eresia al Vicario, e che colui co*m*parendo dimandò chi l' haueua accusato, e di che; perche essendogli detto, che Sandro ero stato; ilquale diceua, che egli teneua l' opinione degli Epicurei, e che l' anima morisse col corpo volle vedere l' acusatore dinanzi al Giudice, onde Sandro comparso, disse; egli è vero, che io ho questa opinione dell' anima di costui, che è vna bestia. Oltre cio non pare a voi, che sia heretico, poi che senza hauere lettere, o apena saper leggere, comenta Da*n*te; e mentoua il suo nome in vano? Dicesi ancora, che egli amò fuor di modo coloro, che egli cognobbe studiosi dell' arte: e che guadagnò assai, ma tutto per hauere poco gouerno, e per trascuratagine, mandò male. Finalmente condottosi vecchio, e disutile, e camina*n*do con due mazze, perche non si reggeua ritto, si morì essendo infermo, e decrepito, d'anni settantotto; & in Ogni Santi di Firenze fu sepolto l'anno 1515.

Nella Guardaroba del S. Duca Cosimo sono di sua mano due teste di femmina in profilo bellissime; Vna dellequali si dice, che fu l' inamorata di Giuliano de' Medici fratello di Lorenzo, e l'altra Madonna Lucrezia de' Tornabuoni moglie di detto Lorenzo. Nel medesimo luogo è similmente di man di Sandro vn Bacco, che alzando con ambe le mani vn barile, se lo pone a boccha, il quale è vna molto graziosa figura: E nel duomo di Pisa alla cappella dell' impagliata cominciò vn' assunta, con vn coro d'Angeli, ma poi no*n* gli piacendo la lasciò imperfetta. In S. Francesco di Monte Varchi fece la tauola dell' altar maggiore: E nella Pieue d' Empoli da quella banda, doue è il S. Bastiano del Rossellino, fece due Angeli. E fu egli de' primi, che trouasse di lauorare gli stendardi & altre drapperie, come si dice, di commesse, perche i colori non istinghino, e mostrino da ogni banda il colore del drappo. E di sua mano cosi fatto, è il Baldachino d' Or S. Michele, pieno di Nostre Donne tutte variate, e belle. Il che dimostra quanto cotal modo di fare meglio conserui il drappo, che non fanno i mordenti, che loricidano, e dannogli poca uita, se bene per manco spesa, è piu in uso hoggi il mordente, che altro. Disegnò Sandro bene fuor di modo, e tanto, che dopo lui vn pezzo s' ingegnarono gl' Artefici d' hauere de suoi disegni. E noi nel nostro libro n' habbiamo alcuni, che son fatti con molta practica, e giudizio. Fu copiose di figure nelle storie, come si puo veder ne' ricami del fregio della croce, che portano a processione i frati S. Maria Nouella tutto di suo disegno. Meritò dunque Sandro gran lode in tutte le pitture, che fece, nellequali volle mettere diligenza, e farle co*n* amore, come fece la detta tauola de' Magi di S. Maria Nouella, laquale è marauigliosa. E molto bello ancora un picciol tondo di sua mano; che si vede nel/la camera del Priore degl' Angeli di Firenze, di figure piccole, ma graziose p. 475.
molto, & fatte con bella considerazione. Della medesima grandezza, che è la detta tauola de' Magi, n' ha vna di mano del medesimo, M. Fabio Segni, Gentil' huomo Fiorentino, nella quale è dipinta la Calunnia d'Apelle, bella quanto possa essere. Sotto la quale tauola, laquale egli stesso donò ad Antonio Segni suo amicissimo, si leggono hoggi questi versi di detto M. Fabio.

Indicio quemquam ne falso lædere tentent
Terrarum Reges parua Tabella monet.
Huic similem AEgipti Regi donauit Apelles.
Rex fuit, e dignus munere: munus eo.

APPENDIX II.

BIBLIOGRAPHY OF ORIGINAL DOCUMENTS RELATING TO THE LIFE AND WORKS OF SANDRO BOTTICELLI, WITH THE TEXT OF THE MORE IMPORTANT, FOR THE MOST PART HITHERTO INEDITED.

Doc. I. Firenze: R. Biblioteca Nazionale. Codice Magliabechiano, xiii, 89. "Codice Petrei."

[A paper book in small quarto, containing a collection of miscellaneous pieces in the same hand. This manuscript came to the Biblioteca Magliabechiana in 1784, from the Library of Sen. Carlo Strozzi, where it was marked, N°. 285.

Fol. 38, tergo, to fol. 51, tergo. Notices of Florentine Painters, Sculptors and Architects.

Fol. 52, recto, to fol. 58, recto. Notices of Florentine churches and of the works of art contained in them.

This miscellany appears, from its contents, to have been collected and transcribed by Antonio Petrei, a canon of San Lorenzo, and of the cathedral in Florence. The notices of the Florentine artists, fol. 38, tergo, to fol. 51, tergo, together with those in another manuscript in the Biblioteca Nazionale, at Florence, Codice Magliabechiano, xxv, 636, fol. 73, recto, to fol. 85, tergo, have been derived, independently, from a common source, the lost "Libro di Antonio Billi," as M. Cornelio de Fabriczy has shown in his introduction to these Notices, which he printed in the "Archivio Storico Italiano," Firenze, 1891, Ser. V, Vol. VII, p. 299. Of the "Libro di Antonio Billi" nothing is known; but Antonio Billi seems to have been the author, and not merely the possessor, of the book. It appears from internal evidence, that it was compiled subsequently to 1516, and before 1530. An allusion to a fresco by Bronzino among the notices of the Florentine churches, fol. 52, recto, to fol. 58, recto, shows that Antonio Petrei compiled these notices, and derived the preceding ones from the "Libro di Antonio Belli," subsequently to the year 1465: in 1470 the copyist died. The "Codice Petrei" is far less accurate than the other manuscript, "Codice Magliabechiano," xxv, 636, derived from the "Libro di Antonio Billi;" but in the latter volume the notices relating to Botticelli are wanting. The notices in this manuscript have also been printed by Dr. Carl Frey, in his "Libro di Antonio Billi," Berlin, 1892.]

Fol. 49, tergo.

"Sandro di botticiello fu diciepolo difra filippo, fece da giouanetto nella merc*an*tia una forteza belliss^{a}. Vna tauola ins^{to} marcho allato allaporta d*e*llachiesa amano sinistra et uno s^{to} agostino, in ognis*anct*j nelpilastro del coro dinanzi. Vna tauola in s^{to} spirito di s^{to} *giouan*ni. in s^{to} bernaba una tauola di n*ost*ra Don*n*a et s^{ta} catherina: Vna tauola nelle conuertite. Vna tauola in s^{ta} maria nouella allaporta del mezo. Piu femmine igniude belle piu ch*e* alchuno altro, et a roma nella cap^{la} di sisto iij fecie piu quadri dicose pichole, et in fra laltre uno s^{to} girolamo."

Doc. II. Firenze: R. Biblioteca Nazionale. Codice Magliabechiano, xvii, 17. "Anonimo Gaddiano."

[A paper book in small quarto, written in a single hand, with the exception of a few interpolated passages. This manuscript came to the Biblioteca Magliabechiana in 1755, from the Library of the Gaddi, where it was marked, N°. 564.

Fol. 1, recto, to fol. 37, recto. Notices of antique Painters and Sculptors.

Fol. 43, recto, to fol. 94, recto. Notices of modern Painters, Sculptors and Architects, chiefly Florentine.

Fol. 99, recto, to fol. 108, recto. Notices of works of art in the churches of Rome, in the Certosa of Florence, and in Perugia and Assisi.

Fol. 109, recto, to fol. 128, tergo. Miscellaneous notices: extracts from Landino, and Pliny, rough drafts, &c.

M. Cornelio de Fabriczy, who has printed and annotated the notices of the Florentine artists, &c., fol. 43, recto, to fol. 108, recto, in the "Archivio Storico Italiano," Firenze, 1893, Ser. V, Vol. XIII, pp. 15-94, and pp. 275-334, has shown that they are a compilation by an anonymous writer, probably of the Gaddi family, derived from the Commentary of Lorenzo Ghiberti, the lost "Libro di Antonio Billi," and from other, unknown sources. It appears from internal evidence that the manuscript was compiled subsequently to 1542, and before 1548. The notices which this writer has preserved of Botticelli are singularly copious and correct: with the exception of a few interpolated passages taken from the "Libro di Antonio Billi," they are derived from a source unknown to Vasari; and they contain two anecdotes, and a description of six works, with other particulars, of which that biographer makes no mention. In one instance only, in regard to Botticelli, is the "Anonimo Gaddiano" found tripping, where he attributes to our master the "Cenacolo" of Domenico Ghirlandaio, in the Refectory of the Monastery of Ognissanti. The notices in this manuscript have also been printed by Dr. Carl Frey, in "Il Codice Magliabechiano, cl. xvii. 17," Berlin, 1892.]

Fol. 83, recto.

Sandro di Mariano di va*nn*j filipepi chamato sandro di Botticello pittore fu dicepolo di fra filippo et huomo molto piaceuole et faceto, et nesua tempi erano le sue opere stimate assaj. Et essendo esso vna volta da M*esser* Tomaso soderinj stretto ator moglie gli rispose Vi uoglio dire quello che no*n* e troppe nott*i* passat*e* che mi*n*terue*n*ne, che sognauo hauere tolto moglie, et tanto dolore nepresj che io mi destaj, et p*er* no*n* mj radorme*n*tare p*er* no*n* lo risognare piu mi leuaj et andaj tutta notte p*er* firenze aspasso come u*n* pazo, p*er*ilche intese M*esser* Tomaso [fol. 83, tergo.] che no*n* era terreno da poruj vigna.

Et auno che piu uolte nel ragionare secho gli haueua detto che harebbe uoluto cento lingue gli rispose, tu chiedj piu lingue, et hane la meta più che il bisogno, chiedj ceruello poueretto, che no*n* haj nie*n*te.

Lauoro assaj e infire*n*ze dipinse nella merchata*n*tia la forteza, nella spalliera de sej, che l'altre sono dimano dipiero dell pollaiuuolo [*sic*].

Nella chiesa defratj di sa*n* marcho e disua mano vna gra*n* tauola allato allaporta della chiesa.

Nella chiesa d'ogni santj nel Pilastro dinanzi al coro dipinse in frescho vn s^{to} agostino, al rico*n*tro del sa*n* girolamo fatto a co*n*correnza co*n* Domenicho del grillandaio.

Vna tauola in s^{to} sp^{to} dig^{nj} deb*ar*dj. [Interpolated in the handwriting of the notices taken from the "Libro di Billi."]

Et indetta chiesa [*i.e.* d'Ognissanti. Lacuna in original.]

Et nel refettorio di dettj frattj edisuamano vncenaculo di Xp̃o co*n* dicepolj ilquale fece nel 1480.

E disua mano i*n*sanb*er*naba latauola dell' altare maggiore di n*ost*ra do*nn*a et s^{ta} caterina.

Et nella chiesa delle suore delle co*n*uertite Dipinse latauola dell' altare maggiore che e [Lacuna in original.]

Vna tauoletta i*n* s^{ta} m*ari*^{a} n^{a} allato allaporta dimezo. [Interpolated from the "Libro di Billi."]

Fol. 84, recto [a half sheet inserted, and written only on one side].

Dipinse nel 1478 nellafacciata doue gia era il bargiello sopra ladoghana, M*esser* Jacopo, franc^{o} et Rinato depazj, et M*esser* franc^{o} saluiatj archiueschouo di Pisa, et duj Jacopi saluiatj, luno fratello et l'altro affine di detto M*esser* franc^{o}, et Bernardo Bandinj, impicchatj p*er* lagola, et Napoleone franzesj impicchato p*er* vn^{o} pie, che sitrouorono nella co*n*giura co*n*tro a Giul^{ao} et Lorenzo de Medicj, 'allj qualj lore*n*zo poi fece aipiedj li epitaffi, et infra l'altrj a Bernardo Bandino che inq*ues*to modo diceua

Son Bernardo Bandinj un nuouo giuda
Traditore micidiale in chiesa io fuj
Ribello p*er* aspettare morte piu cruda.

Et e disua mano nel Palazo de Signorj sopra laschala che ua alla catena listoria de 3 magi.

Dipinse et storio vn Dante in cartapecora al^{zo} dip^{ro} franc^{o} de Medicj, il che fu cosa marauigliosa tenuto.

Fol. 85, recto. Et [in] santa maria nouella dipinse vna tauoletta di altare che e acanto alla porta del mezo, de magi che vj sono piu p*er*sone ritratte alnaturale.

In santa Maria maggiore e di sua mano v*n*^{o} sa*n* bastiano intauola, che e invna colo*n*na, il quale fece dj Gie*n*naio nel 1473.

In sa*n* piero gattolinj la tauola dell' altare magg^{re} che sono [Lacuna in original.]

In s^{to} spirito e disua mano nella capella de Bardj latauola dell altare dove edipinto vn^{a} n*ost*ra donna et v*n*^{o} sa*n* Giova*nn*j batt^{a}.

Piu fe*m*mine gnude Bellissime.

[An index-hand shows that the notices on fol. 84, recto, are to be inserted here.]

A castello in casa il Sr Giova*nn*j demedicj piu quadrj Dipinse che sono delle piu belle opere che facessj.

In Roma dipinse anchora et fecessj una tauola dj magi che fu la piu [*sic*] opera che maj facessj.

Et nella cappella di sixto fece 3 faccie o quadrj. [In margin : Dimandarne.]

Et fece assaj opere picchole bellissime, et in fra l'altre v*n* san girolamo op*er*a singulare.

Doc. III. Firenze: R. Archivio di Stato. Arch. delle Decime. Quartiere, Santa Maria Novella; Gonfalone, Unicorno: Campione 1431, N°. verde 404, fol. cccclxxxvij, tergo. Denunzia of "Mariano dj Vannj conciatore."

Doc. IV. Firenze: R. Archivio di Stato. Arch. delle Decime. Quartiere, Santa Maria Novella; Gonfalone, Unicorno: Campione 1433, N°. verde 494, fol. 312, recto. Denunzia of "Mariano digiouannj chonciatore dichuoia."

Doc. V. Firenze: R. Archivio di Stato. Arch. delle Decime. Quartiere, Santa Maria Novella; Gonfalone, Unicorno: Filza 1451, prima, N°. verde 705, fol. 762, recto.

+ Alnome dj djo adj 17 daghost° 1451
Q' S° m^a n^a g^e chorno.
Mariano dj vannj damideo cho*n*ciatore dj choiame
Non*n*e ebbe maj graueza.
Sustanze
No*n* si truoua nulla dj vasente siche abbiate p*er*
rachomanda p*er* la pace dj .... [Lacuna in original.]

Doc. VI. Firenze: R. Archivio di Stato. Idem, fol. 237, recto. Denunzia of "Jacopo dj Giouan*n*j co*n*ciatore di chuoia."

Doc. VII. Firenze: R. Archivio di Stato. Arch, delle Decime. Quartiere, Santa Maria Novella; Gonfalone, Unicorno: Filza 1457, seconda, N°. verde 814. Denunzia N°. 340. [Omissis.]

[On the folio preceding this Denunzia is written :] ad*j* 28 d*j* feb*r*ajo *recho* Botticello sensale. [*i.e.* 28 Feb. 1457-8.]

✠ ihs

Dinanzi dauoj signjori vficjali delchatasto portata djmarjano djuannj choncjatore djquoja quartjere santa ma*r*ja nouella ghonfalone liochorno e p*r*ima

Vnachasa laquale tenevo p*er*mjo abita*re* quartjere santa + [Croce] gonfalone bue laquale chasa edjmona bjcje donnafu di meo mej della quale si pagha *fiorinj* 16 lanno confina da *prim°* elchomune dasechondo e $\frac{1}{3}$ giouannj dj tadde° charuccj da $\frac{1}{4}$ andrea dj b*er*to linaiuolo laquale chasa apigionaj adetto p*r*egio ep*er* *in*sino aogni santj p*r*ossimo 1458 a b*er*nardo djsan martelljnj che *in*sino a detto tenpo laueuo attenere: tolsi vna chasa p*er* mjo abitare posta nel quartjere dj santa marja novella gonfalone lionrosso laqualpaga *fiorinj*. xi lanno ede dj njcholo dj b*r*anchazio ruccjellaj laquale finj eltenpo aognjsantj passato 1457 chonfina dap*rim°* elchomvne sechondo e $\frac{1}{3}$ nicholo sop*r*adetto $\frac{1}{4}$ filip*p*o dj b*r*anchazio allatolta p*er* suo abitare doue abito: e vna chasa posta nelpopolo djsanpiero achareggi nellaquale sta lamja famigla o partte dessa laquale ho affitto da *ser* njcholo ualentjnj pep*r*egio dj *fiorinj* 6 lanno chonfina da p*rim°* esechondo *ser* njcholo detto $\frac{1}{3}$ simone ghorj quarto chomune sanza sustanze potete *in*tendere ho atorre chasa apigione: epiu ho vnabottegha doue choncjo elchojame ap*p*ie delponte asanta trjnjta quartjere santo sp*irito* laquale edjgiovannj dj sandro chapponj dellaquale pagho l*ire* 40 lan*n*o chonfina da p*rim°* esechondo elchomune $\frac{1}{3}$ giovanj detto $\frac{1}{4}$ m^a pichina madre dagnjolo elorenzo .... vettorj.

truovomj debito chongiovannj djpagholo rucjellaj e chonpagnj [&c., &c. Note in margin: "creditorj som*m*ano l*ire* 496 p*iccio*lj", estimated at] *fiorinj* 124.

E piu truouo chegiovannj mjo figlolo *in* suo nome p*ropri°* addare glinfraschritti d*anari* [&c., &c. Three items amounting to fiorini 52.]

D*e* auere tramme egiovannj [&c., &c. Note in margin: "som*m*ano tuttj q*u*estj debitorj l*ire* 612 p*iccio*lj, istimatj *fiorinj cent°*."]

truovomj deta dannj 65 cholla mja arte posso pocho fare.
ladonna mja deta dannj 53.
giovannj mjo figlolo sensale almo*n*te detta dannj 37: Antonio mjo figlolo sta allorafo aueua

dj salaro *fiorinj* 25 lanno hora quando addafare sta p*er*lauorante traghone pochutjle : Simone mjo figlolo detta dannj 14 mandolo annapoli chonpagholo rucjellaj : sandro mjo figlolo detta dannj 13 sta allegare [*sic*] ede malsano.

truouomj vna fancjulla deta dannj 15 sanza dote o p*r*encjpio : vnaltra deta dannj 10 chetenpo ara *fiorinj* 200 dj dote.

E piu lanera mogle dj giovannj mjo figlolo deta danni 19 : edan*ne* detto giovannj vna fancjulla abalia dj mesi 5 dalle elmese *fiorino* 1°. sono boche 10.

D*e* auere da quegli fecjano pocho chonto [&c., &c.] Questj dj sopra sono tuttj falljtj.

D*e* auere giovannj mjo figluolo dj piu tempo fa dj senserje [&c., &c. Note in margin: "Som*m*ano tuttj q*u*estj debit*or*[i] *lire* 665 p*iccio*lj istimatj *fiorini* 100."]

+ Conposto p*er* partito degluficialj ad*j* xiij digiennaio 1458 p*er* ogni sua sustanza i*n* *soldj* tre ao*ro* dichatasto rogato s*er* domenicho loro not*aro*.

[Another copy of this Denunzia, written in the same hand, apparently that of Giovanni, detto Il Botticello, is contained in another volume of Portate of the year 1457, Santa Maria Novella, Unicorno, N° verde 815, N° 340. This second copy differs materially from the foregoing, only in the following particulars. The age of Antonio di Mariano, omitted above, occurs after the words "sta allorafo," thus, "deta dannj 28:" and the passage relating to Sandro stands thus, "Sandro mjo figlolo deta dannj 13 sta all . . ere ede malsano." The "all" of the last word but two occurs at the end of a line, and the "ere" at the beginning of the next; some letters being inadvertently omitted. The scribe had evidently intended to write "allegere."]

Doc. VIII. Firenze: R. Archivio di Stato. Balie, N°. 39 bis. "liber siue Quar*ter*nus officialium p*ro*curator*um* et Sindicor*um* super rebus et negotijs pactior*um*." 1480-1482.

Fol. 157, recto. Minute of the sale by auction of certain lands and houses of Renato de' Pazzi, at which "Johannes marianj vocatus botticello" was an unsuccessful bidder.

Doc. IX. Firenze: R. Archivio di Stato. Arch. dell' Arte della Seta, N°. 8. Matricule dal 1433, al 1474. Matriculation of Antonio di Mariano, fol. 13.

Doc. X. Firenze: R. Galleria degli Uffizi. Archivio. "Libro di Ricordi" of Neri di Biccidi, dal 1453 al 1475.

[A paper book in large quarto, in the holograph of the painter, formerly in the Biblioteca Strozziana. An account of this manuscript is given by the Florentine commentators of Vasari, ed. Sansoni, Vol. II, p. 69.]

Doc. XI. Firenze: R. Archivio di Stato. Arch. dell' Accademia di Belle Arti, N°. 2. The "Libro Rosso," a paper book of accounts, in a vellum cover, of the "Compagnia di San Luca," inscribed, "Debitori, e Creditori, e Ricordi. Libro Rosso. 1472-1520."

Fol. 14, tergo.

m cccc lxx ij

Alesandro dimariano dett° Botticello de dare p*e*lla grazia fatta Adj 17 g*i*ugno 1472 *soldj* sej p*er* K° dognj debit° auessj chondetta arte p*er* i*n*sino ad*j* p*rim*° di luglio 1472 chome i*n* quest° ac*arta* 2	*lire* —	*soldj* 6 —
Ede dare p*e*lla oferta deld*j* d*j* sant° lucho ad*j* 18 dottob*re* 1472 *soldj* cinque E p*er* ognj anno e p*e*llo presente anno 1472	*lire* —	*soldj* 5 —
Ede dare p*e*lla soue*n*zione deluogho earte e p*er* ognj anno *soldj* sedicj e qualj depaghare ognj mese *soldj* 1° d*anarj* 4 Ep*e*llo p*re*se*n*te anno i*n*chomincat° ad*j* p*rim*° diluglio 1472 *soldj* 16	*lire* —	*soldj* 16 —
Ede dare p*e*lla i*m*posta fatta ad*j* 18 dottob*re* 1472 *soldj* cinque p*er* penonj detronbettj	*lire* —	*soldj* 5 —

Fol. 15, recto.

m cccc lxx ij

Alesandro dimariano dett° Bottjcello d*i*pintore de auere *soldj* sej port° chontantj apiero zucherj chama*r*lingho asua e*n*trata ac*arta* 16	*lire* —	*soldj* 6 —
Ede auere ad*j* 18 dottob*re* 1472 *soldj* cinque pagho cho*n*ta*ntj* p*e*lla ferta di dett° anno aentrata detta ac*arta* 16	*lire* —	*soldj* 5 —
Ede auere *soldj* cinque d*anarj* quatro pagho chontantj p*er* parte della souenzione dellarte apiero zucherj K° asua entrata ac*arta* 16	*lire* —	*soldj* 5 d*anarj* 4

Ede auere ad*j* 7 difeb*r*aio 1472 *soldj* noue e p*er* noj a Giovannj dido-menicho fatauole dabacho post° *in* quest° chegiouannj de dare ac*arta* 143*	*lire* — *soldj* 9 —
Ede auere adj 4 giugnjo 1473 l*ire* vna alib*ro* della souenzione ac*arta* 5 aentrata del K° ac*arta*	*lira* 1[a] —
Ede auere ad*j* 24 d*j* settenb*re* *soldj* dua d*anarj* viij pagho aljb*ro* vatorno ac*arta* 5 aent*rat*[a] del k°	*lire* — *soldj* 2 d*anarj* 8
Ede auere ad*j* 18 dottob*re* *soldj* cinque pagho p*er* el terchietto	*lire* — *soldj* 5 —

[* *Vide* cross entry, at fol. 143, verso, of the same volume.]

Fol. 144, tergo, and 145, recto, [omissis.]

Chont° delle chandele date eld*j* disanta maria chandellaia ad*j* 2 di feb*r*aio 1472.

[This account begins with a list of the candles offered by the Master and the Chamberlain of the Hospital of S. Maria Nuova, the Notary and the Steward of the "Arte degli Speziali," &c.; then follows the list of those candles offered by the members of the "Compagnia di San Luca," which I here transcribe, with a comment of my own in a parallel column. The document is of value, since it preserves the names of the foremost master-painters then working in Florence; not only of the artists whose works have come down to us, but of the merely successful tradesmen of whom memorials are only to be found in records of this kind.]

Capitanj della chonpagnja d*is*[ant]° l[uch]°		[Captains of the Company of St. Luke.
Chime*nt*[i] d*i*lore*n*zo rossellj dipintore [1[a] chandela]	d. 4	Clemente, younger brother of Cosimo Rosselli, painter; *vide* Vasari, ed. Sansoni, iii, 192, notes.
Jac° d*i*piero damilano	d. 4	Jacopo di Piero di Antonio di Baldo, painter in the Via dei Servi.
Franc° djlorenzo djuia djsanghallo	d. 4	Francesco di Lorenzo, painter in the Via di S. Gallo.
Domen*ic*° a*nt*° targhonaio	d. 4	Domenico Antonio di Matteo, painter and targe-maker, in the Corso degli Adimari.
Consiglierj.		Counsellors.
Baldo djpiero piccinj	d. 3	Baldo di Piero Piccini, painter in Via dei Pellicciai.
Ant° d*i*mariano filipepj battiloro	d. 3	Antonio, elder brother of Botticelli, goldbeater.
lorenzo djpiero acchugho	d. 3	Lorenzo di Piero Accughi, painter.
Domen*ic*° d*i*zenobj d*i*pintore		Domenico di Zenobi, painter, "alla parte ghuelfa," in the Via delle Terme.
Camarlingho		Chamberlain.
Andrea d*i*marcho della robbja	d. 3	Andrea, the nephew of Luca della Robbia, carver.
proued*i*tore		Steward.
Chosimo d*i*lorenzo rossellj dipintore	d. 2	Cosimo Rosselli, painter, at Santa Maria in Campo.
Gljuominj del chorpo		The Men of the Body.
Ant° d*i*jachopo delpollaiuolo	d. 2	Antonio Pollaiuoli, painter and goldsmith.
Andrea deluerrocchio	d. 2	Andrea Verrocchio, painter and carver.
Alessandro dimariano dipintore	d. 2	Sandro Botticelli, painter.
bonaiuto ossaio	d. 2	Buonaiuto di Giovanni, bone-carver, in the Corso.
bartolom*m*eo sargjaio	d. 2	Bartolommeo di Giovanni, painter of stained cloths, "a santa liperata dalla uia de S*er*uj," Piazza del Duomo.
bartolom*m*eo targhonajo	d. 2	Bartolommeo, brother of Antonio, di Matteo, targe-maker in the Corso degli Adimari.
barnardo dj franc° battiloro	d. 2	Bernardo di Francesco di Giovanni, goldbeater in Via Porta Rossa.
Chimentj dj piero raffaellj	d. 2	Clemente di Piero Raffaelli, painter in Via dei Pellicciai.
Domenicho djniccholaio dipintore	d. 2	Domenico di Niccolaio, cassone-painter in Borgo SS. Apostoli.
Domenicho djbartolomeo battiloro	d. 2	Domenico di Bartolommeo, goldbeater in Via Porta Rossa.
Franc° dant° delchericho miniatore	d. 2	Francesco d'Antonio del Cherico, miniaturist; Vasari ii, 521 and 522, notes.
S*er* Giouannj d*i* domenicho deuetrj	d. 2	Ser Giovanni di Domenico, glass-painter (vetraio) and priest: the writer has, apparently, confused his name with that of Giovanni di Biagio de' Vetrj, glass-painter.

Gesue dj santj	d. 2	Giosuè di Santi, painter, in the Via di S. Gallo; Vasari, ii, 88, notes.
Gherardo miniatore	d. 2	Gherardo, miniaturist, mosaicist, &c., organist of S. Egidio; Vasari, iii, 237.
Giouannj delle tauole daabbacho	d. 2	Giovanni di Domenico, "fa letavole dabacho," maker of arithmetic tables.
Jachopo dj piero piccinj	d. 2	Jacopo, brother of Baldo, di Piero Piccini, painter, at S. Giovanni.
lionardo delbene d*i*pintore	d. 2	Leonardo del Bene, painter, at Santa Maria Verzaia.
lorenzo randellj d*i*pintore	d. 2	Lorenzo di Piero Randelli, painter in Borgo SS. Apostoli.
lore*n*zo dj gjouannj dj nofrj djpintore	d. 2	Lorenzo di Giovanni, painter, at the corner of the Via dei Servi.
Marcho del buono djpintore	d. 2	Marco del Buono, called Il Marchino, painter, in Borgo SS. Apostoli, disciple of Andrea del Castagno; Vasari, ii, 682.
Marcho djfilippo d*i*pintore	d. 2	Marco di Filippo, painter, in the Corso degli Adimari.
Matt*i*o targhonaio nelchorso	d. 2	Matteo di Bartolommeo, targe-maker, in the Corso degli Adimari.
Mattio del mae*s*tro ant° djpintore	d. 2	Matteo del Maestro Antonio Calvelli, painter.
Nerj d*i* bicci djpintore	d. 2	Neri, the son of the painter Bicci di Lorenzo, painter, in Via Porta Rossa; Vasari, ii, 69, notes.
Piero d*i* lorenzo zuccherj djpintore	d. 2	Piero di Lorenzo Pratese, partner of Pesellino, in the Corso degli Adimari; Vasari, iii, 43, notes.
Piero del masaio d*i*pintore	d. 2	Piero del Massaio, painter, at S. Maria in Campo.
Domenicho di tomaso delle grillande dj-pintore	d. 2	Domenico Ghirlandaio, painter.
Giouannj di bonaiuto ossajo	d. 2	Giovanni, son of Buonaiuto di Giovanni, bone-carver, in the Corso.
lucha dagnjolo fantasia	d. 2	Luca d'Agnolo Fantasia, painter.
Richardo d*i* benedetto d*i* *ser* ruccho dj-pintore	d. 2	Riccardo di Benedetto di Ser Rucco, painter, in Borgo SS. Apostoli.
Ant° delbianco djpintore	d. 2	Antonio del Bianco, painter.
fruosino dipiero djpintore	d. 2	Fruosino di Piero, painter, in the Corso degli Adimari.]

Fol. 14, tergo.

1482

Alesandro dimariano de dare ad*j* 25 d*j* nouenb*re* *soldj* djecj *per* tanto aposto debitore tuttj gluominj della cho*m*pagnia *per* partjto fatto alib*ro* departitj ac*arta* 35 — l*ire* — *soldj* 10 —

Fol. 15, recto.

1482

Alessandro dimariano dipintore detto botticello de auere adj 25 di-nouemb*re* *soldj* diecj alentrata i*n* *quest*ᵃ *carta* 200* — l*ire* — *soldj* 10 —

[* *Vide* cross entry, at fol. 200, recto, of the same volume.]

Fol. 122, tergo.

1503

Sandro dimariano divannj dedare add*j* 17 dottobre *soldj* xvij d*anarj* 4 sono p*er*le pintature [*sic.* dipingiture] delanno auenire cho-minciato detto d*j* efinito chome seghue ad*anarj* 4 lasetimana — l*ire* — *soldj* 17 d*anarj* 4

E add*j* 18 dottobre 1504 *soldj* sette p*er*la festa — l*ire* — *soldj* 7

1505

E de dare adj 18 dottobre 1505 soldj 17 danarj 4 equalj sono epi*n*tj [*sic.* dipinti] delan*no* — l*ire* — soldj 17 d*anarj*

E de dare adj detto *soldj* 7 p*er*la festa — l*ire* — *soldj* 7 d*anarj*

Fol. 123, recto.

1503

Sandro dimaria[no] dichontro deauere addj 18 dottobre *soldj* xvij d*anarj* 4 1504 sono *per* pintj [*sic.* dipinti] pagho delanno passato — l*ire* — *soldj* 17 d*anarj* 4

1505

E de auere adj 18 dottobre 1505 ljre una e soldj quatro danarj 4 *per* gratje delsuo debjto } *lire* 1 *soldj* 4 *danarj* 4

Doc. XII. Pisa: R. Archivio di Stato. Arch. dell' Opera del Duomo. Nº. 443. Ricordanze, dal 1469 al 1475.

Fol. 130, tergo. + Mccc° Lxxiiij°. [Pisan style.]

Sandro botticella dipintore dafirense *fiorino* vno *largho* loquale silidie percheuenne dafirense auedere doue auea ad*i*pingnere Jncamposanto *per* Jnsino adj 27 digennaio. *lire* 5 *soldj* 10 —
postj aspese dop*era* *in* *quest°*, *charta* 136.

Fol. 136, tergo. M cccc° Lxxv adj 30 di maggio.

E adj detto *lire* cinque *soldj* diecj Jn *fiorino* vno *largho* ebbe sandro delbotticella dipintore quando uenne apisa chesacordo poj conlop*era* adipingniere Jncamposanto chome app*are* *in* *quest°*, *charta* 130. *lire* 5 *soldj* 10 *danarj* —

Doc. XIII. Pisa: R. Archivio di Stato. Arch. dell' Opera del Duomo. Nº. 145. Entrata e Uscita, del 1475.

Fol. 70, tergo. adj 20 di settenbre [1475, Pisan style.]

A Sandro detto Botticella dipintore *lire* cento tre*n*ta *soldj* diecj sono *per* *par*te didipintura duna storia cominciata Induomo alla capp*ella* dellancoronata chellastoria dellassensione dinostra donna, laquale fa *per* vno paragone che piacendo apoj adipingniere Incanposanto.
posto alle ricordanse F, *charta* 8. *lire* 130 *soldj* 10

Doc. XIV. Firenze: R. Biblioteca Riccardiana. Codice 1935. "Sepolcrario della Chiesa di S. Mª. Novella, di Fire*n*ze; copiato diligentemente dall' originale, che è appresso i PP^ri^ della medesima chiesa, da me P. Gaetano Martini [&c.] anno Domini MDCCXXVIIII."

[It appears from the inscription on p. 9, that the original was compiled "Anno domini MDCXVII," when Niccolò Sermartelli was prior.]

p. 68 Altare de Vecchietti.

Frà due Porte, cioè frà la Porta d*e*l mezzo, e la Porta uerso S. Benedetto, altare d*e*lla Nunziata d*e*lla famiglia de Vecchietti il quale anticamᵉ fù eretto da Gio. Lami cittad° Fiorentino in sieme con un sepolcro di marmo sotto il Titolo d*e*ll' Epifania, e chiamauasi l' Altare de magi p*er*che era stata dipinta nell' Ancona da Sandro Botticelli Pittore eccellentissimo la storia de tre magi, opera marauigliosa tenuta da tutti, la quale in rifare detta Altare fù da Fabio Mandragoni spagnolo leuata e messa nel suo Palazzo, che poco lontano dalla detta Chiesa laueua fabbricato, et in quello scambio ui fece fare quella che dipresente si uede, doue da Santi di Tito Pittore rarissimo fù dentroui dipinto la Vergine annunziata dall' Angelo. Questo Altare fù la prima uolta fatto di ricchissimi marmi, e nobilissⁱ Intagli ornato dal soprascritto Lami il quale doppo p*er*uenne nella famiglia dei Fedini. Costoro dopo hauerlo tenuto molti anni lo uenderono a Fabio mandragoni, che poi rifece l'Altare guastando il Vecchio *per* seguitare l'ordine d*e*lli Altari, ricoprendo con gli Scalini dell' Altare la sepoltura d*e*l primo fondatore di Casa Lami, p*er*farci dinanzi la sua, conforme a che haueuano fatto gli altri Padroni d*e*lli Altari, i quali in raccomodare la Chiesa posono i loro sepolcri dinanzi ai loro Altari; la qual cosa non seguì p*er*che la cagion non sò, e lo uendè a Bernardo di Gio. Vecchietti conpatto di leuar l' Arme di Casa sua et in uece di quella lasciarci porre quella de Vecchietti come al presente uediamo.

La sopra*de*tta tauola [*i. e.* da Santi di Tito] fù fatta fare dai Vecchietti quando finirono d*e*l tutto la dª Cappella lasciata imperfetta dal Mandragoni.

[The arms of "Lami ò d*e*l Lama" are emblazoned on p. 69: Or, a chevron gules.]

Doc. XV. Firenze: R. Archivio di Stato. Arch. delle Decime. Quartiere, San Giovanni; Gonfalone, Leon d'Oro: Campione, 1480, Nº. verde 1016, fol. 402, recto. Denunzia of Lorenzo and Giovanni, di Pierfrancesco de' Medici. [Excerpta.]

Fol. 412, tergo. Vn podere posto allolmo achastello p*o*p*o*lo disamichele luogho detto aluiuaio co*n* sua uochabolj & co*n*finj, et chonun palagio dasignore et chono*r*to murato, et chonsua apartene*n*ze dimasserizie, el quale tegnamo *per* nostro habitare et *per* nostro vso, co*m*perato *in*sino lan*no* 1477 da Niccholo dandrea dilotteringho della stufa, charta fatta *per* *ser* Giovan*n*j daromena [&c.]

Doc. XVI. Firenze: R. Archivio di Stato. Arch. della Guardaroba, Nº. 198. "Inventarj di Palazzi e Ville." [Without continuous pagination. Excerpta.]

p. 1, 1598. Inuentario di tutti le maseritie, e altro, le quali si trouano al presente, nel palazzo di castello [&c.].

Nel salotto, doue magnia il gra*n* Duca.

1 quadro grande intauola dipintoui tre dee che ballano, e cupido sopra, e merchurio, e altre fiure senza adorn[to] anticho.

p. 2, Camera del gra*n* duca, terrena.
1 quadro grande in tela, anticho, dipintoui una uenere, sopra una nicchia, con altre fiure con ador[to] dorato.

p. 21, Nel salone del palazzo vecchio.
1 quadro grande anticho, in tela, dipintoui una donna e un centauro, con cornice dorate.

Inuentario di piu robe e maseritie lequali sono nel palazzo demedici in uia largha [&c.] comi*n*ciato q[to] dj 18 di Lug[o] 1598.

1 quadro grande in tela con cornicie dorat*a* dipintoui dentro lidea pallade.

1 quadro grande in tela, con cornicette dorate, dipintoui li dio pan con altre fiure nude, cosa bella e anticho.

Doc. XVII. Firenze: R. Archivio di Stato. Arch. della Guardaroba. N°. 537. "Inuentario e Rassegna della Guardaroba e Palazzo della Villa di castello [&c.] cominciato questo di 14 di Aprile 1638." [Excerpta.]

Fol. 1, tergo. Nel salotto, che segue [la Sala del Palazzo Vecchio], e uolta a man' manca con la finestra in sul Prato p*er* dinanzi de' Viuai.

Vn quadro in tauola alto b*raccia* 4 largo b*raccia* 3 con cornicie d'albero tinto di noce filettato e profilato d'oro entroui dipinto una femmina grande al naturale, che piglia un Centauro p*er* i Capelli, con la man diritta, e con la manca tiene un pillo d'arme in ast*a*.

Vn Quadro in tauola anticho alto b*raccia* 4 largo b*raccia* 6 con cornice d'albero tinto di noce filettato e rabeschato d'oro entroui dipinto piu femmine, che parte ballano con un cupido p*er* aria con arco in mano, e da una parte Mercurio.

Vn Quadro in tela anticho alto b*raccia* 3½ largo b*raccia* 5, entroui dipinto una Venere in mare sopra un nicchio con altre figure, con cornice d'albero tinto di noce filettato, e rabeschato d'oro.

Doc. XVIII. Firenze: R. Archivio di Stato. Partiti e Deliberazioni dei Signori Otto del 1478. Vol. 48, fol. 35, tergo. [Excerpta.]

Die xxj Julij 1478.

It*em* s*er*uatis &c. deliberauer*un*t et sta*n*tiauer*un*t
Sandro boticelli pro eius labore in pinge*n*do proditores *florenos* quadraginta lar*gos*, &c.

Doc. XIX. Firenze: R. Archivio di Stato. Dieci di Balia: Carteggio, Missivi, Registri, N°. 9. "Lettere dei Dieci di Balia, da Dicembre a Marzo, 1478." Copy of letter addressed to Tommaso Soderini, at Venice, and dated 9th February, 1478-1479.

Fol. 146, recto.

Doc. XX. Firenze: R. Archivio di Stato. Arch. delle Decime. Quartiere, Santa Maria Novella; Gonfalone, Unicorno: Campione, 1480, N°. verde 1010, fol. 244, recto. [Omissis.]

Dal 69 L[o] corno [c.] 669 da chonto di mariano di vannj p*er* suo uso.
Al 95 n[o] 79 indetto G[o] accho[nto] dj beninchasa elorenzo digiovannj p*er* suo vso.
Dal 69 L[o] corno c. 669 daconto dimarian*n*o detto in iij partite che sono pez. 8 equj dicono pez. vij in 4 partite [&c.].
Al 95 n[o] 79 in chont[o] dj dettj dj sopra [&c.]

[January, 1480-1.] + 1480. q[e]. s. M[a]. n[a] gonfalone lionjchorno

Mariano di vanni p*er*lo adjetro choncjatore di quoja ov*er*o galigajo ebbe dj chatasto s*oldj* 8 e d*anarj* ⅙ l*ire* 2 s*oldj* 12 d*anarj* 4.

Le sustanze didetto mariano divannj una chasa p*er* nostro abitare posta nella via nvova popolo santa lucja dongnisantj da p*rim*[o] via dasechondo lorenzo . . . . choregiajo da sechondo el p*ri*ore dj san pagholo e p*r*ima era giuliano manierj da ⅓ *ser* nastagio da ¼ lo spedale de vespuccj o voglamo dire bigallo ⅕ simone dj petro guiducci.

Due pezi diterra lavoratja posta nel popolo dj santa marja a peretola luogo detto gua*n* djlagio [&c.]

Due pezi djterra avna tenere di staiora 23 o cjrcha posta nel detto popolo luogo detto alisola [&c.]

Uno pezo djterra dj staiora 5½ posta nel popolo dj santa marja a peretola luogo detto ildjmesticho [&c.] vnaltro pezo djterra *in* detto luogo dj stajora iiij[o] [&c.]

Unpezo djterra posta nel popolo dj santa marja a peretola ov*er*o sanmartjno a sesto dj staiora 7 [&c.] tutte le sop*ra*dette terre lavora Antonjo di nencjone e frategli sono achatastate i*n* iij [partite] staja 72 digrano ebarili 13 dj vino i*n*circha hora lo a rechato astaja 90 e barili x djvino il grano merichato elvino pagho vettura cosa bella.

staja 90
barili 10
F*iorinj* 236 s*oldj* 7 d*anarj* 10

Benj alienatj

benj alienatj dal 70 i*n* qua una chasetta posta nel popolo dj sanfriano [&c.]

Fol. 244, tergo.

Una chasa venduta posta i*n*detto popolo i*n*sulchanto dj via maffia allato aquella di sop*ra* [&c.] venderonsi djnovenb*re* ov*ero* djcjenb*re* 1470 [&c.] tutti questi benj cjremasono 1464 cherano diachopo djgiovannj choncjatore djquoia fratello djdetto marjano chonpiu i*n*charichi p*er*che dette chase si venderono.

E piu lascjo p*er*testamento p*er*petuo ongnanno si desse l*ire* 10 p*er*vna piatanza a frati dellos*er*vanza djsanfranc*esc*° chechosi se os*er*vata edassi ados*er*vare sotto pena.

Ep*er*che siamo moltjplichatj i*n*famigla tengo una chasa allato alla mja che delp*ri*°re dj sanpagholo pagho lanno f*iorinj* 9 dj sug° dj pigione chea emedesimj chonfinj dj sop*ra*.

Marjano nostro detta dannj 86 enonfa piu nvlla.

M*onn*ª vangiolista chongnjata di detto marjano esirocchia djnostra madre emogle fu damjde° fratello djnostro padre dannj 70.

Giovannj mjo figlolo deta dannj 60 sensale djm*onte* fugia.

beninchasa suo figlolo deta dannj 19 sta arroma chosalutatj p*er* anchora piu tosto mi chosta cheutile.

Amide° figlolo didetto giovannj detta dannj 16 sta albancho e p*er*anchora nonna salarjo.

Jachopo figlolo deldetto dannj 14 sta alla squola.

Alessandra dannj x figlola deldetto sanza dota.

Agnoletta detta dannj 8 figlola deldetto sanza dota.

Nannina deta dannj 5 figlola del detto sanza dota.

Smeralda deta dunmese sanza dota.

Antonjo di marjano deta dannj 51 fu horafo ora sta abolongnja eva vendendo lib*ri* i*n* forma eda duchatj 2. ilmese elle spese.

la donna djdetto antonjo si truova grossa dj 7 mesi anome bartolomea figlola cheffu dj filip*p*o spiglati.

lisabetta sua figlola detta dannj 9 sanza dota.

Mariano suo figlolo deta danni 7.

bartolomeo suo figlolo deta dannj 5.

Era restato la donna dj giovannj M*onn*a nera figlola cheffu dj beninchasa di manno dechori.

Fol. 245, recto.

Simone djmarjano deta dannj 40 i*n* circha sanza aviamiento anapoli.

Sandro djmarjano deta dannj 33 edjpintore lavora i*n*chasa quando evole.

una fancjulla tengho chello djqui a 3 annj amarjtare.

Sono i*n* tutto bocche — b*occh*ᵉ 20.

tengo afitto un podere chello tolsi Rispetto alla morja olloattenere annj 2. posto nel popolo djsanpiero achareggj chedjricchardo dj papi d*i*michino paghone lanno l*ire* 30. la*rghe* dap*rim*° via da ij via da ⅓ giuliano dj s*er* simone Mannej da ¼ Redj djfranc*esc*° i*n*ghirramj elquale Ricchardo abita p*er*la estagione apisa.

Som*ma* lap*rim*ª fac*cia* dele sue sustanze inq*uest*°	F*iorinj* 336 . 7 . 10
Abatesi 5 p*erc*° dele sue sustanze de fiorinj 336 . 7 . 10 fanno	f*iorinj* 16 . 16 . 4
Abatesi p*er* pigione dele chase tenghino	f*iorinj* 128 . 11 . 6
	[Fiorinj] 145 . 7 . 10

Accanza*no* f*iorinj* 191. a 7 p*er* c° fanno e R*endit*ª f*iorinj* xiij s*oldj* vii d*anarj* v.

Abatti p*er* deliberazio*ne* degluficiali rochato s*er* nicholo ferrinj . . . il 2 dottob*re* 1481 l*ire* dieci p*icciolj* p*er* vnapietanza afrati disanfranc*esc*° dasaminiato p*er*testame*n*to diJacopo di vannj amidej rochato s*er* Girolamo dant° pascholinj sotto di 18 difeb*r*aio 1462.

Somma la Rendita f*iorinj* 10 s*oldj* 17 d*anarj* 5 aoro.

Doc. XXI. Firenze: R. Archivio di Stato. Idem, fol. 303, recto. Denunzia of Ser Nastagio Vespucci.

Doc. XXII. Roma: Archivio Segreto Vaticano. Notae Camerales etc.

sub Sixto IV et Innocent VIII ab an. 1480 ad 1496. Tom. 586, fol. 15, tergo. Contract for the Frescoes in the Sistine Chapel, at Rome.

Locatio picture Capelle magne nove palacii apostolici, sive deputacio ad ipsam depingendam.

Die XXVII Octobris 1481. Rome in camera apostolica, pontificatus sanctissimi in christo patris et domini nostri domini Sixti pape IIII anno undecimo. Rome in palacio apostolico honorabilis vir dominus Johannis Petri de Dulcibus de Florencia habitator Rome superstans sive commissarius fabrice palacii apostolici agens ut dixit de mandato et ex commissione sanctissimi domini nostri pape sibi facta presentibus me notario publico et testibus infrascriptis, gratis etc. conduxit sive locavit ac conducit sive locat providis viris Cosmo Laurentii Phylippi Rosselli, Alexandro Mariani, et Dominico Thomasii Corradi de Florencia, et Petro Christofori Castri Plebis Perusine diocesis depictoribus Rome comorantibus picturam capelle magne nove dicti palacii apostolici a capite altaris inferius, videlicet decem istorias testamenti antiqui et novi cum cortiniis inferius, ad depingendum bene diligenter et fideliter melius quo poterunt per ipsos et eorum quemlibet et familiares suos prout inceptum est. Et convenerunt ac promiserunt ipsi depictores eidem domino Johanni Petri superstanti locatori nomine dicti sanctissimi domini nostri pape dictas decem istorias cum earum cortinis ut predicitur depingere et finere hinc ad quintamdecimam diem mensis marcii proxime futuri cum precio solution[is] et extimation[is] ad quam seu quod extimabuntur istorie iam facte in dicta capella per eosdem depictores, sub pena quinquaginta ducatorum auri de camera pro quolibet eorundem contrafaciente, quam penam sponte sibi imposuerunt et ad quam si contrafacient incidi voluerunt et volunt, que pena aplicari debeat fabrice dicte capelle etc. Et pro predictis omnibus et singulis ipsi depictores obligarunt se et omnia eorum et cuiuslibet ipsorum bona presentia et futura, et quilibet eorum tenetur pro alio contrafacie[n]te et predicta non observante sive observantibus etc. in meliori et strictiori forma camere etc. Sub[mi]cerunt se etc. Renunciarunt etc. Constituerunt procuratores etc. Et iuraverunt etc. Fiat in ampliori forma etc. Et etiam ex pacto fuerunt concordes quod quedam obligacio per dictos depictores alias facta dicto Johanni Petri superstanti super pecuniis per eos receptis et recipiendis ratione dicte depicture maneat in suo valore et robore etc. Presentibus venerabilibus viris dominis Marino de Monte alto et Baptista de Spello camere apostolice notariis pro testibus et me Johanne Gerones eiusdem Camere notario rogato.

[Printed by Domenico Gnoli, in the "Archivio Storico dell' Arte," Anno VI, 1893, p. 128, and again more correctly, by Dr. Ernst Steinman, in "Die Sixtinische Kapelle," München, 1901, Vol. I, p. 633.]

Doc. XXIII. Firenze: R. Archivio di Stato. Deliberazioni degli Operai del Palazzo della Signoria; dal 1478 al 1483. Filza 14. [Excerpta.]

Fol. 13, recto. Die 5 mens*is* octob*ris* 1482

Sup*ra*dict*j* op*er*arij simul adunati in sufficie*n*tj nu*mer*o co*n*gregatj in cam*era* armor*um* dict*j* palatij s*er*uatis s*er*uandis &c. et obtento p*ar*tito p*er* quinq*ue* fabas nigras s*ecundu*m ord*inem* dederu*n*t et locaueru*n*t Vigore legis p*ropter*ea edite p*er* opportuna consilia s*ub* die 31 mens*is* augustj p*roxime* p*re*teritj p*ro* finalj co*n*clusione Dominicho tomasj d*e*lgrilla*n*daio pictorj p*resent*j et ricipie*n*tj &c. faciam [*sic*] sale palatij pop*u*lj flor*entin*j versus doanam ad facie*nd*a*m* et pinge*nd*a*m* i*m*magine*m* s*an*c*t*j zenobij et aliar*um* i*m*magin*um* p*ro* ornando dict*j* palatij soluand*um* salariu*m* s*ecundu*m ord*inem* Cum pacto &c. q*uod* dict*j* op*er*arij no*n* tene*a*ntur [fol. 13, tergo] ad aliquam solutione*m* fienda*m* d*ic*to dominicho sed solui debeat de operarijs dict*j* co*mmun*is ad id p*ropter*ea deputatis Cum exigetur ab illis ad quos p*er*tinet et ordinatum est p*er* oportuna consilia et e*ss*ent pecunie exacte Rogans &c.

Dict*a* [d]ie 5 octob*ris* 1482

Item ut supra adunatj &c. deder*unt* et locaueru*n*t Vigore dict*e* legis s*upra*s*crip*to dominicho et sandro marianj pictorib*us* p*resen*t*ibus* et recip*ientibus* &c. faciam [*sic*] sale audientie d*omin*or*um* dict*j* palatij ad pingend*um* et ornand*um* pro ornamen*t*o dict*j* palatij cu*m* pattis p*ro*mission*ibus* &c. et o*mni*b*us* content*is* i*nfrascriptis* locata s*upra*s*crip*to dominicho &c.

It*em* ut sup*ra* adunati &c. deder*unt* et locaueru*n*t pietro v*ocat*o perugino et blaxio ant*on*ij tuccj pictorib*us* facia*m* [*sic*] sale palatij dict*orum* d*omin*or*um* v*er*sus plateam V*idelicet* facia*m* [*sic*] finestiare*m* ad faciend*um* et pingend*um* p*ro* ornamen*t*o dict*j* palatij soluend*um* salarium ut i*n* s*upra*s*crip*ta deliberatione de dominicho d*e*lgrillandaio co*n*tinet*ur* &c. Rogans &c.

It*em* ut sup*ra* adunatj & deder*unt* et locaueru*n*t facie*m* putei dict*e* sale piero Jacobj d*e*l pollaiuolo picto*rj* ad faciend*um* et pingend*um* p*ro* ornamento dict*j* palatij soluend*um* salariu*m* ut in s*upra*s*crip*ta prima delib*er*atione de domenicho delgrilla*n*daio continet*ur* rogans &c.

Fol. 14, recto. Die 31 mens*is* decembris 1482

Sup*ra*dictj op*er*arij congregatj in camera armor*um* i*n* nu*mer*o sufficientj [&c.] Item s*er*uatis s*er*uandis concess*er*unt filippo fratris filippi l*icet* absentj v*idelicet* ad pingendum eam partem qua*m* alias locauerant perugino pictorj et pro illo p*re*tio et cum illis conditionibus et qualitatib*us* p*ro*ut d*ict*o perugino locauerant Locationem aut*em* dicto perugino factam reuocauerunt.

[Printed by Johan Gaye, in the "Carteggio inedito d'Artisti," Vol. I, p. 578.]

Doc. XXIV. Milano: R. Archivio di Stato. Sezione storica, Autografi, Pittori: Sec. xv e varietà.

[On one side of a single sheet, without date, or other indication. c. 1485-90.]

Sandro di Botticelli pictore Excellen[mo] in tauola, et in muro: le cose sue hano aria virile et sono cum optima ragione, et integra proportione.

Philippino di Frate Philippo optimo discipulo del sopra dicto, et figliolo del piu singulare maestro de tempi suoi: le sue cose hano aria piu dolce, non credo che habiano tanta arte.

El Perusino Maestro singulare, et maxime in muro: le sue cose hano aria angelica et molto dolce.

Domenico de Grilandaio bono maestro in tauola, e piu in muro: le cose sue hano bona aria, et e homo expediticco, et che conduce assai lauoro.

Tutti questi predicti maestri hano facto proua di loro ne la capella di papa Syxto excepto che philippino. Ma tutti poi allospedaletto del M[co] Laur[o] e la palma e quasi ambigua.

[Printed by Herr Müller-Walde: "Beiträge zur Kenntnis des Leonardo da Vinci," in the "Jahrbuch der Königlich Preussischen Kunstsammlungen," Berlin, 1897, Vol. XVIII, p. 165.]

Doc. XXV. Firenze: Archivio privato del Conte Francesco Guicciardini. Libro di Entrata e Uscita e Quaderno di cassa di Giovanni d'Agnolo de' Bardi, segnato B, dal 1484 al 1487.

Fol. 35, recto. Lunedì, adì vij di febraio [1484-5]. Alla chappella di Santo Spirito fior. ventiquattro, sol. viij, den. v, a oro larghi, per fior. 23, sol. 10 larghi d'oro in oro, paghati a Giuliano da San Gallo lengnaiuolo, portò contanti: e sono per intaglio del fornimento della tavola fatta per Sandro del Botticello, e d'achordo. fior. xxiiij, s. viij, d. v.

Fol. 39, tergo. Mercholidì adì iij d'Aghosto [1485]. A chappella di Santo Spirito fior. settantotto, sol. xv a oro larghi, per fior. 75 d'oro in oro, paghati a Sandro del Botticello, a lui contanti: che fior. 2 sono per azurro, e fior. 38 per l'oro e mettitura della tavola, e fior. 35 pel suo pennello; d'achordo. fior. lxxviij, s. xv, d. —

[Printed by Signor Igino Benvenuto Supino, in his "Sandro Botticelli," Florence, 1899, p. 83, note.]

Doc. XXVI. Firenze: R. Archivio di Stato. Arch. delle Decime. Quartiere, Santa Maria Novella; Gonfalone, Leon Bianco: Campione, 1480, N°. verde 1013, fol. 380, recto. Denunzia of Giovambattista di Francesco Tornabuoni.

. . . Vno podere posto nelpopolo e piuiere disant[o] stefano i*n* pane luogho detto chiasso amascierellj co*n* casa da S*ignore* ellauoratorj co*n*finato dap*rim*[o] uia E 2 lore*n*zo demedicj E 3 tomaso lottierj.

Doc. XXVII. Firenze: R. Archivio di Stato. Arch. della Guardaroba, N° 826. "1675 Adi 14 9bre. Inuentario de Mobilj e Masserizie dell'Eredità del Ser[mo] e R*ev*[mo] sig[re] Principe Card[le] Leopoldo di Toscana, cominciata questo di suddetto." [Excerpta.]

Fol. 77, tergo.

377 / ·M· Vn Quadro in Tauola Tondo a Diametro di b*raccia* 2 — dipintoui la mad[na] in Ginocchionj con sei Angiolini attorno, che l'adorano, e Giardino in Lontananza, di mano del Botticelli, con adornamento Intagliato dorato antico confestoni di frutte attorno.

379 / ·M· Vn Quadro in Tauola, tondo, Diametro di b*raccia* 2⅓ dipintoui la mad[na] a sedere, con Banbino in Collo, con sei Angioli di piu che mezza figura uno de quali ha un giglio in mano, di mano del Botticelli, con ador[na]mento Intag[to] e dorato inparte con fondo Turchino.

Doc. XXVIII. Firenze: R. Biblioteca Nazionale. Cod. II, IV, 324. (Magliabechiano, Cl. xxv, N°. 574).

[A collection of various pieces of the fifteenth, sixteenth, and seventeenth centuries, bound together. From the Strozzi Library.

Fol. 122 to fol. 135. An account of a Joust, imperfect at the beginning and end, and without date or other indication: but from internal evidence, it appears to be a description of the famous Tourney held at Florence in 1475, since Piero, the son of Lorenzo, Il Magnifico, born 15th February, 1471-2, is said to have been present, aged three years. An abstract of this document is printed by Prof. Giuseppe Mazzatinti, in his "Inventario dei Manoscritti della R. Biblioteca Nazionale Centrale di Firenze," Forlì, 1899, &c., Vol. II, pp. 219-221.]

Fol. 122, recto. G*i*uliano di piero dicosimo demedici i*n* sua conpagnia. [&c.] Fol. 122, tergo. Vncauallo coue*r*tato di tafecta alexa*n*dri*no* frappato & fra*n*giato i*n*torno tucta dipi*n*ta di bro*n*coni duliuo & fiame difuocho. Era sopra ildecto cauallo vno armato di tucto arme, Et i*n* capo aueua v*no* mazochio i*n* capo di brucoli dorpello cu*m* pe*n*ne a sua diuisa, portaua i*n*ma*no* vna aste gra*n*de dipi*n*ta dazurro suui vno ste*n*dardo di taffecta alexa*n*drino frappato & fra*n*giato i*n*tor*no* ch*e* nella su*m*mjta era vnsole et nelmezo diq*ue*sto ste*n*dardo era vna figura gra*n*de simigliata a pallas uestita duna ueste doro fine i*n* fino amezo leganbe, Et disocto vna ueste biancha onbreggiata doro macinato Et u*no* paio distiualecti azurri i*n* gamba, laquale teneua in pie i*n* su due fia*m*me di fuocho et delle decte fia*m*me usciua fia*m*me ch*e* ardeua*no* rami duliuo ch*e* era*no* dal mezo i*n* giu dello ste*n*dardo ch*e* dalmezo i*n* su erano rami senza fuocho, h[a]ueua i*n* capo vna celata bru*n*ita alla*n*ticha Esuoi capelli tucti atrecciati ch*e* ventolaua*no*, Teneua dect*a* pallas nella mano dirict*a* vna lancia da giostra, Et nella ma*no* ma*n*cha loscudo di medusa, et apresso adecta figura vnprato adorno difiori diuarij colori ch*e* nusciua vno ceppo duliuo conu*no* ramo gra*n*de alquale era legato v*no* dio damore cu*m* lema*n*i dirieto cu*m* cord*o*ni doro, Et apiedi aueua archo turcasso et saecte rocte, Era co*m*messo nelramo dulino doue staua legato lodio damore vno brieue dilectere alla fra*n*zese doro ch*e* diceua*no* lasans par, lasopradect*a* pallas guardaua fisame*n*te nelsole ch*e* era sop*r*[a] allei.

Doc. XXIX. Firenze: R. Archivio di Stato. Carteggio Mediceo innanzi il principato. Inventory of the goods of Lorenzo de' Medici, Il Magnifico. 1492. [Excerpta.]

[Begins] "qvesto Lib*ro* dinue*n*tarij e chopiato da unalt*r*[o] i*n*ve*n*tario elq*u*[a]le fu fatto alla morte del Mag[co] L[zo] demedicj chopiate p*er* me p*r*etesimone di stagio dall*e* pozze oggi q*uest*[o] 23 didicemb*re* 1512 p*er* chommissione di Lorenzo dip*ier*[o] demedicj."

Fol. 1, recto. Inuentario del palagio .... posto in sulchanto della via largha

Fol. 42, tergo. Nella Cam[a] dipiero.

Vno panno i*n* uno i*n*tauolato messo d*or*[o] alto br*accia* 4 i*n* circha & la*rgho* br*accia* 2 entrovj una fighura di pa .... [blank in original] et co*n* 1° schudo dand*r*esse [?] & vna lancia darcho dimano disand*r*[o] di botticello *fiorinj* 10 —

Fol. 48, recto. Nellanticham[a] dip*ier*[o].

Vna lettiera saluaticha dib*raccia* 4 Lu*n*gha co*n*p*r*edelle atorno dinocie & tarsie & mazze et sachone *fiorinj* —

Vno sopracielo adetto Letto didetta anticham[a] dipi*n*touj vna fortuna dimano disandr[o] dibotticello

[A great part of this inventory has been printed by M. Eugène Müntz in "Les Collections des Médicis au xve Siècle," Paris et Londres, 1888.]

Doc. XXX. Firenze: R. Archivio di Stato. Carteggio Mediceo innanzi il principato: Filza 104: Lettered: "Jnuentari di Casa Medici." A collection of Inventories of the fifteenth and sixteenth centuries, bound together. [Excerpta.]

N° 24.

Fol. 1, recto.

Inue*n*tario della diuis[a] fatta p*er*noj Matteo diualerio epiero dinicolo fioreglj p*er*consegn*i*are La parte aciascheduno tocha cioe apierfranc[o] di Lorenzo demedicj e Giovannj di giouannj demedicij lequale cose saranno discritte cosa per cosa insu li infrascrittj foglj e quaderno

Fol. 2, recto. [Anno] 1516.

I*n* Camera Seconda i*n*sulsalotto terreno

1ª figura conuna minerva ej° centaur°

N° 40. [An inventory of 5 leaves, without title, or endorsement; but in the same hand as, and apparently the first draft of, N° 24.]

Fol. 1, recto.
I*n* Camera seconda i*n*sulsalotto alato alla [Camera] bella terrenª

1ª figura conuna minerva e ce*n*tauro i*n* tela e asse drito.

Doc. XXXI. Firenze: R. Archivio di Stato. Arch. dei Corporazioni Religiose soppresse da Leopoldo I. Badia di Settimo. Filza C, xviii, 18, Sec. T. "Memorie del Monasterio di Settimo dal tempo che ui entrorno Li Monaci Cisterciensi, che fu l'Anno 1236. raccolte da varij fragmenti di piu scritture antiche p*er* me D. Ignatio Signorini." [Excerpta.]

Fol. 56, recto.
1480 La Chiesa di Cestello p*er* l'antichità minacciando rouina fu pensiero de Monaci cercar modo di riedificarla, e p*er*che il Monj^{rio} no*n* laueua il modo p*er* tutta la dª spesa, procurovono trouar' amici e amoreuoli del Conuento che souuenissero p*er* dª fabrica.

Addi 26 Marzo, si dette principio alla Cappella Maggiore [&c.] Molti altri Cittadini presero l'assunto di fabbricar' ciascuno di loro vna Cappella, come vi vede dal lib*ro* de Benefattori, et in pochi anni fu ridotta a p*er*fetione.

Fol. 57, recto.
1483 Addi 16 Giugno, finita era la Cappella grande di Cestello [&c.]

Fol. 59, tergo.
1488 Si andauano p*er*fettionando le Cappelle di Cestello da diuersi Cittadini, e q° Anno....
.. Da Benedetto di S*er* Giouanni Guardi fu fatta la 5 Cappella dalla dª. banda del Boschetto, e spese d*ucati* 58 d'*or*°, e fece anco fare la tauola da Sandro Botticelli, che valse d*ucati* 30, oue era dipinto il Misterio dell' Annu*n*tiatione di Maria, e l'Altare fu consecrato dal soprad° Vesc° Vasionen*se* [fr. Benedetto Pagagnotti, suffraganeo dell' Archiuescouo di Firenze,] li 26 Giug° 1490.

[These notices, which are cited by Signor Milanese in his notes to Vasari, ed. Sansoni, Vol. III, p. 314, note, have chiefly been drawn from the following document, the original "Libro de' Benefattori" to which Signorini alludes.]

Doc. XXXII. Firenze: R. Archivio di Stato. Arch. dei Corporazioni Religiose soppresse da Leopoldo I. Monasterio di Cestello. Filza C, xviii, 96. "Libro de Benefattori del Monasterio di Cestello in Pinti." [Excerpta.]

Fol. 1, recto.
1480 [&c.] In questo libro si scrierranno tutti eprecipuj benefattorj delmonasterio disanta maria magdalena dellordine dicestello infirençe, e sito nella via detta dipinti, et popolo disanpier magiore, et maxime efondatorj delle chappelle didetta chiesa et altrj ornatorj didetta chiesa emonasterio [&c.]

Fol. 7, recto. 1488
Adi 19 dimarço 1488 benedetto dis*er* giouannj guardj fecie fare vna chappella efondare incestello difirençe la sechonda ama*n*ritta quando si entra i*n* chiesa echiamasi la chappella della nuntiata, espese p*e*lle mie mani cioe p*er* me don ant° nelmurare didetta chappella duchatj cinquanta cioe cholla finestra uetriata, et piu spese nella tauola didetta chappella ducati trenta che fu dimano disandro botticello.

esiamo obligati apregare iddio p*e*lluj ep*er*sui passati si chome benefattorj delnostro monasterio: altro partichulare none p*er*insino aora.

Adj 26 digiugno 1490 fra benedetto pagagnottj vescouo diuasone esuffraganeo fiore*n*tino *con*secro laltare dibenedetto guardj edette ogni anno i*n*dett° di cent° di dip*er*dono cioe eldi della festa dis*ancto* giouanni et paulo martirj et chosi tutte lesolemnita dinostra donna nellaquale titolo dett° altare ogni di qvaranta di dip*er*dono et chosi tutte ledomeniche diquaresima eldi dis*ancta* maria magdalena et di s*ancto* bernardo e tutte ledomeniche dellanno ec.

E adi 24 dimarço 1490 fecie vno paliotto didomaschino biancho p*er* dett° suo altare.

A 18 digiugno co*m*pero 1° paio dica*n*deglieri*n*j diferro per la sua cappella.

Doc. XXXIII. Firenze: R. Archivio di Stato; Arch. dei Conventi soppressi. N° grosso 103, San Marco; N° 85, Repertorio di obblighi di Messe, dal 1552, al 1606: N° 1.

[Part I, under month of December: the entry appears to be one of the first entries made when the book was begun, *c.* 1525.]

\+ · yħs · Maria

Perpetuj Dicembre

Delprefato mese di dicembre/ Noi habiamo ad Celebrare vno officio dimortj/ ogni anno alla Cappella dellarte diportasancta maria ch*e* si chiama la Cappella di S*ancto* Alò/ p*er*lanime di quelli p*er*chi ci e facta la limosina ch*e* disobto sidira. Et p*er* sapere lorigine/ Ladicta Cappella/ e/ delme*m*bro didecta Arte/ che sono gli oreficj. Et loro feciono vno Calice dargen*t*o tucto co*n* larme loro ch*e* e vna Cuppa; Et disopra nella testudin*e* della cappella e lamedesima arme et i*n*sieme larme dellarte. Dipoi essen*d*o molto antiquata/ et hauendo larte p*er*legge facta dala Com*m*unita difirenze aessere protectrice delno*str*o Conuen*t*o, Insegno dich*e*, Tengono vna bandiera co*n*la loro i*n*segna eldj disanmarco appiccata ala dicta Cappella/ Et viene il corpo dellarte ad offerta co*n*loro torchiettj alla no*str*a chiesa Jndicta festiuita disanma*r*co/ Et se p*er* mal tempo no*n* potessino venir*e* ma*n*dan° lacera Essendo facta nellarte certa prouisione lanno 1488 o alt*r*° piu uero tempo co*n* piena aucto[ta]; et vno officio di Conseruatorj/ fu statuito che p*er* gratitudine dellofficiar*e* decta cappella ch*e* fan*n*o efratj et p*er* dicto officio/ larte ci paghj ogni an*n*o p*er* elemosina lire qvara*n*ta p*icc*iolj, Et uogliono che di Cinq*ue* annj Jn cinq*ue* annj / si habi afar*e* la rafferma didi*ct*a elemosina da Consolj che p*er* tempi saran*n*o/ Et cosi sempre si obserua

[In a later hand.] Lobligo e finito p*er*ch*e* e data a Brandolini.

p*icc*iolj f*iorinj* — l*ire* 40 *soldj* —

Et la dicta Arte oltre ad q*uest*° fece latauola Jnch*e* spese duc[ti] Cento doro lar*ghi* et ilgraticulato et arricciatura/ et ma*n*tiene quella a sua spese

E dipoi statuto che sia p*er*petuo senza la co*n*firmatione qui*n*quenne

Et piu statuto ch*e* p*e*rla lampade habiamo ogni an*n*o vno barile dolio

[In a later hand:]

Questo dj 23 d'Ap*r*ile 1575 fu prorogato p*er* 5 anni co*n* co*n*ditione ch*e* si facci intendere loro q*uando* si fa l'off°:

[Printed by M. Jacques Mesnil, " Quelques Documents sur Botticelli," in the " Miscellanea d'Arte," Firenze, 1903, Vol. I, p. 90.]

Doc. XXXIV. Firenze: R. Archivio di Stato. Arch. dell' Arte della Seta, detta di Por Santa Maria, N° 1.

Fol. 304 tergo.

IN DEI NO*M*I*N*E Ame*n* Anno dominj ab eius salutifera Incarnatione Millesimo Quatuorcentesimo Nonagesimo Indict*ione* viij & die xxviiij mensis ap*r*ilis obtemta fuit i*nfrascrip*ta prouisio p*er* Consulas & Consiliarios dicte artis p*er* xviij fabas nigras no*n* obstante una alba. [Here follow various resolutions regarding the sensali, or brothers, of the guild.]

Fol. 305, tergo.

I*tem* Essendo padrone & hauendo gliuominj dellarte la cura & custodia della chiesa dis° Marco difirenze & hauendouj etiam una Cappella & ordinato lassegnamen*t*o dimurarla & adornarla & in parte e/

Officio a S° Marcho.

Et perch*e* efratrj didetta chiesa in uerita co*n* sollecitudine uidichano messe & co*n*tinue se exercitano p*er*la salute dellanime & maxime de benefattorj & atteso alloro honesta uita & anche alla loro pouerta p*er* tanto si statuisce & ordina p*er* Annj cinque p*r*oximj ch*e* delle Tratte degliaguagli didette sensali si faranno ogni anno del mese dagosto: Elproueditore habbi haritenere fra tutti l*ire* 40 p*iccioli per* l*ira* & s*oldo second*° gliaguali e quali delmese dottobre poi ognianno Conmi*n*ciando a ottobre p*r*oximo si mandino adetti fratri dette l*ire* 40 p*er* una piatanza / e loro sieno tenuti affare ognianno vno officio demorti p*er*lanima de benefattorj didetta arte e ildi e sabbi aterminare p*er* Consolj ch*e* per t*em*po saranno/ Et ch*e* lariten*t*ione sa affare questo anno si facci eltutto delle l*ire* 40 & di poi ogni quatro mesi elterzo delle dette l*ire* 40/

Die xxvj ap*r*ilis 1491 p*er* Consules & Consiliarios fuit dict*a* prouisio p*r*orogata p*er* x annos sequendos im*m*ediate finitis dict*is* quinq*ue* annis. in Libro p*rouisionum* S[to] A, c. 133.

Die 14 dece*m*bris 1503 fuit p*r*orogat*a* per alios x a*n*nos immediate seque*n*dos s*opra scrit*tis i*n* lib° p*r*ouisionu*m* B, c. 2.

Doc. XXXV. Firenze: Archivio dell' Opera di Santa Maria del Fiore. Deliberazioni, dal 1486 al 1491, fol. 68 e 77, &c. Deliberations con-

cerning the designs submitted for the façade of the Duomo, 12 February, 1489-90, and 5 January, 1490-91.

[First printed by the Florentine commentators of Vasari, ed. Le Monnier, 1846-70, Vol. VII, p. 243.]

Doc. XXXVI. Firenze: Archivio dell' Opera di Santa Maria del Fiore. Deliberazioni, dal 1486 al 1491.

Fol. 49, tergo. Die XVIIJ Maij MCCCCLXXXXI.

Sp[les] & dignissimi viri Antonius Paganellus et Thomas Minerbectus Op*er*arii opere S*ancte* Marie floris ciuitat*is* floren*tie*, una cu*m* Sp*ectabilibus* Viris Prouisorib*us* ordinam*en*tor*um* d*ic*te artis, v*idelicet* Roggerio Nicolai de Corbinellis, Franc*isc*[o] Antonii Thaddei, et Laur*enti*[o] Petri Cosme de Medicis, ... delib*er*au*er*unt, et delib*er*ando locau*er*unt

Dominico & David } fr*atr*ibus carnalib*us* & filijs Thomasii Corradi Grillandai, ciuib*us* et pictoribus Florentinis, ibidem tunc p*resen*tib*us* pro una parte, et

Sandro Mariani Botticello pictori & Gherardo Joannis Miniatori et Sociis } ibidem et*iam* p*resen*tib*us* &c. pro alia dimidia,

Ad faciendum pro d*ic*ta opera de musayco in cappella S*anctj* Zenobii sita in d*ic*ta eccl*esia* S*ancte* Marie floris de flor*enti*[a], duas partes ex quatuor testudinis & seu celi dicte cappelle, v*idelicet* duos Spiculos ex quattuor Capelle iam dicte, et cuilib*et* d*ic*tar*um* partium unu*m* ex dictis Spiculis cum illius figuris pro eo p*re*tio illis t*em*p*o*ribus modis & formis, et prout & sicut visum erit operariis presentibus & pro tempore existent*ibus* dict*e* op*ere*, non obstant*ibus* &c.

[The foregoing was first printed by the Florentine commentators of Vasari, ed. Le Monnier' 1846-70, Vol. VI, p. 339.]

Fol. 138, tergo. [Operarii stantiauerunt]
MCCCCLXXXXI die XXV Augusti,
Sandro Mariani Botticelli pro parte Musayci conficiendj i*n* Cappella S*anctj* Zenobii
floreni — l*ibre* 20 [solidi] 4

Fol. 139, tergo. MCCCCLXXXXI,
Die XXIIJ Decembr*is*,
Dominico & Dauid Thome Grillandar*um* mag*ist*ris Musayci pro parte laborer*ij* pro musayco conficiendo i*n* Cappella S*anctj* Zenobij
floreni 70 l*ibre* 89 [solidi] 18

Sandro Mariani, Gherardino, Monti } Magistris Musaici pro d*ic*ta causa ut s*upra*
floreni 47 l*ibre* — [solidi] 15

Doc. XXXVII. Firenze: Archivio dell' Opera di Santa Maria del Fiore. Deliberazioni, dal 1491 al 1498.

Fol. 1, recto. [Operarii deliberauerunt]
MCCCCLXXXXJ [*i.e.* 1491-2]

Die d*ic*ta [VIJ Januarij] Item q*uod* cuidam camere uacuo in parte superiori domus opere fiat clauis et sera, et consignetur Guidoni Baldouinecto p*ro* ibidem conficiendo stucchum pro Musaico cappelle S*anctj* Zenobii et hoc fiat p*er* totam diem Lune nouam p*resen*tis mens*is*, o*mn*i oppositione uacante. Pro camera *pro* Stucho conficiendo.

Fol. 66, recto. [Operarii stantiauerunt]
MCCCCLXXXXIJ, Die XXX[a] Junij
Dom[co] Dauid } Thomasii magistris musayci pro parte laborerij quod f*acit*u*r* pro cappella s*an*cti Zenobii
floreni 21 l*ibre* — [solidi] 10

Gherardo Monti } magistris Musaici pro parte labor*erii* facit*ur* pro cappella S*ancti* Zenobii
floreni 2 l*ibre* — [solidi] 10

Fol. 68, tergo.
Die XVIIJ Decembr*is* 1492
Gherardo Monti } Joannis, Sandro Mariani } magistris Musayci pro parte Musayci facti in Capella S*anctj* Çenobii
floreni 31 l*ibre* 35 [solidi] 11

contra Dominicum & Marioctum

Fol. 21, recto. [Operarii deliberauerunt,]
MCCCCLXXXXIIJ, [*i.e.*, 1493-4.]

D*ict*a die [XIJ[a] Martii] Item q*uod* Dominicus Gregorii & Marioctus de Vulparia & eorum ministri intelligant*ur* remoti ab eorum exercitio si per tota*m* p*re*se*n*tem Diem non non [*sic*] aptau*er*i*n*t palcu*m* p*ro* musayco ita ut Gherardus et Montes possint ibidem laborare.

floreni 10 Gherardo & Monti mag*is*tris Musayci &c.

Fol. 21, tergo. MCCCCLXXXXIIJ [*i.e.*, 1493-4].

Dicta die [XX[a] Martii] Item quod soluantur *florenos* decem lar*gos* auri in auro Gherardo & Monti miniatoribus & mag*ist*ris musayci pro computo dicti musayci et ponant*ur* debitores dicte su*m*me in quaternio prouisoris.

Doc. XXXVIII. Firenze: R. Archivio di Stato. Carteggio Mediceo innanzi il principato. Filza 68, carta 316. Letter addressed by Michelagnolo Buonarroti, in Rome, to Lorenzo di Pier Francesco de' Medici; dated 2 July, 1496, and endorsed, "Sandro dibottjcello infirenze."

[First printed by Michelangiolo Gualandi, in his "Memorie Originali di Belle Arti," Bologna, 1840, ser. iii, p. 112; and again more correctly in "Le Lettere di Michangelo Buonarroti, pubblicate coi Ricordi ed i contratti Artistici, per cura di Gaetano Milanesi," Firenze, 1875, p. 375: also by the Florentine commentators of Vasari, ed. Le Monnier, vol. xii, p. 339, and ed. Sansoni, vol. vii, p. 343.]

Doc. XXXIX. Firenze: R. Archivio di Stato. Arch. delle Decime. Quartiere, Santa Croce; Gonfalone, Lion Nero: Campione, 1480, N° verde 1005. [Omissis.]

Fol. 17, recto.

Ant° dinerj dant° disengna g*u*idj abita nellp*opol*° disarromeo ene laq*uartier*[e] disanta + ghonfalon[e] leonero [&c.]

Sustanze

Vna chasa chonvna chasetta allato e tutte p*er*mio vso estato mio piutempo essenp*re* lachasa allachasetta stato p*er* nostro vso chonllorto vochabolj echonfinj cioe daprimo uia second° zanobj daddiacietto terzo rede difranc° norj ♀ donato dibonifazio.

Vnpoderuzzo [&c.] posto nelp*opol*° epieujere disanguisto [&c.]

Bocche

Ant° dinerj dant° disengna g*u*idj deta dannj 21 nonnisto abbottegha riparomj alauolta albancho debartolinj cioe dannj 21

M[a] Nanna mja m[a]dre dannj 47

Marietta mja sirocchia dannj 14

Vna fante detta disop*ra* [disalario *fiorinj* 7 lanno]

Som*ma* lasustanza chome apare nellafacia dila	*fiorinj* 460 . 15 . 6
Abati djma*n*tenere la posessionj dj *fiorinj* 445 s*oldj* 15 d*anarj* 6 a 5 p*er*c°	*fiorinj* 22 . 5 . 9
	fiorinj 438 . 9 . 9

Restano lesustanze *fiorinj* 438 s*oldj* 9 d*anarj* 9 che a 7 p*er*c° fan*no* dj R*endit*[a] *fiorinj* 30 s*oldj* 13 d*anarj* 10.

Doc. XL. Firenze: R. Archivio di Stato. Arch. della Grascia, N° 5. "Libro P° Nero dei Morti di Firenze," dal 1457, al 1501. [Excerpta.]

Fol. 160, recto. 1481

Mariano chojajo Riposto inognjssantj Adj XX dj febbraio 1481.

Fol. 229, recto. MCCCC°LXXXX°IJ

M[a] nera donna di Giouannj di botticiello R[a] inongnj santj Adj 5 difeb*r*aio.

Fol. 239, recto. MCCCCLXXXXIIJ

Giouannj di mariano vochato botticello riposto i*n* ongnj sa*n*tj adj 30 di ma*r*zo.

Doc. XLI. Firenze: R. Archivio di Stato. Arch. dei Contratti, Rogiti di Ser Giovanni di Ser Marco di Tommaso da Romena; Protocollo dal 25 Gen. 1491-2, al 24 Nov. 1496. Segnato G. 433.

Fol. 97, recto. 1494 Jndic*tione* 12

In dei no*mine* Am*en* Anno do*min*j *nost*ri yħu xp̄i abeius salutifera *in*carnatio*ne* mill*esimo* quadri*ngentesimo* nonagesi*mo* quarto Jndic*tione* xij et die dicianouo me*n*sis aprilis Actu*m* flor*entie in* p*op*ulo s*ancte* m[e] in ca*m*po p*resentibus ser* Cetto bernardi s*er* cetti deloro et pierozzo castellani pierozzi decastellanis ciuib*us* flore*n*tinis testib*us* &c.

R[dus] uir d*ominus* Be*r*nardus dellauolta hospitalarius et rector hospitalis s*anct*e m[e] noue deflor*entia pro* alimonia et s*ubste*n*tatione* paup*erum* et i*n*fermor*um* dicti hospitalis et uigore cui*uscumque* auctoritatis et lice*n*tie d*ict*o hospitalario et seu hospitali qu*omodo*lib*et con*cesse etc. et p*ro* utilitate d*ict*i hospitalis et o*mn*i modo &c. dedit et co*n*cessit &c. ad liuellu*m* seu emphiteosim pe*r*petua*m* Sandro olim Mariani va*n*nis amidej defilipepis egregio pictorj ciui flore*n*tino p*op*uli s*ancte* lucie o*mnium* s*anctorum* deflor*entia pres*enti et recipi*enti* p*r*ose et Antonio et Simone eius fratribus et f*ilij*s olim d*ict*i Marianj et p*ro* filijs masculis Joannis Mariani ol*im* eius fratris et p*ro* [filijs masculis] ip*sorum* sandri Antonij et Simonis et d*ict*or*um* filior*um* dicti Jo*a*nnis nepotu*m* ex fra*tre* dicti Sandri et cuiuslib*et* eor*um* filijs et desce*n*de*n*tib*us* masculis l*egiti*mis et naturalib*us* pe*r*linea*m* masculina*m* i*n*pe*r*petuu*m* desce*n*de*n*tib*us* v*idelicet* primo p*ro* d*ict*o Sandro et eius filijs et desce*n*de*n*tib*us* masculis post*ea* successiue p*ro* dictis eius fratrib*us* et nepotib*us* et eor*um* et cui*us*lib*et* eor*um* f*ilij*s et desce*n*de*n*tib*us* masculis pe*r*linea*m* p*redict*am alter alterj succede*n*do Vnum podere cu*m* domo p*ro*do*min*o et terris laboratiuis uineatis oliuatis et fructatis po*situm in* p*op*ulo s*ancti* sepulcri co*munitatis* flor*entie* p*r*ope et ex*tra* porta*m* s*ancti* fridianj deflor*entia* co*n*finat*um* ap[o] uia aij[o] petrifilippi depa*n*dolfinis aiij[o] Jacobj delcaualierj & aiiij[o] ol*im* fratrum mo*n*tis oliuetj

i*nfra* p*r*ed*ict*os co*n*fino*s* uel al*ios* &c. p*ro* p*r*etio utilis dominij dicti poderis florenor*um* ce*n*tu*m* q*u*inq*u*agi*n*ta q*u*inq*ue* l*argorum* bono*rum* nitidor*um* adgabella*m* d*ict*i co*n*ductoris et p*ro* an*n*uo canone seu liuello vnius paris caponu*m* et cu*m* saluis et modificatio*n*ibus inf*rascript*is quod quide*m* p*r*etiu*m* flo*renorum* 155 l*argorum* fuit co*n*fess*um* etc. se h*ab*uisse et recepisse ad*ict*o Sandro co*n*ductore p*r*ed*ict*o et de eo uocauit se b*en*e pagatu*m* &c. et p*r*omisit &c. sup*er* d*ict*is bo*n*is &c. no*n* mouere lite*m* p*r*ed*ict*a defe*n*dere &c. abo*mn*i ho*min*e &c. cu*m* pactis utilib*us* et al*ias* req*ui*sitis &c. saluis inf*rascript*is &c. Et eco*n*uerso d*ict*us Sander co*n*ductor p*r*ed*ict*us suo no*min*e p*ropr*io et iure et no*min*e o*mnium* et sing*ulorum* eor*um* p*ro*quib*us* ut sup*ra* co*n*dux*it* p*ro*quib*us* et quolib*et* eoru*m* et*iam* derato p*r*omisit et q*uod* obse*r*uabu*n*t &c. et o*mn*i mo*d*o &c. p*r*omisit d*ict*o d*omin*o Be*r*nardo hospitalario p*r*ed*ict*o d*ictum* podere et bo*n*a tenere ut bo*n*a p*er* eu*m* ut sup*ra* co*n*ducta etc. et p*ro* alio no*n* co*n*fiteri &c. et uti arbitris boni uiri &c. [fol. 97, tergo] et dare et tradere d*ict*o hospitali quolib*et* an*n*o deme*n*se augustj vnu*m* par caponu*m* p*ro* d*ict*o an*n*uo canone siue liuello sine exceptio*ne* d*ict*aq*ue* bo*n*a meliorare et quib*us*lib*et* etc an*n*is dura*n*te p*res*enti co*n*cessio*n*e recognoscere d*ict*a bona p*r*od*ict*o hospitali et te*m*pore hui*us*mo*d*i recognitio*n*is siue nouatio*n*is soluere d*ict*o hospitali solidos ugi*n*tj et p*r*ed*ict*a fecer*u*nt cu*m* hijs legib*us* et pactis v*idelicet* q*uod* d*ict*o co*n*ductori uel alijs p*ro*quib*us* ut sup*ra* co*n*dux*it* u*e*l alicui eor*um* no*n* liceat d*ict*a bo*n*a mo*d*o aliq*u*o alienare u*e*l adlo*n*gu*m* te*m*pus locare sine exp*r*essa lice*n*tia d*ict*i hospitalarij u*e*l eius subcessoris p*ro* te*m*pore existe*n*tis et q*uod* si ip*s*e u*e*l alij p*r*ed*ict*i cessauer*i*nt pe*r*trie*n*niu*m* co*n*tinuu*m* i*n*solutio*ne* d*ict*i canonis siue liuellj u*e*l dicta bo*n*a alienauerint u*e*l adlo*n*gu*m* te*m*pus locaueri*n*t q*uod* tu*n*c et eo casu ip*s*i et quilib*et* eor*um* cada*n*t abo*mn*i eor*um* iure et d*ict*a bo*n*a cu*m* o*mn*i eor*um* meliorame*n*to facto et facie*n*do cada*n*t et cecidisse i*n*telliga*n*tur i*ncom*miss*um* et reuerta*n*tur pleno iure add*ictum* hospitale et cu*m* pacto &c. q*uod* finita linea p*r*ed*ict*a ita q*uod* p*r*ed*ict*i p*ro*quib*us* ut sup*ra* facta est d*ict*a co*n*cessio u*e*l aliq*u*is eor*um* no*n* sup*er*si*n*t uiui i*n*humanis q*uod* tu*n*c et eo casu d*ict*a bo*n*a cu*m* d*ict*o o*mn*i meliorame*n*to reuerta*n*t*ur* add*ictum* hospitale et quod in o*mn*i casu reuersio*n*is dictor*um* bonor*um* add*ictum* hospitale liceat et licitu*m* sit d*ict*o hospitalario et alteri cui*uscumque* eius s*u*bcessori p*ro*te*m*pore existe*n*ti d*ictum* podere et bo*n*a cu*m* d*ict*is o*mnibus* suis meliora*mentis* p*r*opria auctoritate capere etc. Que o*mn*ia etc. p*r*omis*er*u*n*t &c. actendere &c. sub pena dupli &c. q*ue* pena &c. p*ro*quib*us* &c. obl*igauerunt* &c. renu*mp*tia*ntes* &c. et*iam* quib*us* &c. guara*ntigia* &c. roga*ntes* &c.

Conductio Sandri ad liuellum.

dat*a* fides ut hic simoni f*ra*tri olim dictj Sandri.

Doc. XLII. Firenze: R. Archivio di Stato. Arch. delle Decime. Quartiere, Santa Maria Novella; Gonfalone, Unicorno: Campione 1498, N°. verde 73. Fol. 75, recto.

Quartiere dj S[a] m[a] novella
Ghonfalone delliochorno.

Alesandro esimone djmarjano divan*n*j filipepj delpopolo disanta lucia dognjsantj abitano inchaxa dibeninchasa & lorenzo filipepj loro nipotj disse lagravezza delan*n*o 1481 Inmariano di van*n*j filipepj chonciatore diq*u*oia overo ghalighaio

Substanzia.

per la veduta degl[i] uficialj per larendit[a] fiorinj due soldj xvii danarj —

Vna chasa dasigniore posta nelpopolo disansipolchro foradella porta asan frjano chon istaiora xij Incircha divignia vecchia & parte posticcj efrutata laquale chasa chomperamo per pregio di fiorini 156 larghi digrossj areda maschulina dasanta marja nuova charta per mano diser giovannj dimarcho daromena notaro djdetto spedale sono dj 19 dj aprile 1494 chonfina da prim[a] esechonda via pierfilippo pandolfinj & daterza via Jachopo delchavaliere elfratello chalzaiuolj & daquarta via lechave overo efratj dimonte oliveto & piualtrj chonfinj ladetta vignia lalavora lorenzo dasansipolchro, sta Indetta chasa anostre spese.

Al 1532. In Alexandro Antinorj g[o] d[o] s[to] sp[o] n[o] 191 per ent[a] difiorinj 2.17—

Rende lanno

vino barilj iiij[o]

fichj ealtre frutta staj[a] ij

Incharichj

Paghasi ognj anno allo spedale dj s[ta] marja nova para uno dichapponj

fiorinj 2 . 17 —

Somma lentrat[a] di quest[a] schritta fiorinj due soldj xvii danarj v a fiorinj due soldj vii danarj vj aoro Larghj di gross[i] tocchaglj soldj iiii[o] danarj viiii Larghj di x[a]

fiorinj — 4 . 9 Larghj

Adi 15 di dicembre 1525 abbattosi di quest[a] posta soldj 4 danarj 9 larghj posti inconto di Nicc[o] di Thomaso antinori gon[e] drago sancto spirito come nella scritta del monte N[o] 52½ sidice pero sicancella et resta nulla.

Doc. XLIII. Firenze: R. Archivio di Stato. Idem, fol. 81, recto. Denunzia of Antonio di Mariano Filipepi. [Excerpta.]

Sutanzie nula

Antonj[o] dimariano divannj filipepj delpopolo dj Santa Lucia dognj santtj abitto inuna chasa apigione che della chiesa dj San pagholo overo prioria djdetta chiesa pagho lano fiorinj 9 disugiello chonfina daprima via lavia nuova ij via amona madalena vedova donna fu dant[o] morelj iij via rede djgiovannj djmariano djvannj filipepj iiij via Ser ant[o] dj Ser gnastagio vespuccj.

detto ant[o] eatore apupilj nono altro esercizio evechio.

Doc. XLIV. Firenze: R. Archivio di Stato. Idem, fol. 178, recto. Denunzia of "Beninchasa e lorenzo di giovannj di marjano filipepj." [Excerpta.]

Vna chasa per nostro abitare posta . . . nella via nuova da prim[a] esechonda via santo pagholo & da terza via lorenzo chorregiaio eda quarta via ser nastagio vespuccj & da quinta via la miserichordja ebighallo eda sesta via simone di pietro ghuiduccj.

Al 1532 in Giovannj suo suc[o] n[o] 125 per vso

[This Denunzia is written in the same hand as that of Sandro and Simone, at fol. 75, recto.]

Doc. XLV. Firenze: R. Archivio di Stato. Idem, fol. 95, recto. Denunzia of "Ser Antonio Amerigo [e] Bernardo frateglj et figluolj dj ser Nastagio dj ser Amerigo Vespuccj." [Excerpta.]

Vna chasa . . . posta . . . nel popolo dj sancta lucia dognissantj et nella via Nuova alla quale da primo detta via nuoua aij[o] chiasso a iij Simone dj petro guiduccj a iiij[o] glj heredj dj Mariano dj vannj Galigaio a v[o] fratj dj Settimo Tegnalla per nostro abitare.

Doc. XLVI. Firenze: R. Biblioteca Nazionale. Codici dei Conventi Soppressi, San Marco, J, 10, 32. Le Giornate di Ser Lorenzo Violi.

[Begins] Fol. 1, recto. Apologia per modo di Dialogo In defensione delle cose predicate dal Reu[do] Padre Fra Hieronimo Sauonarola da Ferrara dell' ordine de Predicatori In Firenze.

Fol. 41, tergo. . . . lui [Doffo Spini, capo e guida dei Compagnacci,] usaua molto in bottega di un dipintore che si chiamaua Sandro di Botticello huomo molto noto nella città per essere allora de primi ecc[ti] Pittori che ci fussino, et in bottega sua era sempre un accademia di scioperati, come uno ne era il prefato Doffo equiui piu uolte ragionando in su la morte delfrate Doffo disse che non fu mai intentione loro mettere il frate di S. fran[co] nel fuoco, e che lo assicurorno di quest[o], ma bastaua loro che gli facessi giuocho tanto che col dilungare la cosa loro uenissino à loro intento di spegnier queste cose del frate, e leuarlo di qua, Donde che parlandone cosi Doffo piu uolte in detta bottega di Sandro, e sendoui ancora presente Simone frat[lo] di detto pittore, ne fece memoria nella sua cronica cioe a un suo libro doue il prefato Simone descriue tutte lecose notabili di quelli tempi, eparendoli che questo detto di Doffo fussi danotarlo per scoprir lauerità che era occulta di questa materia lo scrisse à questo suo libro legato in asse che è come una Cronichetta delle cose occorrenti in quei tempi in Italia, et io ho uisto detto libro, e letto.

[The greater portion of the "Terza Giornata" in which this passage occurs, as well as other passages of this inedited work, were printed in the Appendix to Professor Villari's "Storia di Girolamo Savonarola," ed. 1861, Vol. II, pp. clxxviii and xxv.]

Doc. XLVII. Firenze: R. Biblioteca Nazionale. Codici dei Conventi soppressi, N° 1501, G, 2: Isidori S., Ep. Hispalens, "Imagine del Mondo", &c., Cod. chartac. in fol., saec. xv., proveniente dalla Badia di Ripoli.

A miscellany of original and translated pieces in the handwriting of Antonio di Tuccio Manetti.

Fol. 115, recto. Following the sixth item in the collection, "Pistola di mes*sere* francescho petrarcha Responsiua alla Comunita difirenze," is this memorandum:

Ap*r*esso scriuero j° Capitolo dij^a^ lett*er*^a^ chescrisse daRoma Simone dimariano botticellj a g*i*ouan*n*i suo fratello afirenze didj xvij dagosto 1482.

Jerj Mando nostr° S^e^ vna lett*er*^a^ allegiere amo*n*sig*nor*e diNoara chegliscriue Mes*ser*e Marchion*n*e merch*ante* della Magnia huo*mo* degnio difede ebene conosciuto quj i*n*corte Echonta come i*n* Buemmia sono apparitj spiritj i*n*forma humana, Ecitano lepersone aessere i*n*fra tredj i*n* una selua chome dauantj auno loro p*r*incipale; Equalunque no*n* uiua muore i*n* capo ditre dj, Equellj ch*e* vivan*n*o tornano poj et nonsan*n*o raco*n*tare nulla come smemoratj. Equestj spiritj no*n*citano senone ereticj ch*e* uene assaj. Questo mipare uno grande miracolo seglie vero. Jo o pure visto la lettera, Econosco ess*er*e dimano di Mes*ser*e Marchion*n*e, huo[mo] difede & p*r*aticho, Eda anche dentrata 8 Jn x̃ [10 migliaia] diduc*atj*. Elbonciano costi lochonoscie Eq*u*antj mercatantj visono et presto sara diqua.

Doc. XLVIII. Firenze: R. Archivio di Stato. Arch. dei Conventi soppressi. N°. grosso 98, Santa Maria di Monticelli in Firenze; N°. 54.

[Begins] Questo libro sara chiamato debit*ori* e credit*ori* del nostro munist° dimonticeglj fuorj della porta asampiero ghattolino [&c. dal Giugno 1494, al Dicembre 1497.]

c. 173, debitore.

Sandro dimariano dipintore dedare addi 14 digiugnio 1496 *fiorinj* quattro larg*hj* doro porto chonta*n*tj v*no* suo carçone Sono p*er* parte della dipintura debbe fare neldormitoro appare auscit*a* ac*arta* 127 — *lire* 26 *soldj* 16 *danarj* —

E dedare addi 7 diluglio *fiorinj* quattro larg*hj* doro porto chonta*n*tj u*no* suo carçone ausc*ita* 127 — *lire* 26 *soldj* 16 *danarj* —

E dedare addi 20 detto *fiorinj* duo larg*hj* doro porto luj detto chontantj ausc*ita* 128 — *lire* 13 *soldj* 8 *danarj* —

E dedare addi 14 daghosto 1496 *fiorinj* cinq*ue* larg*hj* doro porto iac° chonta*n*tj ausc*ita* 128 — *lire* 33 *soldj* 10 *danarj* —

E dedare addi 19 detto *fiorinj* cinq*ue* larg*hj* doro porto chonta*n*tj iac° di franc° suo carçone Sono p*er* ogni suo resto della dipintura cia fatto disanfranc° ausc*ita* 129 *lire* 33 *soldj* 10 *danarj* —

c. 173, creditore.

Sandro dimariano dipintore dichontro de auere addi 20 dottob*re* 1496 *fiorinj* uentj larghj doro inoro Sono p*er* resto duno san francescho cia dipinto nel nostro dormitoro nella fabrica posto la detta fabrica debba dare Inq*uest*° [acarta] 199 — *lire* 134 *soldj* — *danarj* —

c. 199, debitore. m° cccc lxxxxvj La fabrica . . . . dedare addi 20 detto *lire* 134 fatte buone asandro dipintore Sono p*er* resto duno san francescho cia dipinto nel nostro dormitoro nuouo posto detto sandro debba auere Inq*uest*° ac*arta* 173 — *lire* 134 *soldj* — *danarj* —

Doc. XLIX. Firenze: R. Archivio di Stato. Carteggio Mediceo innanzi il Principato; 1^a^ Miscellania, Lett^ra^ 201.

[On a single, half sheet.]

fassj fede pe me basino asandro Botjcello dop*ere* cinquanta sette/ ca [*sic* ? ch'a] quj cho tre dipitorj as*oldj* 14 luno. e vno dj sedicj opere as*oldj* 10 e lido vino/ E vno fatore as*oldj* 7 eldj che a opere djciotto. fatte uoj ora/ adj 3 dj luglio 1497. Basino achas[t]ello.

lire 39 . 18 —
8 —
6 . 6
lire 54 . 4

[Endorsed:] Spezabile mro lionado strozj Jn *f*ire*n*ze

[Cited by M. Pierre Gauthiez, in "Lorenzaccio," Paris, 1904, pp. 19 and 411, note.]

Doc. L. Firenze: R. Archivio di Stato. Arch. dei Contratti. Rogiti di Ser Giovannj di Ser Antonio di Giovannj Carsidonj, Protocollo dal 8 marzo 1491-2, al 24 Aprili 1500.

Fol. 215, tergo.

Anno 1497, Indictione xv°.

promissio de non offendendo

Item postea dicto anno indictione & die xviij° februarij actum ut supra presentibus domino Jacob° deburgo & nicholao martinj Testibus &c.

Antonius Migloris deguidoctis ciuis florentinus promisit mihi notario infrascripto &c. quod Sander Marianj alias dj botticello pictor non offendat &c. Filippum dominicj delcaualiere calzaiuolum & casu quo ipsum offenderit soluere &c. loco pene &c. florenos 50 largos pro dimidio officio otto &c. & pro alia parte offense pro quibus omnibus &c. obligavit &c. Renumptians &c. pro quarantigia &c. Rogans &c.

Item postea &c. presentibus ser bartolome° banbello & luca pierantoni' familiaribus &c.

Dominicus Antoni' dominicj de burgho a Sancto lorenzo promisit mihj notario ut supra recipienti quod dictus filippus dominicj bartolome' delcaualiere non offendat &c. dictum Sandrum marjanj botticellj & casu quo offenderit soluere &c. florenos 50 largos ut supra pro quibus &c. obligavit &c. Renumptians &c. pro guarantigia &c. Rogans &c.

Doc. LI. Firenze: R. Archivio di Stato. Arch. delle Decime. Quartiere, San Giovanni; Gonfalone, Drago: Campione 1480, N° verde 1018.

Fol. 39, recto. Denunzia of Antonio di Migliori di Tommaso Guidotti.

Doc. LII. Firenze: R. Archivio di Stato. Arch. delle Decime. Quartiere, San Giovanni; Gonfalone, Drago: Campione 1498, N° verde 110.

Fol. 70, recto. Denunzia of Monna Lisa, widow of Antonio Guidotti, and of Antonio her son.

Doc. LIII. Firenze: R. Archivio di Stato. Arch. dell' Arte dei Medici e degli Speziali, N°. 10. Matricule dal 1491 al 1523. Matriculation of "Alexandro di Mariano di botticello."

Fol. 38, recto. Die 15 nouembris 1499.

Al detto libro [i.e. Libro Biancho,] Ac. 229.

Alexander marianj botticellj pictor uolens uenire ad magistratum dicte artis & poni & scribi in matricula dicte artis jnter alios in dicta arte matriculatos &c. promisit & jurauit &c.
Debet soluere florenos sex sigillj.
[Printed by Dr Carl Frey, in "Die Loggia dei Lanzi zu Florenz," Berlin, 1885, p. 345.]

Doc. LIV. Firenze: R. Archivio di Stato. Arch. delle Decime. Quarticrc, Santa Maria Novella; Gonfalone, Unicorno: Campione 1498, N°. verde 73, fol. 548, recto. Denunzia of "Messer Guidantonio di giouannj vespuccj." [Excerpta.]

Fol. 550, recto. Adj vj dj Febraio 1500.
Vna casa posta nelpopolo disan michele bisdominj, compro dallarte delcambio. Conto dj v djma^r zo 1498. Rogato Ser Michele dasancta + [Croce].

Doc. LV. Roma: Archivio Segreto Vaticano, Politicorum. XLVII, fol. 338 e seg. Estratto della Cronaca di Simone Filipepi. Printed at length by P. Villari, and E. Casanova, in their "Scelta di Prediche e Scritti di Fra Girolamo Savonarola, con nuovi documenti intorno alla sua vita." Firenze, 1898, p. 453, &c.

p. 507. Copierò quì appresso un ricordo che io feci fino alli 2 di novembre 1499. Alessandro di Mariano Filipepi, mio fratello, uno de' buon pittori, che habbia havuto a questi tempi la nostra città, alla presenza mia, sendo in casa al fuoco, circa tre hore di notte, narrò come quel giorno, nella sua bottega in casa di Sandro, ero stato a ragionamento con Doffi Spini sopra i casi di f. Girolamo. Et in effetto, interrogandolo Sandro, perché sapeva che detto Doffo era stato uno de' principali, che sempre s'erano trovati ad essaminarlo, che li dicesse la pura verità, che peccati trovassero in fra Girolamo, onde meritasse fargli cosí vituperosa morte; dove che all' hora gli rispose Doffo:—Sandro, hotti io a dire il vero? non gli trovammo mai, non che peccato mortale, ma né anco veniale se gli trovò.—All' hore Sandro gli disse: Perchè lo faceste voi morire cosí vituperosamente?—Rispose:—E' non fu' io; ma ne fu causa Benozzo Federighi. Et se non si faceva morire questo profeta et gli suoi compagni, et gli havesse rimandati a San Marco, il popolo ci harebbe messo a sacco noi et tagliati tutti a pezzi. La cosa era ita tanto avanti, che cosi determinammo per nostro scampo, che morissero.—Poi accaddero tra loro dell' altre parole, che non bisogna replicarle.

Doc. LVI. Firenze: R. Biblioteca Nazionale. Biblia Sacra, Basilea, 1491. A gloss on the 11th and 12th chapters of the Book of the Apocalypse, written by Fra Girolamo Savonarola, on the margins of a printed copy of the Vulgate.

[Cap.] XIm. *Calamus:* idest scripturarum discretio uel predicationis. *Metire templum:* idest ecclesiam vt non eadem omnibus sed diuersis diuersa predices. *altare:* christus crucifixus, vt scilicet facias quod omnes eum sequantur, sed non uno modo. *atrium:* falsi christiani. *datum est:* idest computatum cum infidelibus. *ciuitatem:* ecclesiam. 42 [i.e. *mensibus quadraginta duobus*]: idest tribus annis cum dimidio. *duobus:* enoc & elie. [*diebus*] *mille*, &c.: idest tribus annis cum dimidio. Sed dies hic nominat quia lucem predicant ueritatis &c. *ignis:* idest predicatio que eos ad ignem condemnabit. *celum:* sacras scripturas. *conuertendi* &c.: eo modo quo dictum est Isaie, Vade exceca &c. *in sanguinem:* peccatorum. *percutere:* idest percutiendam denuntiare. *bestia:* antichristus. *de abysso:* de peccatoribus. *terremotus:* tribulatio magna in qua. *decima pars ciuitatis cecidit:* idest qui non seruarunt decem precepta puncti sunt a deo cum antichristo. *7 milia:* idest perfecti in malitia. hi ergo non pertinent ad nouem ordines angelorum, sed punientur cum capite suo. *in sedibus suis:* idest in sibi commissis. *& qui eras:* non dicit & qui venturus es: quia iam presentem habebant: & tempus post hoc non erit amplius. *tempus mortuorum:* scilicet advenit. *iudicari:* idest ut iudicentur a te.

et apertum est: hec est 4a uisio in qua describitur bellum christi totius & totius antichristi, & precedentibus uisionibus pendet. *templum:* ecclesie mysteria. *in celo:* in ecclesia triumphanti. *arca:* christus & eius mysteria. *in templo:* in ecclesia militante & tu*n*c ceperunt apostoli predicare.

[Cap. XII.] *mulier:* ecclesia. *sole:* iustitie. *luna:* uolubilitas rerum. *corona:* sancti. *in capite:* in christo. *in utero habens:* scilicet uerbum dei. *capita 7:* uniuersos principes: licet 7 capitalia uitia. *cornua x:* idest arma contraria decem preceptis. *diademata:* uictorias de subuersione multorum. *cauda:* que scilicet operit turpia, idest deceptiones quibus operit peccata ne uideatur malus &c. 3am *partem:* idest omnes demones sequentes. *in terram:* in terrenos. *Et draco* &c. Nota quod hec est 4a uisio in qua ponit bella bonorum & malorum. hic ergo descriptis personis describit causum belli & intentionem bellantium. *paritura:* scilicet christum in cordibus hominum. *raptus est*, &c.: quotidie rapitur dum mentes fidelium subleuat ostendens eis gloriam suam. *ad thronum eius:* ad iudiciariam potestatem. *fugit:* scilicet sequendo christum ad solitudinem contemplationis. *diebus:* quia in lumine est. *mille:* ob contemplationem perfectam. *200:* ob duplicem caritatem. *60:* ob perfectione operum. *et factus est*, &c.: angeli & demones pugnant propter electos, &c. *neque locus:* quia in electis non habet locum nam & a limbo liberantur. *serpens:* propter astutiam. *dyabolus:* deorsum cadens. *Sathanas:* aduersarius. *in terra:* in terrenos. *accusabat:* idest accusabiles eos reddebat. *et postquam*, &c.: Cum uidisset Dyabolus fundatas ecclesias per orbem; iratus est ualde; & per hereticos ac falsos fratres & cetera uitia cepit persequi ecclesiam iam tyrannis destructis. *ale due:* uite due, actiua & contemplatiua; licet duo precepta caritatis. *per tempus:* per unum annum. *& tempora:* per duos. *& dimidium temporis:* idest anni. et nota quod tempus christi & antichristi quantum ad proprias personas est trium annorum cum dimidio; et significat totum tempus eorum a principio mundi usque ad finem quo ad corpus mysticum utriusque. *ex ore:* idest mala suasione. *aquam:* doctrinam falsam; licet concupicentias carnis. *terra:* christus uel maria. *os suum:* ad preces; licet christus precepit ut hec aqua anihilaretur. *super arena:* super terrenos fluctuantes.

DOC. LVII. Mantova: Archivio Gonzaga; 13 Via Roberto Ardigò, *già* Ginnasio.

F. II. 9. Copialettere della Marchesa Isabella Gonzaga, dal 29 Luglio 1502, al 30 gennaio 1503. Sub die.

[La Marchesa a] Francisco Malateste.

Francisco: Desiderando nui hauere nel Camerino n*ostr*o picture ad historia de li ex*cellenti* pictori ch*e* sono al p*rese*nte in italia: fra quali el perusino e Famoso: volemo che tu sij cum lui:

usando sel te parrera il megio de qualch*e* suo amico: et uedi sel vole acceptare la impresa di Farne uno quadro cu*m* la historia o inuenctione ch*e* nui gli daremo et le Figure andaran*no* picole si come sciai ch*e* sono le altre ch*e* sono in di*c*to Camerino et acceptan*do* lo asumto de *scr*ivirne: intenderai quello ch*e* vorra di mercede: et se presto se metteria a lauoro ch*e* nui puoi gli mandaressimo le mesure del quadro cu*m* la Fantasia n*ostr*a et cum diligentia ne renderai resposta.

Mant*ue* XV septembris 1502.

E. Esterni, N° XXVIII, 3.

[Francesco Malatesta alla Marchesa Isabella Gonzaga.]

Illma madona mia. Ho uisto qua*n*to la S. V. me scriue ch*e* deba ricerchare del p*er*usino famoso depi*n*tore p*er* hauere quella desiderio de hauere pictura dj sua mano. Ritrouo ch*e* esso e de presenti asiena a lauorare et non e p*er* uenire fina octo o dieci ziorni. Venuto ch*e*l sia p*ar*laro co*n* luj et usaro ogni dilige*n*tia acio ch*e*l toglia lo asu*m*pto di uoler seruire la S. V. Vero e ch*e*l me facto jnte*n*dere ch*e* le h*om*o longo, e p*er* m*od*o dj parlare quasi maj no*n* finisse op*er*a ch*e*l Come*n*za, ta*n*ta e la longheza sua.

Me e stato p*ar*lato de uno altro famoso depi*n*tore el qual anchora luj molto me e laudato, ch*e* se chiama philipo de fra philipino et ho uoluto parlare con luj, el qual me ha ditto ch*e*l no*n* poria dar pri*n*cipio atal op*er*a de questi sei mesi p*er* essere occupato circha altri lauorerj, et che forse poj finiti q*ue*sti el poria seruir la S. V.

Vno altro alexandro botechiella molto me stato laudate et p*er* optimo depi*n*tore, et p*er* h*om*o ch*e* serve volo*n*tera, et no*n* ha del velupo Come li s*oprascrip*ti, al qual io ho facto p*ar*lare, et q*ue*sto tal dice ch*e*l toria lo asumpto de p*rese*nti et seruiria di bona uoglia la S. V. Me p*ar*so de tutti darne noticia ala p*re*fata S. V. acio ch*e* q*ue*lla possa far electione di q*ue*llo ch*e* piu li piacera, ala qual di Continuo me rachoma*n*do.

flore*n*tie 23 septe*m*bris 1502.

E. Ill^me. D.

S*er*uitor francischus de Malatestis etc.

[Endorsed:]

Ala Illma et ecc^ma Madana e patrona mia Madona Marchesana de mantua,
Mantue.

[Printed by Willelmo Braghirolli, among his "Notizie e documenti inediti intorno a Pietro Vannucci, detto Il Perugino," in the "Giornale di Erudizione Artistica," Perugia, 1872, Vol. II, Fasc. VI, pp. 159-160.]

Doc. LVIII. Firenze: R. Biblioteca Laurenziana. Plut. 39, Cod. 40. "Ugolini Verini Carmina & alia." [Variously dated from 1488 to 1491.]

Lib. III, fol. 26 tergo.

"De pictoribus et scultoribus florentinis, qui pri[s]cis grecis equiperari possint."

Doc. LIX. Firenze: Archivio dell' Opera di Santa Maria del Fiore. Deliberazioni. 25 Gennaio, 1503-4. Deliberations concerning the choice of a site for the "David" of Michelangelo.

Printed by Johan Gaye, in the "Carteggio inedito d'Artisti," Vol. III, p. 455; and again, more correctly, among the "Contratti" appended to "Le Lettere di Michelangelo Buonarroti," ecc. Firenze, 1875, p. 620.

Doc. LX. Firenze: R. Archivio di Stato. Arch. della Grascia, N°. 6. Libri dei Morti di Firenze. Libro 2do, dal 1506, al 1560. [Excerpta.]

Fol. 329, recto.

+ 1510 di maggio.

Sandro dib*art*^mo * dipintore R° in ognisantj adj 17 detto.

[* Scribe's error for "Botticello."]

Doc. LXI. Firenze: R. Archivio di Stato. Arch. dell' Arte dei Medici e degli Speziali, N°. 248. "Libbro de Morti dell' Arte delli speciali, seg^to. E." Dal 1505, al 1511. [Excerpta.]

Fol. 45, tergo.

Maggio 1510

Sandro di Botticello dipintore adj 17 R° i*n*ognjsanctj.

Doc. LXII. Firenze: R. Archivio di Stato. Arch. dei Conventi soppressi. N°. grosso 126, Sant' Elizabetta delle Convertite; N°. 62, Libro di Ricordi del Monastero, dal 1451, al 1620.

fol. lxiiij recto.

yhs

1493. Ricordo come oggi questo di 19 difebraio 1493 Jo m*agist*ro nicholaio dafirenze priore delco*n*uento dis*anct*o sp*irit*o oriueduto elconto dellauenerabile religiosa Suora Alexandra badessa delmonasterio delle co*n*uertite della capella della chiesa i*n* magisterio i*n* fondame*n*tj i*n* calcina i*n* rena i*n* ghiaia i*n* matonj i*n* pianelle i*n* legname i*n* ferrame*n*tj digrate inaco*n*cime della altare cioe uno dossale lapredella j*n* [? &] una corona & contando *fiorinj* quat° doro dati alproueditore dellopera & finalme*n*te inogni & qualu*nque* cosa ueduta p*er*me diligenteme*n*te la lasom*m*a di fiorinj cento venti uno doro inoro come sidimostra p*er* sua conti alsuo quaderno partita p*er* partita. *fiorinj* 121.

Uno desco & finestre.

[This "ricordo" is followed by four pages of detailed accounts, fol. lxviij tergo, to fol. lxx recto, relating to the erection of the "capella," or chapel of the high altar, of the church, and the new dormitory. From the debit side of these accounts, the following entries are taken:]

Fol. lxviij recto, Spese fatte nella capella 1491.

Suora Alexandra Badessa delle co*n*vertite deau*er*e le i*n*frascripte spese uedute p*er* me m*agist*ro nicholaio priore delco*n*uento dis*anct*o sp*irit*o Imp*ri*ma lire settanta soldi quat° am*agist*ro giouanni scorbachia p*er* fondame*n*ti della capella . . . .

E de au*er*e fiorini quaranta dette am° giouanni detto p*er* suo magisterio di detta capella . . . .

E de au*er*e fiorini noue e mezo doro inoro dati afranc° dipintore p*er*la corona dellaltare legname oro & facitura . . . .

E de au*er*e lire diciasette dati p*er*uno dossale & p*er* una predella p*er* la capella . . . .

Fol. lxx recto.

Suora Alexandra Badessa delmunisterio delle co*n*uertite de au*er*e p*er* spese fatte i*n* chiesa & neldormitorio nuouo da di 30 daprile 1493 p*er*insino adi 31 doctobre 1493 fiorini cento octanta uno doro inoro dati am*agist*ro Jacopo muratore p*er* suo magisterio della chiesa & dormitorio . . . .

E de au*er*e adi 25 didice*m*bre 1494 aiacopo dipintore ch*e* dipinse glialtarj cioe delcrocifisso & della uergine maria p*er* sua faticha & dipintura ualsono lire noua*n*ta una.

E de aue*re* p*er*insino adidetto lire quat° soldi sedici dati aiacopo dipi*n*tore p*er* oro & calcina p*er* dettj altarj.

[Cited by M. Jacques Mesnil, in the "Miscellanea d'Arte," Firenze, 1903, Vol. I, p. 97.]

Doc. LXIII. Firenze: R. Archivio di Stato. Arch. della Guardaroba, N°. 28. "Inuentario della guardaroba e delle robbe ch*e* sono per el Palazzo di S. Ec^a^ Illma inuentariate . . . . questo dj xxv d'ottobr*e* 1553." [Excerpta.]

Fol. 29, tergo. Nella prima stanza della Guardaroba secreta.

1° Ritratto di bacco in tela alta 3 bra*ccia* co*n* sua cornice.

Fol. 30, recto.

1° Quadro pittoui Madonna Lucretia di piero de Medici co*n* cornice dorata.

Doc. LXIV. Firenze: R. Arch. di Stato. Arch. della Guardaroba, N°. 521. "Questo Libro . . . seg^to^ A è L'Inuent*ari*° Orig*ina*^le^ della Guardaroba del' Ser^mo^ Gran Duca Ferd*inand*° sec^do^ di Toscana, . . . cominc*ia*^to^ q*ues*to di 16 di sett*emb*^re^ 1637." [Excerpta.]

Fol. 128, recto [Palazzo della Signoria]. In su'l Terazzo grande che risponde in su'l Cortile. Vn' Quadro in tela alto b*raccia* uno e $\frac{3}{4}$, dipintoui a' Olio di mano del' Botticelli creduto tale un' Soldato armato in atto di ferire un' Giouane con una donna che lo ritiene con cornice d' Albero.

Vn' Quadro in tela dipintoui a' olio di mano del Botticelli una Galatea Ignuda con Zeffiro e' altre figure, alto b*raccia* uno e' $\frac{3}{4}$, e' largo b*raccia* uno $\frac{1}{3}$, con cornice d' Albero.

Fol. 173, tergo. Nel Salone grande de Gigli alato alla Guardaroba.

Vn' quadro in tela lungo b*raccia* dua e $\frac{1}{2}$ incirca, drentoui dipinto un' Bacco Antico ingnudo che beue al Barile, e piscia in un' oricio [*sic.* orcio] con adornam^to^ ordinario.

Doc. LXV. Firenze: R. Archivio di Stato. Arch. della Guardaroba, N°. 136. Fol. 128, recto. "Copia degli Inventari della guardaroba del Casino et villa della Magia del Ecc^{mo} S^{re} Do*n*. Ant° Medicj." [Excerpta.]

Fol. 129, recto. Inuentario della Guardaroba della Casa e Palazzo del Casino, a custodia di Piero Elmi cominciato oggi questo di 8 di Marzo 1587.

Fol. 153, tergo.
Nella Galleria.
Dua quadretti lunghi $\frac{3}{4}$ alti $\frac{o}{3}$ [di un braccio], con Piu figure drentoui, di mano del botticello, ornamento di noce intag^{to} edorato, in uno Il transito, ein uno lo sposalitio, della mad*onn*^{a}.

Fol. 154, recto.
Vno quadro intauola con una Natiuita di N.S. con magi disse di mano del botticelli, alto b*raccia* 1$\frac{o}{4}$, largo b*raccia* 1$\frac{3}{4}$ inc^{a}, con ornamento di legno intag^{to} edorato.

INDEX

By Richard Stapleford